T0213698

Lecture Notes in Computer Science 10005

Commenced Publication in 1973
Founding and Former Series Editors:
Gerhard Goos, Juris Hartmanis, and Jan van Leeuwen

More information about this series at http://www.springer.com/series/7410

Liqun Chen · Jinguang Han (Eds.)

Provable Security

10th International Conference, ProvSec 2016
Nanjing, China, November 10–11, 2016
Proceedings

 Springer

Editors
Liqun Chen
University of Surrey
Guildford
UK

Jinguang Han
Nanjing University of Finance
  and Economics
Nanjing
China

ISSN 0302-9743   ISSN 1611-3349 (electronic)
Lecture Notes in Computer Science
ISBN 978-3-319-47421-2   ISBN 978-3-319-47422-9 (eBook)
DOI 10.1007/978-3-319-47422-9

Library of Congress Control Number: 2016953218

LNCS Sublibrary: SL4 – Security and Cryptology

Printed on acid-free paper

This Springer imprint is published by Springer Nature
The registered company is Springer International Publishing AG
The registered company address is: Gewerbestrasse 11, 6330 Cham, Switzerland

Preface

The 10th International Conference on Provable Security (ProvSec 2016) was held in Nanjing, P.R. China, November 10–11, 2016. The conference was organized by Nanjing University of Finance and Economics.

The conference program consisted of two invited talks and 23 contributed papers. We would like to express our special thanks to the distinguished keynote speakers, Colin Boyd from the Norwegian University of Science and Technology and Jens Groth from University College London, who gave very enlightening talks.

Out of 79 submissions from 16 countries, 23 papers were selected, presented at the conference, and are included in these proceedings. The accepted papers cover a range of topics in the field of provable security research, including attribute/role-based cryptography, data in cloud, searchable encryption, key management, encryption, leakage analysis, and homomorphic encryption.

The success of this event depended critically on the help and hard work of many people, whose help we gratefully acknowledge. First, we heartily thank the Program Committee and the additional reviewers, listed on the following pages, for their careful and thorough reviews. Most of the papers were reviewed by at least three people, and many by four or five. Significant time was spent discussing the papers. Thanks must also go to the hard-working shepherds for their guidance and helpful advice on improving a number of papers. We also thank the general chair for the excellent organization of the conference.

We also sincerely thank the authors of all submitted papers. We further thank the authors of accepted papers for revising papers according to the various reviewer suggestions and for returning the source files in good time. The revised versions were not checked by the Program Committee, and so authors bear final responsibility for their contents. We would also like to thank the Steering Committee and local Organizing Committee.

Thanks are due to the staff at Springer for their help in producing the proceedings. We further thank the developers and maintainers of the EasyChair software, which greatly helped simplify the submission and review process.

November 2016

Liqun Chen
Jinguang Han

Organization
Provable Security 2016

Nanjing, P.R. China
November 10–11, 2016

General Chair

Jie Cao   Nanjing University of Finance and Economics, China

Program Chairs

Liqun Chen   University of Surrey, UK
Jinguang Han   Nanjing University of Finance and Economics, China

Steering Committee

Feng Bao   Huawei, Singapore
Xavier Boyen   Queensland University of Technology, Australia
Joseph K. Liu   Monash University, Australia
Yi Mu   University of Wollongong, Australia
Josef Pieprzyk   Queensland University of Technology, Australia
Willy Susilo   University of Wollongong, Australia

Program Committee

Man Ho Au   Hong Kong Polytechnic University, SAR China
Joonsang Baek   Khalifa University of Science,
                               Technology and Research, UAE
Zhenfu Cao   East China Normal University, China
Aniello Castiglione   University of Salerno, Italy
Liqun Chen   University of Surrey, UK
Xiaofeng Chen   Xidian University, China
Yu Chen   Chinese Academy of Sciences, China
Céline Chevalier   Université Panthéon-Assas Paris II, France
Kim-Kwang   University of Texas at San Antonio, USA
   Raymond Choo
Sherman S.M. Chow   Chinese University of Hong Kong, SAR China
Nico Döttling   University of California, Berkeley, USA
Georg Fuchsbauer   École normale supérieure, France
David Galindo   University of Birmingham, UK
Jinguang Han   Nanjing University of Finance and Economics, China
Qiong Huang   South China Agricultural University, China

Xinyi Huang	Fujian Normal University, China
Sorina Ionica	University of Picardie Jules Verne, France
Kwangjo Kim	KAIST, Republic of Korea
Alptekin Küpçü	Koç University, Turkey
Jiguo Li	Hohai University, China
Yingjiu Li	Singapore Management University, Singapore
Kaitai Liang	Manchester Metropolitan University, UK
Xiaodong Lin	University of Ontario Institute of Technology, Canada
Joseph Liu	Monash University, Australia
Zhe Liu	University of Waterloo, Canada
Rongxing Lu	University of New Brunswick, Canada
Masahiro Mambo	Kanazawa University, Japan
Mark Manulis	University of Surrey, UK
Bart Mennink	KU Leuven, Belgium
Chris Mitchell	Royal Holloway, University of London, UK
Atsuko Miyaji	Osaka University, Japan
Yi Mu	University of Wollongong, Australia
Tatsuaki Okamoto	NTT, Japan
Thomas Peters	École normale supérieure, France
Christophe Petit	University of Oxford, UK
Josef Pieprzyk	Queensland University of Technology, Australia
Yogachandran Rahulamathavan	Loughborough University in London, UK
Kui Ren	State University of New York at Buffalo, USA
Reza Reyhanitabar	NEC Laboratories Europe, Germany
Dominique Schröder	Saarland University, Germany
Willy Susilo	University of Wollongong, Australia
Qiang Tang	University of Luxembourg, Luxembourg
Cong Wang	City University of Hong Kong, SAR China
Huaxiong Wang	Nanyang Technological University, Singapore
Jian Weng	Jinan University, China
Qianhong Wu	Beihang University, China
Shouhuai Xu	University of Texas at San Antonio, USA
Chung-Huang Yang	National Kaohsiung Normal University, Taiwan
Guomin Yang	University of Wollongong, Australia
Wun-She Yap	Universiti Tunku Abdul Rahman, Malaysia
Xun Yi	RMIT University, Australia
Siu Ming Yiu	The University of Hong Kong, SAR China
Yong Yu	Shaanxi Normal University, China
Tsz Hon Yuen	Huawei, Singapore
Fangguo Zhang	Sun Yat-sen University, China
Futai Zhang	Nanjing Normal University, China
Rui Zhang	Chinese Academy of Sciences, China
Yuan Zhang	Nanjing University, China
Zongyang Zhang	AIST, Japan
Jianying Zhou	Institute for Infocomm Research, Singapore

Organizing Chairs

Zhiang Wu	Nanjing University of Finance and Economics, China
Futai Zhang	Nanjing Normal University, China
Jiguo Li	Hohai University, China

Publication Chairs

Zhan Bu	Nanjing University of Finance and Economics, China
Muhammad Khurram Khan	King Saud University, Kingdom of Saudi Arabia

Publicity Chairs

Jiageng Chen	Huazhong Normal University, China
Ali El Kaafarani	University of Oxford, UK

Registration Chair

Changjian Fang	Nanjing University of Finance and Economics, China

Additional Reviewers

Ang, Yang
Arita, Seiko
Biswas, Bhaskar
Blazy, Olivier
Dong, Changyu
Dong, Xiaolei
Dupont, Pierre-Alain
El Kaafarani, Ali
Etemad, Mohammad
Ezerman, Martianus Frederic
Ferrara, Anna Lisa
Fleischhacker, Nils
Futa, Yuichi
Gong, Junqing
Haiyang, Xue
Hassanzadeh-Nazarabadi, Yahya
Hou, Lin
Huang, Jianye
Huang, Yan
Jiang, Peng
Kai, He
Kuwakado, Hidenori
Lai, Jianchang

Lai, Russell W.F.
Lee, Hyung Tae
Li, Hongbo
Li, Huige
Li, Ximing
Lin, Changlu
Liu, Jia-Nan
Liu, Jianghua
Liu, Ximing
Liu, Yuejun
Liu, Yunwen
Mamun, Mohammad
Michel, Christoph
Minelli, Michele
Ning, Jianting
Nguyen, Khoa
Omote, Kazumasa
Pellegrino, Giancarlo
Russell, Paulet
Sasaki, Yu
Su, Chunhua
Taheri-Boshrooyeh, Sanaz
Tan, Gaosheng

Tan, Syh-Yuan
Tan, Xiao
Vizár, Damian
Wang, Hao
Wang, Jianfeng
Wang, Licheng
Wang, Qin
Wang, Wei
Wang, Xiuhua
Wang, Yilei
Wang, Yuyu
Xiao, Yuting
Xie, Congge
Xie, Shaohao
Xue, Haiyang
Yang, Rupeng
Yang, Wenjie

Yang, Xu
Yang, Xuechao
Yau, Wei-Chuen
Yu, Gang
Yu, Jingyue
Zhang, Huang
Zhang, Kai
Zhang, Liting
Zhang, Shiwei
Zhang, Tao
Zhang, Yinghui
Zhao, Yongjun
Zheng, Haibin
Zhong, Lin
Zhou, Jun
Zhou, Xingguang

Contents

Attribute/Role-Based Cryptography

Accountable Ciphertext-Policy Attribute-Based Encryption Scheme Supporting Public Verifiability and Nonrepudiation

Gang Yu[1,2,3(✉)], Zhenfu Cao[1(✉)], Guang Zeng[2,3],
and Wenbao Han[2,3]

[1] School of Computer Science and Software Engineering,
East China Normal University, Shanghai, China
gyu1010@126.com, zfcao@sei.ecnu.edu.cn
[2] State Key Laboratory of Mathematical Engineering
and Advanced Computing, Zhengzhou, China
sunshine_zeng@sina.com, wbhan@netease.net
[3] Information Science and Technology Institute, Zhengzhou, China

Abstract. Ciphertext-policy attribute-based encryption, denoted by CP-ABE, is a promising extension of identity-based encryption which enables fine-grained data access control by taking a set of attributes as users' public key. However, owing to the fact that an attribute set may be shared by multiple users, malicious users dare to share their decryption keys to others for profits. Furthermore, the central authority is able to issue arbitrary decryption keys for any unauthorized users. To prevent these two kinds of key abuses in CP-ABE system, we propose an accountable CP-ABE scheme which allows any third party to publicly verify the identity embedded in a leaked decryption key, allows an auditor to publicly check whether a malicious user or the authority should be responsible for an exposed decryption key, and the malicious user or the authority can't deny it. The proposed accountable CP-ABE scheme supports any LSSS realizable access structures. At last, the confidentiality and public verifiability of the proposed scheme can be proved to be tightly related to the atomic CP-ABE scheme and the signature scheme that it composed from.

Keywords: Attribute-based encryption · Accountability · White-box traceability · Key abuse

1 Introduction

Cloud computing has emerged as a promising enterprise IT architecture which is attracting more and more enterprises and individuals to move their applications and database into the public cloud for remote data sharing or outsourced delegation computation. While the convenient provided by cloud storage, concerns on the privacy of sensitive data are hindering its large scale applications in industry. Encryption before outsourcing has been considered as an essential method to protect privacy from inside and outside attack. However, due to complex key management mechanism and poor

© Springer International Publishing AG 2016
L. Chen and J. Han (Eds.): ProvSec 2016, LNCS 10005, pp. 3–18, 2016.
DOI: 10.1007/978-3-319-47422-9_1

scalability, traditional data encryption cannot meet the requirements for various online applications that own a large amount of users.

To protect the privacy of data shared on a cloud storage platform with fine-grained access control, Sahai and Waters [1] introduced the concept of attribute-based encryption (ABE), which is envisioned as a promising one-to-many public key encryption primitive. Depending on where the access policy is embedded, ABE can be divided into two types: key-policy attribute-based encryption (KP-ABE) and ciphertext-policy attribute-based encryption (CP-ABE). This paper deals with CP-ABE where access policies are embedded into ciphertexts and decryption keys are associated with attributes.

In CP-ABE, a user can decrypt a ciphertext only if the attribute set associated with his/her decryption key satisfies the access structure embedded in the ciphertext. However, due to the fact that an attribute set may be shared by multiple users which means a decryption key may be shared by multiple users, it is difficult to find out who shares decryption privileges to others. Without worrying about being traced, a malicious user is willing to share his decryption key to get illegal profits. On the other hand, a semi-trusted authority may illegally generate and distribute a valid decryption key that associated with an honest user to other unauthorized users.

Thus, the key abuse problem in CP-ABE includes two kinds: illegal key sharing among users and illegal key distribution of a semi-trust authority. To securely deploy an ABE-based access control systems, the property of accountability, which should guarantee that the identity of a shared decryption key can be publicly verified and the authority's misbehavior should be prevented, is essential.

1.1 A Motivating Story

Take a video on demand (VOD) company for example, it employs a cloud storage system and encrypts the database using a CP-ABE scheme before outsourcing. Each user that pays fees for bundles of channels is assigned with attributes, such as {"NBC", "CCTV", "BBC", etc.}. And a user whose attributes satisfy the access policy over the outsourced data could decrypt the ciphertext and get access to the videos in the cloud. A CP-ABE system is enough for this scenario if all the parties are honest. However, for profits a user with attributes {"NBC", "CCTV"} may want to share his decryption key with other unauthorized users; on the other hand, the cloud storage service provider may issue illegal decryption keys that related to an honest user with attributes {"NBC", "CCTV"} to unauthorized users. In such cases, the VOD Company will suffer severe financial loss without effective ways to forbid these two kinds of key abuses. Accountable CP-ABE, in which a third party can publicly trace the identity of a shared decryption key and an auditor can rule that a malicious user or the authority shared the decryption key, rather than a pure CP-ABE scheme is more suitable for such a scenario.

1.2   Our Contribution

In this paper, we propose an accountable CP-ABE scheme, denoted by CP-AABE, with public verifiability and nonrepudiation. The main features of the CP-AABE scheme can be described as follows.

(1) Direct traceability. The identity of a user is embedded into the decryption key which is essential for the decryption process. Thus, the identity is regarded as an essential part of the decryption key, and anybody can easily learn the identity of an exposed decryption key, i.e. the proposed CP-AABE scheme can achieve direct white-box traceability.

(2) Public verifiability. The signature of identity signed by the authority is also embedded into the decryption key. Thus, any third party can easily check whether an exposed decryption key relates to an identity or not by verifying the validity of the authority's signature only with public parameters, i.e. the proposed scheme can provide the property of public verifiability.

(3) Nonrepudiation. The proposed CP-AABE scheme can also provide the property of nonrepudiation that a malicious user or the authority can't deny his/her misbehavior. Based on a short signature of partial decryption key signed by the user, an auditor can check whether a leaked decryption key is shared by a malicious user or illegally distributed by the semi-trust authority.

1.3   Related Works

Since Goyal *et al.* [2] gave the definition and security notions of KP-ABE, many KP-ABE and CP-ABE schemes have been proposed [3–13] aiming at better expressiveness, efficiency or security.

Depending on whether a decryption key or decryption equipment is shared, traceability can be divided into two types: white-box traceability and black-box traceability. In 2013, Liu *et al.* [14] gave a white-box traceable CP-ABE supporting any monotone access structures. Based on the large universe ABE scheme proposed by [10], in 2015 Ning *et al.* [15] gave a white-box traceable CP-ABE supporting flexible attributes. Besides these white-box traceable CP-ABE, in 2011, Li *et al.* [16] gave a multi-authority black-box traceable ABE supporting AND gate with wildcards access policy; in 2013, Liu, Cao and Wong [17] proposed a black-box traceable CP-ABE system which supports any monotone access structures.

Above ABE schemes with white-box traceability or black-box traceability can only trace the identity of an exposed decryption key and can't prove whether it is shared by a malicious user or the central authority. Thus ABE with traceability is still not sufficient for application in industry. In 2009, to prevent key abuse of both user and the central authority, Li *et al.* [18] gave an accountable ABE to prevent illegal key sharing among colluding users supporting AND gate with wildcards access policy. However, we show that it fails to prevent a malicious user to share his/her decryption privileges to others. In 2015, Ning *et al.* [19] proposed an accountable ABE supporting white-box traceability and public auditing based on ZK-POK of the discrete log of a random element

R_U. Owning to no essential binding between the random R_U and a user, a user still can deny the random R_U doesn't belong to him/her.

Another branch of ABE research considers the applications in concrete systems such as cloud computing [20] and personal health record [21]. Recently, Li *et al.* [22] and Li *et al.* [23] proposed two searchable ABE schemes.

In this paper, based on the signature of partial decryption key signed by user and the signature of the identity signed by the authority, we give an accountable CP-ABE scheme with the property of public traceability and nonrepudiation.

1.4   Main Techniques

To realize accountability, the main idea of our construction is to embed undeniable information of both user and the authority into the decryption key. On one hand, to realize public verifiability of user, a signature scheme inspired by [24] is used to embed a signature of user's identity into the decryption key. On the other hand, to achieve nonrepudiation, a signature [25] of partial decryption key signed by user is also embedded into the decryption key. Additional user information embedded in the decryption key will lead to unsuccessful decryption because no user information is included in the ciphertexts. We use the orthogonal property of bilinear pairing in composite order groups to offset the user information embedded in the decryption key.

In detail, the decryption key is in the form of $U,\ \sigma, K = g^s,\ K' = g^{\alpha h}g^{as}$, $K'' = g_2^\beta (u' \prod_{i \in \mu} u_i)^s \sigma^s,\ K_i = H_i^s, \forall att_i \in S$, where $h = H(\sigma, K, U)$, U denotes a user's identity, σ denotes a short signature for K. The purpose of the additional one-way Hash function $h = H(\sigma, K, U)$ is to bind the identity U, signature σ, and partial decryption K together and prevent an adversary from modifying the identity embedded in $K'' = g_2^\beta (u' \prod_{i \in \mu} u_i)^s \sigma^s$ using a random mask.

The orthogonal property of bilinear pairing in composite order groups such that $\forall h_i \in \mathbb{G}_i, h_j \in \mathbb{G}_j, i \neq j,\ e(h_i, h_j) = 1$ is used to offset the identity embedded in the decryption key, such as $K'' = g_2^\beta (u' \prod_{i \in \mu} u_i)^s \sigma^s$, which will never appear in the ciphertexts.

1.5   Organizations

Section 2 introduces the preliminaries, including the linear secret sharing scheme (LSSS), and the CDH assumption in composite order bilinear groups. Section 3 gives the formal definition of CP-AABE with public verifiability and nonrepudiation and its security model. Section 4 gives a concrete construction of CP-AABE. Section 5 gives the security results and performance analyses. Finally, Sect. 6 presents a brief conclusion.

2 Preliminaries

2.1 Linear Secret Sharing Schemes

Definition 1. Let $\mathcal{P}$ be a set of parties and $\mathbb{W}$ be a matrix of size $l \times k$. Let $\rho :$ $\{1, \cdots, l\} \to \mathcal{P}$ be a map that maps a row of $\mathbb{W}$ to a party in $\mathcal{P}$ for labeling. A secret sharing scheme for access structure $(\mathbb{W}, \rho)$ over a set of parties $\mathcal{P}$ is a linear secret sharing scheme, if it consists of following two polynomial-time algorithms.

Share $(\mathbb{W}, \rho)$: inputting a secret $s \in \mathbb{Z}_p$ to be shared, it sets $\vec{v} = (s, y_2, \cdots y_k)$, where $y_2, \cdots y_k \in_R \mathbb{Z}_p$, and it outputs shares $\lambda_{\rho(i)} = \mathbb{W}_i \cdot \vec{v}$ belonging to party $\rho(i)$ for $i = 1$ to l, where $\mathbb{W}_i$ is the i-th row of $\mathbb{W}$.

Recon $(\mathbb{W}, \rho)$: inputting S that satisfies $(\mathbb{W}, \rho)$, it outputs reconstruction constants $\{(i, w_i)\}_{i \in I}$ such that $\sum_{i \in I} w_i \lambda_{\rho(i)} = s$, where $I = \{i | \rho(i) \in S\}$.

2.2 Bilinear Pairings in Composite Order Groups

Let $\mathbb{G}, \mathbb{G}_T$ be two cyclic groups of order $N = p_1 p_2$, where p_1, p_2 are two big primes. A bilinear pairings $e : \mathbb{G} \times \mathbb{G} \to \mathbb{G}_T$ is a map such that: (1) Bilinear: $\forall g, h \in \mathbb{G}$, $a, b \in \mathbb{Z}_N$, $e(g^a, h^b) = e(g, h)^{ab}$. (2) Non-degenerate: $\exists g \in \mathbb{G}$ such that $e(g, g)$ has order N in $\mathbb{G}_T$. (3) e can be efficiently computed.

Note. Let $\mathbb{G}_{p_1}$, $\mathbb{G}_{p_2}$ denote two subgroups of order p_1, p_2 in $\mathbb{G}$. These subgroups are "orthogonal" to each other under the bilinear pairings e, i.e. $\forall h_i \in \mathbb{G}_{p_i}, h_j \in \mathbb{G}_{p_j}, i \neq j$, there is $e(h_i, h_j) = 1_{\mathbb{G}_T}$, where $1_{\mathbb{G}_T}$ is the identity element of $\mathbb{G}_T$.

2.3 CDH Problem in Composite Order Bilinear Group

Let $\mathbb{G}$ be a cyclic group of order $N = p_1 p_2$, $\mathbb{G}_{p_1}$, $\mathbb{G}_{p_2}$ denote two subgroups of order p_1, p_2 in $\mathbb{G}$ and g_1, g_2 denote two random generators of $\mathbb{G}_{p_1}, \mathbb{G}_{p_2}$ respectively, the CDH problem in $\mathbb{G}$ is: input $g_1^c, g_2^c, g_1^d, g_2^d$, where $c, d \in_R \mathbb{Z}_N^*$, output $(g_1 g_2)^{cd}$.

3 Accountable Ciphertext-Policy Attribute-Based Encryption

3.1 Definition

An accountable ciphertext-policy attribute-based encryption scheme, denoted by CP-AABE, consists of following seven polynomial time algorithms.

Setup. Inputting a security parameter λ, the central authority (CA) generates the master secret key *MSK* and system public parameters *PK* including the description of attribute universe $\mathbb{U}$.

sExtract. Inputting system public parameters *PK*, identity U generates a signing secret key x_U and public key P_U, it keeps x_U secretly and publishes public key P_U.

dExtract. Interaction between the CA and user is needed in this algorithm. Given the master key MSK, public parameters PK and an attributes set $S \subseteq \mathbb{U}$ for an identity U, CA generates partial decryption key K for identity U and secretly distributes it to U. U generates a signature σ of K using its signing secret key x_U, and sends σ to CA secretly. At last, CA outputs the full decryption key $SK_{U,S}$.

Encrypt. Inputting public parameters PK, a message M and an access structure $\mathbb{W}$ over $\mathbb{U}$, it outputs a ciphertext $CT_\mathbb{W}$.

Decrypt. Inputting public parameters PK, a decryption key $SK_{U,S}$, and a ciphertext $CT_\mathbb{W}$ along with access structure $\mathbb{W}$, it outputs a plaintext M or a reject symbol $\perp$.

Verify. Inputting public parameters PK and a decryption key $SK_{U,S}$, it outputs an identity U or an invalid symbol $\perp$.

Audit. Inputting public parameters PK, a leaked decryption key $SK_{U,S}$ and a decryption key $SK'_{U,S}$ provided by user U, an auditor returns an identity (U or CA) or a reject symbol $\perp$.

3.2   Security Models for CP-AABE

Confidentiality for ciphertext. The indistinguishability under adaptive chosen plaintext attack in the selective model (denoted by IND-s-CPA), of CP-AABE is defined through the following game between a challenger $\mathcal{C}$ and an adversary $\mathcal{A}$.

Init. $\mathcal{A}$ outputs the target access structure $\mathbb{W}^*$ that will be used to create the challenge ciphertext.

Setup. $\mathcal{C}$ executes the Setup (λ) algorithm, gives the public key PK to $\mathcal{A}$ and keeps the master secret key MSK to itself.

Phase 1. $\mathcal{A}$ is given access to the following oracles which will be simulated by $\mathcal{C}$.

- sExtract oracle: Given an identity U, $\mathcal{C}$ returns secret key x_U to $\mathcal{A}$.
- dExtract oracle: Given an attributes set S and identity U, $\mathcal{C}$ returns $SK_{U,S}$ to $\mathcal{A}$.

Challenge. $\mathcal{A}$ outputs two messages M_0, M_1 of equal length. $\mathcal{C}$ flips a random coin $b \in_R \{0,1\}$ and generates $CT^* \leftarrow \text{Encrypt}(PK, M_b, \mathbb{W}^*)$ for $\mathbb{W}^*$ and M_b. At last, $\mathcal{C}$ returns the challenge ciphertext CT^* to $\mathcal{A}$.

Phase 2. $\mathcal{A}_1$ continues adaptively to make queries as in Phase 1 except the Extract queries for any S satisfying $S \in \mathbb{W}^*$, and Decrypt oracle queries for CT^* with any $\mathbb{W}$ satisfying $\mathbb{W}^* \subset \mathbb{W}$. $\mathcal{C}$ returns corresponding answers as in Phase 1.

Guess. $\mathcal{A}$ outputs a guess bit $b' \in \{0,1\}$ and wins the game if $b' = b$. The advantage of $\mathcal{A}$ is defined to be $Adv(\mathcal{A}) = |\Pr[b' = b] - 1/2|$.

Public verifiability for the identity of a decryption key (dishonest user game)

The public verifiability for identity of a decryption key of CP-AABE is defined through following game between a challenger C and an adversary A.

Setup. C executes the Setup (λ) algorithm, gives the public key PK to A and keeps the master secret key MSK to itself.

Query Phase. A is allowed to make polynomial time of sExtract and dExtract queries.

- sExtract oracle: Given an identity U, C returns secret key x_U to A.
- dExtract oracle: Given an attributes set S and identity U, C returns $SK_{U,S}$ to A.

Forgery Phase. A outputs a decryption key SK_{U^*,S^*} for some U^*, S^*. A wins if SK_{U^*,S^*} can pass through the verify algorithm and SK_{U^*,S^*} isn't from a dExtract query on S^*, U^*. The advantage of A is defined as $Adv(A) = \Pr[A \, wins]$.

Nonrepudiation for a decryption key (dishonest authority game)

The nonrepudiation for a decryption key in CP-AABE is defined by following game between a challenger C and an adversary A.

Setup. C executes the Setup (λ) algorithm, gives the public key PK to A and keeps the master secret key MSK to itself.

Query Phase. A is allowed to make polynomial sExtract and dExtract queries.

- sExtract oracle: Given an identity U, C returns secret key x_U to A.
- dExtract oracle: Given an attributes set S and identity U, C returns $SK_{U,S}$ to A.

Forgery Phase. A outputs a decryption key SK_{U^*,S^*} for some U^*, S^*. A is not allowed to make a sExtract query for U^*. A wins if SK_{U^*,S^*} can pass through the audit algorithm. The advantage of A is defined as $Adv(A) = \Pr[A \, wins]$.

4 A Concrete CP-AABE Construction

Setup: Given a security parameter λ, CA selects two cyclic groups $\mathbb{G}, \mathbb{G}_T$ of order $N = p_1 p_2$, where p_1, p_2 are two distinct primes; CA selects a random generator g of $\mathbb{G}_{p_1}$, where $\mathbb{G}_{p_1}$ is a subgroup of order p_1 in $\mathbb{G}$; CA chooses a bilinear pairings $e : \mathbb{G} \times \mathbb{G} \to \mathbb{G}_T$. For each attribute $att_i \in \mathbb{U}$, CA chooses $h_i \in_R \mathbb{Z}_N^*$ and sets $H_i = g^{h_i}$. CA chooses $\alpha, a \in_R \mathbb{Z}_{p_1}^*, \beta \in_R \mathbb{Z}_{p_2}^*, g_2 \in_R \mathbb{G}_{p_2}, u' \in_R \mathbb{G}_{p_1}$ and a n_u-dimensional vector $\mathbb{V} = (u_i)_{n_u}$, where $u_i \in_R \mathbb{G}_{p_1}$ and $n_u \in \mathbb{Z}_N$ is the bit length of identity; CA chooses two secure Hash functions $G : \mathbb{G}_{p_1} \times \mathbb{G}_{p_1} \to \mathbb{G}_{p_1}, H : \mathbb{G}_{p_1} \times \mathbb{G}_{p_1} \times \{0, 1\}^* \to \mathbb{Z}_{p_1}^*$. At last, CA keeps $MSK = (g^\alpha, \beta)$ secretly as the master key, and publishes system public key: $PK = (\mathbb{G}, \mathbb{G}_T, N, e, g, g_2, g^a, e(g, g)^\alpha, e(g_2, g_2)^\beta, u', \mathbb{V}, \{H_i = g^{h_i}, \forall att_i \in \mathbb{U}\}, G, H)$.

sExtract: Identity U randomly chooses $x_U \in_R \mathbb{Z}_N$ as his private key, and computes $P_U = g^{x_U}$ as his public key.

dExtract: Let U be a bit string of length n_u representing an identity id and $u[i]$ denote the i-th bit of U. Let $\mu \subset \{1, \cdots, n_u\}$ be the set of indices i such that $u[i] = 1$. The full decryption key $SK_{U,S} = (U, \sigma, K, K', K'', \{K_i : \forall att_i \in S\})$ of identity U with attributes S can be generated as follows.

- CA chooses $s \in_R \mathbb{Z}_N$ and computes $K = g^s$; if $K = g^s$ hasn't been issued for identity U, CA secretly sends K to identity U.
- Receiving K, U computes a short signature $\sigma = G(K, P_U)^{x_U}$ and sends σ to CA secretly.
- CA verifies the validity of σ by $e(\sigma, g) = e(G(K, P_U), P_U)$. If it holds, CA computes $K' = g^{\alpha h} g^{as}$, $K'' = g_2^\beta (u' \prod_{i \in \mu} u_i)^s \sigma^s$, $K_i = H_i^s, \forall att_i \in S$, where $h = H(\sigma, K, U)$.

Encrypt: Given a plaintext $M \in \mathbb{G}_T$ and an access structure $(\mathbb{W}, \rho)$, where $\mathbb{W}$ is a $l \times k$ matrix and ρ is a map from each row $\mathbb{W}_j$ of $\mathbb{W}$ to an attribute $att_{\rho(j)}$. The ciphertext $CT_{(\mathbb{W}, \rho)} = (C, C', C'', \{C_i, D_i\}_{i \in [l]})$ can be generated as follows.

- randomly chooses a vector $\vec{v} = (r, y_2, \cdots, y_k) \in_R (\mathbb{Z}_N^*)^k$, and $r_1, \cdots, r_l \in_R \mathbb{Z}_N^*$;
- computes $C = M \cdot e(g, g)^{\alpha r} \cdot e(g_2, g_2)^{\beta r}$, $C' = g^r$, $C'' = g g_2^r$;
- for $i = 1$ to l, computes $\lambda_i = \mathbb{W}_i \cdot \vec{v}$, $C_i = g^{a\lambda_i} H_{\rho(i)}^{-r_i}, D_i = g^{r_i}$.

Decrypt: Given $CT_{(\mathbb{W}, \rho)}$, a user U with attributes set S' that satisfies the access structure $(\mathbb{W}, \rho)$ can get $\{\omega_i : i \in I\}$ such that $\sum_{i \in I} \omega_i \mathbb{W}_i = (1, 0, \ldots, 0)_k$, where $I = \{i : att_{\rho(i)} \in S'\}$, and then it retrieves the message as follows.

$$M = C\left(\frac{(\prod_{i \in I_e} e(C_i, K)e(D_i, K_{\rho(i)}))^{\frac{\omega_i}{h}} e(K, (u' \prod_{i \in \mu} u_i)\sigma)}{e(C', K')^{\frac{1}{h}} e(C'', K'')}\right), \text{ where } h = H(\sigma, K, U),$$

Verify: Given a decryption key $SK_{U,S} = (U, \sigma, K, K', K'', \{K_i : \forall att_i \in S\})$ and public parameters PK, any third party can verify whether $SK_{U,S}$ associates with U or not as follows.

- checks equations $e(K'', g) = e(K, (u' \prod_{i \in \mu} u_i)\sigma)$, $e(K'', g_2) = e(g_2, g_2)^\beta$ and $e(K', g) = e(g, g)^{\alpha h} e(g^a, K)$ hold or not, where $h = H(\sigma, K, U)$. If one of them doesn't hold, returns a reject symbol $\bot$;
- else, lets $S' \subset S$ denote the set of attributes that satisfy $e(K_i, g) = e(K, H_i)$. If S' is empty, then returns a reject symbol $\bot$; else returns the identity U that $SK_{U,S'} = (U, \sigma, K, K', K'', \{K_i : \forall att_i \in S'\})$ related to.

Audit: If identity U denies the ownership of $SK_{U,S'}$ which could pass the Public verify algorithm.

- an auditor checks whether the equation $e(\sigma, g) = e(G(K, P_U), P_U)$ holds or not, if it doesn't hold, returns a reject symbol $\perp$;
- else, identity U is asked to submit his decryption key $SK'_{U,S} = (U, \sigma, K, \tilde{K}', \tilde{K}'', \{\tilde{K}_i : \forall att_i \in S\}) = (U, \sigma, K, \tilde{K}', \tilde{K}'', \{\tilde{K}_i : \forall att_i \in S\})$ that is related to K. The auditor runs the verify algorithm to check whether $SK'_{U,S}$ associates with U or not. If so, the auditor ruled that $SK_{U,S'}$ is illegally distributed by CA; else, ruled that $SK_{U,S'}$ is shared by U.

5   Discussion

5.1   Security Results

The proposed CP-AABE scheme can be proved IND-s-CPA secure based on the security of the atomic CP-ABE scheme [6] by Theorem 1, and can provide the public verifiability based on the unforgeability of the atomic signature scheme [24] in Theorem 2, and can provide nonrepudiation based on the unforgeability of a short signature [25] by Theorem 3

Theorem 1. *If there is an adversary $\mathcal{A}$ that can break IND-s-CPA security of the CP-AABE scheme with advantage ε, there will be an adversary $\mathcal{A}_1$ with the same advantage ε that can break the encryption scheme proposed by B. Waters [6].*

Proof. We will prove that an adversary $\mathcal{A}_1$ against BW-CPABE can be used to construct an adversary $\mathcal{A}$ against CP-AABE as follows, the challenger $\mathcal{C}$ needs to simulate the queries from $\mathcal{A}$ or $\mathcal{A}_1$.

Setup. $\mathcal{C}$ selects two cyclic groups $\mathbb{G}_{p_2}, \mathbb{G}_{T_2}$ of prime order p_2, a generator h of $\mathbb{G}_{p_2}$; $\mathcal{C}$ chooses an efficient bilinear pairings $e_2 : \mathbb{G}_{p_2} \times \mathbb{G}_{p_2} \to \mathbb{G}_{T_2}$; $\mathcal{C}$ chooses $\beta \in_R \mathbb{Z}^*_{p_2}$, $g_2 \in_R \mathbb{G}_{p_2}$. $\mathcal{C}$ chooses $u' \in_R \mathbb{G}_{p_1}$ and a vector $\mathbb{V} = (u_i)_{n_u}$ where $u_i \in_R \mathbb{G}_{p_1}$, $n_u \in \mathbb{Z}_N$ is the bit length of an identity U. $\mathcal{C}$ also gets the public parameters $(\mathbb{G}_{p_1}, \mathbb{G}_{T_1}, p_1,$ $e_1, g, e_1(g, g)^\alpha, g^a, \{H_i = g^{h_i}, \forall att_i \in \mathbb{U}_e\})$ of scheme BW-CPABE generated by running the Setup algorithm of BW-CPABE. Then $\mathcal{C}$ sets $N = p_1 p_2$, $\mathbb{G} = \mathbb{G}_{p_1} \otimes \mathbb{G}_{p_2}$, $\mathbb{G}_T = \mathbb{G}_{T_1} \otimes \mathbb{G}_{T_2}$, $e = e_1 \circ e_2 : \mathbb{G} \times \mathbb{G} \to \mathbb{G}_T$ such that $e(PQ, P'Q') = e_1(P, P') \cdot e_2(Q, Q')$ for $\forall P, P' \in \mathbb{G}_{p_1}, Q, Q' \in \mathbb{G}_{p_2}$. $\mathcal{C}$ chooses two hash functions: $G : \mathbb{G}_{p_1} \times \mathbb{G}_{p_1} \to \mathbb{G}_{p_1}$, $H : \mathbb{G}_{p_1} \times \mathbb{G}_{p_1} \times \mathbb{G}_{p_1} \to \mathbb{Z}^*_{p_1}$. $\mathcal{C}$ gives $PK = (\mathbb{G}, \mathbb{G}_T, N, e, g,$ $g_2, e(g, g)^\alpha, e(g_2, g_2)^\beta, g^a, u', \mathbb{V}, \{H_i = g^{h_i}, \forall att_i \in \mathbb{U}\}, G, H)$ to $\mathcal{A}$ and keeps α, β secretly. $\mathcal{C}$ also gives $(\mathbb{G}_{p_1}, \mathbb{G}_{T_1}, p_1, e_1, g, e_1(g, g)^\alpha, g^a, \{H_i = g^{h_i}, \forall att_i \in \mathbb{U}_e\})$ to $\mathcal{A}_1$.

Phase 1. $\mathcal{A}_1$ is given access to the following oracle which will be simulated by $\mathcal{C}$.

- dExtract oracle: Given a set of attributes set $S \subset \mathbb{U}$ with $U = u' \prod_{i \in \mu} u_i$ from $\mathcal{A}_1$, $\mathcal{C}$

first generates $SK_{U,S} = (U, \sigma, K, K', K'', \{K_i : \forall att_i \in S\})$ by running the dExtract algorithm and returns $\bar{K} = K$, $\bar{K}' = K' g^{\alpha - \alpha h}$, $\bar{K}_i = K_i, \forall att_i \in S$, where $h = H(\sigma, K, U)$ to $\mathcal{A}_1$.

Challenge. $\mathcal{A}_1$ outputs two messages M_0, M_1 of equal length along with target access structure $\mathbb{W}^*$, $\mathcal{C}$ flips a random coin $b \in_R \{0, 1\}$, and generates the ciphertext $CT_{(\mathbb{W}^*, \rho)} = (C, C', C'', \{C_i, D_i\}_{i \in [l]})$ of M_b by running the Encrypt algorithm and $\mathcal{C}$ returns $\bar{CT}_{(\mathbb{W}^*, \rho)} = (\bar{C} = \frac{C}{e(g_2, g_2)^{\beta r}}, \bar{C}' = C', \bar{C}_i = C_i, \bar{D}_i = D_i)$ to $\mathcal{A}_1$.

Phase 2. $\mathcal{A}_1$ continues adaptively to make queries as in Phase 1 except the Extract queries for any S satisfying $S \in \mathbb{W}^*$, and Decrypt oracle queries for CT^* with any $\mathbb{W}$ satisfying $\mathbb{W}^* \subset \mathbb{W}$. $\mathcal{C}$ returns corresponding answers as in Phase 1.

Guess. $\mathcal{A}$ outputs b', then $\mathcal{A}_1$ also outputs b'.

As can be seen from above simulation, a challenger $\mathcal{C}$ can indistinguishably simulate all the queries asked from $\mathcal{A}_1$. Thus, if there is an adversary $\mathcal{A}$ that has advantage ε to have a correct guess $b' = b$ then, $\mathcal{A}_1$ similarly has advantage ε to break the BW-CPABE scheme.

Theorem 2. *If adversary $\mathcal{A}$ against the CP-AABE, which makes at most q_e dExtract oracle queries, can generate a forged decryption key with advantage ε, there is a challenger $\mathcal{C}$ can solve the CDH problem in the composite order group with advantage at least:* $\frac{1}{4q_e(n_u+1)}\varepsilon$.

Proof. The public verifiability of CP-AABE is based on the unforgeability of the signature of identity embedded in the decryption key. We will prove that a more general signature scheme is unforgeable, and the signature scheme used in CP-AABE is one of its special cases.

Setup. Given a security parameter λ, CA selects two cyclic groups $\mathbb{G}, \mathbb{G}_T$ of order $N = p_1 p_2$, where p_1, p_2 are two distinct primes; CA selects two random generators g, g' of $\mathbb{G}_{p_1}, \mathbb{G}_{p_2}$ respectively, where $\mathbb{G}_{p_1}, \mathbb{G}_{p_2}$ are subgroups of order p_1, p_2 in $\mathbb{G}$; CA chooses an efficient bilinear pairings $e : \mathbb{G} \times \mathbb{G} \to \mathbb{G}_T$. For each $att_i \in \mathbb{U}$, CA chooses $h_i \in_R \mathbb{Z}_N^*$ randomly and sets $H_i = g^{h_i}$. CA chooses $\alpha, a, \beta \in_R \mathbb{Z}_N^*$, $g_1, u' \in_R \mathbb{G}_{p_1}$, $g_2, v' \in_R \mathbb{G}_{p_2}$ and two vectors $\mathbb{V}_1 = (u_i)_{n_u} \in (\mathbb{G}_{p_1})^{n_u}, \mathbb{V}_2 = (v_i)_{n_u} \in (\mathbb{G}_{p_2})^{n_u}$, where n_u denotes the bit length of identity U. CA chooses a secure hash function $H : \mathbb{G}_{p_1} \times \mathbb{G}_{p_1} \times \mathbb{G}_{p_1} \to \mathbb{Z}_N^*$. The master key $MSK = g^\alpha, (g_1 g_2)^\beta, a$, the system public key is: $PK = (\mathbb{G}, \mathbb{G}_T, N, e, g, g', g_1, g_2, e(g, g)^\alpha, e(g_1, g)^\beta, e(g_2, g')^\beta, g^a, u', v', \mathbb{V}_1, \mathbb{V}_2, \{H_i, \forall att_i \in \mathbb{U}\}, H)$.

Sign. Let $u[i]$ denote the i-th bit of U and $\mu \subset \{1, \cdots, n_u\}$ be the set of indices i such that $u[i] = 1$. To generate the decryption key $SK_{U,S}$ of U with attributes set S, it randomly chooses $s \in_R \mathbb{Z}_N, \sigma \in_R \mathbb{G}_{p_1}$, and computes:

$$K = g^s g'^s, \quad K' = g^{\alpha h} g^{as}, \quad K'' = (g_1 g_2)^\beta (u'v' \prod_{i \in \mu} u_i v_i)^s \sigma^s, \quad K_i = H_i^s, \forall att_i \in S, \text{ where}$$

$h = H(\sigma, K, U)$.

Verify. Given a signature $SK_{U,S}$ of identity U with attributes S, any party can verify its validity as follows.

$$e(K'', g) = e(g_1, g)^\beta e(K, (u' \prod_{i \in \mu} u_i)\sigma), e(K'', g') = e(g_2, g')^\beta e(K, v' \prod_{i \in \mu} v_i),$$

$$e(K', g) = e(g, g)^{\alpha h} e(g^a, K), e(K_i, g) = e(K, H_i), \forall att_i \in S.$$

If $g_1 = 1_{\mathbb{G}_{p_1}}, v' = v_i = g' = 1_{\mathbb{G}_{p_2}}$, it is the same as that in CP-AABE.

The unforgeability of above signature is based on the CDH problem in composite order bilinear groups. Let $g, g', g^c, g'^c, g^d, g'^d$, where $c, d \in_R \mathbb{Z}_N^*$, is a CDH instance in $\mathbb{G}$, the challenger $\mathcal{C}$ tries to compute $(gg')^{cd}$.

Setup. $\mathcal{C}$ sets $l_u = 2q_e$, chooses an integer k_u such that $0 \le k_u \le n_u, l_u(n_u + 1) < N$. $\mathcal{C}$ chooses $x' \in_R \mathbb{Z}_{l_u}^*$ and a vector $\mathbb{V}_x = (x_i)$ of length $n_u \in \mathbb{Z}_N$, with $x_i \in_R \mathbb{Z}_{l_u}$ for all i. $\mathcal{C}$ chooses $y' \in_R \mathbb{Z}_{l_u}^*$ and a vector $\mathbb{V}_y = (y_i)$ of length $n_u \in \mathbb{Z}_N$, with $y_i \in_R \mathbb{Z}_N$ for all i. $\mathcal{C}$ sets $u' = (g_1)^{-l_u k_u + x'} g^{y'}, u_i = (g_1)^{x_i} g^{y_i}, v' = (g_2)^{-l_u k_u + x'} (g')^{y'}, v_i = (g_2)^{x_i} (g')^{y_i}, g_1 g_2 = (gg')^c, (gg')^\beta = (gg')^d$. The system public key $PK = (\mathbb{G}, \mathbb{G}_T, N, e, g, g', g_1, g_2, e(g, g)^\alpha, e(g_1, g^d), e(g_2, g'^d), g^a, u', v', \mathbb{V}_1, \mathbb{V}_2, \{H_i, \forall att_i \in \mathbb{U}\})$. The master secret key is $g^\alpha, (gg')^{cd}, a$. $\mathcal{C}$ sends public parameters to $\mathcal{A}$.

For simplicity, two functions are defined: $F(U) = x' + \prod_{i \in \mu} x_i - l_u k_u, J(U) = y' + \prod_{i \in \mu} y_i$. Then $(u'v' \prod_{i \in \mu} u_i v_i) = (g_1 g_2)^{F(U)} (gg')^{J(U)}$.

Extract queries. $\mathcal{C}$ does as follows without knowing $(gg')^{cd}$.

- If $F(U) \ne 0 \mod N$, $\mathcal{C}$ can choose $r_u, r_\sigma \in_R \mathbb{Z}_N^*$ and compute:

$$K = ((gg')^c)^{-1/F(U)} (gg')^{r_u}, K' = g^{\alpha h} ((g)^c)^{-\frac{a}{F(U)}} g^{ar_u},$$

$$K'' = ((gg')^c)^{-\frac{J(U)}{F(U)}} (u'v' \prod_{i \in \mu} u_i v_i)^{r_u} g^{cr_\sigma} g^{\frac{-r_\sigma}{F(U)}},$$

$$K_i = ((g)^c)^{-h_i/F(U)} g^{h_i r_u}, \text{ where, } h = H(\sigma, K, U)$$

It can be verified that $SK_{U,S}$ generated in such a way is valid and is indistinguishable from the keys generated by a true challenger to adversary $\mathcal{A}$, since

$$K = ((gg')^c)^{-1/F(U)} (gg')^{r_u} = (gg')^{r_u - c/F(U)}$$

$$K' = g^{\alpha h} ((g)^c)^{-a/F(U)} g^{ar_u} = g^{\alpha h} (g^a)^{r_u - c/F(U)}$$

$$K'' = ((gg')^c)^{\frac{-J(U)}{F(U)}} (u'v' \prod_{i \in \mu} u_i v_i)^{r_u} g^{r_u r_\sigma} (g^c)^{\frac{-r_\sigma}{F(U)}}$$

$$= (g_1 g_2)^c (u'v' \prod_{i \in \mu} u_i v_i)^{r_u - \frac{c}{F(U)}} (g^{r_\sigma})^{r_u - \frac{c}{F(U)}}$$

$$K_i = ((g)^c)^{-h_i/F(U)} g^{h_i r_u} = (g^{h_i})^{r_u - c/F(U)}$$

- If $F(U) = 0 \mod N$, $\mathcal{C}$ will abort.

Because the assumption $l_u(n_u + 1) < N$ implies $0 \leq l_u k_u < N$ and $0 \leq x' + \prod\limits_{i \in \mu} x_i < N$,

then $F(U) = 0 \mod N$ implies that $F(U) = 0 \mod l_u$. To make the analysis of the simulation easier, $\mathcal{C}$ will abort whenever $F(U) = 0 \mod l_u$. Hence, $F(U) \neq 0 \mod l_u$ implies $F(U) \neq 0 \mod N$, so $F(U) \neq 0 \mod l_u$ will be a sufficient requirement to ensure that a private key for U can be constructed.

Forgery. If $\mathcal{C}$ does not abort, $\mathcal{A}$ will with probability at least ε return an identity U^*, and a valid forgery SK_{U^*,S^*}. If $F(U^*) \neq 0 \mod N$, $\mathcal{C}$ will abort; else $F(U^*) = 0 \mod N$, $\mathcal{C}$ computes the solution to the given CDH problem as follows.

$$\frac{K''}{(K)^{J(U^*)}} = \frac{(g_1 g_2)^c (u'v' \prod\limits_{i \in \mu} u_i v_i)^{r_u} \sigma^{r_u}}{(gg')^{r_u \cdot J(U^*)} \sigma^{r_u}} = (gg')^{cd}.$$

For the simulation without aborting, all q_e identities of dExtract query should satisfy $F(U) \neq 0 \mod l_u$, and the challenged identity U^* should satisfy $F(U^*) = 0 \mod N$.

Let $U_1, \cdots U_{q_e}$ be the identities appearing in dExtract queries except the challenge identity U^*. Define events $A_i, A^*, i = 1, \cdots, q_e$ as $A_i : F(U_i) \neq 0 \mod l_u$, $A^* : F(U^*) = 0 \mod N$. Then:

$$\Pr[A^*] = \Pr[F(U^*) = 0 \mod N]$$

$$= \Pr[F(U^*) = 0 \mod l_u] \Pr[F(U^*) = 0 \mod N | F(U^*) = 0 \mod l_u] = \frac{1}{l_u} \frac{1}{n_u + 1}$$

$$\Pr[\bigcap_{i=1}^{q_e} A_i | A^*] = 1 - \Pr[\bigcup_{i=1}^{q_e} \neg A_i | A^*] \geq 1 - \sum_{i=1}^{q_e} \Pr[\neg A_i | A^*] \geq 1 - \frac{q_e}{l_u} = \frac{1}{2}$$

Thus:

$$\Pr[\neg abort] = \Pr[\bigcap_{i=1}^{q_e} A_i \cap A^*] = \Pr[\bigcap_{i=1}^{q_e} A_i | A^*] \Pr[A^*] \geq \frac{1}{2} \frac{1}{l_u} \frac{1}{n_u + 1} = \frac{1}{4q_e(n_u + 1)}$$

If the simulation doesn't abort, $\mathcal{A}$ will generate a valid forgery on identity U^* with probability at least ε. Then $\mathcal{C}$ can compute $(gg')^{cd}$ with advantage at least $\frac{\varepsilon}{4q_e(n_u + 1)}$.

Theorem 3. *Based on the unforgeability of the short signature scheme [25], the proposed CP-AABE can provide nonrepudiation.*

Proof. From Theorem 2, an auditor can prove that a leaked decryption key $SK_{U,S} = (U, \sigma, K, K', K'', \{K_i : \forall att_i \in S\})$ relates to identity U. Then, the auditor needs to show whether $SK_{U,S}$ is issued by CA or shared by U. If U denies sharing $SK_{U,S}$, the auditor will ask U to submit his/her decryption key. To prove its innocence, U submits $S\bar{K}_{U,S} = (U, \sigma, K, \bar{K}', \bar{K}'', \{\bar{K}_i : \forall att_i \in S\})$ to the auditor. The auditor checks whether $S\bar{K}_{U,S}$ can pass through the verify algorithm. If it does, the auditor will rule that $SK_{U,S}$ is illegally distributed by CA owing to the one-time use of K. Otherwise, if U can't provide such a decryption key, he can't deny his misbehavior based on the unforgeability of U's short signature of K.

5.2   Comparison

In Table 1, we give the comparison between CP-AABE and related ABE schemes [14, 15, 18, 19]. Firstly, the scheme [14, 15] can't support public verifiability because the relationship between the random elements embedded into decryption key and identity can't be publicly verified; the scheme [18] cannot support white-box traceability as they claimed. A malicious user can easily mask his decryption key such as $d_0' = g_2^{\alpha}(u_0^{ID+ID'} u_0^{H(L_1)} \cdots u_0^{H(L_n)} g_3)^r$, $d_1' = g^r$, $d_2' = ID + ID'$, $d_3' = [L_1, \cdots L_n]$ using a random identity ID'. Clearly, the masked decryption keys have the same decryption privileges with original decryption keys. Secondly, in the scheme [14–19], a user can deny that a shared decryption key belongs to him/her because there isn't any evidence that can prove the leaked decryption key isn't illegally distributed by the authority. Thus, the proposed CP-AABE scheme is the only scheme that can simultaneously support public verifiability and nonrepudiation.

Table 1. Features comparison with other related works

Scheme	White-box trace	Public verify	Nonrepudiation	Access structure	Security
[18]	×	×	×	AND	Selective
[14]	✓	×	×	LSSS	Selective
[15]	✓	×	×	LSSS	Selective
[19]	✓	✓	×	LSSS	Full
CP-AABE	✓	✓	✓	LSSS	Selective

At below, $|U|$ denotes the size of attribute universe; $|S|$ denotes the size of attribute set of a decryption key; $|I|$ denotes the size of attribute set involved in decryption; l denotes the row number of an LSSS matrix; $|V_{ID}|$ denotes the size of identities set in the system; n_u denotes the bit length of an identity; n_p denotes the bit length of an element in group $\mathbb{Z}_p$; n_k denotes the bit length of the secret key of a symmetric cryptography used in [15].

In Table 2, We give the storage cost comparison between CP-AABE and related ABE schemes [14, 15, 19] in terms of length of public key (denoted by PKL), the length of decryption key (denoted by SKL), the length of ciphertext (denoted by CTL)

Table 2. Storage cost comparison with other related works

Scheme	PKL($\mathbb{G}$)	SKL($\mathbb{G}$)	CTL($\mathbb{G}$)	PVL(bit)
[14]	$|U|+4$	$|S|+4$	$2l+3$	$|V_{ID}|(n_u+1)$
[15]	7	$2|S|+4$	$3l+3$	$2(t-1)n_p+2n_k$
[19]	$|U|+6$	$|S|+4$	$2l+5$	0
CP-AABE	$|U|+7$	$|S|+5$	$2l+3$	0

and the storage cost of public verifiability (denoted by PVL) which doesn't include the storage cost of public parameters.

In Table 3, we give the efficiency comparison between CP-AABE and related ABE schemes [14, 15, 19] in terms of pairings computation during decryption (denoted by DE), white-box traceability (denoted by WT), public verifiability (denoted by PV) and nonrepudiation (denoted by NR) stage.

Table 3. Efficiency comparison with other related works

Scheme	DE(e)	WT(e)	PV(e)	NR(e)
[14]	$2|I|+1$	$2|S|+4$	-	-
[15]	$3|I|+1$	$4|S|+4$	-	-
[19]	$2|I|+3$	$2|S|+6$	$2|S|+6$	-
CP-AABE	$2|I|+3$	$|S|+3$	$|S|+3$	$2(|S|+3)$

6   Conclusion

In this paper, we propose an accountable ABE scheme supporting public verifiability and nonrepudiation. The identity related to an exposed decryption key can be publicly verified only with the system parameters. A malicious user cannot deny if he/she shared his/her decryption privileges for profits. The authority also cannot deny if he/she illegally issued a decryption key for unauthorized user. We prove that the proposed CP-AABE scheme is IND-s-CPA secure in the standard model.

Acknowledgment. This work was supported in part by China Postdoctoral Science Foundation 2016M591629, in part by the National Natural Science Foundation of China under Grant 61373154, 61371083, 61411146001, 6163000206 and 6160060473, in part by the Prioritized Development Projects through the Specialized Research Fund for the Doctoral Program of Higher Education of China under Grant 20130073130004, in part by Shanghai High-tech field project under Grant 16511101400, and in part by Natural Science Foundation of Shanghai under Grant 16ZR1409200. The authors would like to thank the anonymous reviewers of this paper for their valuable comments and suggestions.

References

1. Sahai, A., Waters, B.: Fuzzy identity-based encryption. In: Cramer, R. (ed.) EUROCRYPT 2005. LNCS, vol. 3494, pp. 457–473. Springer, Heidelberg (2005)
2. Goyal, V., Pandey, O., Sahai, A., Waters, B.: Attribute-based encryption for fine grained access control of encrypted data. In: Proceedings of the 13th ACM Conference on Computer and Communications Security, pp. 89–98. ACM (2006)
3. Ostrovsky, R., Sahai, A., Waters, B.: Attribute-based encryption with non-monotonic access structures. In: Proceedings of ACM Conference on Computer and Communication Security, pp. 195–203. ACM (2007)
4. Cheung, L., Newport, C.: Provably secure ciphertext-policy ABE. In: Proceedings of ACM Conference on Computer and Communication Security, pp. 456–465. ACM Press (2007)
5. Lewko, A., Okamoto, T., Sahai, A., Takashima, K., Waters, B.: Fully secure functional encryption: attribute-based encryption and (hierarchical) inner product encryption. In: Gilbert, H. (ed.) EUROCRYPT 2010. LNCS, vol. 6110, pp. 62–91. Springer, Heidelberg (2010)
6. Waters, B.: Ciphertext-policy attribute-based encryption: an expressive, efficient, and provably secure realization. In: Catalano, D., Fazio, N., Gennaro, R., Nicolosi, A. (eds.) PKC 2011. LNCS, vol. 6571, pp. 53–70. Springer, Heidelberg (2011)
7. Lewko, A., Waters, B.: New proof methods for attribute-based encryption: achieving full security through selective techniques. In: Safavi-Naini, R., Canetti, R. (eds.) CRYPTO 2012. LNCS, vol. 7417, pp. 180–198. Springer, Heidelberg (2012)
8. Garg, S., Gentry, C., Halevi, S., Sahai, A., Waters, B.: Attribute-based encryption for circuits from multilinear maps. In: Canetti, R., Garay, J.A. (eds.) CRYPTO 2013, Part II. LNCS, vol. 8043, pp. 479–499. Springer, Heidelberg (2013)
9. Hohenberger, S., Waters, B.: Attribute-based encryption with fast decryption. In: Kurosawa, K., Hanaoka, G. (eds.) PKC 2013. LNCS, vol. 7778, pp. 162–179. Springer, Heidelberg (2013)
10. Rouselakis, Y., Waters, B.: Practical constructions and new proof methods for large universe attribute-based encryption. In: Proceedings of the 2013 ACM SIGSAC Conference on Computer and Communications Security, pp. 463–474. ACM Press (2013)
11. Hohenberger, S., Waters, B.: Online/Offline attribute-based encryption. In: Krawczyk, H. (ed.) PKC 2014. LNCS, vol. 8383, pp. 293–310. Springer, Heidelberg (2014)
12. Horváth, M.: Attribute-based encryption optimized for cloud computing. In: Italiano, G.F., Margaria-Steffen, T., Pokorný, J., Quisquater, J.-J., Wattenhofer, R. (eds.) SOFSEM 2015-Testing. LNCS, vol. 8939, pp. 566–577. Springer, Heidelberg (2015)
13. Qin, B., Deng, H., Wu, Q., et al.: Flexible attribute-based encryption applicable to secure e-healthcare records. Int. J. Inf. Secur. **14**(6), 499–511 (2015)
14. Liu, Z., Cao, Z., Wong, D.: White-box traceable ciphertext-policy attribute-based encryption supporting any monotone access structures. IEEE Trans. Inf. Forensics Secur. **8**(1), 76–88 (2013)
15. Ning, J., Dong, X., Cao, Z., et al.: White-box traceable ciphertext-policy attribute-based encryption supporting flexible attributes. IEEE Trans. Inf. Forensics Secur. **10**(6), 1274–1288 (2015)
16. Li, J., Huang, Q., Chen, X., Chow, S., Wong, D., Xie, D.: Multi-authority ciphertext-policy attribute-based encryption with accountability. In: Proceedings of the 6th ACM Symposium Information, Computer and Communication Security, pp. 386–390. ACM Press (2011)

17. Liu, Z., Cao, Z., Wong, D.: Black-box traceable CP-ABE: how to catch people leaking their keys by selling decryption devices on ebay. In: Proceedings of the ACM SIGSAC Conference on Computer and Communications Security, pp. 475–486. ACM Press (2013)

18. Li, J., Ren, K., Kim, K.: A2BE: Accountable attribute-based encryption for abuse free access control. IACR Cryptology ePrint Archive, 2009:118

19. Ning, J., Dong, X., Cao, Z., Wei, L.: Accountable authority ciphertext-policy attribute-based encryption with white-box traceability and public auditing in the cloud. In: Pernul, G., et al. (eds.) ESORICS. LNCS, vol. 9327, pp. 270–289. Springer, Heidelberg (2015). doi:10.1007/978-3-319-24177-7_14

20. Li, J., Yao, W., Zhang, Y., Qian, H., Han, J.: Flexible and fine-grained attribute-based data storage in cloud computing. IEEE Trans. Serv. Comput. doi:10.1109/TSC.2016.2520932

21. Qian, H., Li, J., Zhang, Y., Han, J.: Privacy preserving personal health record using multi-authority attribute-based encryption with revocation. Int. J. Inf. Secur. **14**(6), 487–497 (2015)

22. Li, J., Shi, Y., Zhang, Y.: Searchable ciphertext-policy attribute-based encryption with revocation in cloud storage. Int. J. Commun. Syst. doi:10.1002/dac.2942

23. Li, J., Lin, X., Zhang Y., Han, J.: KSF-OABE: outsourced attribute-based encryption with keyword search function for cloud storage. IEEE Trans. Service Comput. doi:10.1109/TSC.2016.2542813

24. Paterson, K.G., Schuldt, J.C.: Efficient identity-based signatures secure in the standard model. In: Batten, L.M., Safavi-Naini, R. (eds.) ACISP 2006. LNCS, vol. 4058, pp. 207–222. Springer, Heidelberg (2006)

25. Boneh, D., Lynn, B., Shacham, H.: Short signatures from the weil pairing. In: Boyd, C. (ed.) ASIACRYPT 2001. LNCS, vol. 2248, pp. 514–532. Springer, Heidelberg (2001)

An Efficient and Expressive Ciphertext-Policy Attribute-Based Encryption Scheme with Partially Hidden Access Structures

Hui Cui[1(✉)], Robert H. Deng[1], Guowei Wu[1], and Junzuo Lai[2]

[1] School of Information Systems,
Singapore Management University, Singapore, Singapore
{hcui,robertdeng,gwwu}@smu.edu.sg
[2] Department of Computer Science, Jinan University, Guangzhou, China
pwdlaijunzuo@163.com

Abstract. A promising solution to protect data privacy in cloud storage services is known as ciphertext-policy attribute-based encryption (CP-ABE). However, in a traditional CP-ABE scheme, a ciphertext is bound with an explicit access structure, which may leak private information about the underlying plaintext in that anyone having access to the ciphertexts can tell the attributes of the privileged recipients by looking at the access structures. A notion called CP-ABE with partially hidden access structures [14,15,18,19,24] was put forth to address this problem, in which each attribute consists of an attribute name and an attribute value and the specific attribute values of an access structure are hidden in the ciphertext. However, previous CP-ABE schemes with partially hidden access structures only support access structures in AND gates, whereas a few other schemes supporting expressive access structures are computationally inefficient since they are built from bilinear pairings over the composite-order groups. In this paper, we focus on addressing this problem, and present an expressive CP-ABE scheme with partially hidden access structures in prime-order groups.

Keywords: Cloud storage · Ciphertext-policy attribute-based encryption · Access structures · Data privacy · Access control

1 Introduction

With the explosive growth of information, there is an increasing demand for outsourcing data to cloud storage services due to its economical scale. However, no user would like to store documents containing sensitive information to a public cloud with no guarantee for security or privacy. A promising solution to provide data privacy while sharing data in cloud is using an encryption mechanism such that data owners upload their data in encrypted forms to the cloud and share them with users having the required credentials (or attributes). One encryption technique that meets this requirement is called ciphertext-policy attribute-based

© Springer International Publishing AG 2016
L. Chen and J. Han (Eds.): ProvSec 2016, LNCS 10005, pp. 19–38, 2016.
DOI: 10.1007/978-3-319-47422-9_2

Table 1. Comparisons of CP-ABE schemes with partially hidden access structures

Schemes	Anonymity of hidden access structures	Expressiveness of access structures	Type of bilinear group	Security	Unbounded attribute names
[19]	partially hidden	AND gates	prime	selective	no
[18]	partially hidden	AND gates	prime	selective	yes
[14]	partially hidden	AND gates	composite	full	no
[15]	partially hidden	LSSS	composite	full	no
[24]	partially hidden	AND gates	prime	selective	yes
Our scheme	partially hidden	LSSS	prime	selective	yes

encryption (CP-ABE) [3], in which a user's private key issued by an attribute authority (AA) is associated with a set of attributes, a message is encrypted under an access structure (or access policy) over a set of attributes by the data owner, and a user can decrypt the ciphertext using his/her private key if and only if his/her attributes satisfy the access policy ascribed to this ciphertext.

Though a ciphertext in a traditional CP-ABE scheme (e.g., [3,7,16,23]) does not directly tell the identities of its recipients, an access structure in the cleartext is attached to the ciphertext, and thus anyone who sees a ciphertext may be able to deduce certain private information about the encrypted message or the privileged recipients of the message. Let us consider the cloud storage system, which is used by a hospital to store electrical medical records (EMRs) of patients. In this system, the hospital encrypts an EMR using CP-ABE under an access structure "(Patient: NR005289 AND Hospital: City Hospital) OR (Doctor: Cardiologist AND Hospital: General Hospital)", and then uploads the ciphertext together with the access policy to the cloud. The access policy requires that a patient identified by NR005289 at City Hospital or any Cardiologist at General Hospital can decrypt the ciphertext to obtain the EMR, from which it can be easily inferred that a person in City Hospital with a patient number NR005289 is suffering a heart problem. This information leakage is definitely not expected by the cloud users, and thus it is necessary to design CP-ABE schemes that can hide access structures.

It is known from [15] that a CP-ABE scheme with hidden access structures can be built from attribute-hiding Inner-product Predicate Encryption (IPE) [13], but this will result in an increase in the size for an arbitrary access structure in the transformation. Also, it is inefficient to implement CP-ABE schemes with fully hidden access structure from attribute-hiding IPE [16]. With the goal of having a trade off between fully hidden access structures and efficiency of CP-ABE, partially hidden access structures [14,15,18,19,24] were embedded in CP-ABE schemes to mitigate the computational cost. However, the schemes in [14,18,19,24] can only be applied to access structures expressed in AND gates. The construction in [15] supports expressive access structures but is built from pairings over the composite-order groups, and "a Tate pairing on a 1024-bit composite-order elliptic curve is roughly 50 times slower than the same pairing on a comparable prime-order curve, and this performance gap will only get worse at higher security levels" [9]. Though there exist several techniques [9] to convert pairing-based schemes from composite-order groups to prime-order groups, there is still a significant performance degradation due to the required size of the special vectors [21]. Therefore, it is desirable to construct an expressive CP-ABE scheme with partially hidden access structures using pairings in the prime-order groups.

In this paper, we focus on designing an expressive CP-ABE scheme in the prime-order groups which can hide attribute values from access structures. We compare our CP-ABE scheme with partially hidden access structures to others in the literature in Table 1. It is straightforward to see that our construction is comparable to the existing ones in that it allows unbounded attribute names, supports expressive access structures and is built in the prime-order groups.

1.1 Challenges and Our Contributions

In the real world, the attribute values always contain more sensitive information than the generic attribute names. For example, the attribute values "Cardiologist" and "NR005289" are more sensitive than the attribute names "Doctor" and "Patient", respectively. Due to this observation, a notion called CP-ABE with partially hidden access structures [15,19] was proposed which divides each attribute into an attribute name and an attribute value, and hides attribute values associated with an access structure included in a ciphertext. That is, instead of a full access structure, a partially hidden access structure (e.g., "(Patient: * AND Hospital: *) OR (Doctor: * AND Hospital: *)") which consists of only attribute names without attribute values is attached to a ciphertext.

We build a CP-ABE scheme with partially hidden access structures from the large universe CP-ABE scheme proposed by Rouselakis and Waters [21], which is an unbounded CP-ABE scheme supporting expressive access policies in the prime-order groups. A naive approach to construct a CP-ABE scheme with partially hidden access structures is simply removing the attribute names from the access structure in the Rouselakis-Waters scheme. However, the resulting scheme suffers off-line dictionary attacks[1]. Therefore, the key challenge here is to modify the Rouselakis-Waters scheme [21] such that its access structure is partially hidden and secure against off-line dictionary attacks. Thanks to the "randomness splitting" technique [6], we build a CP-ABE scheme where the sensitive attribute values are hidden to a computationally bounded adversary by performing some sort of blinding through splitting each attribute value into two randomized complementary components. Thus, though the ciphertext and access structure still contain information about generic attribute names, attribute values are protected from off-line dictionary attacks.

However, since an attribute name in practice may correspond to a number of attribute values, a ciphertext with hidden attribute values raises another issue: given solely attribute names associated with an access structure in a ciphertext, how could a user know he/she is a privileged recipient or not? One solution to this

---

[1] We will show how an off-line dictionary attack works in Sect. 4.

problem is to also encrypt a publicly known message such as the unity element "1" in addition to the encryption of the real data, all under the same access structure [15,24], but this almost doubles the size of the original ciphertext, which is undesirable to a cloud storage system who prefers to save storage space. To reduce the storage cost of cloud services, we simply make a commitment to the encrypted message, and thus a user can know whether he/she has access to the encrypted data by checking whether the decryption result is consistent with the given commitment of the underlying message.

In a nutshell, the differences between our construction of CP-ABE with partially hidden access structure and the Rouselakis-Waters CP-ABE scheme are threefold. Firstly, we perform a "linear splitting" technique [6] on various portions of a ciphertext to overcome the off-line dictionary attacks. Secondly, we re-randomize the key components upon each attribute to make the linear splitting methodology feasible for all attribute values appearing in the ciphertext. Thirdly, we make a commitment to the message to allow a user to check whether he/she is a privileged recipient of a ciphertext without knowing the attribute values ascribed to the ciphertext.

1.2   Related Work

Sahai and Waters [22] introduced a notion called attribute-based encryption (ABE), and then Goyal et al. [11] formulated key-policy ABE (KP-ABE) and CP-ABE as two complimentary forms of ABE. In a CP-ABE system, the private keys are associated with the sets of attributes and the ciphertexts are associated with the access policies, while the situation is reversed in a KP-ABE system. Nevertheless, we believe that KP-ABE is less flexible than CP-ABE because the access policy is determined once the user's attribute-based private key is issued. Bethencourt, Sahai and Waters [3] proposed the first CP-ABE construction, but it was secure under the generic group model. Cheung and Newport [7] presented a CP-ABE scheme that was proved to be secure under the standard model, but it only supported the AND access structures. A CP-ABE system under more advanced access structures was proposed by Goyal et al. [10] based on the number theoretic assumption. Rouselakis and Waters [21] built a large universe CP-ABE system under the prime-order groups to overcome the limitation that the size of the attribute space is polynomially bounded. The cryptographic primitive of CP-ABE with partially hidden access structures was introduced by Nishide et al. [19], but their construction only admitted admissible access structures expressed in AND gates and is selectively secure. Following the work in [19], Li et al. [18] extended the construction with an additional property as user accountability. With the aim of improving efficiency in [18,19], Zhang et al. [24] presented a methodology to reduce the computational overhead in the decryption, but their construction still did not support advanced access structures. Lai, Deng and Li [14] put forth a fully secure CP-ABE scheme with partially hidden access structures, but it only supports restricted access structures as in [18,19]. Later, Lai, Deng and Li proposed [15] a fully secure CP-ABE scheme which can partially hide access structures of any boolean formulas, but it was built from bilinear pairings in the composite-order groups.

1.3   Organization

The remainder of this paper is organized as follows. In Sect. 2, we briefly review the notions and definitions relevant to this paper. In Sect. 3, after depicting the framework for CP-ABE with partially hidden access structures, we present its security model. In Sect. 4, we give a concrete expressive and unbounded CP-ABE scheme with partially hidden access policies and analyze its security and performance. We conclude the paper in Sect. 5.

2   Preliminaries

In this section, we review some basic cryptographic notions and definitions that are to be used in this paper.

2.1   Bilinear Pairings and Complexity Assumptions

Let G be a group of prime order p that is generated from g. We define $\hat{e} : G \times G \to G_1$ to be a bilinear map if it has the following properties [5]:

- Bilinear such that for all $g \in G$, and $a, b \in Z_p$, we have $\hat{e}(g^a, g^b) = \hat{e}(g, g)^{ab}$
- Non-degenerate such that $\hat{e}(g, g) \neq 1$.

We say that G is a bilinear group if the group operation in G is efficiently computable and there exists a group G_1 and an efficiently computable bilinear map $\hat{e} : G \times G \to G_1$ as above.

Decisional $(q-1)$ Assumption [21]. The decisional $(q-1)$ problem is that for any probabilistic polynomial-time algorithm, given $\overrightarrow{y} =$

$$
\begin{aligned}
& g, g^{\mu}, \\
& g^{a^i}, g^{b_j}, g^{\mu \cdot b_j}, g^{a^i b_j}, g^{a^i / b_j^2} \ \forall \ (i, j) \in [q, q], \\
& g^{a^i / b_j} && \forall \ (i, j) \in [2q, q] \text{ with } i \neq q+1, \\
& g^{a^i b_j / b_{j'}^2} && \forall \ (i, j, j') \in [2q, q, q] \text{ with } j \neq j', \\
& g^{\mu a^i b_j / b_{j'}}, g^{\mu a^i b_j / b_{j'}^2} && \forall \ (i, j, j') \in [q, q, q] \text{ with } j \neq j',
\end{aligned}
$$

it is difficult to distinguish $(\overrightarrow{y}, \hat{e}(g, g)^{a^{q+1} \mu})$ from $(\overrightarrow{y}, Z)$, where $g \in G$, $Z \in G_1$, $a, \mu, b_1, ..., b_q \in Z_p$ are chosen independently and uniformly at random.

Decisional Linear Assumption [4]. The decisional linear problem is that for any probabilistic polynomial-time algorithm, given $g, g^{x_1}, g^{x_2}, g^{x_1 x_3}, g^{x_2 x_4}$, it is difficult to distinguish $(g, g^{x_1}, g^{x_2}, g^{x_1 x_3}, g^{x_2 x_4}, g^{x_3 + x_4})$ from $(g, g^{x_1}, g^{x_2}, g^{x_1 x_3}, g^{x_2 x_4}, Z)$, where $g, Z \in G$, $x_1, x_2, x_3, x_4 \in Z_p$ chosen independently and uniformly at random.

2.2   Access Structures and Linear Secret Sharing

We review the the notions of access structures and linear secret sharing schemes [17,23] as follows.

Access Structures. Let $\{P_1, ..., P_n\}$ be a set of parties. A collection $\mathbb{A} \subseteq 2^{\{P_1,...,P_n\}}$ is monotone if $\forall B, C$: if $B \in \mathbb{A}$ and $B \subseteq C$, then $C \subseteq \mathbb{A}$. An (monotone) access structure is a (monotone) collection $\mathbb{A}$ of non-empty subsets of $\{P_1, ..., P_n\}$, i.e., $\mathbb{A} \subseteq 2^{\{P_1,...,P_n\}} \setminus \{\emptyset\}$. The sets in $\mathbb{A}$ are called the authorized sets, and the sets that are not in $\mathbb{A}$ are called the unauthorized sets.

Linear Secret Sharing Schemes (LSSSs). Let P be a set of parties. Let $\mathbb{M}$ be a matrix of size $l \times n$. Let $\rho : \{1, ..., l\} \to P$ be a function that maps a row to a party for labeling. A secret sharing scheme Π over a set of parties P is a linear secret-sharing scheme over Z_p if

1. the shares for each party form a vector over Z_p;
2. there exists a matrix $\mathbb{M}$ which has l rows and n columns called the share-generating matrix for Π. For $x = 1, ..., l$, the x-th row of matrix $\mathbb{M}$ is labeled by a party $\rho(i)$, where $\rho : \{1, ..., l\} \to P$ is a function that maps a row to a party for labeling. Considering that the column vector $v = (\mu, r_2, ..., r_n)$, where $\mu \in Z_p$ is the secret to be shared and $r_2, ..., r_n \in Z_p$ are randomly chosen, then $\mathbb{M}v$ is the vector of l shares of the secret μ according to Π. The share $(\mathbb{M}v)_i$ belongs to party $\rho(i)$.

It has been noted in [17] that every LSSS also enjoys the linear reconstruction property. Suppose that Π is an LSSS for access structure $\mathbb{A}$. Let $\mathbf{A}$ be an authorized set, and define $I \subseteq \{1, ..., l\}$ as $I = \{i | \rho(i) \in \mathbf{A}\}$. Then the vector $(1, 0, ..., 0)$ is in the span of rows of matrix $\mathbb{M}$ indexed by I, and there exist constants $\{w_i \in Z_p\}_{i \in I}$ such that, for any valid shares $\{v_i\}$ of a secret μ according to Π, we have $\sum_{i \in I} w_i v_i = \mu$. These constants $\{w_i\}$ can be found in polynomial time with respect to the size of the share-generating matrix $\mathbb{M}$ [2].

On the other hand, for an unauthorized set $\mathbf{A}'$, no such constants $\{w_i\}$ exist. Moreover, in this case it is also true that if $I' = \{i | \rho(i) \in \mathbf{A}'\}$, there exists a vector $\vec{w}$ such that its first component w_1 is any non zero element in Z_p and $< \mathbb{M}_i, \vec{w} > = 0$ for all $i \in I'$, where $\mathbb{M}_i$ is the i-th row of $\mathbb{M}$ [21].

Boolean Formulas [17]. Access policies can also be described in terms of monotonic boolean formulas. LSSS access structures are more general, and can be derived from representations as boolean formulas. There are standard techniques to convert any monotonic boolean formula into a corresponding LSSS matrix. The boolean formula can be represented as an access tree, where the interior nodes are AND and OR gates, and the leaf nodes correspond to attributes. The number of rows in the corresponding LSSS matrix will be the same as the number of leaf nodes in the access tree.

3   System Architecture and Security Model

In this section, we describe the framework and security model of ciphertext-policy attribute-based encryption with partially hidden access structures.

3.1   Framework

A CP-ABE scheme with partially hidden access structures consists of four algorithms: setup algorithm Setup, attribute-based private key generation algorithm KeyGen, encryption algorithm Encrypt and decryption algorithm Decrypt.

- Setup(1^λ) $\to$ ($pars$, msk). Taking the security parameter λ as the input, this algorithm outputs the public parameter $pars$ and the master private key msk for the system. This algorithm is run by the AA.
- KeyGen($pars$, msk, $\mathbf{A}$) $\to K_{\mathbf{A}}$. Taking the public parameter $pars$, the master private key msk and an attribute set $\mathbf{A}$ as the input, this algorithm outputs an attribute-based private key $K_{\mathbf{A}}$ over the attribute set $\mathbf{A}$. This algorithm is run by the AA.
- Encrypt($pars$, M, ($\mathbb{M}$, ρ, $\{A_{\rho(i)}\}$)) $\to$ CT. Taking the public parameter $pars$, a message M and an access structure ($\mathbb{M}$, ρ, $\{A_{\rho(i)}\}$) where the function ρ associates the rows of $\mathbb{M}$ to generic attribute names, and $\{A_{\rho(i)}\}$ are the corresponding attribute values as the input. Let $\mathbb{M}$ be an $l \times n$ matrix as the input, this algorithm outputs a ciphertext CT. This algorithm is run by the data owner.
- Decrypt($pars$, CT, $\mathbf{A}$, $K_{\mathbf{A}}$) $\to M/\bot$. Taking the public parameter $pars$, a ciphertext CT and an attribute-based private key $K_{\mathbf{A}}$ associated to an attribute set $\mathbf{A}$ as the input, this algorithm outputs either the message M when the private key $K_{\mathbf{A}}$ satisfies the access structure, or a symbol $\bot$ otherwise. This algorithm is run by the user.

We require that a CP-ABE scheme with partially hidden access structures is correct, meaning that for all messages M, all attribute sets $\mathbf{A}$ and access structures ($\mathbb{M}$, ρ, $\{A_{\rho(i)}\}$) with authorized $\mathbf{A}$ satisfying ($\mathbb{M}$, ρ, $\{A_{\rho(i)}\}$), if ($pars$, msk) $\leftarrow$ Setup(1^λ), $K_{\mathbf{A}} \leftarrow$ KeyGen($pars$, msk, $\mathbf{A}$), CT $\leftarrow$ Encrypt($pars$, M, ($\mathbb{M}$, ρ, $\{A_{\rho(i)}\}$)), then Decrypt($pars$, CT, $\mathbf{A}$, $K_{\mathbf{A}}$) = M.

3.2   Security Definitions

A CP-ABE scheme with partially hidden access structures should ensure confidentiality and anonymity. Below we elaborately describe the security definitions for these two requirements one by one.

Confidentiality. Assuming that the adversary makes the key generation queries adaptively, we define the security model for confidentiality by the following game between a challenger algorithm $\mathcal{C}$ and an adversary algorithm $\mathcal{A}$, based on the security model of indistinguishability under chosen-plaintext attacks (IND-CPA) for CP-ABE [23].

- Setup. Algorithm $\mathcal{C}$ runs the setup algorithm, and gives the public parameter *pars* to algorithm $\mathcal{A}$ and keeps the master private key *msk*.
- Phase 1. Algorithm $\mathcal{A}$ makes the key generation queries to algorithm $\mathcal{C}$. Algorithm $\mathcal{A}$ sends an attribute set $\mathbf{A}_i$ to algorithm $\mathcal{C}$. Algorithm $\mathcal{C}$ responds by returning the corresponding key $K_{\mathbf{A}_i}$ to algorithm $\mathcal{A}$.
- Challenge. Algorithm $\mathcal{A}$ chooses two messages M_0^* and M_1^* of the same size, and an access structure $(\mathbb{M}^*, \rho^*, \{A_{\rho(i)}^*\})$ with the constraint that the key generation queries $\{K_{\mathbf{A}_i}\}$ in Phase 1 do not satisfy the access structure $(\mathbb{M}^*, \rho^*, \{A_{\rho(i)}^*\})$. The challenger chooses a random bit $\beta \in \{0,1\}$, and sends algorithm $\mathcal{A}$ a challenge ciphertext CT^* which is an encryption of M_β^* under the access structure $(\mathbb{M}^*, \rho^*, \{A_{\rho(i)}^*\})$.
- Phase 2. Algorithm $\mathcal{A}$ continues issuing the key generation queries on attribute sets $\mathbf{A}_i$ with the constraint that they do not satisfy the access structure in the challenge phase. Algorithm $\mathcal{C}$ responds as in Phase 1.
- Guess. Algorithm $\mathcal{A}$ makes a guess β' for β, and it wins the game if $\beta' = \beta$.

Anonymity. Anonymity prevents an adversary from distinguishing a ciphertext under one access matrix associated with one attribute set from a ciphertext under the same access matrix associated with another attribute set. In the anonymity game, the adversary is given the public parameter, as well as the access to the key generation oracle, and its goal is to guess which of two attribute sets satisfying the same access matrix generates the ciphertext in the challenge phase, without being given either of the private keys associated with the two attribute sets. Below we define the the game of anonymity under chosen-plaintext attacks (ANON-CPA) between a challenger algorithm $\mathcal{C}$ and an adversary algorithm $\mathcal{A}$.

- Setup. Algorithm $\mathcal{C}$ runs the setup algorithm, and gives the public parameter *pars* to algorithm $\mathcal{A}$ and keeps the master private key *msk*.
- Phase 1. Algorithm $\mathcal{A}$ makes the key generation query to algorithm $\mathcal{C}$. Algorithm $\mathcal{A}$ sends an attribute set $\mathbf{A}_i$ to algorithm $\mathcal{C}$. Algorithm $\mathcal{C}$ responds by returning the corresponding key $K_{\mathbf{A}_i}$ to algorithm $\mathcal{A}$.
- Challenge. Algorithm $\mathcal{A}$ chooses a message M^* and an access matrix $(\mathbb{M}^*, \rho^*)$ which can be satisfied by attribute sets $\{A_{\rho(i)}^*\}_0$ and $\{A_{\rho(i)}^*\}_1$ with the constraint that there are no key generation queries $\{K_{\mathbf{A}_i}\}$ in Phase 1 that can satisfy $(\mathbb{M}^*, \rho^*, \{A_{\rho(i)}^*\}_0)$ and $(\mathbb{M}^*, \rho^*, \{A_{\rho(i)}^*\}_1)$. The challenger chooses a random bit $\beta \in \{0,1\}$, and sends algorithm $\mathcal{A}$ a challenge ciphertext CT^* which is an encryption of M^* under the access structure $(\mathbb{M}^*, \rho^*, \{A_{\rho(i)}^*\}_\beta)$.
- Phase 2. Algorithm $\mathcal{A}$ continues issuing the key generation queries to algorithm $\mathcal{C}$. Algorithm $\mathcal{C}$ responds as in Phase 1 with the constraint that the attributes of the key generation queries satisfying $(\mathbb{M}^*, \rho^*, \{A_{\rho(i)}^*\}_0)$ and $(\mathbb{M}^*, \rho^*, \{A_{\rho(i)}^*\}_1)$ are disallowed. Algorithm $\mathcal{C}$ responds as in Phase 1.
- Guess. Algorithm $\mathcal{A}$ makes a guess β' for β, and it wins the game if $\beta' = \beta$.

Algorithm $\mathcal{A}$'s advantage in the above two games are defined as $\Pr[\beta = \beta'] - 1/2$. We say that a CP-ABE scheme with partially hidden access structures is indistinguishable (or anonymous) under the chosen-plaintext attacks if all probabilistic polynomial time (PPT) adversaries have at most a negligible advantage in the security parameter λ. In addition, a CP-ABE scheme with partially hidden access structures is said to be selectively indistinguishable (or anonymous) if an Init stage is added before the Setup phase where algorithm $\mathcal{A}$ commits to the challenge access structure $(\mathbb{M}, \rho, \{A_{\rho(i)}\})$.

4 Ciphertext-Policy Attribute-Based Encryption Scheme with Partially Hidden Access Structures

In this section, we give a concrete construction of a CP-ABE scheme with partially hidden access structures, and analyze its security and performance.

4.1 Attribute Value Guessing Attack

Below we briefly review the encryption algorithm of the CP-ABE scheme in [21], and show that there is an attribute value guessing attack to such a construction.

Encrypt. This algorithm takes the public parameter $pars$, a message M and an LSSS access structure $(\mathbb{M}, \rho)$ where the function ρ associates the rows of $\mathbb{M}$ to attributes as the input. Let $\mathbb{M}$ be an $l \times n$ matrix. It randomly chooses a vector $\overrightarrow{v} = (\mu, y_2, ..., y_n) \in Z_p^n$. These values will be used to share the encryption exponent μ. For $i = 1$ to l, it calculates $v_i = \overrightarrow{v} \cdot \mathbb{M}_i$, where $\mathbb{M}_i$ is the vector corresponding to the i-th row of $\mathbb{M}$. In addition, it randomly chooses β, z_1, ..., $z_l \in Z_p$, and outputs a ciphertext $CT = \left(C, D, \{(C_i, D_i, E_i)\}_{i \in [1,l]}\right)$.

$$C = \hat{e}(g,g)^{\alpha\mu}, \; D = g^{\mu}, \; C_i = w^{v_i} v^{z_i}, \; D_i = g^{z_i}, \; E_i = (u^{\rho(i)} h)^{-z_i},$$

where g, u, h, v, w, $\hat{e}(g,g)^{\alpha}$ belong to the public parameter $pars$.

Attack. Given a ciphertext $CT = \left(C, D, \{(C_i, D_i, E_i)\}_{i \in [1,l]}\right)$, an adversary can easily determine whether an attribute value A_i used in the ciphertext by checking whether $\hat{e}(E_i, g) = \hat{e}(u^{A_i} h, D_i^{-1})$ holds. Clearly, this scheme cannot achieve anonymity.

4.2 Construction

On the basis of the large universe CP-ABE scheme proposed in [21], we present a CP-ABE scheme which can partially hide the access structures in the prime-order groups. Let G be a bilinear group of a prime order p with a generator g. Denote $\hat{e} : G \times G \rightarrow G_1$ by the bilinear map.

- Setup. This algorithm takes the security parameter λ as the input. It randomly chooses a group G of prime order p with a generator g. Also, it randomly chooses u, h, v, $w \in G$, $d_1, d_2, d_3, d_4, \alpha \in Z_p$, and computes $g_1 = g^{d_1}$, $g_2 = g^{d_2}$, $g_3 = g^{d_3}$, $g_4 = g^{d_4}$. The public parameter is $pars = (H, g, u, h, w, v, g_1, g_2, g_3, g_4, \hat{e}(g,g)^{\alpha})$ where H is a collision resistent hash function that maps an element in G_1 to an element in $\{0,1\}^t$ with t being the security parameter such that the concatenate elements in Z_p are represented in t bits, and the master private key is $msk = (d_1, d_2, d_3, d_4, g^{\alpha})$.

- KeyGen. This algorithm takes the public parameter $pars$, the master private key msk and an attribute set $\mathbf{A}$[2] as the input. Let k be the size of $\mathbf{A}$, and A_1, ..., $A_k \in Z_p$ be the attribute values of $\mathbf{A}$. It randomly chooses r, r', r_1, ..., r_k, r'_1, ..., $r'_k \in Z_p$, and outputs the attribute-based private key $K_{\mathbf{A}} = (K_1, K_2, \{K_{i,1}, K_{i,2}, K_{i,3}, K_{i,4}, K_{i,5}\}_{i \in [1,k]})$ over a set of attributes $\mathbf{A}$ as

$$K_1 = g^\alpha w^{d_1 d_2 r + d_3 d_4 r'}, \quad K_2 = g^{r d_1 d_2 + r' d_3 d_4},$$

$$K_{i,1} = ((u^{A_i} h)^{r_i} v^{-r})^{d_2}, \ K_{i,2} = ((u^{A_i} h)^{r_i} v^{-r})^{d_1}, \ K_{i,3} = g^{d_1 d_2 r_i + d_3 d_4 r'_i},$$

$$K_{i,4} = ((u^{A_i} h)^{r'_i} v^{-r'})^{d_4}, \ K_{i,5} = ((u^{A_i} h)^{r'_i} v^{-r'})^{d_3}.$$

- Encrypt. This algorithm takes the public parameter $pars$, a message $M \in Z_p$ and an LSSS access structure $(\mathbb{M}, \rho, \{A_{\rho(i)}\})$[3] as the input. It randomly chooses a vector $\overrightarrow{v} = (\mu, y_2, ..., y_n) \in Z_p^n$. These values will be used to share the encryption exponent μ. For $i = 1$ to l, it calculates $v_i = \overrightarrow{v} \cdot \mathbb{M}_i$, where $\mathbb{M}_i$ is the vector corresponding to the i-th row of $\mathbb{M}$. Then, it randomly chooses γ, $s_{i,1}$, ..., $s_{i,l}$, $s_{1,2}$, ..., $s_{l,2}$, z_1, ..., $z_l \in Z_p$, and outputs a ciphertext $CT = ((\mathbb{M}, \rho), C, D, E, \{(C_i, D_{i,1}, D_{i,2}, E_{i,1}, E_{i,2}, F_i)\}_{i \in [1,l]})$, where

$$C = (M||\gamma) \oplus H(\hat{e}(g, g)^{\alpha\mu}), \ D = g^\mu, \ E = g^M h^\gamma,$$

$$C_i = w^{v_i} v^{z_i}, \ D_{i,1} = g_1^{z_i - s_{i,1}}, \ D_{i,2} = g_3^{z_i - s_{i,2}},$$

$$E_{i,1} = g_2^{s_{i,1}}, \ E_{i,2} = g_4^{s_{i,2}}, \ F_i = (u^{A_{\rho(i)}} h)^{-z_i}.$$

- Decrypt. This algorithm takes the public parameter $pars$, a ciphertext $((\mathbb{M}, \rho), C, D, E, \{(C_i, D_{i,1}, D_{i,2}, E_{i,1}, E_{i,2}, F_i)\}_{i \in [1,l]})$ and a private key $K_{\mathbf{A}}$ for an attribute set $\mathbf{A}$ as the input. It calculates $I_{\mathbb{M}, \rho}$ from $(\mathbb{M}, \rho)$, which is a set of minimum subsets of attributes satisfying $(\mathbb{M}, \rho)$. Denote by $\{w_i \in Z_p\}_{i \in \mathcal{I}}$ a set of constants such that if $\{v_i\}$ are valid shares of any secret μ according to $\mathbb{M}$, then $\sum_{i \in \mathcal{I}} w_i v_i = \mu$. For an $\mathcal{I} \in I_{\mathbb{M}, \rho}$, it computes

$$\frac{\hat{e}(D, K_1)}{\prod_{i \in \mathcal{I}} (\hat{e}(C_i, K_2) \hat{e}(D_{i,1}, K_{i,1}) \hat{e}(E_{i,1}, K_{i,2}) \hat{e}(F_i, K_{i,3}) \hat{e}(D_{i,2}, K_{i,4}) \hat{e}(E_{i,2}, K_{i,5}))^{w_i}}$$

$$= \frac{\hat{e}(g, g)^{\alpha\mu} \hat{e}(g^\mu, w)^{r_1 d_1 d_2} \hat{e}(g^\mu, w)^{r_2 d_3 d_4}}{\prod_{i \in I} (\hat{e}(g, w^{v_i})^{d_1 d_2 r_1 + d_3 d_4 r_2})^{w_i}} = \hat{e}(g, g)^{\alpha\mu}, \quad \frac{C}{H(\hat{e}(g, g)^{\alpha\mu})} = M||\gamma.$$

If $g^M h^\gamma = E$, it outputs M. Otherwise, it outputs $\perp$.

Remarks. In the above construction, the term E, computed using a commitment scheme [20], is added to the ciphertext such that a user can easily ascertain whether he/she is a privileged recipient by checking the decryption result via the given E. Note that according to the binding property of the commitment scheme [8], each E can only be obtained from a unique pair of M and γ, which

[2] Note that each attribute is denoted as $N_i = A_i$, where N_i is the generic name of an attribute and A_i is the corresponding attribute value.

[3] For the details about how to convert a boolean formula into an equivalent LSSS matrix, please refer to [17].

guarantees the correctness of decryption, in spite of the fact that the user has no idea whether his/her attribute set satisfies the access structure ascribed the ciphertext before performing decryption.

4.3   Security Proof

Theorem 1. *Assuming that the $(q-1)$ assumption holds in G, and the decisional linear assumption holds in G, then the above system is selectively indistinguishable and anonymous.*

Proof. At a hight level, the proof is reduced via a sequence of games by concluding that these games are computationally indistinguishable from each other. For succinct description, we remove the access structure related elements from the ciphertext. Denote $\left(C^*, D^*, E^*, \{(C_i^*, D_{i,1}^*, D_{i,2}^*, E_{i,1}^*, E_{i,2}^*, F_i^*)\}_{i \in [1,l]}\right)$ by the challenge ciphertext given to the adversary during an attack in the real world. Let Z be a random element of G_1, and $\{Z_{i,1}\}$, $\{Z_{i,1}'\}$ be sets of random elements of G. We define a sequence of games $\mathrm{Game}_0, \mathrm{Game}_1, ..., \mathrm{Game}_l, \mathrm{Game}_{l+1}, ..., \mathrm{Game}_{2l+1}$ that differ on which challenge ciphertext is given by the challenger to the adversary, where Game_0 is the original game, Game_1 changes the term C^* to Z, and Game_2 to Game_{l+1} change the $D_{i,1}^*$ term to $Z_{i,1}$ one by one for $i \in [1, l]$, and Game_{l+2} to Game_{2l+1} change the $E_{i,1}^*$ term to $Z_{i,1}'$ one by one for $i \in [1, l]$.

- Game_0: The challenge ciphertext is $\mathrm{CT}_0^* = \left(C^*, D^*, E^*, \{(C_i^*, D_{i,1}^*, D_{i,2}^*, E_{i,1}^*, E_{i,2}^*, F_i^*)\}_{i \in [1,l]}\right)$.
- Game_1: The challenge ciphertext is $\mathrm{CT}_1^* = \left(Z, D^*, E^*, \{(C_i^*, D_{i,1}^*, D_{i,2}^*, E_{i,1}, E_{i,2}, F_i^*)\}_{i \in [1,l]}\right)$.
- Game_2: The challenge ciphertext is $\mathrm{CT}_2^* = \left(Z, D^*, E^*, (C_1, Z_{1,1}, D_{1,2}^*, E_{1,1}^*, E_{1,2}^*, F_1^*), \{(C_i^*, D_{i,1}^*, D_{i,2}^*, E_{i,1}^*, E_{i,2}^*, F_i^*)\}_{i \in [2,l]}\right)$.
- $\cdots \cdots$
- Game_{l+1}: The challenge ciphertext is $\mathrm{CT}_{l+1}^* = \left(Z, D^*, E^*, \{(C_i, Z_{i,1}, D_{i,2}^*, E_{i,1}^*, E_{i,2}^*, F_i^*)\}_{i \in [1,l]}\right)$.
- Game_{l+2}: The challenge ciphertext is $\mathrm{CT}_{l+2}^* = \left(Z, D^*, E^*, (C_1^*, Z_{1,1}, Z_{1,1}', E_{1,1}^*, E_{1,2}^*, F_1^*), \{(C_i^*, Z_{i,1}, D_{i,2}^*, E_{i,1}^*, E_{i,2}^*, F_i^*)\}_{i \in [2,l]}\right)$.
- $\cdots \cdots$
- Game_{2l+1}: The challenge ciphertext is $\mathrm{CT}_{2l+1}^* = \left(Z, D^*, E^*, \{(C_i^*, Z_{i,1}, Z_{i,1}', E_{i,1}^*, E_{i,2}^*, F_i^*)\}_{i \in [1,l]}\right)$.

To complete the proof, we will show that the games $\mathrm{Game}_0, \mathrm{Game}_1, ..., \mathrm{Game}_{2l+1}$ are computationally indistinguishable.

Lemma 1. *Assuming that the $(q-1)$ assumption holds in G, then there is no adversary that distinguishes between the games Game_0 and Game_1.*

Proof. Assume that there exists an adversary algorithm $\mathcal{A}$ that can distinguish Game_0 from Game_1. Then we can build a challenger algorithm $\mathcal{C}$ that solves the $(q-1)$ problem.

– Init. Algorithm $\mathcal{A}$ gives algorithm $\mathcal{C}$ a challenge access structure $(\mathbb{M}^*, \rho^*, \{\rho(i)^*\})^4$, where $\mathbb{M}^*$ is an $l \times n$ matrix.

– Setup. Algorithm $\mathcal{C}$ randomly chooses $d_1, d_2, d_3, d_4 \in Z_p$, and computes $g_1 = g^{d_1}$, $g_2 = g^{d_2}$, $g_3 = g^{d_3}$, $g_4 = g^{d_4}$. Then, it randomly chooses a hash function $H\colon G_1 \to \{0,1\}^t$, $\tilde{\alpha}, \tilde{u}, \tilde{v}, \tilde{h} \in Z_p$, In addition, it implicitly sets $\alpha = a^{q+1} + \tilde{\alpha}$, and outputs the rest of the public parameter as $g = g$, $w = g^a$,

$$v = g^{\tilde{v}} \cdot \prod_{(j,j') \in [l,n]} (g^{a^{j'}/b_j})^{\mathbb{M}^*_{j,j'}}, \quad u = g^{\tilde{u}} \cdot \prod_{(j,j') \in [l,n]} (g^{a^{j'}/b_j^2})^{\mathbb{M}^*_{j,j'}},$$

$$h = g^{\tilde{h}} \cdot \prod_{(j,j') \in [l,n]} (g^{a^{j'}/b_j^2})^{-\rho^*(j)\mathbb{M}^*_{j,j'}}, \quad \hat{e}(g,g)^{\alpha} = \hat{e}(g^a, g^{a^q}) \cdot \hat{e}(g,g)^{\tilde{\alpha}}.$$

– Phase 1 and Phase 2. In both phases, algorithm $\mathcal{C}$ has to output the private keys for attribute sets $\mathbf{A} = \{A_1, ..., A_{|\mathbf{A}|}\}$ issued by algorithm $\mathcal{A}$.

Since $\mathbf{A}$ does not satisfy $(\mathbb{M}^*, \rho^*, \{\rho(i)^*\})$, there exists a vector $\vec{w} = (w_1, ..., w_n)^{\perp} \in Z_p^n$ such that $w_1 = -1$, $(\mathbb{M}_i^*, \vec{w}) = 0$ for all $i \in I = \{i | i \in [l] \wedge \rho(i)^* \in \mathbf{A}\}$. Algorithm $\mathcal{B}$ computes $\vec{w}$ using linear algebra. In addition, it randomly chooses $\tilde{r}, \tilde{r}' \in Z_p$, implicitly sets

$$r = \tilde{r} + w_1 a^q + w_2 a^{q-1} + ... + w_n a^{q+1-n} = \tilde{r} + \sum_{i \in [n]} w_i a^{q+1-i},$$

$$r' = \tilde{r}' + w_1 a^q + w_2 a^{q-1} + ... + w_n a^{q+1-n} = \tilde{r} + \sum_{i \in [n]} w_i a^{q+1-i},$$

and computes

$$K_1 = g^{\alpha} w^{d_1 d_2 r + d_3 d_4 r'}$$
$$= (g^{a^{q+1}} g^{\tilde{\alpha}})(g^{a\tilde{r}} \prod_{i \in [n]} g^{w_i a^{q+2-i}})^{d_1 d_2} (g^{a\tilde{r}'} \prod_{i \in [n]} g^{w_i a^{q+2-i}})^{d_3 d_4},$$

$$K_2 = g^{d_1 d_2 r + d_3 d_4 r'}$$
$$= (g^{\tilde{r}} \prod_{i \in [n]} (g^{a^{q+1-i}})^{w_i})^{d_1 d_2} (g^{\tilde{r}'} \prod_{i \in [n]} (g^{a^{q+1-i}})^{w_i})^{d_3 d_4}.$$

Then it computes

$$v^{-r} = v^{-\tilde{r}} \cdot \prod_{i \in [n]} (g^{a^{q+1-i}})^{-\tilde{v} w_i}$$
$$\cdot \prod_{\substack{(i,j,j') \in [n,l,n] \\ i \neq j'}} (g^{a^{q+1+j'-i}/b_j})^{-w_i \mathbb{M}^*_{j,j'}} \prod_{\substack{j \in [l] \\ \rho(j) \notin \mathbf{A}}} g^{(\vec{w} \cdot \mathbb{M}_j^*) a^{q+1}/b_j},$$

$$v^{-r'} = v^{-\tilde{r}'} \cdot \prod_{i \in [n]} (g^{a^{q+1-i}})^{-\tilde{v} w_i}$$
$$\cdot \prod_{\substack{(i,j,j') \in [n,l,n] \\ i \neq j'}} (g^{a^{q+1+j'-i}/b_j})^{-w_i \mathbb{M}^*_{j,j'}} \prod_{\substack{j \in [l] \\ \rho(j) \notin \mathbf{A}}} g^{(\vec{w} \cdot \mathbb{M}_j^*) a^{q+1}/b_j}.$$

---

[4] For notation simplicity, we use $\{\rho(i)^*\}$ to replace $\{A^*_{\rho(i)}\}$ in the rest of the proof.

where the last parts cannot be directly calculated, so it must be canceled by the $(u^{A_i}h)^{r_i}$, $(u^{A_i}h)^{r'_i}$ parts.

Therefore, for all $i \in [|\mathbf{A}|]$, algorithm $\mathcal{C}$ randomly chooses $\tilde{r}_i \in Z_p$, and implicitly sets

$$r_i = \tilde{r}_i + (\tilde{r} \cdot \sum_{\substack{i' \in [l] \\ \rho^*(i') \notin \mathbf{A}}} \frac{b_j}{A_i - \rho^*(i')} + \sum_{\substack{j,i' \in [n,l] \\ \rho^*(i') \notin \mathbf{A}}} \frac{w_j b_{i'} a^{q+1-j}}{A_i - \rho^*(i')}),$$

$$r'_i = \tilde{r}'_i + (\tilde{r}' \cdot \sum_{\substack{i' \in [l] \\ \rho^*(i') \notin \mathbf{A}}} \frac{b_j}{A_i - \rho^*(i')} + \sum_{\substack{j,i' \in [n,l] \\ \rho^*(i') \notin \mathbf{A}}} \frac{w_j b_{i'} a^{q+1-j}}{A_i - \rho^*(i')}).$$

and computes

$$g^{r_i} = g^{\tilde{r}_i} \cdot \prod_{\substack{i' \in [l] \\ \rho^*(i') \notin \mathbf{A}}} (g^{b_{i'}})^{\frac{\tilde{r}}{A_i - \rho^*(i)}} \cdot \prod_{\substack{(k',i') \in [n,l] \\ \rho^*(i') \notin \mathbf{A}}} (g^{b_{i'} a^{q+1-k'}})^{\frac{w_{k'}}{A_i - \rho^*(i')}},$$

$$(u^{A_i}h)^{r_i} = (u^{A_i}h)^{\tilde{r}_i} \cdot (\frac{g^{r_i}}{g^{\tilde{r}_i}})^{\tilde{u}A_i + \tilde{h}} \cdot \prod_{\substack{(i',j,j') \in [l,l,n] \\ \rho^*(i) \notin \mathbf{A}}} (g^{b_{i'} a^{j'}/b_j^2})^{\frac{\tilde{r}(A_i - \rho^*(j))\mathbb{M}^*_{j,j'}}{A_i - \rho^*(i')}}$$

$$\cdot \prod_{\substack{(k',i',j,j') \in [n,l,l,n] \\ \rho^*(i') \notin \mathbf{A},(j \neq i',k' \neq j')}} \left(g^{\frac{b_{i'} a^{q+1+j'-k'}}{b_j^2}} \right)^{\frac{A_i - \rho^*(j)w_{k'}\mathbb{M}^*_{j,j'}}{A_i - \rho^*(i')}}$$

$$\cdot \prod_{\substack{j \in [l] \\ \rho^*(j) \notin \mathbf{A}}} g^{\frac{(\vec{w} \cdot \mathbb{M}^*_j)a^{q+1}}{b_j}},$$

$$(u^{A_i}h)^{r'_i} = (u^{A_i}h)^{\tilde{r}'_i} \cdot (\frac{g^{r'_i}}{g^{\tilde{r}'_i}})^{\tilde{u}A_i + \tilde{h}} \cdot \prod_{\substack{(i',j,j') \in [l,l,n] \\ \rho^*(i) \notin \mathbf{A}}} (g^{b_{i'} a^{j'}/b_j^2})^{\frac{\tilde{r}(A_i - \rho^*(j))\mathbb{M}^*_{j,j'}}{A_i - \rho^*(i')}}$$

$$\cdot \prod_{\substack{(k',i',j,j') \in [n,l,l,n] \\ \rho^*(i') \notin \mathbf{A},(j \neq i',k' \neq j')}} \left(g^{\frac{b_{i'} a^{q+1+j'-k'}}{b_j^2}} \right)^{\frac{A_i - \rho^*(j)w_{k'}\mathbb{M}^*_{j,j'}}{A_i - \rho^*(i')}}$$

$$\cdot \prod_{\substack{j \in [l] \\ \rho^*(j) \notin \mathbf{A}}} g^{\frac{(\vec{w} \cdot \mathbb{M}^*_j)a^{q+1}}{b_j}}.$$

Therefore, algorithm $\mathcal{C}$ can output the private key $K_{\mathbf{A}} = (K_1, K_2, \{K_{i,1}, K_{i,2}, K_{i,3}, K_{i,4}, K_{i,5}\}_{i \in [1,k]})$ for an attribute set $\mathbf{A}$ as required.

– Challenge. Algorithm $\mathcal{A}$ sends algorithm $\mathcal{C}$ a message M^*. Algorithm $\mathcal{C}$ randomly chooses $\gamma \in Z_p$, computes

$$C^* = (M^* || \gamma) \oplus H(Z \cdot \hat{e}(g, g^s)^{\tilde{\alpha}}), \quad D^* = g^s, \quad E^* = g^{M^*} h^{\gamma}.$$

Then it implicitly sets $\overrightarrow{v} = (s, sa + \tilde{y}_2, sa^2 + \tilde{y}_3, ..., sa^{n-1} + \tilde{y}_n)$, where $\tilde{y}_2$, ..., $\tilde{y}_n \in Z_p$, and

$$v_i = \sum_{j\in[n]} \mathrm{M}^*_{i,j} sa^{j-1} + \sum_{j=2}^{n} \mathrm{M}^*_{i,j}\tilde{y}_j = \sum_{j\in[n]} \mathrm{M}^*_{i,j} sa^{j-1} + \tilde{v}_i$$

for each row $i \in [l]$.

Additionally, it implicitly sets $z_i = -sb_i$, and computes

$$C^*_i = w^{v_i} v^{z_i} = w^{\tilde{v}_i} \cdot \prod_{j\in[n]} g^{\mathrm{M}^*_{i,j} sa^j} \cdot (g^{sb_i})^{-\tilde{v}} \cdot \prod_{(i',j')\in[l,n]} g^{\frac{-\mathrm{M}^*_{i',j'} a^{j'} sb_i}{b_{i'}}}$$

$$= w^{\tilde{v}_i} \cdot (g^{sb_i})^{\tilde{v}} \cdot \prod_{\substack{(i',j')\in[l,n] \\ i'\neq i}} (g^{sa^{j'} b_i / b_{i'}})^{-\mathrm{M}^*_{i',j'}},$$

$$F^*_i = (u^{\rho^*(i)} h)^{z_i} = (g^{sb_i})^{-(\tilde{u}\rho^*(i)+\tilde{h})} \cdot \left(\prod_{(i',j')\in[l,n]} g^{\frac{(\rho^*(i)-\rho^*(i'))\mathrm{M}^*_{i',j'} a^{j'}}{b_{i'}^2}} \right)^{-sb_i}$$

$$= (g^{sb_i})^{-(\tilde{u}\rho^*(i)+\tilde{h})} \cdot \prod_{\substack{(i',j')\in[l,n] \\ i'\neq i}} (g^{\frac{sa^{j'} b_i}{b_{i'}^2}})^{-(\rho^*(i)-\rho^*(i'))\mathrm{M}^*_{i',j'}},$$

$$D^*_{i,1} = g_1^{z_i - s_{i,1}} = (g^{-sb_i})^{d_1} \cdot g^{-d_1 s_{i,1}}, \quad E^*_{i,1} = g_2^{s_{i,1}} = g^{d_2 s_{i,1}},$$

$$D^*_{i,2} = g_3^{z_i - s_{i,2}} = (g^{-sb_i})^{d_3} \cdot g^{-d_3 s_{i,2}}, \quad E^*_{i,2} = g_4^{s_{i,2}} = g^{d_4 s_{i,2}},$$

where $s_{i,1}, s_{i,2} \in Z^*_p$. Therefore, algorithm $\mathcal{C}$ outputs the ciphertext $CT^* = \left(C^*, D^*, E^*, \{(C^*_i, D^*_{i,1}, D^*_{i,2}, E^*_{i,1}, E^*_{i,2}, F^*_i)\}_{i\in[1,l]} \right)$ as required.

– Guess. Algorithm $\mathcal{A}$ outputs a guess β' for β to guess which game algorithm $\mathcal{C}$ has been playing, and algorithm $\mathcal{C}$ forwards β' as its own answer to the $(q-1)$ assumption.

If $Z = \hat{e}(g,g)^{sa^{q+1}}$, then algorithm $\mathcal{A}$'s view of this simulation is identical to the original game, because $C^* = (M^*||\gamma) \oplus H(Z \cdot \hat{e}(g,g^s)^{\tilde{\alpha}}) = (M^*||\gamma) \oplus H(Z \cdot \hat{e}(g,g)^{\alpha s})$. On the other hand, if Z is a random term of G_1, then all the information about the message M^* is hidden in the challenge ciphertext. Therefore the advantage of algorithm $\mathcal{A}$ is 0. As a result, if algorithm $\mathcal{A}$ distinguishes game Game_0 from game Game_1 with a non-negligible probability, then algorithm $\mathcal{C}$ has a non-negligible advantage in breaking the $(q-1)$ assumption.

Lemma 2. *Assuming that the decisional linear assumption holds in G, then there is no adversary that distinguishes between the games Game_{j+1} and Game_j for $j \in [1, l]$.*

Proof. Assume that there exists an adversary algorithm $\mathcal{A}$ that can distinguish Game_j from Game_{j+1}. Then we can build a challenger algorithm $\mathcal{C}$ that solves the decisional linear assumption.

- Init. Algorithm $\mathcal{A}$ gives algorithm $\mathcal{C}$ a challenge access structure $(\mathbb{M}^*, \rho^*, \{\rho(i)^*\})$, where $\mathbb{M}^*$ is an $l \times n$ matrix.
- Setup. Algorithm $\mathcal{C}$ randomly chooses $d_3, d_4, y, \tilde{w}, \tilde{v}, \alpha \in Z_p$, and computes $g_3 = g^{d_3}, g_4 = g^{d_4}$. Then, it sets $d_1 = x_2, d_2 = x_1$, and outputs the public parameter as $pars = (H, g, u, h, w, g_1, g_2, g_3, g_4, \hat{e}(g,g)^\alpha)$ where H is hash function that maps from G_1 to $\{0,1\}^t$ as follows.

$$g = g, \quad w = g^{\tilde{w}}, \quad g_1 = g^{x_2}, \quad g_2 = g^{x_1}, \quad g_3 = g^{x_3}, \quad g_4 = g^{x_4},$$
$$v = g^{\tilde{v}}, \quad u = g^{x_2\alpha}, \quad h = g^{-x_2\alpha A_{l'}^*}g^y, \quad \hat{e}(g,g)^\alpha = \hat{e}(g,g)^\alpha.$$

- Phase 1 and Phase 2. To answer an attribute-based private key query on a set of attributes $\mathbf{A} = \{A_1, ..., A_k\}$, algorithm $\mathcal{C}$ randomly chooses $r, r', r_1, ..., r_k, r_1', ..., r_k' \in Z_p$, implicitly sets

$$\tilde{r} = \frac{r\alpha(A_i - A_{l'}^*)}{\alpha(A_i - A_{l'}^*)x_2 + y}, \quad \tilde{r}' = r' + \frac{yx_1 r}{d_3 d_4(\alpha(A_i - A_{l'}^*)x_2 + y)},$$
$$r_i = \frac{\tilde{r}_i(\alpha(A_i - A_{l'}^*)x_2 + y) - \tilde{v}\tilde{r}}{\alpha(A_i - A_{l'}^*)}, \quad r_i' = \tilde{r}_i' - \frac{yx_1\tilde{r}_i - x_1\tilde{r}\tilde{v}}{d_3 d_4(\alpha(A_i - A_{l'}^*))},$$

and computes

$$K_1 = g^\alpha K_2^{\tilde{w}} = g^\alpha w^{d_1 d_2\tilde{r} + d_3 d_4\tilde{r}'}, \quad K_2 = (g^{x_1})^r g^{r'd_3 d_4} = g^{d_1 d_2\tilde{r} + d_3 d_4\tilde{r}'},$$
$$K_{i,1} = (g^{x_1})^{\alpha(A_i - A_{l'}^*)r_i} = ((u^{A_i}h)^{\tilde{r}_i}v^{-\tilde{r}})^{d_2},$$
$$K_{i,2} = (g^{x_2})^{\alpha(A_i - A_{l'}^*)r_i} = ((u^{A_i}h)^{\tilde{r}_i}v^{-\tilde{r}})^{d_1},$$
$$K_{i,4} = g^{\frac{yx_1 r_i - x_1 r\tilde{v}}{d_3}}(u^{A_i}h)^{d_4 r_i'}(v^{-r'})^{d_4} = ((u^{A_i}h)^{\tilde{r}_i'}v^{-\tilde{r}'})^{d_4},$$
$$K_{i,5} = g^{\frac{yx_1 r_i - x_1 r\tilde{v}}{d_4}}(u^{A_i}h)^{d_3 r_i'}(v^{-r'})^{d_3} = ((u^{A_i}h)^{\tilde{r}_i'}v^{-\tilde{r}'})^{d_3},$$
$$K_{i,3} = (g^{x_1})^{r_i}g^{r_i'd_3 d_4} = g^{d_1 d_2\tilde{r}_i + d_3 d_4\tilde{r}_i'}.$$

- Challenge. Algorithm $\mathcal{A}$ sends algorithm $\mathcal{C}$ a message M^*. Algorithm $\mathcal{C}$ randomly chooses a vector $\overrightarrow{v} = (\mu, y_2, ..., y_n) \in Z_p^n$. Also, for $i \in [1, l]$ and $i \neq l$, algorithm $\mathcal{C}$ randomly chooses $\gamma, s_{i,1}, s_{i,2}, z_i \in Z_p, \mu \in Z_p$. Algorithm $\mathcal{C}$ implicitly sets $z_l = x_3 + x_4, s_{l,1} = x_3$, and computes

$$C^* = H(\hat{e}(g,g)^{\alpha\mu}) \oplus (M^*||\gamma), \quad D^* = g^\mu, \quad E^* = g^{M^*}h^\gamma,$$
$$C_l^* = w^{v_l}Z^{\tilde{v}} = w^{v_l}v^{z_l}, \quad D_{l,1}^* = g^{x_2 x_4} = g_1^{z_l - s_{l,1}},$$
$$D_{l,2}^* = Z^{d_3}g^{-d_3 s_{l,2}} = g_3^{z_l - s_{l,2}}, \quad E_{l,1}^* = g^{x_1 x_3} = g_2^{s_{l,1}},$$
$$E_{l,2}^* = g_4^{s_{l,2}}, \quad F_l^* = Z^y = (u^{\rho(l)}h)^{-z_l},$$
$$\forall i \neq l \in [1, l] \quad C_i^* = w^{v_i}v^{z_i}, \quad D_{i,1}^* = g_1^{z_i - s_{i,1}}, \quad E_{i,2}^* = g_4^{s_{i,2}},$$
$$E_{i,1}^* = g_2^{s_{i,1}}, \quad D_{i,2}^* = g_3^{z_i - s_{i,2}}, \quad F_i^* = (u^{\rho(i)}h)^{-z_i},$$

where $v_l = \overrightarrow{v} \cdot \mathbb{M}_l, v_i = \overrightarrow{v} \cdot \mathbb{M}_i, s_{l,2} \in Z_p$. Therefore, algorithm $\mathcal{C}$ outputs the ciphertext $\mathrm{CT}^* = (C^*, D^*, E^*, \{(C_i^*, D_{i,1}^*, D_{i,2}^*, E_{i,1}^*, E_{i,2}^*, F_i^*)\}_{i \in [1,l]})$ as required.

- Guess. Algorithm $\mathcal{A}$ outputs a guess β' for β.

On the one hand, if $Z = g^{x_3+x_4}$, then algorithm $\mathcal{A}$'s view of this simulation is identical to the original game. On the other hand, if Z is randomly chosen from G, then algorithm $\mathcal{A}$'s advantage is nil. Therefore, if algorithm $\mathcal{A}$ can distinguish game Game_j from game Game_{j+1} with a non-negligible probability, algorithm $\mathcal{B}$ has a non-negligible probability in breaking the decisional linear assumption.

Lemma 3. *Assuming that the decisional linear assumption holds in G, then the advantage of an adversary that can distinguish between the games Game_{j+l+1} and Game_{j+l} for $j \in [1, l]$ is negligible.*

Proof. This proof follows almost the same as that of Lemma 2, except that the simulation is done over the parameters g_3 and g_4 instead of g_1 and g_2.

This completes the proof of Theorem 1.

4.4   Performance Evaluation and Implementation

Denote l by the number of attributes in an access structure, k by the size of an attribute set possessed by each user, χ_1 by the number of elements in $I_{\mathbb{M},\rho} = \{\mathcal{I}_1, ..., \mathcal{I}_{\chi_1}\}$, χ_2 by $|\mathcal{I}_1| + ... + |\mathcal{I}_{\chi_1}|$. Table 2 shows the sizes of the public parameter, the master private key, the ciphertext, the attribute-based private key (i.e., storage complexity) of our expressive CP-ABE scheme supporting partially hidden access structures, where $|\mathbb{A}|$ is the size of the access structure. Note that our scheme is measured in terms of the number of elements in the prime-order groups. According to the analysis in [12], in terms of the pairing-friendly elliptic curves, prime-order groups have a clear advantage in the parameter sizes over composite-order groups. Table 3 gives the computational costs incurred by the encryption and decryption algorithms in the scheme proposed in this paper. Since regarding the same security level, composite-order groups are several orders of magnitude slower than the prime-order groups [21], and the performance gap will get worse with the increase of security level [9], it is not difficult to see that our expressive CP-ABE scheme with partially hidden access structures in the prime-order groups becomes very competitive.

Table 2. The storage overheads in our proposed scheme.

Public parameter	Master private key	Private key	Ciphertext	Group oder
11	5	$5k + 3$	$6l + 3 + |\mathbb{A}|$	prime

We implement the proposed CP-ABE scheme with partially hidden access structures in Charm [1][5], which is a framework developed to facilitate rapid

---

[5] For the explicit information on Charm, please refer to [1]. Note that since it has been clearly shown in [12,21] that the efficiency of schemes in composite-order groups is much worse than that of schemes in prime-order groups, we will not implement those schemes in composite-order groups (e.g., [15]).

Table 3. The computational costs in our proposed scheme, "Expo" and "Multi" denote the exponentiation and multiplication calculation, respectively.

Encrypt			Decrypt		
Multi	Expo	Pairing	Multi	Expo	Pairing
$2l + 1$	$8l + 4$	0	$\leq 5\chi_2 + 2\chi_1$	$\leq \chi_2 + 2\chi_1$	$\leq 6\chi_2 + \chi_1$

prototyping of cryptographic schemes and protocols. Since all Charm routines are designed under the asymmetric groups, our construction is transformed into the asymmetric setting before the implementation. That is, three groups G, $\hat{G}$ and G_1 are used and the pairing $\hat{e}$ is a function from $G \times \hat{G}$ to G_1. Notice that it has been stated in [21] that the assumptions and the security proofs in the symmetric groups can be converted to the asymmetric setting in a generic way. Our experiments are run on a desktop computer with Intel Core i5 − 3470T CPU (4 core 3.20 GHz) and 4 GB RAM running Linux Kernel 3.13.0, which is installed with Charm-0.43 and Python 3.4 for the implementation. Also, we install the PBC library of version 0.5.14 and OpenSSL library of version 1.02 for underlying cryptographic operations.

We simulate the algorithms of the proposed scheme over four elliptic curves: SS512 (a symmetric curve with a 512-bit base field), MNT159 (an asymmetric curve with a 159-bit base field), MNT201 (an asymmetric curve with a 201-bit

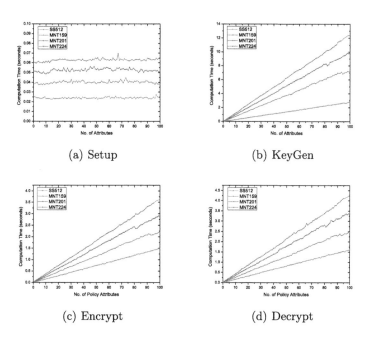

(a) Setup

(b) KeyGen

(c) Encrypt

(d) Decrypt

Fig. 1. Performance of our expressive CP-ABE scheme with partially hidden access structures

base field) and MNT224 (an asymmetric curve with a 224-bit base field), which provide security levels of 80-bit, 80-bit, 100-bit and 112-bit, respectively.

In Fig. 1, the performance of the proposed CP-ABE scheme with partially access structures is shown in terms of four algorithms: the setup algorithm Setup (Fig. 1-(a)), the attribute-based private key generation algorithm KeyGen (Fig. 1-(b)), the encryption algorithm Encrypt (Fig. 1-(c)) and the decryption algorithm Decrypt (Fig. 1-(d)). It is not difficult to see from Fig. 1 that SS512 has the best performance, while MNT224 has the most expensive computational cost among all four curves. For each curve, the computation time for the setup algorithm is immutable with the maximum number of attributes allowed in the system, the computation time for the key generation algorithm increases linearly with the size of attribute set, whilst the computation time for the encryption and decryption algorithms grows linearly with the complexity of the access policy. In addition, in our experiments, the computation time of decrypting a ciphertext ranges from 0.30 s to 0.80 s for a ciphertext with an access policy of 20 attributes and a private key with 20 attributes, and this result is acceptable to most applications in practice.

5   Conclusions

A promising solution for preserving data privacy in cloud services is called ciphertext-policy attribute-based encryption (CP-ABE) [22], where data owners upload their data in encrypted forms to the cloud and share them with users with the specified credentials or attributes. In a standard CP-ABE scheme, every ciphertext is attached with an access structure in a cleartext which may leak sensitive information about the recipients and the encrypted message. To address this problem, the notion of CP-ABE with partially hidden access structures [14,15,18,19,24] was introduced such that the concrete attribute values in access structures are hidden from the public view. Unfortunately, existing CP-ABE schemes with partially hidden access structures [14,15,18,19,24] either only support restricted access structures or are built in the inefficient composite-order bilinear groups. Motivated by this observation, in this paper, we presented a CP-ABE scheme with partially hidden access structures in the prime-order groups, supporting access structures in monotonic boolean formulas expressed as LSSSs. Also, we formally proved its security, and evaluated its efficiency.

Acknowledgments. This research work is supported by the Singapore National Research Foundation under the NCR Award No. NRF2014NCR-NCR001-012.

References

1. Akinyele, J.A., Garman, C., Miers, I., Pagano, M.W., Rushanan, M., Green, M., Rubin, A.D.: Charm: a framework for rapidly prototyping cryptosystems. J. Cryptographic Eng. **3**(2), 111–128 (2013)
2. Beimel, A.: Secure Schemes for Secret Sharing and Key Distribution. Ph.D. thesis, Israel Institute of Technology, Israel Institute of Technology, June 1996

3. Bethencourt, J., Sahai, A., Waters, B.: Ciphertext-policy attribute-based encryption. In: 2007 IEEE Symposium on Security and Privacy (S&P 2007), 20–23, Oakland, California, USA, pp. 321–334. IEEE Computer Society, May 2007
4. Boneh, D., Boyen, X., Shacham, H.: Short group signatures. In: Franklin, M. (ed.) CRYPTO 2004. LNCS, vol. 3152, pp. 41–55. Springer, Heidelberg (2004)
5. Boneh, D., Franklin, M.: Identity-based encryption from the weil pairing. In: Kilian, J. (ed.) CRYPTO 2001. LNCS, vol. 2139, pp. 213–229. Springer, Heidelberg (2001)
6. Boyen, X., Waters, B.: Anonymous hierarchical identity-based encryption (without random oracles). In: Dwork, C. (ed.) CRYPTO 2006. LNCS, vol. 4117, pp. 290–307. Springer, Heidelberg (2006)
7. Cheung, L., Newport, C.C.: Provably secure ciphertext policy ABE. In: Proceedings of the ACM Conference on Computer and Communications Security, CCS , Alexandria, Virginia, USA, October 28–31, pp. 456–465. ACM (2007)
8. Fischlin, M., Fischlin, R.: Efficient non-malleable commitment schemes. J. Cryptology **24**(1), 203–244 (2011)
9. Freeman, D.M.: Converting pairing-based cryptosystems from composite-order groups to prime-order groups. In: Gilbert, H. (ed.) EUROCRYPT 2010. LNCS, vol. 6110, pp. 44–61. Springer, Heidelberg (2010)
10. Goyal, V., Jain, A., Pandey, O., Sahai, A.: Bounded ciphertext policy attribute based encryption. In: Aceto, L., Damgård, I., Goldberg, L.A., Halldórsson, M.M., Ingólfsdóttir, A., Walukiewicz, I. (eds.) ICALP 2008, Part II. LNCS, vol. 5126, pp. 579–591. Springer, Heidelberg (2008)
11. Goyal, V., Pandey, O., Sahai, A., Waters, B.: Attribute-based encryption for fine-grained access control of encrypted data. In: Proceedings of the 13th ACM Conference on Computer and Communications Security, CCS, Alexandria, VA, USA, October 30 - November 3, vol. 5126. LNCS, pp. 89–98. Springer (2006)
12. Guillevic, A.: Comparing the pairing efficiency over composite-order and prime-order elliptic curves. In: Jacobson, M., Locasto, M., Mohassel, P., Safavi-Naini, R. (eds.) ACNS 2013. LNCS, vol. 7954, pp. 357–372. Springer, Heidelberg (2013)
13. Katz, J., Sahai, A., Waters, B.: Predicate encryption supporting disjunctions, polynomial equations, and inner products. J. Cryptology **26**(2), 191–224 (2013)
14. Lai, J., Deng, R.H., Li, Y.: Fully secure cipertext-policy hiding CP-ABE. In: Bao, F., Weng, J. (eds.) ISPEC 2011. LNCS, vol. 6672, pp. 24–39. Springer, Heidelberg (2011)
15. Lai, J., Deng, R.H., Li, Y.: Expressive CP-ABE with partially hidden access structures. In: 7th ACM Symposium on Information, Compuer and Communications Security, ASIACCS 2012, pp. 18–19. ACM, Seoul, Korea, May 2–4 2012
16. Lewko, A., Okamoto, T., Sahai, A., Takashima, K., Waters, B.: Fully secure functional encryption: attribute-based encryption and (hierarchical) inner product encryption. In: Gilbert, H. (ed.) EUROCRYPT 2010. LNCS, vol. 6110, pp. 62–91. Springer, Heidelberg (2010)
17. Lewko, A., Waters, B.: Decentralizing attribute-based encryption. In: Paterson, K.G. (ed.) EUROCRYPT 2011. LNCS, vol. 6632, pp. 568–588. Springer, Heidelberg (2011)
18. Li, J., Ren, K., Zhu, B., Wan, Z.: Privacy-aware attribute-based encryption with user accountability. In: Samarati, P., Yung, M., Martinelli, F., Ardagna, C.A. (eds.) ISC 2009. LNCS, vol. 5735, pp. 347–362. Springer, Heidelberg (2009)
19. Nishide, T., Yoneyama, K., Ohta, K.: Attribute-based encryption with partially hidden encryptor-specified access structures. In: Bellovin, S.M., Gennaro, R., Keromytis, A.D., Yung, M. (eds.) ACNS 2008. LNCS, vol. 5037, pp. 111–129. Springer, Heidelberg (2008)

20. Pedersen, T.P.: Non-interactive and information-theoretic secure verifiable secret sharing. In: Feigenbaum, J. (ed.) CRYPTO 1991. LNCS, vol. 576, pp. 129–140. Springer, Heidelberg (1992)

21. Rouselakis, Y., Waters, B.: Practical constructions and new proof methods for large universe attribute-based encryption. In: ACM SIGSAC Conference on Computer and Communications Security, CCS 2013, pp. 463–474. ACM, Berlin, Germany, November 4–8 2013

22. Sahai, A., Waters, B.: Fuzzy identity-based encryption. In: Cramer, R. (ed.) EURO-CRYPT 2005. LNCS, vol. 3494, pp. 457–473. Springer, Heidelberg (2005)

23. Waters, B.: Ciphertext-policy attribute-based encryption: an expressive, efficient, and provably secure realization. In: Catalano, D., Fazio, N., Gennaro, R., Nicolosi, A. (eds.) PKC 2011. LNCS, vol. 6571, pp. 53–70. Springer, Heidelberg (2011)

24. Zhang, Y., Chen, X., Li, J., Wong, D.S., Li, H.: Anonymous attribute-based encryption supporting efficient decryption test. In: 8th ACM Symposium on Information, Computer and Communications Security, ASIA CCS 2013, pp. 511–516. ACM, Hangzhou, China - May 08–10 2013

Ciphertext-Policy Attribute Based Encryption Supporting Access Policy Update

Yinhao Jiang$^{(\boxtimes)}$, Willy Susilo, Yi Mu, and Fuchun Guo

Centre for Computer and Information Security Research,
School of Computing and Information Technology,
University of Wollongong, Wollongong, Australia
{yj971,wsusilo,ymu,fuchun}@uow.edu.au

Abstract. Attribute-based encryption (ABE) allows one-to-many encryption with static access control. In many occasions, the access control policy must be updated and the original encryptor might be required to re-encrypt the message, which is impractical, since the encryptor might be unavailable. Unfortunately, to date the work in ABE does not consider this issue yet, and hence this hinders the adoption of ABE in practice. In this work, we consider how to efficiently update access policies in Ciphertext-policy Attribute-based Encryption (CP-ABE) systems without re-encryption. We introduce a new notion of CP-ABE supporting access policy update that captures the functionalities of attribute addition and revocation to access policies. We formalize the security requirements for this notion, and subsequently construct two provably secure CP-ABE schemes supporting AND-gate access policy with constant-size ciphertext for user decryption. The security of our schemes are proved under the Augmented Multi-sequences of Exponents Decisional Diffie-Hellman assumption.

Keywords: Attribute-based encryption · Access policy update · Ciphertext-policy

1 Introduction

Attribute-based encryption (ABE) enforces encrypted data to be decrypted with a secure access control mechanism that the assigned attributes must satisfy the access policies associated with ciphertext and private keys. ABE has become a promising cryptographic primitive providing one-to-many encryption. The notion of ABE was put forth by Sahai and Waters [22] with the original notion called *fuzzy IBE*, and subsequently followed by many othere works. In the notion of ABE, there are two variants, namely Ciphertext-policy Attribute-based Encryption (CP-ABE) and Key-policy Attribute-based Encryption (KP-ABE), depending on the location of the access policy. In the former, the access policy is embedded in the ciphertext, whilst in the latter, the access policy is embedded in the private keys. We note that KP-ABE is less flexible than CP-ABE because in KP-ABE, once a users private key is issued the access policy is also

© Springer International Publishing AG 2016
L. Chen and J. Han (Eds.): ProvSec 2016, LNCS 10005, pp. 39–60, 2016.
DOI: 10.1007/978-3-319-47422-9_3

determined, which makes the encryption more difficult as the encryptor needs to compare recipients access policies to all other users to choose a proper set of attributes for the ciphertext. In a CP-ABE system, users' keys are labelled with sets of descriptive attributes and distributed from a trusted key generation authority. Ciphertexts in the system are assigned specific access policies stating what attributes are required for its decryption. In such a system, a ciphertext can be decrypted by a user's key only if the set of attributes associated with the user's key satisfies its access policy.

When using CP-ABE to distribute a message to a specific set of users, the encryptor simply constructs an access policy such that the receivers can only decrypt the ciphertext if they have the set of attributes that satisfy the access policy. The encryptor can just merely encrypt the message with the access policy, and then upload it to the storage server. The storage server does not need to be trusted by receivers but it functions as a proxy, which performs the task that is assigned a priori. Unfortunately, to date, there is no CP-ABE that supports changes of access policies of ciphertexts. We note that this is a highly desirable feature as situation can change from time to time, and without the ability to update the access policy, CP-ABE cannot be adopted in practice. Hence, an efficient update mechanism over access policies of ciphertexts must be enabled.

One may think that the above question can be solved trivially by requesting encryptors to re-encrypt the messages when the access policies are updated. Unfortunately, this approach is very impractical and unusable, since encryptors may not even be available during the access policy update. Alternatively, the Ciphertext-policy Attribute-based Proxy Re-encryption (CP-AB-PRE) system may be employed for access policy update as showed in Fig. 1. The CP-AB-PRE works as follows. When an access control authority has decided to update access policies of certain range of ciphertexts, he uses his own private key to generate a re-encryption key for each ciphertext from the old access policy to a new access policy, and uploads all the re-encryption keys to a proxy to modify the ciphertext. When the proxy receives the re-encryption key, it first checks if the attribute set of the owner of the re-encryption key satisfies the access policy of the ciphertext needed to be re-encrypted. If it does, then it proceeds with the re-encryption. We note that much effort have been put into developing and enhancing Attribute-based Proxy Re-encryption (AB-PRE) including CP-AB-PRE, and this solution is powerful and strong. What AB-PRE provides is an efficient mechanism of re-encryption, to wit to output the result of decrypting and encrypting to a new access policy without actually decrypting the ciphertext or knowing the plaintext, which can provide access policy update but with the restriction that the re-encryptor needs to generate valid re-encryption keys. Nevertheless, when the amount of involved ciphertexts rises, it becomes inefficient for the update initiator to generate all re-encryption keys and the upload bandwidth may also be limited, let alone it is unnecessarily that the initiator's private key should be able to decrypt all involved ciphertexts which then require some other users whose private key can decrypt to help re-encrypting. It can be seen that to update

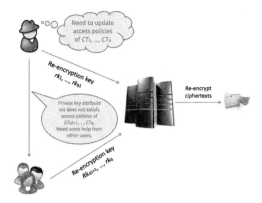

Fig. 1. An example of user updating access policies of ciphertexts employing PRE

access policies for a large amount of ciphertexts will exceeds the capability of AB-PRE who specializes in re-encryption.

1.1 Our Contribution

In this work, we aim to equip the notion of Attribute-based Encryption (ABE) with access policy update. We present the notion of Ciphertext-policy Attribute Based Encryption supporting Access Policy Update (CP-ABE-APU). In our setting, the encryptor will produce encrypted data together with components used for access policy update and send them to a third party, which provides distributed storage servers and functions as access policy update proxy. This third party does not need to be trusted; it will store encrypted data for users accessing and execute access policy update algorithm as requested, which does not give it the ability of decrypting any ciphertexts. We present a new security model to capture these requirements, together with two constructions supporting AND-gate access policy provably secure under augmented assumptions. In our CP-ABE-APU constructions, the ciphertext consists of 3 group elements and the components used for access policy update consist of $n - s - 1$ and t group elements for attribute addition and revocation, respectively, where in the construction for attribute addition the AND-gate access policy consists of s attributes in a ciphertext and there are n attributes in total, and in the construction for attribute revocation the maximum revocation number for a ciphertext is t (Table 1). The components for access policy update will only be stored in storage servers, which makes the ciphertext sent to users for decryption of constant size of 3. We also present the proofs of security of our constructions as well as proofs of intractability of augmented assumptions.

1.2 Related Work

After the notion of Attribute-based Encryption (ABE) was introduced by Sahai and Waters [22], Goyal et al. [9] proposed the first KP-ABE system, in which

Table 1. Comparison between two constructions supporting access policy update

Scheme	Update operation	Attr. universe	Attr. in policy/Max. revocation	Ciphertext for user	Ciphertext for server
Con. 1	Addition	n	s	3	$n - s + 2$
Con. 2	Revocation	n	t	3	$t + 3$

ciphertexts are associated with attributes, and secret keys are associated with access policies. Later, Bethencourt, Sahai and Waters [2] defined a complementary notion indicated in [22], i.e. CP-ABE, but it is proven to be secure in generic group models. Cheung and Newport [6] presented the first CP-ABE construction whose security proof was given in the standard model, which allows the access policies to be a single AND-gate of attributes with values of positive, negative and wildcards. Goyal et al. [8] constructed a CP-ABE scheme but with large key size. Waters [25] designed efficient and expressive CP-ABE systems supporting any monotonic access structure. Attrapadung et al. [1] proposed an efficient CP-ABE for threshold access policy with constant-size ciphertexts, which adopted an algorithm Aggregate from [7] for their decryption algorithm. Later on, Waters [26] proposed the first deterministic finite automata-based functional encryption system in which access policy can be expressed by arbitrary-size regular language. Note that there are also some variants of traditional ABE in the literature, such as [13,20,21,27].

The above schemes are only selectively secure except for [2] being proven in the generic group model. Lewko et al. [11] introduced the dual system encryption technology into the ABE cryptographic setting to convert one of the CP-ABE systems proposed in [25] to achieve fully security with some loss of expressiveness. Later, Lewko and Waters [12] introduced a new method to capture full security without jeopardizing the expressiveness by employing the selective proof technique into the dual system encryption technology.

The proxy re-encryption scheme was first formalized by Blaze, Bleumer, and Strauss [3]. With the concept of ABE and PRE combined, Liang et al. [17] proposed the first CP-AB-PRE scheme based on the CP-ABE scheme [21] supporting non-monotonic access structures. Then Luo et al. [18] proposed another CP-AB-PRE scheme with multi-value positive attributes. Aside from this, Seo et al. [23] proposed a CP-AB-PRE scheme which has constant paring operation latency. Liang et al. constructed CP-AB-PRE schemes [14–16] proven secure in CCA security model.

Recently, Susilo et al. [24] introduced a new notion of recipient-revocable identity-based broadcast encryption scheme. In their scheme, the encryptor produces and sends ciphertexts to a proxy for broadcasting, which will also be able to revoke some identities from the original set of recipients without the knowledge the plaintext.

1.3   Roadmap

The rest of this paper is organized as follows. In Sect. 2, we present some definitions and background that will be used throughout this paper. In Sect. 3, we briefly review bilinear groups and complexity assumption that are used in this paper. We present our CP-ABE scheme that supports attribute addition in Sect. 4, together with its security analysis. Sect. 5 deals with CP-ABE that supports attribute revocation, as well as its security analysis. We presented the analysis of the intractability of the hard problem that is used to analyze our schemes in Sect. 6. The analysis is done in the generic group model. Finally, we conclude the work in Sect. 7.

2   Definitions

We first give formal definitions for the security of Ciphertext-policy Attribute Based Encryption supporting Access Policy Update. Then we give background information on pairings and complexity assumptions.

2.1   Access Structure [6]

Generally speaking, an access structure on attributes is a rule $\mathbb{A}$ that returns either 0 or 1 given an attribute set W. We say that W satisfies $\mathbb{A}$ iff $\mathbb{A}$ answers 1 on W. Access structures may be Boolean expressions, threshold trees, etc.

In this paper, we focus on access structures that consist of a single AND gate whose inputs are attributes. This is denoted $\mathbb{A} = \bigwedge_{\mathsf{at} \in S} \mathsf{at}$, where S is a subset of the attribute universe $\mathcal{P}$ and every at is an attribute in $\mathcal{P}$. Given an attribute set W, $\mathbb{A}$ answers 1 iff for all $\mathsf{at} \in S$, $\mathsf{at} \in W$. Thus, W satisfies $\mathbb{A}$ iff $S \subseteq W$. Since AND-gates are sufficient in many application scenarios, our approach retains significant potential.

2.2   CP-ABE Supporting Access Policy Update Definition

A ciphertext-policy attribute-based encryption system supporting attribute addition consists of five algorithms: Setup, Encrypt, KeyGen, Update and Decrypt.

Setup($1^\lambda, \mathcal{P}$). The setup algorithm takes input the attribute universe $\mathcal{P}$ as well as the implicit security parameter. It outputs the public parameters params and a master secret key msk.

Enc(params, M, $\mathbb{A}$). The encryption algorithm takes in the public parameters params, the message M, and an access structure $\mathbb{A}$ over the universe of attributes. It will output a ciphertext CT such that only users whose private keys associated with attribute sets which satisfy the access structure $\mathbb{A}$ can decrypt M. We assume that the ciphertext implicitly contains $\mathbb{A}$.

KeyGen(msk, W). The key generation algorithm takes as input the master secret msk and a set of attributes W. It outputs a private key sk associated with W.

Update(params, CT, opt, $\mathcal{U}$). The addition algorithm takes as input the public parameters params, a ciphertext CT for an access policy $\mathbb{A} = \bigwedge_{\mathrm{at} \in S}$ at, an operation indicator opt $=$ Add or Revoke and a set of attributes $\mathcal{U}$ with $\mathcal{U} \cap S = \emptyset$ if opt $=$ Add or $\mathcal{U} \subset S$ if opt $=$ Revoke. It outputs a new ciphertext CT' for the new access policy $\mathbb{A}' = \bigwedge_{\mathrm{at} \in S \cup \mathcal{U}}$ or $\bigwedge_{\mathrm{at} \in S \setminus \mathcal{U}}$ according to opt.

Dec(params, CT, sk). The decryption algorithm takes as input the public parameters PK, a ciphertext CT for an access structure $\mathbb{A}$, and a private key sk associated with a set of attributes W. If the attribute set W satisfies the access structure $\mathbb{A}$ then the algorithm will decrypt the ciphertext and return a message M.

Selective CPA Security Model for CP-ABE Supporting Access Policy Update. We now give the security definition for CP-ABE system – Indistinguishability under selective chosen plaintext attacks (IND-sCPA security, for short). This is described by a security game between a challenger and an adversary for a security parameter $\lambda \in \mathbb{N}$. The game proceeds as follows:

Init. The challenger defines an attribute universe $\mathcal{P}$ of size n and gives it to the adversary $\mathcal{A}$. $\mathcal{A}$ chooses a challenge access structure $\mathbb{A}^*$ of one attribute set $S \subset \mathcal{P}$ with $s = |S|$, and gives it to the challenger.

Setup. The challenger runs the Setup algorithm and gives the public parameters params to the adversary.

Phase 1. The adversary queries the challenger for private keys corresponding to sets of attributes W_1, ..., W_{q_1} with the restriction that none of these satisfies the access policy $\mathbb{A}^*$.

Challenge. The adversary declares two equal length messages M_0 and M_1 as well as a attribute set $\mathcal{U}^*$ with $t = |\mathcal{U}^*|$ and $\mathcal{U}^* \subset S$ or $\mathcal{U}^* \cap S = \emptyset$ according to "opt" $=$ Add or "opt" $=$ Revoke respectively. The challenger flips a random coin $\beta \in \{0,1\}$, and encrypts M_β with $\mathbb{A}' = \bigwedge_{\mathrm{at} \in S \setminus \mathcal{U}^*}$ at for "opt" $=$ Add or $\mathbb{A}' = \bigwedge_{\mathrm{at} \in S \cup \mathcal{U}^*}$ at for "opt" $=$ Revoke, producing $CT^* = \mathsf{Enc}(\mathsf{params}, \mathbb{A}^*, M_\beta)$. It gives CT^* to the adversary if $\mathcal{U}^* = \emptyset$, otherwise $CT' = \mathsf{Update}(\mathsf{params}, CT^*, opt, \mathcal{U}^*)$.

Phase 2. The adversary queries the challenger for private keys corresponding to sets of attributes W_{q_1+1}, ..., W_q with the same restriction that none of these satisfies the access policy $\mathbb{A}^*$.

Guess. The adversary outputs a guess β' for β.

The advantage of an adversary in winning this game is defined to be

$$\mathsf{Adv}^{\mathsf{IND\text{-}sCPA}}_{\mathcal{A},\mathsf{CP\text{-}ABE\text{-}AA}} = |\Pr[\beta' = \beta] - \frac{1}{2}|.$$

Definition 1. *A ciphertext-policy attribute-based encryption system supporting access policy update is selective chosen-plaintext attack secure if all polynomial time adversaries have at most a negligible advantage in this security game.*

It is worth noticing that our newly defined security model has two different types of attackers considered.

1. When $\mathcal{U}^* = \emptyset$, the challenge ciphertext CT^* is the direct result of encryption algorithm without any involvement of access policy update algorithm. It can be seen that this is essentially the property of IND-sCPA security for CP-ABE schemes that an adversary who does not hold a private key associated with a set of attributes satisfying the challenge access policy cannot distinguish which submitted message was encrypted as the challenge ciphertext.
2. When $\mathcal{U}^* \neq \emptyset$, the challenge ciphertext CT' is the result of updating $\mathcal{U}^*$ from $\mathbb{A}'$ of the ciphertext of encrypted M_β. It can be seen that in this situation it prevents the type of attackers who obtain private keys associated with any attributes satisfying access policy before update from learning anything about the plaintext.

3 Pairings and Complexity Assumption

Our construction will make use of groups with bilinear maps [5], and two new computational assumptions, that fit into the General Diffie-Hellman Exponent framework proposed by Boneh, Boyen and Goh [4].

3.1 Bilinear Maps

Let $\mathbb{G}_1$, $\mathbb{G}_2$ and $\mathbb{G}_T$ be three cyclic groups of prime order p. A bilinear map $e(\cdot, \cdot)$ is a map $\mathbb{G}_1 \times \mathbb{G}_2 \rightarrow \mathbb{G}_T$ such that for any generators $g_1 \in \mathbb{G}_1$, $g_2 \in \mathbb{G}_2$ and $a, b \in \mathbb{Z}_p$, the following three conditions hold:

1. *Bilinearity.* $e(g_1^a, g_2^b) = e(g_1, g_2)^{ab}$.
2. *Non-degeneracy.* $e(g_1, g_2) \neq 1$.
3. *Computability.* There exists efficient algorithms to compute all group operations as well as the bilinear map $e(\cdot, \cdot)$.

A bilinear map group system is a tuple $\mathbb{S} = (p, \mathbb{G}_1, \mathbb{G}_2, \mathbb{G}_T, e(\cdot, \cdot))$, composed of objects as described above.

In our construction, an arbitrary bilinear map group system is adopted, without any specific additional property. In particular, it does not require $\mathbb{G}_1$ and $\mathbb{G}_2$ to be distinct or equal. Neither does it need an efficient isomorphism from $\mathbb{G}_1$ to $\mathbb{G}_2$, and vice versa.

3.2 Complexity Assumption

The security of our schemes are reduced to the hardness of a problem, which we called the *augmented multi-sequence of exponents decisional Diffie-Hellman problem*. The problems are modified from the (l, m, t)-aMSE-DDH problem defined in [10], of which the generic complexity is covered by the general Diffie-Hellman exponent theorem due to Boneh, Boyen and Goh [4], as the problem lies in the scope of their framework.

First we introduce the assumption which our CP-ABE-AA scheme is reduced to. Let $\mathbb{S} = (p, \mathbb{G}_1, \mathbb{G}_2, \mathbb{G}_T, e(\cdot, \cdot))$ be a bilinear map group system. Let g_0 be a generator of $\mathbb{G}_1$ and h_0 be a generator of $\mathbb{G}_2$. Let n, s be two integers. The first (n, s)-*augmented multi-sequence of exponents decisional Diffie-Hellman* $((n, s)$-aMSE-DDH$_A)$ *problem* related to $\mathbb{S}$ is as follows:

Input. The vector $\overrightarrow{x}_n = (x_1, \ldots, x_n)$ defines the coprime polynomials, of which the components are pairwise distinct elements of $\mathbb{Z}_p$,

$$f(X) = \prod_{i=1}^{n-s} (X + x_i), \quad g(X) = \prod_{i=n-s+1}^{n} (X + x_i),$$

the values

$$\begin{cases} g_0, g_0^{\gamma}, \ldots, g_0^{\gamma^{n-2}}, \quad g_0^{\kappa \cdot \gamma \cdot f(\gamma)}, & (1.1) \\ g_0^{\alpha}, g_0^{\alpha \cdot \gamma}, \ldots, g_0^{\alpha \cdot \gamma^{n-s+1}}, & (1.2) \\ g_0^{\omega \cdot \gamma}, \ldots, g_0^{\omega \cdot \gamma^{n-1}}, & (1.3) \\ h_0, h_0^{\gamma}, \ldots, h_0^{\gamma^{s-2}}, & (1.4) \\ h_0^{\kappa \cdot g(\gamma)}, h_0^{\kappa \cdot \gamma \cdot g(\gamma)}, \ldots, h_0^{\kappa \cdot \gamma^{n-s} \cdot g(\gamma)}, & (1.5) \\ h_0^{\alpha}, h_0^{\alpha \cdot \gamma}, \ldots, h_0^{\alpha \cdot \gamma^{n}}, & (1.6) \\ h_0^{\omega}, h_0^{\omega \cdot \gamma}, \ldots, h_0^{\omega \cdot \gamma^{s-1}}, & (1.7) \end{cases}$$

where κ, ω, α, γ are unknown random elements of $\mathbb{Z}_p$, element $T_b = e(g_0, h_0)^{\kappa \cdot f(\gamma)} \in \mathbb{G}_T$ and a random group element $T_{1-b} \in \mathbb{G}_T$ while b is a fair coin.

Output. a bit b'. The problem is correctly solved if the output is $b' = b$.

The following statement is a corollary of Theorem A.2 in [4]. It provides an intractability bound in the generic model, but in groups equipped with pairings. We emphasize on the fact that, whereas the assumption has several parameters, it is non-interactive, and thus easily falsifiable [19].

Corollary 1 (Generic Security). *For any probabilistic algorithm $\mathcal{B}$ that makes at most q_G queries to the oracles performing group operations in $\mathbb{G}_1, \mathbb{G}_2, \mathbb{G}_T$ and the bilinear map $e(\cdot, \cdot)$, its advantage in solving (n, s)-aMSE-DDH$_A$ problem is bounded as*

$$\mathsf{Adv}_{\mathcal{B}}^{(n,s)\text{-aMSE-DDH}_A}(\lambda) \leq \frac{(q_G + 5n + 3)^2 \cdot d}{2p}$$

where $d = 2n$.

Second, we introduce the assumption for our CP-ABE-AR scheme. Let $\mathbb{S} = (p, \mathbb{G}_1, \mathbb{G}_2, \mathbb{G}_T, e(\cdot, \cdot))$ be a bilinear map group system. Let g_0 be a generator of $\mathbb{G}_1$ and h_0 be a generator of $\mathbb{G}_2$. Let n, s be two integers. The second (n, s)-*augmented multi-sequence of exponents decisional Diffie-Hellman* $((n, s)$-aMSE-DDH$_B)$ *problem* related to $\mathbb{S}$ is as follows:

Input. The vector $\vec{x}_n = (x_1, \dots, x_n)$ defines the coprime polynomials, of which the components are pairwise distinct elements of $\mathbb{Z}_p$,

$$f(X) = \prod_{i=1}^{n-s} (X + x_i), \quad g(X) = \prod_{i=n-s+1}^{n} (X + x_i),$$

the values

$$
\begin{cases}
g_0, g_0^{\gamma}, \dots, g_0^{\gamma^{n-2}}, \quad g_0^{\kappa \cdot \gamma \cdot f(\gamma)}, & (2.1) \\
g_0^{\alpha}, g_0^{\alpha \cdot \gamma}, \dots, g_0^{\alpha \cdot \gamma^{2n-s}}, & (2.2) \\
g_0^{\omega \cdot \gamma}, \dots, g_0^{\omega \cdot \gamma^{n-1}}, & (2.3) \\
h_0, h_0^{\gamma}, \dots, h_0^{\gamma^{s-2}}, & (2.4) \\
h_0^{\kappa \cdot g(\gamma)}, & (2.5) \\
h_0^{\alpha}, h_0^{\alpha \cdot \gamma}, \dots, h_0^{\alpha \cdot \gamma^n}, & (2.6) \\
h_0^{\omega}, h_0^{\omega \cdot \gamma}, \dots, h_0^{\omega \cdot \gamma^{s-1}}, & (2.7)
\end{cases}
$$

where κ, ω, α, γ are unknown random elements of $\mathbb{Z}_p$, element $T_b = e(g_0, h_0)^{\kappa \cdot f(\gamma)} \in \mathbb{G}_T$ and a random group element $T_{1-b} \in \mathbb{G}_T$ while b is a fair coin.

Output. a bit b'. The problem is correctly solved if the output is $b' = b$.

Corollary 2 (Generic Security). *For any probabilistic algorithm $\mathcal{B}$ that makes at most q_G queries to the oracles performing group operations in $\mathbb{G}_1, \mathbb{G}_2, \mathbb{G}_T$ and the bilinear map $e(\cdot, \cdot)$, its advantage in solving (n, s)-aMSE-DDH$_\mathcal{B}$ problem is bounded as*

$$\mathsf{Adv}_{\mathcal{B}}^{(n,s)\text{-aMSE-DDH}_B}(\lambda) \leq \frac{(q_G + 5n + s + 4)^2 \cdot d}{2p}$$

where $d = 2(2n - s)$.

4   CP-ABE Supporting Attribute Addition Construction

In this section, we shall present our ciphertext-policy attribute-based encryption scheme that supports access policy update with operation indicator $opt = \mathsf{Add}$.

Before presenting the description of our scheme, we introduce the adopted algorithm $\mathsf{Aggregate}$ of [7] for the decryption process. This algorithm is given for group elements in $\mathbb{G}_T$ [7], but it can be seen that it works in any group of prime order.

$\mathsf{Aggregate}(\{g^{\frac{r}{\gamma + x_i}}, x_i\}_{1 \leq i \leq n})$. The algorithm takes in values $\{g^{\frac{r}{\gamma + x_i}}, x_i\}_{1 \leq i \leq n}$, where $g^{\frac{r}{\gamma + x_i}} \in \mathbb{G}_1$, $r, \gamma \in \mathbb{Z}_p$ are unknown and x_i's are pairwise distinct. It outputs the value $\mathsf{Aggregate}(\{g^{\frac{r}{\gamma + x_i}}, x_i\}_{1 \leq i \leq n}) = g^{\frac{r}{\prod_{i=1}^{n} (\gamma + x_i)}} \in \mathbb{G}_1$.

4.1 Description

Setup($1^\lambda, \mathcal{P}$). The PKG chooses a suitable encoding τ sending each attribute in $\mathcal{P}$ onto (different) elements $\tau(\mathsf{at}) = \delta \in \mathbb{Z}_p$. It also chooses a bilinear group system $\mathbb{S} = (p, \mathbb{G}_1, \mathbb{G}_2, \mathbb{G}_T, e(\cdot, \cdot))$. It picks at random two generators g of $\mathbb{G}_1$ and h of $\mathbb{G}_2$. Then, the PKG picks at random $\alpha, \gamma \in \mathbb{Z}_p$ and sets $u = g^{\alpha\gamma}$, and $v = e(g^\alpha, h)$.

The master secret key is then $\mathsf{msk} = (g, \alpha, \gamma)$ and the public parameters are

$$\mathsf{params} = \left(\mathcal{P}, n, u, v, h, \{h^{\alpha\gamma^i}\}_{i=0,\ldots,n}, \tau \right).$$

KeyGen($\mathsf{params}, W, \mathsf{msk}$). Given any subset $W \subset \mathcal{P}$ of attributes, the PKG picks $r \in \mathbb{Z}_p$ at random, computes $sk_W = \left(\{g^{\frac{r}{\gamma + \tau(\mathsf{at}_i)}}\}_{\mathsf{at}_i \in W}, h^{\frac{r-1}{\gamma}} \right)$.

Enc($\mathsf{params}, M, \mathbb{A}$). Given an AND-gate access structure of a set of attributes $S \subset \mathcal{P}$ with $s = |S|$, and a message $M \in \mathbb{G}_T$, the sender picks at random $\kappa \in \mathbb{Z}_p$ and computes

$$\begin{cases} E_0 = h^{\kappa \cdot \alpha \cdot \prod_{\mathsf{at} \in S}(\gamma + \tau(\mathsf{at}))}, E_1 = E_0^\gamma, \ldots, E_{n-s} = E_{n-s-1}^\gamma \\ C_1 = u^{-\kappa}, \\ C_M = v^\kappa \cdot M \end{cases}$$

The ciphertext sent from its encryptor to the storage server is then $CT_{\mathsf{server}} = (E_0, \ldots, E_{n-s}, C_1, C_M)$ while the part of $CT = (E_0, C_1, C_M)$ will be accessed by users for decryption.

Update($\mathsf{params}, CT, \text{"add"}, \mathcal{U}$). Given a ciphertext CT with an AND-gate access structure of attribute set S and a set of attributes $\mathcal{U} = \{\mathsf{at}_1', \ldots, \mathsf{at}_t'\}$ with $t = |\mathcal{U}|$ and $\mathcal{U} \cap S = \emptyset$, the proxy adds attributes in $\mathcal{U}$ to the AND-gate access structure of the ciphertext CT as follows.

Let $F(x)$ be the polynomial in x as $F(x) = \prod_{\mathsf{at}' \in \mathcal{U}}(x + \tau(\mathsf{at}')) = f_t x^t + f_{t-1} x^{t-1} + \cdots + f_0$.

Compute $E_0' = E_0^{F(\gamma)} = \prod_{i=0}^t E_i^{f_i}$. Then new ciphertext is then $CT' = (E_0', C_1, C_M)$ with its AND-gate access structure $\mathbb{A}'$ of attribute set $S \cup \mathcal{U}$.

Dec($\mathsf{params}, CT, sk_W$). Any user with a set of attributes W such that $W \models \mathbb{A}$ can use the private key to decrypt the ciphertext.

First, the user computes $e(g, h)^{\kappa \cdot \alpha \cdot r}$ as follows. The user computes

$$\mathsf{Aggregate}(\{g^{\frac{r}{\gamma + \tau(\mathsf{at}_i)}}, \tau(\mathsf{at}_i)\}_{\mathsf{at}_i \in S}) = g^{\frac{r}{\prod_{\mathsf{at}_i \in S_1} \gamma + \tau(\mathsf{at}_i)}}.$$

With the output the user then computes $e(g, h)^{\kappa \cdot \alpha \cdot r} = e(g^{\frac{r}{\prod_{\mathsf{at}_i \in S_1} \gamma + \tau(\mathsf{at}_i)}}, E_0)$. After that, the user computes $e(g, h)^{\kappa \cdot \alpha} = e(C_1, h^{\frac{r-1}{\gamma}}) \cdot e(g, h)^{\kappa \cdot \alpha \cdot r}$. Finally, the user recovers the message $M = \frac{C_M}{e(g, h)^{\kappa \cdot \alpha}}$.

4.2 Security Analysis

In this section, we are going to prove that our CP-ABE-AA scheme is secure against selective chosen-ciphertext attack, assuming that the (n, s)-aMSE-DDH$_A$ problem is hard to solve.

Theorem 1. *Let λ be an integer. For any adversary $\mathcal{A}$ against the* IND-sCPA *security of our CP-ABE-AA encryption scheme $\mathcal{S}_{AA}$, for an attribute universe $\mathcal{P}$ of size n, and a challenge setS with $s = |S|$, there exists an algorithm B of the (n, s)-aMSE-DDH$_A$ problem, such that*

$$\mathsf{Adv}_{\mathcal{B}}^{(n,s)\text{-aMSE-DDH}_A}(\lambda) \geq \mathsf{Adv}_{\mathcal{A},\mathcal{S}_{AA}}^{\text{IND-sCPA}}(\lambda).$$

Proof. We now give the details of the simulation. From now on, we will denote by W_S the subset $W \cap S$.

Init. $\mathcal{B}$ defines an attribute universe $\mathcal{P} = \{\mathsf{at}_1, \ldots, \mathsf{at}_n\}$ of cardinal n. $\mathcal{A}$ gives $\mathcal{B}$ the challenge access structure $\mathbb{A}^*$ defined by an AND-gate policy $\bigwedge_{\mathsf{at} \in S}$ at where $S \subset \mathcal{P}$ of respective cardinal s. Here we assume $S = \{\mathsf{at}_{n-s+1}, \ldots, \mathsf{at}_n\}$.

Setup. The algorithm $\mathcal{B}$ defines $g := g_0^{f(\gamma)}$, $h := h_0$. $\mathcal{B}$ then can compute

- the value $u = g^{\alpha\gamma} = g_0^{\alpha\gamma \cdot f(\gamma)}$ with line (1.2) of its input values, since the exponent $\alpha \cdot \gamma \cdot f(\gamma)$ is a linear combination of $\{\alpha, \alpha \cdot \gamma, \ldots, \alpha \cdot \gamma^{n-s+1}\}$ and $\mathcal{B}$ knows the coefficients of the exponent polynomial.
- the value $v = e(g, h)^\alpha = e(g_0^{\alpha \cdot f(\gamma)}, h_0)$ with line (1.2) and line (1.4).
- elements in $\{h^{\alpha\gamma^i} = h_0^{\alpha \cdot \gamma^i}\}_{i=0,\ldots,n}$ with line (1.6).
- The encoding τ is defined as $\tau(\mathsf{at}_i) = x_i$ for $i = 1, \ldots, n$. It can be seen that the encodings of the first $n - s$ elements are the opposite of the roots of $f(X)$, the encodings of the attributes in S are the opposite of roots of $g(X)$.

Finally, $\mathcal{B}$ sends to $\mathcal{A}$ the simulated public parameters: $\left(u, v, h, \{h^{\alpha\gamma^i}\}_{i=0,\ldots,n}, \tau\right)$.

Phase 1. The adversary $\mathcal{A}$ makes private key queries. To respond to a query on attribute set $W \subset \mathcal{P}$, where $W \not\models \mathbb{A}^*$, the algorithm $\mathcal{B}$ must produce a tuple of the form $\left(\{g^{\frac{r}{\gamma + \tau(\mathsf{at})}}\}_{\mathsf{at} \in W}, h^{\frac{r-1}{\gamma}}\right)$.

Observe that since $W \not\models \mathbb{A}^*$ all allowed queries must satisfy $|W_S| < s$. $\mathcal{B}$ defines the polynomial $Q_{W_S}(X) = \begin{cases} 1 & |W_S| = 0 \\ \lambda_i \cdot \prod_{\mathsf{at} \in W_S}(X + \tau(\mathsf{at})) & |W_S| > 0 \end{cases}$, where $\lambda = \left(\prod_{A \in \omega_S} \tau(\mathsf{at})\right)^{-1}$, and simulates a private key for W as follows:

$\mathcal{B}$ picks at random y_W in $\mathbb{Z}_p$, and defines $r := (1 + \omega y_W \gamma) Q_{W_S}(\gamma)$. $\mathcal{B}$ then computes the elements for sk_W:

- For any attribute $\mathsf{at} \in W$, $g^{\frac{r}{\gamma + \tau(\mathsf{at})}} = g_0^{\omega\gamma y_W \cdot \frac{f(\gamma)Q_{W_S}(\gamma)}{\gamma + \tau(\mathsf{at})}} \cdot g_0^{\frac{f(\gamma)Q_{W_S}(\gamma)}{\gamma + \tau(\mathsf{at})}}$. Since an attribute $\mathsf{at} \in W$ can be in W_S or $\mathcal{P} \setminus S$, $(\gamma + \tau(\mathsf{at})) | f(\gamma) Q_{W_S}(\gamma)$. The first factor can be computed with line (1.3) as its exponent is a polynomial in γ of degree at most $n-1$, and the second factor can be computed with line (1.1) as its exponent is a polynomial in γ of degree at most $n-2$.

- The value $h^{\frac{r-1}{\gamma}} = h_0^{\omega y w\, Q_{W_S}(\gamma)} \cdot h_0^{\frac{Q_{W_S}(\gamma)-1}{\gamma}}$, where the first factor can be computed from line (1.7) and the second factor can be computed from line (1.4), since $Q_{W_S}(\gamma)$ is a polynomial with independent term 1 by its definition, thus $\frac{Q_{W_S}(\gamma)-1}{\gamma}$ is a linear combination of $\{1, \gamma, \ldots, \gamma^{s-2}\}$.

Challenge. Once $\mathcal{A}$ sends to $\mathcal{B}$ the two messages M_0 and M_1 as well as an update attribute set $\mathcal{U}^*$, $\mathcal{B}$ flips a coin $\beta \in \{0,1\}$, and sets $C_M^* = T_0 \cdot M_\beta$. To simulate the rest of the challenge ciphertext, $\mathcal{B}$ implicitly defines the randomness for the encryption as $\kappa^* = \kappa/\alpha$, and sets $E_0^* = h^{\kappa^* \alpha \cdot g(\gamma)} = h_0^{\kappa \cdot g(\gamma)}$ which is given in line (1.5) as well as $E_1^*, \ldots, E_{n-s}^*$. To complete the ciphertext, B computes $C_1^* = u^{-\kappa^*} = g_0^{-\kappa\gamma f(\gamma)}$ from line (1.1). $\mathcal{B}$ gives $\mathcal{A}$ the challenge ciphertext $CT^* = (E_0^*, E_1^*, \ldots, E_{n-s}^*, C_1^*, C_M^*)$.

Phase 2. After the challenge step $\mathcal{A}$ may make other key extraction queries, which are answered as before.

Guess. $\mathcal{A}$ outputs a β'. If $\beta' = \beta$, $\mathcal{B}$ outputs 0; otherwise $\mathcal{B}$ outputs 1.

Probability Analysis

Let $\mathcal{I} = (\overrightarrow{x}_n, \gamma, \kappa, \omega, \alpha, T_b, T_{1-b})$ be the input of the algorithm $\mathcal{B}$ and the adversary $\mathcal{A}$ break our CP-ABE scheme with advantage $\mathsf{Adv}_{\mathcal{A}, \mathcal{S}_{AA}}^{\mathsf{IND\text{-}sCPA}}(\lambda)$. Below we analyse the simulation in two cases.

Case 1 ($\mathcal{U}^* = \emptyset$). Let $\kappa = \kappa^* \cdot \alpha$. One can verify that in this case, $E_0^* = h_0^{\kappa \cdot g(\gamma)} = h^{\kappa^* \cdot \alpha \cdot \prod_{\text{at} \in S}(\gamma + \tau(\text{at}))}$ and $C_1^* = g_0^{-\kappa \cdot \gamma \cdot f(\gamma)} = g_0^{-\kappa^* \cdot \alpha \cdot \gamma \cdot f(\gamma)} = u^{-\kappa^*}$. As for the C_M^*, we also note that if $b = 0$, $T_0 = e(g0, h0)^{\kappa f(\gamma)}$, then $C_M^* = e(g_0, h_0)^{\kappa f(\gamma)}$. $M_\beta = e(g^\alpha, h)^{\kappa^*} \cdot M_\beta = v^{\kappa^*} \cdot M_\beta$. Therefore, the simulation of $\mathcal{B}$ is perfect, and the adversary $\mathcal{A}$ will guess the bit β with its advantage. Hence, if $b = 0$ we have

$$|\Pr[\mathcal{B}(\mathcal{I}) = 0|b = 0] - \frac{1}{2}| = \mathsf{Adv}_{\mathcal{A}}^{\mathsf{IND\text{-}sCPA}}(\lambda).$$

Else, if $b = 1$ and T_0 is uniformly random in $\mathbb{G}_T$, C_M^* is uniformly random and independent in $\mathbb{G}_T$, and the value of β is independent from $\mathcal{A}$'s view as well,

$$\Pr[\mathcal{B}(\mathcal{I}) = 0|b = 1] = \frac{1}{2}.$$

Thus, we have the advantage of $\mathcal{B}$ in solving the (n, s)-aMSE-DDH$_\mathcal{B}$ problem in Case 1 is

$$\mathsf{Adv}_{\mathcal{B}}^{(n,s)\text{-}\mathsf{aMSE_B\text{-}DDH}}(\lambda) = |\Pr[\mathcal{B}(\mathcal{I}) = 0|b = 0] - \Pr[\mathcal{B}(\mathcal{I}) = 0|b = 1]|$$
$$\geq \mathsf{Adv}_{\mathcal{A}}^{\mathsf{IND\text{-}sCPAwAR}}(\lambda).$$

Case 2 ($\mathcal{U}^* = \{\text{at}_1', \text{at}_2', \ldots, \text{at}_t'\} \neq \emptyset$). In this case, we first show that how a challenge ciphertext should be produced in a real game. Formally, the correct procedures are as follows.

Let $S' = S \setminus \mathcal{U}^*$. The encryption algorithm $\mathsf{Enc}(\mathsf{params}, \mathbb{A}' = \bigwedge_{\mathsf{at} \in S'} \mathsf{at}, M_\beta)$ is run to get CT^*. More precisely, it picks a randomness $\kappa' \in \mathbb{Z}_p$ and computes,

$$CT^* = (E_0^*, E_1^*, \cdots, E_{n-s+t}^*, C_1^*, C_M^*)$$
$$= (h^{\kappa' \cdot \alpha \cdot \prod_{\mathsf{at} \in S'} (\gamma + \tau(\mathsf{at}))}, \ldots, h^{\kappa' \cdot \alpha \cdot \gamma^{n-s+t} \cdot \prod_{\mathsf{at} \in S'} (\gamma + \tau(\mathsf{at}))}, u^{-\kappa'}, v^{\kappa'} \cdot M).$$

The Addition algorithm $\mathsf{Add}(\mathsf{params}, CT^*, \mathcal{U}^*)$ is run to add the attribute set $\mathcal{U}^*$ to the access policy of the ciphertext CT^*. It processes as follows.

Let $F^*(x)$ be the polynomial in x as $F^*(x) = \prod_{\mathsf{at}' \in \mathcal{U}^*} (x + \tau(\mathsf{at}')) = f_t^* x^t + f_{t-1}^* x^{t-1} + \cdots + f_0^*$.

Compute $E_0'^* = (E_0^*)^{F^*(\gamma)} = \prod_{i=0}^t (E_i^*)^{f_i^*}$.

Finally, the challenge ciphertext in a real game is produced $CT' = (E_0'^*, C_1^*, C_M^*)$.

Now we assume that the randomness κ' used in producing CT^* is defined as $\kappa' \cdot \alpha = \kappa$. The challenge ciphertext CT' turns out to be as follows,

$$C_M^* = M_\beta \cdot v^{\kappa'} = M_\beta \cdot v^{\frac{\kappa}{\alpha}},$$

$$E_0'^* = h^{\kappa' \cdot \alpha \cdot \prod_{\mathsf{at} \in S} (\gamma + \tau(\mathsf{at}))} = h^{\kappa \cdot \prod_{\mathsf{at} \in S} (\gamma + \tau(\mathsf{at}))} = h_0^{\kappa \cdot g(\gamma)},$$

$$C_1^* = u^{-\kappa'} = g_0^{\kappa \cdot \gamma \cdot f(\gamma)}.$$

It can be seen that if $b = 0$, $T_0 = e(g_0, h_0)^{\kappa \cdot f(\gamma)}$, the challenge ciphertext in a real game is exactly the same as the simulated challenge ciphertext. The simulated game would be a perfect simulation if it can be proved that the setting of κ' is indistinguishable from a real random value from the view of $\mathcal{A}$. It will suffice as κ is random to $\mathcal{A}$. Thus, if $b = 0$ we have

$$|\Pr[\mathcal{B}(\mathcal{I}) = 0 | b = 0] - \frac{1}{2}| = \mathsf{Adv}_{\mathcal{A}, \mathcal{S}_{AA}}^{\mathsf{IND\text{-}sCPA}}(\lambda).$$

On the other hand, if $b = 1$ and T_0 is a random element from $\mathbb{G}_T$, C_M^* is random and independent from the view of $\mathcal{A}$,

$$|\Pr[\mathcal{B}(\mathcal{I}) = 0 | b = 1] = \frac{1}{2}.$$

Thus, we have the advantage of $\mathcal{B}$ in solving the (n, s)-$\mathsf{aMSE\text{-}DDH}_B$ problem in Case 2 is

$$\mathsf{Adv}_{\mathcal{B}}^{(n,s)-\mathsf{aMSE_B\text{-}DDH}}(\lambda) = |\Pr[\mathcal{B}(\mathcal{I}) = 0 | b = 0] - \Pr[\mathcal{B}(\mathcal{I}) = 0 | b = 1]|$$
$$\geq \mathsf{Adv}_{\mathcal{A}, \mathcal{S}_{AA}}^{\mathsf{IND\text{-}sCPAwAR}}(\lambda).$$

This completes the proof. $\qquad\qquad\qquad\qquad\qquad\qquad\qquad\qquad\qquad\quad \square$

5   CP-ABE Supporting Attribute Revocation Construction

In this section, we shall present our ciphertext-policy attribute-based encryption scheme that supports access policy update with operation indicator $opt = $ Revoke.

5.1 Description

Setup($1^\lambda, \mathcal{P}$). The PKG selects a suitable encoding τ sending each attribute in $\mathcal{P}$ onto different elements $\tau(\mathsf{at}) = \delta \in \mathbb{Z}_p$. It also chooses a bilinear group system $\mathbb{S} = (p, \mathbb{G}_1, \mathbb{G}_2, \mathbb{G}_T, e(\cdot, \cdot))$. It picks at random two generators g of $\mathbb{G}_1$ and h of $\mathbb{G}_2$. Then, the PKG picks at random $\alpha, \gamma \in \mathbb{Z}_p$ and sets $\{u_i = g^{\alpha \gamma^i}\}_{i=1\ldots n}$, and $v = e(g^\alpha, h)$.

The master secret key is then $\mathsf{msk} = (g, \alpha, \gamma)$ and the public parameters are

$$\mathsf{params} = \left(\mathcal{P}, n, \{u_i\}_{i=1,\ldots,n}, v, h, \{h^{\alpha \gamma^i}\}_{i=0,\ldots,n}, \tau \right).$$

KeyGen($\mathsf{params}, W, \mathsf{msk}$). Given any subset $W \subset \mathcal{P}$ of attributes, the PKG picks $r \in \mathbb{Z}_p$ at random, computes $sk_W = \left(\{g^{\frac{r}{\gamma + \tau(\mathsf{at}_i)}}\}_{\mathsf{at}_i \in W}, h^{\frac{r-1}{\gamma}} \right)$.

Enc($\mathsf{params}, M, \mathbb{A}, l$). Given an AND-gate access structure of a set of attributes $S \subset \mathcal{P}$ with $s = |S|$, a message $M \in \mathbb{G}_T$ and an extra input which is a maximum revocation number $l \leq s$, the sender picks at random $\kappa \in \mathbb{Z}_p$ and computes

$$\begin{cases} E_0 = h^{\kappa \cdot \alpha \cdot \prod_{\mathsf{at} \in S}(\gamma + \tau(\mathsf{at}))} \\ C_1 = u_1^{-\kappa}, \ldots, C_{l+1} = u_{l+1}^{-\kappa}, \\ C_M = v^\kappa \cdot M \end{cases}$$

The ciphertext sent from its encryptor to the storage server is then $CT_{\mathsf{server}} = (E_0, C_1, \ldots, C_{t+1}, C_M)$ while the part of $CT = (E_0, C_1, C_M)$ will be access by users for decryption.

Update($\mathsf{params}, CT, \text{``revoke''}, \mathcal{U}$). Given a ciphertext $CT = (E_0, C_1, \ldots, C_{t+1}, C_M)$ for an AND-gate access structure $\mathbb{A} = \wedge_{\mathsf{at} \in S}\mathsf{at}$, a revocation attribute set $\mathcal{U} = \{\mathsf{at}'_1, \ldots, \mathsf{at}'_t\} \subseteq S$ with $t \leq l$ and the public parameters params, the revocation update algorithm works as follows.

Let $F(x)$ be the polynomial in x as

$$F(x) = \frac{1}{\prod_{\mathsf{at}' \in \mathcal{U}} \tau(\mathsf{at}')} \prod_{\mathsf{at}' \in \mathcal{U}} (x + \tau(\mathsf{at}')) = f_t x^t + f_{t-1} x^{t-1} + \cdots + f_0.$$

Compute

- $C'_M = C_M \cdot e(\prod_{i=1}^{t} C_i^{-f_i}, h) = M \cdot e(g^{\kappa \cdot \alpha \cdot \sum_{i=0}^{t} f_i \gamma^i}, h) = M \cdot v^{\kappa \cdot F(\gamma)}$,
- $E'_0 = E_0^{\frac{1}{\prod_{\mathsf{at}' \in \mathcal{U}} \tau(\mathsf{at}')}} = h^{\kappa \cdot \alpha \cdot \prod_{\mathsf{at} \in S \setminus \mathcal{U}}(\gamma + \tau(\mathsf{at})) \cdot F(\gamma)}$,
- $C'_1 = \prod_{i=1}^{t+1} C_i^{f_{i-1}} = g^{-\kappa \cdot \alpha \cdot \gamma \cdot F(\gamma)} = u_1^{-\kappa \cdot F(\gamma)}$.

The new ciphertext is then $CT = (E'_0, C'_1, C'_M)$ with new randomness $\kappa \cdot F(\gamma)$.

Dec($\mathsf{params}, CT, sk_W$). Any user with a set of attributes W such that $W \models \mathbb{A}$ can use the private key to decrypt the ciphertext.

First, the user computes $e(g, h)^{\kappa \cdot \alpha \cdot r}$ as follows. The user computes

$$\mathsf{Aggregate}(\{g^{\frac{r}{\gamma+\tau(\mathsf{at}_i)}}, \tau(\mathsf{at}_i)\}_{\mathsf{at}_i \in S_1}) = g^{\frac{r}{\prod_{\mathsf{at}_i \in S_1} \gamma+\tau(\mathsf{at}_i)}}.$$

With the output the user computes $e(g, h)^{\kappa \cdot \alpha \cdot r} = e(g^{\frac{r}{\prod_{\mathsf{at}_i \in S_1} \gamma+\tau(\mathsf{at}_i)}}, E_0)$. After that, the user computes $e(g, h)^{\kappa \cdot \alpha} = e(C_1, h^{\frac{r-1}{\gamma}}) \cdot e(g, h)^{\kappa \cdot \alpha \cdot r}$. Finally, the user recovers the message $M = \frac{C_M}{e(g,h)^{\kappa \cdot \alpha}}$.

5.2 Security Analysis

In this section, we prove that our scheme is secure against selective chosen-ciphertext attack, assuming that the (n, s)-aMSE-DDH$_B$ problem is hard to solve.

Theorem 2. *Let λ be an integer. For any adversary $\mathcal{A}$ against the IND-sCPA security of our CP-ABE-AR encryption scheme $\mathcal{S}_{AR}$, for an attribute universe $\mathcal{P}$ of size n, and a challenge set S with $s = |S|$, there exists an algorithm B of the (n, s)-aMSE-DDH$_B$ problem, such that*

$$\mathsf{Adv}_{\mathcal{B}}^{(n,s)\text{-aMSE-DDH}_B}(\lambda) \geq \mathsf{Adv}_{\mathcal{A}, \mathcal{S}_{AR}}^{\mathsf{IND\text{-}sCPA}}(\lambda).$$

We now give the details of the simulation.

Init. $\mathcal{B}$ defines an attribute universe $\mathcal{P} = \{\mathsf{at}_1, \ldots, \mathsf{at}_n\}$ of cardinal n. $\mathcal{A}$ gives $\mathcal{B}$ the challenge access structure $\mathbb{A}^*$ defined by an AND-gate policy $\bigwedge_{\mathsf{at} \in S} \mathsf{at}$ where $S \subset \mathcal{P}$ of respective cardinal s. Here we assume $S = \{\mathsf{at}_{n-s+1}, \ldots, \mathsf{at}_n\}$.

Setup. The algorithm $\mathcal{B}$ defines $g := g_0^{f(\gamma)}$, $h := h_0$. $\mathcal{B}$ then can compute

- the values $u_i = g^{\alpha \gamma^i} = g_0^{\alpha \gamma^i \cdot f(\gamma)}$ with line (2.2) of its input values, since the exponent $\alpha \cdot \gamma^i \cdot f(\gamma)$ is a linear combination of $\{g_2(\gamma) \cdot \alpha, \ldots, g_2(\gamma) \cdot \alpha \cdot \gamma^{2n-s}\}$ and $\mathcal{B}$ knows the coefficients of the exponent polynomial.
- the value $v = e(g, h)^\alpha = e(g_0^{\alpha \cdot f(\gamma)}, h_0)$ with line (2.2) for $g_0^{\alpha \cdot f(\gamma)}$ and line (2.4) for h_0.
- elements in $\{h^{\alpha \gamma^i} = h_0^{\alpha \cdot \gamma^i}\}_{i=0,\ldots,n}$ with line (2.6).
- The encoding τ is defined as $\tau(\mathsf{at}_i) = x_i$ for $i = 1, \ldots, n$. It can be seen that the encodings of the first $n - s$ elements are the opposite of the roots of $f(X)$, the encodings of the attributes in S are the opposite of roots of $g(X)$.

Finally, $\mathcal{B}$ sends to $\mathcal{A}$ the simulated public parameters: $\left(u, v, h, \{h^{\alpha \gamma^i}\}_{i=0,\ldots,n}, \tau\right)$.

Phase 1. The adversary $\mathcal{A}$ makes private key queries. To respond to a query on attribute set $W \subset \mathcal{P}$, where $W \not\models \mathbb{A}^*$, the algorithm $\mathcal{B}$ must produce a tuple of the form $\left(\{g^{\frac{r}{\gamma+\tau(\mathsf{at})}}\}_{\mathsf{at} \in W}, h^{\frac{r-1}{\gamma}}\right)$.

Observe that since $W \not\models \mathbb{A}^*$ all allowed queries must satisfy $|W_S| < s$. $\mathcal{B}$ defines the polynomial $Q_{W_S}(X) = \begin{cases} 1 & |W_S| = 0 \\ \lambda_i \cdot \prod_{\mathsf{at} \in W_S}(X + \tau(\mathsf{at})) & |W_S| > 0 \end{cases}$, where $\lambda = \left(\prod_{A \in \omega_S} \tau(\mathsf{at})\right)^{-1}$, and simulates a private key for W as follows:

$\mathcal{B}$ picks at random y_W in $\mathbb{Z}_p$, and defines $r := (1 + \omega y_W \gamma) Q_{W_S}(\gamma)$. $\mathcal{B}$ then computes the elements for sk_W:

- For any attribute at $\in W$, $g^{\frac{r}{\gamma + \tau(\text{at})}} = g_0^{\omega \gamma y_W \cdot \frac{f(\gamma) Q_{W_S}(\gamma)}{\gamma + \tau(\text{at})}} \cdot g_0^{\frac{f(\gamma) Q_{W_S}(\gamma)}{\gamma + \tau(\text{at})}}$. Since an attribute at $\in W$ can be in W_S or $\mathcal{P} \setminus (S)$, $(\gamma + \tau(\text{at})) | f(\gamma) g_2(\gamma) Q_{W_S}(\gamma)$. The first factor can be computed with line (2.3) as its exponent is a polynomial in γ of degree at most $n - 1$, and the second factor can be computed with line (2.1) as its exponent is a polynomial in γ of degree at most $n - 2$.

- The value $h^{\frac{r-1}{\gamma}} = h_0^{\omega y_W Q_{W_S}(\gamma)} \cdot h_0^{\frac{Q_{W_S}(\gamma)-1}{\gamma}}$, where the first factor can be computed from line (2.7) and the second factor can be computed from line (2.4), since $Q_{W_{S_1}}(\gamma)$ is a polynomial with independent term 1 by its definition, thus $\frac{Q_{W_S}(\gamma)-1}{\gamma}$ is a linear combination of $\{1, \gamma, \ldots, \gamma^{s-2}\}$.

Challenge. Once $\mathcal{A}$ sends to $\mathcal{B}$ the two messages M_0 and M_1 as well as a attribute set $\mathcal{U}^*$ with $t = |\mathcal{U}^*|$ and $\mathcal{U}^* \cap S = \emptyset$ including all attributes needed to be revoked, $\mathcal{B}$ flips a coin $\beta \in \{0, 1\}$, and sets $C_M^* = T_0 \cdot M_\beta$. To simulate the rest of the ciphertext components, $\mathcal{B}$ sets $E_0^* = h_0^{\kappa \cdot g(\gamma)}$ which is given in line (2.5). Then, B computes $C_1^* = (g_0^{\kappa \gamma f(\gamma)})^{-1}$ from line (2.1). $\mathcal{B}$ gives $\mathcal{A}$ the challenge ciphertext $CT^* = (E_0^*, C_1^*, C_M^*)$.

Here we observe that

if $\mathcal{U}^* = \emptyset$, $t = 0$ $\mathcal{B}$ should output to the adversary $CT = \text{Enc}(\text{params}, \mathbb{A}^*, 0, M_\beta) = (E_0, C_1, C_M)$ for access structure $\mathbb{A}^*$, of which the challenge ciphertext matches the form;

if $\mathcal{U}^* \neq \emptyset$ $\mathcal{B}$ should output $CT' = \text{Revoke}(\text{params}, \text{Enc}(\text{params}, \mathbb{A}', t, M_\beta), \mathcal{U}^*) = (E_0', C_1', C_M)$ for access structure $\mathbb{A}^*$, of which the challenge ciphertext matches the form as well.

Phase 2. After the challenge step $\mathcal{A}$ may make other key extraction queries, which are answered as before.

Guess. $\mathcal{A}$ outputs a β'. If $\beta' = \beta$, $\mathcal{B}$ outputs 0; otherwise $\mathcal{B}$ outputs 1.

Probability Analysis

Let $\mathcal{I} = (\overrightarrow{x}_n, \gamma, \kappa, \omega, \alpha, T_b, T_{1-b})$ be the input of the algorithm $\mathcal{B}$ and the adversary $\mathcal{A}$ break our CP-ABE scheme with advantage $\text{Adv}_{\mathcal{A}}^{\text{IND-sCPA}}(\lambda)$. Below we analyse the simulation in two cases.

Case 1 ($\mathcal{U}^* = \emptyset$). Let $\kappa^* = \kappa \cdot \alpha$. One can verify that in this case, $E_0^* = h_0^{\kappa \cdot g(\gamma)} = h^{\kappa^* \cdot \alpha \cdot \gamma \cdot \prod_{\text{at} \in S}(\gamma + \tau(\text{at}))}$ and $C_1^* = g_0^{-\kappa \cdot \gamma \cdot f(\gamma)} = g_0^{-\kappa^* \cdot \alpha \cdot \gamma \cdot f(\gamma)} = u_1^{-\kappa^*}$. As for the C_M^*, we also note that if $b = 0$, $T_0 = e(g_0, h_0)^{\kappa f(\gamma)}$, then $C_M^* = e(g_0, h_0)^{\kappa f(\gamma)} \cdot M_\beta = e(g^\alpha, h)^{\kappa^*} \cdot M_\beta = v^{\kappa^*} \cdot M_\beta$. Therefore, the simulation of $\mathcal{B}$ is perfect, and the adversary $\mathcal{A}$ will guess the bit β with its advantage. Hence, if $b = 0$ we have

$$|\Pr[\mathcal{B}(\mathcal{I}) = 0 | b = 0] - \frac{1}{2}| = \text{Adv}_{\mathcal{A}}^{\text{IND-sCPA}}(\lambda).$$

Else, if $b = 1$ and T_0 is uniformly random in $\mathbb{G}_T$, C_M^* is uniformly random and independent in $\mathbb{G}_T$, and the value of β is independent from $\mathcal{A}$'s view as well,

$$\Pr[\mathcal{B}(\mathcal{I}) = 0 | b = 1] = \frac{1}{2}.$$

Thus, we have the advantage of $\mathcal{B}$ in solving the (n, s)-aMSE-DDH$_B$ problem in Case 1 is

$$\mathsf{Adv}_{\mathcal{B}}^{(n,s)-\mathsf{aMSE_B}-\mathsf{DDH}}(\lambda) = |\Pr[\mathcal{B}(\mathcal{I}) = 0 | b = 0] - \Pr[\mathcal{B}(\mathcal{I}) = 0 | b = 1]|$$
$$\geq \mathsf{Adv}_{\mathcal{A}}^{\mathsf{IND}-\mathsf{sCPAwAR}}(\lambda).$$

Case 2 $(\mathcal{U}^* \neq \emptyset)$. In this case, we first show how a challenge ciphertext should be produced in a real game. Formally, the correct procedures are as follows.

Let $S' = \mathcal{U}^* \cup S$. The encryption algorithm $\mathsf{Enc}(\mathsf{params}, \mathbb{A}' = \bigwedge_{\mathsf{at} \in S'} \mathsf{at}, t, M_\beta)$ is run to get CT^*. More precisely, it picks a randomness $\kappa' \in \mathbb{Z}_p$ and computes,

$$CT^* = (E_0^*, C_1^*, \cdots, C_{t+1}^*, C_M^*)$$
$$= (h^{\kappa' \cdot \alpha \cdot \prod_{\mathsf{at} \in S_1}(\gamma + \tau(\mathsf{at}))}, u_1^{-\kappa'}, \ldots, u_{t+1}^{-\kappa'}, C_M = v^{\kappa'} \cdot M).$$

The revocation algorithm $\mathsf{Revoke}(\mathsf{params}, CT^*, \mathcal{U}^*)$ is run to revoke the attribute set $\mathcal{U}^*$ from the access policy of the ciphertext CT^*. It processes as follows.

Let $F(x)$ be the polynomial in x as

$$F(x) = \frac{1}{\prod_{\mathsf{at}' \in \mathcal{U}^*} \tau(\mathsf{at}')} \prod_{\mathsf{at}' \in \mathcal{U}^*} (x + \tau(\mathsf{at}')) = f_t x^t + f_{t-1} x^{t-1} + \cdots + f_0.$$

Compute $C_M' = C_M \cdot e(\prod_{i=1}^l C_i^{f_i}, h) = M_\beta \cdot v^{\kappa' \cdot F(\gamma)}$.

Compute $E_0' = E_0^{\frac{1}{\prod_{\mathsf{at}' \in \mathcal{U}} \tau(\mathsf{at}')}} = h^{\kappa' \cdot \alpha \cdot F(\gamma) \cdot \prod_{\mathsf{at} \in S}(\gamma + \tau(\mathsf{at}))}$.

Compute $C_1' = \prod_{i=1}^{l+1} C_i^{f_{i-1}} = u_1^{-\kappa' \cdot F(\gamma)}$.

Finally, the challenge ciphertext in a real game is produced $CT' = (E_0', C_1', C_M')$.

Now we assume that the randomness κ' used in producing CT^* is defined as $\kappa' = \frac{\kappa}{\alpha} \cdot \frac{1}{F(\gamma)}$. Then let $\kappa^* = \kappa/\alpha$ and the challenge ciphertext CT' turns out to be as follows,

$$C_M' = M_\beta \cdot v^{\frac{\kappa}{\alpha}} = M_\beta \cdot v^{\kappa^*},$$

$$E_0' = h^{\kappa \cdot \prod_{\mathsf{at} \in S}(\gamma + \tau(\mathsf{at}))} = h^{\kappa^* \cdot \alpha \cdot \gamma \cdot \prod_{\mathsf{at} \in S}(\gamma + \tau(\mathsf{at}))},$$

$$C_1' = u_1^{\frac{-\kappa}{\alpha}} = u_1^{\kappa^*}.$$

It can be seen that if $b = 0$, $T_0 = e(g_0, h_0)^{\kappa \cdot f(\gamma)}$, the challenge ciphertext in a real game is exactly the same as the simulated challenge ciphertext. The simulated game would be a perfect simulation if it can be proved that the setting of κ' is indistinguishable from a real random value from the view of $\mathcal{A}$. It will suffice as κ is random to $\mathcal{A}$. Thus, if $b = 0$ we have

$$\left| \Pr[\mathcal{B}(\mathcal{I}) = 0 | b = 0] - \frac{1}{2} \right| = \mathsf{Adv}_{\mathcal{A}, \mathcal{S}_{AR}}^{\text{IND-sCPA}}(\lambda).$$

On the other hand, if $b = 1$ and T_0 is a random element from $\mathbb{G}_T$, C_M^* is random and independent from the view of $\mathcal{A}$, $\Pr[\mathcal{B}(\mathcal{I}) = 0 | b = 1] = \frac{1}{2}$. Thus, we have the advantage of $\mathcal{B}$ in solving the (n, s)-aMSE-DDH$_B$ problem in Case 2 is

$$\mathsf{Adv}_{\mathcal{B}}^{(n,s)-\text{aMSE}_B\text{-DDH}}(\lambda) = |\Pr[\mathcal{B}(\mathcal{I}) = 0 | b = 0] - \Pr[\mathcal{B}(\mathcal{I}) = 0 | b = 1]|$$
$$\geq \mathsf{Adv}_{\mathcal{A}, \mathcal{S}_{AR}}^{\text{IND-sCPAwAR}}(\lambda).$$

This completes the proof. □

6 Intractability of (n, S)-aMSE-DDH Assumptions

In this section, we provide the analysis of the intractability of (n, s)-aMSE-DDH problem. The intractability analysis is based on the analysis in the generic group model in [7].

6.1 Notations

For simplicity, we scope the problem to bilinear map group systems in the symmetric case ($\mathbb{G}_1 = \mathbb{G}_2 = \mathbb{G}$). Let then $\mathbb{S} = (p, \mathbb{G}, \mathbb{G}, \mathbb{G}_T, e(\cdot, \cdot))$ be a bilinear map group system. Let $g \in \mathbb{G}$ be a generator of $\mathbb{G}$, and set $g_T = e(g, g) \in \mathbb{G}_T$. Let s, m be two positive integers and $P, Q \in \mathbb{F}_p[X_1, \ldots, X_m]^s$ be two lists containing s m-variate polynomials over $\mathbb{F}_p$. Thus, P and Q can be written as $P = (p_1, p_2, \ldots, p_s)$ and $Q = (q_1, q_2, \ldots, q_s)$, and impose that $p_1 = q_1 = 1$. For any function $h : \mathbb{F}_p \to \Omega$ and vector $(x_1, \ldots, x_m) \in \mathbb{F}_p^m$, the notation $h(P(x_1, \ldots, x_m))$ stands for $(h(p_1(x_1, \ldots, x_m)), \ldots, h(p_s(x_1, \ldots, x_m))) \in \Omega^s$.

We use a similar notation for the s-tuple Q. Let $f \in \mathbb{F}_p[X_1, \ldots, X_m]$. It is said that f depends on (P, Q), which we denote by $f \in \langle P, Q \rangle$, when there exists a linear decomposition $f = \sum_{1 \leq i, j \leq s} a_{i,j} \cdot p_i \cdot p_j + \sum_{1 \leq i \leq s} b_i \cdot q_i$, where $a_{i,j}, b_i \in \mathbb{Z}_p$. Let P, Q be as above and $f \in \mathbb{F}_p[X_1, \ldots, X_m]$. The (P, Q, f)-General Diffie-Hellman Exponent problems are defined as follows.

Definition 2 ((P, Q, f)-GDHE [4]). *Given the tuple*

$$H(x_1, \ldots, x_m) = \left(g^{P(x_1, \ldots, x_m)}, g_T^{Q(x_1, \ldots, x_m)} \right) \in \mathbb{G}^s \times \mathbb{G}_T^s,$$

compute $g^{f(x_1, \ldots, x_m)}$.

Definition 3 ((P, Q, f)-GDDHE). *Given* $H(x_1, \ldots, x_m) \in \mathbb{G}^s \times \mathbb{G}_T^s$ *as above, and* $T \in \mathbb{G}_T$, *decide whether* $T = g^{f(x_1, \ldots, x_m)}$.

We refer to [4] for a proof that (P, Q, f)-GDHE and (P, Q, f)-GDDHE have generic security when $f \notin \langle P, Q \rangle$. We will prove that our construction is secure by first exhibiting the polynomials P, Q and f involved in the security proofs, and then by showing that $f \notin \langle P, Q \rangle$.

6.2 (n, S)-aMSE-DDH

In this section, we prove the intractability of distinguishing the two distributions involved in the (n, s)-aMSE-DDH$_A$ problem (cf. Corollary 1, Sect. 3.2). The proof of the intractability of the (n, s)-aMSE-DDH$_B$ problem (cf. Corollary 2, Sect. 3.2) is similar to that for Corollary 1, and hence, we omit it.

Proof (Proof of Corollary 1) To wrap up Corollary 1, we need to show that (n, s)-aMSE-DDH$_A$ problem fits in the framework of Theorem A.2 in [4]. As mentioned above, we consider our problem in the weakest case $\mathbb{G}_1 = \mathbb{G}_2 = \mathbb{G}$ and pose $g_0 = g, h_0 = g^\beta$. Our problem can be reformulated as (P, Q, F)-GDDHE where

$$P = \begin{pmatrix} 1, \gamma, \ldots, \gamma^{n-2}, \\ \kappa \cdot \gamma \cdot f(\gamma), \\ \alpha, \alpha \cdot \gamma, \ldots, \alpha \cdot \gamma^{n-s+1}, \\ \omega' \cdot \gamma, \omega \cdot \gamma^2, \ldots, \omega\gamma^{n-1}, \\ \beta, \beta \cdot \gamma, \ldots, \beta \cdot \gamma^{s-2}, \\ \beta\kappa \cdot g(\gamma), \beta\kappa \cdot \gamma \cdot g(\gamma), \ldots, \beta\kappa \cdot \gamma^{n-s} \cdot g(\gamma), \\ \beta\alpha, \beta\alpha \cdot \gamma, \ldots, \beta \cdot \alpha \cdot \gamma^n \\ \beta\omega, \beta\omega \cdot \gamma, \ldots, \beta\omega \cdot \gamma^n, \end{pmatrix}$$

$$Q = (1)$$
$$F = \beta\kappa \cdot f(\gamma).$$

We need to prove the independence of F from $\langle P, Q \rangle$. By making all possible products of two polynomials from P which are multiples of $\beta\kappa$, we want to prove that the sum of any polynomials from the list R below does not lead to F:

$$R = \begin{cases} \beta\kappa \cdot \gamma \cdot A(\gamma)f(\gamma) \\ \beta\kappa \cdot B(\gamma)g(\gamma) \\ \beta\kappa \cdot \gamma \cdot B(\gamma)g(\gamma) \\ \vdots \\ \beta\kappa \cdot \gamma^{s-2} \cdot B(\gamma)g(\gamma) \end{cases}$$

where A, B are polynomials in γ.

After simplifying the list R, it can be seen that if F is not independent of $\langle P, Q \rangle$ we can then derive $\gamma \cdot f(\gamma)$ from following list: $R' = \begin{cases} \gamma \cdot A(\gamma)f(\gamma) \\ B'(\gamma)g(\gamma) \end{cases}$ where A, B' are polynomials in γ with $0 \leq \deg A \leq s - 2, 0 \leq \deg B' \leq n + s - 4$.

Thus, we have the following equation:

$$f(\gamma) = \gamma \cdot A(\gamma)f(\gamma) + B'(\gamma)g(\gamma)$$

which can then be re-written into $(1 - \gamma \cdot A(\gamma))f(\gamma) = B'(\gamma)g(\gamma)$ where $1 - \gamma \cdot A(\gamma) \neq 0$, $\deg B_1(\gamma) \leq n + s - 4$. Since f and g are coprime, we must have $g(\gamma)|(1 - \gamma \cdot A(\gamma))$. However, $\deg(1 - \gamma \cdot A(\gamma)) < \deg g(\gamma)$ will result in $1 - \gamma \cdot A(\gamma) = 0$, which contradicts with the fact $1 - \gamma \cdot A(\gamma) \neq 0$. $\square$

7   Conclusion

In this paper, we considered the problem of access policy update in ABE schemes, which make the ABE schemes become practical. When an ABE scheme is not equipped with efficient access policy update, it cannot be used in practice as policy update is an essential feature in the dynamic environment. We outlined some trivial solutions including using AB-PRE system, and also pointed out the difference between access policy update and ciphertext re-encryption, which showed the importance of a general efficient access policy update mechanism. We presented notions of ciphertext-policy attribute-based encryption supporting attribute addition and revocation, and subsequently presented two new CP-ABE schemes featured with functionalities of adding and revoking attributes, respectively. We also proposed a new selective CPA model for CP-ABE with these new features. Finally, we also proved the security of our schemes. The proposed schemes are proven secure against selective CPA under the assumptions that the augmented Multi-Sequence of Exponents Decisional Diffie-Hellman (aMSE-DDH) problems are hard. The intractability of the aMSE-DDH problems is proved in generic group model within the frame work of General Diffie-Hellman Exponent problem in [4]. It remains an open problem to obtain a scheme integrated with efficient access policy update mechanism supporting more expressive access policies which can be proven secure under a more general computational assumption.

Acknowledgement. This work is partially supported by ARC Project (DP130101383).

References

1. Attrapadung, N., Herranz, J., Laguillaumie, F., Libert, B., De Panafieu, E., Ràfols, C.: Attribute-based encryption schemes with constant-size ciphertexts. Theoret. Comput. Sci. **422**, 15–38 (2012)
2. Bethencourt, J., Sahai, A., Waters, B.: Ciphertext-policy attribute-based encryption. In: IEEE Symposium on Security and Privacy, SP 2007, pp. 321–334. IEEE (2007)
3. Blaze, M., Bleumer, G., Strauss, M.: Divertible protocols and atomic proxy cryptography. In: Nyberg, K. (ed.) EUROCRYPT 1998. LNCS, vol. 1403, pp. 127–144. Springer, Heidelberg (1998). doi:10.1007/BFb0054122
4. Boneh, D., Boyen, X., Goh, E.-J.: Hierarchical identity based encryption with constant size ciphertext. In: Cramer, R. (ed.) EUROCRYPT 2005. LNCS, vol. 3494, pp. 440–456. Springer, Heidelberg (2005). doi:10.1007/11426639_26
5. Boneh, D., Franklin, M.: Identity-based encryption from the weil pairing. In: Kilian, J. (ed.) CRYPTO 2001. LNCS, vol. 2139, pp. 213–229. Springer, Heidelberg (2001). doi:10.1007/3-540-44647-8_13
6. Cheung, L., Newport, C.: Provably secure ciphertext policy abe. In: Proceedings of the 14th ACM Conference on Computer and Communications Security, pp. 456–465. ACM (2007)
7. Delerablée, C., Pointcheval, D.: Dynamic threshold public-key encryption. In: Wagner, D. (ed.) CRYPTO 2008. LNCS, vol. 5157, pp. 317–334. Springer, Heidelberg (2008)

8. Goyal, V., Jain, A., Pandey, O., Sahai, A.: Bounded ciphertext policy attribute based encryption. In: Aceto, L., Damgård, I., Goldberg, L.A., Halldórsson, M.M., Ingólfsdóttir, A., Walukiewicz, I. (eds.) ICALP 2008. LNCS, vol. 5126, pp. 579–591. Springer, Heidelberg (2008). doi:10.1007/978-3-540-70583-3_47

9. Goyal, V., Pandey, O., Sahai, A., Waters, B.: Attribute-based encryption for fine-grained access control of encrypted data. In: Proceedings of the 13th ACM Conference on Computer and Communications Security, pp. 89–98. ACM (2006)

10. Herranz, J., Laguillaumie, F., Ràfols, C.: Constant size ciphertexts in threshold attribute-based encryption. In: Nguyen, P.Q., Pointcheval, D. (eds.) PKC 2010. LNCS, vol. 6056, pp. 19–34. Springer, Heidelberg (2010). doi:10.1007/978-3-642-13013-7_2

11. Lewko, A., Okamoto, T., Sahai, A., Takashima, K., Waters, B.: Fully secure functional encryption: attribute-based encryption and (hierarchical) inner product encryption. In: Gilbert, H. (ed.) EUROCRYPT 2010. LNCS, vol. 6110, pp. 62–91. Springer, Heidelberg (2010). doi:10.1007/978-3-642-13190-5_4

12. Lewko, A., Waters, B.: New proof methods for attribute-based encryption: achieving full security through selective techniques. In: Safavi-Naini, R., Canetti, R. (eds.) CRYPTO 2012. LNCS, vol. 7417, pp. 180–198. Springer, Heidelberg (2012)

13. Li, J., Ren, K., Zhu, B., Wan, Z.: Privacy-aware attribute-based encryption with user accountability. In: Samarati, P., Yung, M., Martinelli, F., Ardagna, C.A. (eds.) ISC 2009. LNCS, vol. 5735, pp. 347–362. Springer, Heidelberg (2009)

14. Liang, K., Au, M.H., Liu, J.K., Susilo, W., Wong, D.S., Yang, G., Yu, Y., Yang, A.: A secure and efficient ciphertext-policy attribute-based proxy re-encryption for cloud data sharing. Future Gener. Comput. Syst. **52**, 95–108 (2015)

15. Liang, K., Au, M.H., Susilo, W., Wong, D.S., Yang, G., Yu, Y.: An adaptively CCA-secure ciphertext-policy attribute-based proxy re-encryption for cloud data sharing. In: Huang, X., Zhou, J. (eds.) ISPEC 2014. LNCS, vol. 8434, pp. 448–461. Springer, Heidelberg (2014)

16. Liang, K., Fang, L., Susilo, W., Wong, D.: A ciphertext-policy attribute-based proxy re-encryption with chosen-ciphertext security. In: 2013 5th International Conference on Intelligent Networking and Collaborative Systems (INCoS), pp. 552–559. IEEE (2013)

17. Liang, X., Cao, Z., Lin, H., Shao, J.: Attribute based proxy re-encryption with delegating capabilities. In: Proceedings of the 4th International Symposium on Information, Computer, and Communications Security, pp. 276–286. ACM (2009)

18. Luo, S., Hu, J., Chen, Z.: Ciphertext policy attribute-based proxy re-encryption. In: Soriano, M., Qing, S., López, J. (eds.) ICICS 2010. LNCS, vol. 6476, pp. 401–415. Springer, Heidelberg (2010)

19. Naor, M.: On cryptographic assumptions and challenges. In: Boneh, D. (ed.) CRYPTO 2003. LNCS, vol. 2729, pp. 96–109. Springer, Heidelberg (2003)

20. Nishide, T., Yoneyama, K., Ohta, K.: Attribute-based encryption with partially hidden encryptor-specified access structures. In: Bellovin, S.M., Gennaro, R., Keromytis, A., Yung, M. (eds.) ACNS 2008. LNCS, vol. 5037, pp. 111–129. Springer, Heidelberg (2008). doi:10.1007/978-3-540-68914-0_7

21. Ostrovsky, R., Sahai, A., Waters, B.: Attribute-based encryption with non-monotonic access structures. In: Proceedings of the 14th ACM Conference on Computer and Communications Security, pp. 195–203. ACM (2007)

22. Sahai, A., Waters, B.: Fuzzy identity-based encryption. In: Cramer, R. (ed.) EUROCRYPT 2005. LNCS, vol. 3494, pp. 457–473. Springer, Heidelberg (2005). doi:10.1007/11426639_27

23. Seo, H.J., Kim, H.W.: Attribute-based proxy re-encryption with a constant number of pairing operations. J. Inf. Commun. Convergence Eng. **10**(1), 53–60 (2012)
24. Susilo, W., Chen, R., Guo, F., Yang, G., Mu, Y., Chow, Y.W.: Recipient revocable identity-based broadcast encryption. In: ASIACCS (2016)
25. Waters, B.: Ciphertext-policy attribute-based encryption: an expressive, efficient, and provably secure realization. In: Catalano, D., Fazio, N., Gennaro, R., Nicolosi, A. (eds.) PKC 2011. LNCS, vol. 6571, pp. 53–70. Springer, Heidelberg (2011). doi:10.1007/978-3-642-19379-8_4
26. Waters, B.: Functional encryption for regular languages. In: Safavi-Naini, R., Canetti, R. (eds.) CRYPTO 2012. LNCS, vol. 7417, pp. 218–235. Springer, Heidelberg (2012)
27. Zhang, Y., Chen, X., Li, J., Wong, D.S., Li, H.: Anonymous attribute-based encryption supporting efficient decryption test. In: Proceedings of the 8th ACM SIGSAC Symposium on Information, Computer and Communications Security, pp. 511–516. ACM (2013)

Universally Composable Cryptographic Role-Based Access Control

Bin Liu[⊠] and Bogdan Warinschi

University of Bristol, Bristol, UK
bin.liu@bristol.ac.uk, bogdan@cs.bris.ac.uk

Abstract. In cryptographic access control sensitive data is protected by cryptographic primitives and the desired access structure is enforced through appropriate management of the secret keys. In this paper we study rigorous security definitions for the cryptographic enforcement of Role Based Access Control (RBAC). We propose the first *simulation-based* security definition within the framework of Universal Composability (UC). Our definitions are natural and intuitively appealing, so we expect that our approach would carry over to other access models.

Next, we establish two results that clarify the strength of our definition when compared with existing ones that use the game-based definitional approach. On the positive side, we demonstrate that both read and write-access guarantees in the sense of game-based security are implied by UC security of an access control system. Perhaps expected, this result serves as confirmation that the definition we propose is sound.

Our main technical result is a proof that simulation-based security requires impractical assumptions on the encryption scheme that is employed. As in other simulation-based settings, the source of inefficiency is the well known "commitment problem" which naturally occurs in the context of cryptographic access control to file systems.

Keywords: Universal composability · cRBAC · Game-based security

1 Introduction

Access control is one of the cornerstones of computer security. It comprises mechanisms and techniques that ensure that subjects (users, processes, etc.) get access only to the objects (files, memory locations, etc.) in a way that preserves the privacy/integrity of the objects per some access policy that is in place. Traditional access control mechanisms rely on reference monitors. Since monitors need to be permanently on-line and have to be executed in trust domains outside the control of the data owner(s), this has limitations that directly affect scalability and deployability of applications.

A solution to this problem employs cryptography and is based on a simple and elegant idea: protect the objects using cryptographic primitives (i.e. encryption to guarantee privacy and signatures for integrity) and then enforce the desired security policies by providing the right secret keys to the right parties. This type

© Springer International Publishing AG 2016
L. Chen and J. Han (Eds.): ProvSec 2016, LNCS 10005, pp. 61–80, 2016.
DOI: 10.1007/978-3-319-47422-9_4

of implementation eliminates the need for an on-line monitor: the objects being protected can be made publicly available in encrypted form and access is only provided to the users that have the right secret keys.

SECURITY MODELS FOR CRYPTOGRAPHIC ACCESS CONTROL. Much of the prior work in this area was concerned with designing access control systems from basic cryptographic primitives [2, 8–11, 15, 18] and/or designing new primitives tailored for the problem of access control [14, 17, 23, 24]. For the most part, the security of cryptographic access control systems was only heuristically studied. Yet, precise definitions are particularly important in this area: recent constructions employ complex cryptographic primitives for which the level of security is not always easy to ascertain and for which it is important to understand how they fit within the higher level systems that employ them. For instance, in attribute based encryption there is a sizable gap between security against adversaries that decide statically the keys they will attack and those that take this decision adaptively. Which of these types of schemes should be used in access control systems to ensure security requires rigorous definitions of what such systems aim to achieve and proofs that a given security level suffices.

Throughout the literature, rigorous models that look at the security of systems for access control have only sporadically been developed and were usually concerned with particular schemes or applications [1, 6, 7, 19]. Security models for broader frameworks have only recently been developed [3, 13]. One line of work in this direction is due to Ferrara et al. who consider cryptographic enforcement of Role-Based Access Control models [12, 13]. Specifically, they define a general syntax for cryptographic RBAC schemes (cRBAC in short), propose a security model that captures privacy guarantees for objects protected with such a system, and suggest an implementation based on predicate-encryption (PE).

The models proposed by Ferrara et al. use the so-called *game-based* approach. Here, the model formalizes the interaction between an adversary and the system and rigorously clarifies what is a security breach, e.g. as an event that occurs during the execution. The appeal of this approach is its relative simplicity: executions consider stand-alone scenarios where the system is in complete isolation from other systems and the different security goals (e.g. privacy and integrity of sensitive data) are treated independently from one another. At the same time, simplicity is also cause of some concern. Since the security games must specify precisely the information that an adversary can obtain when attacking the scheme, threats from arbitrary environments may not always be appropriately captured. Similarly, individual treatment of security properties may overlook unwanted interaction since oftentimes security properties are contradictory. Furthermore, it may not always be possible to exhaustively enumerate the different properties that one may desire from a system.

In this paper we consider a definitional alternative that does not suffer from the above shortcomings. Under this paradigm, called *simulation-based* approach, security is defined by comparing a system with an idealized version and demands that the real execution of a system reveals at most as much information is revealed by an ideal version of the system. As a consequence of this definition, the real system inherints *all* of the security properties of the ideal one, so there is no need to enumerate security properties separately. One important class of simulation-based security considers executions determined by an arbitrary environment (tasked, e.g. to provide inputs to the system), so security in this sense is *composable* in the sense that it is preserved in any environment in which the system is employed [4,20,22]. Unfortunately, simulation security is often difficult to establish and impose stringent restrictions on the implementations which rule out construction with no obvious weakness or, at the very least, require inefficient realizations [5,25]. In particular, the only attempt at a simulation-based definition for access control is the work of Halevi, Karger, and Naor [19] who provide such a security notion for access control in distributed file storage. Their definition is for a specific system rather than for a general model as the one developed in this paper.

OUR CONTRIBUTION. The observation that motivates this paper is that simulation-based security with composability properties is an excellent fit for the context of cryptographic access control. Such systems involve multiple parties, are quite complex and need to satisfy several security requirements (e.g. both individual and joint privacy for the protected objects). Moreover, by their raison d'être, access control systems need to maintain their security properties when employed within higher level protocols. Below, we overview our results.

Security definition. We start with the formalization of an ideal functionality that captures the security guarantees expected from a cryptographic RBAC system. Our functionality reflects directly the semantics associated to RBAC systems [26]. Roughly speaking, the functionality keeps track of all of the operations performed on the system and maintains the induced access control matrix; user requests to access files are then granted/refused based on this matrix. Security in the sense that we define requires that an adversary cannot do more against the concrete implementation than it can do against the functionality. This requirement essentially says that the implementation enforces the expected semantics of the RBAC system. Technically, to show security one needs to construct a *simulator* which can simulate the complete view that an adversary has against the real system but only from access to the information that the ideal functionality provides.

We note that our approach should work for any other model that benefits from a precise semantics with an induced access control matrix.

Relation with game-based definitions. Next, we study the relation between the existent game-based security notions and the level of security that our definition entails. It is generally believed that, for the same task, simulation-based security is stronger than game-based security, even if only because the former is suppose to capture *all* of the security properties expected of a system. Indeed, we show that our notion of security entails both security with respect to read access (the game-based variant introduced in [13]) and write access (the game-based variant introduced in [12]). While expected these types of results help build confidence in the definitions.

Lower-bounds for UC-secure cRBAC. Our main result is a gap between simulation-security and game-based security. More precisely, we show that it is impossible for a cryptographic RBAC system to be UC-secure. In technical terms, we show that the so-called commitment problem [5] occurs in the context of access control. Roughly, the problem is that the simulator required by the security definition needs to produce valid looking encryptions of the objects that are protected without actually knowing the actual content of these objects (e.g. files). The problem is that when the adversary gains access to such a file (e.g. by corrupting a user who has access to this file), the simulator needs to produce a decryption key that explains the ciphertext as an encryption of some particular content which the simulator did not know when the ciphertext was created.

In a bit more detail, our proof proceeds in two steps. First, we provide a generic construction of a universally composable non-interactive communication protocol (NICP) out of any universally composable cRBAC system. A classical result by Nielsen shows that such schemes do not exist if no setup assumptions are in place [25]. Nielsen's result does not apply directly in our setting since our construction of a NICP inherits several assumptions that are in place for the cRBAC system; in particular, it requires a publicly available file-system and secure channels between some of the parties. We bypass this difficulty by extending Nielsen's impossibility result to settings that involve these setup assumptions whenever their use are restricted in certain ways, and argue that these restrictions are natural in access control.

2   Preliminaries

In this section, we give a brief overview of Canetti's UC framework [4], provide some background of the Role-Based Access Control and recall Ferrara et at.'s notion of cryptographic Role-Based Access Control.

THE UNIVERSAL COMPOSABILITY (UC) FRAMEWORK. The UC framework is based on the *"real-world/ideal-world"* paradigm, which originates in Goldreich, Micali and Wigderson's paper [16]. The basic idea of this paradigm is to show that the execution of a real-world protocol emulates a process which carries out the given task in an idealised way: all the participants securely provide their individual inputs to a trusted party, who then locally computes the outputs and provide them to the participants according to the specification of the task. The emulation property essentially requires that every possible damage caused by an adversary against the real system can also be simulated by an adversary (the simulator) in the ideal world. Since an adversary cannot really break the idealised protocol, the real-world protocol should also be secure.

This paradigm has been further developed by the UC framework. In the UC framework, the trusted party of the ideal process is modelled as an entity called *ideal functionality* and denoted by $\mathcal{F}$. In addition to handling the inputs obtained repeatedly from the parties and generating the prescribed outputs, $\mathcal{F}$ is allowed to interact with the adversary, in a way that captures the allowed leakage of the protocol. To provide security guarantee under composition, the UC framework introduces an adversarial entity called the *environment* $\mathcal{Z}$, which represents all possible settings in which the protocol can be executed. $\mathcal{Z}$ acts as an interactive distinguisher which aims to tell if it is interacting with the real protocol or with the ideal one. In the process, the environment is allowed to exchange information with the adversary, to provide inputs to the participants of it choice and to obtain outputs from them. A protocol Π is said to securely realize the functionality $\mathcal{F}$, if for any adversary $\mathcal{A}$, there exists a simulator $\mathcal{S}$ such that no environment can distinguish between its interactions with parties running Π and $\mathcal{A}$ and the interactions with the ideal process for $\mathcal{F}$ and $\mathcal{S}$.

An special type of adversary is the so-called *dummy adversary* $\mathcal{D}$. This adversary simply delivers the messages from the environment to the parties and forwards the messages from the parties to the environment: this adversary essentially allows the environment to fully control the input/output and the communication between the parties. A simulator that works for the dummy adversary essentially gives rise to a simulator for any other adversary.

An important concept in the UC framework is the *hybrid model*, an execution setting which is a mix between a real protocol and an idealized setting. Specifically, in an $\mathcal{F}$-hybrid the parties running the protocol can use multiple copies of an ideal functionality $\mathcal{F}$. The extension of the notion of realizing of an ideal functionality in the hybrid model is immediate. In fact, it captures the essence of the general composition theorem specific to UC. If a protocol ρ securely realizes an ideal functionality $\mathcal{G}$ in $\mathcal{F}$-hybrid model and there is a protocol π securely realizes $\mathcal{F}$, then the composed protocol $\rho^{\pi/\mathcal{F}}$ where all the calls to $\mathcal{F}$ are replaced by calls to π securely realizes $\mathcal{G}$. Hence π provides the same security guarantee as the ideal functionality $\mathcal{F}$ even if used within an arbitrary protocol ρ; furthermore the composed protocol $\rho^{\pi/\mathcal{F}}$ still provides the same security guarantee as the ideal functionality $\mathcal{G}$.

One particular application of hybrid models is to capture various communication models. This is achieved by formulating an appropriate ideal functionality $\mathcal{F}$ that represents the abstraction from the communication, then real-world protocols in the communication model can be presented in the $\mathcal{F}$-hybrid model. To exemplify this approach, we present $\mathcal{F}_{\text{SMT}}$, the ideal functionality for secure message transmission (aka secure communication) in Fig. 1. In $\mathcal{F}_{\text{SMT}}$, a sender P_S with input m sends its input to a receiver P_R, while the adversary only learns $|m|$, the length of the message m, and can delay the message delivery. Notice that $\mathcal{F}_{\text{SMT}}$ can only transmit a single message, to transmit multiple messages we need to use multiple instances of $\mathcal{F}_{\text{SMT}}$. We refer to [4] for more details and formal descriptions about the UC framework.

CRYPTOGRAPHIC ROLE-BASED ACCESS CONTROL. Role-based access control (RBAC) is a general access control model that offers many benefits including allowing for fine-grained access controls and simplifying the management of user permissions. Instead of assigning users with the permissions directly, it introduces an indirection namely the roles such that the access control policies are decomposed into two associations: the user-role assignment relation and

---

Functionality $\mathcal{F}_{\text{SMT}}$

$\mathcal{F}_{\text{SMT}}$ proceeds as follows, with a sender P_S, a receiver P_R and an adversary $\mathcal{S}$.

1. Upon receiving an input (**Send**, sid, P_R, m) from P_S, send (**Sent**, sid, P_S, P_R, $|m|$) to the adversary and generate a delayed output (**Sent**, P_S, sid, m) to P_R then halt.

2. Upon receiving (**Corrupt**, sid, P) from $\mathcal{S}$, where $P \in \{P_S, P_R\}$, reveal m to the adversary. If $P = P_S$ and the message has not yet been sent to P_R, then ask $\mathcal{S}$ for a value m' and output (**Sent**, P_S, sid, m') to P_R then halt.

Fig. 1. Ideal functionality for the secure message transmission, $\mathcal{F}_{\text{SMT}}$.

permission-role assignment relation. More formally, at any point a (core) RBAC system is in a state which consists of a set of users U, a set of roles R, a set of permissions P, a relation $UA \subseteq U \times R$ which records the assignment of users to roles and a relation $PA \subseteq P \times R$ which maintains the assignment of permissions to roles. Intuitively, a user u has permission p if there exists a role r such that $(u, r) \in UA$ and $(p, r) \in PA$.

The state of an RBAC system changes dynamically. Throughout the paper we make the simplifying assumption that the set of R of roles is fixed (the assumption reflects the reality that in many organizations the role structure is usually stable). The remaining components of the state change following *administrative commands* of the form $(U', O', P', UA', PA') \leftarrow Cmd((U, O, P, UA, PA), \text{arg})$. We summarize the typical commands and their intended semantics in Fig. 2.

Command	Semantics	Description
AddUser(u)	$U \cup \{u\}$	Add a new user u to the system
DelUser(u)	$U \setminus \{u\}$, $UA \setminus \{(u, r) \in UA \mid r \in R\}$	Remove an existing user u
AddObject(o)	$O \cup \{o\}$	Add a new object o to the system
DelObject(o)	$O \setminus \{o\}, P \setminus \{(o, \cdot)\}$, $PA \setminus \{((o, \cdot), r) \in PA \mid r \in R\}$	Remove an existing object o
AssignUser(u, r)	$UA \cup \{(u, r)\}$	Assign the user u to the role r
DeassignUser(u, r)	$UA \setminus \{(u, r)\}$	Deassign the user u from the role r
GrantPerm(p, r)	$PA \cup \{(p, r)\}$	Grant the permission p to the role r
RevokePerm(p, r)	$PA \setminus \{(p, r)\}$	Revoke the permission p from the role r

Fig. 2. Administrative RBAC commands.

At a high-level, a cryptographic implementation of RBAC (cRBAC) consists of algorithms that implement the administrative commands outlined above, in a way that enforces the desired access matrix of the system. Formal syntax and security for such systems have been introduced by Ferrara et al. for the case where access is only concerned with reading sensitive data [13] and was later extended to also enforcing writing to sensitive files [12]. As in these works, we assume a setting that involves three main entities: a manager, a file system and a set of users. The manager is assumed to be a trusted party and is tasked with carrying out the administrative commands. The file system is publicly-accessible and is assumed to support versioning – users are only allowed to append content to the file system but not delete any data.

More precisely, a cRBAC scheme $\mathcal{CRBAC}$ consists of the following algorithms: Init, AddUser, DelUser, AddObject, DelObject, AssignUser, DeassignUser, GrantPerm, RevokePerm, Update, Write and Read. As suggested above (and by their names) most of the algorithms correspond to the different administrative commands of RBAC. There are three additional algorithms which we describe below. We assume that they define non-interactive multi-party computations which proceeds as follows: first, the manager carries out some local computations according to the RBAC command (including updates to the file system) and produces a set of update messages, one for each of the users. The messages are sent over private channels to users who use it to update their local state. Therefore, these algorithms take as input the locate state of the manager st_M, the RBAC command Cmd and the argument for the command arg as input and output an updated file system fs accordingly, a new state for the manager and a set of update messages $\{msg_u\}_{u \in U}$ for the users. When a user u receives an update message msg_u from the manager, it then executes the Update algorithm with its local state $st[u]$ and the message to update its local state accordingly. The Read and Write are the algorithms that allow users to read/write from the files. Both algorithms take as input the local state of the user $st[u]$, a file name o (potentially some content to be written to the file m) and the state of the file system fs. The Read algorithm should return the content of the file; the Write algorithm should return the content that should be appended to the file system.

3   A UC Security Definition for cRBAC

This section presents a universally composable security definition for cRBAC schemes. We formalize the security requirements of cRBAC schemes by designing an ideal functionality $\mathcal{F}_{\mathrm{CRBAC}}$.

FUNCTIONALITY $\mathcal{F}_{\mathrm{CRBAC}}$. The ideal functionality we present in Fig. 3 captures the intuitive security properties of cRBAC schemes in the way of simply behaving as a server-mediated access control on the files being protected. Very roughly, $\mathcal{F}_{\mathrm{CRBAC}}$ keeps track of every operation performed on the system and maintain the induced access control matrix within, while it preserves that only the authorized access requests will be granted. This is achieved by having $\mathcal{F}_{\mathrm{CRBAC}}$ maintain a built-in database to store the content of every file, along with a symbolic RBAC state of the system. Then it handles every access request according to the RBAC state.

More specifically, $\mathcal{F}_{\mathrm{CRBAC}}$ embodies the essential interfaces of a cRBAC system, including system initialization, RBAC administration and read/write access to the file system. It proceeds as follows. Having received an initialization request with a set of roles R from the manager M, $\mathcal{F}_{\mathrm{CRBAC}}$ initializes an object-indexed

---

Functionality $\mathcal{F}_{\text{CRBAC}}$

$\mathcal{F}_{\text{CRBAC}}$ proceeds as follow, with a manager M, users $u_1, ..., u_n$ and an adversary $\mathcal{S}$.

Initialization: Upon receiving an input (Initialization, sid, R) from M where R is a set of roles, send (Initialization, sid, R) to $\mathcal{S}$, initialize an object-indexed list $FS \leftarrow \emptyset$ and the symbolic RBAC state $(U, O, P, R, PA, UA) \leftarrow (\emptyset, \emptyset, \emptyset, R, \emptyset, \emptyset)$. After that, mark the system as initialized and ignore all the inputs of the form (Initialization, sid, R') for some R' from now on.

RBAC administration: Upon receiving an input (RBAC, sid, cmd, arg) from M where cmd is one of the administrative RBAC commands specified in Fig. 2 and arg is the command-specific arguments, proceed as follows: If the system has not yet been initialized, or the execution of cmd with arg is invalid (e.g. it is considered as invalid if $cmd =$ "GrantPerm" and $arg = (p, r)$, where $r \notin R$), return an error. Otherwise, update the current RBAC state as $(U', O', P', UA', PA') \leftarrow cmd((U, O, P, UA, PA), arg)$ and send (RBAC, sid, cmd, arg) to $\mathcal{S}$.

Write: Upon receiving an input (Write, sid, o, m) from some user u where o is an object and m is some content, if the system has not been initialized or there exists no role r such that both $(u, r) \in UA$ and $((o, \text{write}), r) \in PA$ are satisfied, return an error. Otherwise, set $FS[o] \leftarrow m$ and send (Wrote, $sid, o, |m|$) to $\mathcal{S}$, where $|m|$ is the length of m.

Read: Upon receiving an input (Read, sid, o) from some user u where o is an object, if the system has not been initialized or there exists no role r such that both $(u, r) \in UA$ and $((o, \text{read}), r) \in PA$ are satisfied, return an error. Otherwise, set $m \leftarrow FS[o]$ (if $FS[o]$ stores no content then set m as an empty value), and return m to u.

Corruption: $\mathcal{F}_{\text{CRBAC}}$ is a standard corruption ideal functionality, with the exception that any request for corrupting M will be ignored.

Fig. 3. The cryptographic Role-Based Access control functionality, $\mathcal{F}_{\text{CRBAC}}$.

list fs and the symbolic system RBAC state. Then it notices the adversary that the access control system is initialized with a set of roles R. Once $\mathcal{F}_{\text{CRBAC}}$ is initialized, it ignores the other initialization request afterwards. Having received a request of executing an administrative RBAC command from M, $\mathcal{F}_{\text{CRBAC}}$ checks if the command and its arguments specified in the request are valid. If so, it executes the command symbolically and updates the system RBAC state. The administrative RBAC command can be either of the commands presented in Fig. 2. Having received a request to write some content m on a file o from some arbitrary user u, $\mathcal{F}_{\text{CRBAC}}$ first checks if u has the write permission. If so, it stores m in $fs[o]$ and leaks o and the length of m to the adversary. Having received a request to read the content of a file o from some user u, $\mathcal{F}_{\text{CRBAC}}$ also checks if u has the read permission. If so, $\mathcal{F}_{\text{CRBAC}}$ returns the content stored in $fs[o]$ to u. If $fs[o]$ stores no content, it returns an empty value. With the use of the built-in database, $\mathcal{F}_{\text{CRBAC}}$ guarantees correctness: the content that has been written to a file by an authorized user will be read by a user who is entitled to read that file. $\mathcal{F}_{\text{CRBAC}}$ is a standard corruption ideal functionality, with an exception that

---

Functionality $\mathcal{F}_{\text{VFS}}$

$\mathcal{F}_{\text{VFS}}$ proceeds as follows, running with users $u_1, ..., u_n$, a file system manager M and an adversary $\mathcal{S}$. At the first activation $\mathcal{F}_{\text{VFS}}$ initializes a list L to be empty.

Status: Upon receiving an input (**Status**, sid) from a party P, output (**Content**, sid, L) to P.

Write (user): Upon receiving an input (**Write**, sid, o, c) from some user u, if no record $r \in L$ of the form $(sid, o, \cdot, \cdot)$ exists, set $L \leftarrow L \cup \{(sid, o, 1, c)\}$; Otherwise, set $L \leftarrow L \cup \{(sid, o, ver_m + 1, c)\}$, where $ver_m = max(\{ver | (sid, o, ver, \cdot) \in L\})$. Then send (**Wrote**, sid, o, c) to $\mathcal{S}$ and send (**Updated**, sid) to every user.

Write (manager): Upon receiving an input (**Write**, sid, o, ver, c) from M, if a record $r \in L$ of the form $(sid, o, ver, \cdot)$ exists, modify r as (sid, o, ver, c); Otherwise, set $L \leftarrow L \cup \{(sid, o, ver, c)\}$. Then send (**Wrote**, sid, o, ver, c) to $\mathcal{S}$ and send (**Updated**, sid) to every user.

Remove: Upon receiving an input (**Remove**, sid, o, ver) from M, set $L \leftarrow L \setminus \{(sid, o, ver, c)\}$. Then send (**Removed**, sid, o, ver, c) to $\mathcal{S}$ and send (**Updated**, sid) to every user.

Fig. 4. Ideal functionality for the versioning file storage, $\mathcal{F}_{\text{VFS}}$.

the manager M cannot be corrupted. It captures the reasonable trust on the manager to administrate the access control system.

Several remarks on $\mathcal{F}_{\text{CRBAC}}$ are in order. First, $\mathcal{F}_{\text{CRBAC}}$ is an ideal functionality for the general cryptographic role-based access controls. Due to the purpose of studying the relationship between the previous game-based security notions, $\mathcal{F}_{\text{CRBAC}}$ does not handle any administrative request of adding a new role or removing an existing role. Second, $\mathcal{F}_{\text{CRBAC}}$ only guarantees secure access to the file system and preserves no policy privacy (when handling an administrative request, it simply reveals the command and the arguments to the adversary). There still exists some design choices on policy privacy preserving (e.g. only leaks the executed command but not its arguments), which is left as further study. Third, $\mathcal{F}_{\text{CRBAC}}$ makes no explicit restriction on the form of the file system and the file system is not designed as an individual party of the system. Thus in a real-world cRBAC scheme, the file system should be implemented by the scheme itself. It also captures that the file system does not implement any access control mechanism. Fourth, $\mathcal{F}_{\text{CRBAC}}$ does not have any authentication mechanism on the parties' identities. The authentication is left to the protocols that make calls to $\mathcal{F}_{\text{CRBAC}}$.

Before presenting our definition of universally composable cRBAC system, we first need to transform a cRBAC scheme $\mathcal{CRBAC} = $ (Init, AddUser, DelUser, AddObject, DelObject, AssignUser, DeassignUser, GrantPerm, RevokePerm) into an associated protocol $\Pi_{\mathcal{CRBAC}}$ in the UC setting accordingly. Recall that $\mathcal{CRBAC}$ assumes private channels between the manager and the users. To model this, we let the parties have access to $\mathcal{F}_{\text{SMT}}$, the ideal functionality of secure message transmission which is presented in Fig. 1. Also, $\mathcal{CRBAC}$ makes use of a public-accessible versioning file system. This is modelled by an appropriate functionality $\mathcal{F}_{\text{VFS}}$ which is presented in Fig. 4. $\mathcal{F}_{\text{VFS}}$ proceeds with a set of users and a data manager. Essentially, it serves as an ideal versioning file system which guarantees the correct ordering of the file versions. The users can "write" to the file system by appending new versions to the files instead of overwriting existing contents. The data manager is provided with richer interfaces: it can remove and even rewrite some existing version of a file. All the users in the system can check the current state of the file system by providing a status request to $\mathcal{F}_{\text{VFS}}$, and when any change happens to the file system, the ideal functionality reveals the change to the adversary and also notices the users about the change. These reflect the public-accessible feature of the file system. In addition, any write operation to the file system is done in an anonymous manner, $\mathcal{F}_{\text{VFS}}$ will not reveal information about the identity of the party who carries out the write operation.

For simplification of the protocol presentation, we will also define some shorthand notations. When a party executes some algorithm, it may generate a set of order-preserving instructions to be carried out on the file system. We use $\{info_i\}_{i\in\mathbb{N}}$ to denote this set of instructions. If the party is the manager, each instruction $info_i \in \{info_i\}_{i\in\mathbb{N}}$ can be either $(\texttt{Write}, sid, o, ver, c)$ or $(\texttt{Remove}, sid, o, ver)$, where sid is the session id of $\mathcal{F}_{\text{VFS}}$. If the party is a user, it can only be the form $(\texttt{Write}, sid, o, c)$. A party may also need to come up with a set of order-preserving instructions $\{info_i^{fs\rightarrow fs'}\}_{i\in\mathbb{N}}$ such that after carrying out the instructions on the file system in order, the current state of the file system fs would become fs'. We say a party sends $\{info_i\}_{i\in\mathbb{N}}$ (or $\{info_i^{fs\rightarrow fs'}\}_{i\in\mathbb{N}}$) to $\mathcal{F}_{\text{VFS}}$, it means the party provides every instruction $info_i$ of the set as the input to $\mathcal{F}_{\text{VFS}}$ in order.

We now present the associated protocol $\Pi_{\mathcal{CRBAC}}$ (in Fig. 5) and define universally composable cRBAC scheme.

Definition 1. *Let* $\mathcal{CRBAC} = (\mathsf{Init}, \mathsf{AddUser}, \mathsf{DelUser}, \mathsf{AddObject}, \mathsf{DelObject}, \mathsf{AssignUser}, \mathsf{DeassignUser}, \mathsf{GrantPerm}, \mathsf{RevokePerm})$ *be a cRBAC scheme, we say* $\mathcal{CRBAC}$ *is UC-secure if the associated protocol* $\Pi_{\mathcal{CRBAC}}$ *securely realizes* $\mathcal{F}_{\text{CRBAC}}$ *in* $(\mathcal{F}_{\text{VFS}}, \mathcal{F}_{\text{SMT}})$*-hybrid model and in a setting that the manager never gets corrupted.*

4   UC Security Is Stronger Than Game-Based Security of cRBAC

Based on the transformation above, we study the relation between UC security and game-based security. We treat separately security of read access from that of write access. The security notions of cRBAC scheme with respect to write and read accesses are shown in the Appendix A.

Theorem 1. *Any cRBAC scheme* $\mathcal{CRBAC}$ *which is UC-secure (in* $(\mathcal{F}_{\text{VFS}}, \mathcal{F}_{\text{SMT}})$*-hybrid model) is secure with respect to write accesses.*

Proof sketch. We show that if $\mathcal{CRBAC}$ is not secure with respect to write accesses, then it cannot be UC-secure. Given an adversary $\mathcal{A}_W$ that breaks write security of $\mathcal{CRBAC}$, an environment $\mathcal{Z}$ can distinguish its interactions with parties running $\Pi_{\mathcal{CRBAC}}$ and a dummy adversary, from the ideal process for

---

The Protocol Π_{CRBAC}

The participants: a manger M and a set of users $u_1, ..., u_n$.

initialization: Upon receiving an input (initialization, sid, R) where R is a set of roles, M computes $(st_M, fs, \{msg_u\}_{u \in U}) \leftarrow\!\!{}^{\$} \mathsf{Init}(1^\lambda, R)$. M then invokes an instance of $\mathcal{F}_{\mathrm{VFS}}$ as the data manager with session id (M, sid), parses fs as $\{info_i\}_{i \in \mathbb{N}}$ and sends $\{info_i\}_{i \in \mathbb{N}}$ to $\mathcal{F}_{\mathrm{VFS}}$. If $\{msg_u\}_{u \in U}$ is non-empty, M sends msg_u to every user u using $\mathcal{F}_{\mathrm{SMT}}$.

Administration: Upon receiving an input (RBAC, sid, cmd, arg) where cmd can be either of the administrative commands specified in Fig. 2 and arg is the arguments of the command, M sends (Status, (M, sid)) to $\mathcal{F}_{\mathrm{VFS}}$ to obtain (Content, sid, fs) and then computes $(st'_M, fs', \{msg_u\}_{u \in U}) \leftarrow\!\!{}^{\$} Cmd(st_M, fs, arg)$, where Cmd is the algorithm that implements the administrative command cmd. M sets $st_M \leftarrow st'_M$, and then comes up with $\{info_i^{fs \to fs'}\}_{i \in \mathbb{N}}$. If $\{info_i^{fs \to fs'}\}_{i \in \mathbb{N}}$ is non-empty, M sends $\{info_i^{fs \to fs'}\}_{i \in \mathbb{N}}$ to $\mathcal{F}_{\mathrm{VFS}}$. If $\{msg_u\}_{u \in U}$ is non-empty, M sends msg_u to every user u using $\mathcal{F}_{\mathrm{SMT}}$.

Update: Upon receiving a message (Update, sid, msg_u) from M, a user u computes $st'_u \leftarrow\!\!{}^{\$} \mathsf{Update}(st_u, msg_u)$, where st_u is u's local state (st_u is an empty value when u receives the first update message from M). Then it sets $st_u \leftarrow st'_u$.

Write: Upon receiving an input (Write, sid, o, m), a user u sends (Status, (M, sid)) to $\mathcal{F}_{\mathrm{VFS}}$ to get (Content, sid, fs) and computes $fs' \leftarrow\!\!{}^{\$} \mathsf{Write}(st_u, fs, o, m)$. Then u comes up with $\{info_i^{fs \to fs'}\}_{i \in \mathbb{N}}$ and sends it to $\mathcal{F}_{\mathrm{VFS}}$.

Read: Upon receiving an input (Read, sid, o), a user u sends (Status, (M, sid)) to $\mathcal{F}_{\mathrm{VFS}}$ to get (Content, sid, fs) and then outputs (Read, $sid, \mathsf{Read}(st_u, fs, o)$).

Fig. 5. The Protocol Π_{CRBAC} in $(\mathcal{F}_{\mathrm{VFS}}, \mathcal{F}_{\mathrm{SMT}})$-hybrid model.

$\mathcal{F}_{\mathrm{CRBAC}}$ and a simulator. The idea is, $\mathcal{Z}$ runs a local copy of $\mathcal{A}_W$ and simulates to it the experiment that defines write security of $\mathcal{CRBAC}$ schemes. Then $\mathcal{Z}$ proceeds according $\mathcal{A}_W$'s queries such that the protocol execution is consistent to $\mathcal{A}_W$'s view. Since $\mathcal{A}_W$ is a successful adversary, $\mathcal{Z}$ should be able to write some valid content without having the permission in the real-world execution with non-negligible probability. But in the ideal world, from the specification of $\mathcal{F}_{\mathrm{CRBAC}}$ we can infer that $\mathcal{Z}$ will not be able to write any content to the file system in this case.

Theorem 2. *Any cRBAC scheme $\mathcal{CRBAC}$ which is UC-secure (in $(\mathcal{F}_{\mathrm{VFS}}, \mathcal{F}_{\mathrm{SMT}})$-hybrid model) is secure with respect to read accesses.*

Proof sketch. The proof idea of this theorem is analogous to Theorem 1's. Given an adversary $\mathcal{A}_R$ that breaks secure read access of $\mathcal{CRBAC}$, an environment $\mathcal{Z}$ can tell its interaction with the execution of Π_{CRBAC} and a dummy adversary from the interactions with the ideal process for $\mathcal{F}_{\mathrm{CRBAC}}$ and a simulator. Similarly, $\mathcal{Z}$ runs a local copy of $\mathcal{A}_R$ and simulates to it the experiment that defines read security. Then $\mathcal{Z}$ transforms every query from $\mathcal{A}_R$, which will not lead to a trivial win, into appropriate inputs being provided to the parties and the adversary. By assumption, $\mathcal{Z}$ would be able to distinguish its interactions in the two worlds with the help of $\mathcal{A}_R$.

The full proofs of Theorem 1 and 2 can be found in the full version of this paper.

5   Impossibility of UC-secure cRBAC Scheme

In this section we establish our main result. We show that the level of security demanded by a universally composable cryptographic RBAC system cannot be achieved, even in a setting where a protocol has access to an idealized file system and secure channels between all parties. Our impossibility result is in a setting where the adversary can adaptively corrupt honest protocol participants.

Theorem 3. *There exists no UC-secure cRBAC scheme (in $(\mathcal{F}_{\mathrm{VFS}}, \mathcal{F}_{\mathrm{SMT}})$-hybrid model) with adaptive corruptions.*

Proof: The proof of this theorem proceeds in two steps. First, we show that the existence of any UC-secure cRBAC scheme implies the existence of a universally composable NICP. Specifically, we provide a generic construction of a NICP that securely realizes the functionality $\mathcal{F}_{\mathrm{NCE}}$ of non-committing encryption (which is presented in Fig. 6), from any UC-secure cRBAC scheme. Next, we argue that the resulting communication protocol in fact cannot securely realize $\mathcal{F}_{\mathrm{NCE}}$ – this step is an extension of a well known result by Nielsen to a setting where parties have access to a secure file system and secure channels.

We start by describing the generic construction for the universally composable NICP. Recall that based on our transformation, the associated protocol of a cRBAC scheme works in $(\mathcal{F}_{\mathrm{VFS}}, \mathcal{F}_{\mathrm{SMT}})$-hybrid model and in a setting that the manager never gets corrupted, the resulting communication protocol therefore works in the same hybrid model and makes use of such a trusted party in a restricted way.

Functionality $\mathcal{F}_{\mathrm{NCE}}$

$\mathcal{F}_{\mathrm{NCE}}$ works as follows. It interacts with a message sender P_S, a receiver P_R and an adversary $\mathcal{S}$.

Pre-processing phase: Upon receiving an input $(\texttt{Init}, sid, P_R)$ from P_S, send $(\texttt{Init}, sid, P_S)$ to P_R and send $(\texttt{Init}, sid, P_S, P_R)$ to $\mathcal{S}$. In addition, mark the channel as established.

Communication phase: Upon receiving an input $(\texttt{Send}, sid, P_R, m)$ from P_S, if the channel is not established, ignore the message. Otherwise, send the message $(\texttt{Send}, sid, P_R, m)$ to P_R and reveal $(\texttt{Sent}, sid, P_S, P_R, |m|)$ to $\mathcal{S}$, where $|m|$ is the length of the message.

Corruption: Upon receiving $(\texttt{Corrupt}, sid, P)$ from $\mathcal{S}$ where $P \in \{P_S, P_R\}$, reveal m to $\mathcal{S}$. If $P = P_S$ and the message has not yet been sent to P_R, ask $\mathcal{S}$ for a value m' then output $(\texttt{Sent}, sid, P_S, m')$ to P_R.

Fig. 6. Ideal functionality for the non-committing encryption, $\mathcal{F}_{\mathrm{NCE}}$.

The Protocol Π_{NICP}

The participants: a message sender P_S, a receiver P_R and a trusted party M namely the manager.

Pre-processing phase. M establishes the communication channel for P_S and P_R. In this stage, some content might be written to $\mathcal{F}_{\text{VFS}}$ for the channel set-up.

1. Upon receiving an input $(\texttt{Init}, sid, P_R)$, P_S sends $(\texttt{Init}, sid, P_R)$ to M using $\mathcal{F}_{\text{SMT}}$.

2. Upon receiving a message $(\texttt{Init}, sid, P_R)$ from P_S, M selects a random role r and computes $(st_M, fs, \{st[u_S], st[u_R]\}) \leftarrow^\$ \text{Init}(1^\lambda, \{r\})$, where u_S and u_R are two users to be added to the system. It initializes two lists $msg_S \leftarrow st[u_S]$ and $msg_R \leftarrow st[u_R]$. M then invokes an instance of $\mathcal{F}_{\text{VFS}}$ with session id (M, sid) as the data manager and parses fs as $\{info_i\}_{i \in \mathbb{N}}$. If $\{info_i\}_{i \in \mathbb{N}}$ is non-empty, M sends $\{info_i\}_{i \in \mathbb{N}}$ to $\mathcal{F}_{\text{VFS}}$. After that, M runs a sequence of algorithms which implement the related administrative RBAC commands to add two users u_S, u_R and an object o to the system, to grant the write permission of o to u_S via the role r and to grant the read permission of o to u_R via r. When executing any RBAC command, the state of the file system fs might be updated to fs'. If so, M comes up with $\{info_i^{fs \to fs'}\}_{i \in \mathbb{N}}$ and sends it to $\mathcal{F}_{\text{VFS}}$. When an update message msg for u_S (u_R resp.) is generated, M appends msg to the list msg_S (msg_S resp.). Finally, M sends $(\texttt{Update}, sid, msg_S)$ to P_S, and sends $(\texttt{Update}, sid, msg_R)$ to P_R using $\mathcal{F}_{\text{SMT}}$.

3. Upon receiving a message $(\texttt{Update}, sid, msg_X)$ from M where $X \in \{S, R\}$, the party P_X updates its local state by running the update algorithm $st_X \leftarrow^\$ \text{Update}(st_X, msg)$ on each update message $msg \in msg_X$ in order.

Communication Phase. Once the channel has been established, P_S can send arbitrarily many messages to P_R via $\mathcal{F}_{\text{VFS}}$.

1. Upon receiving an input $(\texttt{Send}, sid, P_R, m)$, P_S sends $(\texttt{Status}, (M, sid))$ to $\mathcal{F}_{\text{VFS}}$ to get $(\texttt{Content}, (M, sid), fs)$, and then computes $fs' \leftarrow^\$ \text{Write}(st_S, fs, o, m)$. Next, P_S comes up with $\{info_i^{fs \to fs'}\}_{i \in \mathbb{N}}$ and sends it to $\mathcal{F}_{\text{VFS}}$.

2. Upon receiving a subroutine output $(\texttt{Updated}, (M, sid))$ from $\mathcal{F}_{\text{VFS}}$, P_R sends $(\texttt{Status}, (M, sid))$ to $\mathcal{F}_{\text{VFS}}$ to get $(\texttt{Content}, (M, sid), fs)$, and then outputs $m' \leftarrow \text{Read}(st_R, fs, o)$.

Fig. 7. The Protocol Π_{NICP} in $(\mathcal{F}_{\text{VFS}}, \mathcal{F}_{\text{SMT}})$-hybrid model.

The communication protocol involves a message sender, a receiver and a trusted party namely the manager. We restrict that there exists no direct communication channel between the sender and the receiver. They have to communicate with each other in an indirect way: after a pre-processing phase in which the manager interacts with the other two parties over secure channels to establish the communication, the sender can send messages to the receiver by writing to the file system and then the receiver performs read operations to get the messages. Notice that the read operation will not bring any change to the file system and the manager only works in the pre-processing phase and does not involve in the communication phase. The communication protocol in fact requires no interaction between the sender and the receiver. Hence it can be considered as non-interactive.

More specifically, let $\mathcal{CRBAC}$ = {Init, AddUser, DelUser, AddObject, DelObject, AssignUser, DeassignUser, GrantPerm, RevokePerm, Update, Write, Read} be a cRBAC scheme. We denote the NICP by Π_{NICP} and present it Fig. 7.

We show that Π_{NICP} securely realizes $\mathcal{F}_{\mathrm{NCE}}$ in $(\mathcal{F}_{\mathrm{VFS}}, \mathcal{F}_{\mathrm{SMT}})$-hybrid model. By assumption, the scheme $\mathcal{CRBAC}$ is UC-secure implies that there exists a simulator $\mathcal{S}$ such that no environment can tell with non-negligible probability whether it interacts with the parties running Π_{CRBAC} in $(\mathcal{F}_{\mathrm{SMT}}, \mathcal{F}_{\mathrm{VFS}})$-hybrid model and a dummy adversary $\mathcal{D}$, or it interacts with the ideal process for $\mathcal{F}_{\mathrm{CRBAC}}$ with $\mathcal{S}$. Then we give the construction of the simulator $\mathcal{S}_{\mathrm{NCE}}$ for Π_{NICP} as follows. $\mathcal{S}_{\mathrm{NCE}}$ internally runs an instance of $\mathcal{S}$. Then it interacts with $\mathcal{S}$ as the environment and simulates to $\mathcal{S}$ the ideal process for $\mathcal{F}_{\mathrm{CRBAC}}$. It proceeds as follow.

1. **Simulating the pre-processing phase.** Upon receiving from $\mathcal{F}_{\mathrm{NCE}}$ a message (Init, sid, P_S, P_R), $\mathcal{S}_{\mathrm{NCE}}$ selects a random role r. It then simulates the pre-processing phase by sending messages to $\mathcal{S}$ sequentially in the name of $\mathcal{F}_{\mathrm{CRBAC}}$ indicating that the cRBAC system is initialized with a role r, a user u_S is granted the write permission of a file o via the role r and another user u_R is granted the read permission of o via r. When the environment requests $\mathcal{S}_{\mathrm{NCE}}$ to provide any information that it can obtain during this phase, including the length of any update message sent from the manager in Π_{NICP} and any content written to $\mathcal{F}_{\mathrm{VFS}}$, $\mathcal{S}_{\mathrm{NCE}}$ then instructs $\mathcal{S}$ to provide the related information and hands it to the environment.

2. **Simulating the communication phase.** Upon receiving from $\mathcal{F}_{\mathrm{NCE}}$ a message (Sent, $sid, P_S, P_R, |m|$), $\mathcal{S}_{\mathrm{NCE}}$ sends (Wrote, $sid', o, |m|$) in the name of $\mathcal{F}_{\mathrm{CRBAC}}$ to $\mathcal{S}$, where $sid' = (M, sid)$. When the environment requests $\mathcal{S}_{\mathrm{NCE}}$ to report the content written to $\mathcal{F}_{\mathrm{VFS}}$, $\mathcal{S}_{\mathrm{NCE}}$ instructs $\mathcal{S}$ to report such content and forwards it as its output.

3. **Party corruption.** When the environment instructs $\mathcal{S}_{\mathrm{NCE}}$ to corrupt P_S (P_R resp.), $\mathcal{S}_{\mathrm{NCE}}$ delivers the corruption message to $\mathcal{F}_{\mathrm{NCE}}$ and also requests $\mathcal{S}$ to corrupt u_S (u_R resp.). If the corruption happens after P_S has ever sent some message to P_R, $\mathcal{S}_{\mathrm{NCE}}$ will also obtain the messages sent so far from $\mathcal{F}_{\mathrm{NCE}}$. Then it provides the obtained information to $\mathcal{S}$ in the name of $\mathcal{F}_{\mathrm{CRBAC}}$. Once $\mathcal{S}$ outputs the internal state of the corrupt party, $\mathcal{S}_{\mathrm{NCE}}$ forwards it to the environment. After that, any message provided by the environment to the corrupt party would be modified as the message for u_S (u_R resp.) accordingly and forwarded to $\mathcal{S}$ (e.g. if the environment instructs the corrupt sender to send some message c, $\mathcal{S}_{\mathrm{NCE}}$ then instructs $\mathcal{S}$ to write the message c to the file o on behave of u_S). Any request from the environment to corrupt the manager will be ignored.

We briefly analyse the validity of $\mathcal{S}_{\mathrm{NCE}}$. Suppose there exists an environment $\mathcal{Z}$ which can tell its interactions with parties running Π_{NICP} in $(\mathcal{F}_{\mathrm{VFS}}, \mathcal{F}_{\mathrm{SMT}})$-hybrid model and a dummy adversary from the interactions with the ideal process for $\mathcal{F}_{\mathrm{NCE}}$ and $\mathcal{S}_{\mathrm{NCE}}$ with non-negligible probability. We show that we can construct an environment $\mathcal{Z}'$ which can tell whether it is interacting with parties running Π_{CRBAC} in $(\mathcal{F}_{VFS}, \mathcal{F}_{SMT})$-hybrid model and a dummy adversary or the interactions with the ideal process for $\mathcal{F}_{CRBAC}$ and the simulator $\mathcal{S}$ with non-negligible probability. The main idea is that $\mathcal{Z}'$ runs an internal copy of $\mathcal{Z}$ towards which it simulates the view of the ideal process for $\mathcal{F}_{NCE}$ and the simulator $\mathcal{S}_{NCE}$. The simulation depends the information that $\mathcal{Z}'$ can obtain during the protocol execution. From the construction of $\mathcal{S}_{NCE}$ above, it can be inferred that every instruction for $\mathcal{S}_{NCE}$ can be broken down to corresponding instructions to $\mathcal{S}$. Also, for the inputs that $\mathcal{Z}$ provides to the dummy parties in the ideal process for $\mathcal{F}_{NCE}$, $\mathcal{Z}'$ can modify them appropriately and provide to the parties it interacts with. Hence we have, in the case that $\mathcal{Z}'$ interacts with the ideal process for $\mathcal{F}_{CRBAC}$ and a simulator $\mathcal{S}$, the simulation $\mathcal{Z}'$ provides to $\mathcal{Z}$ is perfectly identical to the view which $\mathcal{Z}$ expects to see. Then by assumption, $\mathcal{Z}$ can tell its interactions in the two worlds with non-negligible probability, and so can $\mathcal{Z}'$ in this case. Thus, $\mathcal{S}$ cannot be a valid simulator for Π_{CRBAC} which reaches a contradiction. Then we have, if $\mathcal{S}$ is a valid simulator for Π_{CRBAC}, $\mathcal{S}_{NCE}$ is also a valid simulator for Π_{NICP} and therefore Π_{NICP} securely realizes $\mathcal{F}_{NCE}$ in $(\mathcal{F}_{VFS}, \mathcal{F}_{SMT})$-hybrid model.

Now we argue that such a simulator $\mathcal{S}$ in fact does not exist. In [25], it has been shown that no non-interactive communication protocol that securely realizes $\mathcal{F}_{NCE}$ exists in the plain model. However, we cannot apply directly that result to complete our proof, since Π_{NICP} makes use of $\mathcal{F}_{VFS}$, $\mathcal{F}_{SMT}$, albeit in a restricted way. Nonetheless, we show that under these usage restrictions, we can extend Nielsen's result to our setting.

Consider that a Π_{NICP} that securely realizes $\mathcal{F}_{NCE}$ in $(\mathcal{F}_{VFS}, \mathcal{F}_{SMT})$-hybrid model allows the sender to send arbitrarily many messages to the receiver noninteractively (e.g. by performing write operations to the file system). Any real-world adversary that attacks the protocol cannot obtain more than the length of the transmitted message. Consider the following environment $\mathcal{Z}$. After the communication is established between the message sender P_S and the receiver P_R, $\mathcal{Z}$ activates P_S with an input (Send, sid, m) and requests the adversary to report the content c that has been written to some file o of $\mathcal{F}_{VFS}$. Once $\mathcal{Z}$ obtains c, it instructs the adversary to corrupt P_R to obtain its internal state st. Then $\mathcal{Z}$ produces the current state of the file system from the update information provided by the adversary as fs and computes $m' \leftarrow \text{Read}(st, fs, o)$. By assumption $\mathcal{Z}$ should have $m' = m$ except for negligible probability. Then we consider in the ideal-world case, the simulator should be able to come up with c given the length of m by $\mathcal{F}_{NCE}$, and later it should be able to provide the internal state st which is consistent to the transmitted message c when m is available by the time P_R is corrupt. Notice that the ideal functionality $\mathcal{F}_{NCE}$ guarantees correctness on the transmitted message, which means for every message sent by the sender, the receiver should be able to recover the original message except for negligible probability. Hence for Π_{NICP}, there should not exist any local state of the receiver that allows it to decrypt any written content to the file system into two different messages with non-negligible probability each. Otherwise an environment can distinguish its interactions in the two worlds with non-negligible probability. Thus if we fix a file version c, there exists an injective mapping from the underlying messages to the local state of the receiver, which implies that the number of possible internal states st of P_R should be at least the same as the number of the possible messages. Notice that the only way P_R can receive the message from P_S is to execute the Read algorithm to retrieve the current content of o from the file system. The injective mapping will not be affected by executing read operations since (by assumption) Read updates neither the file system nor the local state of P_S. Therefore it is impossible for P_R to use the unchanged local state to receiver arbitrary many message from P_S. Thus we can conclude that Π_{NICP} does not securely realize $\mathcal{F}_{\text{NCE}}$ in $(\mathcal{F}_{\text{VFS}}, \mathcal{F}_{\text{SMT}})$-hybrid model, which contradicts the existence of the simulator $\mathcal{S}$. Hence there exists no UC-secure $\mathcal{CRBAC}$ (in $(\mathcal{F}_{\text{VFS}}, \mathcal{F}_{\text{SMT}})$-hybrid model) with adaptive corruptions.

6   Conclusion

We present a security definition for cryptographic role-based access control in the UC framework. We study its relation with existent game-based notions and show that simulation-based security is strictly stronger. In essence, our results imply that composable simulation-based security for access control may be difficult to achieve to the point that it is impractical[1] Interestingly, similar results were derived empirically in a recent study of the efficiency of cryptographic RBAC based on both standard asymmetric encryption and identity-based encryption schemes [21].

In future work, we plan to study the efficiency implications of UC security for cryptographic access control schemes that hide the access policy that is in place at any given time during the execution of the system.

A   The Security Notions of cRBAC Schemes in [12]

Secure read access. A cRBAC scheme $\mathcal{CRBAC}$ = (Init, AddUser, DelUser, AddUser, AddObject, GrantPerm, RevokePerm, AssignUser, DeassignUser, Update, Read, Write) is said to be secure with respect to read accesses if no user can deduce any content of a file without having the read permission. It is formalized by the experiment $\mathbf{Exp}^{\text{read}}_{\mathcal{CRBAC},\mathcal{A}}$. In the experiment, a random bit is selected at the beginning and the cRBAC system is initialized with a set of roles R. The adversary $\mathcal{A}$ is allowed to request for executing any administrative RBAC command, to take over users, to request an honest user to write some content to a file and to get access to the file system. $\mathcal{A}$ can also specify a file as his challenge and provides two messages, of which one will be written to the file according to the random bit. It can specify multiple challenges and finally output his guess of the bit. To prevent trivial wins, no corrupt user can get read access to any of the challenge files. We say the adversary wins if its guess is correct. A $\mathcal{CRBAC}$ is said to be secure with respect to read accesses if no adversary can win the above experiment with probability significantly better than a half.

---

[1] One possibility which we did not explore in this paper is to rely on additional setup assumptions, e.g. a common reference string, and employ a non-committing encryption scheme.

A predicate $\mathsf{HasAccess}(u,p)$ is used to reflect that symbolically a user u has access to a permission p. It is defined by: $\mathsf{HasAccess}(u,p) \leftrightarrow \exists r \in R : (u,r) \in UA \wedge (p,r) \in PA$.

Definition 2. *A cRBAC scheme $\mathcal{CRBAC}$ is secure with respect to read accesses if for any probabilistic polynomial-time adversary $\mathcal{A}$, we have*

$$\mathbf{Adv}^{read}_{\mathcal{CRBAC},\mathcal{A}}(\lambda) := \Big| \Pr[\mathbf{Exp}^{read}_{\mathcal{CRBAC},\mathcal{A}}(\lambda) \to \mathit{true}] - \frac{1}{2} \Big|$$

is negligible in λ, where $\mathbf{Exp}^{read}_{\mathcal{CRBAC},\mathcal{A}}$ is defined as follows:

$$\begin{array}{l}
\mathbf{Exp}^{read}_{\mathcal{CRBAC},\mathcal{A}}(\lambda) \\
\hline
b \leftarrow_\$ \{0,1\};\ Cr, Ch \leftarrow \emptyset \\
(st_M, fs, \{st[u]\}_{u \in U}) \leftarrow_\$ \mathsf{Init}(1^\lambda, R) \\
b' \leftarrow_\$ \mathcal{A}(1^\lambda : \mathcal{O}_r) \\
Return\ (b' = b)
\end{array}$$

The oracles $\mathcal{O}_r$ to which the adversary has access are specified in Fig. 8.

$\underline{\mathrm{CMD}(arg)}$

$\quad (U', O', P', UA', PA')$
$\qquad \leftarrow Cmd((U, O, P, UA, PA), arg)$
$\quad$ For all $u \in Cr$ and all $o \in Ch$:
$\qquad$ If $\exists r \in R$:
$\qquad\quad (u,r) \in UA' \wedge ((o, read), r) \in PA'$
$\qquad\quad$ then Return $\perp$
$\quad (U, O, P, UA, PA) \leftarrow (U', O', P', UA', PA')$
$\quad (st_M, fs, \{msg_u\}_{u \in U}) \leftarrow_\$ \mathsf{Cmd}(st_M, fs, arg)$
$\quad$ For all $u \in U \setminus Cr$:
$\qquad st[u] \leftarrow \mathsf{Update}(st[u], msg_u)$
$\quad$ Return $(fs, \{msg_u\}_{u \in Cr})$

$\underline{\mathrm{CORRUPTU}(u)}$

$\quad$ If $u \notin U$ then Return $\perp$
$\quad$ For all $o \in Ch$:
$\qquad$ If $\mathsf{HasAccess}(u, (o, \mathbf{read}))$ then
$\qquad\quad$ Return $\perp$
$\quad Cr \leftarrow Cr \cup \{u\}$; Return $st[u]$

$\underline{\mathrm{WRITE}(u, o, m)}$

$\quad$ If $u \notin U$ then Return $\perp$
$\quad$ If $\neg\mathsf{HasAccess}(u, (o, \mathbf{write}))$
$\qquad$ then Return $\perp$
$\quad fs \leftarrow_\$ \mathsf{Write}(st_M, fs, o, m)$
$\quad$ Return fs

$\underline{\mathrm{CHALLENGE}(u, o, m_0, m_1)}$

$\quad$ If $u \notin U$ or $o \notin O$ then
$\qquad$ Return $\perp$
$\quad$ For all $u' \in Cr$:
$\qquad$ If $\mathsf{HasAccess}(u', (o, \mathbf{read}))$
$\qquad\quad$ then Return $\perp$
$\quad$ If $\neg\mathsf{HasAccess}(u, (o, \mathbf{write}))$
$\qquad\quad$ then Return $\perp$
$\quad Ch \leftarrow Ch \cup \{o\}$
$\quad fs \leftarrow_\$ \mathsf{Write}(st_M, fs, o, m_b)$
$\quad$ Return fs

$\underline{\mathrm{FS}(query)}$

$\quad$ If $query = $ "STATE" then
$\qquad$ Return fs
$\quad$ If $query = $ "APPEND$(info)$"
$\qquad$ and $Cr \neq \emptyset$ then
$\qquad\quad fs \leftarrow fs\|info$; Return fs

Fig. 8. Oracles for defining the experiment $\mathbf{Exp}^{read}_{\mathcal{CRBAC},\mathcal{A}}$.

Secure write access. A cRBAC scheme $\mathcal{CRBAC}$ = (Init, AddUser, DelUser, AddUser, AddObject, GrantPerm, RevokePerm, AssignUser, DeassignUser, Update, Read, Write) is said to be secure with respect to write accesses if no user can write some content to a file without having the permission. Particularly, in the case of open-accessible file system, the content wrote by an unauthorized user should not be considered as valid. It is formalized by the experiment $\mathbf{Exp}_{\mathcal{CRBAC},\mathcal{A}}^{write}$. The cRBAC system is initialized with a set of role R. The adversary $\mathcal{A}$ is allowed to request for executing any of the administrative RBAC commands, to corrupt a user, to request an honest user to write some content to a file and to get access to the file system. At some point, $\mathcal{A}$ must output a target file with an honest user's id. It wins if it can write any valid content without the permission(read by the honest user). To prevent trivial wins, from the point when the last write operation to the target file is carried out by an honest user who has the permission till $\mathcal{A}$ generates its output, no corrupt user can get write access to the target file. A $\mathcal{CRBAC}$ is said to be secure with respect to write accesses if no adversary can win in the above experiment with non-negligible probability.

Definition 3. *A cRBAC scheme $\mathcal{CRBAC}$ is secure with respect to write accesses if for any probabilistic polynomial-time adversaries $\mathcal{A}$, we have*

$$\mathbf{Adv}_{\mathcal{CRBAC},\mathcal{A}}^{write}(\lambda) := \Pr\left[\mathbf{Exp}_{\mathcal{CRBAC},\mathcal{A}}^{write}(\lambda) \to 1\right]$$

is negligible in λ, where $\mathbf{Exp}_{\mathcal{CRBAC},\mathcal{A}}^{write}$ is defined as follows:

$\mathbf{Exp}_{\mathcal{CRBAC},\mathcal{A}}^{write}(\lambda)$
$\overline{(U,O,P,UA,PA)} \leftarrow (\emptyset,\emptyset,\emptyset,\emptyset,\emptyset); \ Cr \leftarrow \emptyset$
$(st_M, fs, \{st[u]\}_{u \in U}) \leftarrow\!\!{}^\$ \ \mathsf{Init}(1^\lambda, R)$
$(u^*, o^*) \leftarrow\!\!{}^\$ \ \mathcal{A}(1^\lambda : \mathcal{O}_w)$
If all of the following are satisfied then return 1:
    $- \ u^* \in U \setminus Cr \wedge \mathsf{HasAccess}(u^*, (o^*, \mathbf{read}))$
    $- \ T[o^*] \neq \mathbf{adv} \wedge T[o^*] \neq \mathsf{Read}(st[u^*], o^*, fs))$
Else Return 0

The oracles $\mathcal{O}_w$ to which the adversary has access are specified in Fig. 9.

$\text{CMD}(arg)$

(U, O, P, UA, PA)
$\quad \leftarrow Cmd((U, O, P, UA, PA), arg)$
$(st_M, fs, \{msg_u\}_{u \in U})$
$\quad \leftarrow\!\!\text{\$}\ \mathsf{Cmd}(st_M, fs, arg)$
For all $u' \in Cr$:
$\quad$ For all $o \in O$:
$\qquad$ If $\mathsf{HasAccess}(u', (o, \mathbf{write}))$ then
$\qquad\quad T[o] \leftarrow \mathbf{adv}$
For all $u \in U \setminus Cr$:
$\quad st[u] \leftarrow \mathsf{Update}(st[u], msg_u)$
Return $(fs, \{msg_u\}_{u \in Cr})$

$\text{CORRUPTU}(u)$

If $u \notin U$ then Return $\perp$
For all $o \in O$:
$\quad$ If $\mathsf{HasAccess}(u, (o, \mathbf{write}))$ then
$\qquad T[o] \leftarrow \mathbf{adv}$
$Cr \leftarrow Cr \cup \{u\}$; Return $st[u]$

$\text{WRITE}(u, o, m)$

If $u \in Cr$
$\quad$ then Return $\perp$
If $\neg\mathsf{HasAccess}(u, (o, \mathbf{write}))$
$\quad$ then Return $\perp$
$fs \leftarrow\!\!\text{\$}\ \mathsf{Write}(st[u], fs, o, m)$
For all $u' \in Cr$:
$\quad$ If $\mathsf{HasAccess}(u', (o, \mathbf{write}))$
$\quad$ then Return fs
$T[o] \leftarrow m$; Return fs

$\text{FS}(query)$

If $query = \text{"STATE"}$ then
$\quad$ Return fs
If $query = \text{"APPEND}(info)\text{"}$
$\quad$ and $Cr \neq \emptyset$ then
$\quad fs \leftarrow fs \| info$; Return fs

Fig. 9. Oracles for defining the experiment $\mathbf{Exp}^{\text{write}}_{\mathcal{CRBAC}, \mathcal{A}}$.

References

1. Abadi, M., Warinschi, B.: Security analysis of cryptographically controlled access to XML documents. J. ACM **55**(2), 1–29 (2008)
2. Akl, S.G., Taylor, P.D.: Cryptographic solution to a problem of access control in a hierarchy. ACM Trans. Comput. Syst. **1**(3), 239–248 (1983)
3. Alderman, J., Cid, C., Crampton, J., Janson, C.: Access control in publicly verifiable outsourced computation. IACR Cryptology ePrint Arch. **2014**, 762 (2014)
4. Canetti, R.: Universally composable security: A new paradigm for cryptographic protocols. In: 42nd Annual Symposium on Foundations of Computer Science, FOCS 2001, 14–17, Las Vegas, Nevada, USA, pp. 136–145, October 2001
5. Canetti, R., Fischlin, M.: Universally composable commitments. In: Kilian, J. (ed.) CRYPTO 2001. LNCS, vol. 2139, pp. 19–40. Springer, Heidelberg (2001)
6. Castiglione, A., De Santis, A., Masucci, B., Palmieri, F., Castiglione, A., Huang, X.: Cryptographic hierarchical access control for dynamic structures. IEEE Trans. Inf. Forensics Secur. **11**(10), 2349–2364 (2016)
7. Castiglione, A., De Santis, A., Masucci, B., Palmieri, F., Castiglione, A., Li, J., Huang, X.: Hierarchical and shared access control. IEEE Trans. Inf. Forensics Secur. **11**(4), 850–865 (2016)
8. Chang, Y.-F.: A flexible hierarchical access control mechanism enforcing extension policies. Secur. Commun. Networks **8**(2), 189–201 (2015)
9. Crampton, J.: Practical constructions for the efficient cryptographic enforcement of interval-based access control policies. CoRR, abs/1005.4993 (2010)

10. Crampton, J.: Cryptographic enforcement of role-based access control. In: Degano, P., Etalle, S., Guttman, J. (eds.) FAST 2010. LNCS, vol. 6561, pp. 191–205. Springer, Heidelberg (2011)
11. De Capitani di Vimercati, S., Foresti, S., Jajodia, S., Paraboschi, S., Samarati, P.: Over-encryption: Management of access control evolution on outsourced data. In: VLDB, pp. 123–134. ACM (2007)
12. Ferrara, A.L., Fuchsbauer, G., Liu, B., Warinschi, B.: Policy privacy in cryptographic access control. In: IEEE 28th Computer Security Foundations Symposium, CSF 2015, Verona, Italy, 13–17, pp. 46–60, July 2015
13. Ferrara, A.L., Fuchsbauer, G., Warinschi, B.: Cryptographically enforced RBAC. In: IEEE 26th Computer Security Foundations Symposium, New Orleans, LA, USA, June 26–28, pp. 115–129 (2013)
14. Garg, S., Gentry, C., Halevi, S., Zhandry, M.: TCC 2016-A, Proceedings, Part II, chapter Functional Encryption Without Obfuscation, pp. 480–511. Springer, Heidelberg (2016)
15. Gifford, D.K.: Cryptographic sealing for information secrecy and authentication. Communun. ACM **25**(4), 274–286 (1982)
16. Goldreich, O., Micali, S., Wigderson, A.: How to play any mental game or A completeness theorem for protocols with honest majority. In: Proceedings of the 19th Annual ACM Symposium on Theory of Computing, pp. 218–229. New York, New York, USA (1987)
17. Goyal, V., Pandey, O., Sahai, A., Waters, B.: Attribute-based encryption for fine-grained access control of encrypted data. In: Juels, A., Wright, R.N., De Capitani di Vimercati, S. (eds.) ACM Conference on Computer and Communications Security, pp. 89–98. ACM (2006)
18. Gudes, E.: The design of a cryptography based secure file system. IEEE Trans. Softw. Eng. **6**(5), 411–420 (1980)
19. Halevi, S., Karger, P.A., Naor, D.: Enforcing confinement in distributed storage and a cryptographic model for access control. IACR Cryptology ePrint Archive **2005**, 169 (2005)
20. Hofheinz, D., Shoup, V.: Gnuc: A new universal composability framework. IACR Cryptology ePrint Archive **2011**, 303 (2011)
21. Garrison III, W.C., Shull, A., Lee, A.J., Myers, S.: Dynamic, private cryptographic access control for untrusted clouds: Costs and constructions (extended version). CoRR, abs/1602.09069 (2016)
22. Küsters, R., Tuengerthal, M.: The IITM model: a simple and expressive model for universal composability. IACR Cryptology ePrint Archive **2013**, 25 (2013)
23. Libert, B., Vergnaud, D.: Adaptive-ID secure revocable identity-based encryption. In: Fischlin, M. (ed.) CT-RSA 2009. LNCS, vol. 5473, pp. 1–15. Springer, Heidelberg (2009)
24. Maji, H.K., Prabhakaran, M., Rosulek, M.: Attribute-based signatures. In: Kiayias, A. (ed.) CT-RSA 2011. LNCS, vol. 6558, pp. 376–392. Springer, Heidelberg (2011)
25. Nielsen, J.B.: Separating random oracle proofs from complexity theoretic proofs: the non-committing encryption case. In: Yung, M. (ed.) CRYPTO 2002. LNCS, vol. 2442, pp. 111–126. Springer, Heidelberg (2002). doi:10.1007/3-540-45708-9_8
26. Sandhu, R.S., Coyne, E.J., Feinstein, H.L., Youman, C.E.: Role-based access control models. IEEE Computer **29**(2), 38–47 (1996)

Data in Cloud

ID-based Data Integrity Auditing Scheme from RSA with Resisting Key Exposure

Jianhong Zhang[1]($\boxtimes$), Pengyan Li[1], Zhibin Sun[1], and Jian Mao[2]

[1] College of Sciences, North China University of Technology, Beijing 100144, China
jhzhangs@163.com
[2] School of Electronic and Information Engineering,
Beihang University, Beijing 100019, China
maojian@buaa.edu.cn

Abstract. As an important method, cloud-based data auditing can realize the integrity checking of the outsourced data efficiently. However, the existing public auditing schemes are mainly based on the PKI (public key infrastructure). In this infrastructure, the auditor must validate the certificates of data user before auditing data integrity. Thus, there exist some drawbacks in such infrastructure. (1) It brings the heavy computation burdens on the auditor in the auditing process (2) Complicated management of public key certificate makes the whole auditing protocol inefficient, in particular, in the multi-user setting. To overcome complicated key management and key exposure and reduce computation cost in the auditing process, we propose ID-based data integrity public auditing scheme with forward security in this paper. After a private key of data user is compromised, all previous produced authentication tags still remain valid. And we also show that our construction is provably secure under the RSA assumption with prime exponents. Due to being based on RSA, none of pairing operation is required in any algorithm, it makes that auditing efficiency is greatly improved since the implementations of pairings are much harder than those of exponentiations in a RSA group. The highlight in our scheme is that the auditor's verification cost is constant, it is independent of the number of the challenged set. Comparing with Yu et al.'s scheme, our scheme has more advantages in terms of computation cost and communication overhead. And implementation results also show that our scheme is very practical and suitable for the multi-user setting in the real life.

Keywords: ID-based auditing protocol · The RSA problem · Security proof · Efficiency analysis · Key exposure · Forward security

1 Introduction

As a specialised distributed computing paradigm, cloud computing offers various kinds of computation and storage services to the users via computer networks, and is becoming very popular nowadays. The popularity and widespread use

© Springer International Publishing AG 2016
L. Chen and J. Han (Eds.): ProvSec 2016, LNCS 10005, pp. 83–100, 2016.
DOI: 10.1007/978-3-319-47422-9_5

of cloud computing have brought great convenience for data sharing and data collection. It makes that individuals can not only expediently obtain useful data, but also conveniently achieve data sharing with others.

At present, cloud computing and storage services provide the individuals and enterprises with various capabilities to store and process their data in third-party data centers [4]. Organizations use the cloud in a variety of different service models (SaaS, PaaS, and IaaS) and deployment models (Private, Public, Hybrid, and Community) [18]. Because cloud-based storage services have greatly reduced the burden for local storage management and maintenance, some individuals and enterprises migrate their local data into the cloud. It results in the following cases, which some commercial products such as Google Drive and Dropbox have become very popular for both individuals and enterprises. Nowadays, cloud storage has become a quick profit growth point in cloud computing since it can provide scalable pay as you go and location independent storage services for the users.

However, cloud storage is a double-edged sword, it brings in some new security threats [17]. In the cloud paradigm, after the data are outsourced to the cloud, data users no longer possess these data locally, and they lose physical control over these data. For the data users, the most concern is how to ensure that their data are being correctly stored and maintained. At the same time, cloud servers are not the fully-trusted entity, after they suffer Byzantine failures occasionally, for their own self-interest, they may choose to conceal the data errors from the data users [14]. What is more severe, these cloud servers might neglect to keep or even deliberately delete rarely accessed data that belong to ordinary data users to save storage space. Therefore, it is critical and significant to develop efficient auditing techniques to strengthen data owners' confidence.

To effectively check data integrity remotely, many solutions have been proposed. These solutions are mainly divided into two categories: provable data possession model (PDP) [7] and proof of retrievability model (PoR) [8]. The two solutions can verify the remote data integrity to convince data users that their outsourced data are intactly kept by using spot-checking and digital authentication techniques. However, the underlying ideas of the two approaches differ substantially. PDP only can achieve the data integrity checking while PoR also can recover the original data when data is corrupted but the corruption ratio is within some threshold. According to the above two models, many different schemes [7–11] have been proposed to achieve different functions, such as public auditing, private auditing, dynamic updating. However, the aforementioned schemes are mainly based on complicated public key infrastructure (PKI), where the users' public keys are certified with a public key certificate issued by the certificate authority. However, the complicated key management in PKI brings some inconvenience to the source-constrained data user in the cloud, and also results in heavy verification burden to the third-party auditor (TPA, for short). However, for ID-based cryptosystem, it does not exist the above mentioned problems since data users' public keys in ID-based PKC are their own identities. The identity information can realize self-authentication of the data user, thus it can alleviate the burden of checking tasks in terms of the auditor's computation cost. In particular, in the multi-user setting, it can greatly increase the auditor's auditing efficiency.

The first ID-based data integrity protocol was proposed by Wang *et al.* in [5]. Strictly speaking, their scheme is not genuine ID-based auditing scheme, it should be called as proxy auditing scheme. To construct a genuine ID-based scheme, Zhang *et al.* proposed an efficient ID-based auditing scheme in [15], however, their scheme is only proven secure in the random oracle model. Subsequently, Zhang *et al.* presented an ID-based public auditing scheme in the standard model by using Waters signature in [16]. To the best of our knowledge, most of existing ID-based public auditing schemes are mainly based on the rather new and untested assumptions related to bilinear pairings. And the implementations of pairings are much harder than those of exponentiations in a RSA group. Building an inefficient prototype implementation of pairings is far from straightforward for anyone but an expert, and even then it is often difficult or impossible to generate curves with the desired security parameters. As the most influential public-key encryption algorithm, RSA can resist all known password attack so far, has been recommended for ISO public key data encryption standard. Thus, it has been widely applied in the industry for decades, many companies may have invested in expensive hardware or software implementations of RSA and good pairing implementations are much harder to find, thus they may be reluctant to reinvest in new pairing implementations.

In the real life, it is scarcely possible to guarantee that private key is not compromised since human errors and administration errors might be exploited. Key exposure is a very serious problem, it can result in that all produced signatures by the signer become worthless. To address this problem, once key exposure appears, the corresponding key revocation mechanisms should be invoked immediately to reduce the loss which is from the compromised private key. However, it cannot solve the problem of forgeability of previous signatures fundamentally. In cloud storage, key exposure makes that the validity of the outsourced data faces severe threatens since the compromised private key can be used to generate authentication tags.

Recently, Yu *et al.* proposed an efficient ID-based data integrity auditing scheme from RSA in [1]. Their scheme can achieve higher verifying efficiency. However, it is only suitable for the simple-user setting. And it does not consider key exposure problem. To solve the above problems, in this paper, base on RSA cryptosystem, we propose an ID-based public auditing protocol to achieve data integrity checking. Our contributions are five-folds:

1. We propose a novel ID-based data integrity auditing scheme based RSA cryptosystem. It can simplify the key management and alleviate the burden of the auditor and data users.
2. Our proposed scheme is proven to be secure, the security of the scheme is based on the RSA assumption with prime exponent in the random oracle model.

3. The TPA's computational cost in our scheme is constant in the auditing verification phase.
4. Our protocol can resist replace attack and replay attack in the random oracle model, its security is related to the RSA problem and hash function collusion-resistance.
5. Our scheme supports the property of forward security and does not require any pairing in any stage. And it also can extend to support the data integrity checking in the multi-user setting.

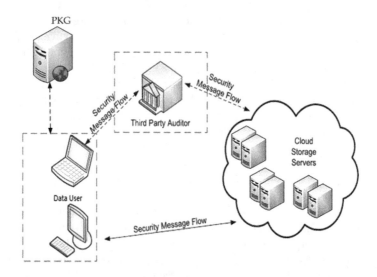

Fig. 1. ID-based cloud storage model in our scheme

2   System Model and Security Requirements

In this section, we will give the system model of ID-based auditing protocol for cloud storage, and define the corresponding security model.

2.1   System Model

For an ID-based auditing protocol, its system model is described as Fig. 1. It consists of four different entities: data users, the third-party auditor (TPA), the cloud server and private key generator (PKG). Their roles are identified as follows:

- Data user: it is an entity which possesses a large amount of data to be outsourced to the cloud for data maintenance and computation. It may be an enterprise or an individual.

- The cloud server: it is an entity which can provide significant storage space and computation capability to store and manage these data. In general, it is an untrusted entity.
- The third-party auditor: it is an entity which has expertise and capabilities that cloud user does not has, and it can realize data integrity auditing service with the cloud servers for the data users.
- Private key generator: it is responsible to produce private key for data users by using the user's identity information.

The intrinsic goal of cloud storage service is to allow data users to outsource their data files to the cloud in order to relieve of the burden of maintaining these data files for data users. However, once these data files are outsourced to the cloud, data users lose physical control over theses data. At the same time, cloud server is not a fully-trusted entity. Thus, it is of very importance for the data user to ensure that their data are being correctly stored and maintained. That is a reason why data users should be equipped with certain security measure so that they can periodically verify the integrity of the outsourced data even without the existence of local copies. For data users, in general, they are the resource-limited entities, it may be a challenge for them to periodically check the integrity of their outsourced data. Therefore, data users can delegate the checking task to a trusted TPA in order to let them free.

2.2 Mathematical Assumption

Definition 1 (the RSA Problem.) Let $N = p \cdot q$ be the product of p and q, where p and q are two k-bit large primes which satisfies $p = 2p' + 1$ and $q = 2q' + 1$ for some primes p' and q'. e^1 is a prime number which is greater than 2^l for some fixed security parameter l and satisfies $gcd(e, \phi(N)) = 1$, where $\phi(N) = 4p'q'$. Let y be a random number in Z_N. We say that an algorithm B solves the RSA problem if it receives an input the tuple (N, e, y) and outputs an element x such that $x^e = y \mod N$.

Definition 2. (ID-based auditing Protocol with Forward security). An ID-based auditing protocol with forward security for cloud storage consists of the following algorithms.

1. **Setup**$(1^k) \rightarrow$ (params, mpk, msk). The algorithm takes as input a security parameter k and outputs the master secret key msk and the master public key mpk of private key generator (PKG) as well the public system parameters *params*.
2. **Extract**$(params, mpk, msk, ID) \rightarrow (sk_{ID}^0)$. The algorithm takes as inputs system parameters *params*, the PKG's secret key msk and the identity information $ID \in \{0,1\}^*$ and outputs the private key sk_{ID}^0 corresponding to the user with identity ID such that this private key is valid at time period $t = 0$.

---

[1] Note that we make a slightly modified version [22, 26] of the original RSA problem definition. Here, we require the exponent to be a prime number.

When we say identity ID_i corresponds to the user's private key s^0_{ID} or vice versa, it means the pair (ID_i, s^0_{ID}) is an input-output pair of Extract algorithm with inputs $param$ and msk.

3. **Update**$(params, sk^t_{ID}, t, ID) \rightarrow (sk^{t+1}_{ID})$. On input a user secret key sk^t_{ID} for a time period t, the algorithm outputs a new user private key sk^{t+1}_{ID} for the time period $t + 1$.

4. **TagGen**(M, sk^t_{ID})$\rightarrow \delta$. The algorithm takes as inputs an outsourced data file M and the private key sk^t_{ID} in time period t. For each data block m_i, it computes a data authentication tag δ_i. It outputs a set of data authentication tag $\delta = (\delta_1, \delta_2, \cdots, \delta_n)$.

5. **Challenge**$(param, ID, Fname) \rightarrow C$. The algorithm takes as inputs system public parameters $param$, the user's identity information ID and the file's name Fname. It outputs a challenge information C.

6. **ProofGen**$(param, ID, C, M, \delta) \rightarrow P$. The algorithm takes as inputs the system parameters $param$, the data file M, the authentication tags δ, and the challenge information C from the auditor. Finally, it outputs a proof information P the challenged blocks.

7. **Verifying**$(C, P, ID, mpk, param) \rightarrow 0/1$. The algorithm takes as inputs system parameters $param$, the proof information P, the user's identity ID, the public key mpk of the PKG, and outputs the auditing result as 1 if the data file M is kept intact, otherwise, it outputs 0.

2.3   Definition of Security Model

Here, we consider each entity's roles in the security mode. PKG is thought of as a trusted authority, it can honestly produce private key for each data user. The TPA (the third-part auditor) is honest but curious, it can reliably perform the audit during the whole process. The cloud server is considered to be a dishonest entity, in other words, it may choose to hide the fact of some data being corrupted for its own reputation. In cloud storage, cloud server is a powerful attacker since it has some information of the outsourced data, we mainly consider that the cloud storage provider (CSP, for short) may launch the following attacks to the TPA in this paper:

1. Forge attack. During the challenging-response procedure between the cloud server and the auditor, the cloud server may forge a proof information P and make P to pass the verification of the auditor.

2. Replace attack. After the challenged data blocks were corrupted, the cloud server may choose another valid and uncorrupted pair of data block and data tag (m_i, δ_i) to replace the challenged pair of data block and data tag (m_j, δ_j). And it can pass the verification the auditor.

3. Replay attack. The cloud server may generate the proof information P from the previous proof information or other information, without retrieving the data user's challenged data.

In cloud, key exposure is a more serious issue since before outsourcing the data, data user needs to produce the corresponding signature on each data block, namely, authentication tag. Once private key of the user is leaked, it may render all previously produced signatures invalid since one cannot distinguish whether a signature is produced prior to the key exposure. Thus, key exposure is a great threat on cloud storage's security. To reduce the damage which is resulted from key exposure, we define an ID-based auditing protocol with forward security. In different cryptographic protocols, forward security has the different meanings depending on security goals for the protocols. In this paper, forward security means unforgeability of authentication tags of data blocks to be valid in previous time periods even if current private key of data user is compromised.

In the following, we give the definition of forward security by an interactive game between the simulator and the adversary.

1. Setup: The simulator B runs Setup(1^k) to obtain system parameters $param$. After that, it returns $param$ the adversary A. And A choose a breakin time t^* and can obtain the private key $s_{ID}^{t^*}$ of the user with identity ID in this phase. At the same time, A knows the total number of time periods T and the current time period t.
2. Extract Oracle: On input a data user's identity ID and a time period t, the private key s_{ID}^t for that time period t is returned.
3. TagGen Oracle: On input a time period t, the data user's identity ID and a data block m, a valid authentication tag ς at time period t is returned.
4. Finally, A outputs an authentication tag ς^*.

A wins this game if $(t^*, m^*, ID, \varsigma^*)$ is a valid authentication tag. The identity ID is not queried Extract Oracle with time period $t < t^*$ and (t^*, m^*, ID) is not queried to TagGen Oracle.

Let Adv_A^{FS} denote the probability of the adversary A which wins the game.

Definition 2 (Forward Security). An ID-based data integrity auditing scheme is forward security if for any probabilistic polynomial-time adversary A, Adv_A^{FS} is negligible.

To construct an efficient and secure ID-based public auditing protocol, the proposed scheme is to achieve the following objectives:

1. Public auditing: anyone is allowed to have the capability to verify the correctness and integrity of the outsourced data in cloud which are stored the users.
2. Blockless verification: The TPA can complete the data integrity verification under the condition that data blocks are unknown during the verification process.
3. Lightweight: the auditing verification should be performed with the minimum communication and computation overhead.
4. Forward security: If the private key of the user ID at time period t is exposed, the produced authentication tags before time period t are not affected.
5. Storage correctness: If the cloud server does not correctly store data users' data as required, then the returned proof information by cloud server cannot pass the auditing verification.

3   Our ID-based Data Integrity Auditing Scheme

In section, we are devoted to the description of our proposed ID-based data integrity auditing scheme, then we analyze the security of the scheme. In our construction, we assume that the validity of the user's private key is divided into T time intervals and these time intervals are public. Our construction consists of the following seven algorithms.

- **Setup**: Taking as input a security parameter 1^k, where $k \in N$, the PKG produces two k-bits large primes $p_0 = 2p' + 1$ and $q_0 = 2q' + 1$, where p' and q' are also big primes. Then it computes the RSA modulus $N_0 = p_0 q_0$. For some two fixed parameter $l, \pi \leq k/20$, the PKG randomly chooses a prime e such that $2^l \leq e \leq 2^{l+1}$ and $GCD(e, \phi(N_0)) = 1$ as well as $2^\pi \leq T \leq 2^{\pi+1}$, where $\phi(N)$ is an Euler Totient Function and T denotes the number of time periods. And it computes $d \in Z_{N_0}$ such that $ed = 1 \mod N_0$. It chooses two hash functions $H_1 : \{0,1\}^* \to \{0,1\}^{l_1}$ and $H_2 : \{0,1\}^* \to Z_{N_0}$, where $l_1 \leq 80$. The system public parameters $Para = \{k, l, e, N_0, H_1, H_2, T\}$ are published and the master secret keys (p_0, q_0, d) are kept secretly.
- **Extract**: For a user U with identity $ID \in \{0,1\}^*$, when it requests for the private key at time period t, where $0 \leq t \leq T$, the PKG uses its master secret key d to compute the user's private key $s_{ID}^t = H_1(ID)^{d^{T+1-t}} \mod \phi(N_0)$, note that in the initial phase of extract t is set 0. Finally, it sends s_{ID}^t to the user U via a secure channel.
- **Update**: Taking as inputs s_{ID}^t and a time period t, if $t + 1 \leq T$, then the user's private key is updated as

$$s_{ID}^{t+1} = (s_{ID}^t)^e$$

otherwise, it outputs "⊥" which means that the user's private key has expired.
- **TagGen**: To outsource a data file M to the cloud at time period t, a user U with identity ID does the following steps:
  1. For the user U, it randomly picks a secure signature algorithm Σ with key pair (sk, pk).
  2. Let M the outsourced file, first of all, it is split into $M = M_1 || M_2 || \cdots || M_n$ such that $M_i \leq 2^k$ for $i = 1, 2 \cdots, n$.
  3. Let $\tau = FName || n || ID_i$ where n is the number of data blocks, $FName$ is a file name and ID is the identity information of the user. Then it sets $sig = \tau || \Sigma.sign_{sk}(\tau)$ as file's identification.
  4. For data file $FName$, it randomly chooses $r \in Z_N$ to compute $R = r^{e^{T+1-t}}$ and for $i = 1$ to n, the authentication tag of data block M_i is computed as follows:

$$\zeta_i = r^{H_2(FName||R||index_i)} (H_1(ID)^{d^{T+1-t}})^{M_i} \mod N_0.$$

  Let $\zeta = \{\zeta_i\}_{i=1,\cdots,n}$
  5. Finally, the user uploads $\{M, t, \zeta, R, \tau, sig\}$ to the cloud and deletes the local storage, note that t denotes time period.

- **Challenge**: To produce the challenge information, the TPA does the following ones:
    1. First, it requests the cloud server for data integrity auditing on the user U's data file $FName$.
    2. Upon receiving this request, the cloud server first returns (τ, sig, t) to the TPA.
    3. Then the TPA first verifies whether time period t is valid. Then it verifies the validity of signature sig by using $\Sigma.verify(\tau, pk)$. If it fails, then aborts it; otherwise, it executes next step.
    4. It chooses a subset $I \subseteq \{1, 2, \cdots, n\}$ and computes the challenge subset $Q = (j, v_j)_{j \in I}$ where $v_j \in 2^k$. And send the challenge information $chall = \{Q, FName, ID\}$ to the cloud server.
- **ProofGen**: Upon receiving the challenge information $chall$, the cloud server computes as follows:
    1. It computes $\delta = \prod_{j \in I} \zeta_j^{v_j} \mod N_0$.
    2. Then it calculates $\mu = \sum_{j \in I} v_j \cdot M_j$.
    3. the resultant proof information $Prf = (\delta, R, \mu)$ is returned to the TPA.
- **Verifying**: Upon receiving proof information Prf, it does the following steps:
    1. It computes $H = \sum_{j \in I} v_j H_2(FName||R||index_j)$.
    2. Then, it checks whether the following equation holds.

$$\delta^{e^{(T+1-t)}} \stackrel{?}{=} R^H \cdot H_1(ID)^\mu \mod N_0 \tag{1}$$

If the equations above hold, it means that the outsourced data file is well maintained. Otherwise, the data file is corrupted. Note that in practice, $\mu \cdot e^{T-t}$ can be computed by cloud server.

Correctness: In the following, we will show the correctness of our construction based on Eq. 1 in time period t:

$$
\begin{aligned}
\delta^{e^{(T+1-t)}} &= (\prod_{j \in I} \zeta_j^{v_j})^{e^{(T+1-t)}} \\
&= (\prod_{j \in I} r^{H_2(FName||R||index_j)v_j} \cdot H_1(ID)^{d^{T+1-t} \cdot v_j \cdot M_j})^{e^{(T+1-t)}} \\
&= (\prod_{j \in I} (r^{v_j H_2(FName||R||index_j)})^{e^{(T+1-t)}} \cdot H_1(ID)^{v_j M_j}) \\
&= (R)^{\sum_{j \in I} v_j H_2(FName||R||index_j)} \cdot H_1(ID)^\mu \\
&= (R)^H \cdot H_1(ID)^\mu
\end{aligned}
$$

For simplicity, we omit all $\mod N_0$ operation in the above equations reasoning. Obviously, if the proof information is honestly produced by the cloud server, it must pass the verification checking.

3.1 Discussion

For an auditing scheme, it should support the data auditing of multiple users, and consume computation cost as less as possible. From the above Eq. 1, we find that only the right side of equation is related to the user's identity information. To support data auditing in the multi-user setting, the proof information should be format $(\delta, R_1, \cdots, R_n, \mu)$. When the auditor verifies the data integrity, it should satisfies

$$\delta^{e^{T+1-t}} \overset{?}{=} ((\prod_{i=1}^{n} R_i))^{H_i} \cdot \prod_{i=1}^{n} H_1(ID_i)^{\mu} \mod N$$

where $H_i = \sum_{j \in I_i} v_j H_2(FName_i \| R_i \| index_j)$ and $\bigcup_i^n I_i = I$.

We can know that the right side of the above equation is a multi-exponentiation computation. To speed up computation, we can adopt fast algorithm for multi-exponentiation. We collectively refer to the multi-exponentiation methods described in [6].

3.2 Forward Security

Forward security is an important cryptographic notion, it can preserve the validity of past signatures when the current private key is compromised. Thus, it can reduce the loss which is resulted from key exposure. In our scheme, if the user's private key s_{ID}^t at time period t is compromised, then the produced authentication tags before time period t are not affected. For forward security of the proposed scheme, its security proof is given in Theorem 3.

3.3 Security Proof

In order to prove the unforgeability of the proof information in our proposed construction, we first show that it is computationally difficult to forge the user's private key s_{ID}^t in time period t.

Theorem 1. If the user's private key s_{ID}^t can be forged by the probabilistic polynomial time adversary Adv, then we can construct an algorithm B which is able to solve the RSA problem or inverse of hash function.

Proof. Here, we classify the adversaries into the outsider attackers and the insider attackers. If an outsider attacker outputs a user's private key $s_{ID^*}^t = H_1(ID^*)^{d^{(T+1-t)}}$, it means that it can solve the instance $(N, e, y = H_1(ID^*))$ of the RSA problem. Because

$$\begin{aligned} y &= y^{(ed)^{(T+1-t)}} \\ &= (H_1(ID^*)^{d^{(T+1-t)}})^{e^{(T+1-t)}} \\ &= (s_{ID^*}^t)^{e^{(T+1-t)}} \end{aligned} \tag{2}$$

Then $(s_{ID^*}^t)^{e^{(T-t)}}$ is the solution of the instance (N, e, y) of the RSA problem.

For the insider attackers, without loss of generality, we assume that the user i and the user j are two insider attackers, they have their own private keys $s_{ID_i}^t = H_1(ID_i)^{d^{(T+1-t)}}$ and $s_{ID_j}^t = H_1(ID_j)^{d^{(T+1-t)}}$. If they collude to output private key $s_{ID^*}^t = d^{(T+1-t) \cdot H_1(ID^*)}$ of the user with identity ID^* at time period t, it means that

$$H_1(ID^*) = H_1(ID_i)^a \cdot H_1(ID_j)^b, \tag{3}$$

where a, b are two integers which should be known for user i and user j. However, it is equivalent to solve the inverse of hash function to find ID^* which satisfies Eq. (3). Obviously, it is in contradiction with the difficulty of solving the inverse of hash function. □

Theorem 2. If there exists a probabilistic polynomial time adversary Adv that successfully convinces the TPA to accept the fake proof information for a corrupted file with non-negligible probability, then we can use Adv to solve the RSA problem problem with non-negligible probability.

Proof. Suppose that there exists an adversary produces a faked proof information which can pass verification auditing, then we are going to construct a PPT algorithm B to solve the instance of the RSA problem. First of all, let us recall the RSA problem: (N, e, y) is an instance of the RSA problem as stated in Definition 1. At the same time, B randomly selects an interrupt time point $\hat{t}, 1 \leq \hat{t} \leq T$, it means that the breakin period happens at $\hat{t}$ or later.

To play this game, B simulates the following oracles.

H_1-**Oracle.** When the adversary A makes H_1-query with identity ID_i, B first checks whether ID_i exist in the H_1-list which is initially empty. It exists, B returns h_{ID_i} to the adversary A. Otherwise, B tosses a biased coin $\beta_i \in \{0, 1\}$ so that $\beta_i = 0$ with probability η and $\beta = 1$ with probability $1 - \eta$. If $\beta_i = 0$, then B sets $h_{ID_i} = x_i^{e^{T+1}} \mod N$, where x_i is a random number of Z_N; Otherwise, it sets $h_{ID_i} = y^{e^{T+1-\hat{t}}} x_i^{e^{T+1}} \mod Z_N$. After B sends h_{ID_i} to A, it adds $(ID_i, h_{ID_i}, x_i, \beta_i)$ in the H_1-list.

H_2-**Oracle.** The adversary A can ask for H_2-Oracle with $(FName, R, ID_i, index_j)$, B randomly picks $\rho_{ij} \in Z_{N_0}$ to set $H_2(FName||R||ID_i||index_j) = \rho_{ij}$ and return ρ_{ij} to the adversary. Finally, it also adds $(FName, R, ID_i, index_j, \rho_{ij})$ in the H_2-list which is initially empty.

Extract Oracle. When A makes the Extract-query with identity ID_i at time period t, B first looks up ID_i in the H_1-list. If the corresponding $\beta_i = 0$, then B computes its private key at time period t as $s_{ID_i}^t = x_i^{e^t} \mod N$. If $\beta_i = 1$ and $t < \hat{t}$, then B aborts it. Otherwise, it computes $s_{ID_i}^t = y^{e^{t-\hat{t}}} x_i^{e^t} \mod N$ as the private key of the user with identity ID_i at time t. Finally, it sends $s_{ID_i}^t$ to the adversary A.

TagGen Oracle. When the adversary A asks for a TagGen Orale with (m, ID_i) in the time period t. B simulate as follows:

1. If $\beta_i = 0$ or $t \geq \hat{t}$, B can retrieve the corresponding private key by querying Extract-Oracle. Then it computes authentication tag (R, ς) of data block m by using its private key.
2. If $\beta_i = 1$ or $t < \hat{t}$, B randomly chooses $r \in Z_N$ to compute $R = r^{e^{T+1-t}} \cdot H_1(ID_i)^{-1} \mod N$ and $\varsigma = r^m \mod N$. And let $H_2(FName||R||ID_i||index) = m$ and add $(FName||R||ID_i||index, m)$ in the H_2-list.
3. Finally, it returns (R, ς) to the adversary.

Prove. B and the adversary A executes an interactive challenge-response protocol where B acts as the TPA and A behaves as the cloud server. A can obtain the auditing result at the end of the protocol.

Output. The adversary A outputs a fake proof information $prf' = (\delta', R, \mu')$ at time period $t^* < \hat{t}$, $prf' \neq prf$, and prf' can pass the verification algorithm, where $prf = (\delta, R, \mu)$ is a valid proof information which is produced by the honest cloud server. As the valid proof information, prf should satisfy the verification algorithm, thus, we can obtain the following equation:

$$\delta^{e^{(T+1-t)}} = R^H \cdot H_1(ID)^\mu \mod N \tag{4}$$

Because the fake proof information prf' can also pass verification algorithm, prf' should satisfy

$$\delta'^{e^{(T+1-t)}} = R^H \cdot H_1(ID)^{\mu'} \mod N \tag{5}$$

Due to $\mu \neq \mu'$, we set $\triangle\mu = \mu - \mu'$. By Eqs. 4 and 5, we can obtain

$$(\delta/\delta')^{e^{(T+1-t)}} = H_1(ID)^{\mu-\mu'} \mod N \tag{6}$$

Note δ'^{-1} is able to be solved by Bezout's identity, namely, there are two numbers $a \cdot \delta' + b \cdot N = 1$.
Because $H_1(ID) = y^{e^{T+1-\hat{t}}} x_i^{e^{T+1}} \mod N$, the above Eq. 6 can be rewrote as

$$(\delta/\delta')^{e^{(T+1-t)}} = (y^{e^{T+1-\hat{t}}} x_i^{e^{T+1}})^{\mu-\mu'} \mod N$$

$$\Downarrow$$

$$\left(\frac{\delta}{\delta' \cdot x_i^{e^{t(\mu-\mu')}}}\right)^{e^{(T+1-t)}} = (y^{e^{T+1-\hat{t}}})^{\mu-\mu'} \mod N$$

$$\Downarrow$$

$$\left(\frac{\delta}{\delta' \cdot x_i^{e^{t(\mu-\mu')}}}\right)^{e^{(\hat{t}-t)}} = y^{\mu-\mu'} \mod N$$

If $gcd(e^{(\hat{t}-t)}, \triangle\mu) = 1$, it means that there exists two integers a and b such that $ae^{(\hat{t}-t)} + b\triangle\mu = 1$, then we have

$$y = y^{ae^{(\hat{t}-t)}+b\triangle\mu}$$

$$= y^{ae^{(\hat{t}-t)}} \cdot \left(\frac{\delta}{\delta' \cdot x_i^{e^{t(\mu-\mu')}}}\right)^{be^{(\hat{t}-t)}}$$

$$= \left(y^a \cdot \left(\frac{\delta}{\delta' \cdot x_i^{e^{t(\mu-\mu')}}}\right)^b\right)^{e^{(\hat{t}-t)}}$$

Let $x^* = \left(y^a \cdot \left(\frac{\delta}{\delta' \cdot x_i^{e^{t(\mu-\mu')}}}\right)^b\right)$, then we have $(x^*)^{e^{\hat{t}-t}} = y$. Thus $(x^*)^{e^{\hat{t}-t-1}}$ is the solution of the given instance of the RSA problem.

If $gcd(e^{(\hat{t}-t)}, \triangle\mu) \neq 1$, then it means that $\triangle\mu$ can divide e, that is to say, $\triangle\mu \equiv 0 \mod e$, since the least factor of $e^{(\hat{t}-t)}$ is e. Thus, the probability of $gcd(e^{(T+1-t)H_1(ID)}, \triangle\mu \cdot v) \neq 1$ is at most

$$\frac{(\hat{t}-t)}{2^k}.$$

Due to $k \geq 256$, the probability of the event occurs is less than $\frac{(\hat{t}-t)}{2^k}$ which is negligible. Thus, we think $gcd(e^{(\hat{t}-t)}, \triangle\mu) = 1$.

As is known to all, It is hard to solve the RSA problem with large exponents. Thus, there does not exist an adversary which can output a fake proof information to pass the verification algorithm.

$\square$

Theorem 3. If there exists an adversary which can break forward security of our scheme. Then, with non-negligible probability, the RSA problem can be solved.

Proof. Suppose that (N_0, e, y) is an instance of the RSA problem as stated in Definition 1. We will construct a PPT algorithm B which makes use of the adversary Adv to solve the RSA problem. In the following game, B can simulate all the above oracles in Theorem 2 and answer Adv's queries.

In the setup phase, the adversary Adv can obtain the public key (N_0, e). Then it can interact with B in an arbitrary way to obtain a series of data block signature pairs $(m_i, \varsigma_i)_{i=1,\cdots,q_t}$. At the same time, we provide all hashing oracles to answer the adversary Adv's hashing queries. Let us define the adversary Adv to break in the system at time period t^* and learn the user ID's private key $s_{ID}^{t^*}$. Finally, the adversary Adv outputs a forged data block/signature pair at time period $t < t^*$ which is not in $(m_i, \varsigma_i)_{i=1,\cdots,q_t}$ with non-negligible probability,

By adopting standard rewind technique, B rewinds to the point just before returning the answer of the H_2 query, and returns another answer to this particular query. For convenient illustration, let $\delta' = (R', \varsigma', m')$ denote the first forged signature by Adv at time period t^*, $\delta'' = (R'', \varsigma'', m')$ be another forged signature by Adv at time period t^*. If Adv successes, then they should satisfy

$$\varsigma'^{e^{T+1-t^*}} = R'^{h'} \cdot H_1(ID)^{m'} \mod N$$

and

$$\varsigma''^{e^{T+1-t^*}} = R''^{h''} \cdot H_1(ID)^{m'} \mod N$$

where $R' = R''$, $h' = H_2(FName\|R'\|index^*)$ and $h'' = H_2(FName\|R''\| index^*)$.

Dividing the above two equations, we have

$$(\frac{\varsigma'}{\varsigma''})^{e^{T+1-t^*}} = R'^{h'-h''}$$

Now, setting $R' = v^{e^{T+1-t^*}} y^\beta$ for $v \in Z_{N_0}$ and $\beta \in [1, 2^k]$ as well as $\Delta h = h' - h''$, then we have

$$(\frac{\varsigma'}{\varsigma''})^{e^{T+1-t^*}} = (v^{e^{T+1-t^*}} y^\beta)^{\Delta h} \tag{7}$$

By reorganizing the above Eq. 7, we yields

$$(\frac{\varsigma'}{\varsigma'' \cdot v^{\Delta h}})^{e^{T+1-t^*}} = y^{\beta \Delta h}$$

Because e is a prime number, we have $gcd(e, \beta \Delta h) = 1$. By using extended Euclidean algorithm, we can find $a, b \in Z_{N_0}$ to satisfy $a \cdot e^{T+1-t^*} + b \cdot \beta \Delta h = 1$. Thus, B can output $\chi^{e^{T+1-t^*}} = y$ where

$$\chi = y^a \cdot (\frac{\varsigma'}{\varsigma'' \cdot v^{\Delta h}})^b$$

It means that the RSA problem is solved. $\qquad\square$

Theorem 4. Our proposed auditing protocol can resist the Replace Attack from the cloud server.

Proof. To resist replace attack, we must make that the cloud server is not able to pass the auditing verification by replacing a specified block and its tag, with another block and its corresponding tag. If the challenged data blocks m_l or its authentication tag ς_l is corrupted in cloud server, the proof information, which is returned by cloud server, cannot pass the auditing since the verification equation may not hold. Therefore, cloud server may launch the replace attack to try to pass the audit.

It chooses another pair of data block and data authentication tag (m_k, ς_k) to replace the corrupted one (m_l, ς_l). Then, it computes

$$\delta^* = (\varsigma_k)^{v_l} \cdot \prod_{j \in I, i \neq l} \varsigma_j^{v_j}, \quad \mu^* = v_l M_k + \sum_{j \in I, j \neq l} v_j \cdot M_j$$

Then, the left hand of the verification equation can be transformed as

$$(\delta^*)^{e^{T+1-t}}$$

$$= [(\zeta_k)^{v_l} \cdot \prod_{j\in I, i\neq l} \zeta_j^{v_j}]^{e^{T+1-t}}$$

$$= (R^{H_2(FName||R||index_k)}(H_1(ID))^{M_k})^{v_l} \cdot$$

$$\prod_{i\in I, i\neq l} (R^{H_2(FName||R||index_i)}H_1(ID))^{M_i v_i} \mod N$$

$$= R^{\sum_{i\in I} H_2(FName||R||index_i)+(H_2(FName||R||index_k)-H_2(FName||R||index_l))} \cdot H_1(ID)^{\mu^*}$$

If the auditing verification can be passed, it means that $H_2(FName ||R||index_k) = H_2(FName||R||index_l)$. However, $index_l \neq index_k$, it is impossible for

$$H_2(FName||R||index_k) = H_2(FName||R||index_l)$$

due to collision resistance of hash function. Thus, the proof from the cloud server cannot pass the auditing.   □

4   Performance Analysis

To achieve 80-bit security parameter, in our scheme, we set k to be 512bits, thus, the size of modulus N is 1024 bits. In the RSA cryptosystem, the size of public parameter e has the important influence on the whole system. Increasing the size of the RSA key will make that the generation of signature becomes slower. Thus, we set the public parameter e which satisfies $2^l \leq e \leq 2^{l+1}$ in our scheme, where $l = 20$. Furthermore, for system public parameters in our scheme, they only consist of some security parameters, a key pair and two hash functions. In the TagGen phase and Verifying phase, any pairing operation is not required.

In the following, we analyze our scheme's perform by making a comparison of our scheme and Yu et al.'s scheme in [1]. Our experiment is conducted using C on a system with an Intel Core 2 processor running at 2.4 GHz, 768 MB RAM, and a 7200 RPM Western Digital 250 GB Serial ATA drive with an 8 MB buffer. All algorithms are implemented using the Miracl Library [3].

Let us assume that 1GB data are stored to the cloud, these data are divided into n data blocks. To fairly compare, the size of the split data block is set as 4KB, thus the size of the index is $|n| = 18$ bits. In the Setup phase, to produce public system parameters, the time costs are 0.166s and 0.1521s in Yu et al.'s scheme and our proposed scheme, respectively. The main difference of time cost between the two scheme is the reason that two pseudo-random functions are introduced in Yu et al.'s scheme. In the Extract algorithm, the time costs to produce private key of the user with identity ID are 5.32 milliseconds in Yu et al.'s scheme and our proposed scheme.

In the TagGen phase, to outsourced 1G data to the cloud, the user needs to split these data into n data blocks, and to compute authentication tag for each data block. As for Yu et al.'s scheme and our scheme, the comparison of their computation costs and communication overhead is shown in Table 1.

Table 1. Comparison of our scheme and Yu et al.'s scheme in the TagGen

	Computation cost	Communication overhead (bits)
Yu et al.'s scheme	$(2n + 2)C_E + (n + 1)C_M + S$	$|M| + |H_1| + (n + 1)|Z_{N_0}|$
Our scheme	$2nC_E + nC_M$	$|M| + n|Z_{N_0}|$

Where C_E denotes exponentiation operator in Z_{N_0} or Z_N, S is time to setup public parameters of RSA and C_M is multiplication operator in Z_{N_0} or Z_N. $|M|$ denotes the length of the outsourced data, H_1 denotes the length of hash function H_1, $|Z_{N_0}|$ is the length of element in Z_{N_0}.

By simulating, we find that it takes 928.576 s to produce these authentication tag of data blocks in Yu et al.'s scheme. However, it needs to take 790.432 s these authentication tags in our scheme when $T = 50$ and $t = 0$. In our scheme, the time to compute authentication tag is influenced by time period T. The reason to produce authentication tag is that the user needs to produce a suit of new public parameters of RSA system.

The average time for the user to compute authentication tags with different choices of time period T is shown in Table 2.

Table 2. The average time for the user to compute authentication tags

	$T = 50$	$T = 100$	$T = 150$	$T = 200$
Times (s)	790.432	970.121	1197.332	1389.732

In the Verifying phase, the auditor's computation cost changes with the number of the challenged blocks. And the probability of detecting error block is also influenced by the number of the challenged blocks. The more the number of the challenged blocks is, the more the auditor's computation cost is and the higher the probability of detecting error block is. Because the probability of detecting error block can be denoted as follows:

$$1 - (1 - \frac{|C|}{n})^{|I|}$$

where $|C|$ denotes the number of the corrupted data blocks and $|I|$ is the number of the challenged blocks. For 1,000,000 data blocks, if the probability of the corrupted data is 1 %, then to obtain 99 % probability of detecting error data, the required challenged data blocks only needs 460 blocks. When the challenged block is 350 blocks, the probability of detecting error data can achieve 95 %.

In the Verifying phase, to verify data integrity, the auditor's computation costs in our scheme and Yu et al.'s scheme are shown in Table 3.

Obviously, our scheme has the advantages over Yu *et al.*'s scheme in terms of computational cost and communication overhead. In our scheme, it is independent of the challenged set in terms of the TPA's computational cost. At the

Table 3. Comparison of our scheme and Yu et al.'s scheme in the Verifying phase

	Computation cost	Communication overhead	Forward security
Yu et al.'s scheme	$(|I| + 4)C_E + (|I| + 1)C_M$	$|H_1| + 2|Z_{N_0}| + |\mu|$	NO
Our scheme	$3C_E + 1C_M$	$2|Z_{N_0}| + |\mu|$	Yes

same time, our scheme can provide forward security. When we set $T = 50$ and the challenged blocks is 300 blocks, our implement shows that cloud server and the auditor need to take 25.43 ms and 239.54 ms respectively to produce and verify the proof in Yu $et\ al.$'s scheme, however, cloud server and the auditor only need to take 22.43 ms and 205.94 ms in our scheme.

According to the statement above, no matter computational cost or communication overhead, our scheme has many advantages over Yu $et\ al.$'s scheme. At the same time, our proposed scheme can support forward security and be applied to the multi-user setting.

5 Conclusion

In this paper, based on RSA cryptosystem we propose a novel ID-based data integrity auditing mechanism with forward security, which does not only eliminate the complicated certificate management in traditional PKI-based PDP or PoR schemes, but also support forward security. At the same time, it also can easily been extended into the multi-user setting. And we show that the proposed scheme can resist malicious cloud server attack, replace attack and replay attack. The security of the scheme is related to the hardness of RSA problem with prime exponent in the random oracle model. By comparing with Yu et al.'s scheme, the our scheme has more advantages in terms of computational cost and communication overhead. It is the future problem how to achieve privacy-preserving in the context of data processing.

Acknowledgments. This work was supported by Beijing Municipal Natural Science Foundation (Nos: 4162020,4132056) and The importation and development of High-Caliber Talents project of Beijing municipal Institutions (CIT&TCD201304004).

References

1. Yong, Y., Xue, L., Au, M.H., Susilo, W., Ni, J., Zhang, Y.F., et al.: Cloud data integrity checking with an identity-based auditing mechanism from RSA. Future Gen. Comput. Syst. **62**, 51–53 (2016). doi:10.1016/j.future.2016.02.003
2. May, P., Ehrlich, H.-C., Steinke, T.: ZIB structure prediction pipeline: composing a complex biological workflow through web services. In: Nagel, W.E., Walter, W.V., Lehner, W. (eds.) Euro-Par 2006. LNCS, vol. 4128, pp. 1148–1158. Springer, Heidelberg (2006)
3. M.I.R.A.C.L. library, Shamus Software Ltd., 94 Shangan Road, Ballymun, Dublin, Ireland

4. Czajkowski, K., Fitzgerald, S., Foster, I., Kesselman, C.: Grid information services for distributed resource sharing. In: 10th IEEE International Symposium on High Performance Distributed Computing, pp. 181–184. IEEE Press, New York (2001)
5. Wang, H.: Identity-based distributed provable data possession in multicloud storage IEEE T. Serv. Compsut. **8**(2), 328–340 (2015)
6. ElGamal, T.: A public-key cryptosystem and a signature scheme based on discrete logarithms. IEEE Trans. Inf. Theor. **31**, 469–472 (1985)
7. Ateniese, G., Burns, R., Curtmola, R., Herring, J., Kissner, L., Peterson, Z., Song, D.: Provable data possession at untrusted stores. In: Proceedings 14th ACM Conference Computer and Communications Security (CCS 2007), pp. 598–609 (2007)
8. Juels, A., Kaliski, B.S.: PORs: proofs of retrievability for large files. In: Proceedings 14th ACM Conference Computer and Communications Security (CCS 2007), pp. 584–597 (2007)
9. Wang, Q., Wang, C., Ren, K., Lou, W., Li, J.: Enabling public auditability and data dynamics for storage security in cloud computing. IEEE Trans. Parallel Distrib. Syst. **22**(5), 847–859 (2011)
10. Zhang, Y., Blanton, M.: Efficient dynamic provable possession of remote data via balanced update trees. In: Proceedings 8th ACM SIGSAC Symposium Information, Computer and Communications Security (ASIACCS 2013), pp. 183–194 (2013)
11. Zheng, Q., Xu, S.: Fair and dynamic proofs of retrievability. In: Proceedings First ACM Conference Data and Application Security and Privacy (CODASPY 2011), pp. 237–248 (2011)
12. Stefanov, E., Dijk, M.V., Oprea, A., Jules, A.: Iris: A Scalable Cloud File System with Efficient Integrity Checks, Report /585, Cryptology ePrint Archive (2011)
13. Gritti, C., Susilo, W., Plantard, T.: Efficient dynamic provable data possession with public verifiability and data privacy. In: Foo, E., Stebila, D. (eds.) ACISP 2015. LNCS, vol. 9144, pp. 395–412. Springer, Heidelberg (2015)
14. Wang, Q., Wang, C., Ren, K., Lou, W., Li, J.: Enabling public auditability and data dynamics for storage security in cloud computing. IEEE Trans. Parallel Distrib. Syst. **22**(5), 847–859 (2011)
15. Jianhong, Z., Qiaocui, D.: Efficient ID-based public auditing for the outsourced data in cloud storage. Inf. Sci. **344**, 1–14 (2016)
16. Zhang, J., Li, P., Mao, J.: IPad: ID-based public auditing for the outsourced data in the standard model. Cluster Comput. **19**(1), 127–138 (2016)
17. Ren, K., Wang, C., Wang, Q.: Security challenges for the public cloud. IEEE Internet Comput. **16**(1), 69–73 (2012)
18. Understanding the Cloud Computing Stack: SaaS, PaaS, IaaS. https://support.rackspace.com/white-paper/understanding-the-cloud-computing-stack-saas-paas-iaas/

Efficient Dynamic Provable Data Possession from Dynamic Binary Tree

Changfeng Li[1] and Huaqun Wang[2(✉)]

[1] Nanjing University of Finance and Economics, Nanjing, China
[2] Nangjing University of Posts and Telecommunications, Nanjing, China
wanghuaqun@aliyun.com

Abstract. In order to ensure the remote data integrity in cloud storage, provable data possession (PDP) is of crucial importance. For most clients, dynamic data operations are indispensable. This paper proposes an efficient dynamic PDP scheme for verifying the remote dynamic data integrity in an untrusted cloud storage. Our dynamic PDP scheme is constructed from dynamic binary tree and bilinear pairings, supporting the dynamic data operations, such as, insertion, deletion, modification. From the computation cost, communication cost, and storage cost, our proposed dynamic PDP scheme is efficient. On the other hand, our proposed concrete dynamic PDP scheme is provably secure.

Keywords: Cloud computing · Dynamic provable data possession · Binary tree

1 Introduction

By using cloud computing, the clients are relieved of the burden for storage management and data processing. Thus, the clients save the capital expenditure on hardware, software, and personnel maintenances, *etc.* In cloud computing, the clients outsource their computing and storage to remote cloud server (CS). At the same time, the clients also face the risks of confidentiality, integrity and availability of data and service. Since the clients do not store these data locally, it is especially vital to ensure their remote data integrity. In 2007, Ateniese *et al.* proposed an important remote data integrity checking primitive: PDP [1]. It is a probabilistic remote data integrity checking primitive. For PDP, the verifier can efficiently check remote data integrity with a high probability. Following Ateniese *et al.*'s pioneering work, Shacham and Waters presented the proof of retrievability (POR) scheme [2].

For most clients, their stored data is dynamic. The clients may frequently insert or delete or modify their remote data. Thus, dynamic PDP is indispensable to ensure remote dynamic data integrity. On the other hand, the dynamic

H. Wang—This work is partly supported by the Natural Science Foundation of China through projects (61272522), by the Program for Liaoning Excellent Talents in University through project (LR2014021), and by the Natural Science Foundation of Liaoning Province (2014020147).

L. Chen and J. Han (Eds.): ProvSec 2016, LNCS 10005, pp. 101–111, 2016.
DOI: 10.1007/978-3-319-47422-9_6

PDP scheme must be efficient for capacity-limited end devices. Zheng *et al.* proposed the fair and dynamic POR [3]. Then, Ateniese *et al.* proposed dynamic PDP model and designed the concrete scheme although it does not support insert operation [4]. In 2009, based on the skip list, Erway *et al.* designed a full-dynamic PDP scheme which supports the insert operation [5]. In 2013, Etemad *et al.* proposed the transparent, distributed, and replicated dynamic PDP scheme [6]. Cash *et al.* proposed the dynamic proofs of retrievability via oblivious RAM [7]. On the other hand, dynamic remote data public auditability has also been studied [8–10].

Tree is an important storage structure for the remote block data. In 2013, Zhang *et al.* propose a dynamic provable scheme via balanced update tree [11]. Zhang *et al.* propose a verifiable dynamic provable data possession scheme by developing a variant authenticated 2–3 tree [12]. Shi *et al.* pointed out that Cash *et al.*'s scheme [7] is mostly of theoretical interest because it employs oblivious RAM as a black box. They also pointed out Stefanov *et al.*'s scheme has a large audit cost. Finally, they proposed a dynamic proof of retrievability scheme with constant client storage whose bandwidth cost is comparable to a Merkle hash tree [13]. Tate *et al.* proposed multi-user dynamic proofs of data possession by using trusted hardware [14].

Until now, the proposed dynamic PDP schemes are inefficient. When a novel block is inserted, many blocks have to change their index and create novel tags. It will incur heavy cost. It is an open problem to keep the other block-tag pairs unchanged even if the novel block is inserted.

1.1 Contributions

The main contributions of this work are summarized below: (1) We present a dynamic binary tree construction method which yields an efficient dynamic PDP scheme; (2) Based on the bilinear pairing and our proposed dynamic binary tree, a concrete private dynamic PDP scheme is designed. (3) Our private dynamic PDP scheme can detect the dishonest client's invalid data.

1.2 Paper Organization

This paper is organized below. Section 2 presents the construction method of dynamic binary tree. It comprises of insertion and deletion. Section 3 gives the models of dynamic PDP: system model, security model and the definition of dynamic PDP scheme. Based on the dynamic binary tree, Sect. 4 propose a concrete dynamic PDP scheme. The performance analysis is also given in this section. Section 5 analyzes the proposed dynamic PDP scheme's security. Finally, Sect. 6 gives the conclusion.

2 Dynamic Binary Tree

In order to realize the remote data integrity checking, the corresponding tag T_i must be generated and uploaded for every block m_i. In our scheme, the tag T_i relates to m_i and the leaf node index l_i. From the procedures Insertion and Deletion, the leaf nodes' index will keep constant after dynamic operations. When the data blocks are stored on the leaf nodes, these blocks' leaf node index will also keep constant after the dynamic operations. Thus, when some blocks are inserted, the other block-tag pairs will be unchanged. This dynamic binary tree can be used to support our private dynamic PDP scheme.

2.1 Binary Tree

A simple binary tree can be depicted in Fig. 1. The top node R (level 0) is the root of the tree. R has two children $1L$ and $1R$ (level 1). Continuously, $1L$ has two children 1 and 2; $1R$ has two children 3 and 4 (level 2). The level 2 is the bottom level which will store the clients' remote data. Specially, denote R's left child as 0 and right child as 1. 0's left child is 00 and right child is 01. 1's left child is 10 and right child is 11. Generally, every node's index is its parent's index plus 0 if it is the left child or plus 1 if it is the right child. Thus, Fig. 1 can be rewritten as Fig. 2. In the Fig. 2, every inner node has two elements: index and leaf node number. For example, the root node R has 4 children which lie on the bottom level. R's left child has 2 children which lie on the bottom level. R's right child has 2 children which lie on the bottom level. In the dynamic binary tree, the bottom nodes may be deleted or modified. On the other hand, some novel nodes can be inserted at any place on the bottom level. On the bottom level, the 4 leaf nodes's indexes are 00, 01, 10, 11, respectively.

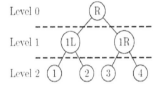

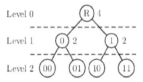

Fig. 1. Binary tree

Fig. 2. Binary tree with index and leaf node number

2.2 Insertion

When a leaf node N_i is inserted after another leaf node N, the binary tree can be updated below:

1. From the node N, the left child and the right child are created and become the leaf nodes. Their parent node N becomes the inner-node.
2. The inner node N's index keeps unchanged and N's left child has the same index as the node N. N's right child's index is N's index plus 1.
3. The inner node N's leaf node number is 2. N's parent, grandfather, until to the root R, add their original leaf node number to 1 which is their new leaf node number.
4. The other nodes' index and leaf node number keep unchanged.

An inner node $< l, v >$ is associated with its index l and its leaf node number v. The leaf node only has the index, *i.e.*, it is denoted as l.

2.3 Deletion

Let a leaf node N's index be l'. Let N's parent node N_p be $< l, v >$. Let N's brother leaf node be l''. When l' is deleted, the binary tree can be updated below:

1. The parent node $< l, v >$ is substituted by the index l'' without the leaf node number. The parent node becomes the leaf node.
2. The two leaf nodes l' and l'' are deleted.
3. N_p's parent, grandfather, until to the root R, subtract 1 from their original leaf node number. The difference values are their new leaf node number.
4. The other inner nodes' index and leaf node number keep unchanged. The other leaf nodes' index keeps unchanged.

3   Model of Dynamic PDP

In our dynamic PDP, there exist two different entities: client and CS. Client's massive data will be stored in CS. CS has significant storage space and computation resource which are used to process the clients' data.

Definition 1 (Dynamic PDP). *Dynamic PDP scheme consists of the phases below. They can be performed in the PPT (probabilistic polynomial time).*

1. *$KeyGen(1^k) \rightarrow (sk, pk)$. Input a security parameter 1^k, it outputs the secret/public key pair (sk, pk). By using $KeyGen(1^k)$, the client gets his secret/public key pair (sk_c, pk_c) and CS gets his secret/public key pair (sk_s, pk_s).*
2. *$TagGen(sk_c, pk_c, pk_s, m) \rightarrow T_m$. Input (sk_c, pk_c), pk_s and the message block m, it outputs the tag T_m.*
3. *$VryTag(sk_s, pk_s, pk_c, m, T_m) \rightarrow$ accept or reject. Input the block-tag pair (m, T_m), CS's secret/public key pair (sk_s, pk_s), the client's public key pk_c, it outputs accept or reject. accept denotes the block-tag pair is valid and reject denotes the block-tag pair is invalid.*
4. *$PreUpdate(sk_c, pk_c, pk_s, F, info, M_e) \rightarrow \{e(F), e(info), e(M'_e)\}$. Input (sk_c, pk_c), pk_s, the file block F, the update information $info$, the previous metadata M_e, it outputs the encoded version of the file $e(F)$, $e(info)$, and the new metadata $e(M'_e)$. At last, the client sends $e(F), e(info)$ to CS and stores M'_e locally.*
5. *$PerUpdate(sk_s, pk_c, pk_s, F_{i-1}, M_{i-1}, e(F), e(info)) \rightarrow \{U, P_U, F_i, M_i\}$. Input pk_c, (sk_s, pk_s), the previous version of the stored file F_{i-1}, the metadata M_{i-1} and the query $(e(F), e(info))$, it outputs the new version of the file F_i and the metadata M_i, along with the update report U and its proof P_U. CS stores F_i, M_i and sends (U, P_U) to the client.*

6. $VryUpdate(sk_c, pk_c, pk_s, F, info, M_e, U, P_U) \rightarrow accept$ or $reject$. Input (sk_c, pk_c), pk_s, $(F, info)$, M_e and (U, P_U), it outputs accept or reject. accept denotes CS's update response is valid. reject denotes CS's update response is invalid.

7. $Challenge(sk_c, pk_c, pk_s, M_e) \rightarrow chal$. Input (sk_c, pk_c), pk_s, M_e, it outputs the challenge chal to CS.

8. $Prove(sk_s, pk_s, pk_c, F_i, M_i, chal) \rightarrow V$. Input (sk_s, pk_s), pk_c, the latest version of the file F_i and the metadata M_i, and chal, it outputs the proof V to the client.

9. $Verify(sk_c, pk_c, pk_s, M_e, chal, V) \rightarrow accept$ or $reject$. Input (sk_c, pk_c), pk_s, M_e, chal, and the proof V, it outputs accept or reject. accept means that CS still keeps the file intact. reject means some challenged blocks are corrupted.

Definition 2. *A dynamic PDP scheme is secure against any untrusted PPT CS if the probability that any such CS wins the dynamic PDP game below is negligible. The untrusted CS is the adversary $\mathcal{A}$. The client is the challenger $\mathcal{C}$. The dynamic PDP game is played between $\mathcal{C}$ and $\mathcal{A}$ below:*

1. *KeyGen: $\mathcal{C}$ runs $KeyGen(1^k) \rightarrow (sk_c, pk_c)$ and gets its own secret/public key pair (sk_c, pk_c). $\mathcal{A}$ runs $KeyGen(1^k) \rightarrow (sk_s, pk_s)$ and gets its own secret/public key pair (sk_s, pk_s). The public keys pk_c and pk_s are made public.*

2. *First-phase Queries: $\mathcal{A}$ adaptively makes a lot of different queries to $\mathcal{C}$. Each query can be one of the following:*
   (a) *Update queries. $\mathcal{A}$ sends the update query to $\mathcal{C}$ adaptively. $\mathcal{C}$ responds $\mathcal{A}$ according to the query.*
   (b) *Hash queries. $\mathcal{A}$ can make hash queries adaptively. $\mathcal{C}$ returns the corresponding hash values to $\mathcal{A}$.*
   (c) *Tag queries. $\mathcal{A}$ makes block-tag pair queries adaptively. For a block query m_i, $\mathcal{C}$ computes the tag $T_i \leftarrow TagGen(sk_c, m_i)$ and sends it to $\mathcal{A}$.*
   Without loss of generality, let (m_i, T_i) be the queried block-tag pair or updated block-tag pair where $i \in \mathbb{I}_1$.

3. *Challenge: $\mathcal{C}$ generates a challenge chal for $\mathcal{A}$. Let the challenged block subscript set satisfy $\{i_1, i_2, \cdots, i_l\} \nsubseteq \mathbb{I}_1$, where l is a positive integer. $\mathcal{A}$ is required to provide a possession proof for the blocks $m_{i_1}, m_{i_2}, \cdots, m_{i_l}$.*

4. *Second-Phase Queries. Similar to the First-Phase Queries. Let (m_i, T_i) be the queried (Update queries or Tag queries) and responded block-tag pairs where the subscript $i \in \mathbb{I}_2$ and $\mathbb{I}_2$ is the queried and responded block-tag pair subscript set in Second-Phase. The restriction is that $\{i_1, i_2, \cdots, i_l\} \nsubseteq \mathbb{I}_1 \cup \mathbb{I}_2$.*

5. *Forge: $\mathcal{A}$ computes the remote data possession proof V for the blocks indicated by chal and outputs V.*

We say that a dynamic PDP scheme satisfies unforgeability against the untrusted CS if the adversary $\mathcal{A}$ wins the dynamic PDP game with negligible probability.

4   The Proposed Dynamic PDP Scheme

4.1   Bilinear Pairings

Let $\mathcal{G}_1$ and $\mathcal{G}_2$ be two cyclic multiplicative groups with the same prime order q. Let $e : \mathcal{G}_1 \times \mathcal{G}_1 \to \mathcal{G}_2$ be a bilinear map [15,16] which satisfies the following properties:

1. Bilinearity: $\forall g_1, g_2 \in \mathcal{G}_1$ and $a, b \in \mathcal{Z}_q$, $e(g_1{}^a, g_2{}^b) = e(g_1, g_2)^{ab}$.
2. Non-degeneracy: $\exists g_4, g_5 \in \mathcal{G}_1$ such that $e(g_4, g_5) \neq 1_{\mathcal{G}_2}$.
3. Computability: $\forall g_6, g_7 \in \mathcal{G}_1$, there is an efficient algorithm to calculate $e(g_6, g_7)$.

Definition 3 (CDH problem). *Let g be the generator of $\mathcal{G}_1$. Given $g, g^a, g^b \in \mathcal{G}_1$ for randomly chosen $a, b \in \mathcal{Z}_q$, calculate $g^{ab} \in \mathcal{G}_1$.*

Definition 4 (DDH problem). *Let g be the generator of $\mathcal{G}_1$. Given $(g, g^a, g^b, \hat{g}) \in \mathcal{G}_1^4$ for randomly chosen $a, b \in \mathcal{Z}_q^*$, decide whether $g^{ab} \stackrel{?}{=} \hat{g}$.*

In the paper, the chosen group $\mathcal{G}_1$ satisfies that CDH problem is difficult but DDH problem is easy. The DDH problem can be solved by using the bilinear pairings. Thus, $(\mathcal{G}_1, \mathcal{G}_2)$ are also defined as GDH (Gap Diffie-Hellman) groups.

4.2   The Concrete Dynamic PDP Scheme

Initially, suppose the maximum number of the stored block-tag pairs is $\hat{n}$. Let f be a pseudo-random function, Ω be a trapdoor function whose first parameter is the trapdoor, π be a pseudo-random permutation, and h be a cryptographic hash function which are given below.

$$f : \mathcal{Z}_q^* \times \{1, 2, \cdots, \hat{n}\} \to \mathcal{Z}_q^*, \quad \Omega : \mathcal{G}_1^* \times \{1, 2, \cdots, \hat{n}\} \to \mathcal{Z}_q^*$$
$$h : \mathcal{Z}_q^* \to \mathcal{G}_1^*, \quad \pi_{\bar{n}} : \mathcal{Z}_q^* \times \{1, 2, \cdots, \bar{n}\} \to \{1, 2, \cdots, \bar{n}\}$$

The client will upload the large message M to CS. In order to generate the corresponding tags, M (maybe encoded by using error-correcting code or encryption algorithm) is divided into n blocks $(m_1, m_2, \cdots, m_n)$ where $m_i \in \mathcal{Z}_q^*$. Without loss of generality, we denote $M = (m_1, m_2, \cdots, m_n)$. CS picks a random number $sk_s \in \mathcal{Z}_q^*$ as its secret key and computes its public key $pk_s = g^{sk_s}$. The client picks a random number $sk_c \in \mathcal{Z}_q^*$ as its secret key and computes its public key $pk_c = g^{sk_c}$. The client also picks a random point $u \in \mathcal{G}_1$ and makes u public.

TagGen(sk_c, pk_c, pk_s, m_i): The client creates the full binary tree with the depth $\lceil \log_2 n \rceil$. From the left, we denote the i-th leaf node index as l_i. For the block m_i which will be stored on the i-th leaf node, the client computes $W_i = \Omega(pk_s^{sk_c}, l_i)$, $T_i = (h(W_i)u^{m_i})^{sk_c}$. Client outputs the block-tag pair (m_i, T_i).

The above procedure is performed n times and all the block-tag pairs are generated. The client uploads $\Sigma = \{(m_1, T_1), \cdots, (m_n, T_n)\}$ to CS. CS creates the full binary tree with the depth $\lceil \log_2 n \rceil$ which is the same as the client's full binary tree. CS stores the block-tag pair (m_i, T_i) on the i-th leaf node from the left whose index is l_i.

$VryTag(sk_s, pk_s, pk_c, m_i, T_i)$: CS searches for the i-th leaf node from the left and gets its index l_i.

1. CS computes $\hat{W}_i = \Omega(pk_c^{sk_s}, l_i)$;
2. CS verifies whether $e(T_i, g) = e(h(\hat{W}_i)u^{m_i}, pk_c)$ holds: if it holds, CS accepts and stores it on the i-th leaf node from the left; otherwise, CS rejects it.

$PreUpdate(sk_c, pk_c, F, info, M_e)$: The client prepares to update the block. The update information is denoted as $info$ (e.g., delete block, insert block, modify block). In order to simplify the procedure, the encoding and encrypting are omitted. Then, the client performs the procedures below:

1. If the update is insertion, the client updates its dynamic binary tree according to Sect. 2.B: insertion. Suppose F is inserted after the leaf node l_N. From the updated dynamic binary tree, the client gets the index l_{N+1} which is after the leaf node l_N. The client computes

$$W_{N+1} = \Omega(pk_s^{sk_c}, l_{N+1}), \ T_{N+1} = (h(W_{N+1})u^F)^{sk_c}$$

   The client outputs the block-tag pair (F, T_F). The original metadata M_e is also modified into the latest metadata M_e'. The client uploads $(F, T_F, info)$ to CS.
2. If the update is deletion, the client updates its dynamic binary tree according to Sect. 2.C: deletion. The original metadata M_e is updated into the latest metadata M_e'. The client uploads $(F, info)$ to CS.
3. If the update is modification, i.e., the block-tag pair (m_i, T_i) is modified into (F, T_F) on the same leaf node with the same index l_i. The client computes

$$W_i = \Omega(pk_s^{sk_c}, l_i), \ T_F = (h(W_i)u^F)^{sk_c}$$

   The client outputs the block-tag pair (F, T_F). The original metadata M_e is also updated into the latest metadata M_e'. The client uploads $(F, T_F, info)$ to CS.

$PerUpdate(pk_c, pk_s, sk_s, F, info, T_F)$: Upon receiving the updating query, the corresponding leaf node (which will be inserted or modified or deleted) can be fleetly searched by using the inner node's parameter v (i.e., the number of the leaf node which are the inner node's children), CS performs the procedures below:

1. If the update is insertion, CS updates its dynamic binary tree according to Sect. 2.B: insertion. Suppose F is inserted after the leaf node with the index l_N. CS gets the index l_{N+1} which is after the leaf node l_N.
   (a) If (F, T_F) can pass $VryTag$, CS stores them on the leaf node with the index l_{N+1}. Then, CS sends the insertion verification information and the corresponding signature $(Info_U, Sign_{sk_s}(Info_U))$ to the client.
   (b) If (F, T_F) can not pass the insertion verification $VryTag$, CS rejects them.

2. If the update is modification and (F, T_F) can pass $VryTag$, CS substitutes (F, T_T) for (m_i, T_i) whose index is l_i. Then, CS sends the modification verification information and the corresponding signature $(Info_U, Sign_{sk_s}(Info_U))$ to the client.
3. If the update is deletion, CS updates its dynamic binary tree according to Sect. 2.B: deletion. Then, CS deletes the corresponding block-tag pair. CS sends the deletion verification information and the corresponding signature $(Info_U, Sign_{sk_s}(Info_U))$ to the client.

$VryUpdate(\{(Info_U, Sign_{sk_s}(Info_U))\})$: Upon receiving the CS's update response $(Info_U, Sign_{sk_s}(Info_U))$ on the update query $(F, T_F, info)$, where T_F is empty for the deletion, the client verifies CS's signature for the update. If it can pass the verification, the client accepts CS's update response; otherwise, the client rejects CS's update response and sends the same query again.

$Challenge(sk_c, pk_c, pk_s, M_c)$: In order to check the remote data integrity, the client sends the challenge $chal = (c, k_1, k_2)$ to CS, where $1 \le c \le \hat{n}, k_1, k_2 \in \mathcal{Z}_q$.

$Prove(sk_s, pk_s, pk_c, \Sigma, chal)$: Suppose that $\hat{n}$ block-tag pairs are stored in CS. Upon receiving the challenge $chal = (c, k_1, k_2)$, CS computes: $v_i = \pi_{\hat{n}}(k_1, i), a_i = f(k_2, i)$, for $1 \le i \le c$; $T = \prod_{i=1}^{c} T_{v_i}^{a_i}$, $\hat{m} = \sum_{i=1}^{c} a_i m_{v_i}$. CS outputs $V = (\hat{m}, T)$ and sends V to the client.

$Verify(sk_c, pk_c, pk_s, M_e, chal, V)$: Upon receiving the response V from CS, based on the challenge $chal$ and the stored metadata, the client performs the procedures below:

1. For $1 \le i \le c$, the client computes: $v_i = \pi_{\hat{n}}(k_1, i), a_i = f(k_2, i)$;
2. From the left, the client searches for the v_i-th $(1 \le i \le c)$ leaf node from the stored dynamic binary tree. Then, the client gets the corresponding leaf node index l_{v_i} for all v_i $(1 \le i \le c)$;
3. For all v_i $(1 \le i \le c)$, the client computes $W_{v_i} = \Omega(pk_s^{sk_c}, l_{v_i})$ and checks

$$e(T, g) \stackrel{?}{=} e(\prod_{i=1}^{c} h(W_{v_i})^{a_i} u^{\hat{m}}, pk_c)$$

If it holds, the client outputs "accept"; otherwise the client outputs "reject".
4. When CS's response can not pass the client's verification, the client will perform the same challenge many times. If the responses still cannot pass the verification, the client will connect the CS provider to inform it this situation. CS provider will censor the client's stored data and retrieve the lost data from the offline backup. If CS provider fails, the client and the CS provider will evaluate the loss and discuss the reparation according to the loss severity.

Correctness: A dynamic PDP scheme must be workable and correct. That is, if the client and CS are honest and follow the specified procedures, the response V can pass the client's verification. The correctness is given below:

$$e(T, g) = e(\prod_{i=1}^{c} T_{v_i}^{a_i}, g) = e(\prod_{i=1}^{c} (h(W_{v_i}) u^{m_i})^{sk_c f(k_2, i)}, g)$$
$$= e((\prod_{i=1}^{c} h(W_{v_i})^{a_i}) u^{\hat{m}}, pk_c)$$

4.3   Performance Analysis

First, we analyze the performance of our proposed dynamic PDP scheme from the computation cost and communication cost. We compare our dynamic PDP scheme with the other up-to-date dynamic PDP schemes.

Table 1. Comparison of computation cost

Protocols	Wang [9]	Zhu [10]	Ours
TagGen	$\hat{n}(2C_{exp} + 1C_{mul})$	$(s + 2\hat{n})C_{exp} + \hat{n}C_{mul}$	$2\hat{n}C_{exp} + \hat{n}C_{mul}$
Prove	$cC_{exp} + (c-1)C_{mul}$	$cC_{exp} + (c-1)C_{mul}$	$cC_{exp} + (c-1)C_{mul}$
Verify	$4C_e + (c+1)C_{exp}$	$3C_e + (c+s)C_{exp}+$	$2C_e + (c+1)C_{exp}+$
	$+cC_{mul}$	$(c+s-2)C_{mul}$	cC_{mul}

Computation: Suppose there are $\hat{n}$ block-tag pairs will be stored in CS. The challenged block number is c. We will consider the computation overhead in the different phases. The multiplication, exponentiation and bilinear pairings contribute most computation cost on the group $\mathcal{G}_1$. Compared with them, the other operations are faster and computation cost is small, such as Hash function, permutation, *etc.* Thus, we only consider the multiplication, exponentiation and bilinear pairings on the group $\mathcal{G}_1$. In the phase *TagGen*, the client performs $2\hat{n}$ exponentiation ($pk_s^{sk_c}$ can be finished in the precomputation once for all) and $\hat{n}$ multiplication on $\mathcal{G}_1$. In the phase of *VryTag*, CS will perform 1 exponentiation, $\hat{n}$ multiplication and $2\hat{n}$ bilinear pairing on $\mathcal{G}_1$. In the phase *PreUpdate*, for one time, the average computation cost is $\frac{1}{4}(3+3) = 1.5$ exponentiation and $\frac{1}{4}(1+1) = 0.5$ multiplication. In the phase *PerUpdate*, for one time, CS performs 1 signature operation and a *VryTag* operation. In the phase *VryUpdate*, the client needs to verify a signature. In the phase of *Prove*, CS will perform c exponentiation on $\mathcal{G}_1$. In the phase of *Verify*, the client will perform c multiplication, $c+1$ exponentiation and 2 pairings ($pk_s^{sk_c}$ can be finished in the precomputation). On the other hand, in 2011, Wang et al. proposed the first dynamic remote data public auditability scheme in cloud computing [9]. In 2013, Zhu et al. proposed the dynamic audit services for outsourced storages in clouds [10]. The computation comparison can be summarized in Table 1. In Table 1, C_{mul} denotes the time cost of multiplication, C_{exp} denotes the time cost of exponentiation on the group $\mathcal{G}_1$, and C_e denotes the time cost of bilinear pairing. In the above comparison, we omit the computation cost in the phase *VryTag*. In order to guard against the dishonest clients to upload invalid block-tag pairs, CS verifies every block-tag pair. Our scheme has this property while Wang et al.'s scheme [9] and Zhu et al.'s scheme [10] have not this property. Thus, we omit *VryTag* in the above comparison. Our dynamic PDP scheme has lower computation cost.

Communication: In dynamic PDP scheme, the communication cost mainly comes from the block-tag uploading, remote data integrity query and response. We give our dynamic PDP scheme's communication overhead below. For $\hat{n}$ blocks, all the block-tag pairs length is $\hat{n}(|\mathcal{G}_1| + \log_2 q)$. In the phase Prove, the client sends the challenge $chal = (c, k_1, k_2)$ to CS, $i.e.$, the communication overhead is $\log_2 \hat{n} + 2\log_2 q$. In the response, CS responds 1 element in $\mathcal{G}_1$ and 1 element in $\mathcal{Z}_q^*$ to the client, $i.e.$, the communication overhead is $|\mathcal{G}_1| + \log_2 q$. On the other hand, Wang et al. [9] and Zhu et al. [10] proposed two different dynamic provable data possession scheme. Compared with these two schemes, our dynamic PDP scheme is more efficient in the communication cost. The communication comparison can be summarized in Table 2. In Table 2, $1|\mathcal{G}_1|$ denotes the bit length of one element in $\mathcal{G}_1$, $1|\mathcal{G}_2|$ denotes the bit length of one element in $\mathcal{G}_2$ and $1|\mathcal{Z}_q|$ denotes the bit length of one element in $\mathcal{Z}_q$. Our dynamic PDP scheme has lower communication cost.

Table 2. Comparison of communication cost (bits)

Protocols	Wang [9]	Zhu [10]	Ours
Tag	$(\hat{n} + 1)|\mathcal{G}_1|$	$(\hat{n} + 1)\log_2 \hat{n} + (s + \hat{n})|\mathcal{G}_1|$ $+\hat{n}(k + 1)$	$\hat{n}|\mathcal{G}_1|$
Chal	$c(\log_2 \hat{n} + \log_2 q$	$c(\log_2 \hat{n} + \log_2 q)$	$\log_2 \hat{n} + 2\log_2 q$
Response	$\log_2 \hat{n} + (c+2)|\mathcal{G}_1| + O(c)$	$2|\mathcal{G}_1| + 1|\mathcal{G}_2| + s\log_2 q$	$1|\mathcal{G}_1| + 1\mathcal{Z}_q$

Private PDP and Convertibility: From the phase *VryTag*, we know CS can identify the invalid block-tag pairs. On the other hand, in the phase *Verify*, the client's secret key sk_c is needed. Thus, only the client can perform his own data's PDP. Our proposed dynamic PDP scheme is private PDP scheme. In the verification, the crucial element is $pk_s^{sk_c}$ which can only be computed by the client and the cloud server. When the client makes the crucial element $pk_s^{sk_c}$ public, every entity can perform the process of verification. Thus, our scheme can be converted into public PDP scheme.

5   Security Analysis

Theorem 1. *The proposed dynamic PDP scheme is existentially unforgeable in the random oracle model if the CDH problem on $\mathcal{G}_1$ is hard.*

The detailed proof process is omitted due to the page limit.

Theorem 2. *Suppose that $\hat{n}$ block-tag pairs are stored, $\bar{d}$ block-tag pairs are modified or are not correctly updated, and c block-tag pairs are challenged. Then, our proposed dynamic PDP scheme is $(\frac{\bar{d}}{\hat{n}}, 1 - (\frac{\hat{n}-\bar{d}}{\hat{n}})^c)$-secure, i.e.,*

$$1 - (\frac{\hat{n} - \bar{d}}{\hat{n}})^c \le P_X \le 1 - (\frac{\hat{n} - c + 1 - \bar{d}}{\hat{n} - c + 1})^c$$

where P_X denotes the probability of detecting the dishonest CS.

The detailed proof process is omitted due to the page limit.

6   Conclusion

Based on the dynamic binary tree, this paper proposes a private dynamic PDP scheme. From the comparison of communication cost and computation cost, our proposed private dynamic PDP scheme is efficient.

References

1. Ateniese, G., Burns, R., Curtmola, R., Herring, J., Kissner, L., Peterson, Z., Song, D.: Provable data possession at untrusted stores. In: Capitani, D., di Vimercati, S., Syverson, P. (eds.) CCS 2007, pp. 598–609. ACM Press, New York (2007)
2. Shacham, H., Waters, B.: Compact proofs of retrievability. In: Pieprzyk, J. (ed.) ASIACRYPT 2008. LNCS, vol. 5350, pp. 90–107. Springer, Heidelberg (2008)
3. Zheng, Q., Xu, S.: Fair and dynamic proofs of retrievability. In: CODASPY 2011, pp. 237–248. ACM Press, New York (2011)
4. Ateniese, G., Di Pietro, R., Mancini, L.V., Tsudik, G.: Scalable and efficient provable data possession. In: Liu, P., Molva, R. (eds.) SecureComm 2008, pp. 9:1–9:10. ACM Press, New York (2008)
5. Erway, C.C., Küpçü, A., Papamanthou, C., Tamassia, R.: Dynamic provable data possession. ACM Trans. Inf. Syst. Secur. **17**(4), 15 (2015)
6. Etemad, M., Küpçü, A.: Transparent, distributed, and replicated dynamic provable data possession. In: Jacobson, M., Locasto, M., Mohassel, P., Safavi-Naini, R. (eds.) ACNS 2013. LNCS, vol. 7954, pp. 1–18. Springer, Heidelberg (2013)
7. Cash, D., Küpçü, A., Wichs, D.: Dynamic proofs of retrievability via oblivious RAM. In: Johansson, T., Nguyen, P.Q. (eds.) EUROCRYPT 2013. LNCS, vol. 7881, pp. 279–295. Springer, Heidelberg (2013)
8. Yang, K., Jia, X.: An efficient and secure dynamic auditing protocol for data storage in cloud computing. IEEE Trans. Parallel Distrib. Syst. **24**(9), 1717–1726 (2013)
9. Wang, Q., Wang, C., Li, J., Ren, K., Lou, W.: Enabling public verifiability and data dynamics for storage security in cloud computing. In: Backes, M., Ning, P. (eds.) ESORICS 2009. LNCS, vol. 5789, pp. 355–370. Springer, Heidelberg (2009)
10. Zhu, Y., Ahn, G., Hu, H., Yau, S., An, H., Chen, S.: Dynamic audit services for outsourced storages in clouds. IEEE Trans. Serv. Comput. **99**, 1 (2011)
11. Zhang, Y., Marina, B.: Efficient dynamic provable possession of remote data via balanced update trees. In: ASIA CCS 2013, pp. 183–194. ACM Press, New York (2013)
12. Wang, J., Liu, S.: Dynamic provable data possession with batch-update verifiability. In: ICADE 2012, pp. 108–113. IEEE Press, New Jersey (2012)
13. Shi, E., Stefanov, E., Papamanthou, C.: Practical dynamic proofs of retrievability. In: ACM CCS, pp. 325–336 (2013)
14. Tate, S.R., Vishwanathan, R., Everhart, L.: Multi-user dynamic proofs of data possession using trusted hardware. In: 3rd ACM CODASPY, pp. 353–364. ACM Press, San Antonio (2013)
15. Boneh, D., Lynn, B., Shacham, H.: Short signatures from the weil pairing. In: Boyd, C. (ed.) ASIACRYPT 2001. LNCS, vol. 2248, pp. 514–532. Springer, Heidelberg (2001)
16. Boneh, D., Franklin, M.: Identity-based encryption from the weil pairing. In: Kilian, J. (ed.) CRYPTO 2001. LNCS, vol. 2139, pp. 213–229. Springer, Heidelberg (2001)

Identity-Based Batch Provable Data Possession

Fucai Zhou[1]([✉]), Su Peng[2], Jian Xu[1], and Zifeng Xu[1]

[1] Software College, Northeastern University, Shenyang, China
{fczhou,xuj}@mail.neu.edu.cn, dk@tnimdk.com
[2] School of Computer Science and Engineering,
Northeastern University, Shenyang, China
supeng@stumail.neu.edu.cn

Abstract. Provable Data Possession (PDP) is a technique for checking whether data is correctly stored in remote servers without retrieving the entire data. For many previous PDP schemes, correctly choosing public key for clients relies on the security of Public Key Infrastructure (PKI), but PKI itself still faces many kinds of security vulnerabilities. In addition, the verification of certificates introduces heavy computation and communication cost. In this paper, we propose an Identity-Based Batch Provable Data Possession (ID-BPDP) scheme to eliminate the certificate management. Meanwhile, to the best of our knowledge, it is the first identity-based provable data possession scheme supporting batch verification for multiple owners and multiple clouds simultaneously to reduce computation cost greatly. Our scheme is provably correct and secure based on bilinear pairings and the hardness assumption of Computational Diffie-Hellman problem, and our analyses/simulations show that the scheme is able to verify the integrity of data efficiently.

Keywords: Provable data possession · Identity-Based cryptography · Batch proving · Bilinear pairings

1 Introduction

With the rapid development of cloud computing, for users possessing large amount of data, it is much cheaper to store the data in remote cloud storage servers than maintaining all the data locally. The outsourced data may not be accessed frequently, but may consist of important information such as scientific research data and archived files that have been collected for decades of years. However, users are not able to control outsourced data directly. Although storage service providers may apply general protections for data storage services, such as transporting data using secure protocols, encrypting data, setting firewalls and so on, the security of data is still doubtable because of system failures and other irresistible factors [1]. In addition, storage service providers are also assumed to be untrusted. Consider this scenario: a data owner uploaded a new version of data, but the server lost updated blocks. Later, when the owner wants to retrieve the data, the server cheats the owner by providing an outdated version.

© Springer International Publishing AG 2016
L. Chen and J. Han (Eds.): ProvSec 2016, LNCS 10005, pp. 112–129, 2016.
DOI: 10.1007/978-3-319-47422-9_7

1.1 Motivation and Related Work

To resolve the problems mentioned above, the most straightforward method is downloading entire data from the cloud storage server to check the integrity. However, in nowadays, this solution is completely infeasible due to extremely large size of data. Provable Data Possession (PDP) was first proposed by Ateniese *et al.* [2] to provide probabilistically accurate verification of data integrity with low computation and communication cost. Following Ateniese *et al.*'s pioneering work, many PDP schemes have been proposed [3–20,22]. Among these works, [3] by Curtmola *et al.* is a multiple replica provable data possession scheme. [5] by Ateniese *et al.* is a dynamic PDP scheme but does not support insert operation. In order to support the insert operation, Erway *et al.* proposed a full-dynamic PDP scheme [6]. [7,9,10,13] allow a data owner to delegate the remote integrity checking to a third party. [11] by Wang is a proxy PDP scheme in public clouds. [12] by Zhu *et al.* is a cooperative PDP scheme in multicloud storage. [15–17,19,20] make corrections to the security issues of some previously proposed PDP schemes. [18] by Wang *et al.* is a PDP scheme supporting efficient user revocation. However, in these schemes, to confirm if the data is uploaded by a certain user, the verifier needs to retrieve the correct public keys of users from Public Key Infrastructure (PKI). PKI ensures authenticity of public keys while introduces some other problems. On the one hand, every user needs to check its validity before using a public key. On the other hand, the managements of certificates, such as delivery, renewal and revocation, need large costs of computation and storage. To make it worse, PKI itself still faces many kinds of security vulnerabilities [21].

To eliminate the implementation of PKI, in 2015, Wang [22] proposed the first Identity-based Distributed Provable Data Possession (ID-DPDP) scheme. However, the scheme only supports verification for single owner and multiple clouds simultaneously. When the verifier checks the integrity of many owners' data, he must do the verification for many times which invokes expensive computation cost.

1.2 Contributions

We proposed a novel Identity-Based Batch Provable Data Possession (ID-BPDP) scheme. Without the implementation of PKI, ID-BPDP eliminates the resource-consuming certificate management. Meanwhile, ID-BPDP supports batch verification for multiple owners and multiple clouds simultaneously to reduce the computation cost greatly, especially in large-scale cloud storage systems. ID-BPDP also reduces computation cost for data owners while generating tags of data blocks and therefore it is especially suitable for data owners with limited computation power.

1.3 Paper Organization

The rest of this paper is organized as follows. Section 2 reviews some preliminaries of this paper. Section 3 presents the definitions of system model and security model of our scheme. Section 4 proposes the detailed construction of our scheme. Section 5 gives the analyses of our scheme in terms of computation and communication costs. Section 6 proves the security of our scheme. Finally, Sect. 7 concludes this paper.

2 Preliminaries

In this section, we review bilinear pairings and CDH problem.

2.1 Bilinear Pairings

Let $\mathcal{G}_1$ and $\mathcal{G}_2$ be two cyclic multiplicative groups with a same prime order q and let g be a generator of $\mathcal{G}_1$. Let $e : \mathcal{G}_1 \times \mathcal{G}_1 \to \mathcal{G}_2$ be a bilinear map [23] which satisfies the following properties:

1. Bilinearity. $\forall u, v \in \mathcal{G}_1$ and $a, b \in \mathcal{Z}_q$, $e(u^a, v^b) = e(u, v)^{ab}$.
2. Non-degeneracy. $e(g, g) \neq 1_{\mathcal{G}_2}$.
3. Computability. $\forall u, v \in \mathcal{G}_1$, There exists an efficient algorithm to compute $e(u, v)$.

2.2 CDH Problem on $\mathcal{G}_1$

Let $\mathcal{G}_1$ be a cyclic multiplicative group with a prime order q and let g be a generator of $\mathcal{G}_1$. Given g, g^a, $g^b \in \mathcal{G}_1$ for randomly chosen $a, b \in \mathcal{Z}_q$, compute $g^{ab} \in \mathcal{G}_1$.

3 Definitions

In this section, we present the system model and security model of our scheme.

3.1 System Model

Our scheme involves four entities: The private key generator (PKG), the data owners (owners), the batch verifier (verifier) and the cloud servers (clouds). The PKG outputs the corresponding private keys when received the identities of the owners. The owners create the data and store their data in the clouds. The batch verifier is a trusted third party to provide batch verification service for the owners. The clouds store the owners' data and provide data access to the owners and, maybe, the other data users.

Furthermore, we assume that every owner possesses a large amount of data comprised of file blocks and stores the blocks in several clouds. The clouds split each block into smaller sectors with a same number and a same size.

Before presenting the definition of our scheme, we first define some notations as listed in Table 1.

Table 1. Notations

Notations	Descriptions
mpk	Master public key
msk	Master private key
DO_i	The i-th owner
CS_j	The j-th cloud
ID_i	DO_i's ID
sk_i	DO_i's private key
M_{ijk}	The k-th block of DO_i stores in CS_j
s	The sector number
F_{ijkl}	The l-th sector of the k-th block of DO_i stores in CS_j
m_{ijk}	Linear combination of $\{F_{ijkl}\}$
σ_{ijk}	M_{ijk}'s tag
c_i	Number of challenged blocks of DO_i
O	Set of indexes of owners selected by verifier
C	Set of indexes of challenged clouds
$chal$	Challenge token of all owners
$chal_j$	Challenge token forwarded to CS_j
P_j	Proof of CS_j

Definition 1 (Identity-Based Batch Provable Data Possession). *The ID-BPDP scheme is comprised of six procedures:*

1. $\mathsf{Setup}(1^k) \to (params, mpk, msk)$. *The procedure is run by the PKG. It takes as input the security parameter k and outputs the public parameters, the master public key mpk and the master private key msk.*
2. $\mathsf{Extract}(params, msk, ID_i) \to sk_i$. *The procedure is run by the PKG. It takes as input the public parameters and the i-th owner DO_i's identity ID_i and outputs the corresponding private key sk_i.*
3. $\mathsf{TagGen}(params, ID_i, sk_i, mpk, \{M_{ijk}\}) \to \{\sigma_{ijk}\}$. *The procedure is run by each owner. M_{ijk} denotes the k's block of DO_i stores in the j-th cloud CS_j and $\{M_{ijk}\}$ denotes all the blocks of DO_i. Each M_{ijk} is comprised of s sectors, i.e., $M_{ijk} = \{F_{ijkl} \mid l = 1, \ldots, s\}$. It takes as input the public parameters, DO_i's identity ID_i, DO_i's private key sk_i, the master public key mpk and $\{M_{ijk}\}$ defined above and outputs the corresponding set of tags $\{\sigma_{ijk}\}$.*
4. $\mathsf{Challenge}(\{(i, j, k)\}) \to (chal, \{chal_j\})$. *The procedure is run by the verifier. It takes as input the set of indexes $\{(i, j, k)\}$ of $\{M_{ijk}\}$ and outputs the challenge token $chal$ by selecting some blocks. Then the verifier splits $chal$ to a set of challenge tokens $\{chal_j\}$ and forwards each $chal_j$ to the corresponding j-th cloud. (Note: Some clouds may not be challenged).*
5. $\mathsf{Prove}(params, chal_j, \{ID_i\}, \{\sigma_{ijk}\}, \{M_{ijk}\}) \to P_j$. *The procedure is run by each cloud who receives challenge token. It takes as input the public*

parameters, the challenge token $chal_j$, the set of the owners' IDs $\{ID_i\}$, the tags $\{\sigma_{ijk}\}$ and the blocks $\{M_{ijk}\}$ and outputs the proof P_j for $chal_j$. Then the cloud forwards P_j to the verifier.

6. Verify($params, chal, \{ID_i\}, \{P_j\}, mpk$) $\rightarrow$ $\{0,1\}$. The procedure is run by the verifier. It takes as input the public parameters, the challenge token $chal$, the set of the owners' IDs $\{ID_i\}$, the set of the clouds' proofs $\{P_j\}$ and the master public key mpk and outputs 1 (valid) or 0 (invalid).

3.2   Security Model

We assume the verifier always performs honestly during the verification procedure, but the clouds could be dishonest and may forge tags or proofs to cheat the verifier and the owners.

Definition 2 (Unforgeability of Tags). *A tag is unforgeable if for any probabilistic polynomial adversary $\mathcal{A}$ (malicious clouds), the probability that $\mathcal{A}$ wins the Tag-Forge game on a set of blocks is negligible. The game between the adversary $\mathcal{A}$ and the challenger $\mathcal{C}$ is described as follows:*

1. *Setup. $\mathcal{C}$ runs Setup(1^k) and gets ($params, mpk, msk$). It forwards the public parameters and the master public key ($param, mpk$) to $\mathcal{A}$ but keeps the master private key msk secret.*
2. *Queries. $\mathcal{A}$ adaptively makes Extract and TagGen queries adaptively to $\mathcal{C}$ as follows:*
   (a) *Extract Queries. $\mathcal{A}$ queries the private key of ID_i. By running Extract($params, msk, ID_i$), $\mathcal{C}$ gets the private key sk_i and forwards it to $\mathcal{A}$. Let S_1 denote the set of extracted identities $\{ID_i\}$.*
   (b) *TagGen Queries. $\mathcal{A}$ queries the tags of blocks $\{M_{ijk}\}$. By running TagGen($params, ID_i, sk_i, mpk, \{M_{ijk}\}$), $\mathcal{C}$ gets the tag σ_{ijk} and forwards it to $\mathcal{A}$. Let I_1 denote the set of the TagGen-queried tuples $\{(i,j,k,M_{ijk})\}$.*
3. *Forge. Eventually, $\mathcal{A}$ responds a valid tag $\sigma_{i^*j^*k^*}$ of ID_{i^*} and $(i^*, j^*, k^*, M_{i^*j^*k^*})$ where $ID_{i^*} \notin S_1$ and $(i^*, j^*, k^*, M_{i^*j^*k^*}) \notin I_1$.*

Definition 3 (Unforgeability of Proofs). *A proof is unforgeable if for any probabilistic polynomial adversary $\mathcal{A}$ (malicious clouds), the probability that $\mathcal{A}$ wins the Proof-Forge game on a set of blocks is negligible. The game between the adversary $\mathcal{A}$ and the challenger $\mathcal{C}$ is described as follows:*

1. *Setup. Same as the Tag-Forge game's Setup phase described above.*
2. *First-Phase Queries. Same as the Tag-Forge game's Queries phase described above.*
3. *Challenge. Let S_1 denote the set of the extracted identities $\{ID_i\}$ and let I_1 denote the set of the TagGen-queried tuples $\{(i,j,k,M_{ijk})\}$. $\mathcal{C}$ generates a challenge token $chal^*$ for a set of c^* tuples $\{(i_n^*, j_n^*, k_n^*, M_{i_n^*,j_n^*,k_n^*}) \mid n = 1, \ldots, c^*\}$ where at least one $ID_{i_n^*} \notin S_1$ and for the same i_n^*, $\{(i_n^*, j_n^*, k_n^*, M_{i_n^*,j_n^*,k_n^*})\} \notin I_1$. Then $\mathcal{C}$ forwards $chal^*$ to $\mathcal{A}$.*

4. *Second-Phase Queries. Similar as the First-Phase Queries. Let S_2 denote the set of the extracted identities $\{ID_i\}$ and let I_2 denote the set of the TagGen-queried tuples $\{(i,j,k,M_{ijk})\}$. The restriction is that at least one $ID_{i_n^*} \notin (S_1 \cup S_2)$ and for the same i_n^*, $(i_n^*, j_n^*, k_n^*, M_{i_n^* j_n^* k_n^*}) \notin (I_1 \cup I_2)$.*

5 *Eventually, $\mathcal{A}$ responds a valid proof $P^* = \{P_{j^*}\}$ of $chal^*$.*

Definition 4 (Detection Probability). *Suppose that n block-tag pairs are stored, t block-tag pairs are modified and c block-tag pairs are challenged, the probability of detecting the modification is P_X.*

4 Construction

The architecture of the proposed ID-BPDP scheme is described in Fig. 1 and the construction is detailed as follows:

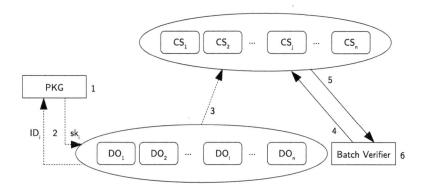

Fig. 1. Architecture of ID-BPDP.

1. Setup$(1^k) \to (params, mpk, msk)$. Given a security parameter k, The PKG chooses two groups $\mathcal{G}_1$ and $\mathcal{G}_2$ with the same order $q > 2^k$ along with a bilinear map $e : \mathcal{G}_1 \times \mathcal{G}_1 \to \mathcal{G}_2$. Let g be a generator of $\mathcal{G}_1$. The PKG also chooses three cryptographic hash functions $H_1 : \{0,1\}^* \to \mathcal{G}_1$, $H_2 : \{0,1\}^* \to \mathcal{Z}_q$, $H_3 : \{0,1\}^* \to \mathcal{G}_1$ and a pseudo-random function $f : \mathcal{Z}_q \times \{1,\ldots,n\} \to \mathcal{Z}_q$. Then the PKG chooses a random number $x \in \mathcal{Z}_q$ as the master private key msk and set g^x as the master public key mpk. The PKG also chooses s random numbers $\{v_l \in \mathcal{Z}_q \mid l = 1,\ldots,s\}$.
2. Extract$(params, msk, ID_i) \to sk_i$. DO_i sets $pk_i = H_1(ID_i)$ as the public key and forwards ID_i to the PKG. The PKG sets $sk_i = pk_i^x$ as DO_i's private key and forwards sk_i to the corresponding owner via a secure channel.
3. TagGen$(params, ID_i, sk_i, mpk, \{M_{ijk}\}) \to \{\sigma_{ijk}\}$. The set $\{M_{ijk}\}$ denotes the k-th block of DO_i will store in CS_j. For each M_{ijk}, the owner sets:

$$m_{ijk} = \sum_{l=1}^{s} v_l F_{ijkl}, \quad h_i = H_2(ID_i), \quad hpk = H_3(mpk).$$

(Note: H_1 and H_2 are different hash functions). DO_i also randomly chooses $u_i \in \mathcal{Z}_q$ and sets the tag $\sigma_{ijk} = (S_{ijk}, T_{ijk})$ of M_{ijk} below:

$$S_{ijk} = g^{u_i}, \ T_{ijk} = sk_i^{m_{ijk}+h_i} \cdot hpk^{u_i}.$$

Then DO_i forwards each M_{ijk} and σ_{ijk} to the corresponding j-th cloud. The tag $\sigma_{ijk} = (S_{ijk}, T_{ijk})$ can be verified by checking whether the following equation holds:

$$e\left(T_{ijk}, g\right) = e(H_1(ID_i)^{\sum_{l=1}^{s} v_l F_{ijkl}+H_2(ID_i)}, mpk)e\left(H_3(mpk), S_{ijk}\right). \quad (1)$$

4. Challenge($\{(i,j,k)\}$) → $(chal, \{chal_j\})$. Suppose that the verifier wants to verify c different blocks. Let $M_{i_n j_n k_n}(1 \le n \le c, (i_n, j_n, k_n) \in \{(i,j,k)\})$ denote the k_n-th blocks of the i_n-th owner stores in the j_n-th cloud to be verified, the verifier forms a challenge token $chal = (I, K)$ with $I = \{(i_n, j_n, k_n) \mid n = 1, \ldots, c\}$ and $K = \{\kappa_{i_n} \mid n = 1, \ldots, c\}$ with each random temporary key $\kappa_{i_n} \in \mathcal{Z}_q$. Then the verifier splits $chal$ to a set of challenge tokens $\{chal_j\}$ and each $chal_j = (I_j, K_j)$ with $I_j = \{(i_n, j, k_n)\} \subseteq I$ and $K_j = \{\kappa_{i_n} \mid (i_n, j_n, k_n) \in I_j$ and for $\forall n_1, n_2$ with $n_1 \neq n_2, i_{n_1} \neq i_{n_2}\} \subseteq K$ (avoid sending duplicated or unneeded keys to reduce communication cost) for each challenged cloud j. (Note: Some clouds may not be challenged). The verifier forwards each $chal_j$ to the corresponding j-th cloud. Let C denote the set of indexes $\{j\}$ of the challenged clouds, we have $\cup_{j \in C} I_j = I$ and for $\forall j_1, j_2 \in C$ and $j_1 \neq j_2, I_{j_1} \cap I_{j_2} = \emptyset$.

5. Prove($params, chal_j, \{ID_i\}, \{\sigma_{ijk}\}, \{M_{ijk}\}$) → P_j. Each cloud who receives the challenge token $chal_j = (I_j, K_j)$ with $I_j = \{(i_n, j, k_n)\} \subseteq I$ and $K_j = \{\kappa_{i_n} \mid (i_n, j_n, k_n) \in I_j$ and for $\forall n_1, n_2$ with $n_1 \neq n_2, i_{n_1} \neq i_{n_2}\} \subseteq K$ computes $\{r_n\} = \{f_{\kappa_{i_n}}(i_n, j, k_n)\}$ and generates the proof $P_j = (S_j', T_j', \{F_{ijl}' \mid (i,j,k) \in I_j\})$ of the challenged blocks $\{M_{i_n j k_n}\}$ with tags $\{\sigma_{i_n j k_n} = (S_{i_n j k_n}, T_{i_n j k_n})\}$ by setting:

$$S_j' = \prod_{chal_j} S_{i_n j k_n}^{r_n}, \ T_j' = \prod_{chal_j} T_{i_n j k_n}^{r_n}, \ F_{ijl}' = \sum_{chal_j, i_n = i} F_{i_n j k_n l} \cdot r_n.$$

Then the cloud forwards P_j to the verifier.

6. Verify($params, chal, \{ID_i\}, \{P_j\}, mpk$) → $\{0, 1\}$. Let O denote the set of indexes $\{i\}$ of the owners selected by the verifier. After received all the proofs of the challenged clouds, with the challenge token $chal = (I, K)$ with $I = \{(i_n, j_n, k_n) \mid n = 1, \ldots, c\}$ and $K = \{\kappa_{i_n} \mid n = 1, \ldots, c\}$, the verifier computes $\{r_n\} = \{f_{\kappa_{i_n}}(i_n, j_n, k_n) \mid n = 1, \ldots, c\}$ and outputs 1 (valid) or 0 (invalid) by checking whether the following equation holds:

$$e\left(\prod_{j \in C} T_j', g\right) = e\left(\prod_{i \in O} H_1(ID_i)^{\sum_{j \in C} \sum_{l=1}^{s} v_l F_{ijl}' + H_2(ID_i) \sum_{i_n = i} r_n}, mpk\right)$$

$$\cdot e\left(H_3(mpk), \prod_{j \in C} S_j'\right). \quad (2)$$

4.1   Correctness

Now we show the correctness of our scheme. If the PKG, the owners, the verifier and the clouds run all the procedures described above correctly, according to formula (2), we have:

$$e\left(\prod_{i\in O} H_1(ID_i)^{\sum_{j\in C}\sum_{l=1}^{s} v_l F'_{ijl}}, mpk\right) = e\left(\prod_{j\in C}\prod_{chal_j} H_1(ID_{i_n})^{m_{i_njk_n}\cdot r_n}, mpk\right)$$

$$= e\left(\prod_{j\in C}\prod_{chal_j} sk_{i_n}^{m_{i_njk_n}\cdot r_n}, g\right),$$

$$e\left(\prod_{i\in O} H_1(ID_i)^{H_2(ID_i)\sum_{i_n=i} r_n}, mpk\right) = e\left(\prod_{j\in C}\prod_{chal_j} H_1(ID_{i_n})^{H_2(ID_{i_n})\cdot r_n}, mpk\right)$$

$$= e\left(\prod_{j\in C}\prod_{chal_j} sk_{i_n}^{h_{i_n}\cdot r_n}, g\right),$$

and:

$$e\left(H_3(mpk), \prod_{j\in C} S'_j\right) = e\left(hpk, \prod_{j\in C}\prod_{chal_j} S_{i_njk_n}^{r_n}\right)$$

$$= e\left(\prod_{j\in C}\prod_{chal_j} hpk^{u_{i_n}\cdot r_n}, g\right).$$

Then the right hand side (RHS) of formula (2) can be expressed as:

$$RHS = e\left(\prod_{j\in C}\prod_{chal_j} sk_{i_n}^{m_{i_njk_n}\cdot r_n}, g\right) e\left(\prod_{j\in C}\prod_{chal_j} sk_{i_n}^{h_{i_n}\cdot r_n}, g\right)$$

$$= e\left(\prod_{j\in C}\prod_{chal_j} T_{i_njk_n}^{r_n}, g\right)$$

$$= e\left(\prod_{j\in C} T'_j, g\right).$$

5   Performance Analysis

In this section, we analyze the performance of our proposed ID-BPDP scheme from the computation and the communication costs and compare them with other up-to-date PDP protocols.

5.1   Computation

We compare the computation cost between our scheme and Yang [14], Wang's Panda [18] and Wang's ID-DPDP [22]. Yang [14] and Wang's Panda [18] support multi-owner-and-multi-cloud verification, while Wang's ID-DPDP [22] is the first ID-based PDP scheme. We summarize the result in Table 2.

Table 2. Comparison of Computation Cost - Multiple Owners ($n_1, n_2 > 1$)

Schemes	TagGen	Prove	Verify	ID-Based
Yang [14]	$n(s+1)C_{exp}$	$n_1 s C_e + (c + n_1 s)C_{exp}$	$(n_1+1)C_e + cC_{exp}$	No
Wang's Panda [18]	$2nC_{exp}$	cC_{exp}	$(n_1+1)C_e + (n_1 + c)C_{exp}$	No
Wang's ID-DPDP [22]	$n(s+1)C_{exp} + nsC_h$	$cC_{exp} + csC_h$	$2n_1 C_e + (c + n_1 s)C_{exp}$	**Yes**
Our ID-BPDP	nC_{exp}	$(c+2n_1 n_2)C_{exp}$	$3C_e + n_1 C_{exp}$	Yes

Notes:

1. C_{exp} denotes the time cost of single exponentiation on the group $\mathcal{G}_1$, C_{mul} denotes the time cost of single multiplication on the group $\mathcal{G}_1$, C_e denotes the time cost of single bilinear pairing; C_h denotes the time cost of single hash operation on the blocks, n denotes the total number of blocks, s denotes the sector number, c denotes the total number of challenged blocks, n_1 denotes the number of owners selected by the verifier, n_2 denotes the number of challenged clouds.
2. Bilinear pairings and exponentiations on $\mathcal{G}_1$ and hash operations on blocks contribute most computation cost. Compared with them, computation cost of multiplications on $\mathcal{G}_1$, multiplications and additions on $\mathcal{Z}_q$, multiplications on $\mathcal{G}_2$ and other hash operations is negligible. Meanwhile, other hash operations can be done once for all. Therefore, we do not consider them in the computation analysis. For the same reason, we do not consider the computation cost of Challenge operation.
3. Because Wang's ID-DPDP [22] does not support multi-owner-and-multi-cloud verification, we assume that the computation repeats for several times that is equal to n_1, but for each loop, the blocks number is n/n_1 and the challenged blocks number is c/n_1.
4. In the Prove operation of our scheme, notice that:

$$S'_j = \prod_{chal_j} S^{r_n}_{i_n j k_n} = \prod_{i \in O} (g^{u_i})^{\sum_{i_n=i}^{} r_n},$$

with this, we can avoid some exponentiations.

Analysis:
In the comparison of computation cost with multiple owners, our scheme has the fastest TagGen and Verify operations than those of the other schemes when more than one owners selected by the verifier, even we set $s = 1$. Independent to the increasing number of the owners selected by the verifier, our scheme needs only three pairing operations to verify all the proofs.

Our Prove operation is slightly slower than that of Wang's ID-DPDP [22], but considering the strong computation power of cloud servers, it is still acceptable.

Meanwhile, our scheme does not suffer from resource-consuming certificate management.

5.2   Communication

We compare the communication cost between our scheme and Yang [14], Wang's Panda [18] and Wang's ID-DPDP [22]. We summarize the result in Table 3.

Table 3. Comparison of Communication Cost - Multiple Owners $(n_1, n_2 > 1)$

Schemes	Challenge	Prove	ID-Based
Yang [14]	$c(\log_2 n + \log_2 q)$	$n_2(2\mathcal{G}_1)$	No
Wang's Panda [18]	$c(\log_2 n + \log_2 q)$	$n_1 n_2(2\mathcal{G}_1) + 2c\log_2 n$	No
Wang's ID-DPDP [22]	$(n_1 + c)\log_2 n$ $+(2n_1 + n_1 n_2)\log_2 q$	$n_1(n_2+1)(1\mathcal{G}_1+s\log_2 q)$	**Yes**
Our ID-BPDP	$\mathbf{c\log_2 n + d\log_2 q}$	$n_2(2\mathcal{G}_1) + n_1 n_2 s \log_2 q$	**Yes**

Notes:

1. d satisfies $\max(n_1, n_2) \le d \le \min(n_1 n_2, c)$, $1\mathcal{G}_1$ denotes the size of one element of $\mathcal{G}_1$ in bits, n denotes the total number of blocks, s denotes the sector number, c denotes the total number of challenged blocks, n_1 denotes the number of owners selected by the verifier, n_2 denotes the number of challenged clouds.
2. Because Wang's ID-DPDP [22] does not support multi-owner-and-multi-cloud verification, we assume that the computation repeats for several times that is equal to n_1, but for each loop, the blocks number is n/n_1 and the challenged blocks number is c/n_1.
3. In Wang's ID-DPDP [22], the communication cost includes four parts: Challenge1, Challenge2, Response1 and Response2. We sum Challenge1 and Challenge2 to Challenge, sum Response1 and Response2 to Prove in Table 3.

Analysis:
In the comparison of communication cost with multiple owners, it is obvious that our Challengeoperation has the smallest communication cost in the compared schemes. Although Wang's ID-DPDP [22] applies pseudo-random permutation

to reduce the communication cost between the verifier and the combiner, but if we take the communication cost between the combiner and the clouds into consideration, the total cost is still larger than that of our scheme. Furthermore, it is difficult to implement a trusted combiner in practice.

The communication cost of our Prove operation is slightly smaller than that of Wang's ID-DPDP [22].

Meanwhile, our scheme does not suffer from resource-consuming certificate management.

5.3   Simulation

We simulate our scheme and Wang's ID-DPDP [22] and compare the computation and communication cost between them under the same environment described as follows:

1. A desktop PC with the following hardware and software settings:
   (a) CPU: Intel Pentium G2030 @ 3.00 GHz;
   (b) Physical Memory: 8 GB DDR3 @ 1333 MHz;
   (c) OS: Linux with kernel 3.16.0-4-amd64;
   (d) Development Environment: GCC v4.9.2 with GMP Library v6.0.0 [24], PBC Library v0.5.14 [25] and OpenSSL 1.0.1k [26].
2. Security parameters: type A curve [25] with 1024-bit group order; Hash functions implemented in PBC Library [25] and pseudo-random functions (permutations) implemented with SHA-256 and AES-256 in OpenSSL [26].

The simulation demonstrated that our schemes reduces computation cost for TagGen and Verify greatly. Our scheme is slightly slower than Wang's ID-DPDP [22] in Prove, but the difference is constant along with the increases of the challenged blocks. The communication cost of our scheme is slightly smaller than that of Wang's ID-DPDP [22].

The detail of our simulation will be given in the extended version.

6   Security Analysis

We first prove the universal unforgeability of our scheme in this section. The proof comprises two parts: single tag is universally unforgeable (Definition 2); proof for blocks is universally unforgeable (Definition 3). Then we estimate the probability of detecting the modification (Definition 4).

Theorem 1. *If a probabilistic polynomial adversary $\mathcal{A}$ wins the Tag-Forge game in Definition 2 with an unnegligible probability ϵ, then there exists a polynomial adversary $\mathcal{B}$ solves the CDH problem on $\mathcal{G}_1$ with an unnegligible probability $\frac{(q_E+q_T)^{(q_E+q_T)}}{(q_E+q_T+1)^{(q_E+q_T+1)}}\epsilon$ after $\mathcal{A}$ makes q_E Extract queries and q_T TagGen queries.*

Proof. We define the interactions between $\mathcal{A}$ and $\mathcal{B}$ in the random oracle model by utilizing the technique proposed by Coron [27]. Adversary $\mathcal{A}$ is given $(g, g^a, g^b) \in \mathcal{G}_1^3$. Its goal is to output $g^{ab} \in \mathcal{G}_1$. $\mathcal{B}$ simulates the challenger and interacts with $\mathcal{A}$ as follows:

1. Setup. $\mathcal{B}$ sets $mpk = g^a$ while a keeps secret. It forwards mpk to $\mathcal{A}$.
2. H_1-Oracle. At any time, $\mathcal{A}$ can query the random oracle H_1. To respond to these queries, $\mathcal{B}$ maintains a list of tuples H_1-list $= \{(ID_I, d_I, y_I, H_{1,I})\}$ as explained below. When $\mathcal{A}$ queries the oracle H_1 at ID_I, $\mathcal{B}$ responds as follows:
   (a) If $(ID_I, *, *, *) \in H_1$-list, $\mathcal{B}$ retrieves the tuple $(ID_I, d_I, y_I, H_{1,I})$ and responds with $H_{1,I}$, i.e., $H_1(ID_I) = H_{1,I}$.
   (b) Otherwise, $\mathcal{B}$ picks a bit $d_I \in \{0, 1\}$ according to a bivariate distribution function: $\Pr[d_I = 0] = \delta, \Pr[d_I = 1] = 1 - \delta$. Here δ is a fixed probability which will be determined later. Based on d_I, $\mathcal{B}$ responds as follows:
      i. If $d_I = 0$, $\mathcal{B}$ independently picks a random y_I, computes $H_{1,I} = g^{y_I}$ and responds with $H_{1,I}$, i.e., $H_1(ID_I) = g^{y_I}$. Then $\mathcal{B}$ adds the tuple $(ID_I, d_I, y_I, H_{1,I})$ to H_1-list.
      ii. If $d_I = 1$, $\mathcal{B}$ independently picks a random y_I, computes $H_{1,I} = g^{by_I}$ and responds with $H_{1,I}$, i.e., $H_1(ID_I) = g^{by_I}$. Then $\mathcal{B}$ adds the tuple $(ID_I, d_I, y_I, H_{1,I})$ to H_1-list.
3. H_2-Oracle. At any time, $\mathcal{A}$ can query the random oracle H_2. To respond to these queries, $\mathcal{B}$ maintains a list of tuples H_2-list $= \{(ID_I, H_{2,I})\}$ as explained below. When $\mathcal{A}$ queries the oracle H_2 at ID_I, $\mathcal{B}$ responds as follows:
   (a) If $(ID_I, *) \in H_2$-list, $\mathcal{B}$ retrieves the tuple $(ID_I, H_{2,I})$ and responds with $H_{2,I}$, i.e., $H_2(ID_I) = H_{2,I}$.
   (b) Otherwise, $\mathcal{B}$ independently picks a random $H_{2,I}$ and responds with $H_{2,I}$, i.e., $H_2(ID_I) = H_{2,I}$. Then $\mathcal{B}$ adds the tuple $(ID_I, H_{2,I})$ to H_2-list.
4. H_3-Oracle. At any time, $\mathcal{A}$ can query the random oracle H_3. To respond to these queries, $\mathcal{B}$ maintains a list of tuples H_3-list $= \{(mpk_I, z_I, H_{3,I})\}$ as explained below. When $\mathcal{A}$ queries the oracle H_3 at mpk_I, $\mathcal{B}$ responds as follows:
   (a) If $(mpk_I, *, *) \in H_3$-list, $\mathcal{B}$ retrieves the tuple $(mpk_I, z_I, H_{3,I})$ and responds with $H_{3,I}$, i.e., $H_3(mpk_I) = H_{3,I}$.
   (b) Otherwise, $\mathcal{B}$ independently picks a random z_I, computes $H_{3,I} = g^{z_I}$ and responds with $H_{3,I}$, i.e., $H_3(mpk_I) = g^{z_I}$. Then $\mathcal{B}$ adds the tuple $(mpk_I, z_I, H_{3,I})$ to H_3-list. Especially, if $mpk_I = mpk$, $\mathcal{B}$ denote the corresponding z_I as z, i.e., $H_3(mpk) = g^z$ and the tuple is (mpk, z, g^z).
5. Extract-Oracle. At any time, $\mathcal{A}$ can query the oracle Extract. To respond to these queries, $\mathcal{B}$ maintains a list of tuples Extract-list $= \{(ID_I, sk_I)\}$ as explained below. When $\mathcal{A}$ queries the oracle Extract at ID_I, $\mathcal{B}$ responds as follows:
   (a) If $(ID_I, *) \in$ Extract-list, $\mathcal{B}$ retrieves the tuple (ID_I, sk_I) and responds with sk_I.
   (b) Otherwise, $\mathcal{B}$ look up H_1-list for the tuple $(ID_I, d_I, y_I, H_{1,I})$. If the tuple does not exist, $\mathcal{B}$ issues a query itself for $H_1(ID_I)$ to ensure that such a tuple exists. Based on d_I, $\mathcal{B}$ responds as follows:
      i. If $d_I = 0$, $\mathcal{B}$ computes $sk_I = (g^a)^{y_I}$ and responds with sk_I. Then $\mathcal{B}$ adds the tuple (ID_I, sk_I) to Extract-list.
      ii. If $d_I = 1$, $\mathcal{B}$ reports failure and the simulation terminates.

6. TagGen-Oracle. At any time, $\mathcal{A}$ can query the oracle TagGen. To respond to these queries, $\mathcal{B}$ maintains a list of tuples TagGen-list$=$ $\{(I, J, K, M_{IJK}, \sigma_{IJK})\}$ as explained below. When $\mathcal{A}$ queries the oracle TagGen at (I, J, K, M_{IJK}), $\mathcal{B}$ responds as follows:

   (a) If $(I, J, K, M_{IJK}, *) \in$ TagGen-list, $\mathcal{B}$ retrieves the tuple $(I, J, K, M_{IJK}, \sigma_{IJK})$ and responds with σ_{IJK}.

   (b) Otherwise, $\mathcal{B}$ looks up H_1-list for the tuple $(ID_I, d_I, y_I, H_{1,I})$. If the tuple does not exist, $\mathcal{B}$ issues a query itself for $H_1(ID_I)$ to ensure that such a tuple exists. Then $\mathcal{B}$ looks up H_2-list for the tuple $(ID_I, H_{2,I})$. If the tuple does not exist, $\mathcal{B}$ issues a query itself for $H_2(ID_I)$ to ensure that such a tuple exists. Then $\mathcal{B}$ looks up H_3-list for the tuple (mpk, z, g^z). If the tuple does not exist, $\mathcal{B}$ issues a query itself for $H_3(mpk)$ to ensure that such a tuple exists. Based on d_I, $\mathcal{B}$ responds as follows:

   i. If $d_I = 0$, $\mathcal{B}$ independently picks a random S_{IJK}, computes

   $$\sigma_{IJK} = (S_{IJK}, (g^a)^{y_I \left(\sum_{l=1}^{s} v_l F_{IJKl} + H_{2,I} \right)} S_{IJK}^z)$$

   and responds with σ_{IJK}. Observe that $(I, J, K, M_{IJK}, \sigma_{IJK})$ satisfies formula (1) and therefore σ_{IJK} is a valid tag on (I, J, K, M_{IJK}). Then $\mathcal{B}$ adds the tuple $(I, J, K, M_{IJK}, \sigma_{IJK})$ to TagGen-list.

   ii. If $d_I = 1$, $\mathcal{B}$ reports failure and the simulation terminates.

7. Forge. Eventually, $\mathcal{A}$ produces a tag $\sigma_{i^*j^*k^*} = (S_{i^*j^*k^*}, T_{i^*j^*k^*})$ on $(i^*, j^*, k^*, M_{i^*j^*k^*})$ such that no Extract query was issued for ID_{i^*} and no TagGen query was issued for $(i^*, j^*, k^*, M_{i^*j^*k^*})$. $\mathcal{B}$ looks up H_1-list for the tuple $(ID_{i^*}, d_{i^*}, y_{i^*}, H_{1,i^*})$. If the tuple does not exist, $\mathcal{B}$ issues a query itself for $H_1(ID_{i^*})$ to ensure that such a tuple exists. Then $\mathcal{B}$ looks up H_2-list for the tuple (ID_{i^*}, H_{2,i^*}). If the tuple does not exist, $\mathcal{B}$ issues a query itself for $H_2(ID_{i^*})$ to ensure that such a tuple exists. Then $\mathcal{B}$ looks up H_3-list for the tuple (mpk, z, g^z). If the tuple does not exist, $\mathcal{B}$ issues a query itself for $H_3(mpk)$ to ensure that such a tuple exists. Based on d_{i^*}, $\mathcal{B}$ responds as follows:

   (a) If $d_{i^*} = 1$, $\mathcal{B}$ reports failure and the simulation terminates.

   (b) If $d_{i^*} = 0$, $(i^*, j^*, k^*, M_{i^*j^*k^*})$ satisfies formula (1), i.e.:

   $$e\left(T_{i^*j^*k^*}, g\right) = e(H_1(ID_{i^*})^{\sum_{l=1}^{s} v_l F_{i^*j^*k^*l} + H_2(ID_{i^*})}, mpk)$$
   $$\cdot e\left(H_3(mpk), S_{i^*j^*k^*}\right).$$

Thus, $\mathcal{B}$ can get:

$$e\left(T_{i^*j^*k^*}, g\right) = e((g^{by_{i^*}})^{\sum_{l=1}^{s} v_l F_{i^*j^*k^*l} + H_{2,i^*}}, g^a) e\left(g^z, S_{i^*j^*k^*}\right)$$
$$= e((g^{ab})^{y_{i^*} \left(\sum_{l=1}^{s} v_l F_{i^*j^*k^*l} + H_{2,i^*} \right)} S_{i^*j^*k^*}^z, g).$$

Finally, $\mathcal{B}$ gets:

$$g^{ab} = (T_{i^*j^*k^*} S_{i^*j^*k^*}^{-z})^{y_{i^*}^{-1} \left(\sum_{l=1}^{s} v_l F_{i^*j^*k^*l} + H_{2,i^*} \right)^{-1}}.$$

Probability Analysis. To evaluate the success probability for $\mathcal{B}$, we analyze the four events needed for $\mathcal{B}$ to succeed:

1. ε_1: $\mathcal{B}$ does not abort as a result of any of $\mathcal{A}$'s Extract queries.
2. ε_2: $\mathcal{B}$ does not abort as a result of any of $\mathcal{A}$'s TagGen queries.
3. ε_3: $\mathcal{B}$ generates a valid tag $\sigma_{i^*j^*k^*} = (S_{i^*j^*k^*}, T_{i^*j^*k^*})$ on $(i^*, j^*, k^*, M_{i^*j^*k^*})$.
4. ε_4: Event ε_3, $d_{i^*} = 1$ for the tuple $(ID_{i^*}, d_{i^*}, y_{i^*}, H_{1,i^*})$ in H_1-list.

$\mathcal{B}$ succeeds if all of these events happen. The probability $\Pr[\varepsilon_1 \wedge \varepsilon_2 \wedge \varepsilon_3 \wedge \varepsilon_4]$ decomposes as:

$$\Pr\left[\varepsilon_1 \wedge \varepsilon_2 \wedge \varepsilon_3 \wedge \varepsilon_4\right] = \delta^{q_E}\delta^{q_T}\epsilon\,(1-\delta) = \delta^{q_E+q_T}(1-\delta)\epsilon.$$

Thus, in the simulation, $\mathcal{B}$ solves the CDH problem on $\mathcal{G}1$ with an unnegligible probability $\delta^{q_E+q_T}(1-\delta)\epsilon$. Furthermore, when $\delta = \frac{q_E+q_T}{q_E+q_T+1}$, the corresponding maximum probability is $\frac{(q_E+q_T)^{(q_E+q_T)}}{(q_E+q_T+1)^{(q_E+q_T+1)}}\epsilon$. This completes the proof.

Theorem 2. *If a probabilistic polynomial adversary $\mathcal{A}$ wins the Proof-Forge game in Definition 3 with an unnegligible probability ϵ, then there exists a polynomial adversary $\mathcal{B}$ solves the CDH problem on $\mathcal{G}_1$ with an unnegligible probability $[\frac{(q_E+q_T)^{(q_E+q_T)}}{(q_E+q_T+c^*)^{(q_E+q_T+c^*)}}]^{c^*-1}c^*\epsilon$ after $\mathcal{A}$ makes q_E Extract queries and q_T TagGen queries. c^* denotes the number of challenged blocks.*

Proof. We define the interactions between $\mathcal{A}$ and $\mathcal{B}$ in the random oracle model by utilizing the technique proposed by Coron [27]. Adversary $\mathcal{A}$ is given $(g, g^a, g^b) \in \mathcal{G}_1^3$. Its goal is to output $g^{ab} \in \mathcal{G}_1$. $\mathcal{B}$ simulates the challenger and interacts with $\mathcal{A}$ as follows:

1. Setup. $\mathcal{B}$ sets $mpk = g^a$ while a keeps secret. It forwards mpk to $\mathcal{A}$.
2. H_1-Oracle, H_2-Oracle, H_3-Oracle, First-Phase Extract-Oracle and First-Phase TagGen-Oracle. Same as H_1-Oracle, H_2-Oracle, H_3-Oracle, Extract-Oracle and TagGen-Oracle in the proof of Theorem 1.
3. Challenge. Let S_1 denote the set of the extracted identities $\{ID_i\}$ and let I_1 denote the set of the TagGen-queried tuples $\{(i, j, k, M_{ijk})\}$. $\mathcal{B}$ generates a challenge token $chal^* = (I^*, K^*)$ with $I^* = \{(i_n^*, j_n^*, k_n^*) \mid n = 1, \ldots, c^*\}$ and $K^* = \{\kappa_n^* \mid n = 1, \ldots, c^*\}$ where at least one $ID_{i_n^*} \notin S_1$ and at least one $(i_n^*, j_n^*, k_n^*, M_{i_n^*j_n^*k_n^*}) \notin I_1$. Then $\mathcal{B}$ forwards it to $\mathcal{A}$.
4. Second-Phase Extract-Oracle and Second-Phase TagGen-Oracle. Same as Extract-Oracle and TagGen-Oracle in the proof of Theorem 1, Let S_2 denote the set of the extracted identities ID_i and let I_2 denote the set of the TagGen-queried tuples $\{(i, j, k, M_{ijk})\}$. The restriction is that at least one $ID_{i_n^*} \notin (S_1 \cup S_2)$ and at least one $(i_n^*, j_n^*, k_n^*, M_{i_n^*j_n^*k_n^*}) \notin (I_1 \cup I_2)$.
5. Forge. Eventually, the adversary $\mathcal{A}$ responds a valid proof $P^* = \{P_{j^*}\} = \{(S_{j^*}', T_{j^*}', \{F_{i^*j^*l}' \mid (i^*, j^*, k^*) \in I^*\})\}$ of $chal^* = (I^*, K^*)$ with $I^* = \{(i_n^*, j_n^*, k_n^*) \mid n = 1, \ldots, c^*\}$ and $K^* = \{\kappa_n^* \mid n = 1, \ldots, c^*\}$. $\mathcal{B}$ looks up H_1-list for the tuples $\{(ID_{i_n^*}, d_{i_n^*}, y_{i_n^*}, H_{1,i_n^*}) \mid n = 1, \ldots, c^*\}$. If some of these tuples

do not exist, $\mathcal{B}$ issues queries itself for $H_1(ID_{i_n^*})$ to ensure that all the tuples exist. Then $\mathcal{B}$ looks up H_2-list for the tuples $\{(\widetilde{ID}_{i_n^*}, H_{2,i_n^*}) \mid n = 1, \ldots, c^*\}$. If some of these tuples do not exist, $\mathcal{B}$ issues queries itself for $H_2(ID_{i^*})$ to ensure that all the tuples exist. Then $\mathcal{B}$ looks up H_3-list for the tuple (mpk, z, g^z). If the tuple does not exist, $\mathcal{B}$ issues a query itself for $H_3(mpk)$ to ensure that such a tuple exists. Based on $\{d_{i_n^*} \mid n = 1, \ldots, c^*\}$, $\mathcal{B}$ responds as follows:

(a) If every $d_{i_n^*} = 0$, $\mathcal{B}$ reports failure and the simulation terminates.

(b) If at least one $d_{i_n^*} = 1$, $\mathcal{B}$ computes $\{r_n^*\} = \{f_{\kappa_n^*}(i_n^*, j_n^*, k_n^*) \mid n = 1, \ldots, c^*\}$. Let O^* denote the set of indexes $\{i^*\}$ and C^* denote the set of indexes $\{j^*\}$. Since P^* is a valid proof, $\{(S'_{j^*}, T'_{j^*}, \{F'_{i^*j^*l} \mid (i^*, j^*, k^*) \in I^*\})\}$ satisfies formula (2), i.e.:

$$e\left(\prod_{j^* \in C^*} T'_{j^*}, g\right)$$

$$= e\left(\prod_{i^* \in O^*} H_1(ID_{i^*})^{\sum_{j^* \in C^*} \sum_{l=1}^{s} v_l F'_{i^*j^*l} + H_2(ID_{i^*}) \sum_{i_n^* = i^*} r_n^*}, mpk\right)$$

$$\cdot e\left(H_3(mpk), \prod_{j^* \in C^*} S'_j\right).$$

For simplicity, let

$$S^* = \prod_{j^* \in C^*} S'_{j^*}, \quad T^* = \prod_{j^* \in C^*} T'_{j^*}.$$

Similar to the analysis of correctness of formula (2), $\mathcal{B}$ has:

$$e(T^*, g) = e\left(\prod_{j^* \in C^*} \prod_{chal_{j^*}^*} H_1(ID_{i_n^*})^{(m_{i_n^*j^*k_n^*} + H_2(ID_{i^*}))r_n^*}, mpk\right)$$

$$\cdot e(H_3(mpk), S^*)$$

$$= e\left(\prod_{n=1}^{c^*} H_1(ID_{i_n^*})^{(m_{i_n^*j^*k_n^*} + H_2(ID_{i^*}))r_n^*}, mpk\right) e(H_3(mpk), S^*).$$

Let $N_0 = \{n \mid (ID_{i_n^*}, d_{i_n^*}, y_{i_n^*}, H_{1,i_n^*}) \in H_1\text{-list}, d_{i_n^*} = 0\}$, $N_1 = \{n \mid (ID_{i_n^*}, d_{i_n^*}, y_{i_n^*}, H_{1,i_n^*}) \in H_1\text{-list}, d_{i_n^*} = 1\}$ with $N_1 \neq \emptyset$, $H^* = m_{i_n^*j^*k_n^*} + H_2(ID_{i^*})$, $\mathcal{B}$ can get:

$$e(T^*, g) = e\left(\prod_{n=1}^{c^*} H_1(ID_{i_n^*})^{H^*r_n^*}, mpk\right) e(H_3(mpk), S^*)$$

$$= e\left(\prod_{n \in N_0} (g^{y_{i_n^*}})^{H^*r_n^*} \cdot \prod_{n \in N_1} (g^{by_{i_n^*}})^{H^*r_n^*}, g^a\right) e(g^z, S^*)$$

$$= e\left(\prod_{n \in N_0} (g^a)^{y_{i_n^*}H^*r_n^*} \cdot \prod_{n \in N_1} (g^{ab})^{y_{i_n^*}H^*r_n^*} \cdot S^{*z}, g\right).$$

Finally, $\mathcal{B}$ gets:

$$g^{ab} = [T^* S^{*-z}(g^a)^{-\sum_{n \in N_0} y_{i_n^*} H^* r_n^*} (\sum_{n \in N_1} y_{i_n^*} H^* r_n^*)^{-1}].$$

Probability Analysis. To evaluate the success probability for $\mathcal{B}$, we analyze the four events needed for $\mathcal{B}$ to succeed:

1. ε_1: $\mathcal{B}$ does not abort as a result of any of $\mathcal{A}$'s Extract queries.
2. ε_2: $\mathcal{B}$ does not abort as a result of any of $\mathcal{A}$'s TagGen queries.
3. ε_3: $\mathcal{B}$ generates a valid proof $P^* = \{P_{j*}\} = \{(S'_{j*}, T'_{j*}, \{F'_{i*j*l} \mid (i^*, j^*, k^*) \in I^*\})\}$ of $chal^* = (I^*, K^*)$ with $I^* = \{(i_n^*, j_n^*, k_n^*) \mid n = 1, \ldots, c^*\}$ and $K^* = \{\kappa_n^* \mid n = 1, \ldots, c^*\}$.
4. ε_4: Event at least one $d_{i_n^*} = 1$ for the tuples $\{(ID_{i_n^*}, d_{i_n^*}, y_{i_n^*}, H_{1,i_n^*}) \mid n = 1, \ldots, c^*\}$ in H_1-list.

$\mathcal{B}$ succeeds if all of these events happen. The probability $\Pr[\varepsilon_1 \wedge \varepsilon_2 \wedge \varepsilon_3 \wedge \varepsilon_4]$ decomposes as:

$$\Pr[\varepsilon_1 \wedge \varepsilon_2 \wedge \varepsilon_3 \wedge \varepsilon_4] = \delta^{q_E} \delta^{q_T} \epsilon(1 - \delta^{c^*}) = \delta^{q_E + q_T}(1 - \delta^{c^*})\epsilon.$$

Thus, in the simulation, $\mathcal{B}$ solves the CDH problem on $\mathcal{G}_1$ with an unnegligible probability $\delta^{q_E + q_T}(1 - \delta^{c^*})\epsilon$. Furthermore, when $\delta = (\frac{q_E + q_T}{q_E + q_T + c^*})^{c^* - 1}$, the corresponding maximum probability is $[\frac{(q_E + q_T)^{(q_E + q_T)}}{(q_E + q_T + c^*)^{(q_E + q_T + c^*)}}]^{c^* - 1} c^* \epsilon$. This completes the proof.

Theorem 3. *Suppose that n block-tag pairs are stored, t block-tag pairs are modified and c block-tag pairs are challenged. Then the probability P_X of detecting the modification satisfies:*

$$1 - (\frac{n - t}{n})^c \le P_X \le (\frac{n - c + 1 - t}{n - c + 1})^c.$$

Proof. Let X be a discrete random variable that is defined to be the number of blocks challenged that match the blocks modified, we have:

$$P_X = \Pr[X \ge 1] = 1 - \Pr[X = 0] = 1 - \frac{n - t}{n} \cdot \frac{n - 1 - t}{n - 1} \cdot \ldots \cdot \frac{n - c + 1 - t}{n - c + 1}.$$

It follows that:

$$1 - (\frac{n - t}{n})^c \le P_X \le (\frac{n - c + 1 - t}{n - c + 1})^c.$$

This completes the proof.

Figure 2 illustrates the probability curve of P_X with $n = 10000$. From this, we know that our scheme has a high modification checking probability.

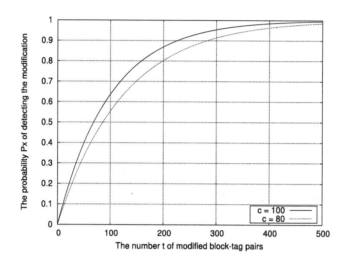

Fig. 2. Probability curve P_X of detecting the modification ($n = 10000$).

7 Conclusion

We proposed a novel Identity-Based Batch Provable Data Possession (ID-BPDP) scheme in this paper. Without implementation of PKI, ID-BPDP eliminates the resource-consuming certificate management. Meanwhile, ID-BPDP supports batch verification for multiple owners and multiple clouds simultaneously to reduce computation cost greatly, especially in large-scale cloud storage systems. ID-BPDP also reduces computation cost for data owners while generating tags of data blocks. We proved that ID-BPDP is correct and secure based on bilinear pairings and the hardness assumption of CDH problem, and our analyses/simulations show that ID-BPDP is able to verify integrity of data efficiently.

References

1. Armbrust, M., Fox, A., Griffith, R., Joseph, A.D., Katz, R.H., Kon-winski, A., Lee, G., Patterson, D.A., Rabkin, A., Stoica, I., Zaharia, M.: A view of cloud computing. Commun. ACM **53**(4), 50–58 (2010)
2. Ateniese, G., Burns, R., Curtmola, R., Herring, J., Kissner, L., Peterson, Z., Song, D.: Provable data possession at untrusted stores. In: Proceedings of CCS, pp. 598–609 (2007)
3. Curtmola, R., Khan, O., Burns, R., Ateniese, G.: MR-PDP: multiple-replica provable data possession. In: Proceedings of ICDCS, pp. 411–420 (2008)
4. Sebé, F., Domingo-Ferrer, J., Martínez-Ballesté, A., Deswarte, Y., Quisquater, J.: Efficient remote data integrity checking in critical information infrastuctures. IEEE Trans. Knowl. Data Eng. **20**(8), 1034–1038 (2008)
5. Ateniese, G., Pietro, R.D., Mancini, L.V., Tsudik, G.: Scalable and efficient provable data possession. In: Proceedings of SecureComm, pp. 1–10 (2008)

6. Erway, C.C., Küpçü, A., Papamanthou, C., Tamassia, R.: Dynamic provable data possession. In: Proceedings of CCS, pp. 213–222 (2009)
7. Wang, C., Wang, Q., Ren, K., Lou, W.: Privacy-preserving public auditing for data storage security in cloud computing. In: Proceedings of IEEE INFOCOM (2010)
8. Zhu, Y., Wang, H., Hu, Z., Ahn, G.J., Hu, H., Yau, S.S.: Efficient provable data possession for hybrid clouds. In: Proceedings of CCS, pp. 756–758 (2010)
9. Wang, Q., Wang, C., Ren, K., Lou, W., Li, J.: Enabling public auditability and data dynamics for storage security in cloud computing. IEEE Trans. Parallel Distrib. Syst. **22**(5), 847–859 (2011)
10. Wang, C., Wang, Q., Ren, K., Cao, N., Lou, W.: Toward secure and dependable storage services in cloud computing. IEEE Trans. Serv. Comput. **5**(2), 220–232 (2012)
11. Wang, H.: Proxy provable data possession in public clouds. IEEE Trans. Serv. Comput. **6**(4), 551–559 (2013)
12. Zhu, Y., Hu, H., Ahn, G.J., Yu, M.: Cooperative provable data possession for integrity verification in multicloud storage. IEEE Trans. Parallel Distrib. Syst. **23**(12), 2231–2244 (2012)
13. Lier, S., Wörsdörfer, D., Gesing, J.: Business models and product service systems for transformable, modular plants in the chemical process industry. In: Meier, H. (ed.) Product-Service Integration for Sustainable Solutions. LNPE, vol. 6, pp. 227–238. Springer, Heidelberg (2013)
14. Yang, K., Jia, X.: An efficient and secure dynamic auditing protocol for data storage in cloud computing. IEEE Trans. Parallel Distrib. Syst. **24**(9), 1717–1726 (2013)
15. Yu, Y., Ni, J., Au, M.H., Liu, H., Wang, H., Xu, C.: Improved security of a dynamic remote data possession checking protocol for cloud storage. Expert Syst. Appl. **41**, 7789–7796 (2014)
16. Yu, Y., Zhang, Y., Ni, J., Au, M.H., Chen, L., Liu, H.: Remote data possession checking with enhanced security for cloud storage. Future Gener. Comput. Syst. **52**, 77–85 (2015)
17. Yu, Y., Au, M.H., Mu, Y., Tang, S., Ren, J., Susilo, W., Dong, L.: Enhanced privacy of a remote data integrity-checking protocol for secure cloud storage. Int. J. Inf. Secur. **14**, 307–318 (2015)
18. Wang, B., Li, B., Li, H.: Panda: public auditing for shared data with efficient user revocation in the cloud. IEEE Trans. Serv. Comput. **8**(1), 92–106 (2015)
19. Yu, Y., Ni, J., Au, M.H., Mu, Y., Wang, B., Li, H.: Comments on a public auditing mechanism for shared cloud data service. IEEE Trans. Serv. Comput. **8**(6), 998–999 (2015)
20. Yu, Y., Li, Y., Ni, J., Yang, G., Mu, Y., Susilo, W.: Comments on "public integrity auditing for dynamic data sharing with multiuser modification". IEEE Trans. Inf. Forensics Secur. **11**(3), 658–659 (2016)
21. Ellison, C., Schneier, B.: Ten risks of PKI: what you're not being told about public key infrastructure. Comput. Secur. J. **16**(1), 1–7 (2000)
22. Wang, H.: Identity-based distributed provable data possession in multicloud storage. IEEE Trans. Serv. Comput. **8**(2), 328–340 (2015)
23. Boneh, D., Franklin, M.: Identity-based encryption from the weil pairing. In: Kilian, J. (ed.) CRYPTO 2001. LNCS, vol. 2139, pp. 213–229. Springer, Heidelberg (2001)
24. The GNU multiple precision arithmetic library. https://gmplib.org
25. The pairing-based cryptography library (PBC). https://crypto.stanford.edu/pbc
26. OpenSSL: cryptography and SSL/TLS Toolkit. http://www.openssl.org
27. Coron, J.-S.: On the exact security of full domain hash. In: Bellare, M. (ed.) CRYPTO 2000. LNCS, vol. 1880, pp. 220–235. Springer, Heidelberg (2000)

Secure Naïve Bayesian Classification over Encrypted Data in Cloud

Xingxin Li, Youwen Zhu$^{(\boxtimes)}$, and Jian Wang

College of Computer Science and Technology,
Nanjing University of Aeronautics and Astronautics, Nanjing 210016, China
lixingxin93@163.com, {zhuyw,wangjian}@nuaa.edu.cn

Abstract. To enjoy the advantage of cloud service while preserving security and privacy, huge data is increasingly outsourced to cloud in encrypted form. Unfortunately, encryption may impede the analysis and computation over the outsourced dataset. Naïve Bayesian classification is an effective algorithm to predict the class label of unlabeled samples. In this paper, we investigate naïve Bayesian classification on encrypted dataset in cloud and propose a secure scheme for the challenging problem. In our scheme, all the computation task of naïve Bayesian classification are completed by the cloud, which can dramatically reduce the burden of data owner and users. Based on the theoretical proof, our scheme can guarantee the security of both input dataset and output classification results, and the cloud can learn nothing useful about the training data of data owner and the test samples of users throughout the computation. Additionally, we evaluate our computation complexity and communication overheads in detail.

Keywords: Cloud security · Naïve Bayesian classification · Privacy

1 Introduction

In recent years, cloud services become more and more prevalent, since they can offer many benefits, such as quick deployment without up-front cost, dynamical allocation and cost reduction. For enjoying the advantages, individuals and organizations are being motivated to centralize their datasets into the convenient pay-as-you-go storage space of cloud service providers, e.g., Amazon, Google, Microsoft. Because the direct physical control will be transferred to cloud service providers while outsourcing data to a remote cloud, it arouses the security and privacy concerns. Thus, the sensitive information of outsourced data has to be encrypted by data owner before they are uploaded to cloud such that no privacy is breached. Meanwhile, some users may want to take advantage of the powerful computation capability of cloud server to analyze the data stored in the cloud for extracting beneficial knowledge and patterns. Nevertheless, encryption will impede the functionality and performance of querying/analyzing over the outsourced dataset in cloud.

© Springer International Publishing AG 2016
L. Chen and J. Han (Eds.): ProvSec 2016, LNCS 10005, pp. 130–150, 2016.
DOI: 10.1007/978-3-319-47422-9_8

Naïve Bayesian classification [16] is an effective algorithm to predict the class label of unclassified samples, which is particularly suitable for high dimensional data classification tasks, such as recommender system [15], text classification [11], medical data analysis [1]. In this paper, we investigate the challenging problem how to make use of cloud service to secure realize naïve bayesian classification on encrypted data. In the past several years, much work [5,10,22] has focused on the privacy-preserving naïve bayesian classification. In the works, they consider the model where database is vertically or horizontally distributed in two or more independent parties, and the participants want to perform naïve bayesian classification for a public or confidential unlabel sample without disclosing private data to each other. In their setting, each participant can access a part of the dataset, and utilize the data to complete the computation. However, in an outsourcing scene, the cloud service providers should access only the encrypted data to protect the privacy of data owner, and the computation task is also completed by the cloud. Thus, we are faced with a different scene from what the previous privacy-preserving naïve bayesian classification schemes consider. Because the cloud can just learn the encrypted results, our problem is much more challenging. Lately, Liu *et al.* [14] propose a privacy-preserving naïve Bayesian classification approach for medical diagnosis, which introduces the cloud to store the encrypted training dataset and compute some probability during training stage. Nevertheless, the users in Liu *et al.*'s scheme must burden heavy computation which does not fit the outsourcing goal well. Besides, if the domain of one dimension of the sample consists of T different values, Liu *et al.*'s scheme will extend the dimension into T new dimensions, because their approach is suitable for binary dimensions only. Hence, Liu *et al.*'s scheme will be low-efficient if the value range of the sample's dimensions is large. In [3], Bost *et al.* propose several secure schemes to support classification over encrypted data, including naïve Bayesian classification. However, the server in [3] is assumed to access the training data set, i.e., Bost *et al.*'s approach cannot protect the training samples from the cloud server.

In this paper, we make use of Paillier homomorphic cryptosystem to encrypt the training dataset of data owner and the unlabeled samples of users. The encrypted data will be outsourced to the cloud for storage and naïve Bayesian classification. All the computation tasks for naïve Bayesian classification will be completed by the cloud in encrypted format. Additionally, the cloud can attain only the encrypted value of the classification result, and only the user can clearly learn the returned class label for his sample. Generally, our main contributions in this paper are as follows.

- We present a secure scheme that can utilize cloud to implement naïve Bayesian classification over encrypted dataset. In our scheme, all the computation task of naïve Bayesian classification are completed by the cloud, which can dramatically reduce the burden of data owner and users.
- In the proposed scheme, we can guarantee the security of both input dataset and output classification results. The cloud can learn nothing useful about the training data set of data owner and the test data of users.

- We theoretically prove the security of our scheme, and provide detailed evaluation on the computation complexity and communication cost.

The remainder of the paper is organized as follows. In Sect. 2, we introduce naïve Bayesian classification, preliminaries, our problem definition and threat model. In Sect. 3, we present our secure scheme in detail. Then, we theoretically prove the security of our scheme, and evaluate our computation and communication cost in Sect. 4. In Sect. 5, we review the related work. At last, we conclude this paper in Sect. 6.

2   Preliminaries and System Model

2.1   Naïve Bayesian Classification

In the area of data mining, naïve Bayesian classification [16] is an effective algorithm to predict the class label of unclassified samples, which is particularly suitable for high dimensional data classification tasks, such as recommender system [15], text classification [11], medical data analysis [1]. We concisely describe naïve Bayesian classification as follows.

Assume S is an unclassified sample, which can be represented by a d-dimensional vector, $S = (S_1, S_2, \cdots, S_d)$. The domain of class label is $\{1, 2, \cdots, \lambda\}$. Let C_S denote the class label of S. Naïve Bayesian classification predicts C_S to be the class with the highest posterior probability. It means

$$C_S = \operatorname*{argmax}_{1 \leqslant i \leqslant \lambda} \left(P(C_S = i | S) \right). \tag{1}$$

That is, $P(C_S = i | S) \geqslant P(C_S = j | S)$, for each $j \in \{1, 2, \cdots, \lambda\}$ and $j \neq i$.

Based on Bayes theorem,

$$P(C_S = i | S) = \frac{P(S | C_S = i) P(C_S = i)}{P(S)}. \tag{2}$$

As can be seen from the Eq. (2), $P(S)$ is the same for each class label $i \in \{1, 2, \cdots, \lambda\}$. Then,

$$C_S = \operatorname*{argmax}_{1 \leqslant i \leqslant \lambda} \left(P(S | C_S = i) P(C_S = i) \right). \tag{3}$$

In naïve Bayesian classification, a simplifying assumption is further made that the values of each attribute are conditionally independent of that of another. It can guarantee

$$P(S | C_S = i) = \prod_{t=1}^{d} P(S_t | C_S = i). \tag{4}$$

$$C_S = \operatorname*{argmax}_{1 \leqslant i \leqslant \lambda} \left(P(C_S = i) \prod_{t=1}^{d} P(S_t | C_S = i) \right). \tag{5}$$

In the Eq. (5), the values of probabilities $P(C_S = i)$ and $P(S_t|C_S = i)$ can be estimated from the training dataset as follows.

$$P(C_S = i) = \frac{m_i}{m},\tag{6}$$

$$P(S_t|C_S = i) = \frac{m_{it}}{m_i},\tag{7}$$

where m is the total number of samples in training dataset, m_i is the number of samples with class label i, and m_{it} is the number of samples whose class label are i and t-th dimension equal to S_t.

In this paper, we will investigate a challenging problem: how to securely harness cloud service to complete the naïve Bayesian classification over encrypted data.

2.2 System Model

As shown in Fig. 1, this paper considers a secure outsourcing system involving a data owner, two non-colluding cloud servers CS_1 and CS_2, several users. Data owner (denoted as Alice) owns a database $\mathbf{D}$ of m labeled samples $\{\mathbf{T}_1, \mathbf{T}_2, \cdots, \mathbf{T}_m\}$. Each sample is a d-dimensional vector, i.e., $\mathbf{T}_i = (T_{i1}, T_{i2}, \cdots, T_{id})$. The class label of $\mathbf{T}_i$ is denoted as C_i, and $C_i \in \{1, 2, \cdots, \lambda\}$. Here, we assume the dataset $\mathbf{D}$ is large enough, in which the number of any class of samples is not less than 1. Suppose (pk, sk) is the key pair of Paillier homomorphic encryption system proposed in [17], where pk is the public key and sk is the secret key. The detail about Paillier is described in Appendix. For $1 \leqslant i \leqslant m$ and $1 \leqslant j \leqslant d$, $E_{pk}(T_{ij})$ and $E_{pk}(C_i)$ are the encrypted values of T_{ij} and C_i, respectively. Let $\mathbf{T}_i'$ denote the encrypted result of $\mathbf{T}_i$, and $\mathbf{D}' = \{\mathbf{T}_1', \mathbf{T}_2', \cdots, \mathbf{T}_m'\}$. For enjoying the advantages of cloud service and relieving himself from expensive local storage and computation cost, Alice plans to

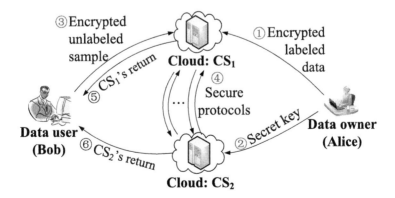

Fig. 1. Architecture of securely outsourcing naïve Bayesian classification over encrypted data

store the encrypted data $\mathbf{D}'$ at CS_1 and outsource her secret key sk to CS_2, in which CS_1 and CS_2 are assumed to be non-colluding. Then, Alice also employs the cloud service providers to securely complete various data analysis tasks over the encrypted dataset. In this paper, we focus on achieving secure naïve Bayesian classification, and leave other tasks for future work.

Suppose each user (denoted as Bob) has an unlabeled sample $\boldsymbol{S} = (S_1, S_2, \cdots, S_d)$, and Bob wants to attain the class label of his data $\boldsymbol{S}$ through the naïve Bayesian classification algorithm based on the dataset of Alice. For the object, Bob will use Alice's public key to encrypt each dimension of $\boldsymbol{S}$, and submit the encrypted sample $\boldsymbol{S}'$ to cloud server CS_1. It should be remarked that Bob cannot access the secret key of Alice.

Finally, the two cloud servers CS_1 and CS_2 will complete naïve Bayesian classification based on the encrypted dataset $\mathbf{D}'$ and the encrypted unlabeled sample $\boldsymbol{S}'$, such that only Bob can learn the classification result.

Now, the challenging problem is how CS_1 and CS_2 can complete the naïve Bayesian classification task taking as inputs $\{\mathbf{D}', \boldsymbol{S}'\}$ and the secret key sk, respectively, while disclosing no privacy of Alice and Bob.

2.3   Threat Model

In this paper, all participants (Alice, Bob and cloud service providers) are assumed to be semi-honest (i.e., honest-but-curious) [9]. Generally speaking, each semi-honest participant will strictly follow the protocol, but try to infer as much information as possible from what he legally receives during the protocol. Additionally, the involved two cloud service providers CS_1 and CS_2 are assumed to be non-colluding. This setting of non-colluding CS_1 and CS_2 has been widely applied in many previous works, such as [8,13,18,19], and they have shown that the assumption is practical and feasible in the real-world. The cloud service providers, for example Amazon and Google, have little motivation to collude, for protecting their business reputation, trade secret, etc.

In [9] (Chap. 7), Goldreich has given a security definition for the semi-honest model. The definition is to ensure that any participant cannot infer more information than what can be deduced from his input and deserved output. Briefly speaking, a protocol is said to be secure against semi-honest adversaries if the view of each participant, namely what each participant learns during the protocol, is computationally indistinguishable with random parameters and the input & output of the participant. Therefore, we will consider the view of each party while analyzing the security of our scheme.

Under the semi-honest model, our security goals include the following three aspects.

- **Privacy of Alice's dataset D**: Neither the cloud nor the user Bob can learn any useful information about every sample in Alice's dataset $\mathbf{D}$.
- **Privacy of Bob's sample S**: Each dimension of the sample $\boldsymbol{S}$ should be private to Bob. Both Alice and the cloud cannot know it.
- **Privacy of Bob's output class label of S**: The output class label should be known to Bob only. Alice and the cloud cannot learn the class label of $\boldsymbol{S}$.

3   Our Proposed Scheme

In this paper, after outsourcing the encrypted dataset $\mathbf{D}'$ and her secret key sk to two non-colluding cloud servers separately, Alice will not implement any computation task again. All the future computation will be completed by the cloud service providers. Our scheme does not require Alice to be online for the classification.

While the user Bob wants to find out C_S, i.e., the class label of his unlabeled sample $\mathbf{S}$, he will encrypt $\mathbf{S}$ into $\mathbf{S}'$ using the public key pk and submit the encrypted value to CS_1. Then, the cloud will complete the naïve Bayesian classification, and each cloud service provider returns an random number to Bob who can easily obtain the class label C_S through a subtraction of the two returned numbers.

Naïve Bayesian classification aims at finding a class label i such that $P(\mathbf{S}|C_S = i)P(C_S = i) \geqslant P(\mathbf{S}|C_S = j)P(C_S = j)$, for any $j \neq i$. For the goal, a straightforward method is to compute $P(\mathbf{S}|C_S = i)P(C_S = i)$ for each $i \in \{1, 2, \cdots, \lambda\}$ and compare them. Obviously, the probabilities are floating-point numbers. Nevertheless, the employed Paillier homomorphic encryption system can encrypt only the non-negative integers in its plaintext space. Here, we convert the probability comparison into the comparison of the product of several integers such that the computation and comparison does not involve any floating-point number.

In naïve Bayesian classification, there is $P(\mathbf{S}|C_S = i)P(C_S = i) = P(C_S = i)\prod_{t=1}^{d} P(S_t|C_S = i)$.

Based on the Eqs. (6) and (7), we have

$$P(\mathbf{S}|C_S = i)P(C_S = i) = \frac{m_i}{m} \prod_{t=1}^{d} \frac{m_{it}}{m_i} = \frac{\prod_{t=1}^{d} m_{it}}{m_i^{d-1}m}. \tag{8}$$

Thus, for any $i, j \in \{1, 2, \cdots, \lambda\}$, $P(\mathbf{S}|C_S = i)P(C_S = i) \geqslant P(\mathbf{S}|C_S = j)P(C_S = j)$ if and only if

$$\frac{\prod_{t=1}^{d} m_{it}}{m_i^{d-1}m} \geqslant \frac{\prod_{t=1}^{d} m_{jt}}{m_j^{d-1}m}. \tag{9}$$

Since m is the same for each i and j, then,

$$m_j^{d-1} \prod_{t=1}^{d} m_{it} \geqslant m_i^{d-1} \prod_{t=1}^{d} m_{jt}. \tag{10}$$

Therefore, we can determine the larger one of $P(\mathbf{S}|C_S = i)P(C_S = i)$ and $P(\mathbf{S}|C_S = j)P(C_S = j)$ through comparing $m_j^{d-1} \prod_{t=1}^{d} m_{it}$ and $m_i^{d-1} \prod_{t=1}^{d} m_{jt}$ in which no floating numbers is involved.

In our scheme, the cloud will find out the class label for unlabeled sample by implementing the comparison shown in the Eq. (10) in encrypted form.

Concretely, our scheme consists of two stages. The first stage will be implemented just once while Alice uploads her encrypted dataset to CS_1. In our first stage, the cloud servers CS_1 and CS_2 will execute a secure computation protocol such that CS_1 attains the encrypted m_i for each $i \in \{1, 2, \cdots, \lambda\}$, and then compute each m_i^{d-1} in encrypted form which is also known to CS_1 only. The second stage will be executed once for each unclassified sample S. In the second stage, the cloud will await users to submit the encrypted unlabeled sample. Upon receiving an encrypted sample S' to classify, the cloud will compute the encrypted value of each m_{it}, based on which the cloud can further compute the classification label of Bob's sample in encrypted form. At last, each cloud service provider returns a random number to Bob, and the latter can locally obtain his class label by a simple subtraction of two clouds' returned numbers. In the following section, we will introduce the two stages of our scheme in detail.

3.1   First Stage: Preparation

In this stage, for each $i \in \{1, 2, \cdots, \lambda\}$, the cloud aims at computing m_i and m_i^{d-1} both in encrypted form. For the goal, CS_1 first computes the λ-dimensional vector $\boldsymbol{W}_k$ for each $1 \leqslant k \leqslant m$. Let W_{ki} denote the i-th dimension of $\boldsymbol{W}_k$. It is required that $W_{ki} = E_{pk}(1)$ if $C_k = i$, otherwise $W_{ki} = E_{pk}(0)$. Besides, no cloud server can learn which W_{ki} is equal to $E_{pk}(1)$, such that the class label of Alice's samples will be well protected throughout the computation. Aroused by the secure frequency protocol in [18], we enable CS_1 to gain each $\boldsymbol{W}_k$ through the following interaction with CS_2.

CS_1 selects random λ non-zero numbers $\{R_{k1}, R_{k2}, \cdots, R_{k\lambda}\}$ in the plaintext space of Paillier homomorphic encryption system, and a random permutation Π_k of λ numbers. Then, CS_1 computes $X_{ki} = E_{pk}(R_{ki}(C_k - i)) = \left(E_{pk}(C_k)E_{pk}(i)^{N-1}\right)^{R_{ki}}$ for $1 \leqslant i \leqslant \lambda$, and sends the randomly-permutated vector $\Pi_k(\boldsymbol{X}_k) = \Pi_k(X_{k1}, X_{k2}, \cdots, X_{k\lambda})$ to CS_2. The latter will decrypt the λ dimensions of the vector, and return CS_1 a λ-dimensional vector $\boldsymbol{Y}_k = (Y_{k1}, Y_{k2}, \cdots, Y_{k\lambda})$ where $Y_{ki} = E_{pk}(1)$ if the decrypted result of the i-th dimension of $\Pi_k(\boldsymbol{X}_k)$ is zero, otherwise $Y_{ki} = E_{pk}(0)$. At last, CS_1 can obtain $\boldsymbol{W}_k = \Pi_k^{-1}(\boldsymbol{Y}_k)$. Here, Π_k^{-1} denotes the inverse permutation to Π_k. It is to say that $C_k = i$ if and only if $R_{ki}(C_k - i) = 0$. Thus, $\boldsymbol{W}_k$ can be correctly computed by the approach above. $\boldsymbol{W}_k$ will be used not only to compute each $E_{pk}(m_i)$ in this stage, but also to classify in the second stage. It should be remarked that neither CS_1 nor CS_2 can learn any plaintext hidden in $\boldsymbol{W}_k$.

After acquiring all $\boldsymbol{W}_k$, CS_1 can locally calculate the encrypted value of each m_i using the method shown in the following equation $E_{pk}(m_i) = \prod_{k=1}^{m} W_{ki}$ Further, we propose a novel secure and efficient approach enabling CS_1 to get $E_{pk}(m_i^{d-1})$. For each $i \in \{1, 2, \cdots, \lambda\}$, CS_1 randomly selects a non-zero numbers P_i, and sends $E_{pk}(m_iP_i)$ to CS_2 where $E_{pk}(m_iP_i) = E_{pk}(m_i)^{P_i}$ based on the homomorphic property. Then, CS_2 decrypts $E_{pk}(m_iP_i)$, and returns $E_{pk}\left((m_iP_i)^{d-1}\right)$ to CS_1. At last, CS_1 can compute $E_{pk}(m_i^{d-1}) = E_{pk}\left((m_iP_i)^{d-1}\right)^{Q_i}$ where $Q_i = P_i^{1-d} \bmod N$.

Protocol 1. First Stage: computing $E_{pk}(m_i^{d-1})$

Input: CS_1 holds $\{E_{pk}(C_1), E_{pk}(C_2), \cdots, E_{pk}(C_m)\}$. CS_2 has the secret key (decryption key) sk.

Output: CS_1 obtains $E_{pk}(m_i^{d-1})$ for each $i \in \{1, 2, \cdots, \lambda\}$.

1: **for** $k = 1$ to m **do**
2:     CS_1 randomly selects λ non-zero numbers $\{R_{k1}, R_{k2}, \cdots, R_{k\lambda}\}$ where $R_{ki} \in \mathbb{Z}_N^*$.

3:     CS_1 generates a random permutation of λ numbers Π_k.
4:     CS_1 computes the λ-dimensional vector $\boldsymbol{X}_k = (X_{k1}, X_{k2}, \cdots, X_{k\lambda})$ such that, for each $i \in \{1, 2, \cdots, \lambda\}$,

$$X_{ki} = \left(E_{pk}(C_k) E_{pk}(i)^{N-1} \right)^{R_{ki}}. \tag{11}$$

5:     CS_1 uses Π_k to permute $\boldsymbol{X}_k$, and sends $\Pi_k(\boldsymbol{X}_k)$ to CS_2.
6:     CS_2 decrypts $\Pi_k(\boldsymbol{X}_k)$, and sets the λ-dimensional vector $\boldsymbol{Y}_k = (Y_{k1}, Y_{k2}, \cdots, Y_{k\lambda})$ as follows.

$$Y_{ki} = \begin{cases} E_{pk}(1), & \text{if the plaintext hidden in the } i\text{-th dimension of } \Pi_k(\boldsymbol{X}_k) \text{ is } 0, \\ E_{pk}(0), & \text{otherwise.} \end{cases} \tag{12}$$

7:     CS_2 sends the vector $\boldsymbol{Y}_k$ to CS_1.
8:     CS_1 uses Π_k^{-1} (i.e., the inverse permutation to Π_k) to compute $\boldsymbol{W}_k = \Pi_k^{-1}(\boldsymbol{Y}_k)$.
9: **end for**
10: **for** $i = 1$ to λ **do**
11:     CS_1 computes $E_{pk}(m_i) = \prod_{k=1}^m W_{ki}$. Here, W_{ki} denotes the i-th dimension of $\boldsymbol{W}_k$.
12:     CS_1 selects a random non-zero number $P_i \in \mathbb{Z}_N^*$, then computes $E_{pk}(m_i P_i) = E_{pk}(m_i)^{P_i}$, and sends $E_{pk}(m_i P_i)$ to CS_2.
13:     CS_2 uses the secret key sk to decrypt $E_{pk}(m_i P_i)$, then calculates $(m_i P_i)^{d-1}$, and returns $E_{pk}\left((m_i P_i)^{d-1} \right)$ to CS_1.
14:     CS_1 figures out $E_{pk}(m_i^{d-1}) = E_{pk}\left((m_i P_i)^{d-1} \right)^{Q_i}$ where Q_i equals to $(P_i^{1-d} \bmod N)$.
15: **end for**

The detailed steps of our first stage is shown in protocol 1. The protocol will be executed only once while Alice submits her encrypted data to the cloud CS_1.

3.2 Second Stage: Computing Class Label for the Encrypted Sample

In this stage, the cloud will complete naïve Bayesian classification for the unlabeled sample of users. While a user Bob wants to find out the class label of his sample $\boldsymbol{S} = (S_1, S_2, \cdots, S_d)$, Bob will encrypt $\boldsymbol{S}$ into $\boldsymbol{S}' = (E_{pk}(S_1), E_{pk}(S_2), \cdots, E_{pk}(S_d))$ and submit the encrypted vector to CS_1. After receiving the encrypted sample $\boldsymbol{S}'$ to classify, the cloud will compute the

---

Protocol 2. Secure CipherText Comparison Protocol (SCTC)

Input: CS_1 holds two encrypted values $E_{pk}(X)$ and $E_{pk}(Y)$. CS_2 has the secret key (decryption key) sk. Suppose $0 \leqslant X, Y < 2^\Omega$.

Output: CS_1 obtains the output $\Gamma = E_{pk}(1)$ if $X \geqslant Y$, otherwise $\Gamma = E_{pk}(0)$. It should be remarked that neither CS_1 nor CS_2 know the comparison result hidden in the output ciphertext Γ.

1: CS_1 selects a random non-zero number $\delta \in \{1, 2, \cdots, 2^{\Omega+1}\}$, and a random number $\phi \in \{0, 1\}$.

2: **if** $\phi = 1$ **then**

3:     CS_1 computes $\Phi = E_{pk}(X)^{2\delta} E_{pk}(Y)^{N-2\delta} E_{pk}(2^{2\Omega+2} + \delta)$,

4: **else**

5:     CS_1 computes $\Phi = E_{pk}(X)^{N-2\delta} E_{pk}(Y)^{2\delta} E_{pk}(2^{2\Omega+2} - \delta)$,

6: **end if**

7: CS_1 sends Φ to CS_2.

8: CS_2 decrypts Φ, and returns Ψ to CS_1 where

$$\Psi = \begin{cases} E_{pk}(1), & \text{if } D_{sk}(\Phi) > 2^{2\Omega+2}, \\ E_{pk}(0), & \text{otherwise.} \end{cases} \tag{13}$$

9: CS_1 attains the output Γ as follows.

$$\Gamma = \begin{cases} \beta^N \Psi, & \text{if } \phi = 1, \\ E_{pk}(1)\Psi^{N-1}, & \text{if } \phi = 0. \end{cases} \tag{14}$$

Here, β is a random number that belongs to $\mathbb{Z}_N^*$.

---

encrypted $E_{pk}(m_{it})$ for each $t \in \{1, 2, \cdots, d\}$, and then securely find out the class label $E_{pk}(C_S)$ where $C_S \in \{1, 2, \cdots, \lambda\}$ can make $P(\mathbf{S}|C_S)P(C_S)$ be the maximum. The framework of our second stage is shown in protocol 3.

Here, m_{it} is the number of Alice's samples which meet the class label is i and the t-th dimension equals to S_t. While computing m_{it}, it needs to securely determine whether the t-th dimension of each sample in $\mathbf{D}$ is equal to S_t for each $t \in \{1, 2, \cdots, d\}$. For the goal, we propose a sub-protocol SCTC (shown in Protocol 2) to securely compare two encrypted numbers $E_pk(X)$ and $E_pk(Y)$.

Based on the proposed SCTC protocol, our second stage computes each $E_{pk}(m_{it})$ $(t = 1, 2, \cdots, d)$ as follows. For each T_{kt} $(k = 1, 2, \cdots, m)$, CS_1 and CS_2 implement SCTC twice such that CS_1 gains A_{kt1} and A_{kt2} which are the encrypted comparison results of $S_t \geqslant T_{kt}$ and $T_{kt} \geqslant S_t$, respectively. Namely, $A_{kt1} = E_{pk}(S_t \geqslant T_{kt})$, $A_{kt2} = E_{pk}(T_{kt} \geqslant S_t)$ (Here, we set TRUE $= 1$ and FALSE $= 0$). Then, $S_t = T_{kt}$ if and only if $D_{sk}(A_{kt1}) = D_{sk}(A_{kt2}) = 1$, i.e., $D_{sk}(A_{kt1}A_{kt2}) = 2$. In our first stage, W_{ki} has be set as $E_{pk}(1)$ if Alice's k-th sample's class label C_k equals to i, otherwise $E_{pk}(0)$. We thus have that the plaintext hidden in $(A_{kt1}A_{kt2}W_{ki})$ equals to 3 if and only if $S_t = T_{kt}$ and $C_k = i$, namely $D_{sk}(A_{kt1}) = D_{sk}(A_{kt2}) = D_{sk}(W_{ki}) = 1$. It is easy to say $1 \leqslant D_{sk}(A_{kt1}A_{kt2}W_{ki}) \leqslant 3$. By employing our SCTC protocol to find out the encrypted comparison result of $D_{sk}(A_{kt1}A_{kt2}W_{ki}) \geqslant 3$

Protocol 3. Second Stage: computing the class label for each S

Input: CS_1 has the following encrypted data $T'_k = (E_{pk}(T_{k1}), E_{pk}(T_{k2}), \cdots, E_{pk}(T_{kd})), 1 \leqslant k \leqslant m$, $\mathbf{W}_k = (W_{k1}, W_{k2}, \cdots, W_{k\lambda}), 1 \leqslant k \leqslant m$, $E_{pk}(m_i^{d-1}), 1 \leqslant i \leqslant \lambda$. CS_2 has the secret key (decryption key). Bob has an unlabeled sample $S = (S_1, S_2, \cdots, S_d)$ to classify.

Output: Bob obtains C_S, i.e., the class label of S using naïve Bayesian classification.

1: Bob encrypts each dimension of S, and sends the encrypted vector $S' = (E_{pk}(S_1), E_{pk}(S_2), \cdots, E_{pk}(S_d))$ to CS_1.

2: **for** $k = 1$ to m **do**

3:    **for** $t = 1$ to d **do**

4:        CS_1 and CS_2 implement $\mathtt{SCTC}(\{E_{pk}(S_t), E_{pk}(T_{kt})\}, \{sk\})$ such that CS_1 obtains

$$A_{kt1} = \begin{cases} E_{pk}(1), & \text{if } S_t \geqslant T_{kt}, \\ E_{pk}(0), & \text{otherwise.} \end{cases} \quad (15)$$

5:        Similarly, CS_1 and CS_2 implement $\mathtt{SCTC}(\{E_{pk}(T_{kt}), E_{pk}(S_t)\}, \{sk\})$ such that CS_1 obtains

$$A_{kt2} = \begin{cases} E_{pk}(1), & \text{if } T_{kt} \geqslant S_t, \\ E_{pk}(0), & \text{otherwise.} \end{cases} \quad (16)$$

6:        **for** $i = 1$ to λ **do**

7:            CS_1 and CS_2 securely implement $\mathtt{SCTC}(\{A_{kt1}A_{kt2}W_{ki}, E_{pk}(3)\}, \{sk\})$ such that CS_1 obtains

$$B_{kti} = \begin{cases} E_{pk}(1), & \text{if } D_{sk}(A_{kt1}A_{kt2}W_{ki}) \geqslant 3, \\ E_{pk}(0), & \text{otherwise.} \end{cases} \quad (17)$$

8:        **end for**

9:    **end for**

10: **end for**

11: **for** $i = 1$ to λ **do**

12:    **for** $t = 1$ to d **do**

13:        CS_1 computes $E_{pk}(m_{it}) = \prod_{k=1}^{m} B_{kti}$.

14:    **end for**

15: **end for**

16: **for** $i = 1$ to λ **do**

17:    CS_1 randomly selects d non-zero numbers $H_{i1}, H_{i2}, \cdots, H_{id} \in \mathbb{Z}_N^*$, and sends the set $\{E_{pk}(m_{i1})^{H_{i1}}, E_{pk}(m_{i2})^{H_{i2}}, \cdots, E_{pk}(m_{id})^{H_{id}}\} to CS_2$.

18:    CS_2 decrypts them, and returns $E_{pk}(\prod_{t=1}^{d} m_{it}H_{it})$ to CS_1.

19:    CS_1 gains $E_{pk}(\prod_{t=1}^{d} m_{it}) = E_{pk}(\prod_{t=1}^{d} m_{it}H_{it})^{G_i}$ where $G_i = \prod_{t=1}^{d} H_{it}^{-1} (\text{mod } N)$.

20: **end for**

21: CS_1 sets $Max_1 = E_{pk}(m_1^{d-1})$, $Max_2 = E_{pk}(\prod_{t=1}^{d} m_{1t})$, and $Ecl = E_{pk}(1)$.

22: **for** $i = 2$ to λ **do**

23:    CS_1 and CS_2 implement $\mathtt{SMRP}()$ protocol (see Protocol 4 for details) that takes as input $\{Ecl, Max_1, Max_2\} \cup \{E_{pk}(i), E_{pk}(m_i^{d-1}), E_{pk}(\prod_{t=1}^{d} m_{it})\}$ and $\{sk\}$, such that CS_1 obtains the updated Ecl, $Max1$ and $Max2$ which satisfy

$$Ecl = \begin{cases} E_{pk}(D_{sk}(Ecl)), & \text{if } \left(m_i^{d-1}D_{sk}(Max_2)\right) \text{ is not less} \\ & \qquad\qquad \text{than } \left(D_{sk}(Max_1)\prod_{t=1}^{d} m_{it}\right), \\ E_{pk}(i), & \text{otherwise.} \end{cases}$$

    $Max_1 = E_{pk}(m_u^{d-1})$, and $Max_2 = E_{pk}(\prod_{t=1}^{d} m_{ut})$ where u denotes $D_{sk}(Ecl)$.

24: **end for**

25: CS_1 selects a random number $\mu_1 \in \mathbb{Z}_N$. Then, CS_1 sends $Ecl * E_{pk}(\mu_1)$ to CS_2, and gives μ_1 to Bob. CS_2 returns $\mu_2 = D_{sk}(Ecl * E_{pk}(\mu_1))$ to Bob.

26: At last, Bob obtains the class label $C_S = \mu_2 - \mu_1$.

and set $B_{kti} = E_{pk}(D_{sk}(A_{kt1}A_{kt2}W_{ki}) \geqslant 3)$, we can ensure $B_{kti} = E_{pk}(1)$ if Alice's k-th sample satisfies its class label is i and t-th dimension equals to S_t,

Protocol 4. Secure Maximum Ratio Protocol (SMRP)

Input: CS$_1$ has two encrypted sets $\{E_{pk}(\alpha), E_{pk}(X_\alpha), E_{pk}(Y_\alpha)\}$ and $\{E_{pk}(\beta), E_{pk}(X_\beta), E_{pk}(Y_\beta)\}$.
CS$_2$ has the secret key (decryption key) sk. Suppose $0 < X_\alpha, X_\beta, Y_\alpha, Y_\beta < 2^\Omega$.

Output: CS$_1$ obtains the output Ecl, Max_1 and Max_2 which satisfy if $X_\beta Y_\alpha \geqslant X_\alpha Y_\beta$ (i.e., the ratio $Y_\alpha/X_\alpha \geqslant Y_\beta/X_\beta$), then $Ecl = E_{pk}(\alpha)$, $Max_1 = E_{pk}(X_\alpha)$ and $Max_2 = E_{pk}(Y_\alpha)$; otherwise $Ecl = E_{pk}(\beta)$, $Max_1 = E_{pk}(X_\beta)$ and $Max_2 = E_{pk}(Y_\beta)$. Neither CS$_1$ nor CS$_2$ can learn the values hidden in the output results Ecl, Max_1 and Max_2.

1: CS$_1$ randomly selects four non-zero number $\theta_1, \theta_2, \theta_3, \theta_4 \in \mathbb{Z}_N^*$, and sends $\{E_{pk}(X_\alpha)^{\theta_1}, E_{pk}(Y_\alpha)^{\theta_2}, E_{pk}(X_\beta)^{\theta_3}, E_{pk}(Y_\beta)^{\theta_4}\}$ to CS$_2$.

2: CS$_2$ decrypts the encrypted values and returns $\{E_{pk}(X_\alpha Y_\beta \theta_1 \theta_4), E_{pk}(X_\beta Y_\alpha \theta_2 \theta_3)\}$ to CS$_1$.

3: CS$_1$ selects a random non-zero number $\delta \in \{1, 2, \cdots, 2^{2\Omega}\}$ and a random number $\phi \in \{0, 1\}$, and then computes $\{\gamma_1, \gamma_2, \gamma_3, \gamma_4\}$ as follows.

4: **if** $\phi = 1$ **then**

5:
$$
\begin{cases}
\gamma_1 = 2\delta(\theta_2 \theta_3)^{-1} \bmod N, \\
\gamma_2 = (N - 2\delta)(\theta_1 \theta_4)^{-1} \bmod N, \\
\gamma_3 = 2^{4\Omega} + \delta, \\
\gamma_4 = 1.
\end{cases}
\tag{18}
$$

6: **else**

7:
$$
\begin{cases}
\gamma_1 = (N - 2\delta)(\theta_2 \theta_3)^{-1} \bmod N, \\
\gamma_2 = 2\delta(\theta_1 \theta_4)^{-1} \bmod N, \\
\gamma_3 = 2^{4\Omega} - \delta, \\
\gamma_4 = N - 1.
\end{cases}
\tag{19}
$$

8: **end if**

9: CS$_1$ selects three random numbers $\omega_1, \omega_2, \omega_3 \in \mathbb{Z}_N$, computes

$$
\begin{cases}
\Phi_1 = E_{pk}(\alpha)^{N-\gamma_4} E_{pk}(\beta)^{\gamma_4} E_{pk}(\omega_1), \\
\Phi_2 = E_{pk}(X_\alpha)^{N-\gamma_4} E_{pk}(X_\beta)^{\gamma_4} E_{pk}(\omega_2), \\
\Phi_3 = E_{pk}(Y_\alpha)^{N-\gamma_4} E_{pk}(Y_\beta)^{\gamma_4} E_{pk}(\omega_3), \\
\Phi_4 = E_{pk}(X_\beta Y_\alpha \theta_2 \theta_3)^{\gamma_1} E_{pk}(X_\alpha Y_\beta \theta_1 \theta_4)^{\gamma_2} E_{pk}(\gamma_3).
\end{cases}
\tag{20}
$$

and sends $\{\Phi_1, \Phi_2, \Phi_3, \Phi_4\}$ to CS$_2$.

10: CS$_2$ decrypts Φ_4, computes $\{\Psi_1, \Psi_2, \Psi_3, \Psi_4\}$ as follows.

11: **if** $D_{sk}(\Phi_4) < 2^{4\Omega}$ **then**

12:
$$
\begin{cases}
\Psi_1 = \Phi_1 R_1^N \bmod N^2, \\
\Psi_2 = \Phi_2 R_2^N \bmod N^2, \\
\Psi_3 = \Phi_3 R_3^N \bmod N^2, \\
\Psi_4 = E_{pk}(1).
\end{cases}
\tag{21}
$$

13: **else**

14:     $\Psi_1 = E_{pk}(0)$, $\Psi_2 = E_{pk}(0)$, $\Psi_3 = E_{pk}(0)$, $\Psi_4 = E_{pk}(0)$.

15: **end if**

Here, R_1, R_2 and R_3 are the random parameters selected from $\mathbb{Z}_N^*$.

16: CS$_2$ returns $\{\Psi_1, \Psi_2, \Psi_3, \Psi_4\}$ to CS$_1$.

17: CS$_1$ sets Ecl, $Max1$ and $Max2$ by the following method.

$$
\begin{cases}
Ecl = \Psi_1 E_{pk}(t) \Psi_4^{N-\omega_1}, \\
Max_1 = \Psi_2 E_{pk}(X_t) \Psi_4^{N-\omega_2}, \\
Max_2 = \Psi_3 E_{pk}(Y_t) \Psi_4^{N-\omega_3}.
\end{cases}
\tag{22}
$$

Here, $t = \alpha$ if $\phi = 1$, otherwise $t = \beta$.

otherwise $B_{kti} = E_{pk}(0)$. That is, m_{it} exactly equals to the number of "1"s hidden in B_{kti} for $k = 1, 2, \cdots, m$. Hence, CS_1 can use B_{kti} to locally compute $E_{pk}(m_{it}) = \prod_{k=1}^{m} B_{kti}$ based on the homomorphic property.

To complete the posterior probability comparison with the Eq. (10), CS_1 needs to further compute $E_{pk}(\prod_{t=1}^{d} m_{it})$. Here, as shown in lines 16 to 20 of Protocol 3, we propose an efficient secure approach to make CS_1 obtain $E_{pk}(\prod_{t=1}^{d} m_{it})$ from $E_{pk}(m_{it})$. In our scheme, CS_1 randomly generates non-zero number $H_{it} \in \mathbb{Z}_N^*$ to preserve m_{it}, and sends $E_{pk}(m_{it} H_{it}) = E_{pk}(m_{it})^{H_{it}}$ to CS_2 for $t = 1, 2, \cdots, d$. Then, CS_2 returns $E_{pk}(\prod_{t=1}^{d} m_{it} H_{it})$ to CS_1, such that the latter can obtain $E_{pk}(\prod_{t=1}^{d} m_{it}) = E_{pk}\left(\prod_{t=1}^{d} m_{it} H_{it}\right)^{G_i}$ where $G_i = \prod_{t=1}^{d} H_{it}^{-1} \bmod N$.

Up to now, CS_1 has gotten $E_{pk}(m_i^{d-1})$ and $E_{pk}(\prod_{t=1}^{d} m_{it})$ for $i = 1, 2, \cdots, \lambda$. At the last phase of our second stage, CS_1 and CS_2 will compute the encrypted class label $E_{pk}(C_S)$ by the mean of Eq. (10). Here, CS_1 first sets the initial values $Ecl = E_{pk}(1)$, $Max_1 = E_{pk}(m_1^{d-1})$ and $Max_2 = E_{pk}(\prod_{t=1}^{d} m_{1t})$. Then, for every $i = 2$ to λ, CS_1 and CS_2 implement SMRP shown in Protocol 4 (we will introduce the SMRP protocol later) such that CS_1 attains an updated Ecl which is $E_{pk}(i)$ if $D_{sk}(Max_1)(\prod_{t=1}^{d} m_{it}) > (m_i^{d-1}) D_{sk}(Max_2)$, or $Ecl_{old} * r^N$ otherwise. Here, Ecl_{old} denotes the value of Ecl before being updated, and $r \in \mathbb{Z}_N^*$ is a random self-blinding parameter of Paillier encryption system. Meanwhile, CS_1 also gains the updated Max_1 and Max_2. Let u denote the plaintext hidden in the updated Ecl, then, the corresponding $Max_1 = E_{pk}(m_u^{d-1})$ and $Max_2 = E_{pk}(\prod_{t=1}^{d} m_{ut})$. It should be remarked that neither CS_1 nor CS_2 can learn any plaintext hidden in Ecl, Max_1 and Max_2.

In [14], Liu et al. lately propose a privacy preserving maximum proto-col (PMAX) to get $E_{pk}(\max\{H_A, H_B\})$ from $E_{pk}(H_A)$ and $E_{pk}(H_B)$. How-ever, PMAX cannot be directly applied to our problem, since we need to compare $D_{sk}(Max_1)(\prod_{t=1}^{d} m_{it})$ and $(m_i^{d-1}) D_{sk}(Max_2)$, i.e., the product of hidden plaintexts. For tackling the challenging problem, we improve PMAX and propose SMRP to support our applications. In our SMRP, we use $\{E_{pk}(\alpha), E_{pk}(X_\alpha), E_{pk}(Y_\alpha)\}$ and $\{E_{pk}(\beta), E_{pk}(X_\beta), E_{pk}(Y_\beta)\}$ to denote the input set of CS_1. Here, α (or β) is a class label, and the corresponding $E_{pk}(m_\alpha^{d-1})$ and $E_{pk}(\prod_{t=1}^{d} m_{\alpha t})$ are $E_{pk}(X_\alpha)$ and $E_{pk}(Y_\alpha)$, respectively. The output, known to CS_1 only, is denoted as $\{Ecl, Max_1, Max_2\}$ which is the first or second input set of CS_1 according to the comparison result of $X_\beta Y_\alpha$ and $X_\alpha Y_\beta$. Remarkably, CS_1 cannot know $\{Ecl, Max_1, Max_2\}$ is his first or second input set, because the encrypted values have been self-blinded with random parameters.

Assume $0 < X_\alpha, X_\beta, Y_\alpha, Y_\beta < 2^\Omega$. For the data privacy, SMRP uses the random $\theta_1, \theta_2, \theta_3, \theta_4 \in \mathbb{Z}_N^*$ to protect X_α, Y_α, X_β, Y_β, and CS_1 sends $\{E_{pk}(X_\alpha)^{\theta_1}, E_{pk}(Y_\alpha)^{\theta_2}, E_{pk}(X_\beta)^{\theta_3}, E_{pk}(Y_\beta)^{\theta_4}\}$ to CS_2 who returns the cipher-text $E_{pk}(X_\alpha Y_\beta \theta_1 \theta_4)$ and $E_{pk}(X_\beta Y_\alpha \theta_2 \theta_3)$ to CS_1. Next, we will introduce the main process to make CS_1 obtain $Ecl = E_{pk}(\alpha)$ if $X_\beta Y_\alpha \geqslant X_\alpha Y_\beta$ holds, or $Ecl = E_{pk}(\beta)$ otherwise. The corresponding output $\{Max_1, Max_2\}$ (which is $\{E_{pk}(X_\alpha), E_{pk}(Y_\alpha)\}$ or $\{E_{pk}(X_\beta), E_{pk}(Y_\beta)\}$) can be achieved by the similar methods. For computing Ecl, CS_1 first selects two random numbers $0 < \delta < 2^{2\Omega}$ and $\omega_1 \in \mathbb{Z}_N$ to protect the private data from CS_2. Then, CS_1 sends CS_2 Φ_1 and Φ_4 which are decided by CS_1's coin-toss $\phi \in \{0,1\}$. If $\phi = 1$, CS_1 sets $\Phi_1 = E_{pk}(\beta - \alpha + \omega_1) = E_{pk}(\alpha)^{N-1}E_{pk}(\beta)E_{pk}(\omega_1)$ and $\Phi_4 = E_{pk}\left(\delta(2X_\beta Y_\alpha + 1 - 2X_\alpha Y_\beta) + 2^{4\Omega}\right)$; otherwise $\Phi_1 = E_{pk}(\alpha - \beta + \omega_1) = E_{pk}(\alpha)E_{pk}(\beta)^{N-1}E_{pk}(\omega_1)$ and $\Phi_4 = E_{pk}\left(\delta(2X_\alpha Y_\beta - 2X_\beta Y_\alpha - 1) + 2^{4\Omega}\right)$. After receiving Φ_4, CS_2 can learn whether $(D_{sk}(\Phi_4) - 2^{4\Omega})$ is larger than 0 or not. Nevertheless, CS_2 does not know it indicates $2X_\beta Y_\alpha + 1 > 2X_\alpha Y_\beta$ or $2X_\alpha Y_\beta > 2X_\beta Y_\alpha + 1$, owing to the confidentiality of CS_1's coin-toss ϕ. According to the value of $D_{sk}(\Phi_4)$, CS_2 sets $\Psi_1 = E_{pk}(0)$ and $\Psi_4 = E_{pk}(0)$ if $D_{sk}(\Phi_4) - 2^{4\Omega} > 0$; otherwise $\Psi_1 = \Phi_1 * R_1^N$ and $\Psi_4 = E_{pk}(1)$. Here, $R_1 \in \mathbb{Z}_N^*$ is a random self-blinding parameter. The intention that CS_2 blinds Φ_1 is to preserve CS_1 from learning whether Ψ_1 and Φ_1 hides the same plaintext or not, and further to keep CS_1 from any information about the class label hidden in the output Ecl. At last, CS_1 computes $\Psi_1\Psi_4^{N-\omega_1}$ which is $E_{pk}(0)$ or $E_{pk}(D_{sk}(\Phi_1) - \omega_1)$, and attains $Ecl = \Psi_1 E_{pk}(\alpha)\Psi_4^{N-\omega_1}$ if his coin-toss $\phi = 1$; otherwise $Ecl = \Psi_1 E_{pk}(\beta)\Psi_4^{N-\omega_1}$. The correctness of Ecl can be guaranteed as follows.

While CS_1's coin-toss $\phi = 1$, CS_1 sends $\Phi_1 = E_{pk}(\beta - \alpha + \omega_1)$ and $\Phi_4 = E_{pk}\left(\delta(2X_\beta Y_\alpha + 1 - 2X_\alpha Y_\beta) + 2^{4\Omega}\right)$ to CS_2. Then, we have $D_{sk}(\Phi_4) - 2^{4\Omega} > 0$ if and only if $2X_\beta Y_\alpha + 1 > 2X_\alpha Y_\beta$, i.e., $X_\beta Y_\alpha \geqslant X_\alpha Y_\beta$. Thus, $\Psi_1\Psi_4^{N-\omega_1}$ will be $E_{pk}(0)$ if $X_\beta Y_\alpha \geqslant X_\alpha Y_\beta$, and CS_1 can obtain $Ecl = \Psi_1 E_{pk}(\alpha)\Psi_4^{N-\omega_1} = E_{pk}(\alpha)$. On the contrary (namely, $X_\beta Y_\alpha < X_\alpha Y_\beta$), $\Psi_1\Psi_4^{N-\omega_1}$ will be $E_{pk}(\beta - \alpha)$, and CS_1 will attain $Ecl = \Psi_1 E_{pk}(\alpha)\Psi_4^{N-\omega_1} = E_{pk}(\beta)$.

While CS_1's coin-toss $\phi = 0$, CS_1 sends $\Phi_1 = E_{pk}(\alpha - \beta + \omega_1)$ and $\Phi_4 = E_{pk}\left(\delta(2X_\alpha Y_\beta - 2X_\beta Y_\alpha - 1) + 2^{4\Omega}\right)$ to CS_2. Then, we have $D_{sk}(\Phi_4) - 2^{4\Omega} > 0$ if and only if $2X_\alpha Y_\beta > 2X_\beta Y_\alpha + 1$, i.e., $X_\alpha Y_\beta > X_\beta Y_\alpha$. Therefore, $\Psi_1\Psi_4^{N-\omega_1}$ will be $E_{pk}(0)$ if $X_\alpha Y_\beta > X_\beta Y_\alpha$, and CS_1 can obtain $Ecl = \Psi_1 E_{pk}(\beta)\Psi_4^{N-\omega_1} = E_{pk}(\beta)$. On the contrary (namely, $X_\beta Y_\alpha \geqslant X_\alpha Y_\beta$), $\Psi_1\Psi_4^{N-\omega_1}$ will be $E_{pk}(\alpha - \beta)$, and CS_1 will attain $Ecl = \Psi_1 E_{pk}(\beta)\Psi_4^{N-\omega_1} = E_{pk}(\alpha)$.

After achieving the final Ecl, CS_1 perturbs it with a random $\mu_1 \in \mathbb{Z}_N$, and sends $Ecl * E_{pk}(\mu_1)$ to CS_2. Then, CS_1 returns μ_1 to Bob, and CS_2 returns $\mu_2 = D_{sk}(Ecl * E_{pk}(\mu_1)) = C_S + \mu_1$ to Bob. At last, Bob can obtain his class label $C_S = \mu_2 - \mu_1$, which correctly completes the naïve Bayesian classification for the sample S.

4   Evaluation

In this section, we prove the security of our scheme, and then analyze our cost in computation and communication.

4.1   Security

We consider the security of our scheme under semi-honest model. That is, each participant is assumed to correctly follow the stated steps. Additionally, we assume CS_1 and CS_2 do not collude with each other. Our scheme can be proved securely through following four theorems.

Theorem 1 *(Security of Protocol 1). Our first stage is secure. Namely, no information about Alice's dataset is disclosed to CS_1 or CS_2 throughout our first stage.*

Theorem 2 *(Security of Protocol 2). Our SCTC protocol is secure. No useful information is disclosed to CS_1 or CS_2.*

Theorem 3 *(Security of Protocol 4). Our SMRP protocol is secure. CS_1 or CS_2 cannot learn or deduce about any information about useful information.*

Theorem 4 *(Security of Protocol 3). Our second stage is secure. No information about Alice's dataset and Bob's query are disclosed to Alice's dataset. And Bob can only obtain the class label.*

The proof process about each theorem above can be found in Appendix.

4.2 Computation and Communication Complexity

In this section, we will analyze our computation cost and communication overheads, respectively. The computation and communication complexity of our scheme is shown in Table 1, where $\mathcal{K}$ is the encryption key size. The detail about computation and communication cost process is shown in Appendix.

Table 1. Computational and communication complexity of our scheme

Approach	Computation cost		Communication
	Encryptions	Exponentiations	
First stage	$O(m\lambda)$	$O(m\lambda)$	$O(m\lambda\mathcal{K})$
SCTC protocol	$O(1)$	$O(1)$	$O(\mathcal{K})$
SMRP protocol	$O(1)$	$O(1)$	$O(\mathcal{K})$
Second stage	$O(m\lambda d)$	$O(m\lambda d)$	$O(m\lambda d\mathcal{K})$

5 Related Work

We simple review the related work as follows. Privacy preserving Bayes classification scheme was first studied in distributed environment where dataet is horizontally partitioned or vertically partitioned. Kantarcioglu *et al.* [10] first devised a privacy-preserving naive Bayes classification for horizontally partitioned data by adopting secure sum protocol [4] and private $\ln x$ protocol [12]. Yang et al. [20] proposed a protocol for vertically partitioned customer data. This privacy-preserving naive Bayes classification was achieved by using the additively homomorphic property of a variant of ElGamal encryption [7]. Yi and Zhang [22] achieved naive Bayes classification over horizontally partitioned data by two non-colluding mixers private $\ln x$ protocol [12]. However, in the privacy-preserving naive Bayes classification on distributed data, each participant can access a part of the dataset. It is not suitable to our outsourcing scene, since the cloud in our problem cannot learn any plaintext of the input dataset.

Recently, with the popularity of cloud computing, many privacy-preserving protocols have been proposed to solve the problem of secure analysis encrypted data in the cloud. Samanthula *et al.* [19] proposed a protocol for secure evaluation of range queries in the cloud computing environment by devising a secure bit-decomposition protocol which can convert an encrypted integer z into encryptions of the individual bits of z. Elmehdwi *et al.* [8] proposed a set of secure primitives which are based on additively homomorphic encryption (e.g., Paillier encryption system [17]) and two non-colluding could servers. These primitive protocols assume there are two non-colluding cloud service providers, one of which stores users' encrypted data and another holds users' secret key. These two non-colluding cloud servers could implement computation tasks by using secure multi-party computation. Elmehdwi *et al.* then use these secure primitives to construct secure k-NN query scheme in [8] and secure k-NN classification scheme in [18]. Liu *et al.* [13] develop some secure protocols for secure similarity evaluation of encrypted trajectories outsourced to the cloud. These secure protocols are implemented based on secure primitives in [8], Paillier homomorphic encryption system and Yao's garbled circuit [9,21]. The recent works [24,25] study secure k-NN query over encrypted data in cloud, but they cannot support secure naïve Bayesian classification. Yuan *et al.* [23] proposed privacy preserving back-propagation neural network over arbitrarily partitioned data. In Yuan *et al.*'s scheme, all parties encrypt data by using BGN homomorphic encryption algorithm [2], which supports one multiplication and multiple addition operations, and upload encrypted data to the cloud. The cloud can implement back-propagation neural network with the help of all parties and the homomorphic property of BGN encryption. Liu *et al.* [14] achieved privacy preserving Bayes classification over encrypted disease data by using additive homomorphic proxy aggregation scheme in [6], Paillier encryption system in [17] and secure multiplication protocol in [8]. Nevertheless, no existing work can outsource the entire computation task of naïve Bayesian classification to cloud.

6   Conclusions

In this paper, we investigated naïve Bayesian classification on encrypted dataset in cloud and proposed a semantically secure scheme for the challenging problem. Our scheme enables all the computation task of naïve Bayesian classification to be completed by the cloud, and thus can dramatically reduce the burden of data owner and users. Besides, our scheme can guarantee the security of both input dataset and output classification results, and the cloud can learn nothing useful about the data of data owner and users. At last, theoretical analysis and evaluation indicated the security and computation/communication complexity of our proposed scheme.

Acknowledgements. We thank the anonymous reviewers and our shepherd, Prof. Xun Yi, for their valuable feedbacks. This work is partly supported by the Natural Science Foundation of Jiangsu Province of China (No. BK20150760), the Fundamental Research Funds for the Central Universities (No. NZ2015108, NS2016094), the China Postdoctoral Science Foundation funded project (No. 2015M571752), and the Natural Science Foundation of China (No. 61472470).

Appendix

Paillier Cryptosystem. Paillier [17] proposed an efficient public key cryptosystem with semantic security (indistinguishability under chosen plaintext attack, IND-CPA). The encryption scheme is additively homomorphic, i.e.,

$$E_{pk}(m_1, r_1) \times E_{pk}(m_2, r_2) = E_{pk}(m_1 + m_2, r_1 r_2), \tag{23}$$

$$E_{pk}(m_1, r_1)^\kappa = E_{pk}(\kappa \times m_1, r_1^\kappa). \tag{24}$$

Here, E denotes the encryption function, m_1 and m_2 are arbitrary messages in plaintext space, pk is the public key, r_1 and r_2 are random parameters for encryption, $E_{pk}(m_1, r_1)$ denotes the encrypted result of m_1 using the random parameter r_1, and κ is a positive integer. In this paper, we also use $E_{pk}(m_1)$ to denote the encrypted value of m_1 while it is unnecessary to emphasize the random parameter. We briefly review the main steps of the encryption system as follows.

Key Generation. Select two large enough primes p and q. Then, the secret key sk is $s = \text{lcm}(p-1, q-1)$, that is, the least common multiple of $p-1$ and $q-1$. The public key pk is (N, g), where $N = pq$ and $g \in \mathbb{Z}_{N^2}^*$ such that $\gcd\left(L(g^s \bmod N^2), N\right) = 1$, that is, the maximal common divisor of $L(g^s \bmod N^2)$ and N is equivalent to 1. Here, $L(x) = (x-1)/N$, the same below.

Encryption. Let m_0 be a number in plaintext space $\mathbb{Z}_N$. Select a random $r \in \mathbb{Z}_N^*$ as the secret parameter, then the ciphertext c_0 of m_0 is $c_0 = g^{m_0} r^N \bmod N^2$.

Decryption. Let $c_0 \in \mathbb{Z}_{N^2}$ be a ciphertext. The plaintext hidden in c_0 is

$$m_0 = \frac{L(c_0^s \bmod N^2)}{L(g^s \bmod N^2)} \bmod N.$$

Paillier homomorphic encryption system is an important secure building block to be used in our scheme. As a probabilistic encryption, Paillier homomorphic encryption system also has the self-blinding property, that is, $E_{pk}(m_0, r_1) * r_2^N = E_{pk}(m_0, r_1 r_2)$ and $m_0 = D_{sk}(E_{pk}(m_0, r_1)) = D_{sk}\left(E_{pk}(m_0, r_1) * r_2^N\right)$ for any $r_2 \in \mathbb{Z}_N^*$.

For simplicity, we also use $E_{pk}(m_0)$ to denote the encrypted result of m_0 while it is no need to emphasize the random parameter r.

Description about SCTC. In SCTC, CS_1 holds the ciphertext $\{E_{pk}(X), E_{pk}(Y)\}$, and CS_2 holds secret key. SCTC enables CS_1 to obtain an output Γ which satisfies $\Gamma = E_{pk}(1)$ if $X \geqslant Y$, otherwise $\Gamma = E_{pk}(0)$. It is remarked that CS_1 and CS_2 cannot know any plaintext hidden in $E_{pk}(X), E_{pk}(Y)$ and Γ throughout SCTC. The main steps of SCTC are as follows.

Assume $0 \leqslant X, Y < 2^\Omega$. We have $0 \leqslant (2X + 1), 2Y < 2^{\Omega+1}$. Besides, $X \geqslant Y$ if and only if $2X + 1 > 2Y$. In SCTC, CS_1 selects a random positive number $\delta < 2^{\Omega+1}$, and sends Φ to CS_2, where Φ equals to the ciphertext $E_{pk}\left(\delta(2X + 1 - 2Y) + 2^{\Omega+2}\right)$ or $E_{pk}\left(\delta(2Y - 2X - 1) + 2^{\Omega+2}\right)$ with the same probability 50%. Here, Φ can be locally achieved by CS_1 using the following equations based on the homomorphic property.

$$E_{pk}\left(\delta(2X + 1 - 2Y) + 2^{\Omega+2}\right) = E_{pk}(X)^{2\delta} E_{pk}(Y)^{N-2\delta} E_{pk}(2^{2\Omega+2} + \delta).$$

$$E_{pk}\left(\delta(2Y - 2X - 1) + 2^{\Omega+2}\right) = E_{pk}(X)^{N-2\delta} E_{pk}(Y)^{2\delta} E_{pk}(2^{2\Omega+2} - \delta).$$

After receiving Φ, CS_2 can learn whether $D_{sk}(\Phi) > 2^{2\Omega+2}$ which indicates the size relationship of $(2X + 1)$ and $2Y$. Nevertheless, CS_2 cannot know it is $2X+1 > 2Y$ or $2Y > 2X+1$, since CS_2 has no idea which value is set as Φ by CS_1. CS_2 tells CS_1 whether $D_{sk}(\Phi) > 2^{2\Omega+2}$ or not in encrypted form $\Psi = E_{pk}(1)$ or $E_{pk}(0)$. At last, CS_1 can obtain the comparison result (in encrypted form) of $2X + 1 > 2Y$ by setting $\Gamma = \Psi$ if selecting the first value as Φ, otherwise $\Gamma = E_{pk}(1 - D_{sk}(\Psi)) = E_{pk}(1)\Psi^{N-1}$ which is just the comparison result of $X \geqslant Y$. During the execution of SCTC, CS_1 can only access the encrypted values $E_{pk}(X), E_{pk}(Y), \Psi$ and Γ. CS_2 can decrypt Φ, but cannot learn useful information about X and Y, owing to the randomness of δ and CS_1's coin-toss ϕ. Thus, the plaintext hidden in the input/output ciphertext will be well protected from both CS_1 and CS_2.

Security Proof. The proof of Theorem 1.

Proof. In the following, we consider the view of CS_1 and CS_2, respectively.

CS_1: In our first stage shown in Protocol 1, CS_1 can access nothing but the encrypted values $E_{pk}(C_k)$, Y_{ki} and $E_{pk}\left((m_i P_i)^{d-1}\right)$ for each $k = 1, 2, \cdots, m$ and $i = 1, 2, \cdots, \lambda$. Thus, CS_1 cannot learn any useful information about the plaintext hidden in the encrypted values, owing to the semantic security (IND-CPA) of Paillier homomorphic encryption system.

CS_2: In Protocol 1, CS_2 holds the secret key sk, and he can also receive $\Pi_k(\boldsymbol{X}_k)$ (for each $k = 1, 2, \cdots, m$) and $E_{pk}(m_i P_i)$ (for each $i = 1, 2, \cdots, \lambda$). Through decrypting, CS_2 can attain $\Pi_k\left(R_{k1}(C_k - 1), R_{k1}(C_k - 2), \cdots, R_{k1}(C_k - \lambda)\right)$ and $m_i P_i$. Because P_i is randomly selected from $\mathbb{Z}_N^*$, CS_2 can learn nothing about m_i (in this paper, we have assumed $m_i > 0$). For each C_k, it has $1 \leqslant C_k \leqslant \lambda$, thus it must be one and only one $R_{ki}(C_k - i)$ equals to 0 for all $i \in \{1, 2, \cdots, \lambda\}$. Due to the randomness of R_{ki}, CS_2 can only know some $R_{ki}(C_k - i) = 0$, i.e., some i meets $C_k - i = 0$. Nevertheless, CS_2 does not know which i satisfies $R_{ki}(C_k - i) = 0$, on account of the random permutation Π_k. Therefore, CS_2 can learn nothing during our first stage.

To sum up, no information about Alice's dataset is disclosed to CS_1 or CS_2 throughout our first stage. Our first stage is secure. It completes our proof of Theorem 1.

The proof of Theorem 2.

Proof. We consider the view of CS_1 and CS_2 as follows.

CS_1: In SCTC protocol, i.e., Protocol 2, CS_1 can obtain the values $E_{pk}(X)$, $E_{pk}(Y)$ and Ψ in total. All the three values are the ciphertext of Paillier homomorphic encryption system. Based on its semantic security (IND-CPA), CS_1 cannot learn any useful information about the plaintext hidden in the encrypted values $E_{pk}(X)$, $E_{pk}(Y)$ and Ψ.

CS_2: In Protocol 2, CS_2 can receive Φ only. After decrypting Φ, CS_2 can get $\left(\delta(2X+1-2Y)+2^{2\Omega+2}\right)$ or $\left(\delta(2Y-2X-1)+2^{2\Omega+2}\right)$ with the same probability 50 %. Nevertheless, δ is a random number holden by CS_1. Thus, CS_2 can learn no useful information about X or Y from the decrypted result of Φ.

In all, our SCTC is secure, which completes the proof of Theorem 2.

The proof of Theorem 3.

Proof. Our SMRP protocol, namely Protocol 4, also consists of two participants: CS_1 and CS_2. We will consider their view during the protocol, respectively.

CS_1: In Protocol 4, in addition to the input of himself, CS_1 can attain the set $\{E_{pk}(X_\alpha Y_\beta \theta_1 \theta_4), E_{pk}(X_\beta Y_\alpha \theta_2 \theta_3)\}$ and $\{\Psi_1, \Psi_2, \Psi_3, \Psi_4\}$. From the former encrypted data set, CS_1 can infer nothing, because of the semantic security (IND-CPA) of Paillier homomorphic encryption system.

For Ψ_i $(i = 1, 2, 3)$, it is either $E_{pk}(0)$ or a blinded Φ_i. It is easy to say CS_1 cannot efficiently distinguish Ψ_i from any other value in ciphertext space, based on the semantic security.

Additionally, $\Psi_4 = E_{pk}(1)$ or $E_{pk}(0)$. Hence, CS_1 cannot deduce any plaintext hidden in Ψ_4, owing to the security of Paillier encryption system.

CS_2: In SMRP protocol, CS_2 can access secret key and the encrypted value set $\{E_{pk}(X_\alpha \theta_1), E_{pk}(Y_\alpha \theta_2), E_{pk}(X_\beta \theta_3), E_{pk}(Y_\beta \theta_4)\}$, $\{\Phi_1, \Phi_2, \Phi_3, \Phi_4\}$. Because of the randomness of $\{\theta_1, \theta_2, \theta_3, \theta_4\}$, the values $\{X_\alpha, Y_\alpha, X_\beta, Y_\beta\}$ can be securely protected from CS_2.

By decrypting $\{\Phi_1, \Phi_2, \Phi_3\}$, CS_2 can get the set $\{\beta - \alpha + \omega_1, X_\beta - X_\alpha + \omega_2, Y_\beta - Y_\alpha + \omega_3\}$ or $\{\alpha - \beta + \omega_1, X_\alpha - X_\beta + \omega_2, Y_\alpha - Y_\beta + \omega_3\}$ with the same probability 50 %. Since the random $\omega_1, \omega_2, \omega_3 \in \mathbb{Z}_N$, CS_2 can learn nothing about $\{\alpha, \beta, X_\alpha, X_\beta, Y_\alpha, Y_\beta\}$.

From Φ_4, CS_2 can obtain $\delta(2X_\beta Y_\alpha + 1 - 2X_\alpha Y_\beta) + 2^{4\Omega}$ or $\delta(2X_\alpha Y_\beta - 2X_\beta Y_\alpha - 1) + 2^{4\Omega}$ with 50 % probability both. Since the random δ is holden by CS_1, CS_2 cannot learn any useful information by decrypting Φ_4.

Overall, CS_1 or CS_2 can learn nothing useful about $\{\alpha, \beta, X_\alpha, X_\beta, Y_\alpha, Y_\beta\}$, thus SMRP protocol is secure, and we complete the proof of Theorem 3.

The proof of Theorem 4.

Proof. Our second stage involves three participants: CS_1, CS_2, Bob. We will consider the view of them, respectively.

Bob: Apart from his unlabeled sample S, Bob only can receive μ_1 and μ_2 from the cloud. μ_1 is a random selected by CS_1, and $\mu_2 = D_{sk}(Ecl) + \mu_1$. Then, Bob can obtain nothing but $D_{sk}(Ecl)$ which is just the class label of his sample S using naïve Bayesian classification. That is, Bob can learn nothing about the data of Alice.

CS_1: Apart from employing SCTC and SMRP, there is a **for** loop (line 16 to 20) in our second stage shown in Protocol 3. In the **for** loop, CS_1 can access nothing but $E_{pk}(\prod_{t=1}^d m_{it}H_{it})$. Thus, CS_1 cannot learn any useful information about the data of Alice and Bob, based on the security of SCTC, SMRP, and Paillier encryption system.

CS_2: Similarly, CS_2 can only gain secret key and $E_{pk}(m_{it}H_{it})$ for each $t = 1$, $2, \cdots, d$. Here, each H_{it} is randomly selected by CS_1 from $\mathbb{Z}_N^*$. Therefore, every m_{it} can be well preserved from CS_2.

In all, our second stage can ensure that Bob can obtain only the class label of his sample, and the cloud can learn nothing useful about the data of Alice and Bob. Our second stage is thus secure, which completes the proof of Theorem 4.

The analysis procedure of computation and communication complexity in detail are shown as follow.

Computation Complexity. In Protocol 1 (namely our first stage), Eqs. (11) and (12) need to be done $m\lambda$ times, which leads to $m\lambda$ encryptions and $2m\lambda$ exponentiations. From lines 10 to 15, λ encryptions and 4λ exponentiations are performed to calculate all $E_{pk}(m_i^{d-1})$ (for $i = 1, 2, \cdots, \lambda$). Based on the above analysis, the total computation complexity of Protocol 1 is bounded by $O(m\lambda)$ encryptions and $O(m\lambda)$ exponentiations.

In SCTC protocol, two encryptions and exponentiations are performed to compute Φ (line 3 and line 5). In addition, considering Eq. (13) acquires one encryption and Eq. (14) needs one exponentiation, the total computation complexity of SCTC Protocol is bounded by $O(1)$ encryptions and $O(1)$ exponentiations.

In SMRP protocol, one encryption and four exponentiations are performed to compute ciphertext multiplication from lines 1 to 8. The rest part of this protocol needs five encryptions and fourteen exponentiations to acquire the maximum of two ciphertexts. Therefore, the total computation complexity of SMRP Protocol is bounded by $O(1)$ encryptions and $O(1)$ exponentiations as well.

In Protocol 3 (namely our second stage), SCTC protocol (line 4 and line 7) is performed $m(\lambda+2)d$ times to get the comparative result of multiple ciphertexts. From lines 16 to 20, it takes one encryption and $d+1$ exponentiations to compute multiple ciphertext multiplication. From lines 22 to 24, SMRP protocol (line 23) needs to be done $\lambda - 1$ times. Based on the aforementioned analysis, SCTC protocol is bounded by $O(1)$ encryptions and $O(1)$ exponentiations. Besides, the SMRP protocol is also bounded by $O(1)$ encryptions and $O(1)$ exponentiations.

Therefore, the total complexity of Protocol 3 is bounded by $O(m\lambda d)$ encryptions and $O(m\lambda d)$ exponentiations.

Communication Complexity. In our first stage, i.e., Protocol 1, CS_1 needs to send $m + 1$ λ-dimensional vectors to CS_2 who returns CS_1 $m + 1$ corresponding λ-dimensional vectors. Considering all the data transferred between two clouds are in encrypted form, the whole communication complexity in first stage is bounded by $O(m\lambda\mathcal{K})$ bits, where $\mathcal{K}$ is the encryption key size.

In SCTC protocol, there is only two ciphertexts transferred between CS_1 and CS_2, which means communication complexity in SCTC protocol is bounded by $O(\mathcal{K})$ bits.

In SMRP protocol, the number of ciphertexts sent by CS_1 and CS_2 is seventeen. Thus, the communication complexity in this protocol is bounded by $O(\mathcal{K})$ bits.

In our second stage (namely Protocol 3), SCTC protocol needs to be done $m(\lambda + 2)d$ times, which leads to $2m(\lambda + 2)d$ ciphertexts transferred between CS_1 and CS_2. In addition, while computing $E_{pk}(\prod_{t=1}^{d} m_{it})$, CS_1 sends λd ciphertexts to CS_2 who returns λ ciphertexts to CS_1. At last, $17(\lambda - 1)$ ciphertexts need to be transmitted between CS_1 and CS_2, while CS_1 and CS_2 implement $\lambda - 1$ times SMRP protocol. Therefore, the communication complexity in Protocol 3 is bounded by $O(m\lambda d\mathcal{K})$ bits.

References

1. Bellazzi, R., Zupan, B.: Predictive data mining in clinical medicine: current issues and guidelines. Int. J. Med. Inform. **77**(2), 81–97 (2008)
2. Boneh, D., Goh, E.-J., Nissim, K.: Evaluating 2-DNF formulas on ciphertexts. In: Kilian, J. (ed.) TCC 2005. LNCS, vol. 3378, pp. 325–341. Springer, Heidelberg (2005). doi:10.1007/978-3-540-30576-7_18
3. Bost, R., Popa, R.A., Tu, S., Goldwasser, S.: Machine learning classification over encrypted data. In: The Network and Distributed System Security Symposium (NDSS), pp. 1–14 (2015)
4. Clifton, C., Kantarcioglu, M., Vaidya, J., Lin, X., Zhu, M.Y.: Tools for privacy preserving distributed data mining. ACM Sigkdd Explorations Newslett. **4**(2), 28–34 (2002)
5. Clifton, C., Vaidya, J., Kantarcioglu, M.: Privacy-preserving naïve Bayes classification. VLDB J. **17**(4), 879–898 (2008)
6. Dong, C., Chen, L., Camenisch, J., Russello, G.: Fair private set intersection with a semi-trusted arbiter. In: Wang, L., Shafiq, B. (eds.) DBSec 2013. LNCS, vol. 7964, pp. 128–144. Springer, Heidelberg (2013)
7. Elgamal, T.: A public key cryptosystem and a signature scheme based on discrete logarithms. IEEE Trans. Inf. Theory **31**(4), 469–472 (1985)
8. Elmehdwi, Y., Samanthula, B.K., Jiang, W.: Secure k-nearest neighbor query over encrypted data in outsourced environments. In: IEEE 30th International Conference on Data Engineering (ICDE), pp. 664–675 (2014)
9. Goldreich, O.: Foundations of Cryptography: Volume II, Basic Applications. Cambridge University Press, Cambridge (2004)

10. Kantarcıoglu, M., Vaidya, J., Clifton, C.: Privacy preserving naive Bayes classifier for horizontally partitioned data. In: IEEE ICDM workshop on privacy preserving data mining, pp. 3–9 (2003)
11. Kim, H.J., Kim, J.U., Ra, Y.G.: Boosting naïve Bayes text classification using uncertainty-based selective sampling. Neurocomputing **67**, 403–410 (2005)
12. Lindell, Y., Pinkas, B.: Privacy preserving data mining. J. Cryptology **15**(3), 36–54 (2002)
13. Liu, A., Zhengy, K., Liz, L., Liu, G., Zhao, L., Zhou, X.: Efficient secure similarity computation on encrypted trajectory data. In: IEEE 31st International Conference on Data Engineering (ICDE), pp. 66–77 (2015)
14. Liu, X., Lu, R., Ma, J., Chen, L., Qin, B.: Privacy-preserving patient-centric clinical decision support system on naive Bayesian classification. IEEE J. Biomed. Health Inform. **20**(2), 655–668 (2016)
15. Lops, P., Gemmis, M.D., Semeraro, G.: Content-based recommender systems: state of the art and trends. In: Recommender Systems Handbook, pp. 73–105 (2011)
16. Mitchell, T.: Machine Learning, 1st edn. McGraw-Hill Science/Engineering/Math, New York (1997)
17. Paillier, P.: Public-key cryptosystems based on composite degree residuosity classes. In: Stern, J. (ed.) EUROCRYPT 1999. LNCS, vol. 1592, pp. 223–238. Springer, Heidelberg (1999)
18. Samanthula, B.K., Elmehdwi, Y., Jiang, W.: k-nearest neighbor classification over semantically secure encrypted relational data. IEEE Trans. Knowl. Data Eng. **27**(5), 1261–1273 (2015)
19. Samanthula, B.K., Jiang, W.: Efficient privacy-preserving range queries over encrypted data in cloud computing. In: IEEE Sixth International Conference on Cloud Computing, pp. 51–58 (2013)
20. Yang, Z., Zhong, S., Wright, R.N.: Privacy-preserving classification of customer data without loss of accuracy. In: Siam International Conference on Data Mining, pp. 92–102 (2005)
21. Yao, A.: How to generate and exchange secrets. In: 27th Annual Symposium on Foundations of Computer Science, pp. 162–167. IEEE (1986)
22. Yi, X., Zhang, Y.: Privacy-preserving naive Bayes classification on distributed data via semi-trusted mixers. Inform. Syst. **34**(3), 371–380 (2009)
23. Yuan, J., Yu, S.: Privacy preserving back-propagation neural network learning made practical with cloud computing. IEEE Trans. Parallel Distrib. Syst. **25**(1), 212–221 (2014)
24. Zhu, Y., Huang, Z., Takagi, T.: Secure and controllable k-nn query over encrypted cloud data with key confidentiality. J. Parallel Distrib. Comput. **89**, 1–12 (2016)
25. Zhu, Y., Wang, Z., Zhang, Y.: Secure k-NN query on encrypted cloud data with limited key-disclosure and offline data owner. In: The 20th Pacific-Asia Conference on Knowledge Discovery and Data Mining, pp. 401–414 (2016)

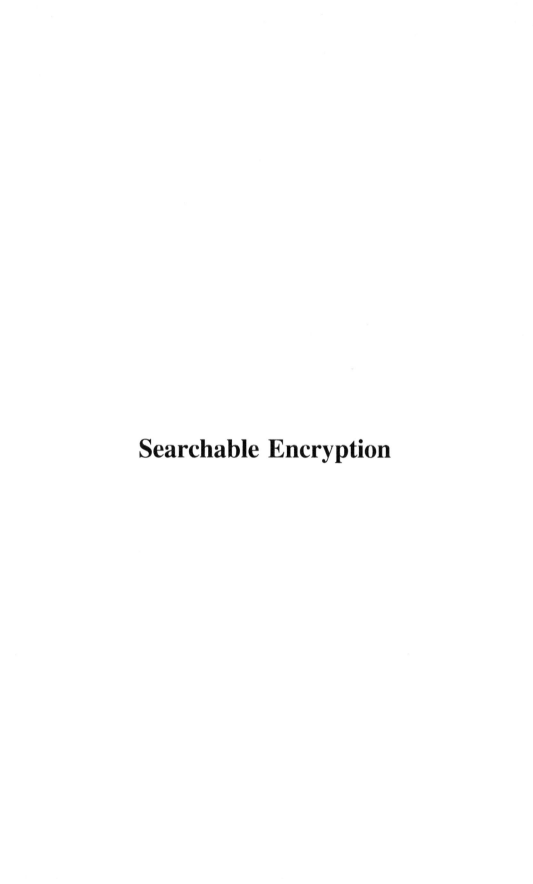

Searchable Encryption

Integrity Preserving Multi-keyword Searchable Encryption for Cloud Computing

Fucai Zhou[1]($\boxtimes$), Yuxi Li[1], Alex X. Liu[2], Muqing Lin[3], and Zifeng Xu[1]

[1] Software College, Northeastern University,
Shenyang 110819, Liaoning, China
fczhou@mail.neu.edu.cn
[2] The Department of Computer Science and Engineering,
Michigan State University, East Lansing, MI 48824, USA
[3] The College of Information Science and Engineering, Northeastern University,
Shenyang 110819, Liaoning, China

Abstract. Searchable symmetric encryption is an efficient way to perform keyword search over encrypted data in cloud storage. However, most existing methods do not take into account the integrity verification of the search result. Moreover, existing methods can only verify the integrity of single-keyword search results, which cannot meet the requirements of multi-keyword conjunctive search. To address this problem, we proposed a multi-keyword searchable encryption scheme with an authentication mechanism that can efficiently verify the integrity of search results. The proposed scheme is based on the searchable symmetric encryption and adopts the bilinear map accumulator to prove the correctness of set operations. It supports multiple keywords as input for conjunctive search and gives the server the ability to prove the integrity of the search result to the user. Formal proofs show that the proposed scheme is unforgeable and adaptive secure against chosen-keyword attacks. To the best of our knowledge, this is the first work that can authenticate the multi-keyword search result over encrypted data.

Keywords: Conjunctive keyword search · Integrity authentication · Searchable encryption · Secure cloud storage

1 Introduction

Cloud computing is an innovative Internet-based computing paradigm that enables cloud users to move out their data and applications to a remote cloud in order to deploy scalable and elastic services on demand without having to provision a data center. However, while cloud computing has many advantages, it has not been widely used. According to a survey lunched by Twin Strata in 2015, only 38 % of organizations would like to put their inactive data stored in public cloud; about 24 % of users were using cloud storage for data backup, archiving and disaster recovery. This shows that the issue of data security [1, 2] is one of the major obstacles to the promotion of cloud

© Springer International Publishing AG 2016
L. Chen and J. Han (Eds.): ProvSec 2016, LNCS 10005, pp. 153–172, 2016.
DOI: 10.1007/978-3-319-47422-9_9

storage. Since the user's data is outsourced to distributed cloud servers, the service provider can easily access the data.

To prevent data from being maliciously accessed by cloud providers, data owners tend to encrypt their private data before outsourcing to the cloud, and they only share the decryption key to other authorized users. Although this method can protect the privacy of the data, it brings the data retrieve problems. This limitation has motivated many researches on advanced searchable encryption schemes that enable searching on the encrypted data while protecting the confidentiality of the data and queries.

The solution of searchable encryption that first proposed by Song et al. [3] provides a way to perform efficient keyword searches over encrypted data. Promoted by Song's pioneering work, many efforts have been devoted to construct more efficient searchable symmetric encryption (SSE) schemes, such as [4–8] and [9]. A SSE scheme allows users to encrypt their data using symmetric encryption, and then uses files and keywords to create the encrypted index for further searches. When the user wants to retrieve some files, he needs to choose a keyword and use it to generate a search request. After that, the server uses this special request to search over its internal data structure. At last, the server finds all the files related to that keyword and returns the file collection to the user. Besides performing successful searches, the privacy feature of the SSE also ensures that, given encrypted files, encrypted indexes and a series of search requests, the server cannot learn any useful information about the files and the keywords.

The solutions above are single-keyword oriented, which are inefficient in practice since the searches may return a very large number of files, such as when searching in a remote-stored email archive. The works in [10–12] and [13] extend the search primitive to the multi-keyword conjunctive search, which avoid this limitation and are more practical for real world scenarios.

To the best of our knowledge, few works consider the searchable encryption and the search authentication together. Kamara et al. [14] presented a cryptographic cloud storage system which combines an adaptive secure searchable symmetric encryption scheme with a search authenticate mechanism to allow the user to verify the integrity of the search result. They used a simple Merkle tree structure [15] and a pre-computed basis to authenticate the given dataset. Kurosawa and Ohtaki [16] introduced the definition of UC-security and proposed a verifiable SSE scheme that allows the user to detect search result's integrity.

Our Contribution. In this paper, we present a dynamic integrity preserving multi-keyword searchable encryption scheme, enabling search authentication in multi-keyword searchable encryption schemes to fulfill the practical needs. We reduce the multi-keyword search (MSE) problem to the single-keyword case by performing a search for each individual keyword and doing the intersection between each resultant file sets to get the final result. To lower the communication overhead during a search, the intersection of each keyword's search result is computed at the server side. The only thing that the user needs to do is to receive the final result and verify its integrity.

Thus, our approach should meet the following requirements: (1) the server is able to take multiple keywords as input, and give the final result directly; (2) for the server that honestly executes the search algorithm, a valid proof can be formed and pass the verification; no one can generate a valid proof for a maliciously modified search result and still pass the verification. Theoretical basis of proposed solution is inspired by the authenticated data structure in [17] to verify set operations on out sourced sets.

We use dynamic SSE to realize the single-keyword search and use Merkle tree as the base data structure to prove the correctness of the intersection. Based on them, our scheme maintains the adaptive chosen-keyword security and is unforgeable against adaptive adversaries.

2   Definition and Security Model

2.1   Definitions

We consider the scenario that consists of two types of entities. One of them is the user that owns the data, and the other is the cloud storage provider, as known as the server, which provides storage services to the user. The dynamic MSE scheme allows a user to encrypt his data and outsource the encrypted data to the server. After uploading the encrypted data, the user only needs to store a secret key and an authenticated data state, regardless of the file number and size, i.e., the user's storage overhead is constant size. User can later generate search requests using single or multiple keywords and submit to the server. Given a search request, the server searches over the encrypted data and returns the set of encrypted files and a corresponding proof. The correctness of this search result can be verified by the user, using this result and proof. User can also dynamically update the file set on demand after the first uploading. The main system architecture is showed in Fig. 1.

Fig. 1. Integrity preserving search over encrypted data

While using multiple keywords in a search, we define the search result to be the intersection of the sets generated by searching for each individual keyword. Concretely speaking, the question we discussed in this paper is the conjunctive keyword search. We use "token" to describe the request sent by user. Since our scheme is dynamic, there are two additional tokens, the add token and the delete token. The formal definition of our scheme is defined as follows.

Definition 1. *A dynamic MSE scheme is a tuple of eight polynomial-time algorithms and protocols* MSE = (Gen, Setup, SrchToken, Search, Verify, Dec, Add/Update, Del/Update) *such that:*

$K \leftarrow$ Gen(1^k): *is a probabilistic algorithm run by the user that takes a security parameter* 1^k *as input, outputs a secret key K.*

$(\gamma, \mathbf{c}, st, \alpha) \leftarrow$ Setup$(K, \delta, \mathbf{f})$: *is a probabilistic algorithm run by the user that takes the secret key K, an index δ and a set of files $\mathbf{f}$ as input, outputs an encrypted index γ, a set of ciphertexts $\mathbf{c}$, a data state st and an authenticated structure α.*

$\tau_s \leftarrow$ SrchToken(K, W): *is a deterministic algorithm run by the user that takes as input the secret key K and a set of words W, outputs search token τ_s.*

$(\mathbf{I}_W, \pi) \leftarrow$ Search$(\alpha, \gamma, \mathbf{c}, \tau_s)$: *is a deterministic algorithm run by the server that takes as input the authenticated structure α, the encrypted index γ, the set of ciphertexts $\mathbf{c}$ and the search token τ_s, outputs a set of file identifiers $\mathbf{I}_W$, and a proof π.*

$b \leftarrow$ Verify$(K, st, \tau_s, \mathbf{I}', \pi)$: *is a deterministic algorithm run by the user that takes as input the secret key K, the data state st, a search token τ_s, a set of file identifiers $\mathbf{I}'$ and a proof π, outputs 1 as accept or 0 as reject.*

$f \leftarrow$ Dec(K, c): *is a deterministic algorithm run by the user to decrypt a ciphertext c, outputs a plaintext file f.*

$(U : st'; \ S : \alpha', \gamma', \mathbf{c}') \leftarrow$ Add/Update$(U : K, \delta_f, f, st; \ S : \alpha, \gamma, \mathbf{c})$: *is an interactive protocol run between the user U and the server S to **add** file to the file set.*

$(U : st'; \ S : \alpha', \gamma', \mathbf{c}') \leftarrow$ Del/Update$(U : K, \delta_f, f, st; \ S : \alpha, \gamma, \mathbf{c})$: *is an interactive protocol run between the user U and the server S to **delete** file from the file set.*

2.2   Security Model

We consider the server to be an un-trusted entity, which may deliberately steal or sabotage the user's data, or ignore some special files in the search result. Intuitively, an integrity preserving searchable encryption scheme should meet the following security features: (1) the encrypted files and data structures on the server side should not leak any information about the files to the server; (2) the search requests generated by the user should not leak any information about the keywords he uses; (3) for a fallacious result, the server cannot produce a valid proof and pass the user's verification.

Dynamic CKA2-Secure. This security requirement characterizes the feature that the scheme does not leak any information to the adversary except those defined in the leakage functions. The security definition will be parameterized by the four leakage functions $\mathcal{L}_1 \sim \mathcal{L}_4$. The adversary is allowed to be adaptive, i.e., its queries could base on the previous results. Let $\mathcal{A}$ be a stateful adversary that executes the server-side algorithm, "game" represent the interaction between $\mathcal{A}$ and user or simulator, "view" represent all the information that $\mathcal{A}$ can collect during the game. We assume that, $\mathcal{A}$ can choose the encrypted message, and then generates the queries by interacting with the user adaptively. Therefore, in our security definition, the "view" of $\mathcal{A}$ should only contain the information specified by $\mathcal{L}_1, \mathcal{L}_2, \mathcal{L}_3$ and $\mathcal{L}_4$ in a simulated way.

Definition 2. *Given the dynamic MSE scheme described in Definition 1, describe $\mathcal{A}$ as a stateful adversary, $\mathcal{S}$ as a stateful simulator, $\mathcal{L}_1, \mathcal{L}_2, \mathcal{L}_3, \mathcal{L}_4$ as stateful leakage functions. Consider the following games:*

$\mathrm{Real}_{\mathcal{A}}(1^k):$
  $K \leftarrow \mathrm{Gen}(1^k)$
  $(\delta, \mathbf{f}) \leftarrow \mathcal{A}(1^k)$
  $(\gamma, \mathbf{c}, st, \alpha) \leftarrow \mathrm{Setup}(K, \delta, \mathbf{f})$
  for $1 \le i \le q$
   $\{W_i, f_i, f_i'\} \xleftarrow[\text{each time}]{\text{one query}} \mathcal{A}(\alpha, \gamma, \mathbf{c}, \tau_1, \dots \tau_{i-1}, c_1, \dots c_{i-1})$
   $\tau_i \xleftarrow{\mathcal{A}} \mathrm{SrchToken}(K, W_i)$, or
   $(U : st'; \mathcal{A} : \tau_i, c_i) \xleftarrow{\mathcal{A}} \mathrm{Add/Update}(U : K, \delta_f, f, st; \mathcal{A})$, or
   $(U : st'; \mathcal{A} : \tau_i) \xleftarrow{\mathcal{A}} \mathrm{Del/Update}(U : K, \delta_f, f, st; \mathcal{A})$
  output $b \leftarrow \mathcal{A}(\alpha, \gamma, \mathbf{c}, \tau_1, \dots, \tau_q, c_1, \dots c_q)$

$\mathrm{Ideal}_{\mathcal{A}, \mathcal{S}}(1^k):$
  $(\delta, \mathbf{f}) \leftarrow \mathcal{A}(1^k)$
  $(\tilde{\alpha}, \tilde{\gamma}, \tilde{\mathbf{c}}) \leftarrow \mathcal{S}^{\mathcal{L}_1(\delta, \mathbf{f})}(1^k)$
  for $1 \le i \le q$
   $\{W_i, f_i, f_i'\} \xleftarrow[\text{each time}]{\text{one query}} \mathcal{A}(\tilde{\alpha}, \tilde{\gamma}, \tilde{\mathbf{c}}, \tilde{\tau}_1, \dots \tilde{\tau}_{i-1}, \tilde{c}_1, \dots \tilde{c}_{i-1})$
   $\tilde{\tau}_i \xleftarrow{\mathcal{A}} \mathcal{S}^{\mathcal{L}_2(\delta, \mathbf{f}, W_i)}(1^k)$, or
   $(\mathcal{S} : st'; \mathcal{A} : \tilde{\tau}_i, \tilde{c}_i) \xleftarrow{\mathcal{A}} \mathrm{Add/Update}(\mathcal{S}^{\mathcal{L}_3(\delta, \mathbf{f}, f_i)}(1^k); \mathcal{A})$, or
   $(\mathcal{S} : st'; \mathcal{A} : \tilde{\tau}_i) \xleftarrow{\mathcal{A}} \mathrm{Del/Update}(\mathcal{S}^{\mathcal{L}_4(\delta, \mathbf{f}, f_i)}(1^k); \mathcal{A})$
  output $b \leftarrow \mathcal{A}(\tilde{\alpha}, \tilde{\gamma}, \tilde{\mathbf{c}}, \tilde{\tau}_1, \dots, \tilde{\tau}_q, \tilde{c}_1, \dots \tilde{c}_q)$

 The dynamic MSE scheme is $(\mathcal{L}_1, \mathcal{L}_2, \mathcal{L}_3, \mathcal{L}_4)$-secure against adaptive dynamic chosen-keyword attacks if for all PPT adversary $\mathcal{A}$, there exist a probabilistic polynomial time simulator $\mathcal{S}$ such that:

$$\left| \mathbf{Pr}\left[\mathrm{Real}_{\mathcal{A}}(1^k) = 1\right] - \mathbf{Pr}\left[\mathrm{Ideal}_{\mathcal{A}, \mathcal{S}}(1^k) = 1\right] \right| \le \mathbf{negl}(1^k),$$

where $\mathbf{negl}(1^k)$ is a negligible function with input 1^k.

Unforgeability. We use game $\mathrm{Forge}_{\mathcal{A}}(1^k)$ to describe our scheme's unforgeability. In the unforgeability game, the adversary interacts with a user that honestly executes the scheme. User initializes his data structures using the data provided by the adversary. After making polynomial times queries, the adversary produces a set of keywords, a wrong search result and a proof to this result. If these outputs pass the user's verification algorithm, the game outputs 1, otherwise it outputs 0. The unforgeability requires that, all PPT adversaries have at most negligible probability to let the game output 1. We give the formal definition as follow.

Definition 3. *Given the dynamic MSE scheme described in Definition 1, for a stateful adversary $\mathcal{A}$, consider the following game:*

$$\text{Forge}_{\mathcal{A}}(1^k):$$
$$\quad K \leftarrow \text{Gen}(1^k)$$
$$\quad (\delta, \mathbf{f}) \leftarrow \mathcal{A}(1^k)$$
$$\quad (\gamma, \mathbf{c}, st, \alpha) \leftarrow \text{Setup}(K, \delta, \mathbf{f})$$
$$\quad \text{for } 1 \le i \le q$$
$$\quad\quad \{W_i, f_i, f_i'\} \xleftarrow[\text{each time}]{\text{one query}} \mathcal{A}(\alpha, \gamma, \mathbf{c}, \tau_1, \dots \tau_{i-1}, c_1, \dots c_{i-1})$$
$$\quad\quad \tau_i \xleftarrow{\mathcal{A}} \text{SrchToken}(K, W_i), \text{ or}$$
$$\quad\quad (\tau_i, c_i) \xleftarrow{\mathcal{A}} \text{Add/Update}(U : K, \delta_{f_i}, f_i, st; \mathcal{A}), \text{ or}$$
$$\quad\quad \tau_i \xleftarrow{\mathcal{A}} \text{Del/Update}(U : K, \delta_{f_i'}, f_i', st; \mathcal{A})$$
$$\quad (W, \mathbf{I'}, \pi) \leftarrow \mathcal{A}(\alpha, \gamma, \mathbf{c}, \tau_1, \dots, \tau_q, c_1, \dots c_q)$$
$$\quad \tau_s \leftarrow \text{SrchToken}(K, W)$$
$$\quad \text{output } b \leftarrow \text{Verify}(K, st', \tau_s, \mathbf{I'}, \pi)$$

where the set $\mathbf{I'} \neq \mathbf{I}_W$. We say the dynamic MSE scheme is unforgeable if for all PPT adversary $\mathcal{A}$, the probability: $\Pr[\text{Forge}_A(1^k) = 1] \le \mathbf{negl}(1^k)$, where $\mathbf{negl}(1^k)$ is a negligible function with input 1^k.

3 Integrity Preserving Multi-keyword Searchable Encryption Scheme

In this section, we first construct a multi-keyword searchable encryption scheme, and then add the search authentication mechanism to it to make the search result's integrity verifiable.

In our construction, the set of files $\mathbf{f}$ along with the inverted indexes δ are the initial input. In contrast to the file index, an inverted index is a set of lists that lead by keywords, and each keyword is followed by a set of files that contain that keyword. The keywords of each file are pre-selected, and can be considered as the outputs of some other algorithms, which won't be discussed here.

3.1 Dynamic Searchable Encryption

In the literature, most searchable encryption schemes use symmetric encryption to improve performance. We follow the prior constructions and build our scheme upon the CPA secure private key encryption [18].

The Fig. 2 shows our dynamic searchable encryption structure that is constructed based on the inverted index. Generally speaking, the lookup table contains all the keywords in the system, and each keyword in the table leads a list that stored in the search array. For example, the list of keyword w_2 starts at address 4 in the array, and the node at address 4 has a pointer that points to address 7, and then address 8. By traversing this list, all files that contain the keyword w_2 can be retrieved. All the nodes are stored at random location in the search array. To support efficient file updating,

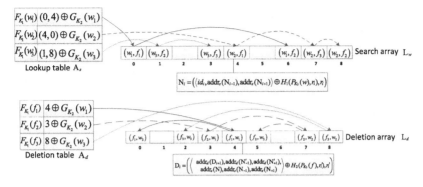

Fig. 2. The schematic search structure

there are also a deletion table and a deletion array. They work the same way, except those lists are led by files.

In order to prevent the server from learning the data, all the tables' entry, all the pointers in the table, and all the nodes in those arrays are encrypted. During a search, given the encrypted keywords, the server first decrypts the pointers in the lookup table and then uses the pointers to find the corresponding file identifiers in the search array. Those keywords remain encrypted throughout the search. Even if the server has searched all those keywords, it can only learn the relationship between the encrypted keywords and the related file identifiers but cannot obtain any useful knowledge about the keywords itself. This could prevent the curious server from learning the files and keywords. A more detailed analysis about this security model will be presented in Sect. 4.

3.2 Making Result Verifiable

In the following content, we discuss the method to make result verifiable. This method can allow a server to prove to a client that it answered a multi-keyword search query correctly.

The method proposed in [14] is a Merkle tree based solution that it computes the accumulated value for each word w, and uses these values as leaves to construct the tree. In a search, the server returns a file set S, and a Merkle tree proof to this set. The user can compute his own accumulated value using the files in S, and use it to perform the Merkle tree verification. If the newly computed root equals to the original one, then the result is correct and can be accepted by the user.

However, while switching to the multiple keywords setting, this solution is obsolete to prove the correctness of the intersection of the results. The server could only generate the proof for each set separately. These sets and proofs must be transferred to the user side to be verified, and subsequently the intersection of these sets could be computed by the user. Obviously, the communication complexity is linear and may have performance problems when the sets are very large.

The reasonable way to address this problem is to let the server compute the intersection, and give the user final result directly. In this case, the correctness of the intersection operation should be proved. We use the bilinear-map accumulator to realize this functionality. The bilinear-map accumulator [19] is an efficient tool to provide proofs of membership for elements that belong to a set. Let $s \in \mathbb{Z}_p^*$ be a randomly chosen trapdoor. The accumulator accumulates elements in $\mathbb{Z}_p$, and outputs an element in $\mathbb{G}$. For a set of elements $\mathcal{X}$ in $\mathbb{Z}_p$, the accumulation value $acc(\mathcal{X})$ is defined as:

$$acc(\mathcal{X}) = g^{\prod_{x \in \mathcal{X}} (x+s)} \tag{1}$$

Without knowing the trapdoor s, the value $acc(\mathcal{X})$ can also be constructed using $\mathcal{X}$ and the pre-computed $(g, g^s, \ldots, g^{s^q})$, where $q \geq \#\mathcal{X}$. The proof of subset containment of a set $\mathcal{S} \subseteq \mathcal{X}$ is the witness $(\mathcal{S}, \mathcal{W}_{\mathcal{S},\mathcal{X}})$ where:

$$\mathcal{W}_{\mathcal{S},\mathcal{X}} = g^{\prod_{x \in \mathcal{X} - \mathcal{S}} (x+s)} \tag{2}$$

Subset containment of $\mathcal{S}$ in $\mathcal{X}$ can be verified by checking:

$$e\left(\mathcal{W}_{\mathcal{S},\mathcal{X}}, g^{\prod_{x \in \mathcal{S}} (x+s)}\right) = e(acc(\mathcal{X}), g) \tag{3}$$

The security of the bilinear-map accumulator relies on the bilinear q-Strong Diffie-Hellman assumption.

Intuitively, the correctness of the intersection could be defined as follows: given a set $\mathbf{I}$ and a series of sets $S_1, \ldots, S_n$, $\mathbf{I}$ is the correct intersection of $S_1, \ldots, S_n$ if and only if the following conditions hold:

1. The subset condition: $(\mathbf{I} \subseteq S_1) \wedge \cdots \wedge (\mathbf{I} \subseteq S_n)$.
2. The completeness condition: $(S_1 - \mathbf{I}) \cap \cdots \cap (S_n - \mathbf{I}) = \emptyset$.

The subset condition is easy to understand, because as the intersection, the set $\mathbf{I}$ must be included in each set S_i. We use Merkle tree to authenticate the value $acc(S_i)$. For all $w \in \mathbf{w}$, the values $acc(\mathbf{f}_w)$ are computed according to (1), then the tree is constructed using these values as leaves.

Since the user does not store those accumulated values, the server should first generates Merkle tree proofs for each $acc(S_i)$. It's then straight forward to produce the subset witness $(\mathbf{I}, \mathcal{W}_{\mathbf{I},S_i})$ in (2) for each set S_i. Given the $acc(S_i)$ and the witness $(\mathbf{I}, \mathcal{W}_{\mathbf{I},S_i})$, the validity of the value $acc(S_i)$ should be first verified using Merkle tree proofs, then the subset containment relationship could be checked by performing the verifications according to the equation in (3).

The completeness condition is also necessary since the set $\mathbf{I}$ must contain all the common elements. To construct the completeness proof, we define the polynomial:

$$P_i(s) = \prod_{f \in S_i - \mathbf{I}} (s + id(f))$$

The following result is based on the extended Euclidean algorithm over polynomials and provides verification for checking the completeness of set intersection.

Lemma 1. *The set* **I** *is complete if and only if there exist polynomials* $q_1(s), \ldots, q_n(s)$ *such that* $q_1(s)P_1(s) + \cdots + q_n(s)P_n(s) = 1$ *where* $P_i(s)$ *is defined above. Suppose* **I** *is not the complete set, then there exist at least one common factor in* $P_1(s), \ldots, P_n(s)$. *Thus there are no polynomials* $q_1(s), \ldots, q_n(s)$ *to satisfy* $q_1(s)P_1(s) + \cdots + q_n(s)P_n(s) = 1$.

The formal analysis will be given in Sect. 4.

3.3   Explicit Construction

Let $\Pi = (\text{Gen}, \text{Enc}, \text{Dec})$ be a private-key encryption system. $F : \{0,1\}^k \times \{0,1\}^* \to \{0,1\}^k$, $G : \{0,1\}^k \times \{0,1\}^* \to \{0,1\}^*$, $P : \{0,1\}^k \times \{0,1\}^* \to \{0,1\}^k$ be pseudo-random functions. Let $H_1 : \{0,1\}^* \to \{0,1\}^*$, $H_2 : \{0,1\}^* \to \{0,1\}^*$ and $H_3 : \{0,1\}^* \to \{0,1\}^k$ be collision-resistant hash functions. Let $z \in \mathbb{N}$ be the initial size of the free list, and $\mathbf{0}$ be a series of 0's. Choose bilinear pairing parameters $(p, \mathbb{G}, \mathcal{G}, e, g)$.

  Gen(1^k) : Randomly choose three k - bit strings K_1, K_2, K_3 and generate $K_4 \leftarrow \Pi.\text{Gen}(1^k)$. Choose $s \in \mathbb{Z}_p^*$ at random and output $K = (K_1, K_2, K_3, K_4, s)$ as the private keys. Compute $(g, g^s, g^{s^2}, \ldots, g^{s^q})$ as public parameters where q should be large enough, i.e., should at least satisfy $q \geq \max\{\#\mathbf{f}_w\}_{w \in \mathbf{w}}$.

  Setup(K, δ, f) :

1. Let A_s and A_d be arrays of size $|\mathbf{c}|/8 + z$ and let T_s and T_d be dictionaries of size $\#\mathbf{w}$ and $\#\mathbf{f}$, respectively. Use "free" to represent a k - length word not in **w**. The following step 2 and step 3 should be performed synchronously to set up A_s and A_d at the same time.

2. For every keyword $w \in \mathbf{w}$,

   - Generate a list L_w of $\#\mathbf{f}_w$ nodes $(N_1, \ldots, N_{\#\mathbf{f}_w})$ randomly stored in A_s, set $N_i = (\langle id_i, \text{addr}_s(N_{i-1}), \text{addr}_s(N_{i+1}) \rangle \oplus H_1(P_{K_3}(w), r_i), r_i)$, where id_i is the identity of the ith file in $\mathbf{f}_w$, r_i is a k - bit random string, and $\text{addr}_s(N_{\#\mathbf{f}_w + 1}) = \text{addr}_s(N_0) = \mathbf{0}^{\log \# A_s}$
   - Set $T_s[F_{K_1}(w)] = \langle \text{addr}_s(N_1), \text{addr}_d(N_1') \rangle \oplus G_{K_2}(w)$, where N_1' is the dual of N_1, which has the same (f_1, w) pair as node N_1.

3. For each file f in $\mathbf{f}$,

   - Create a list L_f of $\#f$ dual nodes $(D_1, \ldots, D_{\#f})$ $(N_1, \ldots, N_{\#\mathbf{f}_w})$ randomly stored in the deletion array A_d. Each node D_i is associated with a word w, and a corresponding node N in L_w. Let N_{+1} be the node after N in L_w, and N_{-1} be the node before N in L_w. Define D_i as:

$$D_i = \left(\left\langle \begin{array}{c} \mathrm{addr}_d(D_{i+1}), \mathrm{addr}_d(N'_{-1}), \mathrm{addr}_d(N'_{+1}), \\ \mathrm{addr}_s(N), \mathrm{addr}_s(N_{-1}), \mathrm{addr}_s(N_{+1}) \end{array} \right\rangle \oplus H_2(P_{K_3}(f), r'_i), r'_i \right),$$

where r'_i is a random k - bit string, $\mathrm{addr}_d(D_{\#f+1}) = 0^{\log \#A_d}$

- Store a pointer to the first node of L_f in the deletion table by setting:

$$T_d[F_{K_1}(f)] = \mathrm{addr}_d(D_1) \oplus G_{K_2}(f)$$

4. Generate the free list L_{free} by choosing z at random in A_s and in A_d. Let $(F_1, \ldots, F_z)$ and $(F'_1, \ldots, F'_z)$ be the free nodes in A_s and A_d, respectively. Set: $T_s[\text{free}] = \langle \mathrm{addr}_s(F_1), 0^{\log \#A_s} \rangle$, and for $1 \le i \le z$, set $A_s[\mathrm{addr}_s(F_i)] = \langle 0^{\log \#f}, \mathrm{addr}_s(F_{i+1}), \mathrm{addr}_d(F'_i), 0^k \rangle$, where $\mathrm{addr}_s(F_{z+1}) = 0^{\log \#A_s}$.
5. Fill the remaining entries of A_s and A_d with random strings.
6. For $1 \le i \le \#\mathbf{f}$, let $c_i \leftarrow \Pi.\mathrm{Enc}_{K_4}(f_i)$.
7. For all $w \in \mathbf{w}$, form the leaf node by letting $\theta_w = \left\langle F_{K_1}(w), g^{\prod_{f \in t_w}(s+id(f))} \right\rangle$. Construct a Merkle tree using H_3 with leaves $\mathcal{L} = \{\theta_w\}_{w \in \mathbf{w}}$ permuted in a random order.
8. Output $(\gamma, \mathbf{c}, st, \alpha)$, where $\gamma = (A_s, T_s, A_d, T_d)$, $\mathbf{c} = (c_1, \ldots, c_{\#\mathbf{f}})$, st is the root of the tree, and α is the tree itself.

SrchToken(K, W): For $W = (w_1, \ldots, w_n)$, compute each $\tau_i = (F_{K_1}(w_i), G_{K_2}(w_i), P_{K_3}(w_i))$, then output $\tau_s = (\tau_1, \ldots \tau_n)$.
Search$(\alpha, \gamma, \mathbf{c}, \tau_s)$:

1. For each τ_i in τ_s, parse τ_i as $(\tau_{i,1}, \tau_{i,2}, \tau_{i,3})$,

   - Recover a pointer to the first node of the list by computing $(\alpha_1, \alpha'_1) = T_s[\tau_{i,1}] \oplus \tau_{i,2}$.
   - Lookup node $N_1 = A[\alpha_1]$ and decrypt it using $\tau_{i,3}$, i.e., parse N_1 as (v_1, r_1) and compute $(id_1, 0, \mathrm{addr}_s(N_2)) = v_1 \oplus H_1(\tau_{i,3}, r_1)$. Let $\alpha_2 = \mathrm{addr}_s(N_2)$.
   - For $j \ge 2$, decrypt node N_j as above until $\alpha_{j+1} = 0$.
   - Let $S_i = \{id_1, \ldots, id_t\}$ be the file identifiers revealed in the previous steps.

2. For the sets $S_1, \cdots, S_n$ generated in step 1, let $\mathbf{I}_W = \{id_1, \ldots, id_m\}$ be the intersection, i.e., $\mathbf{I}_W = S_1 \cap S_2 \cap \ldots \cap S_n$. Compute the proofs in the following steps:

   - For $1 \le i \le n$, find the leaf θ_i in α whose first element is $\tau_{i,1}$ and generate the proof t_i. The t_i includes θ_i and all the sibling nodes in the path from the leaf θ_i to the root. Let $\mathcal{T} = \{t_1, \ldots, t_n\}$.
   - For $1 \le i \le n$, form the polynomial: $P_i = \prod_{f \in S_i - \mathbf{I}_w}(s + id(f))$, then use the public parameters $(g, g^s, g^{s^2}, \ldots, g^{s^q})$ to compute the value g^{P_i}. Let $\mathcal{S} = \{g^{P_1}, \ldots, g^{P_n}\}$ be the subset witness.

- Giving the polynomials $\{P_1, \ldots, P_n\}$ generated in step 2, find the polynomials $\{q_1, \ldots, q_n\}$ that satisfying $q_1P_1 + q_2P_2 + \cdots + q_nP_n = 1$. This can be done using extended Euclidean algorithm over polynomials. Let $\mathcal{C} = \{g^{q_1}, \ldots, g^{q_n}\}$ be the completeness witness.

3. Output the result $\mathbf{I}_W$ and the proof $\pi = \{\mathcal{T}, \mathcal{S}, \mathcal{C}\}$.

Verify$(K, st, \tau_s, \mathbf{I}', \pi)$:

1. Parse π as $\{\mathcal{T}, \mathcal{S}, \mathcal{C}\}$ and verify these proofs in the following steps:

- For each proof t_i in $\mathcal{T}$, let θ_i be the corresponding leaf node in t_i. Parse θ_i as $(\theta_{i,1}, \theta_{i,2})$, i.e. $\theta_{i,1} = F_{K_1}(w_i)$ and $\theta_{i,2} = g^{\prod_{f \in t_{w_i}} (s + id(f))}$.Verify if the value $\theta_{i,1}$ equals to $\tau_{i,1}$, where $\tau_{i,1}$ is the first element of τ_i in τ_s. Then verify the proof t_i using the root st.
- For $1 \le i \le n$, parse the leaf node θ_i as $(\theta_{i,1}, \theta_{i,2})$, then perform the subset condition verification by checking: $e(g^{\prod_{k=1}^{m} (s + id_k)}, g^{P_i}) \stackrel{?}{=} e(\theta_{i,2}, g)$, where $(id_1, \ldots .id_m)$ is from $\mathbf{I}'$ and g^{P_i} is element in $\mathcal{S}$.
- Verify the completeness condition by checking: $\prod_{i=1}^{n} e(g^{P_i}, g^{q_i}) \stackrel{?}{=} e(g, g)$, where g^{P_i} is element in $\mathcal{S}$ and g^{q_i} is the corresponding element in $\mathcal{C}$.

2. If all the verifications succeed, then output 1, otherwise output 0.

Dec(K, c): Output $f = \Pi.\text{Dec}_{K_4}(c)$.
Add/Update$(U : K, \delta_f, f, st;\ S : \alpha, \gamma, \mathbf{c})$:
User:
Recover the unique sequence of words $(w_1, \ldots, w_{\#f})$ from δ_f and compute the set $\{F_{K_1}(w_i)\}_{1 \le i \le \#f}$ and send to the server.
Server:

1. For $1 \le i \le \#f$, traverse the Merkel tree α and:

- Find the leaf θ_i in α whose first element is $F_{K_1}(w_i)$.
- Let t_i be the proof in α from θ_i to the root. The proof includes the leaf θ_i, and all the sibling nodes from θ_i to the root.

2. Let $\rho = (t_1, \ldots, t_{\#f})$ and send it to the user.

User:

1. Verify the proofs in $(t_1, \ldots, t_{\#f})$ using st, if fails, output $\perp$ and terminate.
2. For $1 \le i \le \#f$,

- Let θ_i be the leaf in t_i, parse θ_i as $(\theta_{i,1}, \theta_{i,2})$.
- Compute the new leaf node $\theta_i' = (\theta_{i,1}, (\theta_{i,2})^{s + id(f)})$.

3. Update the root hash st using $(\theta_1', \ldots, \theta_{\#f}')$ and the information in $(t_1, \ldots, t_{\#f})$.
4. Compute $\tau_a = (F_{K_1}(f), G_{K_2}(f), \lambda_1, \ldots .\lambda_{\#f})$, where for all $1 \le i \le \#f$ ::

$$\lambda_i = \begin{pmatrix} \theta'_{i,1}, \theta'_{i,2}, G_{K_2}(w_i), \langle id(f), \mathbf{0}, \mathbf{0}, \rangle \oplus H_1(P_{K_3}(W_i), r_i), \\ r_i, \langle \mathbf{0}, \mathbf{0}, \mathbf{0}, \mathbf{0}, \mathbf{0}, \mathbf{0} \rangle \oplus H_2(P_{K_3}(f), r'_i), r'_i \end{pmatrix},$$

where r_i and r'_i are random k - bit strings.

5. Let $c_f \leftarrow \text{SKE.Enc}_{K_4}(f)$ and send (τ_a, c_f) to the server, then output the new root st'.

Server:

1. Parse τ_a as $(\tau_1, \tau_2, \lambda_1, \ldots, \lambda_{\#f})$ and return $\bot$ if τ_1 is already in T_d.
2. For $1 \leq i \leq \#f$,

   - Find the first free location φ in A_s, second free location φ_{+1} in A_s, first free location φ' in A_d, and second free location φ'_{+1} in A_d, by computing $(\varphi, \mathbf{0}) = \mathrm{T}_s[\text{free}]$, $(\mathbf{0}, \varphi_{+1}, \varphi') = \mathrm{A}_s[\varphi]$ and $(\mathbf{0}, \varphi_{+2}, \varphi'_{+1}) = \mathrm{A}_s[\varphi_{+1}]$.
   - Update the search table by setting $\mathrm{T}_s[\text{free}] = (\varphi_{+1}, \mathbf{0})$.
   - Recover N_1's address α_1 by computing $(\alpha_1, \alpha'_1) = \mathrm{T}_s[\lambda_i[1]] \oplus \lambda_i[3]$.
   - Parse $\mathrm{N}_1 = \mathrm{A}_s[\alpha_1]$ as (v_1, r_1), then update N_1's back pointer point by setting: $\mathrm{A}_s[\alpha_1] = (v_1 \oplus \langle \mathbf{0}, \varphi, \mathbf{0} \rangle, r_1)$.
   - Store the new node at location φ and modify its forward pointer to N_1 by setting: $\mathrm{A}_s[\varphi] = (\lambda_i[4] \oplus \langle \mathbf{0}, \mathbf{0}, \alpha_1 \rangle, \lambda_i[5])$.
   - Update the search table by setting: $\mathrm{T}_s[\lambda_i[1]] = (\varphi, \varphi') \oplus \lambda_i[3]$.
   - Parse $\mathrm{D}_1 = \mathrm{A}_d[\alpha'_1]$ as (v'_1, r'_1), set $\mathrm{A}_d[\alpha'_1] = (v'_1 \oplus \langle \mathbf{0}, \varphi', \mathbf{0}, \mathbf{0}, \varphi, \mathbf{0} \rangle, r'_1)$.
   - If $i < \#f$, set $\mathrm{A}_d[\varphi'] = (\lambda_i[6] \oplus \langle \varphi'_{+1}, \mathbf{0}, \alpha'_1, \varphi, \mathbf{0}, \alpha_1 \rangle, \lambda_i[7])$.
   - If $i = \#f$, set $\mathrm{A}_d[\varphi'] = (\lambda_i[6] \oplus \langle \mathbf{0}, \mathbf{0}, \alpha'_1, \varphi, \mathbf{0}, \alpha_1 \rangle, \lambda_i[7])$.
   - If $i = 1$, then update the deletion table by setting $\mathrm{T}_d[\tau_1] = \varphi' \oplus \tau_2$.

3. Update the cipher texts by adding c to $\mathbf{c}$.
4. Let $\theta'_i = (\lambda_i[1], \lambda_i[2])$, update the tree α by replacing the leaves $(\theta_1, \ldots, \theta_{\#f})$ with $(\theta'_1, \ldots, \theta'_{\#f})$.
5. Output $(\alpha', \gamma', \mathbf{c}')$, where α' is the updated tree.

Del/Update$(U : K, \delta_f, f, st; S : \alpha, \gamma, \mathbf{c})$:
User:
Recover the unique sequence of words $(w_1, \ldots, w_{\#f})$ from δ_f and compute the set $\{F_{K_1}(w_i)\}_{1 \leq i \leq \#f}$ and send to the server.
Server:

1. For $1 \leq i \leq \#f$, traverse the Merkel tree α and:

   - Find the leaf θ_i in α whose first element is $F_{K_1}(w_i)$.
   - Let t_i be the proof in α from θ_i to the root. The proof includes the leaf θ_i, and all the sibling nodes from θ_i to the root.

2. Let $\rho = (t_1, \ldots, t_{\#f})$ and send it to the user.

User:

1. Verify the proofs in $(t_1, \ldots, t_{\#f})$ using st, if fails, output $\bot$ and terminate.
2. For $1 \leq i \leq \#f$,

- Let θ_i be the leaf in t_i, parse θ_i as $(\theta_{i,1}, \theta_{i,2})$.
- Compute the new leaf node $\theta'_i = (\theta_{i,1}, (\theta_{i,2})^{1/(s+id(f))})$.

3. Update the root hash st using $(\theta'_1, \ldots, \theta'_{\#f})$ and the information in $(t_1, \ldots, t_{\#f})$.
4. Compute $\tau_d = (F_{K_1}(f), G_{K_2}(f), P_{K_3}(f), id(f), \theta'_1, \ldots, \theta'_{\#f})$.
5. Send τ_d to the server, then output the new root st'.

Server:

1. Parse τ_d as $(\tau_1, \tau_2, \tau_3, id, \theta'_1, \ldots, \theta'_{\#f})$.
2. Find the first node of L_f by computing $\alpha'_i = T_d[\tau_1] \oplus \tau_2$.
3. While $\alpha'_i \neq \mathbf{0}$,

   - Parse $D_i = A_d[\alpha'_i]$ as (v'_i, r'_i), decrypt D_i by computing $(\alpha_1, \ldots, \alpha_6) = v'_i \oplus H_2(\tau_3, r'_i)$.
   - Delete D_i by setting $A_d[\alpha'_i]$ to a random string.
   - Find address of the first free node by computing $(\varphi, \mathbf{0}) = T_s[\text{free}]$.
   - Update the first node of the free list in the T_s point to D_i's dual by setting $T_s[\text{free}] = (\alpha_4, \mathbf{0})$.
   - Free D_i's dual by setting $A_s[\alpha_4] = (\mathbf{0}, \varphi, \alpha'_i)$.
   - Let N_{-1} be the node before D_i's dual. Update N_{-1}'s next pointer by setting $A_s[\alpha_5] = (\beta_1, \beta_2, \beta_3 \oplus \alpha_4 \oplus \alpha_6, r_{-1})$, where $(\beta_1, \beta_2, \beta_3, r_{-1}) = A_s[\alpha_5]$. Also, update the pointers of N_{-1}'s dual by setting: $A_d[\alpha_2] = (\beta_1, \beta_2, \beta_3 \oplus \alpha'_i \oplus \alpha_3, \beta_4, \beta_5, \beta_6 \oplus \alpha_4 \oplus \alpha_6, r'_{-1})$, where $(\beta_1, \ldots, \beta_6, r'_{-1}) = A_d[\alpha_2]$.
   - Let N_{+1} be the node after D_i's dual. Update N_{+1}'s previous pointer by setting $A_s[\alpha_6] = (\beta_1, \beta_2 \oplus \alpha_4 \oplus \alpha_5, \beta_3, r_{+1})$, where $(\beta_1, \beta_2, \beta_3, r_{+1}) = A_s[\alpha_6]$. Also, update N_{+1}'s dual's pointers by setting: $A_d[\alpha_3] = (\beta_1, \beta_2 \oplus \alpha'_i \oplus \alpha_2, \beta_3, \beta_4, \beta_5 \oplus \alpha_4 \oplus \alpha_5, \beta_6, r'_{+1})$, where $(\beta_1, \ldots, \beta_6, r'_{+1}) = A_d[\alpha_3]$.
   - Set $\alpha'_i = \alpha_1$.

4. Remove the cipher text corresponding to id from $\mathbf{c}$.
5. Remove τ_1 from T_d.
6. Update the tree α by replacing the leaves $(\theta_1, \ldots, \theta_{\#f})$ with $(\theta'_1, \ldots, \theta'_{\#f})$.
7. Output $(\alpha', \gamma', \mathbf{c}')$, where α' is the updated tree.

4 Security Analysis

4.1 Dynamic CKA2-Secure

In the following, we analyze our dynamic MSE scheme and investigate which information has been leaked during the execution of these algorithms and protocols. The formal definition will be given afterwards.

In our scheme, for each word w_i, the value $F_{K_1}(w_i)$ can be treated as a unique identifier, and we denote it by $id(w_i)$. For each file f_i, there are two identifiers, the $id(f_i)$ in the array A_s and the $F_{K_1}(f_i)$ in the table T_d. Both of them can uniquely represent a file, so for convenience, we do not distinguish between them.

Given the encrypted index $\gamma = (T_s, A_s, T_d, A_d)$, the Merkle tree α and the ciphertexts $\mathbf{c}$, the server can learn the size of A_s, the set $[id(w)]_{w \in \mathbf{w}}$ from T_s, the set $[id(f)]_{f \in \mathbf{f}}$ and the length of each file $[|f|]_{f \in \mathbf{f}}$. We denote these by $\mathcal{L}_1$, i.e.,

$$\mathcal{L}_1(\delta, \mathbf{f}) = \left(\#A_s, [id(w)]_{w \in \mathbf{w}}, [id(f)]_{f \in \mathbf{f}}, [|f|]_{f \in \mathbf{f}} \right).$$

The search operation reveals to the server $id(w)$ for all $w \in W$, and the relationship between $id(w)$ and the identifiers of all files that contains w. We denote these by $\mathcal{L}_2$, i.e.,

$$\mathcal{L}_2(\delta, \mathbf{f}, W) = \left([id(f)]_{f \in \mathbf{f}_w}, id(w) \right)_{\text{for all} w \in W}.$$

In the add protocol, the server can learn the identifier of the file to be added, the length of the file, and the identifiers of the words that belong to the file. In addition, it can tell whether the word w contained in the file is a new word by checking the table T_s. We denote these by $\mathcal{L}_3$, i.e.,

$$\mathcal{L}_3(\delta, \mathbf{f}, f) = \left(id(f), [id(w), \text{apprs}(w)]_{w \in \mathbf{w}_f}, |f| \right),$$

where $\text{apprs}(w)$ is a one bit flag set to 1 if the word w exists in the index before the file f is added, otherwise, it is set to 0.

Similarly, in the delete protocol, the server can learn the identifier of the file to be deleted, and know the relationship between $id(f)$ and those word identifiers. In addition, for each $w \in \mathbf{w}_f$, by removing the word pair (f, w) from the list L_w, the server learns the locations of the pair's neighbors in L_w. We denote these by $\mathcal{L}_4$.

$$\mathcal{L}_4(\delta, \mathbf{f}, f) = \left(id(f), [id(w), \text{prev}(f, w), \text{next}(f, w)]_{w \in \mathbf{w}_f} \right),$$

where $\text{prev}(f, w)$ and $\text{next}(f, w)$ are the file identifiers of the file before and after f in the word list L_w. For the head and the tail of the list, the corresponding value is set $\perp$ to indicate that there are no more nodes before or after this one.

Now we use the following theorem to claim that the construction in Sect. 4 is dynamic CKA2-secure in the random oracle model with the leakage functions described above.

Theorem 1. *If the private-key encryption system Π is CPA-secure, and the F, G and P are pseudo-random functions, then the dynamic MSE scheme is $(\mathcal{L}_1, \mathcal{L}_2, \mathcal{L}_3, \mathcal{L}_4)$-secure against adaptive chosen-keyword attacks in the random oracle model.*

Proof: The primary goal of providing this proof is to construct a PPT simulator $\mathcal{S}$ that can generate the simulated values in the ideal game using the information given in these leakage functions. Those simulated values should be indistinguishable from ones in the real game to any PPT adversary.

Given the information received from $\mathcal{L}_1$, the simulator could determine the length and the structure of encrypted index γ, ciphertexts $\mathbf{c}$ and tree α. Then it can use randomly chosen strings to construct these structures and produce these values as the simulated one $(\tilde{\gamma}, \tilde{\mathbf{c}}, \tilde{\alpha})$. If a PPT adversary can distinguish the tuple $(\tilde{\gamma}, \tilde{\mathbf{c}}, \tilde{\alpha})$ from $(\gamma, \mathbf{c}, \alpha)$ with non-negligible probability then it can break at least one of these properties with non-negligible probability: the CPA security of the encryption scheme; the pseudo-randomness of the PRFs and the elliptic curve discrete logarithm assumption.

Given the information received from $\mathcal{L}_2$, $\mathcal{L}_3$ and $\mathcal{L}_4$, the simulator should respond the simulated search token, the simulated add token and the simulated delete token during the adversary's queries. These steps become more complex due to the fact that simulator needs to track the dependencies between the information revealed by these queries to ensure consistency among these simulated tokens. We define additional assisting structures iA_s, iA_d, iT_s and iT_d in the simulator side to maintain consistency during updation. The simulator uses these assisted structures to record those dependencies that are revealed by $\mathcal{L}_2$, $\mathcal{L}_3$ and $\mathcal{L}_4$ in the queries, and builds internal relationship in iA_s, iA_d, iT_s and iT_d, while the values in $\tilde{\gamma} = (\tilde{A}_s, \tilde{T}_s, \tilde{A}_d, \tilde{T}_d)$ remain random. This gives the simulator the ability to respond the adversary's queries like a real user, except using those simulated values.

Analyze.

1. If the pseudo-randomness of F, G and P holds, then for all PPT adversaries $\mathcal{A}$, there exist negligible value ε_1 such that:

$$\left| \mathbf{Pr}[1 \leftarrow \mathcal{A}(\delta, \mathbf{f}, A_s, T_s, A_d, T_d)] - \mathbf{Pr}\left[1 \leftarrow \mathcal{A}(\delta, \mathbf{f}, \tilde{A}_s, \tilde{T}_s, \tilde{A}_d, \tilde{T}_d)\right] \right| \leq \varepsilon_1.$$

Because each cell in $\tilde{A}_s$ can be recognized as the form $\langle \tilde{N}, \tilde{r} \rangle$ where $|\tilde{N}| = 2\log \#A_s + \log \#\mathbf{f}$ and $|\tilde{r}| = k$. The cell in A_s is $N_i = (\langle id_i, addr_s(N_{i-1}), addr_s(N_{i+1}) \rangle \oplus H_1(P_{K_3}(w), r_i), r_i)$, due to the pseudo-randomness of P and the random oracle H_1, all PPT adversaries $\mathcal{A}\ominus$ cannot distinguish $\tilde{A}_s$ from A_s. Similarly, it cannot distinguish T_s, A_d, T_d with $\tilde{T}_s, \tilde{A}_d, \tilde{T}_d$ if the pseudo-randomness of F, G and P holds. It means the adversary can distinguish the real index A_s, T_s, A_d, T_d from the simulated index $\tilde{A}_s, \tilde{T}_s, \tilde{A}_d, \tilde{T}_d$. Therefore, the probability ε_1 is negligible.

2. Based on the elliptic curve discrete logarithm assumption and the pseudo-randomness of F, any PPT adversary $\mathcal{A}$ cannot distinguish the real leaf nodes $\mathcal{L}$ from the simulated one $\tilde{\mathcal{L}}$, therefore cannot distinguish the tree $\tilde{\alpha}$ from α, since they are generated by these leaves. i.e. there exist negligible value ε_2 such that:

$$|\mathbf{Pr}[1 \leftarrow \mathcal{A}(\delta, \mathbf{f}, \alpha)] - \mathbf{Pr}[1 \leftarrow \mathcal{A}(\delta, \mathbf{f}, \tilde{\alpha})]| \leq \varepsilon_2.$$

Because the pseudo-randomness of F holds, any PPT adversary cannot distinguish the random bits from the output of PRF F. So it cannot distinguish the random bits $\gamma_s(id(w_i))$ with $F_{K_1}(w_i)$. In addition, due to the discrete logarithm assumptions, any PPT adversary cannot can distinguish g^{ω_i} with $g^{\prod_{f \in \mathbf{f}_{w_i}} (s + id(f))}$. As we know, the real

leaf nodes $\mathcal{L}$ from the simulated one $\tilde{\mathcal{L}}$ are: $\tilde{\mathcal{L}} = \{\tilde{\theta}_w\}_{w \in \mathbf{w}} = \{(\tilde{\theta}_{w,1}, \tilde{\theta}_{w,2})\}_{w \in \mathbf{w}} = (\gamma_s(id$
$(w_i)), g^{\omega_i}); \mathcal{L} = \{\theta_w\}_{w \in \mathbf{w}} = \{(\theta_{w,1}, \theta_{w,2})\}_{w \in \mathbf{w}} = (F_{K_1}(w_i), g^{\prod_{f \in \mathbf{t}_{w_i}} (s + id(f))}),$

So $\mathcal{A}$ cannot distinguish $\mathcal{L}$ from $\tilde{\mathcal{L}}$. The tree $\tilde{\alpha}$ and α are build by the collision-resistant hash function H_3 of the leaf nodes, so the adversary cannot distinguish the tree $\tilde{\alpha}$ and α, then ε_2 is negligible.

3. If the private-key encryption system Π is CPA-secure, then for all PPT adversaries $\mathcal{A}$, there exists negligible value ε_3 such that:

$$|\mathbf{Pr}[1 \leftarrow \mathcal{A}(\mathbf{f}, \mathbf{c})] - \mathbf{Pr}[1 \leftarrow \mathcal{A}(\mathbf{f}, \tilde{\mathbf{c}})]| \leq \varepsilon_3.$$

Because the private-key encryption system Π is proved to be CPA secure, so the ciphertexts it produces do not reveal any partial information about the plaintext. So any PPT adversary $\mathcal{A}$ cannot distinguish the ciphertexts that generated by two different inputs using the SKE encryption. As we know, $\tilde{\mathbf{c}}$ and $\mathbf{c}$ are:$\mathbf{c} = (c_1, \ldots, c_{\#\mathbf{f}})$, in which $c_i = \Pi.\mathrm{Enc}_{K_4}(f_i)$; $\tilde{\mathbf{c}} = (\tilde{c}_1, \ldots, \tilde{c}_{\#\mathbf{f}})$, in which $\tilde{c}_i = \Pi.\mathrm{Enc}_{K_4}(0^{|f_i|})$. So $\mathcal{A}$ cannot distinguish $\tilde{\mathbf{c}}$ from $\mathbf{c}$. Therefore, ε_3 is negligible.

In addition, there exists negligible value ε_4 such that:

$$|\mathbf{Pr}[1 \leftarrow \mathcal{A}(\delta, \mathbf{f}, \tau_s)] - \mathbf{Pr}[1 \leftarrow \mathcal{A}(\delta, \mathbf{f}, \tilde{\tau}_s)]| \leq \varepsilon_4$$

Because the pseudo-randomness of F, G, P holds, any PPT adversary cannot distinguish the random bits from the output of PRF F, G, P. So it cannot distinguish $\tilde{\tau}_i = \left(\gamma_s(id(w_i)), \tilde{T}'_s[\gamma_s(id(w_i))] \oplus iT_s(id(w_i)), K_{id(w_i)}\right)$ with $\tau_i = (F_{K_1}(w_i), G_{K_2}(w_i),$ $P_{K_3}(w_i))$, so as $\tau_s = (\tau_1, \ldots \tau_n)$ and $\tilde{\tau}_s = (\tilde{\tau}_1, \ldots \tilde{\tau}_n)$. Therefore, ε_4 is negligible.

In the same way, based on the elliptic curve discrete logarithm assumption and the pseudo-randomness of F, G, P, we have:

$$\left|\mathbf{Pr}\left[1 \leftarrow \mathcal{A}(\delta, \mathbf{f}, \tau_a, c_f)\right] - \mathbf{Pr}\left[1 \leftarrow \mathcal{A}(\delta, \mathbf{f}, \tilde{\tau}_a, \tilde{c}_f)\right]\right| \leq \varepsilon_5,$$

$$\left|\mathbf{Pr}\left[1 \leftarrow \mathcal{A}(\delta, \mathbf{f}, \tau_d)\right] - \mathbf{Pr}\left[1 \leftarrow \mathcal{A}(\delta, \mathbf{f}, \tilde{\tau}_d)\right]\right| \leq \varepsilon_6,$$

where $\varepsilon_5, \varepsilon_6$ are all negligible values.

To sum up, we have the conclusion that for all PPT adversaries $\mathcal{A}$, the output of $\mathrm{Real}_{\mathcal{A}}(1^k)$ and $\mathrm{Ideal}_{\mathcal{A},\mathcal{S}}(1^k)$ are identical, except with negligible probability $\mathbf{negl}(1^k)$, i.e.:

$$\left|\mathbf{Pr}\left[\mathrm{Real}_{\mathcal{A}}(1^k) = 1\right] - \mathbf{Pr}\left[\mathrm{Ideal}_{\mathcal{A},\mathcal{S}}(1^k) = 1\right]\right| \leq \mathbf{negl}(1^k).$$

Therefore our dynamic MSE scheme is $(\mathcal{L}_1, \mathcal{L}_2, \mathcal{L}_3, \mathcal{L}_4)$-secure against adaptive chosen-keyword attacks in random oracle model. □

4.2   Unforgeability

Theorem 2. *If H_3 is collision-resistant hash function and the bilinear q-SDH assumption holds then the dynamic MSE scheme is unforgeable.*

Proof: The main idea to give the proof is that, if there exists a PPT adversary $\mathcal{A}$ such that $\mathrm{Forge}_{\mathcal{A}}(1^k) = 1$, then there exist a PPT simulator $\mathcal{S}$ that breaks at least one of the assumptions : The collision-resistance property of H_3 and the Bilinear q-SDH assumption.

During the game, the simulator $\mathcal{S}$ interacts with $\mathcal{A}$ using real algorithm. Assume after q times queries, $\mathcal{A}$ outputs a set of file identifiers $\mathbf{I}' \neq \mathbf{I}_W$ and a valid proof π. This means the proof $\pi = \{\mathcal{T}, \mathcal{S}, \mathcal{C}\}$ he produces under query W passes all three steps of the verification phase. We categorize the forgery into three types:

Type I forgery: For some word $w_i \in W$, the adversary outputs a different leaf value $\widehat{\theta}_{w_i}$ in Merkle tree proof $\widehat{t}_i$ and passes the verification step 1.

Type II forgery: For some word $w_i \in W$, $\mathbf{I}' \not\subset S_i$. The adversary gives the simulator the real accumulation value in the proof t_i, and outputs a subset witness $\widehat{g}^{P_i}$ that passes the verification step 2.

Type III forgery: The set $\mathbf{I}'$ is a proper subset of $\mathbf{I}_W$. The adversary gives the simulator the real $\mathcal{S} = \{g^{P_1}, \ldots, g^{P_n}\}$, and outputs a completeness witness $\widehat{\mathcal{C}}$ which passes the verification step 3.

It is clear that if $\mathbf{I}' \neq \mathbf{I}_W$ and proof π is valid then one of the above mentioned forgeries must occur. Next we show that the simulator $\mathcal{S}$ can use type I forgery to break the collision-resistance property of H_3, and use type II or III forgeries to break the bilinear q-SDH assumption.

1. The collision-resistance property of H_3

The hash function H_3 is collision-resistance if it is difficult for all PPT adversaries to find two different messages m_1 and m_2, such that $H_3(m_1) = H_3(m_2)$.

First, given the hash function H_3, the simulator $\mathcal{S}$ interacts with the adversary $\mathcal{A}$ according to the game $\mathrm{Forge}_{\mathcal{A}}(1^k)$. If $\mathcal{A}$ wins the game and the Type I forgery occurs, that means for some word $w_i \in W$, $\mathcal{A}$ outputs a different leaf value $\widehat{\theta}_{w_i}$ in Merkle tree proof $\widehat{t}_i$.. Then, the simulator $\mathcal{S}$ verifies the value $\mathcal{A}$ outputs, which passes the verification step 1. Let $\widehat{\theta}_{w_i} = (\widehat{\theta}_{w_i,1}, \widehat{\theta}_{w_i,2})$. Passing the verification step 1 means the following two conditions hold:

- The search key $F_{K_1}(w_i) = \widehat{\theta}_{w_i,1}$.
- The Merkle tree verification using the leaf $\widehat{\theta}_{w_i}$ succeeds.

According to the verification step 1, the adversary $\mathcal{A}$ may only forge the $\widehat{\theta}_{w_i,2}$. Then passing the Merkle tree verification implies that the adversary is able to find the collision of H_3, because it can generate the same root with the modified leaf.

2. Bilinear q-SDH assumption

Given the simulator $\mathcal{S}$ an instance of bilinear q-SDH problem: $(p, \mathbb{G}, \mathcal{G}, e, g)$ and a $(q+1)$-tuple $(g, g^s, \ldots, g^{s^q})$. $\mathcal{S}$ interacts with the adversary $\mathcal{A}$ in the following way.

First, since $\mathcal{S}$ doesn't know the value s in the given bilinear q-SDH instance, it needs to reconstruct the following algorithms which related to s in the game $\text{Forge}_{\mathcal{A}}(1^k)$:

In the algorithm Gen, the simulator $\mathcal{S}$ directly uses $(g, g^s, \ldots, g^{s^q})$ as the public parameters without knowing s, and sends them to the adversary.

And in the algorithm Setup, for the leaf nodes: $\theta_w = \left(F_{K_1}(w), g^{\prod_{f \in \mathfrak{f}_w} (s + id(f))} \right)$, the simulator $\mathcal{S}$ computes the value using $(g, g^s, \ldots, g^{s^q}):g^{\prod_{f \in \mathfrak{f}_w} (s + id(f))}$.

It is worth mentioning that, the simulator $\mathcal{S}$ needs to construct an extra auxiliary data structure $\mathcal{N}$. It stores for each leaf nodes θ_w the polynomial: $n_w = \prod_{f \in \mathfrak{f}_w} (s + id(f))$, which is used to form the add/delete tokens later.

Simulator $\mathcal{S}$ cannot directly compute the value of τ_a in Add/Update protocol. In the Add/Update protocol's user's step 2, when computing the value of the new leaf node θ_i' in τ_a, it first finds $\mathcal{N}$ to find the polynomials n_i that equals $\theta_{i,2}$, then computes the value $g^{n_i \cdot (s + id(f))}$ using $(g, g^s, \ldots, g^{s^q})$. The value $\theta_i' = (\theta_{i,1}, g^{n_i \cdot (s + id(f))})$ is the updated leaf node.

Similarly, in the Del/Update protocol, $\mathcal{S}$ finds the n_i in $\mathcal{N}$ and removes the factor $s + id(f)$ from n_i and then computes the value $g^{n_i / (s + id(f))}$ using $(g, g^s, \ldots, g^{s^q})$ and gets a new leaf node $\theta_i' = (\theta_{i,1}, g^{n_i / (s + id(f))})$.

In this modified game, the values that related to s are computed in a new way. However, it produces same output as it was produced by earlier version of algorithm. So in the adversary $\mathcal{A}$'s view, these values are still valid, it cannot distinguish this game with the original one.

If $\mathcal{A}$ wins the game, and the following two types of forgeries occur, then the simulator $\mathcal{S}$ may solve the given bilinear q-SDH instance.

- If the Type II forgery occurs, i.e., the adversary $\mathcal{A}$ outputs a set $\mathbf{I}' = \{x_1, \ldots, x_m\}$ and a witness $\hat{g}^{P_i}$ for some $w_i \in W$. Let $S_i = \{id_1, \ldots, id_q\}$ be the file identifier set related to the word w_i, then $g^{(s + id_1)(s + id_2) \cdots (s + id_q)}$ is the corresponding accumulation value. Since $\mathbf{I}' \not\subset S_i$, there exists some $1 \leq j \leq m$, such that $x_j \notin S_i$. This means in the equation: $e(g^{\prod_{x \in \mathbf{I}'} (s + x)}, \hat{g}^{P_i}) = e(g^{(s + id_1)(s + id_2) \cdots (s + id_q)}, g)$, $(s + x_j)$ does not divide $(s + id_1)(s + id_2) \cdots (s + id_q)$. Therefore there exists polynomial $Q(s)$ of degree $q - 1$ and constant $c \neq 0$, such that: $(s + id_1)(s + id_2) \cdots (s + id_q) = Q(s)(s + x_j) + c$.

  Then the simulator $\mathcal{S}$ has $e(g, \hat{g}^{P_i})^{(s + x_j) \prod_{x \in \mathbf{I}' \wedge x \neq x_j} (s + x)} = e(g, g)^{Q(s)(s + x_j) + c}$.

  After transformation, it can finally have $e(g, g)^{1/s + x_j} = e(g, \hat{g}^{P_i})^{\prod_{x \in \mathbf{I}' \wedge x \neq x_j} (s + x)}$ $e(g, g)^{-Q(s)})^{1/c}$. This means the simulator $\mathcal{S}$ can solve the instance of bilinear q-SDH problem in polynomial time.

- If the Type III forgery occurs, i.e., the adversary $\mathcal{A}$ outputs a set $\mathbf{I}' = \{x_1, \ldots, x_m\}$ and the completeness witness $\widehat{\mathcal{C}}$. Since the set $\mathbf{I}'$ is the proper subset of $\mathbf{I}_W$, there exists at least one common factor in polynomials $P_1, \ldots, P_n$. We use $(s+x)$ to denote the factor, where $x \notin \mathbf{I}'$. These values can pass the verification step 3 means the following holds: $\prod_{i=1}^{n} e(g^{P_i}, g^{q_i}) = e(g, g)$. And extract $(s+x)$ from each P_i by computing $g^{P'_i} = (g^{P_i})^{1/(s+x)}$, then $\prod_{i=1}^{n} e(g^{P_i}, g^{q_i}) = (\prod_{i=1}^{n} e(g^{P'_i}, g^{q_i}))^{s+x} = e(g, g)$.

Thus the simulator $\mathcal{S}$ can easily form the solution of the instance of bilinear q-SDH problem by computing: $e(g, g)^{1/(s+x)} = \prod_{i=1}^{n} e(g^{P'_i}, g^{q_i})$. This means the simulator can also solve the instance of bilinear q-SDH problem in polynomial time.

The above analyses show that, if the adversary $\mathcal{A}$ could successfully forge a proof, it must have the ability to break at least one of these assumptions above. Therefore we have the conclusion that for all PPT adversaries $\mathcal{A}$, the probability

$$\mathbf{Pr}[\text{Forge}_{\mathcal{A}}(1^k) = 1] \leq \mathbf{negl}(1^k),$$

where $\mathbf{negl}(1^k)$ is a negligible function with input 1^k. Thus our dynamic MSE scheme is unforgeable. □

5 Conclusion

Searchable encryption is an important cryptographic primitive for cloud storage environment. It is well motivated by the popularity of cloud storage services. At the same time, the authentication methods utilized for the search results' verification is a significant supplement that makes the search more reliable and it would greatly promote the development of cloud storage service.

In this paper, we described a searchable encryption scheme which supports multiple keywords search and authentication. The scheme can greatly reduce the communication cost during the search. We demonstrated that, taking into account the security challenges in the cloud storage, our scheme can withstand the chosen-keyword attack carried out by the adaptive adversaries. Proposed scheme also prevents the result from being maliciously altered by those adversaries.

In the future, we will perform a detailed analysis of the security aspects in this paper and investigate the feasibility of designing improved security model to enhance the scheme's security features. Moreover, we will give consideration to the authenticate techniques to achieve more efficiency to meet practical needs.

Acknowledgement. This work was supported in part by the National Science and Technology Major Project under Grant No. 2013ZX03002006, the Liaoning Province Science and Technology Projects under Grant No. 2013217004, the Liaoning Province Doctor Startup Fund under Grant NO. 20141012, the Fundamental Research Funds for the Central Universities under Grant No. N130317002, the Shenyang Province Science and Technology Projects under Grant No. F14-231-1-08, and the National Natural Science Foundation of China under Grant Numbers 61472184, 61321491, 61272546.

172 F. Zhou et al.

References

1. Cachin, C., Keidar, I., Shraer, A.: Trusting the cloud. ACM SIGACT News. **40**(2), 81–86 (2009)
2. Kamara, S., Lauter, K.: Cryptographic cloud storage. In: Sion, R., Curtmola, R., Dietrich, S., Kiayias, A., Miret, J.M., Sako, K., Sebé, F. (eds.) RLCPS, WECSR, and WLC 2010. LNCS, vol. 6054, pp. 136–149. Springer, Heidelberg (2010)
3. Song, D.X., Wagner, D., Perrig, A.: Practical techniques for searches on encrypted data. In: IEEE Symposium on Security and Privacy (S&P 2010), Oakland, California, USA, pp. 44–55. IEEE Computer Society (2010)
4. Goh, E.J.: Secure indexes. cryptology. ePrint Archive, Report 2003/216
5. Chang, Y.-C., Mitzenmacher, M.: Privacy preserving keyword searches on remote encrypted data. In: Ioannidis, J., Keromytis, A.D., Yung, M. (eds.) ACNS 2005. LNCS, vol. 3531, pp. 442–455. Springer, Heidelberg (2005)
6. Curtmola, R., Garay, J., Kamara, S., Ostrovsky, R.: Searchable symmetric encryption: improved definitions and efficient constructions. J. Comput. Secur. **19**(5), 895–934 (2011)
7. Kamara, S., Papamanthou, C., Roeder, T.: Dynamic searchable symmetric encryption. In: Proceedings of CCS 2012, pp. 965–976. ACM (2012)
8. Cash, D., Jaeger, J., Jarecki, S., Jutla, C.S., Krawczyk, H., Rosu, M.C., Steiner, M.: Dynamic searchable encryption in very-large databases: data structures and implementation. I Cryptology ePrint Archive, Report 2014/853
9. Stefanov, E., Papamanthou, C., Shi, E.: Practical dynamic searchable encryption with small leakage. In: Proceedings of the Network and Distributed System Security Symposium (NDSS 2011), 23–26 February 2011, San Diego, California, USA. The Internet Society (2011)
10. Golle, P., Staddon, J., Waters, B.: Secure conjunctive keyword search over encrypted data. In: Jakobsson, M., Yung, M., Zhou, J. (eds.) ACNS 2004. LNCS, vol. 3089, pp. 31–45. Springer, Heidelberg (2004)
11. Ballard, L., Kamara, S., Monrose, F.: Achieving efficient conjunctive keyword searches over encrypted data. In: Qing, S., Mao, W., López, J., Wang, G. (eds.) ICICS 2005. LNCS, vol. 3783, pp. 414–426. Springer, Heidelberg (2005)
12. Byun, J.W., Lee, D.-H., Lim, J.-I.: Efficient conjunctive keyword search on encrypted data storage system. In: Atzeni, A.S., Lioy, A. (eds.) EuroPKI 2006. LNCS, vol. 4043, pp. 184–196. Springer, Heidelberg (2006)
13. Cao, N., Wang, C., Li, M., Ren, K., Lou, W.: Privacy-preserving multi-keyword ranked search over encrypted cloud data. IEEE Trans. Parallel Distrib. Syst. **25**(1), 222–233 (2014)
14. Kamara, S., Papamanthou, C., Roeder, T.: CS2: a searchable cryptographic cloud storage system. TechReport MSR-TR-2011-58, Microsoft Research (2011)
15. Merkle, R.C.: A certified digital signature. In: Brassard, G. (ed.) CRYPTO 1989. LNCS, vol. 435, pp. 218–238. Springer, Heidelberg (1990)
16. Kurosawa, K., Ohtaki, Y.: UC-secure searchable symmetric encryption. In: Keromytis, A.D. (ed.) FC 2012. LNCS, vol. 7397, pp. 285–298. Springer, Heidelberg (2012)
17. Papamanthou, C., Tamassia, R., Triandopoulos, N.: Optimal verification of operations on dynamic sets. In: Rogaway, P. (ed.) CRYPTO 2011. LNCS, vol. 6841, pp. 91–110. Springer, Heidelberg (2011)
18. Katz, J., Lindell, Y.: Introduction to Modern Cryptography. CRC Press, Boca Raton (2014)
19. Nguyen, L.: Accumulators from bilinear pairings and applications. In: Menezes, A. (ed.) CT-RSA 2005. LNCS, vol. 3376, pp. 275–292. Springer, Heidelberg (2005)

Oblivious Keyword Search with Authorization

Peng Jiang[1,2(✉)], Xiaofen Wang[3], Jianchang Lai[2],
Fuchun Guo[2(✉)], and Rongmao Chen[2]

[1] State Key Laboratory of Networking and Switching Technology,
Beijing University of Posts and Telecommunications, Beijing 100876, China
[2] Centre for Computer and Information Security Research,
School of Computing and Information Technology,
University of Wollongong, Wollongong, NSW 2522, Australia
{pj688,fuchun}@uow.edu.au
[3] Centre for Cyber Security and Big Data Research Center,
University of Electronic Science and Technology of China,
Chengdu 611731, Sichuan, China

Abstract. Oblivious keyword search (OKS) allows a user to search and retrieve the data associated with a chosen keyword in an oblivious way. The database supplier issues a trapdoor (used for searching) of a specific keyword chosen by the user while learns nothing about this keyword. In this paper, we propose a new cryptographic primitive called oblivious keyword search with authorization (OKSA). In OKSA, the supplier is able to verify the to-be-search keyword belonging to the authorized keyword set for a user before running the OKS protocol. The proposed OKSA augments the traditional OKS by providing assurance of keyword authorization besides oblivious search. Then we present an OKSA protocol and formally prove its security. The proposed protocol features with one-round (two-pass) interaction and constant size communication cost between the supplier and the user in the transfer phase. Precisely, the communication cost nseeds only four group elements (three group elements for keyword token and proof, and one group element for assigned trapdoor), independent of the size of authorized keyword set.

Keywords: Keyword search · Oblivious transfer · Authorization

1 Introduction

Keyword search is a fundamental database operation. It involves two main parties: a database supplier (or *supplier* for short) who holds a database comprised of a set of data, and a user who wishes to retrieve some pieces of data containing specific keywords. To preserve keyword privacy, searchable encryption [39] was introduced to allow searching on encrypted data without revealing the associated keyword. Searchable encryption can be realized in either symmetric setting or asymmetric setting. Although the symmetric searchable encryption (SSE) enjoys high efficiency [13,17,24,25], it suffers from complicated secret key distribution/management when users want to share data. To resolve this problem,

© Springer International Publishing AG 2016
L. Chen and J. Han (Eds.): ProvSec 2016, LNCS 10005, pp. 173–190, 2016.
DOI: 10.1007/978-3-319-47422-9_10

Boneh et al. introduced a more flexible primitive, namely public key encryption with keyword search (PEKS) [7] that applies the asymmetric encryption setting to enable users to search encrypted data.

Although supporting the keyword privacy in the asymmetric searching, PEKS is unsuitable in database operation where supplier can control users based on keyword while unknowing that keyword. In [30], Ogata and Kurosawa introduced an interesting notion, called oblivious keyword search (OKS). In the OKS protocol, data is encrypted using the associated keyword and all ciphertexts are committed to users. The user generates the token for arbitrary one keyword of his choice and sends the keyword token to the supplier. The supplier then generates the trapdoor with the received token and his master secret key without any restriction. By this, the user can retrieve the data containing the specific keyword. With a two-party oblivious transfer protocol between a supplier and a user, the user is able to get the trapdoor of the chosen keyword without revealing it to the supplier, while learns nothing except the data of his choice.

The OKS protocol solves the problem of the trapdoor generation for an unknown keyword. However, in some special databases, such as databases for commercial secrets and databases for DNA information, data is highly confidential and users may have different retrieving rights according to their classes. That is, the choice of keyword from a user must be in an authorized keyword set defined by the supplier. Precisely, if W is the authorized keyword set for a user, the user can only specify any keyword $w \in W$ and the supplier grants the user with the retrieving right for data associated with w. The supplier is able to verify that the chosen keyword belongs to W but does not know which keyword it is.

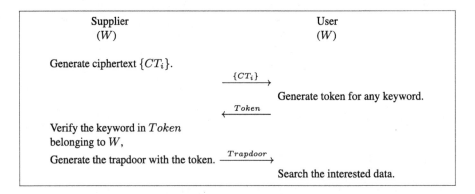

Fig. 1. OKSA framework.

Our Contributions. The contributions of this paper are mainly twofold.

Firstly, we propose a new notion named *oblivious keyword search with authorization* (OKSA), which extends the previous OKS. We systematically study the keyword authorization problem in the oblivious keyword search, where the supplier has an agreed authorized keyword set with each user. In OKSA, the user generates a keyword token for any keyword in the authorized keyword set and thereafter the supplier generates the trapdoor with the received token, his secret key and the authorized keyword set, which is presented intuitively in Fig. 1. Like this, the supplier can know the fact that the to-be-search keyword belongs to the authorized keyword set but cannot distinguish which one it is. Compared with OKS, the OKSA provides authorization verification of the to-be-search keyword besides allowing the user to search data in an oblivious way.

Secondly, we design an OKSA protocol featuring that its communication cost between user and supplier is constant, independent of the size of authorized keyword set. A potential approach to the OKSA protocol is that the supplier encrypts all trapdoors of keywords in W (we assume $|W| = n$) and runs a 1-out-of-n oblivious transfer protocol with the user on each encrypted trapdoor. This requires the linear size communication cost from the supplier to the user. To obtain low communication bandwidth, we employ an aggregation algorithm in trapdoor generation. Then each transfer subphase in this protocol requires constant-size communication cost (i.e. one group element) from the supplier to the user. The keyword token and proof for accountability are also of short size, with two group elements and one group element respectively. Another nice feature is that the proposed OKSA protocol removes computationally expensive cryptographic primitives (e.g. zero-knowledge proof), which are necessary and impractical in the traditional OKS schemes. Finally, we formally prove the security of the proposed OKSA protocol.

1.1 Related Work

Public Key Encryption with Keyword Search. Boneh et al. [7] introduced the notion of PEKS to address weaknesses of SSE and presented a concrete scheme. In their scheme, the searchable ciphertext is created using a keyword and the user's public key. The trapdoor is created using his secret key and keyword for searching. The corresponding encrypted data is returned to the user only when the keyword in the trapdoor matches the keyword in the ciphertext.

Many PEKS variants have been proposed to improve the security or functionality later on. In terms of keyword security, some secure channel free-PEKS (SCF-PEKS) schemes [3,18,34,35] have been proposed to resist keyword guessing attacks. Regarding the search functionality, combinable multi-keyword search using public-key encryption scheme with conjunctive keyword search (PECKS) were achieved in [4,5,8,31,36,37]. To enhance the database system usability, Abdalla et al. [1] constructed the public key encryption with temporary keyword search (PETKS). The transformation from anonymous IBE to public key-based search over encrypted data was given in [11,15]. From perpectives of application, some schemes based on attribute-based encryption (ABE) [38,40,41] were proposed to benefit data search control and some privacy-preserving data search in multi-cloud were presented in [27,28].

Oblivious Transfer. Originally, the notion of oblivious transfer was introduced by Rabin [32], which is a two party protocol between a sender $\mathcal{S}$ and a receiver $\mathcal{R}$. $\mathcal{S}$

has two bits and $\mathcal{R}$ wishes to get one of them satisfying the followings properties: $\mathcal{S}$ does not know which bit $\mathcal{R}$ obtains, and $\mathcal{R}$ does not know any information about the bit that he did not obtain. In an OT system, the most general type is k-out-of-n oblivious transfer (OT_n^k), where $\mathcal{S}$ holds n messages and $\mathcal{R}$ retrieves k of them simultaneously, such that $\mathcal{S}$ does not know which messages $\mathcal{R}$ obtains. There have been many works on oblivious transfer, such as adaptive oblivious transfer [16,26], oblivious transfer with fully simulatable security [12], oblivious transfer with universally composable security [20], oblivious transfer with access control [9] and priced oblivious transfer [2,10]. Some proposed OT_n^k protocols, such as [14,21,29], have ideal communication rounds.

Oblivious Keyword Search. Ogata and Kurosawa [30] introduced the notion of oblivious keyword search to address the user privacy issue in the keyword search, which was based on a two party OT protocol between a supplier and a user. Their OKS employed the blind signature, where the ciphertext is generated by the master secret key of the supplier (denoted by msk) and some keyword, and each trapdoor is transferred from the supplier to the user using msk and the keyword token generated by the user. Rhee et al. [33] presented an oblivious conjunctive keyword search to allow search over boolean combinations of keywords. Freedman et al. [19] considered privacy concerns in keyword search using oblivious evaluation of pseudorandom functions. Zhu and Bao [42] addressed the OKS in the public database by using linear and non-linear oblivious polynomial evaluation. Camenisch et al. [11] proposed the public key encryption with oblivious keyword search (PEOKS) to build a public key encrypted database permitting private information retrieval (PIR), where computationally expensive zero-knowledge proof (ZKP) was employed.

Comparison with OKS [30]. There are some differences in components between the OKS and our OKSA, especially the generation of the keyword token and the trapdoor. Let sk be the secret key of the user, (mpk, msk) be the key pair of the supplier, w be a keyword and W be the authorized keyword set, respectively. We make a comparison of our OKSA with the OKS in terms of notion formulation in Table 1, including the involved parameters and entities, and the component size.

Table 1. Comparisons between Our OKSA and Traditional OKS.

Protocol	Ciphertext	Keyword Token	Trapdoor	Token Size	Trapdoor Size
OKS [30]	w, msk, m	w, mpk, sk (User)	$Token, msk$ (Supplier)	$O(1)$	$O(1)$
OKSA	w_i, mpk, m	$W, mpk, sk, w_i \in W$ (User)	$Token, msk, W$ (Supplier)	$O(1)$	$O(1)$

As shown in Table 1, OKS focuses on a single keyword and its trapdoor size is $O(1)$ for one keyword. When for multiple keywords, the trapdoor size of OKS will be $O(n)$ to achieve the oblivious property. The trapdoor size in OKSA is $O(1)$, independent of the size of the keyword set. OKSA can achieve the efficient oblivious search over a keyword set. Since the keyword set W is involved in trapdoor generation, OKSA provides that the supplier can verify that the to-be-search keyword is in the authorized keyword set (i.e., $w_i \in W$), but cannot distinguish which one w_i is.

Organization. The rest of this paper is organized as follows. In Sect. 2, we give some preliminaries and define the OKSA algorithm, security model and complexity assumptions. We present an efficient OKSA protocol in Sect. 3 and prove its security in Sect. 4. We conclude the paper in Sect. 5.

2   Preliminaries

2.1   Bilinear Pairing

Let $\mathbb{G}, \mathbb{G}_T$ be two cyclic multiplicative groups of the same prime order p, g be the generator of $\mathbb{G}$. A bilinear map is defined as $e : \mathbb{G} \times \mathbb{G} \to \mathbb{G}_T$ which satisfies the following properties [6]:

- Bilinearity: For all $g, h \in \mathbb{G}$ and $a, b \in \mathbb{Z}_p$, we have $e\left(g^a, h^b\right) = e\left(g, h\right)^{ab}$.
- Non-degeneracy: $e(g, g) \neq 1$.
- Computability: It is efficient to compute $e\left(g, h\right)$ for any $g, h \in \mathbb{G}$.

A bilinear group $\mathcal{PG} = (p, \mathbb{G}, \mathbb{G}_T, e)$ is composed of objects described above.

2.2   Algorithm Definition

Our OKSA adopts a two-party interaction between the supplier and the user as [30].

Definition 1. *An oblivious keyword search with authorization consists of the following polynomial time randomized algorithms.*

Setup
The supplier $\mathcal{T}$ takes a security parameter 1^λ and an integer n as input, and outputs the master public/secret key pair (mpk, msk) to establish the system. $\mathcal{T}$ negotiates a keyword set W with each user, where $|W| \leq n$.

Commit
$\mathcal{T}$ takes a message m_i, a keyword w_i and the master public key mpk as input, and outputs the ciphertext CT_i, where each message m_i has its own unique keyword w_i. $\mathcal{T}$ commits all ciphertexts $\{CT_i\}$ to the user $\mathcal{U}$.

Transfer

- $\mathcal{U} \to \mathcal{T}$: $\mathcal{U}$ takes the authorized keyword set W, a specified keyword $w_i' \in W$ and the master public key mpk as input, and outputs the keyword token $\mathbf{P}(w_i')$, the secret key of the user sk and the proof information for accountability Σ. Then $\mathcal{U}$ sends $(\mathbf{P}(w_i'), \Sigma)$ to $\mathcal{T}$. Here, $\mathbf{P}(w_i')$ is computed from sk, w_i', W, mpk. Σ helps $\mathcal{T}$ to verify the accountability, that is, the received token is used to generate a trapdoor for only one keyword in the authorized keyword set.
- $\mathcal{T} \to \mathcal{U}$: $\mathcal{T}$ takes the received keyword token $\mathbf{P}(w_i')$, the authorized keyword set W and the master secret key msk as input. It verifies the accountability by checking $|\mathbf{P}(w_i')| = 1$. and then outputs a trapdoor T to $\mathcal{U}$.
- $\mathcal{U}$: $\mathcal{U}$ takes CT_i, T, sk as input and outputs m_i if $w_i = w_i'$, otherwise, $\bot$.

Correctness. An oblivious keyword search with authorization is correct if the user obtains the message of his choice when all of entities follow the protocol steps above. Also, passing the verification of accountability means that the to-be-generate trapdoor, based on the received token, will be for only one specific keyword and this specific keyword is in the authorized keyword set.

2.3   Security Notions

Based on [7,30], we define security requirements to be user privacy, indistinguishability and accountability. User privacy guarantees that the supplier $\mathcal{T}$ does not learn the to-be-search keyword from the user's token in the i-th Transfer subphase. Indistinguishability guarantees that a malicious user $\mathcal{U}$ cannot distinguish the message and keyword from the ciphertext. Accountability guarantees that the trapdoor the user asks for is for only one keyword in the authorized keyword set.

- (User Privacy.) Given $(\mathbf{P}(w), \Sigma)$ and two keywords w_0, w_1, it is hard to distinguish whether $w = w_0$ or w_1.
- (Indistinguishability.) Given two message-keyword tuples $(m_0, w_0), (m_1, w_1)$ and a ciphertext CT for (m, w), it is hard to distinguish $(m, w) = (m_0, w_0)$ or $(m, w) = (m_1, w_1)$.
- (Accountability.) Given $(\mathbf{P}(W), W, sk)$ satisfying $|W| > 1$, it is hard to generate $(\mathbf{P}(W), \Sigma)$ that passes the verification.

Based on the above requirements, we define the security models via the following games played between a challenger $\mathcal{C}$ and an adversary $\mathcal{A}$. More formally,

User Privacy.

- **Setup.** $\mathcal{C}$ runs the Setup algorithm to generate the system parameter mpk and sends it to $\mathcal{A}$.
- **Challenge.** $\mathcal{A}$ gives two keywords w_0, w_1 to $\mathcal{C}$. $\mathcal{C}$ responds by choosing a coin $\theta \in \{0, 1\}$, setting $w = w_\theta$ and generating $(\mathbf{P}(w), \Sigma)$.
- **Guess.** $\mathcal{A}$ outputs θ' and wins the game if $\theta' = \theta$.

We define $\mathcal{A}$'s advantage as $\mathsf{Adv} = |\Pr[\theta' = \theta] - 1/2|$.

Definition 2. *We say that an OKSA satisfies user privacy if there exists no probabilistic polynomial time adversary to win the above user privacy game with a non-negligible advantage.*

Indistinguishability.

- **Setup.** $\mathcal{C}$ runs the Setup algorithm to generate the system parameter mpk and sends it to $\mathcal{A}$.
- **Phase 1.** $\mathcal{A}$ makes the trapdoor query for the keyword w and $\mathcal{C}$ responds with the trapdoor T.
- **Challenge.** $\mathcal{A}$ gives two same length message-keyword tuples (m_0, w_0), (m_1, w_1) to $\mathcal{C}$ with the restriction that w_0, w_1 have not been issued the trapdoor queries in **Phase 1**. $\mathcal{C}$ responds the challenge ciphertext CT^* for randomly choosing $\theta \in \{0,1\}$.
- **Phase 2.** $\mathcal{A}$ issues more trapdoor queries with the same restriction in **Challenge**, $\mathcal{C}$ responds as **Phase 1**.
- **Guess.** $\mathcal{A}$ outputs θ' and wins the game if $\theta' = \theta$.

We define $\mathcal{A}$'s advantage as $\mathsf{Adv} = |\Pr[\theta' = \theta] - 1/2|$.

Definition 3. *We say that OKSA has indistinguishability against chosen keyword attack if there exists no probabilistic polynomial time adversary to win the above game with a non-negligible advantage.*

Accountability. In OKSA, the verification of accountability is to assure that the to-be-generate trapdoor is for only one authorized keyword. It captures the attack that an adversary $\mathcal{A}$ can forge a proof for a valid keyword token $\mathbf{P}(W')$, where W' is a subset of the authorized keyword set W with $1 < |W'| < |W| \leq n$. Here, the validness means that $\mathcal{A}$ knows W', W, sk of computing $\mathbf{P}(W')$.

- **Setup.** $\mathcal{C}$ runs the Setup algorithm to generate the system parameter mpk and sends it to $\mathcal{A}$.
- **Challenge.** $\mathcal{A}$ outputs $(\mathbf{P}(W'), W, W', sk)$ and 1 for challenge, where $\mathbf{P}(W')$ is generated from W, W', sk, mpk and $|W'| > 1$.
- **Win.** $\mathcal{A}$ outputs $(\mathbf{P}(W'), \Sigma)$ and wins the game if $(\mathbf{P}(W'), \Sigma)$ passes the verification algorithm.

We define $\mathcal{A}$'s advantage as Adv in computing $(\mathbf{P}(W'), \Sigma)$.

Definition 4. *We say that OKSA has accountability if there exists no polynomial time adversary to win the above game with a non-negligible advantage.*

2.4   Assumptions

We define two hard problems to provide foundation for the security of OKSA, i.e., (f, n)-DHE Problem and (f, q)-MSE-DDH Problem. Since (f, n)-DHE Problem has been proposed and analyzed in [22,23], we only give its description and omit its intractability analysis. We refer readers to the corresponding references for details.

Definition 5 (f, n)**-DHE Problem.** Let $\mathbb{G}$ be a group of prime order p, $h \in \mathbb{G}$ and $a \in \mathbb{Z}_p$. Given $h, h^a, \cdots, h^{a^n}$, output $(f(x), h^{f(a)})$, where $f(x) \in \mathbb{Z}_p[x]$ is a polynomial function with $\deg f(x) > n$.

Then we introduce a new hard problem named (f, q)-MSE-DDH Problem, which is slightly modified from MSE-DDH problem while still preserving its hardness. Our (f, q)-MSE-DDH problem is a special instance of general Diffie-Hellman exponent assumptions in [6], and its intractability will be analyzed later on.

Definition 6 (f, q)**-MSE-DDH Problem.** Let $\mathcal{PG}$ be a bilinear map group system and g_0, h_0 be the generators of the group $\mathbb{G}$. We assume two pairwise coprime polynomials f and q with degree $1, n - 1$, respectively, where n is an integer. Given $g_0, g_0^\alpha, g_0^r, h_0^{f(\alpha)}, \cdots, h_0^{\alpha^{n-2}f(\alpha)}, h_0^{f(\alpha)q(\alpha)}, \cdots, h_0^{\alpha^n f(\alpha)q(\alpha)}$, and $Z \in \mathbb{G}_T$, the goal is to distinguish $Z = e(g_0, h_0)^{rq(\alpha)}$ or a random group element in $\mathbb{G}_T$.

Intractability Analysis of (f, q)-MSE-DDH Problem.
The (f, q)-MSE-DDH Problem can be reformulated as D, E, F. Since g_0, h_0 are generators in group $\mathbb{G}$, we suppose $h_0 = g_0^\beta$,

$$D = \begin{pmatrix} 1, & \alpha, & r, \\ \beta f(\alpha), & \cdots, & \beta \alpha^{n-2} f(\alpha), \\ \beta f(\alpha)q(\alpha), & \cdots, & \beta \alpha^n f(\alpha)q(\alpha), \end{pmatrix}$$

$$E = 1,$$

$$F = r\beta q(\alpha).$$

We need to show that F is independent of (D, E), i.e. no coefficients $\{x_{i,j}\}$ and y_1 exist such that $F = \Sigma x_{i,j} d_i d_j + \Sigma y_1 e_1$, where the polynomials d_i, d_j are listed in D and e_1 is listed in E above. By making all possible products of two polynomials from D which are multiples of $r\beta$ to F', we want to prove that no such linear combination F' leads to F,

$$F' = \begin{pmatrix} r\beta f(\alpha), & \cdots, & r\beta \alpha^{n-2} f(\alpha), \\ r\beta f(\alpha)q(\alpha), & \cdots, & r\beta \alpha^n f(\alpha)q(\alpha), \end{pmatrix}$$

Any such linear combination associated with $r\beta$ can be written

$$r\beta f(\alpha)A(\alpha) + r\beta f(\alpha)q(\alpha)B(\alpha) = r\beta q(\alpha),$$

where $A(\alpha), B(\alpha)$ are polynomials with degree deg $A \leq n - 2$ and deg $B \leq n$.

If $B(\alpha) \neq 0$, we have deg $f(\alpha)q(\alpha)B(\alpha) \geq n$. Since deg $(q(\alpha) - f(\alpha)A(\alpha)) \leq n - 1$, we have $B(\alpha) = 0$. We simplify the above equation as $f(\alpha)A(\alpha) = q(\alpha)$, so $f(\alpha)|q(\alpha)$, which contradicts that $f(\alpha)$ and $q(\alpha)$ are comprime. Therefore, there exist no coefficients $\{x_{i,j}\}, y_1$ such that $F = \Sigma x_{i,j}d_i d_j + \Sigma y_1 e_1$ holds, (f, q)-*MSE-DDH Problem* is intractable.

3   Oblivious Keyword Search with Authorization

In this section, we propose an oblivious keyword search with authorization protocol. Our protocol allows the user to obliviously obtain an authorized trapdoor by submitting a keyword token adaptively. It features with constant size communication cost between the supplier and the user. The proposed scheme achieves that $\mathcal{T}$ can generate the trapdoor for any keyword in the authorized keyword set but cannot guess which one it is. Like OKS, OKSA is played between a supplier $\mathcal{T}$ and a user $\mathcal{U}$, and it consists of three phases: Setup, Commit and Transfer. Our OKSA protocol is illustrated in Fig. 2 and its details are as follows.

Setup. $\mathcal{T}$ takes as input a security parameter 1^{λ}, an integer n and $\mathcal{PG} = (p, \mathbb{G}, \mathbb{G}_T, e)$. Then $\mathcal{T}$ chooses generators $g, h \in \mathbb{G}$, random numbers $\alpha, x \in \mathbb{Z}_p$ and computes $g^{\alpha}, h_i = h^{\alpha^{i-1}}$ for $i = 1, 2, \cdots, n + 1$. It picks a cryptographic one-way hash function $H : (\{0, 1\}, \mathbb{G}_T) \to \{0, 1\}^{\ell}$. The master public/secret key pair is

$$mpk = (\mathcal{PG}, H, g, g^{\alpha}, h_1, h_2, \cdots, h_{n+1}), \ msk = \alpha.$$

$\mathcal{T}$ publishes mpk to all and keeps msk private.

Commit. The universal keyword space is denoted as $\mathcal{KS}$ with the size n. Each message has its associated keyword. Given a message $m_i \in \{0, 1\}^{\ell}$ and a keyword $w_i \in \mathcal{KS}$, $\mathcal{T}$ chooses $r_i \in_R \mathbb{Z}_p$ and computes the encrypted message CT_i as

$$CT_i = \left(c_{1i} = g^{r_i(\alpha + w_i)}, c_{2i} = H\left(0, e\left(g, h\right)^{r_i}\right), c_{3i} = H\left(1, e\left(g, h\right)^{r_i}\right) \oplus m_i\right).$$

$\mathcal{T}$ commits all ciphertexts $\{CT_i\}$ to $\mathcal{U}$.

Remark. There is a little difference between our OKSA and traditional OKS [30]. In OKS, the ciphertext is based on the master secret key and only the supplier, who holds msk, can generate it. In our OKSA, the ciphertext is based on the master public key and anyone in the system can generate it.

Transfer. We suppose $\mathcal{T}$ negotiates a unique keyword set W with each user, where $W \subseteq \mathcal{KS}$ and the size of W is denoted as $|W| = k \leq n$.

- $\mathcal{U} \to \mathcal{T}$: Given the authorized keyword set W, a keyword $w_i \in W$ and the master public key mpk, $\mathcal{U}$ picks $s \in_R \mathbb{Z}_p$ as his secret key $sk = s$ and computes the token $\mathbf{P}(w_i)$ and the proof Σ as

$$\mathbf{P}(w_i) = h^{s \prod_{w_j \in W, j \neq i}(\alpha + w_j)},$$

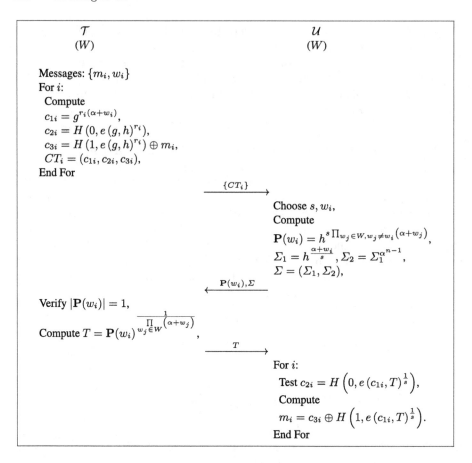

Fig. 2. Oblivious keyword search with authorization protocol.

$$\Sigma = \left(\Sigma_1 = h^{\frac{\alpha+w_i}{s}}, \ \Sigma_2 = \Sigma_1^{\alpha^{n-1}}\right).$$

Then $\mathcal{U}$ sends $(\mathbf{P}(w_i), \Sigma)$ to $\mathcal{T}$.

– $\mathcal{T} \rightarrow \mathcal{U}$: Given the tuple $(\mathbf{P}(w_i), W, \Sigma)$ and the master secret key mpk, $\mathcal{T}$ checks the accountability by the following equations,

$$e\left(\Sigma_2, h^\alpha\right) = e\left(\Sigma_1, h^{\alpha^n}\right),$$

$$e\left(h, h^{\prod_{w_i \in W}(\alpha+w_i)}\right) = e\left(\mathbf{P}(w_i), \Sigma_1\right).$$

If both equations hold, $\mathcal{T}$ accepts the received keyword token is for the trapdoor for one keyword, and we denote it as $|\mathbf{P}(w_i)| = 1$; otherwise, aborts. Given msk and W, $\mathcal{T}$ computes the trapdoor T as

$$T = \mathbf{P}(w_i)^{\frac{1}{\prod_{w_j \in W}(\alpha+w_j)}}.$$

Then $\mathcal{T}$ returns the trapdoor T to $\mathcal{U}$.

– $\mathcal{U}$: Given CT_i, T, sk, $\mathcal{U}$ executes the searching operation by

$$c_{2i} = H\left(0, e\left(c_{1i}, T\right)^{\frac{1}{s}}\right).$$

If the above equation holds, $\mathcal{U}$ continues the decryption operation by

$$m_i = c_{3i} \oplus H\left(1, e\left(c_{1i}, T\right)^{\frac{1}{s}}\right).$$

Correctness. Given the master public secret key pair (mpk, msk) from running Setup algorithm and token/proof tuple $(\mathbf{P}(w_i), \Sigma)$, the correctness of the accountability is verified by the following equations.

$$e\left(\Sigma_2, h^\alpha\right) = e\left(\Sigma_1^{\alpha^{n-1}}, h^\alpha\right)$$
$$= e\left(\Sigma_1, h^{\alpha^n}\right),$$

$$e\left(h, h^{\prod_{w_i \in W}(\alpha + w_i)}\right) = e\left(h^{s\prod_{w_j \in W, j \neq i}(\alpha + w_j)}, h^{\frac{\alpha + w_i}{s}}\right)$$
$$= e\left(\mathbf{P}(w_i), \Sigma_1\right).$$

Given a ciphertext CT_i from running the Commit algorithm, a trapdoor T from running the Transfer algorithm and the secret key of the user sk, the correctness of searching and decryption can be verified by

$$H\left(0, e\left(c_{1i}, T\right)^{\frac{1}{s}}\right) = H\left(0, e\left(g^{r_i(\alpha + w_i)}, h^{\frac{s}{\alpha + w_i}}\right)^{\frac{1}{s}}\right)$$
$$= H\left(0, e\left(g, h\right)^{r_i}\right)$$
$$= c_{2i},$$

$$c_{3i} \oplus H\left(1, e\left(c_{1i}, T\right)^{\frac{1}{s}}\right) = H\left(1, e\left(g, h\right)^{r_i}\right) \oplus m_i \oplus H\left(1, e\left(g^{r_i(\alpha + w_i)}, h^{\frac{s}{\alpha + w_i}}\right)^{\frac{1}{s}}\right)$$
$$= H\left(1, e\left(g, h\right)^{r_i}\right) \oplus m_i \oplus H\left(1, e\left(g, h\right)^{r_i}\right)$$
$$= m_i.$$

4 Security Analysis

We formally analyze the security of our OKSA protocol, which is under the security model defined in Sect. 2.3. The security reduction is based on the hard problems defined in Sect. 2.4. We show the detailed proof process as follows.

4.1 User Privacy

Theorem 1. *The proposed scheme satisfies the unconditional keyword privacy of the token from the user under the Privacy game.*

Proof. Let W be the authorized keyword set and $(\mathbf{P}(w), \Sigma)$ be generated from $w = w_0$. We have the keyword token and proof as

$$\mathbf{P}(w) = h^{s \prod_{w_j \in W, w_j \neq w_0} (\alpha + w_j)},$$

$$\Sigma = \left(\Sigma_1 = h^{\frac{\alpha + w_0}{s}}, \ \Sigma_2 = h^{\frac{\alpha^{n-1}(\alpha + w_0)}{s}} \right).$$

For any distinct keyword w_1, let $s' \in \mathbb{Z}_p$, we implicitly set $s' = s \cdot \frac{\alpha + w_1}{\alpha + w_0}$. We find that the keyword tokens are identical, i.e., $\mathbf{P}(w_0) = \mathbf{P}(w_1)$, which can be verified as

$$\mathbf{P}(w_0) = h^{s \prod_{w_j \in W, w_j \neq w_0} (\alpha + w_j)} = h^{s' \prod_{w_j \in W, w_j \neq w_1} (\alpha + w_j)} = \mathbf{P}(w_1).$$

Suppose $\Sigma' = (\Sigma'_1, \Sigma'_2)$. The proofs of accountability are also identical, i.e., $\Sigma_1 = \Sigma'_1$ and $\Sigma_2 = \Sigma'_2$, which can be verified as

$$\Sigma_1 = h^{\frac{\alpha + w_0}{s}} = h^{\frac{\alpha + w_1}{s'}} = \Sigma'_1,$$

$$\Sigma_2 = h^{\frac{\alpha^{n-1}(\alpha + w_0)}{s}} = h^{\frac{\alpha^{n-1}(\alpha + w_1)}{s'}} = \Sigma'_2.$$

We have $(\mathbf{P}(w_0), \Sigma) = (\mathbf{P}(w_1), \Sigma')$. Since s is randomly chosen from $\mathbb{Z}_p$, we have s' is also universally random in $\mathbb{Z}_p$. The distributions of $(\mathbf{P}(w), \Sigma)$ for both w_0 and w_1 are identical and therefore $\mathcal{A}$ has no advantage in guessing the keyword in $\mathbf{P}(w)$. This completes the proof of **Theorem 1**.

4.2   Indistinguishability

Theorem 2. *The proposed scheme is semantically secure and indistinguishable under the Indistinguishability game in the random oracle model if the (f, q)-MSE-DDH Problem is hard.*

Proof. Suppose there exists an adversary $\mathcal{A}$ who can break the indistinguishability. We can construct an algorithm $\mathcal{B}$ that solves the (f, q)-*MSE-DDH Problem*. That is, given an instance of (f, q)-*MSE-DDH Problem* and $Z \in \mathbb{G}_T$, the goal of $\mathcal{B}$ is to distinguish $Z = e(g_0, h_0)^{rq(\alpha)}$ or a random group element in $\mathbb{G}_T$. $\mathcal{B}$ interacts with $\mathcal{A}$ as follows.

Setup. We assume the universal keyword space as $\mathcal{KS} = \{w_1, w_2, \cdots, w_n\}$. $\mathcal{B}$ chooses w_θ from $\mathcal{KS}$ and its corresponding message is denoted as m_θ. It implicitly sets the polynomials

$$f(\alpha) = \alpha + w_\theta, \quad q(\alpha) = \prod_{w_j \in \mathcal{KS}, w_j \neq w_\theta} (\alpha + w_j).$$

It also sets $g = g_0, h = h_0^{f(\alpha)q(\alpha)}$ and computes $h_i = h_0^{\alpha^{i-1} f(\alpha)q(\alpha)}$. Then $\mathcal{B}$ sends the master public key *mpk* to $\mathcal{A}$, where

$$mpk = (g_0, g_0^\alpha, h_1, h_2, \cdots, h_{n+1}, \mathcal{PG}).$$

H-Query. $\mathcal{B}$ maintains a hash list $L(a_i, X_i, h^i)$, which is initially empty. Upon receiving an H query for (a_i, X_i), if (a_i, X_i) is in the list L, $\mathcal{B}$ returns the corresponding h^i to $\mathcal{A}$. Otherwise, $\mathcal{B}$ sets the hash value h^i as follows.

$$h^i = H(a_i, X_i) = \begin{cases} b_0^i, & \text{if } a_i = 0, \\ b_1^i, & \text{if } a_i = 1, \end{cases}$$

where b_0^i, b_1^i are randomly chosen from $\{0,1\}^\ell$. Then $\mathcal{B}$ adds (a_i, X_i, h^i) to the list and returns h^i to $\mathcal{A}$.

Phase 1. $\mathcal{A}$ chooses a keyword set $W \subseteq \mathcal{KS}$, where $|W| \leq n$. When asking for the trapdoor query for a keyword $w_i \in W$, $\mathcal{A}$ randomly chooses $s \in \mathbb{Z}_p$ as the secret key $sk = s$, and sends (w_i, s) to $\mathcal{B}$.

- If $w_i = w_\theta$, abort.
- If $w_i \neq w_\theta$, $\mathcal{B}$ responds $T = h_0^{sq_i(\alpha)f(\alpha)}$ to $\mathcal{A}$, where $q_i(\alpha) = \frac{q(\alpha)}{\alpha + w_i}$. The trapdoor can be verified

$$T = \mathbf{P}(w_i)^{\frac{1}{\Pi_{w_j \in W}(\alpha + w_j)}} = h^{\frac{s \Pi_{w_j \in W, j \neq i}(\alpha + w_j)}{\Pi_{w_j \in W}(\alpha + w_j)}} = h_0^{\frac{sf(\alpha)q(\alpha)}{\alpha + w_i}} = h_0^{sq_i(\alpha)f(\alpha)}.$$

It is easy to see that $h_0^{q_i(\alpha)f(\alpha)}$ can be computed from elements $h_0^{f(\alpha)}, h_0^{\alpha f(\alpha)}, \cdots, h_0^{\alpha^{n-2}f(\alpha)}$ in the instance.

Challenge. $\mathcal{A}$ sends two tuples $(m_0, w_0), (m_1, w_1)$ to $\mathcal{B}$ for challenge, where the trapdoor for w_0 or w_1 has not been queried.

- If $w_\theta \notin \{w_0, w_1\}$, abort.
- If $w_\theta \in \{w_0, w_1\}$, $\mathcal{B}$ checks whether $(0, Z)$ and $(1, Z)$ are in the list L. If yes, obtains the corresponding hash value and denotes them as b_0^* and b_1^*. Otherwise, $\mathcal{B}$ chooses $b_0^*, b_1^* \in_R \{0,1\}^\ell$ and sets

$$H(0, Z) = b_0^*, \ H(1, Z) = b_1^*.$$

Then $\mathcal{B}$ adds $(0, Z, b_0^*)$ and $(1, Z, b_1^*)$ to the list L. $\mathcal{B}$ responds $\mathcal{A}$ with the challenge ciphertext

$$CT^* = (c_1 = g_0^r, c_2 = b_0^*, c_3 = b_1^* \oplus m_\theta).$$

If $Z = e(g_0, h_0)^{rq(\alpha)}$, one can verify it by implicitly setting $r = r_i f(\alpha)$

$$c_1 = g^{r_i(\alpha + w_\theta)} = g_0^{r_i f(\alpha)} = g_0^r,$$

$$c_2 = H(0, e(g, h)^{r_i}) = H\left(0, e(g_0, h_0)^{rq(\alpha)}\right) = H(0, Z) = b_0^*,$$

$$c_3 = H(1, e(g, h)^{r_i}) \oplus m_\theta = H\left(1, e(g_0, h_0)^{rq(\alpha)}\right) \oplus m_\theta = H(1, Z) \oplus m_\theta = b_1^* \oplus m_\theta.$$

Therefore, CT^* is a valid challenge ciphertext.

If Z is a random element in $\mathbb{G}_T$, the challenge ciphertext CT^* will be random from the $\mathcal{A}$'s view.

Phase 2. $\mathcal{A}$ continues to ask trapdoor queries for w_i with restrictions $w_i \neq w_0, w_1$. $\mathcal{B}$ responds as **Phase 1**.

Guess. $\mathcal{A}$ outputs a guess θ' of θ.

This completes the description of our simulation. We will analyze the advantage of $\mathcal{B}$ to solve the hard problem. Suppose that the total number of trapdoor query is q_T and the size of the keyword space is n. According to the above simulation, we have the probability that $\mathcal{B}$ does not abort is $\Pr[\neg abort] = (1-\frac{1}{n})(1-\frac{1}{n-1})\cdots(1-\frac{1}{n-q_T+1}) = \frac{n-q_T}{n}$. Since w_0, w_1 have not been queried in Phase 1 and Phase 2, we have $q_T \leq n - 2$. Then $\Pr[\neg abort] \geq \frac{2}{n}$. Assume that $\mathcal{A}$'s advantage to break the security game is at least ϵ, then we have $\epsilon_{reduction} = \Pr[\theta' = \theta | Z = e(g_0, h_0)^{rq(\alpha)}] - \Pr[\theta' = \theta | Z \text{ is random}] = \frac{1}{2} + \epsilon - \frac{1}{2} = \epsilon$. Therefore, $\mathcal{B}$'s advantage to solve the (f, q)-MSE-DDH Problem is at least $\epsilon_{\mathcal{B}} = \Pr[\neg abort] \cdot \epsilon_{reduction} = \frac{2}{n}\epsilon$. This completes the proof of **Theorem 2**.

4.3   Accountability

Theorem 3. *The proposed scheme captures the accountability under the Accountability game if the (f, n)-DHE Problem is hard.*

Proof. Suppose there exists an adversary $\mathcal{A}$ who can break the security of accountability. We construct an algorithm $\mathcal{B}$ that solves the (f, n)-DHE Problem. Given a challenge instance of (f, n)-DHE Problem, $\mathcal{B}$ interacts with the adversary as the follows.

Setup. $\mathcal{B}$ sets $\alpha = a$, we have $h_1 = h, h_2 = h^a, \cdots, h_{n+1} = h^{a^n}$, which are from the (f, n)-DHE instance. $\mathcal{B}$ chooses a hash function H as in the real scheme and sends mpk to $\mathcal{A}$, where

$$mpk = (g, g^a, h_1, h_2, \cdots, h_{n+1}, H, \mathcal{PG}).$$

Challenge. The adversary chooses two keyword sets W, W' with restriction $|W'| > 1, |W| \leq n$, and selects a random number $s \in \mathbb{Z}_p$ as the secret key of the user $sk = s$. $\mathcal{A}$ outputs $(\mathbf{P}(W'), W, W', sk)$ and 1 for challenge, where the token is denoted as

$$\mathbf{P}(W') = h^{s \prod_{w_j \in W - W'}(a+w_j)}.$$

Win. The adversary $\mathcal{A}$ outputs $(\mathbf{P}(W'); \Sigma)$ and wins the game if $(\mathbf{P}(W'), \Sigma)$ passes the verification algorithm.

In this case, the proof for accountability should be denoted as

$$\Sigma = \left(\Sigma_1 = h^{\frac{1}{s}\prod_{w_j \in W'}(a+w_j)}, \ \Sigma_2 = \Sigma_1^{a^{n-1}} = h^{\frac{1}{s}a^{n-1}\prod_{w_j \in W'}(a+w_j)}\right).$$

Then the token and its proof can pass the verification as

$$e\left(\Sigma_2, h^a\right) = e\left(\Sigma_1, h^{a^n}\right),$$

$$e\left(h, h^{\prod_{w_i \in W}(a+w_i)}\right) = e\left(\mathbf{P}(W'), \Sigma_1\right).$$

Let $f(x) = \frac{1}{s}x^{n-1}\prod_{w_j \in W'}(x + w_j)$, then $\Sigma = h^{f(a)}$. We have $f(x)$ is a polynomial function with $\deg f(x) > n$. $\mathcal{B}$ outputs $(f(x), \Sigma)$ as the solution to the (f, n)-*DHE Problem*. This completes the proof of **Theorem** 3. Hence we obtain $|W'| = 1, |\mathbf{P}(W')| = 1$.

5   Conclusion

We proposed a new notion namely oblivious keyword search with authorization, where an authorized keyword set is taken into consideration in OKS. In OKSA, the user gets a trapdoor for any keyword in the authorized keyword set in an oblivious way. The supplier can know the fact that the to-be-search keyword is in the authorized keyword set but has no idea about which one it is. We presented an efficient OKSA protocol featured with constant size communication cost in transfer phase. Each transfer subphase in our protocol only needs one-round (two-pass) interaction. By borrowing the property of aggregation algorithm into trapdoor generation, a constant-size trapdoor is issued from the supplier to the user. We gave the formal security proof of the proposed protocol under the security models.

Acknowledgments. This work is supported by BUPT Excellent Ph.D. Students Foundation (Grant No. CX2015312), NSFC (Grant Nos. 61300181, 61502044, 61572390, 61502086), the Fundamental Research Funds for the Central Universities (Grant No. 2015RC23).

References

1. Abdalla, M., Bellare, M., Catalano, D., Kiltz, E., Kohno, T., Lange, T., Malone-Lee, J., Neven, G., Paillier, P., Shi, H.: Searchable encryption revisited: consistency properties, relation to anonymous IBE, and extensions. In: Shoup, V. (ed.) CRYPTO 2005. LNCS, vol. 3621, pp. 205–222. Springer, Heidelberg (2005)
2. Aiello, B., Ishai, Y., Reingold, O.: Priced oblivious transfer: how to sell digital goods. In: Pfitzmann, B. (ed.) EUROCRYPT 2001. LNCS, vol. 2045, pp. 119–135. Springer, Heidelberg (2001). doi:10.1007/3-540-44987-6_8
3. Baek, J., Safavi-Naini, R., Susilo, W.: Public key encryption with keyword search revisited. In: Gervasi, O., Murgante, B., Laganà, A., Taniar, D., Mun, Y., Gavrilova, M.L. (eds.) ICCSA 2008, Part I. LNCS, vol. 5072, pp. 1249–1259. Springer, Heidelberg (2008)
4. Ballard, L., Kamara, S., Monrose, F.: Achieving efficient conjunctive keyword searches over encrypted data. In: Qing, S., Mao, W., López, J., Wang, G. (eds.) ICICS 2005. LNCS, vol. 3783, pp. 414–426. Springer, Heidelberg (2005)

5. Bethencourt, J., Song, D.X., Waters, B.: New constructions and practical applications for private stream searching (extended abstract). In: 2006 IEEE Symposium on Security and Privacy (S&P 2006), pp. 132–139 (2006)
6. Boneh, D., Boyen, X., Goh, E.-J.: Hierarchical identity based encryption with constant size ciphertext. In: Cramer, R. (ed.) EUROCRYPT 2005. LNCS, vol. 3494, pp. 440–456. Springer, Heidelberg (2005)
7. Boneh, D., Di Crescenzo, G., Ostrovsky, R., Persiano, G.: Public key encryption with keyword search. In: Cachin, C., Camenisch, J.L. (eds.) EUROCRYPT 2004. LNCS, vol. 3027, pp. 506–522. Springer, Heidelberg (2004)
8. Boneh, D., Waters, B.: Conjunctive, subset, and range queries on encrypted data. In: Vadhan, S.P. (ed.) TCC 2007. LNCS, vol. 4392, pp. 535–554. Springer, Heidelberg (2007)
9. Camenisch, J., Dubovitskaya, M., Neven, G.: Oblivious transfer with access control. In: Proceedings of the 2009 ACM Conference on Computer and Communications Security, CCS 2009, pp. 131–140 (2009)
10. Camenisch, J., Dubovitskaya, M., Neven, G.: Unlinkable priced oblivious transfer with rechargeable wallets. In: Sion, R. (ed.) FC 2010. LNCS, vol. 6052, pp. 66–81. Springer, Heidelberg (2010)
11. Camenisch, J., Kohlweiss, M., Rial, A., Sheedy, C.: Blind and anonymous identity-based encryption and authorised private searches on public key encrypted data. In: Jarecki, S., Tsudik, G. (eds.) PKC 2009. LNCS, vol. 5443, pp. 196–214. Springer, Heidelberg (2009)
12. Camenisch, J.L., Neven, G., Shelat, A.: Simulatable adaptive oblivious transfer. In: Naor, M. (ed.) EUROCRYPT 2007. LNCS, vol. 4515, pp. 573–590. Springer, Heidelberg (2007)
13. Cash, D., Jarecki, S., Jutla, C., Krawczyk, H., Roşu, M.-C., Steiner, M.: Highly-scalable searchable symmetric encryption with support for boolean queries. In: Canetti, R., Garay, J.A. (eds.) CRYPTO 2013, Part I. LNCS, vol. 8042, pp. 353–373. Springer, Heidelberg (2013)
14. Chen, Y., Chou, J., Hou, X.: A novel k-out-of-n oblivious transfer protocols based on bilinear pairings. IACR Cryptology ePrint Archive 2010, 27 (2010)
15. Chow, S.S.M.: Removing Escrow from identity-based encryption. In: Jarecki, S., Tsudik, G. (eds.) PKC 2009. LNCS, vol. 5443, pp. 256–276. Springer, Heidelberg (2009)
16. Chu, C.-K., Tzeng, W.-G.: Efficient k-Out-of-n oblivious transfer schemes with adaptive and non-adaptive queries. In: Vaudenay, S. (ed.) PKC 2005. LNCS, vol. 3386, pp. 172–183. Springer, Heidelberg (2005)
17. Curtmola, R., Garay, J.A., Kamara, S., Ostrovsky, R.: Searchable symmetric encryption: improved definitions and efficient constructions. In: Proceedings of the 13th ACM Conference on Computer and Communications Security, CCS 2006, pp. 79–88 (2006)
18. Fang, L., Susilo, W., Ge, C., Wang, J.: Public key encryption with keyword search secure against keyword guessing attacks without random oracle. Inf. Sci. **238**, 221–241 (2013)
19. Freedman, M.J., Ishai, Y., Pinkas, B., Reingold, O.: Keyword search and oblivious pseudorandom functions. In: Kilian, J. (ed.) TCC 2005. LNCS, vol. 3378, pp. 303–324. Springer, Heidelberg (2005)
20. Green, M., Hohenberger, S.: Universally composable adaptive oblivious transfer. In: Pieprzyk, J. (ed.) ASIACRYPT 2008. LNCS, vol. 5350, pp. 179–197. Springer, Heidelberg (2008)

21. Guo, F., Mu, Y., Susilo, W.: Subset membership encryption and its applications to oblivious transfer. IEEE Trans. Inform. Forensics Secur. **9**(7), 1098–1107 (2014)
22. Guo, F., Mu, Y., Susilo, W., Varadharajan, V.: http://www.uow.edu.au/fuchun/publications/ACISP13.pdf (2013). full Version
23. Guo, F., Mu, Y., Susilo, W., Varadharajan, V.: Membership encryption and its applications. In: Boyd, C., Simpson, L. (eds.) ACISP. LNCS, vol. 7959, pp. 219–234. Springer, Heidelberg (2013)
24. Jarecki, S., Jutla, C.S., Krawczyk, H., Rosu, M., Steiner, M.: Outsourced symmetric private information retrieval. In: 2013 ACM SIGSAC Conference on Computer and Communications Security, CCS 2013, pp. 875–888 (2013)
25. Kamara, S., Papamanthou, C., Roeder, T.: Dynamic searchable symmetric encryption. In: the ACM Conference on Computer and Communications Security, CCS 2012, pp. 965–976 (2012)
26. Kurosawa, K., Nojima, R.: Simple adaptive oblivious transfer without random Oracle. In: Matsui, M. (ed.) ASIACRYPT 2009. LNCS, vol. 5912, pp. 334–346. Springer, Heidelberg (2009)
27. Li, J., Li, J., Chen, X., Liu, Z., Jia, C.: Privacy-preserving data utilization in hybrid clouds. Future Generation Comp. Syst. **30**, 98–106 (2014)
28. Li, J., Lin, D., Squicciarini, A., Li, J., Jia, C.: Towards privacy-preserving storage and retrieval in multiple clouds. IEEE Trans. Cloud Comput. (2015, to appear)
29. Mu, Y., Zhang, J., Varadharajan, V.: m out of n oblivious transfer. In: Batten, L., Seberry, J. (eds.) ACISP 2002. LNCS, vol. 2384, pp. 395–405. Springer, Heidelberg (2002). doi:10.1007/3-540-45450-0_30
30. Ogata, W., Kurosawa, K.: Oblivious keyword search. J. Complexity **20**(2–3), 356–371 (2004)
31. Park, D.J., Kim, K., Lee, P.J.: Public key encryption with conjunctive field keyword search. In: Lim, C.H., Yung, M. (eds.) WISA 2004. LNCS, vol. 3325, pp. 73–86. Springer, Heidelberg (2005)
32. Rabin, M.O.: How to exchange secrets with oblivious transfer. Technical report TR-81, Aiken Computation Laboratory, Harvard University (2005)
33. Rhee, H.S., Byun, J.W., Lee, D.-H., Lim, J.-I.: Oblivious conjunctive keyword search. In: Song, J.-S., Kwon, T., Yung, M. (eds.) WISA 2005. LNCS, vol. 3786, pp. 318–327. Springer, Heidelberg (2006)
34. Rhee, H.S., Park, J.H., Susilo, W., Lee, D.H.: Improved searchable public key encryption with designated tester. In: Proceedings of the 2009 ACM Symposium on Information, Computer and Communications Security, ASIACCS 2009, pp. 376–379 (2009)
35. Rhee, H.S., Susilo, W., Kim, H.: Secure searchable public key encryption scheme against keyword guessing attacks. IEICE Electron. Express **6**(5), 237–243 (2009)
36. Ryu, E., Takagi, T.: Efficient conjunctive keyword-searchable encryption. In: 21st International Conference on Advanced Information Networking and Applications (AINA 2007), vol. 1, pp. 409–414 (2007)
37. Sedghi, S., van Liesdonk, P., Nikova, S., Hartel, P., Jonker, W.: Searching keywords with wildcards on encrypted data. In: Garay, J.A., De Prisco, R. (eds.) SCN 2010. LNCS, vol. 6280, pp. 138–153. Springer, Heidelberg (2010)
38. Shi, J., Lai, J., Li, Y., Deng, R.H., Weng, J.: Authorized keyword search on encrypted data. In: Kutyłowski, M., Vaidya, J. (eds.) ICAIS 2014, Part I. LNCS, vol. 8712, pp. 419–435. Springer, Heidelberg (2014)
39. Song, D.X., Wagner, D., Perrig, A.: Practical techniques for searches on encrypted data. In: 2000 IEEE Symposium on Security and Privacy, pp. 44–55 (2000)

40. Sun, W., Yu, S., Lou, W., Hou, Y.T., Li, H.: Protecting your right: Attribute-based keyword search with fine-grained owner-enforced search authorization in the cloud. In: 2014 IEEE Conference on Computer Communications, INFOCOM 2014, pp. 226–234 (2014)
41. Zheng, Q., Xu, S., Ateniese, G.: VABKS: verifiable attribute-based keyword search over outsourced encrypted data. In: 2014 IEEE Conference on Computer Communications, INFOCOM 2014, pp. 522–530 (2014)
42. Zhu, H., Bao, F.: Oblivious keyword search protocols in the public database model. Proceedings of IEEE International Conference on Communications, ICC 2007, pp. 1336–1341 (2007)

Efficient Asymmetric Index Encapsulation Scheme for Named Data

Rong Ma[1(✉)] and Zhenfu Cao[1,2]

[1] Shanghai Jiaotong University, Shanghai, China
marong.sjtu@gmail.com
[2] East China Normal University, Shanghai, China
zfcao@sei.ecnu.edu.cn

Abstract. We are studing the problem of searching on hidden index in asymmetric setting. We define a mechanism that enables receiver to provide a token to the server and enables the server to test whether an encapsulated index matches the token without learning anything else about them. We refer to this mechanism as Asymmetric Index Encapsulation. We suggest to using the AIE as the core protocol of anonymous content-oriented networking. A construction of AIE which strikes a balance between efficiency and security is also given. Our scheme is proved secure base on the DBDH/CDH assumption in the random oracle with tight reduction, while the encapsulated header and the token in our system consists of only three elements.

Keywords: Asymmetric index encapsulation scheme · Anonymous content-oriented networking · Asymmetric searchable encryption · Private keyword search

1 Introduction

Named Data. It tends to concern security on named data under untrusted network. There are a variety of purposes for naming the data, for example, name may be treated as index, tag, keyword or label in different scenarios. Let's list some interesting examples of named data below:

- Files stored in cloud server.
- E-mail. The contents of the letter can be seen as data, while the receiver's address or title can be seen as the name of data.
- Named content in Content-Oriented Networking (CON). CON is a candidate for internet architecture designs in next generation. The content-oriented communication paradigm relies on naming the content itself, rather that its location. Content is self-contained, has a unique name, can be retrieved by means of an interest for the name, cached in any arbitrary location, and digitally signed to ensure its integrity and authenticity. We will discuss in more detail later.

© Springer International Publishing AG 2016
L. Chen and J. Han (Eds.): ProvSec 2016, LNCS 10005, pp. 191–203, 2016.
DOI: 10.1007/978-3-319-47422-9_11

We propose an asymmetric index encapsulation (AIE) scheme to provide a way to hide the name except to a party that is given appropriate token. In addition, the token can only be generated from the authorized users and the functionality of the token kept secret even during the match procedure.

In AIE scheme, three parties called "sender", "receiver", "server" are involved. The sender is a party that creates the encapsulated header and sends it to server. The server is a party that stores and forwards headers upon tokens. The receiver is a party that distributes tokens to match the desired header. The term "asymmetric" refers to the fact that sender can be anyone while receiver can only be who owns the token.

Formally, an asymmetric index encapsulation scheme is specified by a quadruple of probabilistic polynomial time algorithms:

- The setup algorithm **Setup** is run by the central authority, takes a security parameter 1^λ and outputs the public system parameters pp together with a master (secret) key mk. The system parameters will be publicly known, while the master key will be known only to the key generation algorithm.
- The index encapsulation algorithm **Enc** is run by the sender, takes as input an index x, outputs a encapsulated header hd_x.
- The token generation algorithm **Gen** is run by the central authority, takes as input the master secrect key mk and an index y, outputs a related token tk_y.
- The test algorithm **Test** is run by the server, takes as input a header hd_x and a token tk_y, and outputs whether tk_y matches hd_x, if they match, returns "1", else returns "0"

1.1   Contribution

New primitive. The first contribution of our paper is in defining a new cryptographic primitive known as asymmetric index encapsulation scheme. There are at least two differences between asymmetric index encapsulation and PEKS or identity-based searchable encryption [6,16]. Firstly, the goal of AIE scheme is to decouple index hiding and searching procedure from encryption scheme. There are independent application scenarios of index encapsulation. Identity based searchable encryption can be replaced by any combination of AIE and anonymous identity based encryption. Secondly, asymmetric index encapsulation scheme does not imply public key encryption or identity based encryption. There are possibility to get better security reduction and efficiency.

New security model. We introduce new adversarial models for AIE. The anonymity model captures the intuitive notion that an adversary should not be able to distinguish between the encapsulated header of two challenge indices of his choice, even if his is allowed to obtain tokens for any other indices. The privacy model requires any token belongs to index x is indistinguishable from a random token if x is choosen from a sufficiently high min-entropy distribution.

New construction. The security of our scheme relies on the DBDH/CDH assumption in prime-order groups and random oracle. An encapsulated header in our system consists of only three elements, while a token in our system also consists of only three elements. Besides the acceptable efficiency in practice, the scheme has tight security reduction against all kind of adversaries. A security reduction is said to be tight when breaking the scheme is exactly as hard as solving the underlying problem.

New application. We embed AIE scheme in the CON to provide comparable anonymity with lower relative overhead. The main idea of our approach is to encapsulate the name of the content/data packet and using token instead of the interest packet. Public executable test algorithm of AIE scheme enables router to retrieve the cached content matching the token from users. This work presents an initial attempt to provide security and anonymity in CON by cryptographic protocol.

1.2   Related Work

Symmetric searchable encryption with adaptive security against chosen-keyword attacks was first considered explicitly in [14], where symmetric index encapsulation was first considered explicitly by [8]. Unlike in asymmetric settings, securely encapsulating a single keyword/index is nearly trivial in symmetric settings. In these schemes and subsequent work [2,4], researchers focus on how to handle full text indices and try to improve efficiency. Another line of work uses deterministic encryption [1,4]. It only provides security for data and queries that have high entropy.

Starting with the work of Boneh, Crescenzo, Ostrovsky and Persiano [6], searchable encryption has also been considered in the public key setting [3,7, 13,21,22]. The early works lack function privacy until the first definition was suggested very recently by Boneh, Raghunathan, Segev [16].

One of the key goals of CON projects is "security by design" [5]. In contrast to todays Internet, where security problems were identified along the way, the research community stresses both awareness of issues and support for features and countermeasures from the outset. To this end, a few of papers investigate various attacks and solutions in CON [9–11]. However, to the best of our knowledge, there is an absence of cryptographic perspective.

1.3   Organization

Preliminaries and notations are recalled in Sect. 2. Definitions of security model are given and discussed in Sect. 3. The application in CON is stated in Sect. 4. The scheme description is presented in Sect. 5. The reduction proofs are shown in following sections respectively.

2   Preliminaries

2.1   Notation

We denote by $\mathbf{X} = (X_1, X_2, \ldots, X_q)$ a joint distribution of q random variables, and by $\mathbf{x} = (x_1, x_2, \ldots, x_q)$ a sample drawn from $\mathbf{X}$. The min-entropy of a random variable X is $\mathbf{H}_\infty(X) = -\log_2(\max_x \Pr[X = x])$. A k-source is a random varibale X with $\mathbf{H}_\infty(X) \geq k$. A (q, k)-block-source is a random varibale $\mathbf{X} = (X_1, X_2, \ldots, X_q)$ where for each $i \in \{1, 2, \ldots, q\}$, $(x_1, \ldots, x_{i-1})$ holds that $X_i|_{X_1=x_1,\ldots,X_{i-1}=x_{i-1}}$ is k-source. The statistical distance between two random variables X and Y over a finite domain S is defined as

$$\mathbf{SD}(X, Y) = \frac{1}{2} \sum_{x \in S} |\Pr[X = x] - \Pr[Y = x]|$$

2.2   Pairing Group

Let **GroupGen** be a probabilistic polynomial-time algorithm taking 1^λ as security parameter and outputs $(\mathbb{G}, \mathbb{G}_T, p, g, e)$ where $\mathbb{G}$ and $\mathbb{G}_T$ are groups of prime order p, $2^\lambda < p < 2^{\lambda+1}$, g is a generator of group $\mathbb{G}$ and $e : \mathbb{G} \times \mathbb{G} \to \mathbb{G}_T$ is a non-degenerate efficiently computable bilinear map. See [12] for a description of the properties of such pairings.

2.3   DBDH and CDH Assumption

Decisional bilinear Diffie-Hellman (BDDH) problem is to distinguish two distributions $\mathcal{P}_{\text{BDH}} = (g^\alpha, g^\beta, g^\gamma, e(g, g)^{\alpha\beta\gamma})$ and $\mathcal{R}_{\text{BDH}} = (g^\alpha, g^\beta, g^\gamma, R)$ for random α, β, γ and R. Computational Diffie-Hellman (CDH) problem is to compute $g^{\alpha\beta}$ provided that g^α and g^β. To state the assumption asymptotically we rely on the bilinear group generator algorithm **GroupGen**(1^λ).

Definition 1. *Let **GroupGen**(1^λ) be a bilinear group generator. The DBDH assumption holds for **GroupGen**(1^λ) if for all probabilistic polynomial-time algorithm $\mathcal{B}$, its BDDH advantage, denoted by*

$$\boldsymbol{Adv}_{\mathcal{B}}^{DBDH}(\lambda) = \left| \Pr[\mathcal{B}(g^\alpha, g^\beta, g^\gamma, e(g, g)^{\alpha\beta\gamma}) = 1] - \Pr[\mathcal{B}(g^\alpha, g^\beta, g^\gamma, R) = 1] \right|$$

*is a negligible function of λ, where the probability is over $(\mathbb{G}, \mathbb{G}_T, p, g, e) \leftarrow$ **GroupGen**(1^λ), $\alpha, \beta, \gamma \leftarrow \mathbb{Z}_p^*$, $R \leftarrow \mathbb{G}_T$.*

Definition 2. *Let **GroupGen**(1^λ) be a bilinear group generator. The CDH assumption holds for **GroupGen**(1^λ) if for all probabilistic polynomial-time algorithm $\mathcal{B}$, its CDH advantage, denoted by*

$$\boldsymbol{Adv}_{\mathcal{B}}^{CDH}(\lambda) = \Pr[\mathcal{B}(g^\alpha, g^\beta) = g^{\alpha\beta}]$$

*is a negligible function of λ, where the probability is over $(\mathbb{G}, \mathbb{G}_T, p, g, e) \leftarrow$ **GroupGen**(1^λ), $\alpha, \beta \leftarrow \mathbb{Z}_p^*$.*

2.4   The Leftover Hash Lemma

Definition 3 (Universal Hash Function). *A collection $\mathcal{H}$ of function H with form $U \rightarrow V$ is universal if for any $x, x' \in U$ such that $x \neq x'$ it holds that*

$$\Pr_{H \leftarrow \mathcal{H}}[H(x) = H(x')] = \frac{1}{|V|}$$

Theorem 1 (Leftover Hash Lemma for block-source, see [16]). *Let $\mathcal{H}$ be a universal collection of functions $H : U \rightarrow V$, let $\mathbf{X} = (X_1, X_2, \ldots, X_q)$ be (q, k)-block-source where $k \geq \log |V| + 2 \log(1/\epsilon) + \Theta(1)$. Then the distribution*

$$(H_1, H_1(X_1), H_2, H_2(X_2), \ldots, H_q, H_q(X_q))$$

where $(H_1, H_2, \ldots, H_q) \leftarrow \mathcal{H}^q$ is ϵq-close to the uniform distribution over $(\mathcal{H} \times V)^q$

3   Definition of Security Models

3.1   Intuition

Before we begin to build our security model formally, it is necessary to identify what attacks AIE should withstand, and what attributes are desirable to have:

- Anonymity of encapsulated header. An AIE scheme is anonymous if $\mathbf{Enc}(pp, x)$ leaks no information about x.
- Privacy of token's functionality. Formalizing such a notion is not straightforward since adversary can mount a guessing attack. If adversary has some knowledge that the token comes from a small set, he can encapsulate each candidate index, and run the legitimate **Test** procedure to learn the function embedded inside the token. We adapt the notion from [16] which requires that $\mathbf{Gen}(mk, y)$ is indistinguishable from a random token if y is chosen from a sufficiently high min-entropy distribution.

We give the precise definitions based on the above discussion.

3.2   Security Model for Anonymity

To capture the anonymity properties formally, A game between a challenger and an adversary $\mathcal{A}$ is defined as follows:

- Setup Phase: The challenger runs **Setup**(1^λ) and sends pp to adversary $\mathcal{A}$, keeps mk to itself.
- Pre-Challenge Phase: In this phase, adversary $\mathcal{A}$ is allowed to make token extraction qurey. The challenger responds the query about index y by sending $\mathcal{A}$ the output of **Gen**(mk, y)
- Challenge Phase: $\mathcal{A}$ submits two indices x_0, x_1, which is restricted to the indices that he did not request in pre-challenge phase. The challenger flips a fair binary coin b and returns **Enc**(pp, x_b) as challenge header.

- Post-Challenge Phase: This phase is repeat of pre-challenge phase. The adversary issues additional adaptive queries with the restriction that he can not request token of x_0 or x_1.
- Guess Phase: Finally, $\mathcal{A}$ submits a guess b' of b. The adversary wins if $b' = b$.

Definition 4 (Anonymity of AIE). *An AIE scheme says anonymous if for any probabilistic polynomial-time algorithm $\mathcal{A}$, it's ANON advantage, denoted by*

$$\boldsymbol{Adv}_{\mathcal{A}}^{ANON}(\lambda) = \left| \Pr[b' = b] - \frac{1}{2} \right|$$

is a negligible function of λ, where the probability is over the random bits used by the challenger and the adversary.

3.3   Security Model for Function Privacy

The following security game parameterized by a distribution D helps us capture properties of token's function privacy:

- Setup Phase. The challenger runs **Setup**(1^λ) and sends both master secret key mk and public parameters pp to adversary $\mathcal{A}$.
- Challenge Phase. In this phase, the challenger samples an indices vector $(x_1, x_2, \ldots, x_q)$ from the distribution **D**, then for every $i \in \{1, 2, \ldots, n\}$, computes $tk_i = \mathbf{Gen}(mk, x_i)$, returns $(tk_1, \ldots, tk_q)$ to $\mathcal{A}$.
- Guess Phase. Finally, $\mathcal{A}$ sumbits a guess of the distribution challenger's used. It outputs "0" standing for uniform distribution, otherwise outputs "1".

Definition 5 (Privacy of AIE). *An AIE scheme says function private if for any probabilistic polynomial-time algorithm $\mathcal{A}$ and any (q, k)-block-source distribution D where q, k is a polynomial of λ, it's PRIV advantage, denoted by*

$$\boldsymbol{Adv}_{\mathcal{A}}^{PRIV}(\lambda) = \left| \Pr[\Psi_D(\lambda) = 1] - \Pr[\Psi_R(\lambda) = 1] \right|$$

is a negligible function of λ where R stands for uniform distribution.

4   Application

Review of CON. Communication in CON adheres to the pull model. End users express interests and fetch data. Data are always named to facilitate search. Interests represent the willingness of the user to retrieve certain data, independently of its location. Content routing relies on content rather that hosts. Content routers are responsible of forwarding interests and forwarding back the associated data. Each router is assumed to have a built-in cache which is expected to be much bigger than today's routers.

CON has some innate privacy friendly features, such as lack of source and destination addresses on contents. However, there are some security and privacy challenges in CON:

- Content privacy. As CON stores data packets and makes it available to anyone that asks for it, the adversary might retrieve confidential content from caches [11].
- Name privacy. Names reveal significantly more information about content than IP addresses. Keeping the name private while ensuring accessibility and routablility is the starting point of our work [10].
- Interest flooding attack. Adversary generates a large number of interests, aiming to overwhelm in routers, in order to prevent them from handling legitimate interests. Since CON interests lack source address, it is difficult to determine the attack originator [9].

Instantiating AIE in CON. Our main idea is to encrypt the content, encapsulate the name and use token instead of the interest packet. Encrypted content, encapsulated header and signature binding the first two compose the anonymous content packet of x. As illustrated in Fig. 1, when a router receives a token for name x and there are no same pending tokens in its cache, it forwards this token to the neighbor routers. When the desired content is returned or there is already an encapsulated header matching this token in the cache, the router forwards it out on all neighbors where the token for x has been received and flushes the corresponding cache entry. The anonymity and token function privacy of AIE ensure that the name is hidden at interest and content packet, while the token unforgeability helps central authority locating who is launching an interest flooding attack.

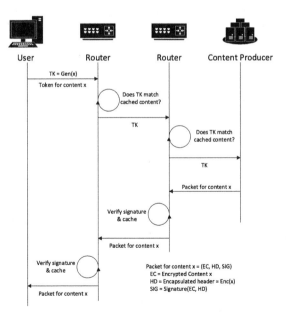

Fig. 1. Instantiating AIE scheme in anonymous CON

Disscusion and Suggestion. Since adversary can mount a guessing attack (exhaustively testing the token by using pairings). We argue the name must be sample from a large enough set. To own reasonable high min-entropy in anonymous CON, we suggest that data provider should assign a complicated name of the encrypted data. Taking advantage of the present of timestamp and hierarchical prefix, it's possible to prevent adversary knowing sensitive information by brute force method.

5 Scheme Construction

In this section, we present an efficient AIE scheme with constant size token and encapsulated header. The design inspiration of our scheme comes from [15,16].

- **Setup**(1^λ): On input security parameter 1^λ, the setup algorithm works as follows:
  1. Generate $(p, \mathbb{G}, \mathbb{G}_T, g, e) \leftarrow \textbf{GroupGen}(1^\lambda)$.
  2. Randomly sample $a \leftarrow \mathbb{Z}_p^*$.
  3. Compute $g_a \leftarrow g^a$.
  4. Choose two cryptographic hash function H and $F : \{0,1\}^\lambda \rightarrow \mathbb{G}$. The security analysis will view H, F as random oracles.
  5. Output a as master key, (g, g_a) as public parameters.
- **Enc**(pp, x): Given x, the index encapsulation algorithm does:
  1. Randomly sample $r \leftarrow \mathbb{Z}_p^*$.
  2. Compute $c \leftarrow g^r$, $T \leftarrow e(g_a, H(x))^r$, $R \leftarrow e(g_a, F(x))^r$.
  3. Output (c, T, R) as an encapsulated header.
- **Gen**(mk, y): On input the master key a and an index y, the token generation algorithm does the following:
  1. If the same query for y is repeated twice, then the same token is provided.
  2. Randomly choose $u, v \leftarrow \mathbb{Z}_p^*$.
  3. Compute $d \leftarrow \left(H(y)^u F(y)^v\right)^a$.
  4. Output and record (d, u, v) as the token of y.
- **Test**(hd, tk): Given an encapsulated header hd and a token tk, the test algorithm does:
  1. Parse hd as (c, T, R), tk_y as (d, u, v).
  2. Check if the following equation holds true:

$$e(c, d) = T^u \cdot R^v,$$

if it holds, output "1", meaning tk matches hd, else output "0".

Correctness. For any index x, we need to guarantee **Test**$(hd_x, tk_x) = 1$, where $hd_x \leftarrow \textbf{Enc}(x, pp)$ and $tk_x \leftarrow \textbf{Gen}(x, \overset{*}{m}k)$. Denoting $hd_x = (c, T, R)$ and $tk_x = (d, u, v)$, that is clear since

$$
\begin{aligned}
e(c, d) &= e\left(g^s, (H(x)^u F(x)^v)^a\right) \\
&= e(g^s, H(x))^{au} e(g^s, F(x))^{av} \\
&= \left(e(g^a, H(x))^s\right)^u \left(e(g^a, F(x))^s\right)^v \\
&= T^u \cdot R^v
\end{aligned}
$$

6   Proof of Anonymity

We use reduction to prove anonymity of our scheme under the DBDH assumption.

Lemma 1. *Suppose there is an adversary $\mathcal{A}$ that can win the anonymity game with advantage $\epsilon(\lambda)$. Then there is a algorithm $\mathcal{B}$ solves the DBDH problem with advantage $\epsilon(\lambda)$.*

Given a tuple (g_a, g_b, g_c, Z), that is either sampled from $\mathcal{P}_{\text{BDH}}$ or from $\mathcal{R}_{\text{BDH}}$. Algorithm $\mathcal{B}$ interacts with adversary $\mathcal{A}$ as follows:

Setup Phase. $\mathcal{B}$ sets up public parameter $pp = g_\alpha$.
Programming the Random Oracle. $\mathcal{B}$ simulates the random oracle for $\mathcal{A}$ as
follows:

    If the same query is repeated twice, then the same return value is provided,
    on issuing a fresh query for $H(x)$, $\mathcal{B}$:
        1. samples $t_1 \leftarrow \mathbb{Z}_p^*$, $t_2 \leftarrow \mathbb{Z}_p^*$
        2. stores tuple (x, t_1, t_2) in table L_H
        3. returns $H(x) = (g_\beta)^{t_1} g^{t_2}$
    On issuing a fresh query for $F(x)$, $\mathcal{B}$:
        1. samples $t_3 \leftarrow \mathbb{Z}_p^*$, $t_4 \leftarrow \mathbb{Z}_p^*$,
        2. stores tuple (x, t_3, t_4) in table L_F,
        3. returns $F(x) = (g_\beta)^{t_3} g^{t_4}$.

Pre-Challenge Phase. On $\mathcal{A}$ issuing a token for index y, algorithm $\mathcal{B}$:
    1. if the same query for y is repeated twice, then the same token is provided,
    2. if $\mathcal{A}$ has not made a query for $H(y)$ and/or $F(y)$, programs $H(y)$ and/or $F(y)$ as mentioned above.
    3. retrieves (y, t_1, t_2) from L_H and (y, t_3, t_4) from L_F
    4. samples $u \leftarrow \mathbb{Z}_p^*$, computes $v \leftarrow -u \cdot t_1 / t_3$. i.e., randomly samples u and v such that $u \cdot t_1 + v \cdot t_2 = 0$
    5. computes $d \leftarrow (g_\alpha)^{ut_2 + vt_4}$
    6. returns (d, u, v)
  (Correctness of simulation). We argue that (d, u, v) is always a proper token corresponding to y since

$$
\begin{aligned}
\left(H(y)^u F(y)^v\right)^\alpha &= \left((g_\beta^{t_1} g^{t_2})^u (g_\beta^{t_3} g^{t_4})^v\right)^\alpha \\
&= \left((g_\beta^{ut_1 + vt_3}) g^{ut_2 + vt_4}\right)^\alpha \\
&= g_\alpha^{ut_2 + vt_4} \\
&= d
\end{aligned}
$$

Challenge Phase. After $\mathcal{A}$ sends x_0 and x_1, algorithm $\mathcal{B}$:
    1. picks a random bit $b \leftarrow \{0, 1\}$
    2. if $\mathcal{A}$ has not made a query for $H(x_b)$ and/or $F(x_b)$, programs $H(x_b)$ and/or $F(x_b)$ as mentioned above.
    3. retrieve (x_b, s_1, s_2) from L_H and (x_b, s_3, s_4) from L_F

4. computes $c \leftarrow g_\gamma$, $T \leftarrow Z^{s_1} e(g_\alpha, g_\gamma)^{s_2}$, $W \leftarrow Z^{s_3} e(g_\alpha, g_\gamma)^{s_4}$
5. returns (c, T, W) as challenge header

Post-Challenge Phase. $\mathcal{B}$ responds as before in pre-challenge phase.

Guess Phase. Finally $\mathcal{A}$ outputs a guess b' of b. $\mathcal{B}$ concludes its own game by outputting a guess as follows. if $b' = b$, $\mathcal{B}$ returns 1, else returns 0.

Analysis of $\mathcal{B}$'s behavior. Denote $\gamma = \log_g g_\gamma$. If Z is sampled from $\mathcal{P}_{\mathrm{BDH}}$, i.e., $Z = e(g_\alpha, g_\beta)^\gamma$, then (c, T, W) is a perfectly legitimate header of x_b since

$$e(g_\alpha, H(x))^\gamma = e(g_\alpha, g_\beta^{s_1} g^{s_2})^\gamma = \left(e(g_\alpha, g_\beta)^\gamma\right)^{s_1} e(g_\alpha, g^{s_2})^\gamma = Z^{s_1} e(g_\alpha, g_\gamma)^{s_2} = T$$

$$e(g_\alpha, F(x))^\gamma = e(g_\alpha, g_\beta^{s_3} g^{s_4})^\gamma = \left(e(g_\alpha, g_\beta)^\gamma\right)^{s_3} e(g_\alpha, g^{s_4})^\gamma = Z^{s_3} e(g_\alpha, g_\gamma)^{s_4} = W$$

Therefore, $\mathcal{B}$ simulates a perfect environment of $\mathcal{A}$, the probability of the evnet $\mathcal{A}$ winning the game is identical to ϵ. However, when Z is uniformly random, the challenge header will not be legitimate. This is not a problem, and indeed, it is crucial to the proof of security.

Lemma 2. *If Z is sampled from uniformly random, the distribution of the b is independent from the adversary's view, so the probablility of event $\mathcal{A}$ winning the game is identical to $1/2$.*

Proof. Consider the joint distribution of the adversary's view. Note that the adversary is not allowed to make a token query for x_0 and x_1, from his view, only $H(x_b)$, $F(x_b)$, T and W may leak information about b. What we need proof is for any fixed g_α, g_β, g_γ, T, W, $H(x_0)$, $F(x_0)$, $H(x_1)$ and $F(x_1)$,

$$\Pr \begin{bmatrix} Z^{r_1} e(g_\alpha, g_\gamma)^{r_2} = T \\ Z^{r_3} e(g_\alpha, g_\gamma)^{r_4} = W \\ g_\beta^{r_1} g^{r_2} = H(x_0) \\ g_\beta^{r_3} g^{r_4} = F(x_0) \end{bmatrix} = \Pr \begin{bmatrix} Z^{r_1} e(g_\alpha, g_\gamma)^{r_2} = T \\ Z^{r_3} e(g_\alpha, g_\gamma)^{r_4} = W \\ g_\beta^{r_1} g^{r_2} = H(x_1) \\ g_\beta^{r_3} g^{r_4} = F(x_1) \end{bmatrix}$$

where the probability is over r_1, r_2, r_3, r_4 and Z. That is clear because the four equations are linear independent since for any fixed T, W, f and h,

$$\Pr \begin{bmatrix} Z^{r_1} e(g_\alpha, g_\gamma)^{r_2} = T \\ Z^{r_3} e(g_\alpha, g_\gamma)^{r_4} = W \\ g_\beta^{r_1} g^{r_2} = h \\ g_\beta^{r_3} g^{r_4} = f \end{bmatrix} = \frac{1}{|\mathbb{G}|^2}$$

That concludes that $\mathcal{A}$ learns nothing about b.

To summarize, when the input tuple is sampled from $\mathcal{P}_{\mathrm{BDH}}$, then adversary's view is identical to its view in a real security game and therefore $\mathcal{A}$ satisfies $|\Pr[b' = b] - 1/2| \geq \epsilon$. When the input tuple is sampled from $\mathcal{R}_{\mathrm{BDH}}$, then $\Pr[b' = b] = 1/2$. Therefore, we have that

$$\mathbf{Adv}_{\mathcal{B}}^{\mathrm{DBDH}}(\lambda) = |\Pr[\mathcal{B}(\mathcal{P}_{\mathrm{BDH}}) = 1] - \Pr[\mathcal{B}(\mathcal{R}_{\mathrm{BDH}}) = 1]| \geq |(1/2 \pm \epsilon) - 1/2|| = \epsilon$$

We present our conclusion as the following statement:

Theorem 2. *The AIE scheme we proposed is anonymous assuming the DBDH assumption holds for the bilinear group generated by **GroupGen**.*

7   Proof of Function Privacy

Proof. Denote View_D by the distribution of $\mathcal{A}$'s view in the game $\Psi_D(\lambda)$, View_R by the distribution of $\mathcal{A}$'s view in the game $\Psi_R(\lambda)$. We prove that View_D is statistically close to View_R even for arbitrary fixed public parameters.

Suppose $\mathcal{A}$ received tokens corresponding to $(x_1, x_2, \ldots, x_q)$ in the challenge phase. As $\mathcal{A}$ knows the master key and having fixed pp, we can assume that View_D is equivalent to

$$\left(u_1, v_1, h_1^{u_1} f_1^{v_1}, \ u_2, v_2, h_2^{u_2} f_2^{v_2}, \ldots, u_q, v_q, h_q^{u_q} f_q^{v_q} \right)$$

where $h_i = H(x_i)$ and $f_i = F(x_i)$ for each $i \in \{1, \ldots, q\}$.

Without loss of generality, we can assume that H and F are injective since they are modeled as random oracle. Assuming that H and F are injective guarantees that for any (q, k)-block-source X over $\{0, 1\}^{\lambda q}$ it holds that $((h_1, f_1), \ldots, (h_q, f_q))$ is also a (q, k)-block-source over $\mathbb{G}^{2q}$.

Note that the collection of functions $\{g_{u,v} : \mathbb{G}^2 \to \mathbb{G}\}_{u,v \in \mathbb{Z}_p^*}$ defined by $g_{u,v}(h, f) = h^u f^v$ is universal (see [19]). This enables us to directly apply the Leftover Hash Lemma on block-source, implying that the statistical distance between View_D and the uniform distribution is negligible in λ. The same holds also for View_R since R is a (q, k)-block-source in particular. This completes the proof of function privacy. We present our conclusion as the following statement:

Theorem 3. *The AIE scheme we proposed is (computational) function privacy under random oracle model.*

8   Conclusion and Future Work

In this article, we have discussed the problem of searching on hidden index in asymmetric setting. We make several contributions including a new primitive, new security definitions, a new construction and a new application. An interesting open problem is to construct AIE schemes for other classes of functions. A possible starting point is to consider simple functionalities, such as wildcard [17] and inner-product testing [18]. Another fascinating open problem is to design a scheme which is secure in the standard model as well as keeps the token size and header size constant. Finally, we leave it as an open problem to design an AIE scheme without pairing.

Acknowledgements. This work is supported in part by the National Natural Science Foundation of China (Grant Nos. 6163000206, 61373154, 61371083, and 61411146001), in part by the Prioritized Development Projects through the Specialized Research Fund for the Doctoral Program of Higher Education of China (Grant No. 20130073130004), in part by Shanghai High-tech field project (Grant No. 16511101400). We also thank Prof. Jiguo Li and Tsz Hon Yuen for the helpful suggestions.

References

1. Bellare, M., Boldyreva, A., O'Neill, A.: Deterministic and efficiently searchable encryption. In: Menezes, A. (ed.) CRYPTO 2007. LNCS, vol. 4622, pp. 535–552. Springer, Heidelberg (2007). doi:10.1007/978-3-540-74143-5_30
2. Cash, D., Tessaro, S.: The locality of searchable symmetric encryption. In: Nguyen, P.Q., Oswald, E. (eds.) EUROCRYPT 2014. LNCS, vol. 8441, pp. 351–368. Springer, Heidelberg (2014). doi:10.1007/978-3-642-55220-5_20
3. Baek, J., Safavi-Naini, R., Susilo, W.: Public key encryption with keyword search revisited. In: Gervasi, O., Murgante, B., Laganà, A., Taniar, D., Mun, Y., Gavrilova, M.L. (eds.) ICCSA 2008. LNCS, vol. 5072, pp. 1249–1259. Springer, Heidelberg (2008). doi:10.1007/978-3-540-69839-5_96
4. Kamara, S., Papamanthou, C., Roeder, T.: Dynamic searchable symmetric encryption. In: ACM Conference on Computer and Communications Security, pp. 965–976 (2012)
5. Compagno, A., Conti, M., Gasti, P., Tsudik, G.: Poseidon: Mitigating interest flooding DDoS attacks in Named Data Networking. In: LCN, pp. 630–638 (2013)
6. Boneh, D., Crescenzo, G., Ostrovsky, R., Persiano, G.: Public key encryption with keyword search. In: Cachin, C., Camenisch, J.L. (eds.) EUROCRYPT 2004. LNCS, vol. 3027, pp. 506–522. Springer, Heidelberg (2004). doi:10.1007/978-3-540-24676-3_30
7. Camenisch, J., Kohlweiss, M., Rial, A., Sheedy, C.: Blind and anonymous identity-based encryption and authorised private searches on public key encrypted data. In: Public Key Cryptography, pp. 196–214 (2009)
8. Goh, E.-J.: Secure Indexes (2004)
9. Paolo, G., Gene, T., Ersin, U., Lixia, Z.: DoS and DDoS in named data networking. In: ICCCN , pp. 1-7 (2013)
10. DiBenedetto, S., Gasti, P., Tsudik, G., Uzun, E.: ANDaNA: Anonymous Named Data Networking Application. In: NDSS 2012 (2012)
11. Abdelberi, C., De Cristofaro, E., Kaafar, M.A., Uzun, E.: Privacy in content-oriented networking: threats and countermeasures. Comput. Commun. Rev. **43**(3), 25–33 (2013)
12. Boneh, D., Franklin, M.K.: Identity-based encryption from the weil pairing. SIAM J. Comput. **32**(3), 586–615 (2003)
13. Abdalla, M., Bellare, M., Catalano, D., Kiltz, E., Kohno, T., Lange, T., Malone-Lee, J., Neven, G., Paillier, P., Shi, H.: Searchable encryption revisited: consistency properties, relation to anonymous IBE, and extensions. J. Cryptology **21**(3), 350–391 (2008)
14. Curtmola, R., Garay, J.A., Kamara, S., Ostrovsky, R.: Searchable symmetric encryption: improved definitions and efficient constructions. J. Comput. Secur. **19**(5), 895–934 (2011)
15. Coron, J.-S.: A variant of Boneh-Franklin IBE with a tight reduction in the random oracle model. Des. Codes Crypt. **50**(1), 115–133 (2009)
16. Boneh, D., Raghunathan, A., Segev, G.: Function-private identity-based encryption: hiding the function in functional encryption. In: Canetti, R., Garay, J.A. (eds.) CRYPTO 2013. LNCS, vol. 8043, pp. 461–478. Springer, Heidelberg (2013). doi:10.1007/978-3-642-40084-1_26
17. Abdalla, M., Birkett, J., Catalano, D., Dent, A.W., Malone-Lee, J., Neven, G., Schuldt, J.C.N., Smart, N.P.: Wildcarded identity-based encryption. J. Crypt. **24**(1), 42–82 (2011)

18. Katz, J., Sahai, A., Waters, B.: Predicate encryption supporting disjunctions, polynomial equations, and inner products. J. Crypt. **26**(2), 191–224 (2013)
19. Carter, L., Wegman, M.N.: Universal classes of hash functions. J. Comput. Syst. Sci. **18**(2), 143–154 (1979)
20. Li, J., Lin, X., Zhang, Y., Han, J.: KSF-OABE: outsourced attribute-based encryption with keyword search function for cloud storage. IEEE Trans. Serv. Comput. **PP**(99), 1 (2016)
21. Li, J., Shi, Y., Zhang, Y.: Searchable ciphertext-policy attribute-based encryption with revocation in cloud storage. Int. J. Commun. Syst. (2015)
22. Yuen, T.H., Zhang, Y., Yiu, S.M., Liu, J.K.: Identity-based encryption with post-challenge auxiliary inputs for secure cloud applications and sensor networks. In: Kutyłowski, M., Vaidya, J. (eds.) ESORICS 2014. LNCS, vol. 8712, pp. 130–147. Springer, Heidelberg (2014). doi:10.1007/978-3-319-11203-9_8

Key Management

Multi-cast Key Distribution: Scalable, Dynamic and Provably Secure Construction

Kazuki Yoneyama[1]([⊠]), Reo Yoshida[2], Yuto Kawahara[2], Tetsutaro Kobayashi[2], Hitoshi Fuji[2], and Tomohide Yamamoto[2]

[1] Ibaraki University, Hitachi, Ibaraki, Japan
kazuki.yoneyama.sec@vc.ibaraki.ac.jp
[2] NTT Secure Platform Laboratories, Musashino, Japan

Abstract. In this paper, we propose a two-round dynamic multi-cast key distribution (DMKD) protocol under the star topology with a central authentication server. Users can share a common session key without revealing any information of the session key to the server, and can join/leave to/from the group at any time even after establishing the session key. Our protocol is scalable because communication and computation costs of each user are independent from the number of users. Also, our protocol is still secure if either private key or session-specific randomness of a user is exposed. Furthermore, time-based backward secrecy is guaranteed by renewing the session key for every time period even if the session key is exposed. We introduce the first formal security definition for DMKD under the star topology in order to capture such strong exposure resilience and time-based backward secrecy. We prove that our protocol is secure in our security model in the standard model.

Keywords: Multi-cast key distribution · Exposure resilience · Star topology · Backward secrecy

1 Introduction

HTML 5 is an emerging technology for next generation web applications [1]. Actually, web browser vendors support this new technology. Google said its Chrome browser would begin blocking Internet ads using Adobe's Flash tech, likely prompting advertisers to abandon the video format [2]. Similarly, Mozilla, the Firefox vendor, is encouraging developers to adopt HTML5 and not to use Flash [3].

In HTML5, we have a simple method using WebRTC [4] for a *full-mesh real time communication topology* [5]. WebRTC provides the confidentiality of real time transport protocol (RTP) [6] by using a key exchange and encrypted transport protocol, DTLS-SRTP [7], which has been suggested in IETF Draft [8]. In order to make the full-mesh encrypted communication topology, WebRTC needs full-mesh DTLS key exchanges to establish all SRTP sessions. In brief, WebRTC clients must exchange the keys with $n - 1$ users in the n clients case.

© Springer International Publishing AG 2016
L. Chen and J. Han (Eds.): ProvSec 2016, LNCS 10005, pp. 207–226, 2016.
DOI: 10.1007/978-3-319-47422-9_12

This is very inefficient. Such key exchange protocols under the mesh topology are generally called group key exchange (GKE).

In this paper, we consider the *star topology* instead of the mesh topology for establishing the session key. In the star topology, each user communicates with a central authentication server, and users do not directly communicate with. Thus, it is possible to reduce costs of clients without depending on n; and therefore, WebRTC clients can do the key exchange part very efficiently. Key exchange protocols under the star (or tree) topology are generally called multi-cast key distribution (MKD) or group key management. Though the star topology can reduce the cost for clients, moving most of the burden to the server makes the server a natural target for a concentrated attack. Thus, the star topology is useful if the system is still secure when some part of secret information of the server is exposed by some attack.

Our Contribution. In this paper, we propose a new *provably secure two-round dynamic* MKD (DMKD) protocol under the star topology with a central authentication server. Because of the star topology, each user does not directly communicate with other users. Instead, the central server communicates with users, and distributes information for establishing the session key. If the server was malicious under the star topology, the session key could be known for the server by impersonating a user. Thus, we suppose that the server is honest-but-curious, and even the server must not know any information of the session key.

Each user has public information, called a *static public key (SPK)*, and the corresponding secret information, called a *static secret key (SSK)*. The SPK is also expected to be certified with user's ID through an infrastructure such as PKI. A user who wants to share a *session key* with other users exchanges *ephemeral public keys (EPKs)* that is generated from the corresponding session-specific randomness, called *ephemeral secret keys (ESKs)*, via the server.

The highlight of our protocol is as follows.

- **Dynamic Group.** Our protocol allows users to share the session key in the dynamic group manner. It means that, after establishing the session key among a group of users in a distribution phase, a set of users can join/leave the group without executing a new distribution phase among the new group. Users generate and keep state information for the join and leave phases at the end of the distribution phase. The join and leave phases of our protocol need smaller computation and communication costs than the distribution phase thanks to state information. Also, since the session key is refreshed after the join/leave phases, any information of the new session key do not exposed to leaving users.
- **Strong Exposure Resilience.** In real-world applications, there are several situations that secret information is exposed. For example, if a pseudo-random number generator implemented in a system is poor, ESKs may be guessed to the adversary. Also, when some devices containing SSKs are lost, then a malicious person may use SSKs to know the session key generated by the owner. Furthermore, the government may order the server to reveal the SSK. Thus, it

is desirable that DMKD protocols are resilient to secret key exposure attacks. Our protocol is secure even if either of SSKs or ESKs used to generate the session key are exposed. We call security when ESKs are exposed *ephemeral key exposure resilience*, and security when SSKs (including the server's) are exposed *strong server key forward secrecy*. To achieve ephemeral key exposure resilience, we use *the twisted pseudo-random function (PRF) trick* [9,10]. Strong server key forward secrecy guarantees even if the adversary is allowed to modify messages in the target session while most of AKE protocols prevent that (i.e., weak forward secrecy). Moreover, our protocol guarantees a distinguished security property, called *time-based backward secrecy*. It means that if the session key is exposed at a time frame, the exposed session key is revoked when a new time frame begins. Time-based backward secrecy is very useful to resist real-time session key exposure attacks like malwares. We achieve time-based backward secrecy by formalizing the notion of the time frame in the security model, and proposing a method to update the session key with a minimum cost.

- **Scalability.** Most of previous GKE protocols are constructed under the mesh topology. A user must combine information from users in order to establish the session key with contributions of all users. Thus, the user needs to broadcast a message to all users (i.e., computation and communication costs depend on the number of users), or the round complexity depends on the number of users. Hence, if we adopt the mesh topology, it is difficult to achieve scalability. On the other hand, our DMKD protocol is constructed under the star topology. Though the server needs computation and communication costs depending on the number of users, users can share the session key with constant costs. The load of the server is actually not a problem because the server can be very powerful in computational resource and communication bandwidth. Conversely, users may have poor resources like a mobile device; and thus, scalability is very important in reality.

Also, we propose a first formal security model for DMKD. Our security model captures the star topology and several exposure resilience. Especially, to grasp time-based backward secrecy, the notion of time frames is formulated to define session freshness.

Related Work. We revisit several related work of this work.

Group Key Exchange. The first provably secure GKE protocol is proposed by Bresson et al. [11]. Their protocol is not dynamic (i.e., the group member is fixed before starting sessions.). Then, several dynamic GKE (DGKE) protocols and security models are proposed [12,13]. These protocols need a linear number of rounds. After that, several constant round DGKE protocols are studied [14–16]. Exposure resilience of GKE protocols is firstly considered in the security model by Manulis et al. [17]. Their model guarantees ephemeral key exposure resilience and weak forward secrecy. This security model is extended by Suzuki and Yoneyama [18] to grasp session state exposure. However, their proposed GKE protocol is not for general group setting but three-party setting. Since these GKE protocols are considered under the mesh topology, costs of users depend on the number of users.

Multicast Key Distribution. Since the main application of MKD is Mobile Ad Hoc Networks (MANET), most of MKD protocols use tree topology. The advantage of the tree-based MKD is that total communication complexity is reduced to $\mathcal{O}(\log n)$. For example, MKD protocols based on logical key hierarchies [19–22] have been well studied. There are few papers studying MKD in the star topology [23–26]. The motivation of previous star topology-based MKD protocols is to reduce the rekeying cost of tree topology-based MKD protocols. Most of these protocols have no formal security proof. Sun et al. [26] propose a provably secure star topology-based MKD protocol. However, their security model does not capture exposure resilience, and their protocol is not scalable because communication complexity for uses depend on the number of users. A formal security model for MKD protocols is introduced by Micciancio and Panjwani [27]. However, their model allows the server to know the session key shared by users. Also, exposure resilience is not considered.

2   Preliminaries

2.1   Notations

Throughout this paper we use the following notations. If Set is a set, then by $m \in_R$ Set we denote that m is sampled uniformly from Set. If **ALG** is an algorithm, then by $y \leftarrow \textbf{ALG}(x; r)$ we denote that y is output by **ALG** on input x and randomness r (if **ALG** is deterministic, r is empty).

2.2   Pseudo-Random Function, and Twisted Pseudo-Random Function Trick

Let κ be a security parameter and $\mathsf{F} = \{F_\kappa : Dom_\kappa \times Kspace_\kappa \rightarrow Rng_\kappa\}_\kappa$ be a function family with a family of domains $\{Dom_\kappa\}_\kappa$, a family of key spaces $\{Kspace_\kappa\}_\kappa$ and a family of ranges $\{Rng_\kappa\}_\kappa$.

Definition 1 (Pseudo-Random Function). *We say that function family* $\mathsf{F} = \{F_\kappa\}_\kappa$ *is the PRF family, if for any PPT distinguisher* $\mathcal{D}$, $|\Pr[1 \leftarrow \mathcal{D}^{F_\kappa(\cdot)}]$ $- \Pr[1 \leftarrow \mathcal{D}^{RF_\kappa(\cdot)}]| \leq negl$, *where* $RF_\kappa : Dom_\kappa \rightarrow Rng_\kappa$ *is a truly random function.*

Next, we show the notion of the twisted PRF [9]. The twisted PRF $tPRF$ is a function that $tPRF : \{0,1\}^\kappa \times Kspace_\kappa^2 \times \{0,1\}^\kappa \rightarrow Rng_\kappa$. We construct $tPRF(a, a', b, b') := F_\kappa(a, b) \oplus F_\kappa(b', a')$ with PRF F_κ, where $a, b' \in \{0,1\}^\kappa$ and $a', b \in Kspace_\kappa$. The twisted PRF is used to guarantee that $tPRF(a, a', b, b')$ looks random even if either (a, a') or (b, b') is exposed.

Lemma 1 (Theorem 1 in [10]). *If* F_κ *is PRF, then*

- $[(a, a'), tPRF(a, a', b, b')]$ *is indistinguishable from* $[(a, a'), R]$ *where* R *is randomly chosen from* Rng_κ, *and*
- $[(b, b'), tPRF(a, a', b, b')]$ *is indistinguishable from* $[(b, b'), R]$ *where* R *is randomly chosen from* Rng_κ.

2.3   Target-Collision Resistant Hash Function

We say a function $TCR : Dom \rightarrow Rng$ is a target-collision resistant (TCR) hash function if the following condition holds for security parameter κ: For any PPT adversary $\mathcal{A}$, $\Pr[x \in_R Dom; x' \leftarrow \mathcal{A}(x) \text{ s.t. } x \neq x' \wedge TCR(x) = TCR(x')] \leq negl$.

2.4   Public Key Encryption

Definition 2 (Syntax for Public Key Encryption Schemes). *A PKE scheme consists of the following 3-tuple* (**Gen, Enc, Dec**)*:*

Gen : *a key generation algorithm which on input* 1^κ, *where* κ *is the security parameter, outputs a pair of public and secret keys* (pk, sk).
Enc : *an encryption algorithm which takes as input public key* pk *and plaintext* m, *outputs ciphertext* CT.
Dec : *a decryption algorithm which takes as input secret key* sk *and ciphertext* CT, *outputs plaintext* m *or reject symbol* $\perp$.

Definition 3 (Chosen-Ciphertext Security for Public Key Encryption). *A PKE scheme is CCA-secure if the following property holds for security parameter* κ; *For any adversary* $\mathcal{A} = (\mathcal{A}_1, \mathcal{A}_2)$, $|\Pr[(pk, sk) \leftarrow \mathbf{Gen}(1^\kappa); (m_0, m_1, state) \leftarrow \mathcal{A}_1^{\mathcal{DO}(sk, \cdot)}(pk); b \in_R \{0, 1\}; CT^* \leftarrow \mathbf{Enc}(pk, m_b); b' \leftarrow \mathcal{A}_2^{\mathcal{DO}(sk, \cdot)}(pk, CT^*, state);$ $b' = b] - 1/2| \leq negl(\kappa)$, *where* $\mathcal{DO}$ *is the decryption oracle which outputs* m *or* $\perp$ *on receiving* CT, *state is state information (possibly including* pk, m_0 *and* m_1*) which* $\mathcal{A}$ *wants to preserve.* $\mathcal{A}$ *cannot submit the ciphertext* $CT = CT^*$ *to* $\mathcal{DO}$.

2.5   Ciphertext-Policy Attribute-Based Encryption

Definition 4 (Syntax for Ciphertext-Policy Attribute-based Encryption Schemes). *A CP-ABE scheme consists of the following 4-tuple* (**Setup, Der, AEnc, ADec**)*:*

$(Params, msk) \leftarrow \mathbf{Setup}(1^\kappa, att)$: *a setup algorithm which on inputs* 1^κ *and* att, *where* κ *is the security parameter and* att *is an attribute universe description, outputs a public parameter* $Params$ *and a master secret key* msk.
$usk_A \leftarrow \mathbf{Der}(Params, msk, A)$: *a key derivation algorithm which on input* $Params$, msk *and attribute* A, *outputs a user secret key* usk_A.
$CT \leftarrow \mathbf{AEnc}(Params, P, m)$: *an encryption algorithm which on input* $Params$, *an access structure* P *and a plaintext* m, *outputs a ciphertext* CT.

$m \leftarrow \mathbf{ADec}(Params, usk_A, CT)$ **:** *a decryption algorithm which on input usk_A and CT, outputs plaintext m if A satisfies P.*

Definition 5 (Chosen-Ciphertext Security for Ciphertext-Policy Attribute-based Encryption). *A CP-ABE scheme is CCA-secure if the following property holds for security parameter κ; For any PPT adversary $\mathcal{A} = (\mathcal{A}_1, \mathcal{A}_2)$, $|\Pr[(Params, msk) \leftarrow \mathbf{Setup}(1^\kappa, att); (m_0, m_1, P^*, s) \leftarrow \mathcal{A}_1^{\mathcal{EO}(Params, msk, \cdot), \mathcal{DO}(Params, usk., \cdot)}(Params);$ $b \in_R \{0,1\};$ $CT^* \leftarrow \mathbf{AEnc}(Params, P^*, m_b);$ $b' \leftarrow \mathcal{A}_2^{\mathcal{EO}(Params, msk, \cdot), \mathcal{DO}(Params, usk., \cdot)}(Params, CT^*, s); b' = b] - 1/2| \leq negl$, where $\mathcal{EO}$ is the key extraction oracle, $\mathcal{DO}$ is the decryption oracle and s is state information that $\mathcal{A}$ wants to preserve from $\mathcal{A}_1$ to $\mathcal{A}_2$. $\mathcal{A}$ cannot submit sets of attributes which satisfy P^* to $\mathcal{EO}$ and the ciphertext CT^* to $\mathcal{DO}$.*

We say a CP-ABE scheme is CPA-secure if $\mathcal{A}$ does not access $\mathcal{DO}$. Also, we say a CP-ABE scheme is selectively secure if the adversary must commit P^* before **Setup**.

2.6   Message Authentication Codes

Definition 6 (Syntax for Message Authentication Codes). *A MAC scheme consists of the following 3-tuple (**MGen**, **Tag**, **Ver**):*

MGen : *a key generation algorithm which on input 1^κ, where κ is the security parameter, outputs a MAC key mk.*

Tag : *a tagging algorithm which on input mk and plaintext m, outputs an authentication-tag σ.*

Ver : *a verification algorithm which on input mk, m and σ, outputs 1 if accepts, 0 otherwise.*

Definition 7 (Unforgeability against Chosen-Message Attacks for Message Authentication Codes). *A MAC scheme is UF-CMA if the following property holds for security parameter κ; For any PPT forger $\mathcal{A}$, $\Pr[mk \leftarrow \mathbf{MGen}(1^\kappa); (m^*, \sigma^*) \leftarrow \mathcal{A}^{\mathcal{MO}(mk, \cdot)}; 1 \leftarrow \mathbf{Ver}(mk, m^*, \sigma^*)] \leq negl$, where $\mathcal{MO}$ is the MAC oracle. $\mathcal{A}$ cannot submit m^* to $\mathcal{MO}$.*

2.7   Decisional Diffie-Hellman Assumption

Definition 8 (Decisional Diffie-Hellman Assumption). *Let p be a prime and let g be a generator of a finite cyclic group G of order p. We define two experiments, $\mathsf{Exp}_{g,p}^{ddh-real}(\mathcal{D})$ and $\mathsf{Exp}_{g,p}^{ddh-rand}(\mathcal{D})$. For a distinguisher $\mathcal{D}$, inputs $(g, A = g^a, B = g^b, C)$ are provided, where $(a, b) \in_R (\mathbb{Z}_p)^2$. $C = g^{ab}$ in $\mathsf{Exp}_{g,p}^{ddh-real}(\mathcal{D})$ and $C = g^c$ in $\mathsf{Exp}_{g,p}^{ddh-rand}(\mathcal{D})$, where $c \in_R \mathbb{Z}_p$. Let $(g, A = g^a, B = g^b, C = g^{ab})$ be the tuple in $\mathsf{Exp}_{g,p}^{ddh-real}(\mathcal{D})$ and $(g, A = g^a, B = g^b, C = g^c)$ be the tuple in $\mathsf{Exp}_{g,p}^{ddh-rand}(\mathcal{D})$. We say that the DDH assumption in G holds for security parameter κ if for any PPT distinguisher $\mathcal{D}$ $|\Pr[\mathsf{Exp}_{g,p}^{ddh-real}(\mathcal{D}) = 1] - \Pr[\mathsf{Exp}_{g,p}^{ddh-rand}(\mathcal{D}) = 1]| \leq negl$.*

3   Security Definition

In this section, we introduce a new security definition of DMKD under the star topology. Our definition captures strong exposure-resilience and time-based forward secrecy. The model is based on [16,18,28].

3.1   Protocol Participants and Initialization

Let $\mathcal{U} := \{U_1, \ldots, U_N\}$ be a set of potential protocol users. Each user U_i is modelled as a PPT Turing machine w.r.t. security parameter κ. For user U_i, we denote static secret (public) key by SSK_i (SPK_i). U_i generates its own keys, SSK_i and SPK_i, and the static public key SPK_i is linked with U_i's identity in some systems like PKI. Each user U_i and the authentication server S are connected by unauthenticated the star topology. That is, they do communications through an unicast channel over an insecure network like the Internet. Users do not directly communicate. S is also modelled as a PPT Turing machine. S has the static secret key by SSK_S and the static public key SPK_S.

3.2   Session and State Information

There are three phases (Dist, Join, Leave) for DMKD. Dist means the session key distribution phase that a new group is established and a session key is generated for users in the group. Join means the user joining phase that a set of new users join an established group and a session key is re-generated for users in the new group. Leave means the user leaving phase that a set of users leave an established group and a session key is re-generated for remaining users in the group. An invocation of a phase is called a *session*. We suppose that a session contains n users $\{U_{i_1}, \ldots, U_{i_n}\}$, where $2 \le n \le N$. Let Π be a phase identifier such that $\Pi \in \{\mathsf{Dist}, \mathsf{Join}, \mathsf{Leave}\}$. A session owned by user instance $U_{i_\ell}^{j_\ell}$ is managed by a tuple $(\Pi, U_{i_\ell}^{j_\ell}, \{U_{i_1}^{j_1}, \ldots, U_{i_n}^{j_n}\})$. $U_{i_\ell}^{j_\ell}$ means the j_ℓ-th instance of U_{i_ℓ}. Sessions owned by user instances $\{U_{i_1}^{j_1}, \ldots, U_{i_{\ell-1}}^{j_{\ell-1}}, U_{i_{\ell+1}}^{j_{\ell+1}}, \ldots, U_{i_n}^{j_n}\}$ are called matching sessions of the session of $U_{i_\ell}^{j_\ell}$. Hereafter, for simplicity, we can describe U_{i_ℓ} as U_i without loss of generality. We suppose that the total number of sessions in the system is ℓ_{max}. We consider the notion of *time frames*. Each user U_i and S communicate to update some state information $state_i$ when the session is firstly executed in a time frame. Hereafter, U_i uses $state_i$ in sessions within the time frame. Also, we consider the session key update based on time frames. Update means the session key update phase that the shared session key is updated when a new time frame begins. If a session key is shared in the Dist/Join/Leave phase in the past time frame, the session key is updated by Update. We note that the session is not changed after Update phase but only the session key is changed. In Dist phase, U_i^j generates ephemeral secret key ESK_i^j and sends ephemeral public key EPK_i^j to S. When S receives all EPK_i^j for $i, j = 1, \ldots, n$, then S returns messages to users. Users and S repeat some rounds, and then users finally share session key SK and complete the session. After completing the session, each user U_i updates $state_i$ to remain necessary information for Update, Join and Leave phases. $state_i$ is passed to another inactivated instance $U_i^{j'}$ to participate in the next activation of Update, Join or Leave phase. Similarly, in Update, Join and Leave phases, users and S execute some interactions, and users update the session key. DMKD consists of many concurrent executions of Dist, Update, Join and Leave phases.

3.3 Adversary

The adversary $\mathcal{A}$, which is modelled as a PPT Turing machine, controls all communications between parties including session activation and registrations of users by performing the following adversary queries.

- Establish(U_i, SPK_i): This query allows $\mathcal{A}$ to introduce a new user. In response, if $U_i \notin \mathcal{U}$ (due to the uniqueness of identities) then U_i with the static public key SPK_i is added to $\mathcal{U}$. Note that $\mathcal{A}$ is not required to prove the possession of the corresponding secret key SSK_i. If a party is registered by a Establish query issued by $\mathcal{A}$, then we call the party *dishonest*. If not, we call the party *honest*.
- Send$(U_i^j, message)$: This query allows $\mathcal{A}$ to send *message* to instance U_i^j. *message* includes $\Pi \in \{\text{Dist}, \text{Join}, \text{Leave}\}$. $\mathcal{A}$ obtains the response from U_i^j. If U_i^j is an inactivated instance and $\Pi = \{\text{Join}, \text{Leave}\}$, $state_i$ is passed to U_i^j.

To capture exposure of secret information, the adversary $\mathcal{A}$ is allowed to issue the following queries.

- SessionReveal(U_i^j): The adversary $\mathcal{A}$ obtains the session key SK for the session owned by U_i^j if the session is completed.
- StateReveal(U_i): The adversary $\mathcal{A}$ obtains current state information $state_i$ of U_i. State information do not include the static secret key.
- ServerReveal: This query allows the adversary $\mathcal{A}$ to obtain static secret key SSK_S of the server S.
- StaticReveal(U_i): This query allows the adversary $\mathcal{A}$ to obtain static secret key SSK_i of the user U_i.
- EphemeralReveal(U_i^j): This query allows the adversary $\mathcal{A}$ to obtain ephemeral secret key ESK_i^j of U_i^j if the session is not completed (i.e., the session key is not established yet).

3.4 Freshness

For the security definition, we need the notion of freshness.

Definition 9 (Freshness). *Let* $\mathsf{sid}^* = (\Pi, U_i^j, \{U_{i_1}^{j_1}, \ldots, U_{i_n}^{j_n}\})$ *be a completed session between honest users* $\{U_1, \ldots, U_n\}$*, which is owned by* U_i^j*. Let* $\overline{\mathsf{sid}}^*$ *be a matching session of* sid^**. We say session* sid^* *is* fresh *if none of the following conditions hold:*

1. *The adversary $\mathcal{A}$ issues either of* SessionReveal(U_i^j) *or* SessionReveal($U_{i'}^{j'}$) *for any* $\overline{\text{sid}}^*$ *in the current time frame,*
2. *The adversary $\mathcal{A}$ issues either of* SessionReveal(U_i^j) *or* SessionReveal($U_{i'}^{j'}$) *for any* $\overline{\text{sid}}^*$ *in the past time frame if $\mathcal{A}$ issues either of* ServerReveal, StaticReveal(U_i) *or* StaticReveal($U_{i'}$),
3. *The adversary $\mathcal{A}$ issues* ServerReveal *before completing* sid*,
4. *The adversary $\mathcal{A}$ makes either of* StateReveal(U_i) *or* StateReveal($U_{i'}$) *in the current time frame or any of its ancestors[1],*
5. *The adversary $\mathcal{A}$ makes either of* StaticReveal(U_i) *before completing* sid* *or* StaticReveal($U_{i'}$) *before completing* $\overline{\text{sid}}^*$ *for any* $\overline{\text{sid}}^*$,
6. *The adversary $\mathcal{A}$ makes both of* StaticReveal(U_i) *and* EphemeralReveal(U_i^j), *and*
7. *The adversary $\mathcal{A}$ makes both of* StaticReveal($U_{i'}$) *and* EphemeralReveal($U_{i'}^{j'}$) *for any* $\overline{\text{sid}}^*$.

We note that if both EphemeralReveal(U_i^j) and StaticReveal(U_i) are posed, then we regard that StateReveal(U_i) in the time frame for instance U_i^j is also posed because $state_i$ in the time frame is trivially derived from ESK_i^j and SSK_i.

3.5   Security Experiment

For the security definition, we consider the following security experiment. Initially, the adversary $\mathcal{A}$ is given a set of honest users and makes any sequence of the queries described above. During the experiment, the adversary $\mathcal{A}$ makes the following query.

– Test(sid*): Here, sid* must be a fresh session. Select random bit $b \in_R \{0, 1\}$, and return the session key held by sid* if $b = 0$, and return a random key if $b = 1$.

The experiment continues until the adversary $\mathcal{A}$ makes a guess b'. The adversary $\mathcal{A}$ *wins* the game if the test session sid* is still fresh and if the guess of the adversary $\mathcal{A}$ is correct, i.e., $b' = b$. The advantage of the adversary $\mathcal{A}$ is defined as $\mathbf{Adv}^{\text{dmkd}}(\mathcal{A}) = \Pr[\mathcal{A} \; wins] - \frac{1}{2}$. We define the security as follows.

Definition 10 (DMKD Security). *We say that a DMKD protocol Π is secure in the DMKD model if the following conditions hold:*

1. *If two honest parties complete matching sessions, then, except with negligible probability, they both compute the same session key.*
2. *For any PPT adversary $\mathcal{A}$, $\mathbf{Adv}^{\text{dmkd}}(\mathcal{A})$ is negligible in security parameter κ for the test session* sid*.

---

[1] We say that $state_i$ is an ancestor of $state_{i'}$ if there exists a path $(state_i, \ldots, state_{i'})$ such that each state in the path is updated to the next one.

3.6   Summary of Our Security Definition

Here, we give an intuition of security properties captured by our security definition.

– **Ephemeral Key Exposure Resilience.** The adversary can obtain ESKs of users by EphemeralReveal queries. From the freshness definition, when the adversary does not pose StaticReveal(U_i) where U_i is the owner of the test session, then the adversary can pose EphemeralReveal(U_i^j) where the j-th session of U_i is the test session. Thus, it guarantees that the session key is still secure even if $ESKs$ used to generate the session key are *totally exposed*.

– **Time-based Backward Secrecy.** The adversary can obtain the session key of the test session by SessionReveal queries if the session key was generated at a past time frame. Generally, if the session key of the test session is exposed, the adversary easily distinguish the real session key from a random key. In our security model, we introduce the notion of the time frame, and consider the Update phase. Thus, when a new time frame begins, the session key may be updated. Hence, it guarantees that the updated session key looks independent from past session keys even in the test session.

– **Strong Server Key Forward Secrecy.** The adversary can obtain both SSKs of users and the server by StaticReveal and ServerReveal queries. From the freshness definition, when the adversary does not pose EphemeralReveal queries for the test session, then the adversary can pose StaticReveal and ServerReveal for users in the test session after completion of the session.[2] Hence, it guarantees that past session keys are still secure even if SSKs of users and the server are exposed. Also, the adversary is allowed to modify messages in the test session (i.e., there is a non-matching session.) regardless of posing StaticReveal or ServerReveal. Thus, while in most of AKE protocols only weak forward secrecy is guaranteed (i.e., the adversary is prohibited to pose StaticReveal for non-matching sessions.), our security guarantees strong forward secrecy.

4   New Dynamic Multi-cast Key Distribution Protocol Under Star Topology

In this section, we show a DMKD protocol under the star topology. In the Dist phase, a group of users shares a session key with the help of the central server. In the Join phase, new users can join the group that previously established the session key with lower costs than executing a Dist phase by the new group members. In the Leave phase, a subset of group users leaves from the group with lower costs than executing a Dist phase by the remaining group members. After establishing the session key, users can update the key at a new time frame. In the

---

[2] If the adversary poses StaticReveal or ServerReveal before completion of the test session, then the session key is trivially distinguished from a random key. Also, it means that the server is honest-but-curious.

Update phase, the server sends information to refresh the session key to users, and users can locally update the key.

For simplicity, we show a simple setting that only one user joins/leaves the group simultaneously. We show the general setting that multiple users can join/leave the group simultaneously in the full paper [29].

4.1   Design Principle

The session key in our protocol is generated from two key materials K_1 and K_2. K_1 guarantees ephemeral key exposure resilience and strong server key forward secrecy, and K_2 guarantees time-based backward secrecy. Here, we give an intuition of the design of our protocol.

The way to share K_1 is based on the ring structure, and is similar to the previous dynamic group key exchange protocol (the YT protocol) [16]. In the YT protocol, each user broadcasts g^{r_i} in Round 1, and computes $g^{r_{i-1}r_i}$ and $g^{r_i r_{i+1}}$. Then, the left key $K_i^{(l)}$ based on $g^{r_{i-1}r_i}$ and the right key $K_i^{(r)}$ based on $g^{r_i r_{i+1}}$ are generated, and each user broadcasts $K_i^{(l)} \oplus K_i^{(r)}$ in Round 2. Also, a representative user generates k, and broadcasts the masked k with his left key to all users. Then, each user can recover the left and right keys for all group members with his/her $K_i^{(l)}$ and $K_i^{(r)}$. Thus, they can share k, and generate K_1 based on k. However, we cannot simply apply the YT protocol to our protocol. First, the YT protocol is insecure if ESKs of users are exposed; that means, ephemeral key exposure resilience is not satisfied. The other problem is scalability. To broadcast messages and to compute k, both communication and computational complexity of each user depend on the number of users; and thus, if the YT protocol is used very large system, the load of users increases. Therefore, achieving both exposure resilience and scalability is not easy task.

We can solve the first problem on ephemeral key exposure resilience by using the twisted PRF trick. We use outputs of the twisted PRF based on the SSK and the ESK instead of all randomness of users in our protocol. From Lemma 1, it is guaranteed that an output of the twisted PRF is indistinguishable from the random value unless both SSK and ESK are exposed. The freshness definition also guarantee that both SSK and ESK are not exposed in the test session. Therefore, our protocol satisfies ephemeral key exposure resilience. Also, we can solve the second problem on scalability thanks to the difference of the network topology. In the YT protocol, each user must communicate with other users directly because of the mesh topology, and all costs inevitably depend on the number of users. On the other hand, in our protocol, each user only communicates with the server because of the star topology. Thus, we can confine commutation depending on the number of users to the server in our protocol. The server only sends a constant number of messages to each user. Therefore, communication and computational complexity of each user do not depend on the number of users; and thus, our protocol is scalable. We note that complexity of the server depends on the number of users, however, it is inevitable and not serious because the server has sufficient computational power and communication bandwidth in reality.

The other key material, K_2, is generated by the server. It is encrypted by a CP-ABE scheme with the access structure that the ID is of the recipient and the time is within the current time frame. Since for every time frame each user receives a new decryption key with attribute of his/her ID and the current time, K_2 can be decrypted if the ID of the recipient is valid and the decryption key is sent at the same time frame. The new decryption key is stored as state information. After generating the session key, when a new time frame begins, the server sends the encrypted form of new K_2 and each user locally updates the session key. Though the adversary can pose StateReveal queries, the freshness definition guarantee that state information of the test session in the current time frame or any of its ancestors is not exposed. Thus, even if the adversary obtains session keys at past time frames, the session key at the current time frame is still secure. Therefore, our protocol satisfies time-based backward secrecy.

4.2   System Setup

S runs the setup algorithm **Setup** of CP-ABE, and generates a public parameter $Params$ and a master secret key msk. Let p be a κ-bit prime, and G be a finite cyclic group of order p with generator g, h. Let $TCR : \{0,1\}^* \rightarrow \{0,1\}^\kappa$ be a TCR hash function. Let $tPRF : \{0,1\}^\kappa \times Kspace_\kappa^2 \times \{0,1\}^\kappa \rightarrow \mathbb{Z}_p$ and $tPRF' : \{0,1\}^\kappa \times Kspace_\kappa^2 \times \{0,1\}^\kappa \rightarrow Kspace_\kappa$ be twisted PRFs. Let $F : \{0,1\}^\kappa \times G \rightarrow \mathbb{Z}_p^2$, $F' : \{0,1\}^\kappa \times \mathbb{Z}_p \rightarrow Kspace_\kappa$ and $F'' : \{0,1\}^\kappa \times Kspace_\kappa \rightarrow \{0,1\}^\kappa$, $F''' : \{0,1\}^\kappa \times Kspace_\kappa \rightarrow \mathbb{Z}_p$ be PRFs. S stores msk as SSK_S, and publishes $(Params, p, G, g, h, TCR, tPRF, tPRF', F, F', F'', F''')$ as SPK_S.

There are N users $U_1 \ldots, U_N$. Each user U_i runs the key generation algorithm of PKE **Gen**, and generates a public key pk_i and a secret key sk_i. Also, U_i generates secret strings for the twisted PRF (st_i, st_i') and (st_S, st_S'), where $st_i, st_S \in_R Kspace_\kappa$ and $st_i', st_S' \in_R \{0,1\}^\kappa$. U_i stores (sk_i, st_i, st_i') as SSK_i, and publishes pk_i as SPK_i.

4.3   Dist Phase

A set of users $U_{i_1}, \ldots, U_{i_n}$ $(n \leq N)$ starts a new session and share a session key. For simplicity, w.l.o.g., we suppose that $(U_{i_1}, \ldots, U_{i_n}) = (U_1, \ldots, U_n)$.

(State Update at New Time Frame) If the session is the first session for U_i at the time frame TF, then for the current time $time$ S generates $usk_i \leftarrow$ **Der**$(Params, msk, A_i)$ with attribute $A_i = (U_i, time)$ and $mk_i \leftarrow$ **MGen**, and computes $CT_i \leftarrow$ **Enc**$_{pk_i}(usk_i, mk_i)$. Then, S sends CT_i to U_i, and U_i obtains $(usk_i, mk_i) \leftarrow$ **Dec**$_{sk_i}(CT_i)$ and updates (usk_i, mk_i) in $state_i$.

(Round 1 for Users) U_i generates $\tilde{r}_i \in_R \{0,1\}^\kappa$, $\tilde{r}_i' \in_R Kspace_\kappa$, $\tilde{k}_i \in_R \{0,1\}^\kappa$, $\tilde{k}_i' \in_R Kspace_\kappa$, $\tilde{s}_i \in_R \{0,1\}^\kappa$ and $\tilde{s}_i' \in_R Kspace_\kappa$ as ESK_i, and computes $r_i = tPRF(\tilde{r}_i, \tilde{r}_i', st_i, st_i')$, $k_i = tPRF(\tilde{k}_i, \tilde{k}_i', st_i, st_i')$ and $s_i = tPRF(\tilde{s}_i, \tilde{s}_i', st_i, st_i')$. Then, U_i computes $R_i = g^{r_i}$ and $c_i = g^{k_i} h^{s_i}$, and sends (R_i, c_i) to S.

(Round 1 for Server) On receiving (R_i, c_i) from all users, S computes $sid = TCR(c_1, \ldots, c_n)$ and chooses a representative user from $(U_1, \ldots, U_n)$. Here, w.l.o.g., we suppose that U_1 is the representative user. For $i \in [1, n]$, S sends (sid, R_{i-1}, R_{i+1}) to U_i. Also, S notices that U_1 is the representative user.

(Round 2 for Users) For $i \in [2, n]$, on receiving (sid, R_{i-1}, R_{i+1}), U_i computes $K_i^{(l)} = F(sid, R_{i-1}^{r_i})$, $K_i^{(r)} = F(sid, R_{i+1}^{r_i})$ and $T_i = K_i^{(l)} \oplus K_i^{(r)}$. Then, U_i computes $\sigma_i \leftarrow \mathbf{Tag}_{mk_i}(R_i, c_i, R_{i-1}, R_{i+1}, k_i, s_i, T_i, U_i, sid)$ and sends $(k_i, s_i, T_i, \sigma_i)$ to S.

On receiving (sid, R_n, R_2), U_1 computes $K_1^{(l)} = F(sid, R_n^{r_1})$, $K_1^{(r)} = F(sid, R_2^{r_1})$, $T_1 = K_1^{(l)} \oplus K_1^{(r)}$ and $T' = K_1^{(l)} \oplus (k_1 \| s_1)$. Then, U_1 computes $\sigma_1 \leftarrow \mathbf{Tag}_{mk_1}(R_1, c_1, R_n, R_2, T_1, T', U_1, sid)$ and sends (T_1, T', σ_1) to S.

(Round 2 for Server) On receiving (T_1, T', σ_1) and $(k_i, s_i, T_i, \sigma_i)$, S verifies $\mathbf{Ver}_{mk_1}(R_1, c_1, R_n, R_2, T_1, T', U_1, sid, \sigma_1)$ and $\mathbf{Ver}_{mk_i}(R_i, c_i, R_{i-1}, R_{i+1}, k_i, s_i, T_i, U_i, sid, \sigma_i)$, and if the verification fails, then aborts. Also, for $i \in [2, n]$, S checks if $c_i = g^{k_i} h^{s_i}$ holds, and if the verification fails, then aborts. S generates $\tilde{k}_S \in_R \{0,1\}^\kappa$, $\tilde{k}'_S \in_R \mathsf{Kspace}_\kappa$, $\tilde{K}_1 \in_R \{0,1\}^\kappa$ and $\tilde{K}'_1 \in_R Kspace_\kappa$ as ESK_S, and computes $k_S = tPRF(\tilde{k}_S, \tilde{k}'_S, st_S, st'_S)$, $K_1 = tPRF'(\tilde{K}_1, \tilde{K}'_1, st_S, st'_S)$ and $k' = (\bigoplus_{2 \le i \le n} k_i) \oplus k_S$. For $i \in [2, n]$, S computes $T'_i = \bigoplus_{1 \le j \le i-1} T_j$. For $i \in [1, n]$, S computes $CT'_i \leftarrow \mathbf{AEnc}(Params, P_i, K_1)$ with access structure $P_i := (ID = U_i) \wedge (time \in TF)$. S computes $\sigma'_1 \leftarrow \mathbf{Tag}_{mk_1}(R_1, c_1, R_n, R_2, T_1, T', U_1, sid, k', CT'_1)$, and sends (k', CT'_1, σ'_1) to U_1. For $i \in [2, n]$, S computes $\sigma'_i \leftarrow \mathbf{Tag}_{mk_i}(R_i, c_i, R_{i-1}, R_{i+1}, k_i, s_i, T_i, U_i, sid, c_1, k', T'_i, T', CT'_i)$, and sends $(c_1, k', T'_i, T', CT'_i, \sigma'_i)$ to U_i.

(Session Key Generation and Post Computation) For $i \in [2, n]$, on receiving $(c_1, k', T'_i, T', CT'_i, \sigma'_i)$, U_i verifies $\mathbf{Ver}_{mk_i}(R_i, c_i, R_{i-1}, R_{i+1}, k_i, s_i, T_i, U_i, sid, c_1, k', T'_i, T', CT'_i, \sigma'_i)$, and if the verification fails, then aborts. U_i computes $K_1^{(l)} = T'_i \oplus K_i^{(l)}$ and $k_1 \| s_1 = T' \oplus K_1^{(l)}$, and checks if $c_1 = g^{k_1} h^{s_1}$ holds, and if the verification fails, then aborts. U_i decrypts $K_1 \leftarrow \mathbf{ADec}_{usk_i}(CT'_i, P_i)$, computes $K_2 = F'(sid, k' \oplus k_1)$, and outputs the session key $SK = F''(sid, K_1) \oplus F''(sid, K_2)$. As state information, U_i adds sid, $H_i^{(l)} = R_{i-1}^{r_i}$, $H_i^{(r)} = R_{i+1}^{r_i}$ and $r = F'''(sid, K_1) \oplus F'''(sid, K_2)$ to $state_i$. On receiving (k', CT'_1, σ'_1), U_1 verifies $\mathbf{Ver}_{mk_1}(R_1, c_1, R_n, R_2, T_1, T', U_1, sid, k', CT'_1, \sigma'_1)$, and if the verification fails, then aborts. U_1 decrypts $K_1 \leftarrow \mathbf{ADec}_{usk_1}(CT'_1, P_1)$, computes $K_2 = F'(sid, k' \oplus k_1)$, and outputs the session key $SK = F''(sid, K_1) \oplus F''(sid, K_2)$. As state information, U_1 adds sid, $H_1^{(l)} = R_n^{r_1}$, $H_1^{(r)} = R_2^{r_1}$ and $r = F'''(sid, K_1) \oplus F'''(sid, K_2)$ to $state_i$.

4.4 Join Phase

A user $U_{i_{n+1}}$ joins an established session by $U_1, \ldots, U_n$. W.l.o.g., we suppose that $U_{i_{n+1}} = U_{n+1}$.

In the Join phase, users U_i for $i \in [2, n-1]$ can reduce computation than the Dist phase. They do not need to compute g^{r_i}. The ring structure to compute K_1 still works because r in $state_i$ is used to connect the ring instead of using r_i.

(State Update at New Time Frame) If the session is the first session for U_i at the time frame TF', then for the current time $time$ S generates $usk_i \leftarrow$ **Der**$(Params, msk, A_i)$ with attribute $A_i = (U_i, time)$ and $mk_i \leftarrow$ **MGen**, and computes $CT_i \leftarrow$ **Enc**$_{pk_i}(usk_i, mk_i)$. Then, S sends CT_i to U_i, and U_i obtains $(usk_i, mk_i) \leftarrow$ **Dec**$_{sk_i}(CT_i)$ and updates (usk_i, mk_i) in $state_i$.

(Round 1 for Users) For $i \in \{1, n, n+1\}$, U_i generates $\tilde{r}_i \in_R \{0,1\}^\kappa$, $\tilde{r}'_i \in_R$ Kspace$_\kappa$, $\tilde{k}_i \in_R \{0,1\}^\kappa$, $\tilde{k}'_i \in_R$ Kspace$_\kappa$, $\tilde{s}_i \in_R \{0,1\}^\kappa$ and $\tilde{s}'_i \in_R$ Kspace$_\kappa$ as ESK_i, and computes $r_i = tPRF(\tilde{r}_i, \tilde{r}'_i, st_i, st'_i)$, $k_i = tPRF(\tilde{k}_i, \tilde{k}'_i, st_i, st'_i)$ and $s_i = tPRF(\tilde{s}_i, \tilde{s}'_i, st_i, st'_i)$. U_i computes $R_i = g^{r_i}$ and $c_i = g^{k_i} h^{s_i}$, and sends (R_i, c_i) to S.

For $i \in [2, n-1]$, U_i generates $\tilde{k}_i \in_R \{0,1\}^\kappa$, $\tilde{k}'_i \in_R$ Kspace$_\kappa$, $\tilde{s}_i \in_R \{0,1\}^\kappa$ and $\tilde{s}'_i \in_R$ Kspace$_\kappa$ as ESK_i, and computes $k_i = tPRF(\tilde{k}_i, \tilde{k}'_i, st_i, st'_i)$ and $s_i = tPRF(\tilde{s}_i, \tilde{s}'_i, st_i, st'_i)$. U_i computes $c_i = g^{k_i} h^{s_i}$, and sends c_i to S.

(Round 1 for Server) On receiving (R_i, c_i) for $i \in \{1, n, n+1\}$ and c_i for $i \in [2, n-1]$, S computes $sid = TCR(c_1, \ldots, c_{n+k})$, and chooses a representative user from $i \in \{1, n, n+1\}$. Here, w.l.o.g., we suppose that U_1 is the representative user. S sends (sid, R_n, R_1) to U_{n+1}. For $i \in \{1, 2\}$, S sends (sid, R_{i-1}) to U_i where $R_0 = R_{n+1}$. For $i \in [3, n-2]$, S sends sid to U_i. Also, S notices that U_1 is the representative user.

(Round 2 for Users) On receiving (sid, R_{n+1}), U_1 computes $K_1^{(l)} = F(sid, R_{n+1}^{r_1})$, $K_1^{(r)} = F(sid, R_1^r)$, $T_1 = K_1^{(l)} \oplus K_1^{(r)}$ and $T' = K_1^{(l)} \oplus (k_1 || s_1)$. U_1 computes $\sigma_1 \leftarrow$ **Tag**$_{mk_1}(R_1, c_1, R_{n+1}, T_1, T', U_1, sid)$, and sends (T_1, T', σ_1) to S.

On receiving (sid, R_1), U_2 computes $K_2^{(l)} = F(sid, R_1^r)$, $K_2^{(r)} = F(sid, g^r)$ and $T_2 = K_2^{(l)} \oplus K_2^{(r)}$. U_2 computes $\sigma_2 \leftarrow$ **Tag**$_{mk_2}(c_2, R_1, k_2, s_2, T_2, U_2, sid)$, and sends $(k_2, s_2, T_2, \sigma_2)$ to S.

For $i \in [3, n-2]$, on receiving sid, U_i computes $\sigma_i \leftarrow$ **Tag**$_{mk_i}(c_i, k_i, s_i, U_i, sid)$, and sends (k_i, s_i, σ_i) to S.

On receiving (sid, R_n), U_{n-1} computes $K_{n-1}^{(l)} = F(sid, g^r)$, $K_{n-1}^{(r)} = F(sid, R_n^r)$ and $T_{n-1} = K_{n-1}^{(l)} \oplus K_{n-1}^{(r)}$. U_{n-1} computes $\sigma_{n-1} \leftarrow$ **Tag**$_{mk_{n-1}}(c_{n-1}, R_n, k_{n-1}, s_{n-1}, T_{n-1}, U_{n-1}, sid)$, and sends $(k_{n-1}, s_{n-1}, T_{n-1}, \sigma_{n-1})$ to S.

On receiving (sid, R_{n+1}), U_n computes $K_n^{(l)} = F(sid, R_n^r)$, $K_n^{(r)} = F(sid, R_{n+1}^{r_n})$ and $T_n = K_n^{(l)} \oplus K_n^{(r)}$. U_n computes $\sigma_n \leftarrow$ **Tag**$_{mk_n}(R_n, c_n, R_{n+1}, k_n, s_n, T_n, U_n, sid)$, and sends $(k_n, s_n, T_n, \sigma_n)$ to S.

On receiving (sid, R_n, R_1), U_{n+1} computes $K_{n+1}^{(l)} = F(sid, R_n^{r_{n+1}})$, $K_{n+1}^{(r)} = F(sid, R_1^{r_{n+1}})$ and $T_{n+1} = K_{n+1}^{(l)} \oplus K_{n+1}^{(r)}$. U_{n+1} computes $\sigma_{n+1} \leftarrow$ **Tag**$_{mk_{n+1}}(R_{n+1}, c_{n+1}, R_n, R_1, k_{n+1}, s_{n+1}, T_{n+1}, U_{n+1}, sid)$, and sends $(k_{n+1}, s_{n+1}, T_{n+1}, \sigma_{n+1})$ to S.

(Round 2 for Server) On receiving (T_1, T', σ_1) from U_1, $(k_i, s_i, T_i, \sigma_i)$ for $i \in \{2\} \cup [n-1, n+1]$ and (k_i, s_i, σ_i) for $i \in [3, n-2]$, S verifies authentication-tags, and if the verification fails, then aborts. Also, for $i \in [2, n+1]$, S checks if $c_i = g^{k_i} h^{s_i}$ holds, and if the verification fails, then aborts. S generates $\tilde{k}_S \in_R \{0,1\}^\kappa$, $\tilde{k}'_S \in_R$ Kspace$_\kappa$, $\tilde{K}_1 \in_R \{0,1\}^\kappa$ and $\tilde{K}'_1 \in_R$ K$space_\kappa$ as ESK_S, and computes $k_S = tPRF(\tilde{k}_S, \tilde{k}'_S, st_S, st'_S)$, $K_1 = tPRF'(\tilde{K}_1, \tilde{K}'_1, st_S, st'_S)$ and

$k' = (\bigoplus_{2 \le i \le n+k} k_i) \oplus k_S$. For $i \in [2, n+1]$, S computes $T_i' = \bigoplus_{1 \le j \le i-1} T_j$, where for $i \in [3, n-1]$, T_i is treated as empty (i.e., $T_3' = \cdots = T_{n-1}'$). For $i \in [1, n+1]$, S computes $CT_i' \leftarrow \mathbf{AEnc}(Params, P_i, K_1)$ with access structure $P_i := (ID = U_i) \wedge (time \in TF)$.

S computes $\sigma_1' \leftarrow \mathbf{Tag}_{mk_1}(R_1, c_1, R_{n+1}, T_1, T', U_1, sid, k', CT_1')$, and sends (k', CT_1', σ_1') to U_1.

S computes $\sigma_2' \leftarrow \mathbf{Tag}_{mk_2}(c_2, R_1, k_2, s_2, T_2, U_2, sid, c_1, k', T_2', T', CT_2')$, and sends $(c_1, k', T_2', T', CT_2', \sigma_2')$ to U_2.

For $i \in [3, n-2]$, S computes $\sigma_i' \leftarrow \mathbf{Tag}_{mk_i}(c_i, k_i, s_i, U_i, sid, c_1, k', T_i', T', CT_i')$, and sends $(c_1, k', T_i', T', CT_i', \sigma_i')$ to U_i.

S computes $\sigma_{n-1}' \leftarrow \mathbf{Tag}_{mk_{n-1}}(c_{n-1}, R_n, k_{n-1}, s_{n-1}, T_{n-1}, U_{n-1}, sid, c_1, k', T_{n-1}', T', CT_{n-1}')$, and sends $(c_1, k', T_{n-1}', T', CT_{n-1}', \sigma_{n-1}')$ to U_{n-1}.

S computes $\sigma_n' \leftarrow \mathbf{Tag}_{mk_n}(R_n, c_n, R_{n+1}, k_n, s_n, T_n, U_n, sid, c_1, k', T_n', T', CT_n')$, and sends $(c_1, k', T_n', T', CT_n', \sigma_n')$ to U_n.

S computes $\sigma_{n+1}' \leftarrow \mathbf{Tag}_{mk_{n+1}}(R_{n+1}, c_{n+1}, R_n, R_1, k_{n+1}, s_{n+1}, T_{n+1}, U_{n+1}, sid, c_1, k', T_{n+1}', T', CT_{n+1}')$, and sends $(c_1, k', T_{n+1}', T', CT_{n+1}', \sigma_{n+1}')$ to U_{n+1}.

(Session Key Generation and Post Computation) For $i \in [2, n+1]$, on receiving $(c_1, k', T_i', T', CT_i', \sigma_i')$, U_i verifies the authentication-tag, and if the verification fails, then aborts. U_i computes $K_1^{(l)} = T_i' \oplus K_i^{(l)}$ where for $i \in [3, n-1]$ $K_1^{(l)} = T_i' \oplus g^r$ and $k_1 || s_1 = T' \oplus K_1^{(l)}$, and checks if $c_1 = g^{k_1} h^{s_1}$ holds, and if the verification fails, then aborts. U_i decrypts $K_1 \leftarrow \mathbf{ADcc}_{usk_i}(CT_i', P_i)$, computes $K_2 = F'(sid, k' \oplus k_1)$, and outputs the session key $SK = F''(sid, K_1) \oplus F''(sid, K_2)$. As state information, U_i updates $r = F'''(sid, K_1) \oplus F'''(sid, K_2)$ in $state_i$. Also, U_n updates $H_n^{(r)} = R_{n+1}^{r_n}$ in $state_n$. U_{n+1} adds sid, $H_{n+1}^{(l)} = R_n^{r_{n+1}}$ and $H_{n+1}^{(r)} = R_1^{r_{n+1}}$ to $state_{n+1}$.

On receiving (k', CT_1', σ_1'), U_1 verifies the authentication-tag, and if the verification fails, then aborts. U_1 decrypts $K_1 \leftarrow \mathbf{ADec}_{usk_1}(CT_1', P_1)$, computes $K_2 = F'(sid, k' \oplus k_1)$, and outputs the session key $SK = F''(sid, K_1) \oplus F''(sid, K_2)$. As state information, U_1 updates sid, $H_1^{(l)} = R_{n+k}^{r_1}$ and $r = F'''(sid, K_1) \oplus F'''(sid, K_2)$ in $state_1$.

4.5 Leave Phase

A user U_j leaves an established session by $U_1, \ldots, U_n$.

In the Leave phase, users $U_i \in \mathcal{I} \setminus \{U_{j-1}, U_j, U_{j_1+1}\}$ can reduce computation than the Dist phase. They do not need to compute g^{r_i}. The ring structure to compute K_1 still works because $H_i^{(l)}$ and $H_i^{(r)}$ in $state_i$ are used to connect the ring instead of using $g^{r_{i-1}r_i}$ and $g^{r_i r_{i+1}}$.

(State Update at New Time Frame) If the session is the first session for U_i at the time frame TF', then for the current time $time$ S generates $usk_i \leftarrow \mathbf{Der}(Params, msk, A_i)$ with attribute $A_i = (U_i, time)$ and $mk_i \leftarrow \mathbf{MGen}$, and computes $CT_i \leftarrow \mathbf{Enc}_{pk_i}(usk_i, mk_i)$. Then, S sends CT_i to U_i, and U_i obtains $(usk_i, mk_i) \leftarrow \mathbf{Dec}_{sk_i}(CT_i)$ and updates (usk_i, mk_i) in $state_i$.

(Round 1 for Users) $U_i \in \{U_{j-1}, U_{j+1}\}$ generates $\tilde{r}_i \in_R \{0,1\}^\kappa$, $\tilde{r}'_i \in_R$ Kspace$_\kappa$, $\tilde{k}_i \in_R \{0,1\}^\kappa$, $\tilde{k}'_i \in_R$ Kspace$_\kappa$, $\tilde{s}_i \in_R \{0,1\}^\kappa$ and $\tilde{s}'_i \in_R$ Kspace$_\kappa$ as ESK_i, and computes $r_i = tPRF(\tilde{r}_i, \tilde{r}'_i, st_i, st'_i)$, $k_i = tPRF(\tilde{k}_i, \tilde{k}'_i, st_i, st'_i)$ and $s_i = tPRF(\tilde{s}_i, \tilde{s}'_i, st_i, st'_i)$. Then, U_i computes $R_i = g^{r_i}$ and $c_i = g^{k_i} h^{s_i}$, and sends (R_i, c_i) to S.
$U_i \in \mathcal{I} \setminus \{U_{j-1}, U_j, U_{j+1}\}$ generates $\tilde{k}_i \in_R \{0,1\}^\kappa$, $\tilde{k}'_i \in_R$ Kspace$_\kappa$, $\tilde{s}_i \in_R \{0,1\}^\kappa$ and $\tilde{s}'_i \in_R$ Kspace$_\kappa$ as ESK_i, and computes $k_i = tPRF(\tilde{k}_i, \tilde{k}'_i, st_i, st'_i)$ and $s_i = tPRF(\tilde{s}_i, \tilde{s}'_i, st_i, st'_i)$. Then, U_i computes $c_i = g^{k_i} h^{s_i}$, and sends c_i to S.

(Round 1 for Server) On receiving (R_i, c_i) from $U_i \in \{U_{j-1}, U_{j+1}\}$ and c_i from $U_i \in \mathcal{I} \setminus \{U_{j-1}, U_j, U_{j+1}\}$, for i such that $U_i \in \mathcal{I} \setminus \{U_j\}$, S computes $sid = TCR(\{c_i\}_{\mathcal{I} \setminus \{U_j\}})$, chooses a representative user from $U_i \in \{U_{j-1}, U_{j+1}\}$. Here, w.l.o.g., we suppose that U_{j-1} is the representative user. S sends (sid, R_{j+1}) to U_{j-1}. S sends (sid, R_{j-1}) to U_{j+1}. Then, S sends sid to $U_i \in \mathcal{I} \setminus \{U_{j-1}, U_j, U_{j+1}\}$. Also, S notices that U_{j-1} is the representative user.

(Round 2 for Users) On receiving (sid, R_{j+1}), U_{j-1} computes $K_{j-1}^{(l)} = F(sid, H_{j-1}^{(l)})$, $K_{j-1}^{(r)} = F(sid, R_{j+1}^{r_{j-1}})$, $T_{j-1} = K_{j-1}^{(l)} \oplus K_{j-1}^{(r)}$ and $T' = K_{j-1}^{(l)} \oplus (k_{j-1} \| s_{j-1})$. U_{j-1} computes $\sigma_{j-1} \leftarrow \mathbf{Tag}_{mk_{j-1}}(R_{j-1}, c_{j-1}, R_{j+1}, T_{j-1}, T', U_{j-1}, sid)$, and sends $(T_{j-1}, T', \sigma_{j-1})$ to S.
On receiving (sid, R_{j-1}), U_{j+1} computes $K_{j+1}^{(l)} = F(sid, R_{j-1}^{r_{j+1}})$, $K_{j+1}^{(r)} = F(sid, H_{j+1}^{(r)})$ and $T_{j+1} = K_{j+1}^{(l)} \oplus K_{j+1}^{(r)}$. U_{j+1} computes $\sigma_{j+1} \leftarrow \mathbf{Tag}_{mk_{j+1}}(R_{j+1}, c_{j+1}, R_{j-1}, k_{j+1}, s_{j+1}, T_{j+1}, U_{j+1}, sid)$, and sends $(k_{j+1}, s_{j+1}, T_{j+1}, \sigma_{j+1})$ to S.
On receiving sid, $U_i \in \mathcal{I} \setminus \{U_{j-1}, U_j, U_{j+1}\}$ computes $K_i^{(l)} = F(sid, H_i^{(l)})$, $K_i^{(r)} = F(sid, H_i^{(r)})$ and $T_i = K_i^{(l)} \oplus K_i^{(r)}$. U_i computes $\sigma_i \leftarrow \mathbf{Tag}_{mk_i}(c_i, k_i, s_i, T_i, U_i, sid)$, and sends $(k_i, s_i, T_i, \sigma_i)$ to S.

(Round 2 for Server) On receiving $(T_{j-1}, T', \sigma_{j-1})$ from U_{j-1} and $(k_i, s_i, T_i, \sigma_i)$ from other users, S verifies the authentication-tag, and if the verification fails, then aborts. Also, for $U_i \in \mathcal{I} \setminus \{U_{j-1}, U_j\}$, S checks if $c_i = g^{k_i} h^{s_i}$ holds, and if the verification fails, then aborts. S generates $\tilde{k}_S \in_R \{0,1\}^\kappa$, $\tilde{k}'_S \in_R$ Kspace$_\kappa$, $\tilde{K}_1 \in_R \{0,1\}^\kappa$ and $\tilde{K}'_1 \in_R$ $K space_\kappa$ as ESK_S, and computes $k_S = tPRF(\tilde{k}_S, \tilde{k}'_S, st_S, st'_S)$ and $K_1 = tPRF'(\tilde{K}_1, \tilde{K}'_1, st_S, st'_S)$. For i such that $U_i \in \mathcal{I} \setminus \{U_{j-1}, U_j\}$, S computes $k' = (\bigoplus\{k_i\}) \oplus k_S$. For i such that $U_i \in \mathcal{I} \setminus \{U_j\}$ and $i < j - 1$, S computes $T'_i = \bigoplus_{1 \le \ell \le i-1, j-1 \le \ell \le n} T_\ell$, where T_j is empty. For i such that $U_i \in \mathcal{I} \setminus \{U_j\}$ and $j + 1 \le i$, S computes $T'_i = \bigoplus_{j-1 \le \ell \le i-1} T_\ell$, where T_j is empty. For $U_i \in \mathcal{I} \setminus \{U_j\}$, S computes $CT'_i \leftarrow \mathbf{AEnc}(Params, P_i, K_1)$ with access structure $P_i := (ID = U_i) \wedge (time \in TF)$.
S computes $\sigma'_{j-1} \leftarrow \mathbf{Tag}_{mk_{j-1}}(R_{j-1}, c_{j-1}, R_{j+1}, T_{j-1}, T', U_{j-1}, sid, k', CT'_{j-1})$, and sends $(k', CT'_{j-1}, \sigma'_{j-1})$ to U_{j-1}.
S computes $\sigma'_{j+1} \leftarrow \mathbf{Tag}_{mk_{j+1}}(R_{j+1}, c_{j+1}, R_{j-1}, k_{j+1}, s_{j+1}, T_{j+1}, U_{j+1}, sid, c_{j-1}, k', T'_{j+1}, T', CT'_{j+1})$, and sends $(c_{j-1}, k', T'_{j+1}, T', CT'_{j+1}, \sigma'_{j+1})$ to U_{j+1}.

For $U_i \in \mathcal{I} \setminus \{U_{j-1}, U_j, U_{j+1}\}$, S computes $\sigma_i' \leftarrow \mathbf{Tag}_{mk_i}(c_i, k_i, s_i, T_i, U_i, sid,$ $c_{j-1}, k', T_i', T', CT_i')$, and sends $(c_{j-1}, k', T_i', T', CT_i', \sigma_i')$ to U_i.

(Session Key Generation and Post Computation) On receiving $(c_{j-1},$ $k', T_i', T', CT_i', \sigma_i')$, $U_i \in \mathcal{I} \setminus \{U_{j-1}, U_j\}$ verifies the authentication-tag, and if the verification fails, then aborts. U_i computes $K_{j-1}^{(l)} = T_i' \oplus K_i^{(l)}$ and $k_{j-1}\|s_{j-1} = T' \oplus K_{j-1}^{(l)}$, and checks if $c_{j-1} = g^{k_{j-1}} h^{s_{j-1}}$ hold, and if the verification fails, then aborts. U_i decrypts $K_1 \leftarrow \mathbf{ADec}_{usk_i}(CT_i', P_i)$, computes $K_2 = F'(sid, k' \oplus k_{j-1})$, and outputs the session key $SK = F''(sid, K_1) \oplus F''(sid, K_2)$. As state information, U_i updates $sid, r = F'''(sid, K_1) \oplus F'''(sid, K_2)$ in $state_i$.

On receiving $(k', CT_{j-1}', \sigma_{j-1}')$, U_{j-1} verifies the authentication-tag, and if the verification fails, then aborts. U_{j-1} decrypts $K_1 \leftarrow \mathbf{ADec}_{usk_{j-1}}(CT_{j-1}',$ $P_{j-1})$, computes $K_2 = F'(sid, k' \oplus k_{j-1})$, and outputs the session key $SK = F''(sid, K_1) \oplus F''(sid, K_2)$. As state information, U_1 updates $sid,$ $r = F'''(sid, K_1) \oplus F'''(sid, K_2)$ in $state_{j-1}$.

Additionally, U_{j-1} updates $H_{j-1}^{(r)} = R_{j+1}^{r_{j-1}}$ in $state_{j-1}$, and U_{j+1} updates $H_{j+1}^{(l)} = R_{j-1}^{r_{j+1}}$ in $state_{j+1}$.

4.6 Update Phase

When a new time frame begins, a set of users $U_{i_1}, \ldots, U_{i_n}$ $(n \le N)$ updates the session key SK shared by them in the Dist/Join/Leave phase at the past time frame to a new session key SK'. For simplicity, w.l.o.g., we suppose that $(U_{i_1}, \ldots, U_{i_n}) = (U_1, \ldots, U_n)$.

(State Update at New Time Frame) If the session is the first session for U_i at the time frame TF, then for the current time $time$ S generates $usk_i \leftarrow \mathbf{Der}(Params, msk, A_i)$ with attribute $A_i = (U_i, time)$ and $mk_i \leftarrow \mathbf{MGen}$, computes $CT_i \leftarrow \mathbf{Enc}_{pk_i}(usk_i, mk_i)$. Then, S sends CT_i to U_i, and U_i obtains $(usk_i, mk_i) \leftarrow \mathbf{Dec}_{sk_i}(CT_i)$ and updates (usk_i, mk_i) in $state_i$.

(Information for Update) S generates $\tilde{K}_1 \in_R \{0,1\}^\kappa$ and $\tilde{K}_1' \in_R Kspace_\kappa$, and computes $K_1 = tPRF'(\tilde{K}_1, \tilde{K}_1', st_S, st_S')$ and $CT_i' \leftarrow \mathbf{AEnc}(Params, P_i,$ $K_1)$ with access structure $P_i := (ID = U_i) \land (time \in TF)$. Then, S sends CT_i' to U_i.

(Session Key Update) On receiving CT_i', U_i decrypts $K_1 \leftarrow \mathbf{ADec}_{usk_i}(CT_i',$ $P_i)$, and outputs the updated session key $SK' = F''(sid, K_1) \oplus SK$.

5 Complexity for Users

5.1 Computational Complexity

We consider dominant operations like modular exponentiations and operations for public key crypto, and ignore other light-weight operations like XORs and operations for secret key crypto.

In the Dist phase, on-line computations (i.e., from Round 1 to post computations) for a user are g^{r_i} and $g^{k_i}h^{s_i}$ for Round 1, $R_{i-1}^{r_i}$ and $R_{i+1}^{r_i}$ for Round 2, and $g^{k_1}h^{s_1}$ and the decryption of CT_i' for the session key generation. In the Join phase, maximum on-line computations for a user are g^{r_i} and $g^{k_i}h^{s_i}$ for Round 1, $R_{i-1}^{r_i}$ and $R_{i+1}^{r_i}$ for Round 2, and $g^{k_1}h^{s_1}$ and the decryption of CT_i' for the session key generation. In the Leave phase, maximum on-line computations for a user are g^{r_i} and $g^{k_i}h^{s_i}$ for Round 1, $R_{i-1}^{r_i}$ for Round 2, and $g^{k_1}h^{s_1}$ and the decryption of CT_i' for the session key generation. In the Update phase, the on-line computation for a user is the decryption of CT_i' for the session key update.

Therefore, for all phases, computational complexity of users is constant for the number of users.

5.2 Communication Complexity

In the Dist phase, sent and received information for a user in on-line (i.e., from Round 1 to post computations) are (R_i, c_i) and (sid, R_{i-1}, R_{i+1}) for Round 1, and $(k_i, s_i, T_i, \sigma_i)$ and $(c_1, k', T_i', T', CT_i', \sigma_i')$ for Round 2. In the Join phase, maximum sent and received information for a user in on-line are (R_i, c_i) and (sid, R_{i-1}, R_{i+1}) for Round 1, and $(k_i, s_i, T_i, \sigma_i)$ and $(c_1, k', T_i', T', CT_i', \sigma_i')$ for Round 2. In the Leave phase, maximum sent and received information for a user in on-line are (R_i, c_i) and (sid, R_{i-1}) for Round 1, and $(k_i, s_i, T_i, \sigma_i)$ and $(c_{j-1}, k', T_{j+1}', T', CT_{j+1}', \sigma_{j+1}')$ for Round 2. In the Leave phase, received information for a user in on-line is CT_i' for the session key update.

Therefore, for all phases, communication complexity of users is constant for the number of users.

6 Security

Theorem 1. *We assume that TCR satisfies the TCR property, tPRF and tPRF' are twisted PRFs, F, F', F'' and F''' are PRFs, (Gen, Enc, Dec) is a CCA-secure PKE, (Setup, Der, AEnc, ADec) is a selective CCA-secure CP-ABE, (MGen, Tag, Ver) is an UF-CMA MAC scheme and the DDH assumption in G holds. Then, our scheme is secure in the DMKD model.*

Here, we show a proof sketch. The proof can be divided four cases: (1) the test session is in the Dist phase, (2) the test session is in the Join phase, (3) the test session is in the Leave phase, and (4) the test session is in the Update phase. For Case (1), (2) and (3), secrecy of the session key is guaranteed by secrecy of K_1. Thus, we use the game hopping proof technique [30], and, finally, K_1 is replaced with a random value. To prevent malicious behaviours of the adversary, we show that the probability that messages in the test session are modified is negligible thanks to the security of PKE and MAC, and the DDH assumption. For Case (4), secrecy of the session key is guaranteed by secrecy of K_2. Thus, K_2 is replaced with a random value similar to other cases. In this case, we rely on the security of CP-ABE to prevent malicious behaviours of the adversary.

We show the proof of Theorem 1 in the full paper [29].

References

1. Berjon, R., Leithead, T., Navara, E.D., O'Connor, E., Pfeiffer, S.: HTML5. In: W3C Working Draft (2012)
2. Marshall, J.: Google chrome will begin blocking flash web ads. In: The Wall Street Journal (2015)
3. Chesters, J.: Mozilla blocks flash, encourages HTML5 adoption. In: InfoQ (2015)
4. Bergkvist, A., Burnett, D.C., Jennings, C., Narayanan, A., Aboba, B.: WebRTC 1.0: real-time communication between browsers. In: InfoQ (2015)
5. Westerlund, M., Wenger, S.: RTP topologies, draft-ietf-avtcore-rtp-topologies-update-10. In: IETF Draft (2015). https://tools.ietf.org/html/draft-ietf-avtcore-rtp-topologies-update-10
6. Schulzrinne, H., Casner, S.L., Frederick, R., Jacobson, V.: RTP: a transport protocol for real-time applications. In: IEFT RFC 3550 (2003)
7. Fischl, J., Tschofenig, H., Rescorla, E.: Framework for establishing a secure real-time transport protocol (SRTP), security context using datagram transport layer security (DTLS). In: IEFT RFC 5763 (2010)
8. Rescorla, E.: WebRTC security architecture, draft-ietf-rtcweb-security-arch-12. In: IETF Draft (2015). https://tools.ietf.org/html/draft-ietf-rtcweb-security-arch-12
9. Fujioka, A., Suzuki, K., Xagawa, K., Yoneyama, K.: Strongly secure authenticated key exchange from factoring, codes, and lattices. Des. Codes Crypt. **76**, 469–504 (2015)
10. Kurosawa, K., Furukawa, J.: 2-pass key exchange protocols from CPA-secure KEM. In: Benaloh, J. (ed.) CT-RSA 2014. LNCS, vol. 8366, pp. 385–401. Springer, Heidelberg (2014). doi:10.1007/978-3-319-04852-9_20
11. Bresson, E., Chevassut, O., Pointcheval, D., Quisquater, J.: Provably authenticated group Diffie-Hellman key exchange. In: Reiter, M.K., Samarati, P., (eds.) CCS 2001, Proceedings of the 8th ACM Conference on Computer and Communications Security, Philadelphia, Pennsylvania, USA, 6–8 November 2001, pp. 255–264. ACM (2001)
12. Bresson, E., Chevassut, O., Pointcheval, D.: Provably authenticated group Diffie-Hellman key exchange — the dynamic case. In: Boyd, C. (ed.) ASIACRYPT 2001. LNCS, vol. 2248, pp. 290–309. Springer, Heidelberg (2001). doi:10.1007/3-540-45682-1_18
13. Bresson, E., Chevassut, O., Pointcheval, D.: Dynamic group Diffie-Hellman key exchange under standard assumptions. In: Knudsen, L.R. (ed.) EUROCRYPT 2002. LNCS, vol. 2332, pp. 321–336. Springer, Heidelberg (2002). doi:10.1007/3-540-46035-7_21
14. Kim, H.-J., Lee, S.-M., Lee, D.H.: Constant-round authenticated group key exchange for dynamic groups. In: Lee, P.J. (ed.) ASIACRYPT 2004. LNCS, vol. 3329, pp. 245–259. Springer, Heidelberg (2004). doi:10.1007/978-3-540-30539-2_18
15. Dutta, R., Barua, R.: Constant round dynamic group key agreement. In: Zhou, J., Lopez, J., Deng, R.H., Bao, F. (eds.) ISC 2005. LNCS, vol. 3650, pp. 74–88. Springer, Heidelberg (2005). doi:10.1007/11556992_6
16. Yang, G., Tan, C.H.: Dynamic group key exchange revisited. In: Heng, S.-H., Wright, R.N., Goi, B.-M. (eds.) CANS 2010. LNCS, vol. 6467, pp. 261–277. Springer, Heidelberg (2010). doi:10.1007/978-3-642-17619-7_19
17. Manulis, M., Suzuki, K., Ustaoglu, B.: Modeling leakage of ephemeral secrets in tripartite/group key exchange. In: Lee, D., Hong, S. (eds.) ICISC 2009. LNCS, vol. 5984, pp. 16–33. Springer, Heidelberg (2010). doi:10.1007/978-3-642-14423-3_2

18. Suzuki, K., Yoneyama, K.: Exposure-resilient one-round tripartite key exchange without random oracles. In: Jacobson, M., Locasto, M., Mohassel, P., Safavi-Naini, R. (eds.) ACNS 2013. LNCS, vol. 7954, pp. 458–474. Springer, Heidelberg (2013). doi:10.1007/978-3-642-38980-1_29
19. Caronni, G., Waldvogel, M., Sun, D., Plattner, B.: Efficient security for large and dynamic multicast groups. In: Proceedings of 7th Workshop on Enabling Technologies (WETICE 1998), Infrastructure for Collaborative Enterprises, 17–19 June 1998, Palo Alto, CAUSA, pp. 376–383. IEEE Computer Society (1998)
20. Canetti, R., Garay, J.A., Itkis, G., Micciancio, D., Naor, M., Pinkas, B.: Multicast security: a taxonomy and some efficient constructions. In: Proceedings IEEE INFO-COM 1999, The Conference on Computer Communications, Eighteenth Annual Joint Conference of the IEEE Computer and Communications Societies, The Future Is Now, New York, NY, USA, 21–25 March 1999, pp. 708–716. IEEE (1999)
21. Waldvogel, M., Caronni, G., Sun, D., Weiler, N., Plattner, B.: The versakey framework: versatile group key management. IEEE J. Sel. Areas Commun. **17**, 1614–1631 (1999)
22. Sherman, A.T., McGrew, D.A.: Key establishment in large dynamic groups using one-way function trees. IEEE Trans. Softw. Eng. **29**, 444–458 (2003)
23. Lin, I., Tang, S., Wang, C.: Multicast key management without rekeying processes. Comput. J. **53**, 939–950 (2010)
24. Saravanan, K., Purusothaman, T.: Efficient star topology based multicast key management algorithm. J. Comput. Sci. **8**(6), 951–956 (2012)
25. Mittal, N., Kumar, V.: An efficient and secure multicast key management scheme based on star topology. Int. J. Comput. Sci. Inf. Technol. **5**(3), 3777–3783 (2014)
26. Sun, H., He, B., Chen, C., Wu, T., Lin, C., Wang, H.: A provable authenticated group key agreement protocol for mobile environment. Inf. Sci. **321**, 224–237 (2015)
27. Micciancio, D., Panjwani, S.: Optimal communication complexity of generic multicast key distribution. In: Cachin, C., Camenisch, J.L. (eds.) EUROCRYPT 2004. LNCS, vol. 3027, pp. 153–170. Springer, Heidelberg (2004). doi:10.1007/978-3-540-24676-3_10
28. Suzuki, K., Yoneyama, K.: Exposure-resilient one-round tripartite key exchange without randomoracles. IEICE Trans. **97**(A), 1345–1355 (2014)
29. Yoneyama, K., Yoshida, R., Kawahara, Y., Kobayashi, T., Fuji, H., Yamamoto, T.: Multi-cast key distribution: scalable, dynamic and provably secure construction. In: Cryptology ePrint Archive: 2016/833 (2016)
30. Shoup, V.: Sequences of games: a tool for taming complexity in security proofs. In: Cryptology ePrint Archive: 2004/332 (2004)

One-Round Attribute-Based Key Exchange in the Multi-party Setting

Yangguang Tian[1]([⊠]), Guomin Yang[1], Yi Mu[1], Kaitai Liang[2], and Yong Yu[3]

[1] School of Computing and Information Technology,
University of Wollongong, Wollongong, NSW 2522, Australia
{ytian,gyang,ymu}@uow.edu.au
[2] School of Computing, Mathematics and Digital Technology,
Manchester Metropolitan University, Manchester M1 5GD, UK
kaitailiang88@gmail.com
[3] School of Computer Science, Shaanxi Normal University, Xi'an 710062, China
yyucd2012@gmail.com

Abstract. Attribute-based authenticated key exchange (AB-AKE) is a useful primitive that allows a group of users to establish a shared secret key and at the same time enables fine-grained access control. A straightforward approach to design an AB-AKE protocol is to extend a key exchange protocol using attribute-based authentication technique. However, insider security is a challenge security issue for AB-AKE in the multi-party setting and cannot be solved using the straightforward approach. In addition, many existing key exchange protocols for the multi-party setting (e.g., the well-known Burmester-Desmedt protocol) require multiple broadcast rounds to complete the protocol. In this paper, we propose a novel one-round attribute-based key exchange (OAKE) protocol in the multi-party setting. We define the formal security models, including session key security and insider security, for OAKE, and prove the security of the proposed protocol under some standard assumptions in the random oracle model.

Keywords: Attribute-based cryptography · One-round key exchange · Multi-party setting · Insider security

1 Introduction

Authenticated key exchange (AKE) protocols are a central building block in many network security standards such as IPSec, TLS/SSL, SSH, and so on. AKE aims to share a common secret key among multiple users over an insecure communication channel, such that the users can authenticate each other by using the respective identities or public keys. AKE has been further explored in the attribute-based context recently [16,26]. Attribute-based AKE (AB-AKE), as a new general form of AKE, enables fine-grained access control between authenticated users. The AB-AKE mechanism is significantly useful in many

© Springer International Publishing AG 2016
L. Chen and J. Han (Eds.): ProvSec 2016, LNCS 10005, pp. 227–243, 2016.
DOI: 10.1007/978-3-319-47422-9_13

real-world applications, such as distributed collaborative systems [16]. In practice, sometimes it is necessary for users to communicate with each other based on their role/responsibility. For instance, an individual user should be allowed to establish a secure communication with another user if and only if the former's role/responsibility can satisfy the latter's expectation.

The anonymity property naturally exists in attribute-based systems since people with different attribute sets may all satisfy an access policy. This brings a security issue for AB-AKE in the multi-party setting where it might be possible that a malicious authorized member can successfully impersonate other authorized members (i.e., insider attacks). Specifically, a malicious user Alice (attacker) attempts to impersonate an honest user Bob to establish a conversion with another user, say Charlie, but the impersonated user Bob was not actually involved in the particular conversion with Charlie. Such an attack is possible due to the inherent anonymous property of attribute-based systems. Therefore, achieving insider security is a non-trivial task for AB-AKE under the multi-party setting. Although there are some existing works on AB-AKE [16,26], they didn't consider the issue of insider attacks in the multi-party setting.

In order to achieve the insider security for AB-AKE in the multi-party setting, in this paper, we propose a novel hybrid signcryption (HSC) scheme to address the issue, where the hybrid signcryption scheme is built on top of a combination of key-policy attribute-based encryption (KP-ABE) [17] and identity-based signature (IBS) [14,19]. In addition to insider security and fine-grained authentication for key exchange, it is also desirable to share a secret key with less communication rounds. Many existing multi-party (or group) AKE protocols, such as the well-known Burmester-Desmedt protocol [12], require mutiple broadcast rounds in order to complete the protocol. In this paper we tackle this problem by making use of the (generic) multilinear maps [10] to establish a session key with only one broadcast round for a group of users.

1.1 This Work

In this paper, we introduce the notion of one-round attribute-based broadcast key exchange in the multi-party setting, allowing all users to agree on a common session key in only one broadcast round. Our contributions are as follows:

1. We present the formal security definitions for OAKE. In particular, we extend the model of [26] to define session key security and propose a new insider security model to capture malicious insider attacks.
2. We introduce a new primitive named hybrid signcryption (HSC), and propose a concrete scheme that is built on top of an identity-based signature scheme and Goyal et al.'s [17] key-policy attribute-based encryption scheme. We also prove that the proposed HSC scheme can achieve existential unforgeability in the random oracle model.
3. We present a one-round AB-AKE protocol in the multi-party setting based on our proposed HSC scheme and the generic multilinear maps [10]. We further prove that the proposed protocol can achieve both session key security and insider security.

1.2   Related Work

Key Exchange. Burmester and Desmedt [12] introduced several key exchange protocols in the multi-party setting, including star-based, tree-based, broadcast-based and cyclic-based protocols. Later, a few generic transformations [8,20, 21] were proposed to convert passive-secure group key exchange protocols into active-secure ones. Bellare and Rogaway [5] introduced the first complexity-theoretic security model for key exchange under the symmetric-key setting. The model was later extended and enhanced under different contexts [3,4,6]. Canetti and Krawczyk [13] later refined the previous models and proposed a new model, known as the CK model, which is widely used in the analysis of many well-known key exchange protocols. Some variants [22,23] of CK model were also proposed to allow an adversary to obtain either long term secret key or ephemeral secret key of the challenge session. In [26] an extension of the eCK (extended CK) model proposed in [23] was introduced for the attribute-based setting. It strengthens the session key security model by allowing adversary to gain access to the master secret key.

Signcryption. Zheng [27] introduced the concept of signcryption that provides an efficient way of achieving both message confidentiality and authenticity. The security of the scheme was later proven in [2]. An et al. [1] formally analyzed three generic constructions of signcryption in the public key setting, namely "encrypt then sign" (*EtS*), "sign then encrypt" (*StE*), and "commit then encrypt and sign" (*CtE&S*). Meanwhile, Haber and Pinkas [18] proposed a combined public key scheme under the joint security model, where encryption schemes and signature schemes shared the common public parameters and secret key. Boyen [11] introduced an efficient identity-based signcryption (IBSC) scheme based on the Boneh–Franklin IBE [9] scheme and the Cha–Cheon IBS [14] scheme.

Attribute-based Cryptography. For achieving fine-grained access control over the encrypted data, Sahai and Waters [25] proposed the fuzzy identity-based encryption, in which users must match at least a certain threshold of attributes before data decryption. Later, two types of attribute-based encryption (ABE) systems were proposed: Key-policy ABE [17] and Ciphertext-policy ABE [7]. In KP-ABE, a ciphertext is labeled with an attribute set, while a secret key is associated with the access structure specifying which ciphertext a user is able to decrypt. The roles of attribute set and access structure are swapped in the CP-ABE context. Inspired by the attribute-based cryptography, several attribute-based signcryption schemes [15,24] have been proposed in the literature where both signing and encryption functions are attribute-based. We should note that such kind of attribute-based signcryption schemes are not suitable for our purpose since they cannot address the insider attacks.

2   Security Models

In this section, we present the security models for OAKE. As mentioned in the introduction, a secure OAKE protocol in the multi-party setting should achieve both session key security and insider security. Below we present the corresponding security models to capture the above requirements. Specifically, the session key security model is a *modified* version of Yoneyama's model [26] which is an extension of eCK model [23] in the attribute-based setting.

States. We define a system user set $\mathcal{U}$ with n users, i.e. $|\mathcal{U}| = n$. We say an oracle Π_U^i may be *used* or *unused*. The oracle is considered as unused if it has never been initialized. Each unused oracle Π_U^i can be initialized with a secret key x. The oracle is initialized as soon as it becomes part of a group. After the initialization the oracle is marked as *used* and turns into the *stand-by* state where it waits for an invocation to execute a protocol operation. Upon receiving such invocation the oracle Π_U^i learns its partner id pid_U^i and turns into a *processing* state where it sends, receives and processes messages according to the description of the protocol. During that stage, the internal state information state_U^i is maintained by the oracle. The oracle Π_U^i remains in the *processing* state until it collects enough information to compute the session key k_U^i. As soon as k_U^i is computed Π_U^i *accepts* and *terminates* the protocol execution meaning that it would not send or receive further messages. If the protocol execution fails then Π_U^i terminates without having accepted.

Partnering. We denote the i-th session established by an user U by Π_U^i, the attribute set of the user by δ_U, and the access structure of the user by Λ_U. Let the partner identifier pid_U^i includes the identities of participating users (including U) in the i-th session established by the user U with the condition that $\forall U_j \in \mathsf{pid}_U^i, \Lambda_U(\delta_{U_j}) = 1$, where δ_{U_j} denotes the attribute set of the user U_j, and $\Lambda_U(\delta_{U_j}) = 1$ means that the attribute set δ_{U_j} is satisfied by the access structure Λ_U. In other words, pid_U^i is a collection of *recognized* participants by the instance oracle Π_U^i. We also define sid_U^i as the unique session identifier belonging to the session i established by the user U. Specifically, $\mathsf{sid}_U^i = (\mathsf{pid}_U^i, \{m_j\}_{j=1}^n)$, where $m_j \in \{0,1\}^*$ is the message transcript among users in pid_U^i. We say two instance oracles Π_U^i and $\Pi_{U'}^j$ are *partners* if and only if $\mathsf{sid}_U^i = \mathsf{sid}_{U'}^j$.

2.1   Session Key Security

We define the session key security model for key-policy AB-AKE protocols, in which each user obtains a secret key associating with his/her access structure from the trusted authority (TA), and establishes a session key depending on the partners' attribute sets. The model is defined via a game between a probabilistic polynomial time (PPT) adversary $\mathcal{A}$ and a simulator $\mathcal{S}$. $\mathcal{A}$ is an active attacker with full control of the communication channel among all the users.

– Setup: $\mathcal{S}$ first generates master public/secret key pair $(\mathcal{K}_0, x_0)$ for the TA and long term secret keys $\{x_i\}_{i=1}^n$ for n users by running the corresponding key generation algorithms, where x_i denotes the secret key of user i, such that x_i $(i \neq 0)$ is corresponding to the access structure Λ_i and identity ID_i of user i. $\mathcal{S}$ also tosses a random coin b which will be used later in the game.
– Training: $\mathcal{A}$ can make the following queries in arbitrary sequence to simulator $\mathcal{S}$.

- Establish: $\mathcal{A}$ is allowed to register a user U' with an access structure Λ'. If a party is registered by the $\mathcal{A}$, then we call the user i *dishonest*; Otherwise, it is *honest*.
- Send: If $\mathcal{A}$ issues a send query in the form of (U, i, m) to simulate a network message for the i-th session of user U, then $\mathcal{S}$ would simulate the reaction of instance oracle Π_U^i upon receiving message m, and returns to $\mathcal{A}$ the response that Π_U^i would generate; If $\mathcal{A}$ issues a send query in the form of $(U,' start', \delta_U)$, then $\mathcal{S}$ creates a new instance oracle Π_U^i and returns to $\mathcal{A}$ the first protocol message under the attribute set δ_U.
- Session key reveal: $\mathcal{A}$ can issue session key reveal query to an accepted instance oracle Π_U^i. If the session is accepted, then $\mathcal{S}$ will return the session key to $\mathcal{A}$; Otherwise, a special symbol '$\perp$' is returned to $\mathcal{A}$.
- Ephemeral secret key reveal: If $\mathcal{A}$ issues an ephemeral secret key reveal query to (possibly unaccepted) instance oracle Π_U^i, then $\mathcal{S}$ will return all ephemeral secret values contained in Π_U^i at the moment the query is asked.
- Long term secret key reveal: If $\mathcal{A}$ issues a long term secret key reveal (or corrupt, for short) query to user i, then $\mathcal{S}$ will return the long term secret key x_i to $\mathcal{A}$.
- Master secret key reveal: If $\mathcal{A}$ issues a master secret key reveal query to TA, then $\mathcal{S}$ will return the master secret key x_0 to $\mathcal{A}$.
- Test: This query can only be made to an accepted and *fresh* (as defined below) session i of a user U. Then $\mathcal{S}$ does the following:
  * If the coin $b = 1$, $\mathcal{S}$ returns the real session key to the adversary;
  * Otherwise, a random session key is drawn from the session key space and returned to the adversary.

  It is also worth noting that $\mathcal{A}$ can continue to issue other queries after the Test query. However, the test session must maintain *fresh* throughout the entire game.

Finally, $\mathcal{A}$ outputs b' as its guess for b. If $b' = b$, then the simulator outputs 1; Otherwise, the simulator outputs 0.

Freshness. We say an *accepted* instance oracle Π_U^i is fresh if $\mathcal{A}$ does not perform any of the following actions during the game:

- $\mathcal{A}$ issues *establish* query, where the new user $U' \in \mathsf{pid}_U^i$;
- $\mathcal{A}$ issues a *session key reveal* query to Π_U^i or its accepted partnered instance oracle $\Pi_{U'}^j$ (if the latter exists);
- $\mathcal{A}$ issues both *long term secret key reveal* query to U' s.t. $U' \in \mathsf{pid}_U^i$ and *ephemeral secret key reveal* query for an instance $\Pi_{U'}^i$ partnered with Π_U^i.
- $\mathcal{A}$ issues *long term secret key reveal* query to user U' s.t. $U' \in \mathsf{pid}_U^i$ prior to the acceptance of instance Π_U^i and there exists no instance oracle $\Pi_{U'}^j$ partnered with Π_U^i.

Note that the *master key reveal query* is equivalent to the *long term secret key reveal* to all users in $\mathcal{U}$.

We define the advantage of an adversary $\mathcal{A}$ in the above game as

$$\mathrm{Adv}_{\mathcal{A}}(k) = \Pr[\mathcal{S} \to 1] - 1/2.$$

Definition 1. *We say an OAKE protocol has* session key security *if for any probabilistic polynomial-time (PPT)* $\mathcal{A}$, $\mathrm{Adv}_{\mathcal{A}}(k)$ *is a negligible function of the security parameter* k.

2.2   Insider Security

Informally, a PPT adversary $\mathcal{A}$ attempts to impersonate one honest user to communicate with other honest users, whereas the impersonated honest user is not actually involved in that conversion. We define the insider security game between a PPT insider adversary $\mathcal{A}$ and a simulator $\mathcal{S}$ as follows.

- Training: $\mathcal{A}$ is allowed to issue establish, send, ephemeral secret key reveal, at most *n-1* long term secret key reveal, and session key reveal queries to the simulator. Let $\mathcal{U}'$ denotes the set of *uncorrupted* users (the established users are excluded from $\mathcal{U}'$). At the end of training stage, $\mathcal{A}$ outputs (U, U', s), such that $U \in \mathcal{U}'$, i.e., U denotes an *impersonated* but honest user who is *not corrupted*, and $U' \in \mathcal{U}$ can be a *corrupted* user who has a used oracle $\Pi_{U'}^s$. Note that $\mathcal{A}$ is not allowed to issue the master key reveal query, otherwise all users are *corrupted*.
- Attack: $\mathcal{A}$ wins the game if all of the following conditions hold.
  - $\Pi_{U'}^s$ accepted, it implies $\mathrm{sid}_{U'}^s$ exist;
  - $U \in \mathrm{pid}_{U'}^s$, it implies $\Lambda_{U'}(\delta_U) = 1$;
  - $m_U \in \mathrm{sid}_{U'}^s$, *but there exists no* Π_U^i which has sent m_U (m_U denotes the message transcript from the user U).

We define the advantage of an adversary $\mathcal{A}$ in the above game as

$$\mathrm{Adv}_{\mathcal{A}}(k) = \Pr[\mathcal{A} \ wins].$$

Definition 2. *We say a OAKE protocol has* insider security *if for any probabilistic polynomial-time (PPT)* $\mathcal{A}$, $\mathrm{Adv}_{\mathcal{A}}(k)$ *is an negligible function of the security parameter* k.

3   OAKE Protocol

In this section, we firstly review the preliminaries and the building blocks that will be used in the proposed hybrid signcryption scheme and the OAKE protocol, and then introduce our constructions.

3.1   Preliminaries

(Generic) Multilinear Maps [10]. It assumes the existence of a group generator g, which takes a security parameter k and the number of levels $\mathcal{K}$ as input, outputs a sequence of groups $(\mathbb{G}_1, \cdots, \mathbb{G}_\mathcal{K})$ with the corresponding canonical generators $(g_1, \cdots, g_\mathcal{K})$, each of them with large prime order q. The multilinear maps $\hat{e} : \mathbb{G}_i \times \mathbb{G}_j \to \mathbb{G}_{i+j} | i, j \geq 1; i + j \leq \mathcal{K}$ satisfies the following relation:

$$\hat{e}(g_i^{\alpha_i}, g_j^{\alpha_j}) = g_{i+j}^{\alpha_i \cdot \alpha_j} : \forall \alpha_i, \alpha_j \in_R \mathbb{Z}_q, i + j \leq \mathcal{K}$$

Bilinear Maps. The bilinear maps (i.e., $\mathcal{K} = 2$) $e : \mathbb{G} \times \mathbb{G} \to \mathbb{G}_T$ has the following properties:

1. Bilinearity: $e(g^{\alpha_i}, g^{\alpha_j}) = e(g, g)^{\alpha_i \cdot \alpha_j} : \forall \alpha_i, \alpha_j \in \mathbb{Z}_q, g \in \mathbb{G}$.
2. Non-degeneracy: $e(g, g) \neq 1$.
3. Computable: There exists an efficient algorithm for computing the bilinear maps.

Note that the maps e is symmetric since $e(g^{\alpha_i}, g^{\alpha_j}) = e(g, g)^{\alpha_i \cdot \alpha_j} = e(g^{\alpha_j}, g^{\alpha_i})$.

$\mathcal{K}$-Multilinear Decisional Diffie-Hellman ($\mathcal{K}$-MDDH) Assumption [10]: Given $g_1, g_1^{c_1}, \cdots, g_1^{c_\mathcal{K}}$ where $c_1, \cdots, c_\mathcal{K} \in_R \mathbb{Z}_q$, we define the advantage of the adversary in solving the $\mathcal{K}$-MDDH problem as

$$\mathsf{Adv}_\mathcal{A}(k) = \Pr[b \in \{0,1\}, \mathcal{A}(g_1^{c_1}, \cdots, g_1^{c_\mathcal{K}}, T_b = g_{\mathcal{K}-1}^{\prod_{i=1}^\mathcal{K} c_i}, T_{1-b} \in \mathbb{G}_{\mathcal{K}-1}) = b].$$

The $\mathcal{K}$-MDDH assumption holds if for any PPT $\mathcal{A}$, $\mathsf{Adv}_\mathcal{A}(k)$ is a *negligible* function of the security parameter k.

Computational Diffie-Hellman (CDH) Assumption [22]: Given $g, g^a, g^b \in \mathbb{G}$ where $a, b \in_R \mathbb{Z}_q$, we define the advantage of the adversary in solving the CDH problem as

$$\mathsf{Adv}_\mathcal{A}^{CDH}(k) = \Pr[\mathcal{A}(g, g^a, g^b) = g^{ab} \in \mathbb{G}].$$

The CDH assumption holds if for any PPT $\mathcal{A}$, $\mathsf{Adv}_\mathcal{A}(k)$ is a *negligible* function of the security parameter k.

3.2   Building Blocks

Key-Policy Attribute-based Encryption Access Structure [17]. Let $\{P_1, \cdots, P_n\}$ be a set of parties. A collection $\Lambda \subseteq 2^{\{P_1, \cdots, P_n\}}$ is monotone if $\forall B, C :$ if $B \in \Lambda$ and $B \subseteq C$ then $C \in \Lambda$. An access structure (i.e., monotone access structure) is a collection of non-empty subsets of $\{P_1, \cdots, P_n\}$ (i.e., $\Lambda \subseteq 2^{\{P_1, \cdots, P_n\}} \setminus \{\phi\}$). The sets in Λ are called the authorized sets, and the sets not in Λ are called the unauthorized sets.

Access Tree Λ [17]. Let Λ be a tree representing an access structure. Each non-leaf node of the tree represents a threshold gate, described by its children and a threshold value. If num_i is the number of children of a node x and k_x is its threshold value, then $1 \leq k_x \leq num_x$. If $k_x = 1$, it is an OR gate; If $k_x = num_x$, it is an AND gate. Each leaf node x of the tree is described by an attribute and a threshold value $k_x = 1$.

We define the parent of the node x in the tree by $parent(x)$, the attribute associates with the leaf node x in the tree by $att(x)$, the ordering between the children of every node x in the tree by $index(x)$ (numbered from 1 to num).

Satisfying An Access Tree. Let Λ be an access tree with root R. The Λ_x denotes the subtree of Λ rooted at the node x (e.g., $\Lambda = \Lambda_R$). If a set of attributes δ satisfies the access tree Λ_x, we denote it as $\Lambda_x(\delta) = 1$. We compute $\Lambda_x(\delta)$ as follows: If x is a leaf node, then $\Lambda_x(\delta)$ returns 1 iff $att(x) \in \delta$; If x is a non-leaf node, evaluate $\Lambda_{x'}(\delta)$ for all children x' of node x. $\Lambda_x(\delta)$ returns 1 iff at least k_x children return 1.

Key-Policy Attribute-Based Encryption Scheme: It consists of four algorithms [17]: KP-ABE=(Setup, KeyGen, Encrypt, Decrypt).

- Setup: The algorithm takes the security parameter k as input, outputs the master public parameters mpk and the master secret key msk.
- KeyGen: The algorithm takes the master secret key msk and an access structure Λ as input, outputs a secret key sk.
- Encrypt: The algorithm takes the master public parameters mpk, a message M and a set of attributes δ as input, outputs a ciphertext C. The C implicitly contains δ.
- Decrypt: The algorithm takes the master public parameters mpk, a ciphertext C and the secret key sk as input, outputs the message M if and only if the attribute set δ satisfies the access structure Λ.

Identity-Based Signature. An identity-based signature (IBS) scheme [14,19] consists of four algorithms: IBS=(Setup, KeyGen, Sign, Verify).

- Setup: The algorithm takes the security parameter k as input, outputs the master public parameters mpk and the master secret key msk.
- KeyGen: The algorithm takes the master secret key msk and an identity ID as input, outputs a secret signing key sk.
- Sign: The algorithm takes a message M and the signing key sk as input, outputs a signature σ on the message M.
- Verify: The algorithm takes the signature σ, the message M and the identity ID as input, outputs 1 if σ is valid on M, otherwise reject.

Hybrid Signcryption. A hybrid signcryption (HSC) scheme consists of four algorithms: HSC=(Setup, KeyGen, Sigcrypt, Unsigncrypt).

- Setup: The algorithm takes the security parameter k as input, and outputs the master key pair (mpk, msk).

- KeyGen: The algorithm takes an identity ID, an access structure Λ and the master secret key msk as input, and outputs the decryption/signing key pair (dk, sk), where dk is corresponding to Λ and sk is corresponding to ID.
- Signcrypt: The randomized algorithm takes the master public key mpk, a message M, a sender's identity ID, the signing key sk and an attribute set δ as input, and outputs a signcryption CT.
- Unsigncrypt: The deterministic algorithm takes the master public key mpk, a signcryption CT, the decryption key dk as input, and outputs the message M and sender's identity ID if CT is valid, otherwise it outputs reject.

We define an unforgeability game between an insider adversary $\mathcal{A}$ and a simulator $\mathcal{S}$ in the multiple party setting, which proceeds as follows:

- Setup: $\mathcal{S}$ runs $(mpk, msk) \leftarrow \mathsf{Setup}(1^k)$, where k is the security parameter, returns mpk to $\mathcal{A}$.
- Training: $\mathcal{A}$ is allowed to issue Signcrypt, Unsigncrypt and KeyGen queries. Note that $\mathcal{S}$ will return the secret key pair (dk, sk) to $\mathcal{A}$ when issuing the KeyGen query.
- Forgery: $\mathcal{A}$ outputs a signcryption CT^* and an access structure Λ^*.
- Outcome: $\mathcal{A}$ wins if all of the following conditions hold.
  - Unsigncrypt$(mpk, CT^*, dk^*) = (M^*, ID^*)$ where dk^* denotes the decryption key corresponding to Λ^*;
  - no KeyGen query was made on ID^*;
  - no Signcrypt query was made on M^* and ID^*.

We define the advantage of the adversary as

$$\mathsf{Adv}_{\mathcal{A}}(k) = \Pr[\mathcal{A} \ wins].$$

Definition 3. *We say that the HSC scheme is* existentially unforgeable under chosen message attacks (EUF-CMA) *if for any PPT* $\mathcal{A}$, $\mathsf{Adv}_{\mathcal{A}}(k)$ *is a* negligible *function of the security parameter* k.

3.3 A Novel Hybrid Signcryption Scheme

We construct a hybrid signcryption scheme based on the KP-ABE scheme proposed in [17]. We define the Lagrange coefficient $\Delta_{i,N}$ for $i \in \mathbb{Z}_q$ and a set, N, of elements in $\mathbb{Z}_q$: $\Delta_{i,N}(x) = \prod_{i \in N}^{j \neq i} \frac{x - j}{i - j}$. The data will be signcrypted under a set δ of n elements of $\mathbb{Z}_q$. The proposed hybrid signcryption scheme works as follows:

- Setup: It takes the security parameter k as input, outputs the master public key $mpk = (g, T_1 = g^{t_1}, \cdots, T_{n+1} = g^{t_{n+1}}, g^{\alpha}, g^{\beta}, e(g, h)^{\alpha}, h \in_R \mathbb{G})$ and the master secret key $msk = (t_1, \cdots, t_{n+1}, \alpha, \beta \in_R \mathbb{Z}_q)$. It also generates hash functions $\mathsf{H}_1 : \{0, 1\}^* \to \mathbb{G}, \mathsf{H}_2 : \mathbb{G}_1 \to \mathbb{G}$ and chooses a pseudo-random generator G. We let N be the set $\{1, 2, \cdots n + 1\}$ and denote the bilinear pairing $e : \mathbb{G} \times \mathbb{G} \to \mathbb{G}_T$. We define a function T as $T(X) = h^{X^n} \cdot \prod_{i=1}^{n+1} T_i^{\Delta_{i,N}(X)}$.

- KeyGen: It takes the identity $ID \in \{0,1\}^*$, the access tree Λ as input, outputs the signing key $sk = H_1(ID)^\beta$ and the decryption key dk.

  1. It chooses a polynomial q_x for each node x (including the leaf nodes) in the tree Λ. These polynomials are chosen in the following way in a top-down manner, starting from the root node R. For each node x in the tree, set the degree d_x of the polynomial q_x to be one less than the threshold value k_x of that node (i.e., $d_x = k_x - 1$). Starting with the root note R, the algorithm will set $q_R(0) = \alpha$. Then it chooses d_R other points of the polynomial q_R randomly to define it completely. For other nodes x, it sets $q_x(0) = q_{parent(x)}(index(x))$ and chooses d_x other points randomly to completely define q_x. We define L as the set of *leaf* nodes in Λ, and proceed as follows:

  2. $\forall l \in L : D_l = h^{q_x(0)} \cdot T(i)^{r_l}, R_l = g^{r_l}$, where $i = att(l)$ and $r_l \in_R \mathbb{Z}_q$ is corresponding to leaf node l in Λ. Set $dk = \{D_l, R_l\}_{l \in L}$.

- Signcrypt: It takes a message $m \in \mathbb{G}_1$ and a set of attributes δ as input, then

  1. Computes $\widehat{C} = (m\|ID) \oplus G(e(g,h)^{\alpha \cdot s}), C = g^s, \{C_i = T(i)^s\}_{i \in \delta}$, where $s \in_R \mathbb{Z}_q$;

  2. Computes $S = sk \cdot H_2(m)^s$;

  3. Outputs the signcryption: $CT = \{\delta, \widehat{C}, C, \{C_i\}_{i \in \delta}, S\}$.

- Unsigncrypt:

  1. We define a recursive algorithm DecryptNode(CT, dk, x), such that dk is associated with an access tree Λ and a node x from Λ.

     • If x is a leaf node, we let $i = att(x)$.

       * If $i \in \delta$, compute

$$
\text{DecryptNode}(CT, dk, x) = \frac{e(D_x, C)}{e(R_x, C_i)}
$$
$$
= \frac{e(h^{q_x(0)} \cdot T(i)^{r_x}, g^s)}{e(g^{r_x}, T(i)^s)}
$$
$$
= \frac{e(h^{q_x(0)}, g^s) \cdot e(T(i)^{r_x}, g^s)}{e(g^{r_x}, T(i)^s)}
$$
$$
= e(g, h)^{s \cdot q_x(0)};
$$

       * If $i \notin \delta$, abort.

     • If x is a non-leaf node, for all nodes z, which are children of x, call DecryptNode(CT, dk, z) and store the output as C_z. Let S_x be an arbitrary k_x-sized set of child nodes z such that $C_z \neq \bot$. If no such set exists, the node is not satisfied and the algorithm aborts. Otherwise, compute:

$$C_x = \prod_{z \in S_x} (e(g,h)^{s \cdot q_z(0)})^{\Delta_{i,S'_x}(0)}$$

$$= \prod_{z \in S_x} (e(g,h)^{s \cdot q_{parent(z)}(index(z))})^{\Delta_{i,S'_x}(0)}$$

$$= \prod_{z \in S_x} e(g,h)^{s \cdot q_x(i) \cdot \Delta_{i,S'_x}(0)}$$

$$= e(g,h)^{s \cdot q_x(0)}.$$

Note that $i = index(z)$, $S'_x = \{index(z) : z \in S_x\}$, and the computation $\Delta_{i,S'_x}(0)$ is computed via the polynomial interpolation according to access tree Λ.

2. If the attribute set associated with the ciphertext satisfies the tree Λ, we get $e(g,h)^{s \cdot q_R(0)} = e(g,h)^{\alpha \cdot s}$, and next compute $(m\|ID) = \widehat{C} \oplus G(e(g,h)^{\alpha \cdot s})$;
3. If $e(S,g) = e(H_1(ID), g^{\beta}) \cdot e(H_2(m), C)$, it returns m; Otherwise, reject.

Lemma 1. *The proposed HSC scheme achieves EUF-CMA security under the CDH assumption.*

Proof. Let $\mathcal{S}_{CDH}$ denotes a Computational Diffie-Hellman problem solver, who is given g, g^a, g^b and aims to find g^{ab}. Let $\mathcal{A}$ denotes a forger against the proposed HSC scheme. $\mathcal{S}_{CDH}$ plays the EUF-CMA security game with $\mathcal{A}$ as follows.

- Setup Stage: Let $\mathcal{K}$ denotes the maximum number of users that will occur in the game. $\mathcal{S}_{CDH}$ randomly selects two indices i and j and guesses that the **Forge** event will happen with regard to user i and the j-th query (denote it by m^*) to the random oracle H_2. $\mathcal{S}_{CDH}$ further sets $g^{\beta} = g^a$, and generates master secret/public keys ($msk = (\alpha, t_1, \cdots, t_{\mathcal{K}+1}), mpk = (T_1 = g^{t_1}, \cdots, T_{\mathcal{K}+1} = g^{t_{\mathcal{K}+1}}, g^{\alpha}, e(g,h)^{\alpha}, h = g^{\theta})$ as in the real scheme. $\mathcal{S}_{CDH}$ finally sends mpk to $\mathcal{A}$. Note that $\theta \in_R \mathbb{Z}_q$ is chosen by $\mathcal{S}_{CDH}$.
- $\mathcal{S}_{CDH}$ answers $\mathcal{F}$'s queries as follows.
  - If $\mathcal{A}$ issues ID_i to random oracle H_1, then $\mathcal{S}_{CDH}$ chooses $b_i \in_R \mathbb{Z}_q$ and returns $g^b \cdot g^{b_i}$ as the public key of user i; Otherwise, $\mathcal{S}_{CDH}$ chooses $b_j \in_R \mathbb{Z}_q$ returns the value g^{b_j} to $\mathcal{F}$.
  - If $\mathcal{A}$ queries the random oracle H_2 with regard to the message m^*, then $\mathcal{S}_{CDH}$ chooses $c_i \in_R \mathbb{Z}_q$ and returns g^{c_i} as the response to $H_2(m^*)$. If $\mathcal{A}$ queries the random oracle H_2 with regard to other messages (e.g., m_i), then $\mathcal{S}_{CDH}$ chooses $c_i \in_R \mathbb{Z}_q$ and returns $g^{c_i - a}$ as the response.
  - If $\mathcal{A}$ issues a KeyGen query for the user i, abort. If $\mathcal{A}$ issues a KeyGen query of a user ID_j (whereby $j \neq i$), $\mathcal{S}_{CDH}$ returns the value $g^{a \cdot b_j}$ as the signing key to $\mathcal{A}$, and further simulates the decryption key exactly same as in the algorithm KeyGen. $\mathcal{A}$ is given both the signing key and the decryption key of the user j.

- $\mathcal{S}_{CDH}$ simulates the Signcrypt oracle for the user i as follows. Firstly, $\mathcal{S}_{CDH}$ chooses $k_i \in_R \mathbb{Z}_q$, generates $\widehat{C} = (m_i \| ID_i) \oplus \mathsf{G}(e(g,h)^{\alpha \cdot (b+k_i)})$, $C = g^{b+k_i}$, $S_i = g^{b \cdot c_i} \cdot g^{a \cdot (b_i - k_i)} \cdot g^{c_i \cdot k_i}$, where the randomness s is implicitly sets as $b + k_i$. Secondly, $\mathcal{S}_{CDH}$ generates $\{C_i\}_{i \in \delta} = \{T(i)^{b+k_i}\}_{i \in \delta}$ using the knowledge of t_i and θ. Finally, $\mathcal{S}_{CDH}$ returns the signcryption $CT = \{\delta, \widehat{C}, C, \{C_i\}_{i \in \delta}\}, S_i\}$ to $\mathcal{A}$. One can verify that the signcryption is valid since $g^{c_i - a} = \mathsf{H}_2(m_i)$ and $e(S_i, g) = e(g^b \cdot g^{b_i}, g^a) \cdot e(g^{c_i - a}, g^{b+k_i})$.

  Note that if $\mathcal{A}$ issues the Signcrypt query for other users, e.g., user l ($l \neq i$), $\mathcal{S}_{CDH}$ can simulate it perfectly since the simulator knows the signing key.
  - If $\mathcal{A}$ issues an Unsigncrypt query, $\mathcal{S}_{CDH}$ answers the query as usual since $\mathcal{S}_{CDH}$ has the knowledge of α.
- If $\mathcal{A}$ successfully forges a signcryption CT^* including a valid forgery $C^* = g^{s^*}$, $S^* = g^{(b+b_i) \cdot a} \cdot \mathsf{H}_2(m^*)^{s^*}$ (notice that the randomness s^* is chosen by $\mathcal{A}$) satisfying the validity check, $\mathcal{S}_{CDH}$ can compute $g^{a \cdot b} = \dfrac{S^*}{C^* \cdot c_i \cdot g^{a \cdot b_i}}$ (c_i is known to $\mathcal{S}_{CDH}$ who programmed the random oracle $g^{c_i} = \mathsf{H}_2(m^*)$) as the solution of the Computational Diffie-Hellman problem.

Probability analysis: Let q_{h_i} denotes the number of queries that $\mathcal{F}$ asks to the random oracles H_i, $i = 1, 2$. If $\mathcal{S}_{CDH}$ guesses the challenge user i and challenge message correctly, then the simulation is perfect. Therefore we have

$$\Pr[\mathbf{Forge}] \leq \mathcal{K} \cdot q_{h_2} \cdot \mathsf{Adv}_{\mathcal{S}}^{CDH}(k).$$

3.4 Our OAKE Protocol

Now we present our proposed one-round authenticated key exchange protocol in the multiple party setting. It works as follows:

- Setup: TA takes the security parameter k and the number of users $\mathcal{K}$ as input, outputs the master public key $mpk = (T_1 = g^{t_1}, \cdots, T_{n+1} = g^{t_{n+1}}, g^{\alpha}, g^{\beta}, e(g,h)^{\alpha}, \{\mathbb{G}, \mathbb{G}_1, \cdots, \mathbb{G}_{\mathcal{K}}\}, \{g, g_1, \cdots, g_{\mathcal{K}}\}, h \in_R \mathbb{G})$ and the master secret key $msk = (t_1, \cdots, t_{n+1}, \alpha, \beta \in_R \mathbb{Z}_q)$. In addition, let $\hat{e} : \mathbb{G}_i \times \mathbb{G}_j \to \mathbb{G}_{i+j}$ denotes the $\mathcal{K}$-linear maps and $e : \mathbb{G} \times \mathbb{G} \to \mathbb{G}_T$ denotes the bilinear maps. TA also generates three hash functions $\mathsf{H}_1 : \{0,1\}^* \to \mathbb{G}$, $\mathsf{H}_2 : \{0,1\}^* \to \mathbb{Z}_q$, $\mathsf{H}_3 : \{0,1\}^* \to \mathbb{G}$. We let N be the set $\{1, 2, \cdots n + 1\}$ and define a function T as $T(X) = h^{X^n} \cdot \prod_{i=1}^{n+1} \cdot T_i^{\Delta_{i,N}(X)}$.
- KeyGen: Run the KeyGen algorithm described in the HSC scheme.
- KeyExchange: User i performs the following steps.
  1. Choose the ephemeral secret key $r_i \in_R \mathbb{Z}_q$, computes $x_i = \mathsf{H}_2(r_i \| dk_i \| sk_i)$ and $m_i = g_1^{x_i}$;
  2. Run the Signcrypt algorithm described in the HSC scheme, but the algorithm sets the randomness as x_i;
  3. Compute $S_i = sk \cdot \mathsf{H}_3(m_i \| ts_i)^{x_i}$, where $ts_i \in_R \mathbb{Z}_q$ is the current timestamp generated by user i;
  4. **Broadcast** the signcryption: $CT = \{ts_i, \delta_i, \widehat{C}, C, \{C_i\}_{i \in \delta}, S_i\}$.

– SharedKey: After receiving the ciphertext $CT_j = \{ts_j, \delta_j, \widehat{C}, C, \{C_j\}_{j \in \delta}, S_j\}$ from user j, user i does the following operations.

1. Check the time-stamp: If $|ts_i - ts_j| > \varrho$ (ts_i is the current time-stamp generated by user i and ϱ denotes the time window), then reject;

2. Run the Unsigncrypt algorithm described in the HSC scheme, then get the message $m_j = g_1^{x_j}$ and ID_j, and verify: If $e(S_j, g) = e(\mathsf{H}_1(ID_j), g^\beta) \cdot e(\mathsf{H}_3(m_j \| ts_j), C)$, it returns m_j; Otherwise, it rejects the session;

3. **Compute** the session key: $SK_i = \hat{\mathsf{e}}(g_1^{x_1}, \cdots, g_1^{x_{i-1}}, g_1^{x_{i+1}}, \cdots, g_1^{x_\mathcal{K}})^{x_i} = g_{\mathcal{K}-1}^{\prod_{j=1}^{\mathcal{K}} x_j}$.

Design Rational. The proposed Hybrid Signcripiton scheme has been used in the OAKE protocol for preventing the insider attacks in the multi-party setting. In addition, the Hybrid Signcryption scheme also ensures the user privacy in the proposed OAKE protocol. More details will be given in the full version of the paper.

4   Security Analysis

Theorem 1. *The proposed OAKE protocol achieves session key security (Definition 1) if the $\mathcal{K}$-MDDH assumption hold in the underlying group $\mathbb{G}_{\mathcal{K}-1}$, the proposed signcryption scheme HSC is EUF-CMA secure.*

Proof. We define a sequence of games G_i, $i = 0, \cdots, 3$ and let Adv_i^{OAKE} denotes the advantage of the adversary in game G_i. Assume that $\mathcal{A}$ activates at most m sessions in each game.

– G_0 This is original game $Game_{\mathcal{A}}^{OAKE}$ for session key security.
– G_1 This game is identical to game G_0 except that $\mathcal{S}$ will output a random bit if **Forge** event happens where $\mathcal{A}$ makes a send query in the form of CT_i, such that S_i is a valid signature of user i who is not corrupted (i.e., no long term key reveal query to user i or master secret key reveal query) when the send query is made, and S_i is not previously generated by the simulator. Therefore we have:

$$\left| \mathsf{Adv}_0^{OAKE} - \mathsf{Adv}_1^{OAKE} \right| \le \Pr[\mathbf{Forge}] \tag{1}$$

Lemma 2. *The **Forge** event happens only with a negligible probability when our proposed signcryption scheme HSC is EUF-CMA secure.*

Let $\mathcal{F}$ denotes a forger against signcryption scheme HSC with EUF-CMA security, who has access to the Signcrypt oracle, the Unsigncrypt oracle and the KeyGen oracle, and aims to forge a valid signature S^*. $\mathcal{F}$ simulates the game for $\mathcal{A}$ as follows.

- Setup Stage: $\mathcal{F}$ sets up the game for $\mathcal{A}$ by creating $\mathcal{K}$ users with the corresponding identity set $\prod_{i=1}^{\mathcal{K}} \{ID_i\}$. $\mathcal{F}$ randomly selects an index i and guesses that the **Forge** event will happen with regard to user i. $\mathcal{F}$ then sends the master public keys and the identity set to $\mathcal{A}$. $\mathcal{F}$ obtains all the user secret keys except the secret key of ID_i via the KeyGen oracle. It is obvious that $\mathcal{F}$ can answer all the queries made by $\mathcal{A}$ except user i. Below we mainly focus on the simulation of user i only.

- $\mathcal{F}$ answers $\mathcal{A}$'s queries as follows.
  * If $\mathcal{A}$ issues a send query in the form of a signcryption CT to user i, then $\mathcal{F}$ will perform the simulation as follows: $\mathcal{F}$ firstly can get the message g_1^x and the identity ID after submitting the received signcryption CT to his Unsigncrypt oracle. If $\mathcal{A}$ makes a send query in the form of an activation request, $\mathcal{F}$ randomly chooses $r_i \in_R \mathbb{Z}_q$ and programs the H_2 oracle to get x_i, computes the message $g_1^{x_i}$ and generates the signcryption CT_i using his Signcrypt oracle on the message $g_1^{x_i} \| ID_i$ and returns CT_i to $\mathcal{A}$.
  * If $\mathcal{A}$ issues an ephemeral secret key reveal query to user i, then $\mathcal{F}$ returns $r_i \in_R \mathbb{Z}_q$ to $\mathcal{A}$.
  * If $\mathcal{A}$ issues long term secret key reveal query to user i or master secret key reveal query, then $\mathcal{F}$ aborts.
  * $\mathcal{F}$ answers the session key reveal query and test query by using the session key it has derived during the protocol simulation described above.
- If a **Forge** event with respect to user i occurs, then $\mathcal{F}$ outputs whatever $\mathcal{A}$ outputs as its own forgery; Otherwise, $\mathcal{F}$ aborts the game. Therefore we have:

$$\Pr[\mathbf{Forge}] \leq \mathcal{K} \cdot \mathsf{Adv}_{\mathcal{F}}^{HSC}(k) \qquad (2)$$

- G_2: This game is identical to game G_1 except the following difference: $\mathcal{S}$ randomly chooses $g \in [1, m]$ as a guess for the index of the test session. $\mathcal{S}$ will output a random bit if $\mathcal{A}$'s test query does not occurred in the g-th session (denote this event by **Guess**). Therefore we have

$$\mathsf{Adv}_1^{OAKE} = m \cdot \mathsf{Adv}_2^{OAKE} \qquad (3)$$

- G_3 This game is identical to game G_2 except that in the test session, we replace the session key $SK = g_{\mathcal{K}-1}^{\Pi_{j=1}^{\mathcal{K}} x_j}$ by a random value $R \in_R \mathbb{G}_{\mathcal{K}-1}$. Below we show that the difference between G_2 and G_3 is negligible under the $\mathcal{K}$-MDDH assumption is hold in the group $G_{\mathcal{K}-1}$.

Let $\mathcal{S}_{\mathcal{K}-MDDH}$ denotes a distinguisher against the $\mathcal{K}$-MDDH assumption, who is given $(g_1^{c_1}, \cdots, g_1^{c_{\mathcal{K}}})$ and aims to distinguish the value $T = g_{\mathcal{K}-1}^{\Pi_{j=1}^{\mathcal{K}} c_j}$ from a random value $R \in_R \mathbb{G}_{\mathcal{K}-1}$. $\mathcal{S}_{\mathcal{K}-MDDH}$ simulates the game for $\mathcal{A}$ as follows.

  - Setup Stage: $\mathcal{S}_{\mathcal{K}-MDDH}$ sets up the game for $\mathcal{A}$ by creating $\mathcal{K}$ users. $\mathcal{S}_{\mathcal{K}-MDDH}$ then generates the master public/secret key pair (mpk, msk) and the secret keys $\{(dk_i, sk_i)\}$ for all the users, where the dk_i is corresponding to an access tree Λ_i and sk_i is corresponding to the identity ID_i of user i. $\mathcal{S}_{\mathcal{K}-MDDH}$ then sends the master public key and the identity set to $\mathcal{A}$.
  - It is easy to see that all queries to a user can be simulated perfectly using the user secret keys. In the g-th (i.e., test) session, $\mathcal{S}_{\mathcal{K}-MDDH}$ sets $m_1 =$

$g_1^{c_1}, \cdots, m_{\mathcal{K}} = g_1^{c_{\mathcal{K}}}$ for all the users which implicitly sets $H(r_i\|dk_i\|sk_i) = c_i$ where r_i denotes the ephemeral key of user i in the g-th session. Since $\mathcal{A}$ is not allowed to ask both ephemeral and long term secret keys of a user in the test session, the simulation is perfect.

- $\mathcal{S}_{\mathcal{K}-MDDH}$ answers the Test query by using its own challenge as the session key of the g-th session.
- If $\mathcal{A}$ wins the game, then $\mathcal{S}_{\mathcal{K}-MDDH}$ outputs that the challenge is $g_{\mathcal{K}-1}^{\Pi_{j=1}^{\mathcal{K}} c_j}$; Otherwise $\mathcal{S}_{\mathcal{K}-MDDH}$ outputs that the challenge is a random element.

If the challenge of $\mathcal{S}_{\mathcal{K}-MDDH}$ is $g_{\mathcal{K}-1}^{\Pi_{j=1}^{\mathcal{K}} c_j}$, then the simulation is consistent with G_2; Otherwise, the simulation is consistent with G_3. If the advantage of $\mathcal{A}$ is significantly different in G_2 and G_3, then $\mathcal{S}_{\mathcal{K}-MDDH}$ can break the $\mathcal{K}$-MDDH assumption. Therefore we have

$$\left|\mathsf{Adv}_2^{OAKE} - \mathsf{Adv}_3^{OAKE}\right| \leq \mathsf{Adv}_{\mathcal{S}_{\mathcal{K}-MDDH}}^{\mathcal{K}-MDDH}(k) \tag{4}$$

It is easy to see that in game G_3, $\mathcal{A}$ has no advantage, i.e.,

$$\mathsf{Adv}_3^{OAKE} = 0 \tag{5}$$

Combining the above results together, we have

$$\mathsf{Adv}_{\mathcal{A}}^{OAKE}(k) \leq \mathcal{K} \cdot \mathsf{Adv}_{\mathcal{F}}^{HSC}(k) + m \cdot \mathsf{Adv}_{\mathcal{S}_{\mathcal{K}-MDDH}}^{\mathcal{K}-MDDH}(k)$$

Theorem 2. *The proposed OAKE protocol achieves insider security (Definition 2) if the proposed signcryption scheme HSC is EUF-CMA secure.*

The proof of insider security can be obtained from the proof of Lemma 2 since if an attacker can break the insider security with a non-negligible probability, then a **Forge** event would occur also with a non-negligible probability. We omit the details of the proof here.

5   Conclusion

In this paper, we proposed a one-round attribute-based key exchange (OAKE) protocol in the multi-party setting. In order to address the insider security issue, we proposed a new primitive named hybrid signcryption which is a combination of attribute-based encryption and identity-based signature. We used this new primitive and the multilinear maps as major building block in constructing our OAKE protocol. We also defined the formal security models for session key security and insider security, and proved the security of the proposed OAKE protocol in the random oracle model.

References

1. An, J.H., Dodis, Y., Rabin, T.: On the security of joint signature and encryption. In: Knudsen, L.R. (ed.) EUROCRYPT 2002. LNCS, vol. 2332, pp. 83–107. Springer, Heidelberg (2002). doi:10.1007/3-540-46035-7_6

2. Baek, J., Steinfeld, R., Zheng, Y.: Formal proofs for the security of signcryption. J. Cryptology **20**(2), 203–235 (2007)
3. Bellare, M., Canetti, R., Krawczyk, H.: A modular approach to the design and analysis of authentication and key exchange protocols (extended abstract). In: Proceedings of the Thirtieth Annual ACM Symposium on the Theory of Computing, pp. 419–428 (1998)
4. Bellare, M., Pointcheval, D., Rogaway, P.: Authenticated key exchange secure against dictionary attacks. In: Preneel, B. (ed.) EUROCRYPT 2000. LNCS, vol. 1807, pp. 139–155. Springer, Heidelberg (2000). doi:10.1007/3-540-45539-6_11
5. Bellare, M., Rogaway, P.: Entity authentication and key distribution. In: Stinson, D.R. (ed.) CRYPTO 1993. LNCS, vol. 773, pp. 232–249. Springer, Heidelberg (1994). doi:10.1007/3-540-48329-2_21
6. Bellare, M., Rogaway, P.: Provably secure session key distribution: the three party case. In: Proceedings of the Twenty-Seventh Annual ACM Symposium on Theory of Computing, pp. 57–66 (1995)
7. Bethencourt, J., Sahai, A., Waters, B.: Ciphertext-policy attribute-based encryption. In: 2007 IEEE Symposium on Security and Privacy (S&P 2007), pp. 321–334 (2007)
8. Bohli, J., Vasco, M.I.G., Steinwandt, R.: Secure group key establishment revisited. Int. J. Inf. Secur. **6**(4), 243–254 (2007)
9. Boneh, D., Franklin, M.: Identity-based encryption from the weil pairing. In: Kilian, J. (ed.) CRYPTO 2001. LNCS, vol. 2139, pp. 213–229. Springer, Heidelberg (2001). doi:10.1007/3-540-44647-8_13
10. Boneh, D., Waters, B.: Constrained pseudorandom functions and their applications. In: Sako, K., Sarkar, P. (eds.) ASIACRYPT 2013. LNCS, vol. 8270, pp. 280–300. Springer, Heidelberg (2013). doi:10.1007/978-3-642-42045-0_15
11. Boyen, X.: Multipurpose identity-based signcryption. In: Boneh, D. (ed.) CRYPTO 2003. LNCS, vol. 2729, pp. 383–399. Springer, Heidelberg (2003). doi:10.1007/978-3-540-45146-4_23
12. Burmester, M., Desmedt, Y.: Efficient and secure conference-key distribution. In: Security Protocols, International Workshop, Cambridge, United Kingdom, 10–12 April 1996, p. 119–129 (1996)
13. Canetti, R., Krawczyk, H.: Analysis of key-exchange protocols and their use for building secure channels. In: Pfitzmann, B. (ed.) EUROCRYPT 2001. LNCS, vol. 2045, pp. 453–474. Springer, Heidelberg (2001). doi:10.1007/3-540-44987-6_28
14. Cha, J.C., Cheon, J.H.: An identity-based signature from gap diffie-hellman groups. In: IACR Cryptology ePrint Archive 2002, vol. 18 (2002)
15. Gagné, M., Narayan, S., Safavi-Naini, R.: Threshold attribute-based signcryption. In: Security and Cryptography for Networks, pp. 154–171 (2010)
16. Gorantla, M.C., Boyd, C., González Nieto, J.M.: Attribute-based authenticated key exchange. In: Steinfeld, R., Hawkes, P. (eds.) ACISP 2010. LNCS, vol. 6168, pp. 300–317. Springer, Heidelberg (2010). doi:10.1007/978-3-642-14081-5_19
17. Goyal, V., Pandey, O., Sahai, A., Waters, B.: Attribute-based encryption for fine-grained access control of encrypted data. In: ACM, CCS 2006, pp. 89–98 (2006)
18. Haber, S., Pinkas, B.: Securely combining public-key cryptosystems. In: CCS 2001, pp. 215–224 (2001)
19. Hess, F.: Efficient identity based signature schemes based on pairings. In: Nyberg, K., Heys, H. (eds.) SAC 2002. LNCS, vol. 2595, pp. 310–324. Springer, Heidelberg (2003). doi:10.1007/3-540-36492-7_20
20. Katz, J., Shin, J.S.: Modeling insider attacks on group key-exchange protocols. In: ACM, CCS 2005, pp. 180–189 (2005)

21. Katz, J., Yung, M.: Scalable protocols for authenticated group key exchange. In: Boneh, D. (ed.) CRYPTO 2003. LNCS, vol. 2729, pp. 110–125. Springer, Heidelberg (2003). doi:10.1007/978-3-540-45146-4_7

22. Krawczyk, H.: HMQV: a high-performance secure diffie-hellman protocol. In: Shoup, V. (ed.) CRYPTO 2005. LNCS, vol. 3621, pp. 546–566. Springer, Heidelberg (2005). doi:10.1007/11535218_33

23. LaMacchia, B.A., Lauter, K.E., Mityagin, A.: Stronger security of authenticated key exchange. In: Provable Security 2007, pp. 1–16 (2007)

24. Rao, Y.S., Dutta, R.: *Expressive* bandwidth-efficient attribute based signature and signcryption in standard model. In: Susilo, W., Mu, Y. (eds.) ACISP 2014. LNCS, vol. 8544, pp. 209–225. Springer, Heidelberg (2014). doi:10.1007/978-3-319-08344-5_14

25. Sahai, A., Waters, B.: Fuzzy identity-based encryption. In: Cramer, R. (ed.) EURO-CRYPT 2005. LNCS, vol. 3494, pp. 457–473. Springer, Heidelberg (2005). doi:10.1007/11426639_27

26. Yoneyama, K.: Strongly secure two-pass attribute-based authenticated key exchange. In: Joye, M., Miyaji, A., Otsuka, A. (eds.) Pairing 2010. LNCS, vol. 6487, pp. 147–166. Springer, Heidelberg (2010). doi:10.1007/978-3-642-17455-1_10

27. Zheng, Y.: Digital signcryption or how to achieve cost(signature & encryption) $\ll$ cost(signature) + cost(encryption). In: Kaliski Jr., B.S. (ed.) CRYPTO 1997. LNCS, vol. 1294, pp. 165–179. Springer, Heidelberg (1997)

Strongly Secure Two-Party Certificateless Key Agreement Protocol with Short Message

Yong Xie[1,2], Libing Wu[1(✉)], Yubo Zhang[1], and Zhiyan Xu[1]

[1] School of Computer Science, Wuhan University, Wuhan 430072, China
{xieyongdian,wu,cszyb,czxzy}@whu.edu.cn
[2] Jingdezhen Ceramic Institute, Jingdezhen 333403, China

Abstract. Key agreement protocol is generic way to establish a secure private conversation over a public network. Recently, certificateless key agreement (CL-KA) protocol has drawn much attention because it not only efficiently eliminates the problems of key escrow and certificate management but also is more suitable for universal wireless communication environment. However, it is a challenge to design a CL-KA protocol to meet security and efficiency requirement concurrently. In this paper, we propose a new two-party CL-KA protocol with short message under GDH and GBDH assumption. We also present a full security proof for the proposed protocol in extended Canetti-Krawczyk (eCK) security model. The performance shows that the proposed protocol can capture the security requirements and is more efficient than similar CL-KA protocol.

Keywords: Certificateless · Key agreement · eCK · Two-party

1 Introduction

Nowadays, people can enjoy a variety of convenient applications and services from various communication networks. The private conversation over public networks has become one of the most important and popular applications. People could launch a private conversation through public networks anywhere and anytime. However, the private conversation encounters a perplexing situation that opportunities and challenges coexist in the public networks because there are more and more security attacks in public networks. To protect conversation privacy, the participants agree on a shared session key firstly, then use the session key to encrypt their following conversation. No one can reveal the conversation without knowing the session key. The process to generate a shared session key is called key agreement. Recent years, many key agreement protocols [1–4] have been proposed to provide secure private conversation for different network environments. To avoid the complex certificate management and the key escrow problem, some researchers have designed CL-KA protocols [5–8] by using certificateless public key cryptography.

Key agreement is executed in an insecure environment, so a CL-KA protocol should first resist all kinds of secure attacks and meet security requirements.

© Springer International Publishing AG 2016
L. Chen and J. Han (Eds.): ProvSec 2016, LNCS 10005, pp. 244–254, 2016.
DOI: 10.1007/978-3-319-47422-9_14

The efficiency of CL-KA protocol is alway another obligatory property, which is more valued in the scenario that power and computation ability is limited. It is well known that security and efficiency are a contradiction for the protocol design. The existing CL-KA protocols may meet security requirement well or efficiency requirement well, but cannot meet both of them. Therefore, it is still a challenge for CL-KA protocol to meet the two requirements simultaneously.

Most recently, Lin proposed a new efficient two-party CL-KA protocol [9]. Lin demonstrated his protocol is provably secure in the eCK security model [10]. Unfortunately, Lin's protocol is insecure against the Type II adversary in eCK security model. A Type II adversary can successfully impersonate any legal users to generate a session key with other legal user at will. The detailed analysis of the attack will be presented in the full-version paper. To solve the problem of Lin's protocol and meet security and efficiency requirements concurrently, we propose an improved two-party CL-KA protocol in this paper. And we also present an in-depth security analysis in eCK security model. The performance analysis shows that the proposed protocol can meet security requirements and incurs less computation cost than Lin's CL-KA protocol.

2 Preliminaries

The eCK security model for the CL-KA protocol is defined as a game played between a challenger $\mathscr{C}$ and an adversary $\mathscr{A}$. In a CL-KA protocol, each participant has three secrets, i.e. partial private key (issued by the KGC), secret value (selected by the user) and ephemeral secret key (selected by the user). Adversary is allowed to reveal two secrets at most. There are two types of adversary in the CL-KA protocol, i.e. Type I adversary $\mathscr{A}_I$ and Type II adversary $\mathscr{A}_{II}$. The capability of the two adversaries are defined as following.

- $\mathscr{A}_I$. It can replace user's secret value with an assigned value. However, it cannot know the master key of the KGC.
- $\mathscr{A}_{II}$. It can know the master key of the KGC and replace user's partial private key, but cannot know any users' secret value.

The adversary $\mathscr{A}$ can access the following oracle queries at will in any order, and the simulator S answers the oracle queries according to the specification of security model.

- CreateUser(i). S generates user i's partial private key, secret value and public key, then sends the public key to $\mathscr{A}$.
- RevealMasterKey: S sends the master key to $\mathscr{A}$.
- RevealPartialKey(i). S returns user i's partial key to $\mathscr{A}$.
- RevealSecertKey(i): S returns user i's secret key to $\mathscr{A}$.
- RevealEphemeralKey($\Pi_{i,j}^t$): S sends user i's ephemeral secret key about session $\Pi_{i,j}^t$ to $\mathscr{A}$, where $\Pi_{i,j}^t$ denotes the tth session between i and j.
- ReplaceKey(i,k_i): S replaces user i's public key with k_i that sent by $\mathscr{A}$.

- RevealSessionKey($\Pi_{i,j}^t$): If $\Pi_{i,j}^t$ has been accepted, S sends the session key to $\mathscr{A}$. Else, S returns $\perp$ to $\mathscr{A}$.
- Send($\Pi_{i,j}^t, m$): $\mathscr{A}$ sends the message m to this oracle and obtains a response according to the protocol specification.

Definition 1 (Matching session). If $\Pi_{i,j}^t$ and $\Pi_{j,i}^s$ have an identical session identity, we says that $\Pi_{i,j}^t$ has a matching session $\Pi_{j,i}^s$.

Once $\mathscr{A}$ has decided to finish the first phase, it will start the second phase by selecting a fresh session $\Pi_{i,j}^t$, and issue the following $Test(\Pi_{i,j}^t)$ queries.

$Test(\Pi_{i,j}^t)$. This oracle query model is used as the indistinguishability between random session keys and the actual key. The session $\Pi_{i,j}^t$ must be fresh. The challenger $\mathscr{C}$ flips a fair coin $b \in \{0,1\}$, then decides by following.

- If $b = 0$, $\mathscr{C}$ sends the actual session key to $\mathscr{A}$.
- If $b = 1$, $\mathscr{C}$ selects a random one from the distribution of session keys.

At last, $\mathscr{A}$ guesses a coin value b' for b. If $\Pi_{i,j}^t$ is fresh and $b' = b$, $\mathscr{A}$ wins the game. Therefore, the advantage of that $\mathscr{A}$ wins the game is defined as $Adv_{\mathscr{A}}(\kappa) = |pr[\mathscr{A} \ \text{win}] - 1/2|$. We say that $\mathscr{A}$ wins the game, if $Adv_{\mathscr{A}}(\kappa)$ is non-negligible.

3   The Proposed Protocol

The new protocol includes five phases, i.e. Setup, Partial private key extraction, Keygen, Message exchange and Key computation. The details of the five phase are described as following.

Setup. Let the security parameter be κ. The KGC selects group $(G_1, +)$ and $(G_2, \times)$ with same prime order q over bilinear paring mapping $e : G_1 \times G_1 \to G_2$ and two secure hash function, $H_1 : \{0,1\}^* \to G_1$, $H_2 : \{0,1\}^* \times \{0,1\}^* \times G_1^3 \times G_2^1 \times G_1^1 \to \{0,1\}^n$, where $n > 0$, P is generator of G_1. Then the KGC selects $s \in Z_q^*$ as its master secret key, compute $P_{pub} = s \cdot P$. At last, the KGC publishes public parameters $pp = \{G_1, G_2, q, P, e, H_1, H_2, P_{pub}\}$.

Partial private key extraction. The KGC computes user's partial private key $D_{ID} = s \cdot H_1(ID)$, where $ID \in \{0,1\}^*$. Then the KGC returns D_{ID} to user in a secure way.

Keygen. user selects $x_{ID} \in Z_q^*$ as secret value and computes $Y_{ID} = x_{ID} \cdot P$.

Message exchange. Assume A and B be the session participants. A selects $r_a \in_R Z_q^*$, and computes $R_A = r_a \cdot P$, then sends message $\{ID_A, R_A, Y_A\}$ to B. B randomly selects $r_b \in Z_q^*$, and computes $R_B = r_b \cdot P$, then sends message $\{ID_B, R_B, Y_B\}$ to A.

Key computation. A and B compute the session key respectively as following.
$$K_{A1} = (x_a + r_a)(Y_B + R_B) = (x_b + r_b)(Y_A + R_A) = K_{B1},$$

$$K_{A2} = e(D_A + r_a \cdot P_{pub}, H_1(ID_B) + R_B)$$
$$= e(D_B + r_b \cdot P_{pub}, H_1(ID_A) + R_A) = K_{B2},$$
$$K_{A3} = r_a \cdot R_B = r_b \cdot R_A = K_{B3},$$
$$sk_A = H_2(ID_A, ID_B, R_A, R_B, K_{A1}, K_{A2}, K_{A3})$$
$$= H_2(ID_A, ID_B, R_A, R_B, K_{B1}, K_{B2}, K_{B3}) = sk_B.$$

At last, A and B compute an identical session key $sk = sk_A = sk_B$.

4 Security Proof

In this section, we prove that our proposed scheme is secure in eCK security model. Let $\mathscr{C}$ be a challenger who can answer an adversary $\mathscr{A}$'s oracle queries to solve a specific problem that defined in the protocol, where $\mathscr{A} \in \{\mathscr{A}_I, \mathscr{A}_{II}\}$. Gap DiffieHellman (GDH) problem and Gap Bilinear Diffie-Hellman (GBDH) problem will be used in the game, which are assumed to be hard in polynomial time [5,11].

4.1 Security Proof on $\mathscr{A}_I$

Theorem 1. The advantage of adversary $\mathscr{A}_I$ against the proposed protocol is negligible under the GDH and GBDH assumption.

Proof. Let κ be the system security parameter. Assume $\mathscr{A}_I$ is PPT bounded adversary, $\mathscr{A}_I$ can invoke κ_p distinct honest participants, and make κ_q distinct hash queries. Every participant could be involved in κ_s sessions. $\mathscr{A}_I$ can distinguish the tested session key from random one only in the following three ways.

- W1. $\mathscr{A}_I$ obtains the session key by guess attack. The probability of outputting a right session key in this way is $\mathcal{O}(1/2^\kappa)$. Therefore, it can be negligible.
- W2. $\mathscr{A}_I$ obtains the session key by key-replication attack. In this way, $\mathscr{A}_I$ queries the session key of other sessions to form a same key with the test session. However, the probability of outputting a right session key in this way is $\mathcal{O}((\kappa - 1)^2/2^\kappa)$. Therefore, it can be negligible too.
- W3. $\mathscr{A}_I$ obtains the session key by forging attack. In this way, $\mathscr{A}_I$ queries H_2-oracle on $H_2(ID_A, ID_B, R_A, R_B, K_1, K_2, K_2)$ in test session, in which the value of K_1, K_2 and K_3 should be computed by $\mathscr{A}_I$.

Next, a challenger $\mathscr{C}$ run $\mathscr{A}_I$'s advantages in distinguishing the tested session key from a random string into an advantage in solving the GDH or GBDH problem. $\mathscr{C}$ simulates the game with $\mathscr{A}_I$. $\mathscr{C}$ chooses two random number $I, J \in [1, \kappa_p]$ and $t \in \kappa_s$, where $I \neq J$. Let $P_0 \leftarrow \gamma \cdot P$, P_0 is the KGC's public key. Assume $\Pi_{I,J}^t$ is the test session in this game, $\Pi_{I,J}^s$ is the matching session if $\Pi_{I,J}^t$ is existing. The probability of the session key being guessed correctly is $\mathcal{O}(\frac{1}{\kappa_p \kappa_s})$. The following six complementary events must be considered in this game.

E1. The matching session $\Pi_{J,I}^S$ exists, and $\mathscr{A}_I$ cannot query both Reveal-EphemeralKey($\Pi_{I,J}^T$) and RevealPartialKey(J).

E2. The matching session $\Pi_{J,I}^S$ exists, and $\mathscr{A}_I$ cannot query both Reveal-EphemeralKey($\Pi_{I,J}^T$) and RevealEphemeralKey($\Pi_{J,I}^S$).

E3. The matching session $\Pi_{J,I}^S$ exists, and $\mathscr{A}_I$ cannot query both Reveal-PartialKey(I) and RevealEphemeralKey($\Pi_{J,I}^S$).

E4. The matching session $\Pi_{J,I}^S$ exists, and $\mathscr{A}_I$ cannot query both Reveal-PartialKey(I) and RevealPartialKey(J).

E5. There is no matching session for $\Pi_{I,J}^T$, and $\mathscr{A}_I$ cannot query both Reveal-EphemeralKey($\Pi_{I,J}^T$) and RevealPartialKey(J).

E6. There is no matching session for $\Pi_{I,J}^T$, and $\mathscr{A}_I$ cannot query both Reveal-PartialKey(I) and RevealPartialKey(J).

Next, the six events in forging attack will be analyzed. At the beginning of each simulation, $\mathscr{C}$ maintains four lists L_{H1}, L_{H2}, L_c and L_s with contents of queries and answers of H_1-oracle, H_2-oracle, Create-oracle, Send-oracle, and Reveal-oracle, which are initial empty list when the game starts, and are consisted of entries with form of (ID_i, H_i), $(ID_i, ID_j, R_i, R_j, K_1, K_2, K_3, sk)$, (ID_i, x_i, Y_i, D_i) and $(\Pi_{i,j}^t, ID_i, ID_j, R_i, R_j, Y_i, Y_j, sk)$.

Event E1. In this event, the ephemeral private key of ID_I and the partial private key of ID_J are chosen by $\mathscr{C}$ in the simulation, which cannot be revealed by $\mathscr{A}_I$.

Given a GBDH problem instance $(U = u \cdot P, V = v \cdot P, P_0 = \gamma \cdot P)$, $\mathscr{C}$ aims to solve GBDH(U, V, P_0) by accessing DBDH oracle, where $u, v \in Z_n^*$ and $P \in G$. Let $Adv_{\mathscr{C}}^{GBDH}(\kappa)$ be the advantage that $\mathscr{C}$ obtains in solving GBDH problem.

Queries. $\mathscr{C}$ begins this phase by answering $\mathscr{A}_I$'s queries as follows.

Create(ID_i). $\mathscr{A}_I$ queries this oracle with ID_i. If $ID_i = ID_J$, $\mathscr{C}$ selects $x_i \in_R Z_n^*$, and calculates $Y_i = x_i \cdot P$, sets $H_1(ID_i) \leftarrow V$, then adds the tuple $(ID_i, x_i, Y_i, \perp)$ and (ID_i, V) to L_c and L_{H1} respectively. Otherwise, $\mathscr{C}$ selects $x_i, h_i \in_R Z_n^*$, and calculates $Y_i = x_i \cdot P$, sets $H_1(ID_i) \leftarrow H_i = h_i \cdot P$, $D_i \leftarrow h_i \cdot P_0$, then adds the tuple (ID_i, x_i, Y_i, D_i) and (ID_i, H_i) to L_c and L_{H1} respectively.

H_1-oracle. $\mathscr{A}_I$ queries this oracle with tuple (ID_i). If this tuple is already in L_{H1}, $\mathscr{C}$ returns H_i to $\mathscr{A}_I$. Else, $\mathscr{C}$ selects $h_i \in_R Z_n^*$, computes $H_i = h_i \cdot P$, then returns H_i to $\mathscr{A}_I$ and adds the entry (ID_i, H_i) to L_{H1}.

H_2-oracle. As $\mathscr{A}_I$ queries this oracle with tuple $(ID_i, ID_j, R_i, R_j, K_1, K_2, K_3)$, $\mathscr{C}$ responds as the following way.

- If the tuple exists in L_{H2}, $\mathscr{C}$ sends the corresponding session key sk to $\mathscr{A}_I$.
- Else If $ID_i = ID_J$. $\mathscr{C}$ looks up L_{H2} for the entry $(ID_i, ID_j, R_i, R_j, *)$. If this entry is already in L_{H2}, $\mathscr{C}$ calculates $\overline{K_2} = \frac{K_2}{e(D_j, H_1(ID_i) + R_i)e(R_j, P_0)^{r_i}}$. Then $\mathscr{C}$ checks whether the tuple $(R_j, H_i, P_0, \overline{K_2})$ meets the oracle $DBDH(*) \rightarrow 1$ when the tuple is the oracle input, and checks whether the equation $K_1 = (x_i + r_i)(Y_j + R_j)$, $K_2 = e(D_j + r_j \cdot P_0, H_1(ID_i) + R_i)$, $K_3 = r_i \cdot R_j$. If they hold, $\mathscr{C}$ adds $(ID_i, ID_j, R_i, R_j, Y_1, Y_2, sk)$ to L_s, where sk is obtained from L_{H2}. Else, $\mathscr{C}$ randomly selects $sk \in \{0,1\}^\kappa$, then adds $(ID_i, ID_j, R_i, R_j, K_1, K_2, K_3, sk)$ to L_{H_2} and sends sk to $\mathscr{A}_I$.

- Else, $\mathscr{C}$ looks for $(ID_i, ID_j, R_i, R_j, *, *, *)$ from L_s. If there exists this tuple, $\mathscr{C}$ gets sk and adds the entry $(ID_i, ID_j, R_i, R_j, K_1, K_2, K_3, sk)$ to L_{H2}. Else, $\mathscr{C}$ randomly selects $sk \in \{0,1\}^\kappa$, then adds $(ID_i, ID_j, R_i, R_j, K_1, K_2, K_3, sk)$ to L_{H2} and sends sk to $\mathscr{A}_I$.

RevealMasterKey. $\mathscr{C}$ terminates this simulation.

RevealStaticKey(ID_i). if $ID_i = ID_J$, $\mathscr{C}$ aborts. Else, $\mathscr{C}$ looks up L_c for $(ID_i, *)$. If there exists this entry $(ID_i, *)$, $\mathscr{C}$ sends the corresponding D_i to $\mathscr{A}_I$, else $\mathscr{C}$ executes create(ID_i) and sends s_i to $\mathscr{A}_I$.

RevealSecretValue(ID_i). $\mathscr{C}$ looks up L_c for $(ID_i, *)$. If there exists this entry $(ID_i, *)$, $\mathscr{C}$ sends the corresponding x_i to $\mathscr{A}_I$, else $\mathscr{C}$ executes create(ID_i) and sends x_i to $\mathscr{A}_I$.

ReplacePublicKey(ID_i, Y_i). $\mathscr{C}$ looks up L_c for $(ID_i, *)$. If there exists this entry $(ID_i, *)$, $\mathscr{C}$ replaces Y_i and x_i with P_i' and x_i' respectively, where $x_i' \in {}_R Z_n^*$ and $Y_i' = x_i' \cdot P$. Else $\mathscr{C}$ executes create(ID_i) with Y_i' and x_i'.

RevealEphemeralKey$(\Pi_{i,j}^t)$. If $\Pi_{i,j}^t = \Pi_{I,J}^T$, $\mathscr{C}$ terminates this simulation. Otherwise, $\mathscr{C}$ sends the ephemeral key to $\mathscr{A}_I$.

RevealSessionKey$(\Pi_{i,j}^t)$. If $\Pi_{i,j}^t = \Pi_{I,J}^T$ or $\Pi_{i,j}^t = \Pi_{J,I}^S$, $\mathscr{C}$ terminates this simulation. Otherwise, $\mathscr{C}$ returns the stored session key to $\mathscr{A}_I$.

Send$(\Pi_{i,j}^t, m)$. When $\mathscr{A}_I$ makes this query, $\mathscr{C}$ responds according to the following situations.

- If $\Pi_{i,j}^t = \Pi_{I,J}^T$, $\mathscr{C}$ sends $R_i = V$ to $\mathscr{A}_I$.
- Else if $ID_i = ID_J$, $\mathscr{C}$ selects $r_i \in {}_R Z_n^*$, and calculates $\overline{K_2}$. Then $\mathscr{C}$ checks whether the tuple $(R_i, H_j, P_0, \overline{K_2})$ meets the oracle $DBDH(*, *, *, *) \rightarrow 1$ when the tuple is the oracle input. If it does, $\mathscr{C}$ get sk from L_{H2} and adds $(ID_i, ID_j, R_i, R_j, sk)$ to L_s. Else, $\mathscr{C}$ randomly selects $sk \in \{0,1\}^\kappa$, then adds $(\Pi_{i,j}^t, ID_i, ID_j, R_i, R_j, Y_i, Y_j, sk)$.
- Else $\mathscr{C}$ responds based on the regulation of protocol.

Test$(\Pi_{i,j}^t)$. $\mathscr{C}$ responds to this query according to the following conditions.

- If $\Pi_{i,j}^t \neq \Pi_{I,J}^S$, $\mathscr{C}$ terminates this simulation.
- Else $\mathscr{C}$ randomly selects $sk \in \{0,1\}^\kappa$ and sends to $\mathscr{A}_I$.

Analysis. If $\mathscr{A}_I$ dose successfully, it should have made queries from H_2-oracle about $(ID_I, ID_J, U, R_J, K_1, K_2, K_3)$ and H_1-oracle about (ID_i, V). To solve the GBDH problem, $\mathscr{C}$ optionally selects a entry from L_{H2} with probability $\mathcal{O}(1/\kappa_p)$. Then $\mathscr{C}$ calculates $\overline{K_2} = \frac{K_2}{e(D_I, V + R_J)e(U, P_0)^{r_J}}$. At last, $\mathscr{C}$ outputs $GBDH(U, V, P_0) = \overline{K_2} = e(P, P)^{uv\gamma}$. The advantage of that $\mathscr{C}$ solves the $GBDH(U, V, P_0)$ problem is $Adv_{\mathscr{C}}^{GBDH}(\kappa) \geq \frac{Adv_{\mathscr{A}_I}(\kappa)}{\kappa_s \kappa_p^2 \kappa_q}$. Because $Adv_{\mathscr{A}_I}(\kappa)$ is assumed to be non-negligible, $Adv_{\mathscr{C}}^{GBDH}(\kappa)$ should be non-negligible. However, it is a contradiction to the GBDH assumption.

Event E2. In this event, the ephemeral private keys of ID_I and ID_J are chosen by $\mathscr{C}$ in the simulation, which cannot be revealed by $\mathscr{A}_I$.

Given a GDH problem instance $(U = u \cdot P, V = v \cdot P)$, $\mathscr{C}$ aims to solve $GDH(U, V)$ by accessing DDH oracle, where $u, v \in Z_n^*$ and $P \in G$. Let $Adv_{\mathscr{C}}^{GDH}(\kappa)$ be the advantage that $\mathscr{C}$ obtains in solving GDH problem.

Queries. In query phase, $\mathscr{C}$ responds to the oracle queries as it does in Event E1 except the follows.

Create(ID_i). $\mathscr{C}$ selects $x_i, h_i \in {}_R Z_n^*$, and calculates $Y_i = x_i \cdot P$, sets $H_1(ID_i) \leftarrow H_i = h_i \cdot P$, $D_i \leftarrow h_i \cdot P_0$, then adds the tuple (ID_i, x_i, Y_i, D_i) and (ID_i, H_i) to L_c and L_{H1} respectively.

H_2-oracle.   As $\mathscr{A}_I$ queries   this   oracle   with   tuple $(ID_i, ID_j, R_i, R_j, K_1, K_2, K_3)$, $\mathscr{C}$ responds as the following way.

- If this tuple has already in L_{H2}, $\mathscr{C}$ sends the corresponding K to $\mathscr{A}_I$.
- Else, $\mathscr{C}$ looks up L_s for the entry $(ID_i, ID_j, R_i, R_j, *)$. If it is already in L_s, $\mathscr{C}$ checks whether (R_i, R_j, K_1) meets the oracle $DDH(*, *, *) \rightarrow 1$ when the tuple is the oracle's input. If it holds, $\mathscr{C}$ adds $(ID_i, ID_j, R_i, R_j, Y_1, Y_2, sk)$ to L_s, where sk is obtained from L_{H2}. Else, $\mathscr{C}$ randomly selects $sk \in \{0,1\}^\kappa$, then adds $(ID_i, ID_j, R_i, R_j, K_1, K_2, K_3, sk)$ to L_{H2} and sends sk to $\mathscr{A}_I$.
- Else. $\mathscr{C}$ randomly selects $sk \in \{0,1\}^\kappa$, then adds $(ID_i, ID_j, R_i, R_j, K_1, K_2, K_3, sk)$ to L_{H2}, and sends sk to $\mathscr{A}_I$.

RevealPartialKey(i). $\mathscr{C}$ looks up L_c for $(ID_i, *)$. If there exists this entry $(ID_i, *)$, $\mathscr{C}$ sends the corresponding D_i to $\mathscr{A}_I$. Else $\mathscr{C}$ executes create(ID_i) and sends D_i to $\mathscr{A}_I$.

RevealEphemeralKey($\Pi_{i,j}^t$). when $\mathscr{A}_I$ makes this query, $\mathscr{C}$ checks $\Pi_{i,j}^t$. If $\Pi_{i,j}^t = \Pi_{I,J}^T$ or $\Pi_{i,j}^t = \Pi_{J,I}^S$, $\mathscr{C}$ terminates this simulation. Otherwise, $\mathscr{C}$ sends the ephemeral key to $\mathscr{A}_I$.

Send($\Pi_{i,j}^t, m$). When $\mathscr{A}_I$ makes this query, $\mathscr{C}$ responds according to the following situations.

- If $\Pi_{i,j}^t = \Pi_{I,J}^T$, $\mathscr{C}$ sends $R_i = U$ to $\mathscr{A}_I$.
- Else if $\Pi_{i,j}^t = \Pi_{J,I}^S$, $\mathscr{C}$ sends $R_i = V$ to $\mathscr{A}_I$.
- Else, $\mathscr{C}$ responds this query based on the regulation of protocol.

Analysis. If $\mathscr{A}_I$ dose successfully, it should have makes queries from H_2-oracle about $(ID_I, ID_J, U, V, K_1, K_2, K_3)$ or $(ID_J, ID_I, V, U, K_1, K_2, K_3)$. To solve the GDH problem, $\mathscr{C}$ optionally selects an entry from L_{H2} with probability $\mathcal{O}(1/\kappa_p)$. Then $\mathscr{C}$ outputs $GDH(U, V) = K_3 = uv \cdot P$. The advantage of that $\mathscr{C}$ solves the $GDH(U, V)$ problem is $Adv_{\mathscr{C}}^{GDH}(\kappa) \geq \frac{Adv_{\mathscr{A}_I}(\kappa)}{\kappa_s \kappa_p^2 \kappa_q}$. Because $Adv_{\mathscr{A}_I}(\kappa)$ is assumed to be non-negligible, $Adv_{\mathscr{C}}^{GDH}(\kappa)$ should be non-negligible. However, it is a contradiction to the GDH assumption.

Event E3. In this event, only the roles of ID_I and ID_J are changed when compared with Event E1. Therefore, $Adv_{\mathscr{C}}^{GBDH}(\kappa)$ in this event can be proved to be non-negligible with the same analysis way of E1 by changing the roles of ID_I and ID_J. For simplicity, the detailed analysis is not presented.

Event E4. In this event, the partial key of ID_I and ID_J are chosen by $\mathscr{C}$ in the simulation, which cannot be revealed by $\mathscr{A}_I$.

Given a GBDH problem instance $(U = u \cdot P, V = v \cdot P, P_0 = \gamma \cdot P)$, $\mathscr{C}$ aims to solve GBDH(U, V, P_0) by accessing DBDH oracle, where $u, v \in Z_n^*$ and $P \in G$. Let $Adv_{\mathscr{C}}^{GBDH}(\kappa)$ be the advantage that $\mathscr{C}$ obtains in solving GBDH problem.

Queries. In query phase, $\mathscr{C}$ responds to the oracle queries as it does in Event E1 except the follows.

Create(ID_i). $\mathscr{A}_I$ queries this oracle with ID_i. If $ID_i = ID_I$, $\mathscr{C}$ selects $x_i \in {}_R Z_n^*$, and calculates $Y_i = x_i \cdot P$, sets $H_1(ID_i) \leftarrow U$, then adds the tuple $(ID_i, x_i, Y_i, \bot)$ and (ID_i, U) to L_c and L_{H1} respectively. Else if $ID_i = ID_J$, $\mathscr{C}$ selects $x_i \in {}_R Z_n^*$, and calculates $Y_i = x_i \cdot P$, sets $H_1(ID_i) \leftarrow V$, then adds the tuple $(ID_i, x_i, Y_i, \bot)$ and (ID_i, V) to L_c and L_{H1} respectively. Otherwise, $\mathscr{C}$ selects $x_i, h_i \in {}_R Z_n^*$, and calculates $Y_i = x_i \cdot P$, sets $H_1(ID_i) \leftarrow H_i = h_i \cdot P$, $D_i \leftarrow h_i \cdot P_0$, then adds the tuple (ID_i, x_i, Y_i, D_i) and (ID_i, H_i) to L_c and L_{H1} respectively.

H_2-oracle. As $\mathscr{A}_I$ queries this oracle with tuple $(ID_i, ID_j, R_i, R_j, K_1, K_2, K_3)$, $\mathscr{C}$ responds as the following way.

- If this tuple has already in L_{H2}, $\mathscr{C}$ sends the corresponding sk to $\mathscr{A}_I$.
- Else If $ID_i = ID_I$ or $ID_i = ID_J$, $\mathscr{C}$ looks up L_{H2} for the entry $(ID_i, ID_j, R_i, R_j, *)$. If it is in L_{H2}, $\mathscr{C}$ calculates $\overline{K_2} = \frac{K_2}{e(r_i \cdot P_0, H_1(ID_j) + R_j) e(H_1(ID_i), P_0)^{r_j}}$. Then $\mathscr{C}$ checks whether the tuple $(H_1(ID_i), H_1(ID_j), P_0, \overline{K_2})$ meets the oracle $DBDH(*, *, *, *) \to 1$ when the tuple is the oracle input. If it holds, $\mathscr{C}$ adds $(ID_i, ID_j, R_i, R_j, Y_1, Y_2, sk)$ to L_s, where sk is obtained from L_{H2}. Else, $\mathscr{C}$ randomly selects $sk \in \{0,1\}^\kappa$, then adds $(ID_i, ID_j, R_i, R_j, K_1, K_2, K_3, sk)$ to L_{H2} and sends sk to $\mathscr{A}_I$.
- Else, $\mathscr{C}$ looks up L_s for the entry $(ID_i, ID_j, R_i, R_j, *)$. If this entry is in L_s, $\mathscr{C}$ gets the sk from L_s and stores $(ID_i, ID_j, R_i, R_j, K_1, K_2, K_3, sk)$ to L_{H2}, where the values of tuple comes form L_s. Else, $\mathscr{C}$ randomly selects $sk \in \{0,1\}^\kappa$, then adds $(ID_i, ID_j, R_i, R_j, K_1, K_2, K_3, sk)$ to L_{H2}.

RevealPartialKey(i). if $ID_i = ID_I$ or $ID_i = ID_J$, $\mathscr{C}$ aborts. Else, $\mathscr{C}$ looks up L_c for $(ID_i, *)$. If there exists this entry $(ID_i, *)$, $\mathscr{C}$ sends the corresponding D_i to $\mathscr{A}_I$, else $\mathscr{C}$ executes create(ID_i) and sends D_i to $\mathscr{A}_I$.

Send$(\Pi_{i,j}^t, m)$. When $\mathscr{A}_I$ makes this query, $\mathscr{C}$ responds according to the following situations.

- If $\Pi_{i,j}^t = \Pi_{J,I}^S$, $\mathscr{C}$ return $H_i = V$ to $\mathscr{A}_I$. Else if $\Pi_{i,j}^t = \Pi_{I,J}^T$, $\mathscr{C}$ return $H_i = U$ to $\mathscr{A}_I$.
- Otherwise, if $ID_i = ID_I$ or $ID_i = ID_J$, $\mathscr{C}$ selects $t_i \in {}_R Z_n^*$, and calculates $\overline{K_2} = \frac{K_2}{e(r_i \cdot P_0, H_1(ID_j) + R_j) e(H_1(ID_i), P_0)^{r_j}}$. Then $\mathscr{C}$ checks whether the tuple $(H_1(ID_i), H_1(ID_j), P_0, \overline{K_2})$ meets the oracle $DBDH(*, *, *, *) \to 1$ when the tuple is the oracle input. If it holds, $\mathscr{C}$ adds $(ID_i, ID_j, R_i, R_j, K_1, K_2, K_3, sk)$ to L_{H2}. Else, $\mathscr{C}$ randomly selects $sk \in \{0,1\}^\kappa$, then adds $(ID_i, ID_j, R_i, R_j, K_1, K_2, K_3, sk)$ to L_{H2}.

- Else, $\mathscr{C}$ responds this query based on the regulation of protocol.

Analysis. If $\mathscr{A}_I$ dose successfully, it should have makes queries from H_2-oracle about $(ID_I, ID_J, R_I, R_J, K_1, K_2, K_3)$ or $(ID_J, ID_I, R_J, R_I, K_1, K_2, K_3)$, and H_1-oracle about (ID_I, U) and (ID_J, V). To solve the GBDH problem, $\mathscr{C}$ optionally selects an entry from L_{H2} with probability $\mathcal{O}(1/\kappa_p)$. Then $\mathscr{C}$ calculates $\overline{K}_2 = \frac{K_2}{e(r_I \cdot P_0, V + R_J)e(U, P_0)^{r_J}}$. At last, $\mathscr{C}$ outputs $GBDH(U, V, P_0) = \overline{K}_2 = e(P, P)^{\gamma uv}$. The advantage of that $\mathscr{C}$ solves the $GBDH(U, V, P_0)$ problem is $Adv_{\mathscr{C}}^{GBDH}(\kappa) \geq \frac{Adv_{\mathscr{A}_I}(\kappa)}{\kappa_s \kappa_p^2 \kappa_q}$. Because $Adv_{\mathscr{A}_I}(\kappa)$ is assumed to be non-negligible, $Adv_{\mathscr{C}}^{GBDH}(\kappa)$ should be non-negligible. However, it is a contradiction to the GBDH assumption.

Event E5. In this Event, there is no matching session for $\Pi_{I,J}^T$. The simulation of this event is similar to Event E4, so we do not repeat here for simplicity.

Event E6. In this Event, there is no matching session for $\Pi_{I,J}^T$. The simulation of this event is similar to Event E1, so we won't go into detail here.

4.2   Security Proof on $\mathscr{A}_{II}$

Theorem 2. The advantage of the adversary $\mathscr{A}_{II}$ against the proposed protocol is negligible under the GDH assumption.

The proof of Theorem 2 is not presented here. The detailed proof is deferred to the full paper due to page constraint.

According to Theorems 1 and 2, we can draw a conclusion that our proposed protocol is a secure in eCK security model under the GDH and GBDH assumption.

5   Performance Analysis

In this section, the proposed protocol is compared with Lin's protocols [9] in terms of security and efficiency.

As for the security comparison, our proposed CL-KA protocol can meet all of the security requirements, while lin's protocol has a fatal security deficiency that it can not resist impersonation attack.

For convenience, let T_b, T_m and T_e denote the time cost for a bilinear pairing operation, a curve point multiplication operation and a exponentiation operation respectively. The other operations are omitted during comparison due to much less than the three former operations. The execution times of the basic operations in Xiong et al.'s experiments [12] are adopted in this paper. The execution time of the three operations, T_b, T_m and T_e, are 5.32 s, 2.45 s and 1.25 s respectively. Therefore, the total time of the Lin's protocol and our proposed protocol are 18.41 s and 12.67 s.

The results of security and computation cost comparison are shown in Table 1 according the former analysis. From Table 1, our proposed CL-KA protocol achieves more advantages than lin's protocol.

Table 1. Performance comparisons

	Lin's protocol [9]	Our protocol
Resist impersonation attack	No	Yes
Resist KCI attack	Yes	Yes
RLESK	Yes	Yes
No key control	Yes	Yes
Forward secrecy	Yes	Yes
Known-key security	Yes	Yes
Resist unknown key share	Yes	Yes
Security model	eCK	eCK
Hardness	GDH	GDH and GBDH
Precomputed cost	$2T_b$	0
Computation cost	$T_b + T_m + T_e$	$T_b + 3T_m$
Total time	18.41 s	12.67 s

6   Conclusion

In this paper, to meet security and efficiency simultaneously, we propose an improved CL-KA protocol with short message over Lin's CL-KA protocol [9]. The proposed protocol overcomes the security deficiencies of Lin's CL-KA protocol. Only one complex bilinear paring operation in the key computation phase and no precomputation is required in the proposed protocol. We also present the security proof in the eCK model under the GDH and GBDH problem. The performance analysis shows the proposed CL-KA protocol can meet all security requirements and incurs less computation cost than Lin's protocol. Due to the paring operation is a complex crypto-operation for mobile devices, our next work is to study strongly secure CL-KA protocol without paring.

References

1. Sun, H., Wen, Q., Zhang, H., Jin, Z.: A strongly secure identity-based authenticated key agreement protocol without pairings under the gdh assumption. Secur. Commun. Netw. **8**(17), 3167–3179 (2015)
2. Choo, K.K.R., Nam, J., Won, D.: A mechanical approach to derive identity-based protocols from Diffie-Hellman-based protocols. Inf. Sci. **281**, 182–200 (2014)
3. Hafizul Islam, S.K., Singh, A.: Provably secure one-round certificateless authenticated group key agreement protocol for secure communications. Wirel. Pers. Commun. **85**(3), 879–898 (2015)
4. Zhu, Z., et al.: Cryptanalysis of pairing-free certificateless authenticated key agreement protocol. IACR Cryptology ePrint Archive, p. 253 (2012)
5. Swanson, C., Jao, D.: A study of two-party certificateless authenticated key-agreement protocols. In: Roy, B., Sendrier, N. (eds.) INDOCRYPT 2009. LNCS, vol. 5922, pp. 57–71. Springer, Heidelberg (2009). doi:10.1007/978-3-642-10628-6_4

6. He, D., Chen, J., Jin, H.: A pairing-free certificateless authenticated key agreement protocol. Int. J. Commun. Syst. **25**(2), 221–230 (2012)
7. Kim, Y.-J., Kim, Y.-M., Choe, Y.-J.: An efficient bilinear pairing-free certificateless two-party authenticated key agreement protocol in the eCK model. arXiv preprint arXiv:1304.0383 (2013)
8. Bala, S., Verma, A.K.: A non-interactive certificateless two-party authenticated key agreement protocol for wireless sensor networks. Int. J. Ad Hoc Ubiquit. Comput. **21**(2), 140–155 (2016)
9. Lin, H.-Y.: Secure certificateless two-party key agreement with short message. Inf. Technol. Contr. **45**(1), 71–76 (2016)
10. LaMacchia, B., Lauter, K., Mityagin, A.: Stronger security of authenticated key exchange. In: Susilo, W., Liu, J.K., Mu, Y. (eds.) ProvSec 2007. LNCS, vol. 4784, pp. 1–16. Springer, Heidelberg (2007)
11. Liu, J.K., Baek, J., Susilo, W., Zhou, J.: Certificate-based signature schemes without pairings or random oracles. In: Wu, T.-C., Lei, C.-L., Rijmen, V., Lee, D.-T. (eds.) ISC 2008. LNCS, vol. 5222, pp. 285–297. Springer, Heidelberg (2008)
12. Xiong, X., Wong, D.S., Deng, X.: Tinypairing: a fast and lightweight pairing-based cryptographic library for wireless sensor networks. In: Wireless Communications and Networking Conference (WCNC 2010), pp. 1–6. IEEE (2010)

Encryption

Integrity Analysis of Authenticated Encryption Based on Stream Ciphers

Kazuya Imamura[1], Kazuhiko Minematsu[2], and Tetsu Iwata[1(✉)]

[1] Nagoya University, Nagoya, Japan
k_imamur@echo.nuee.nagoya-u.ac.jp, iwata@cse.nagoya-u.ac.jp
[2] NEC Corporation, Kawasaki, Japan
k-minematsu@ah.jp.nec.com

Abstract. We study the security of authenticated encryption based on a stream cipher and a universal hash function. We consider ChaCha20-Poly1305 and generic constructions proposed by Sarkar, where the generic constructions include 14 AEAD (authenticated encryption with associated data) schemes and 3 DAEAD (deterministic AEAD) schemes. In this paper, we analyze the integrity of these schemes both in the standard INT-CTXT notion and in the RUP (releasing unverified plaintext) setting called INT-RUP notion. We present INT-CTXT attacks against 3 out of the 14 AEAD schemes and 1 out of the 3 DAEAD schemes. We then show INT-RUP attacks against 1 out of the 14 AEAD schemes and the 2 remaining DAEAD schemes. We next show that ChaCha20-Poly1305 is provably secure in the INT-RUP notion. Finally, we show that 4 out of the remaining 10 AEAD schemes are provably secure in the INT-RUP notion.

Keywords: Authenticated encryption · Stream cipher · Universal hash function · Provable security · Integrity · Releasing unverified plaintext

1 Introduction

Background. An authenticated encryption (AE) scheme is a symmetric encryption primitive where the goal is to achieve both privacy and integrity of plaintexts. Examples of AE include GCM [11], CCM [19], and EAX [6], and they are widely used in practice. There are several ways to construct AE, and the construction by the generic composition (GC), which was formalized by Bellare and Namprempre [3], is to combine existing primitives, one for encryption and the other for authentication, to obtain AE. The security notion for integrity, called INT-CTXT, requires that an adversary is unable to produce a ciphertext that is accepted in verification, where the adversary has access to an encryption oracle. Authenticated encryption with associated data (AEAD) was formalized in [15], where associated data (AD) is the input that is authenticated but not encrypted. Nonce-based encryption was formalized in [16], where a nonce is the input of the scheme which is supposed to be used only once, meaning that it is

© Springer International Publishing AG 2016
L. Chen and J. Han (Eds.): ProvSec 2016, LNCS 10005, pp. 257–276, 2016.
DOI: 10.1007/978-3-319-47422-9_15

not repeated. Implementation of a nonce is non-trivial in practice, and a repeat of a nonce in AEAD is often devastating. To address this issue, deterministic authenticated encryption (DAE) was formalized in [17]. More precisely, DAEAD is DAE that supports AD, which is AE that remains secure without the use of a nonce and does not leak information about a plaintext from a ciphertext, except for the repetition of the input. In this sense DAEAD has the nonce-reuse misuse resistance, but on a downside, DAEAD requires off-line computation. The GC in [3] was refined by Namprempre, Rogaway, and Shrimpton [12] by explicitly treating the use of a nonce.

Another direction of GC was put forward by Sarkar [18], where a stream cipher is used for encryption and a universal hash function is used for authentication. In [18], a total of 17 AEAD/DAEAD schemes are proposed. There are 14 AEAD schemes, called AEAD-$\{1, 2, 2a, 2b, 3, 4, 4a, 4b, 5, 6, 6a, 7, 8, 8a\}$, and 3 DAEAD schemes, called DAEAD-$\{1, 2, 2a\}$. It was proved that all these schemes achieve both privacy and integrity under the assumption that the stream cipher is a pseudo-random function (PRF) and that the hash function is a universal hash function.

Related AEAD which we call ChaCha20-Poly1305 was proposed by Nir and Langley [13]. A stream cipher ChaCha20 [8] is used for encryption and a universal hash function Poly1305 [7] is used for authentication, which were designed by Bernstein. ChaCha20-Poly1305 is practically used in IETF protocols [13]. The scheme is similar to one of the GC called AEAD-2b of [18], but there is a subtle difference and it does not exactly follow the composition. Procter [14] proved that ChaCha20-Poly1305 achieves both privacy and authenticity in the model of [4] under the assumption that ChaCha20 block function is a PRF.

Another security notion called the releasing unverified plaintext (RUP) was formalized by Andreeva et al. [1]. This notion is motivated to cover the situation in which there is not enough memory in decryption devices to store the entire decrypted plaintext and decrypted plaintexts are immediately required in real time. The corresponding integrity notion is called INT-RUP, and the goal of an adversary under the INT-RUP notion is to produce a new ciphertext which is accepted in the verification, where the adversary has access to the oracle that returns unverified plaintexts. We remark that the notion is often referred to as the decryption-misuse setting.

Our Contributions. In this paper, we study the integrity of AEAD and DAEAD based on a stream cipher and a universal hash function in the standard INT-CTXT notion and in the decryption-misuse, INT-RUP notion.

Our results are summarized in Table 1. We first show that there are INT-CTXT attacks against 4 out of 17 schemes in [18], invalidating the original INT-CTXT security claims. In addition to this, we show INT-RUP attacks against 3 out of the 17 schemes, showing a sort of tightness of the original INT-CTXT claims. All our attacks need only a few queries, and are hence practical. Specifically, we show INT-CTXT attacks against AEAD-$\{2a, 4a, 4b\}$ and DAEAD-2a, and INT-RUP attacks against AEAD-2b and DAEAD-$\{1, 2\}$. We note that INT-RUP security is not claimed in [18], as [18] predates [1].

Table 1. INT-CTXT and INT-RUP security of AEAD and DAEAD schemes. The mark ✓ means secure, ✗ means insecure, (✗) follows from the INT-CTXT result, and ? remains open.

Scheme	INT-CTXT	INT-RUP
ChaCha20-Poly1305	✓ ([14])	✓ (Theorem 1)
AEAD-1	✓ ([18, Theorem 20])	✓ (Theorem 2)
AEAD-2	✓ ([18, Theorem 20])	✓ (Theorem 2)
AEAD-2a	✗ (Sect. 4.1)	(✗)
AEAD-2b	✓ ([18, Theorem 20])	✗ (Sect. 4.2)
AEAD-3	✓ ([18, Theorem 20])	✓ (Theorem 2)
AEAD-4	✓ ([18, Theorem 20])	✓ (Theorem 2)
AEAD-4a	✗ (Sect. 4.1)	(✗)
AEAD-4b	✗ (Sect. 4.1)	(✗)
AEAD-5	✓ ([18, Theorem 20])	?
AEAD-6	✓ ([18, Theorem 20])	?
AEAD-6a	✓ ([18, Theorem 20])	?
AEAD-7	✓ ([18, Theorem 20])	?
AEAD-8	✓ ([18, Theorem 20])	?
AEAD-8a	✓ ([18, Theorem 20])	?
DAEAD-1	✓ ([18, Theorem 21])	✗ (Sect. 4.2)
DAEAD-2	✓ ([18, Theorem 21])	✗ (Sect. 4.2)
DAEAD-2a	✗ (Sect. 4.1)	(✗)

A universal hash function, or more precisely an almost XOR universal (AXU) hash function, is used in these schemes, and our observation is that the definition of an AXU hash function does not exclude a case where it has a fixed point, which is the input X and the output Y of the hash function H such that $H_L(X) = Y$ holds independent of the key L. Our INT-CTXT attacks against AEAD-{2a, 4a, 4b} and DAEAD-2a, and INT-RUP attacks against DAEAD-{1, 2} make use of the existence of the fixed point. The INT-RUP attack against AEAD-2b is based on a different observation. We show that an adversary can recover the hash key from the unverified plaintext and hence break the INT-RUP security with probability 1. The attacks are described in Sect. 4. We remark that our attacks imply the existence of a universal hash function that makes these schemes insecure, and the attacks do not imply the non-existence of a universal hash function that makes the schemes secure.

Next, we show that ChaCha20-Poly1305 is INT-RUP secure under the same assumption as Procter. While ChaCha20-Poly1305 is similar to AEAD-2b, there is a difference in the order of the generation of a hash key and a keystream, and this small difference results in the difference in INT-RUP security. Finally, we show that AEAD-$\{1, 2, 3, 4\}$ are INT-RUP secure under the assumption that a stream cipher is a PRF. Our security bounds of these schemes are shown in Sect. 5.

2 Preliminaries

2.1 Notation

We write $\{0,1\}^*$ for the set of all finite bit strings, and for an integer $l \geq 0$, we write $\{0,1\}^l$ for all the l-bit strings. We write ε for the empty string. For $X \in \{0,1\}^*$, $|X|$ is its length in bits. For $X \in \{0,1\}^*$ and an integer l such that $|X| \geq l$, $\mathsf{msb}_l(X)$ denotes the most significant (the leftmost) l bits of X, and $\mathsf{lsb}_l(X)$ denotes the least significant (the rightmost) l bits of X. For $X, Y \in \{0,1\}^*$, their concatenation is written as $X \parallel Y$. The bit string of m zeros is written as $0^m \in \{0,1\}^m$, and m ones is written as $1^m \in \{0,1\}^m$. We write $g \circ f$ for the composite function of two functions f and g, which is defined as $g \circ f(\cdot) = g(f(\cdot))$. For a finite set $\mathcal{X}$, we write $X \xleftarrow{\$} \mathcal{X}$ for a procedure of assigning X an element sampled uniformly at random from $\mathcal{X}$.

2.2 AEAD and DAEAD

Authenticated Encryption with Associated Data (AEAD) [3,15]. The goal of AEAD is to achieve both privacy and integrity of a plaintext, and integrity of associated data. We consider that AEAD consists of three deterministic algorithms, and let AEAD = (AEAD.Enc, AEAD.Dec, AEAD.Ver). Let $K \in \mathcal{K}$ be the underlying secret key that fixes the three algorithms, where $\mathcal{K}$ is the key space. The encryption algorithm AEAD.Enc$_K$ takes input a nonce N, associated data A, and a plaintext M, and outputs a ciphertext C and a tag T. The decryption algorithm AEAD.Dec$_K$ takes input N, A, C, and T, and always outputs M. The verification algorithm AEAD.Ver$_K$ takes input N, A, C, and T, and outputs $\top$ or $\bot$, where $\top$ means that the verification is accepted, and $\bot$ means that the verification is rejected. The correctness requirement must be satisfied, that is, the following requirements are satisfied.

$$\begin{cases} \mathsf{AEAD.Dec}_K(N, A, \mathsf{AEAD.Enc}_K(N, A, M)) = M \\ \mathsf{AEAD.Ver}_K(N, A, \mathsf{AEAD.Enc}_K(N, A, M)) = \top \end{cases}$$

Deterministic AEAD (DAEAD) [17]. DAEAD is AEAD that does not require a nonce. Let DAEAD = (DAEAD.Enc, DAEAD.Dec, DAEAD.Ver), where the encryption algorithm DAEAD.Enc$_K$ takes input A and M, and outputs C and T, the decryption algorithm DAEAD.Dec$_K$ takes input A, C, and T, and outputs M, and the verification algorithm DAEAD.Ver$_K$ takes input A, C, and T, and outputs $\top$ or $\bot$. As in AEAD, the following correctness requirement must be satisfied.

$$\begin{cases} \mathsf{DAEAD.Dec}_K(A, \mathsf{DAEAD.Enc}_K(A, M)) = M \\ \mathsf{DAEAD.Ver}_K(A, \mathsf{DAEAD.Enc}_K(A, M)) = \top \end{cases}$$

2.3   Security Definitions

Ciphertext Integrity. For AEAD and DAEAD, privacy and integrity are the main two security notions. In this paper, we focus on the latter, and describe two notions called INT-CTXT and INT-RUP. INT-CTXT is a standard, classical notion that captures the integrity of ciphertext under chosen ciphertext attacks. INT-RUP considers a more powerful adversary that has access to an oracle that returns unverified plaintexts. We note that INT-RUP is a stronger notion than INT-CTXT, and if a scheme is INT-RUP secure, then it is also INT-CTXT secure.

Definition 1 (INT-CTXT Advantage [3,4]**).** Let $\mathcal{A}$ be an adversary that has access to two oracles $\mathsf{AEAD.Enc}_K$ and $\mathsf{AEAD.Ver}_K$. Then we define the INT-CTXT advantage of $\mathcal{A}$ against AEAD as

$$\mathbf{Adv}_{\mathsf{AEAD}}^{\mathsf{int\text{-}ctxt}}(\mathcal{A}) \stackrel{\text{def}}{=} \Pr[\mathcal{A}^{\mathsf{AEAD.Enc}_K,\mathsf{AEAD.Ver}_K} \text{ forges}],$$

where $K \stackrel{\$}{\leftarrow} \mathcal{K}$ and $\mathcal{A}$ forges is the event that $\mathsf{AEAD.Ver}_K$ returns $\top$ to $\mathcal{A}$. We assume that $\mathcal{A}$ does not repeat a query, and if $\mathcal{A}$ receives a response (C,T) for an encryption query (N, A, M), then $\mathcal{A}$ does not subsequently make a verification query (N, A, C, T). We assume that $\mathcal{A}$ is nonce-respecting with respect to encryption queries, that is, if (N_i, A_i, M_i) denotes the i-th encryption query, then it holds that $N_i \neq N_{i'}$ for any $i \neq i'$.

We note that $\mathcal{A}$ may repeat a nonce within verification queries, may reuse a nonce used for an encryption query as a nonce for a subsequent verification query, and may reuse a nonce used for a verification query as a nonce for a subsequent encryption query.

The INT-CTXT advantage for DAEAD is similarly defined as

$$\mathbf{Adv}_{\mathsf{DAEAD}}^{\mathsf{int\text{-}ctxt}}(\mathcal{A}) \stackrel{\text{def}}{=} \Pr[\mathcal{A}^{\mathsf{DAEAD.Enc}_K,\mathsf{DAEAD.Ver}_K} \text{ forges}].$$

We assume that $\mathcal{A}$ does not repeat a query, and if $\mathcal{A}$ receives a response (C, T) for an encryption query (A, M), then $\mathcal{A}$ does not subsequently make a verification query (A, C, T). Since DAEAD does not take a nonce N as input, $\mathcal{A}$ has no nonce-respecting restriction.

Definition 2 (INT-RUP Advantage [1]**).** Let $\mathcal{A}$ be an adversary that has access to three oracles $\mathsf{AEAD.Enc}_K$, $\mathsf{AEAD.Dec}_K$, and $\mathsf{AEAD.Ver}_K$. Then we define the INT-RUP advantage of $\mathcal{A}$ against AEAD as

$$\mathbf{Adv}_{\mathsf{AEAD}}^{\mathsf{int\text{-}rup}}(\mathcal{A}) \stackrel{\text{def}}{=} \Pr[\mathcal{A}^{\mathsf{AEAD.Enc}_K,\mathsf{AEAD.Dec}_K,\mathsf{AEAD.Ver}_K} \text{ forges}],$$

where $K \stackrel{\$}{\leftarrow} \mathcal{K}$ and $\mathcal{A}$ forges is the event that $\mathsf{AEAD.Ver}_K$ returns $\top$ to $\mathcal{A}$. $\mathcal{A}$ does not repeat a query, and if $\mathcal{A}$ receives a response (C, T) for an encryption query (N, A, M), then $\mathcal{A}$ does not subsequently make a verification query (N, A, C, T). $\mathcal{A}$ is nonce-respecting with respect to encryption queries. However, a nonce can be repeated within decryption queries and within verification queries, and the same nonce can be reused across encryption, decryption, and verification queries.

The INT-RUP advantage of DAEAD is defined as

$$\mathbf{Adv}_{\mathsf{DAEAD}}^{\mathrm{int\text{-}rup}}(\mathcal{A}) \stackrel{\mathrm{def}}{=} \Pr[\mathcal{A}^{\mathsf{DAEAD.Enc}_K, \mathsf{DAEAD.Dec}_K, \mathsf{DAEAD.Ver}_K} \text{ forges}].$$

As in the INT-CTXT definition, since DAEAD does not take a nonce N as input, $\mathcal{A}$ has no nonce-respecting restriction. However, we assume that $\mathcal{A}$ does not repeat a query, and if $\mathcal{A}$ receives a response (C, T) for an encryption query (A, M), then $\mathcal{A}$ does not subsequently make a verification query (A, C, T).

Pseudo-Random Function (PRF). Following [18], we consider a stream cipher as a function $\mathsf{SC} \colon \mathcal{K} \times \{0,1\}^n \to \{0,1\}^\ell$, where $\mathcal{K}$ is the set of keys, n denotes the length of IV in bits, and ℓ is a sufficiently large and fixed integer. For a key $K \in \mathcal{K}$, the corresponding function SC_K takes an IV $N \in \{0,1\}^n$ as input, and outputs the keystream $Z \leftarrow \mathsf{SC}_K(N) \in \{0,1\}^\ell$. Let $\mathrm{Rand}(n, \ell)$ be the set of all functions from $\{0,1\}^n$ to $\{0,1\}^\ell$, and let $\mathcal{A}$ be an adversary. Then we define the PRF-advantage of $\mathcal{A}$ against SC as

$$\mathbf{Adv}_{\mathsf{SC}}^{\mathrm{prf}}(\mathcal{A}) \stackrel{\mathrm{def}}{=} \Pr[K \xleftarrow{\$} \mathcal{K} \colon \mathcal{A}^{\mathsf{SC}_K} \Rightarrow 1] - \Pr[F \xleftarrow{\$} \mathrm{Rand}(n, \ell) \colon \mathcal{A}^F \Rightarrow 1],$$

where $\mathcal{A} \Rightarrow 1$ denotes the event that $\mathcal{A}$ outputs 1.

We note that in the above formalization, SC_K is a function with fixed-input length and fixed-output length, and we assume that the output of SC_K is always ℓ bits. However, in the actual usage of SC_K, we abuse the notation and for instance we write $C \leftarrow M \oplus \mathsf{SC}_K(N)$ to mean $C \leftarrow M \oplus \mathsf{msb}_{|M|}(\mathsf{SC}_K(N))$, or $R \parallel Z \leftarrow \mathsf{SC}_K(N)$, where $|R| = n$ and $|Z|$ is clear from the context (such as the length of the plaintext), to mean $Y \leftarrow \mathsf{SC}_K(N), R \leftarrow \mathsf{msb}_n(Y)$, and $Z \leftarrow \mathsf{lsb}_{|Z|}(\mathsf{msb}_{n+|Z|}(Y))$.

Hash Function. Let $\mathsf{H} \colon \mathcal{L} \times \mathcal{D}_{\mathsf{H}} \to \{0,1\}^n$ be a hash function, where $\mathcal{L}$ is a set of hash keys, $\mathcal{D}_{\mathsf{H}}$ denotes the domain, and n is the length of the output in bits. The function specified by $L \in \mathcal{L}$ is written as H_L.

Let $\{\mathsf{H}_L\}$ be a family of keyed hash functions. For any distinct $X', X \in \mathcal{D}_{\mathsf{H}}$ and any $Y \in \{0,1\}^n$, if the differential probability $\Pr[\mathsf{H}_L(X) \oplus \mathsf{H}_L(X') = Y]$ is at most ϵ, then H_L is defined to be an ϵ-almost-XOR-universal (ϵ-AXU) hash function, where the probability is taken over the choice of $L \xleftarrow{\$} \mathcal{L}$.

There are several examples of an ϵ-AXU hash function for small ϵ, and they include GHASH used in GCM [11] and Poly1305 [7]. For these hash functions, the key length is independent of the input length, and the key space is the set of bit strings of a fixed length. Following [18], we call this type of hash functions Type-I hash functions. There are other examples of an ϵ-AXU hash function where the key length can be as long as the input length, or even longer that that, including UMAC [9]. We call this type of hash functions Type-II hash functions.

We observe that the definition of an ϵ-AXU hash function does not exclude a case where the hash function has a fixed point. That is, there may exist $X \in \mathcal{D}_{\mathsf{H}}$ and $Y \in \{0,1\}^n$ such that $\mathsf{H}_L(X) = Y$ holds independently of the key L, since the requirement is about the differential probability, and the uniformity of a single input is irrelevant of the definition. Indeed, practical hash functions like GHASH and Poly1305 have a fixed point. For GHASH, it takes $(A, C) \in \{0, 1\}^* \times \{0, 1\}^*$ as input and outputs $Y \in \{0, 1\}^n$, and it holds that $\mathsf{GHASH}_L(A, C) = Y$ with probability 1 for $(A, C) = (\varepsilon, \varepsilon)$ and $Y = 0^n$. Poly1305 has the same fixed point. We will exploit the existence of a fixed point in our attacks.

3   Schemes

In this section, we present the specifications of AEAD and DAEAD schemes that are proposed in [18], and ChaCha20-Poly1305 [13].

AEAD in [18]. Let fStr be an arbitrary fixed n-bit string. For instance fStr could be 0^n. AEAD schemes in [18] are specified by a stream cipher SC and a hash function H, and we write AEAD[SC, H] for AEAD that uses SC and H as parameters. We also write AEAD[Rand(n, ℓ), H] for AEAD where we use a random function $F \xleftarrow{\$} \mathrm{Rand}(n, \ell)$ as the stream cipher SC_K. The encryption algorithms of the schemes are defined in Fig. 1. See Fig. 2 for the overall structure of the encryption algorithms. The decryption and verification algorithms are naturally defined and are presented in [10]. We note that these schemes have the convention on the length of the input. Specifically, the encryption algorithms take any plaintext M which is not empty, and $|M| = 0$ is not allowed [18].

We also note that AEAD-$\{1, 2, 2a, 2b, 3, 4, 4a, 4b\}$ use H as a double-input hash function, but AEAD-$\{5, 6, 6a, 7, 8, 8a\}$ use H as a hash function that can take both double-input and single-input. See [18] for more details on this matter.

ChaCha20-Poly1305 [13]. Let $\mathcal{K}_{\mathsf{CC}} = \{0, 1\}^{256}$ and $\mathcal{K}_{\mathsf{Poly}} = \{0, 1\}^{128} \times \{0, 1\}^{128}$. We denote ChaCha20 block function by $\mathsf{CC} \colon \mathcal{K}_{\mathsf{CC}} \times \{0, 1\}^{32} \times \{0, 1\}^{96} \to \{0, 1\}^{512}$, and denote Poly1305 authentication function by $\mathsf{Poly} \colon \mathcal{K}_{\mathsf{Poly}} \times \{0, 1\}^* \to \{0, 1\}^{128}$. The functions specified by $K \in \mathcal{K}_{\mathsf{CC}}$ and $(r, s) \in \mathcal{K}_{\mathsf{Poly}}$ are written as CC_K and $\mathsf{Poly}_{r,s}$, respectively. We write CC&Poly for ChaCha20-Poly1305.

With these functions, the encryption algorithm of ChaCha20-Poly1305 is defined in Fig. 3. See Fig. 4 for the overall structure of the encryption algorithm. See [7, 8] for further details of the specifications of ChaCha20 and Poly1305.

Observe the similarity to AEAD-2b. $\mathsf{SC}_K(N)$ in AEAD-2b corresponds to $\mathsf{CC}_K(0, N), \mathsf{CC}_K(1, N), \ldots, \mathsf{CC}_K(\lceil |M|/512 \rceil, N)$, where (L, R) in AEAD-2b corresponds to (r, s) in ChaCha20-Poly1305. The difference is that L is taken from the rightmost bits of $\mathsf{SC}_K(N)$, thus the starting position can be moved depending on the length of M, while s is always taken from the same position.

DAEAD in [18]. The encryption algorithms of DAEAD schemes are defined in Fig. 5. See Fig. 6 for the overall structure. We note that the basic idea of DAEAD schemes follows the SIV construction in [17].

4   Negative Results

In this section, we show that AEAD-$\{2a, 4a, 4b\}$ and DAEAD-2a are not INT-CTXT secure and that AEAD-2b and DAEAD-$\{1, 2\}$ are not INT-RUP secure. Our forgery attacks against these schemes are presented in Figs. 7 and 8.

AEAD-1.$\text{Enc}_{K,L}(N,A,M)$	AEAD-2.$\text{Enc}_{K,K'}(N,A,M)$	AEAD-2a.$\text{Enc}_K(N,A,M)$
1. $R \parallel Z \leftarrow \text{SC}_K(N)$ 2. $C \leftarrow M \oplus Z$ 3. $T \leftarrow \text{H}_L(A,C) \oplus R$ 4. **return** (C,T)	1. $L \leftarrow \text{SC}_K(K')$ 2. $R \parallel Z \leftarrow \text{SC}_K(N)$ 3. $C \leftarrow M \oplus Z$ 4. $T \leftarrow \text{H}_L(A,C) \oplus R$ 5. **return** (C,T)	1. $K' \leftarrow \text{msb}_n(\text{SC}_K(\text{fStr}))$ 2. $L \leftarrow \text{SC}_K(K')$ 3. $R \parallel Z \leftarrow \text{SC}_K(N)$ 4. $C \leftarrow M \oplus Z$ 5. $T \leftarrow \text{H}_L(A,C) \oplus R$ 6. **return** (C,T)

AEAD-3.$\text{Enc}_{K,L}(N,A,M)$	AEAD-4.$\text{Enc}_{K,K'}(N,A,M)$	AEAD-4a.$\text{Enc}_K(N,A,M)$
1. $R \parallel Z \leftarrow \text{SC}_K(N)$ 2. $C \leftarrow M \oplus Z$ 3. $T \leftarrow \text{H}_L(A,M) \oplus R$ 4. **return** (C,T)	1. $L \leftarrow \text{SC}_K(K')$ 2. $R \parallel Z \leftarrow \text{SC}_K(N)$ 3. $C \leftarrow M \oplus Z$ 4. $T \leftarrow \text{H}_L(A,M) \oplus R$ 5. **return** (C,T)	1. $K' \leftarrow \text{msb}_n(\text{SC}_K(\text{fStr}))$ 2. $L \leftarrow \text{SC}_K(K')$ 3. $R \parallel Z \leftarrow \text{SC}_K(N)$ 4. $C \leftarrow M \oplus Z$ 5. $T \leftarrow \text{H}_L(A,M) \oplus R$ 6. **return** (C,T)

AEAD-2b.$\text{Enc}_K(N,A,M)$	AEAD-4b.$\text{Enc}_K(N,A,M)$
1. $R \parallel S \leftarrow \text{SC}_K(N)$ 2. Parse S as $Z \parallel L$ where $|Z| = |M|$ 3. $C \leftarrow M \oplus Z$ 4. $T \leftarrow \text{H}_L(A,C) \oplus R$ 5. **return** (C,T)	1. $R \parallel S \leftarrow \text{SC}_K(N)$ 2. Parse S as $Z \parallel L$ where $|Z| = |M|$ 3. $C \leftarrow M \oplus Z$ 4. $T \leftarrow \text{H}_L(A,M) \oplus R$ 5. **return** (C,T)

AEAD-5.$\text{Enc}_{K,L}(N,A,M)$	AEAD-6.$\text{Enc}_{K,K'}(N,A,M)$	AEAD-6a.$\text{Enc}_K(N,A,M)$
1. $V \leftarrow \text{H}_L(A,N)$ 2. $R \parallel Z \leftarrow \text{SC}_K(V)$ 3. $C \leftarrow M \oplus Z$ 4. $T \leftarrow \text{H}_L(C) \oplus R$ 5. **return** (C,T)	1. $L_1 \parallel L_2 \leftarrow \text{SC}_K(K')$ 2. $V \leftarrow \text{H}_{L_1}(A,N)$ 3. $R \parallel Z \leftarrow \text{SC}_K(V)$ 4. $C \leftarrow M \oplus Z$ 5. $T \leftarrow \text{H}_{L_2}(C) \oplus R$ 6. **return** (C,T)	1. $K' \leftarrow \text{msb}_n(\text{SC}_K(\text{fStr}))$ 2. $L_1 \parallel L_2 \leftarrow \text{SC}_K(K')$ 3. $V \leftarrow \text{H}_{L_1}(A,N)$ 4. $R \parallel Z \leftarrow \text{SC}_K(V)$ 5. $C \leftarrow M \oplus Z$ 6. $T \leftarrow \text{H}_{L_2}(C) \oplus R$ 7. **return** (C,T)

AEAD-7.$\text{Enc}_{K,L}(N,A,M)$	AEAD-8.$\text{Enc}_{K,K'}(N,A,M)$	AEAD-8a.$\text{Enc}_K(N,A,M)$
1. $V \leftarrow \text{H}_L(A,N)$ 2. $R \parallel Z \leftarrow \text{SC}_K(V)$ 3. $C \leftarrow M \oplus Z$ 4. $T \leftarrow \text{H}_L(M) \oplus R$ 5. **return** (C,T)	1. $L_1 \parallel L_2 \leftarrow \text{SC}_K(K')$ 2. $V \leftarrow \text{H}_{L_1}(A,N)$ 3. $R \parallel Z \leftarrow \text{SC}_K(V)$ 4. $C \leftarrow M \oplus Z$ 5. $T \leftarrow \text{H}_{L_2}(M) \oplus R$ 6. **return** (C,T)	1. $K' \leftarrow \text{msb}_n(\text{SC}_K(\text{fStr}))$ 2. $L_1 \parallel L_2 \leftarrow \text{SC}_K(K')$ 3. $V \leftarrow \text{H}_{L_1}(A,N)$ 4. $R \parallel Z \leftarrow \text{SC}_K(V)$ 5. $C \leftarrow M \oplus Z$ 6. $T \leftarrow \text{H}_{L_2}(M) \oplus R$ 7. **return** (C,T)

Fig. 1. Pseudocode of the encryption algorithms of AEAD schemes [18]

Before describing the details of our attacks, we present the following proposition showing that the fixed point can be "moved" to any desired point without changing the value of ϵ.

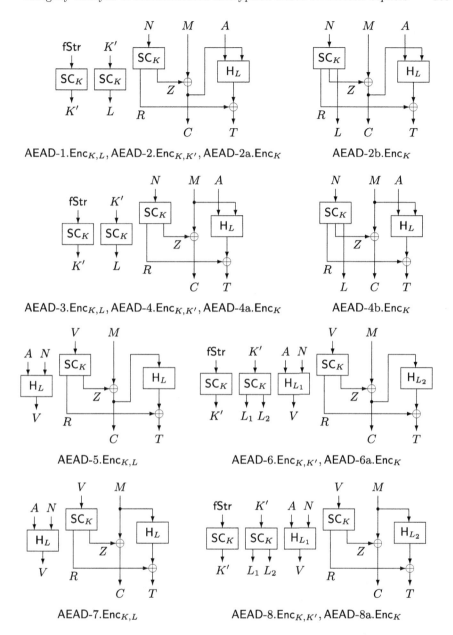

Fig. 2. Illustration of the encryption algorithms of AEAD schemes [18]. In AEAD-2 and AEAD-4, $L = \mathsf{SC}_K(K')$. In AEAD-2a and AEAD-4a, $L = \mathsf{SC}_K(\mathsf{msb}_n(\mathsf{SC}_K(\mathsf{fStr})))$. In AEAD-6 and AEAD-8, $L_1 \parallel L_2 = \mathsf{SC}_K(K')$. In AEAD-6a and AEAD-8a, $L_1 \parallel L_2 = \mathsf{SC}_K(\mathsf{msb}_n(\mathsf{SC}_K(\mathsf{fStr})))$.

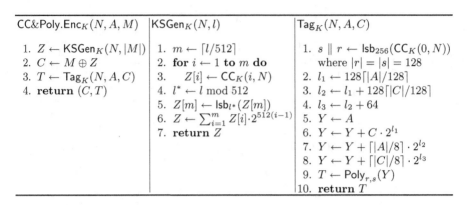

$\mathsf{CC\&Poly.Enc}_K(N, A, M)$	$\mathsf{KSGen}_K(N, l)$	$\mathsf{Tag}_K(N, A, C)$
1. $Z \leftarrow \mathsf{KSGen}_K(N, \lvert M\rvert)$	1. $m \leftarrow \lceil l/512\rceil$	1. $s \parallel r \leftarrow \mathsf{lsb}_{256}(\mathsf{CC}_K(0, N))$
2. $C \leftarrow M \oplus Z$	2. **for** $i \leftarrow 1$ **to** m **do**	$\quad$ where $\lvert r\rvert = \lvert s\rvert = 128$
3. $T \leftarrow \mathsf{Tag}_K(N, A, C)$	3. $\quad Z[i] \leftarrow \mathsf{CC}_K(i, N)$	2. $l_1 \leftarrow 128\lceil\lvert A\rvert/128\rceil$
4. **return** (C, T)	4. $l^* \leftarrow l \bmod 512$	3. $l_2 \leftarrow l_1 + 128\lceil\lvert C\rvert/128\rceil$
	5. $Z[m] \leftarrow \mathsf{lsb}_{l^*}(Z[m])$	4. $l_3 \leftarrow l_2 + 64$
	6. $Z \leftarrow \sum_{i=1}^{m} Z[i]\cdot 2^{512(i-1)}$	5. $Y \leftarrow A$
	7. **return** Z	6. $Y \leftarrow Y + C \cdot 2^{l_1}$
		7. $Y \leftarrow Y + \lceil\lvert A\rvert/8\rceil \cdot 2^{l_2}$
		8. $Y \leftarrow Y + \lceil\lvert C\rvert/8\rceil \cdot 2^{l_3}$
		9. $T \leftarrow \mathsf{Poly}_{r,s}(Y)$
		10. **return** T

Fig. 3. Pseudocode of the encryption algorithm of ChaCha20-Poly1305. The arithmetics are usual integer addition and multiplication.

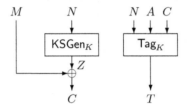

Fig. 4. Illustration of the encryption algorithm of ChaCha20-Poly1305

$\mathsf{DAEAD\text{-}1.Enc}_{K,L}(A, M)$	$\mathsf{DAEAD\text{-}2.Enc}_{K,K'}(A, M)$	$\mathsf{DAEAD\text{-}2a.Enc}_K(A, M)$
1. $V \leftarrow \mathsf{H}_L(A, M)$	1. $L \leftarrow \mathsf{SC}_K(K')$	1. $K' \leftarrow \mathsf{msb}_n(\mathsf{SC}_K(\mathsf{fStr}))$
2. $T \leftarrow \mathsf{msb}_n(\mathsf{SC}_K(V))$	2. $V \leftarrow \mathsf{H}_L(A, M)$	2. $L \leftarrow \mathsf{SC}_K(K')$
3. $Z \leftarrow \mathsf{SC}_K(T)$	3. $T \leftarrow \mathsf{msb}_n(\mathsf{SC}_K(V))$	3. $V \leftarrow \mathsf{H}_L(A, M)$
4. $C \leftarrow M \oplus Z$	4. $Z \leftarrow \mathsf{SC}_K(T)$	4. $T \leftarrow \mathsf{msb}_n(\mathsf{SC}_K(V))$
5. **return** (C, T)	5. $C \leftarrow M \oplus Z$	5. $Z \leftarrow \mathsf{SC}_K(T)$
	6. **return** (C, T)	6. $C \leftarrow M \oplus Z$
		7. **return** (C, T)

Fig. 5. Pseudocode of the encryption algorithms of DAEAD schemes [18]

Proposition 1. *Let* $\widetilde{\mathsf{H}}_L \colon \mathcal{D}_{\mathsf{H}} \to \{0,1\}^n$ *be a hash function,* $\varphi \colon \mathcal{D}_{\mathsf{H}} \to \mathcal{D}_{\mathsf{H}}$ *be an injective function, and* $c \in \{0,1\}^n$ *be a constant. Let* $\mathsf{H}_L \colon \mathcal{D}_{\mathsf{H}} \to \{0,1\}^n$ *be a hash function, where* $\mathsf{H}_L(X) = \widetilde{\mathsf{H}}_L(\varphi(X)) \oplus c$. *If* $\{\widetilde{\mathsf{H}}_L\}$ *is* ϵ-*AXU, then* $\{\mathsf{H}_L\}$ *is* ϵ-*AXU.*

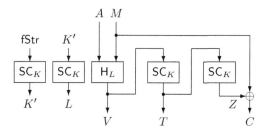

Fig. 6. Illustration the encryption algorithms of DAEAD schemes [18]. In DAEAD-2, $L = \mathsf{SC}_K(K')$. In DAEAD-2a, $L = \mathsf{SC}_K(\mathsf{msb}_n(\mathsf{SC}_K(\mathsf{fStr})))$.

INT-CTXT attack against AEAD-2a

1. $(C_1, T_1) \leftarrow$ AEAD-2a.$\mathsf{Enc}_K(N_1, A_1, M_1)$ where $(N_1, A_1, M_1) \leftarrow (\mathsf{fStr}, A_0, M_0)$
2. **if** $C_1 = C_0$ **then**
3. $K' \leftarrow T_1$
4.   **if** $K' \neq \mathsf{fStr}$ **then**
5. $(C_2, T_2) \leftarrow$ AEAD-2a.$\mathsf{Enc}_K(N_2, A_2, M_2)$ where $(N_2, A_2, M_2) \leftarrow (K', A_0, M_0)$
6.   **if** $C_2 = C_0$ **then**
7. $L^* \leftarrow T_2$; $T^* \leftarrow \mathsf{H}_{L^*}(A^*, C^*) \oplus K'$
8. $\top \leftarrow$ AEAD-2a.$\mathsf{Ver}_K(N^*, A^*, C^*, T^*)$ where $N^* \leftarrow \mathsf{fStr}$
9.   **else**
10. $L^* \leftarrow \mathsf{fStr}$; $T^* \leftarrow \mathsf{H}_{L^*}(A^*, C^*) \oplus \mathsf{fStr}$
11. $\top \leftarrow$ AEAD-2a.$\mathsf{Ver}_K(N^*, A^*, C^*, T^*)$ where $N^* \leftarrow \mathsf{fStr}$

INT-CTXT attack against AEAD-4a

1. $(C_1, K') \leftarrow$ AEAD-4a.$\mathsf{Enc}_K(N_1, A_1, M_1)$ where $(N_1, A_1, M_1) \leftarrow (\mathsf{fStr}, A_0, M_0)$
2. **if** $K' \neq \mathsf{fStr}$ **then**
3. $(C_2, L^*) \leftarrow$ AEAD-4a.$\mathsf{Enc}_K(N_2, A_2, M_2)$ where $(N_2, A_2, M_2) \leftarrow (K', A_0, M_0)$
4. **else**
5. $L^* \leftarrow K'$
6. $T^* \leftarrow \mathsf{H}_{L^*}(A^*, M^*) \oplus K'$ where $|M^*| \leq |M_0|$
7. $\top \leftarrow$ AEAD-4a.$\mathsf{Ver}_K(N^*, A^*, M^* \oplus \mathsf{msb}_{|M^*|}(M_1 \oplus C_1), T^*)$ where $N^* \leftarrow \mathsf{fStr}$

INT-CTXT attack against AEAD-4b

1. $(C_0, R) \leftarrow$ AEAD-4b.$\mathsf{Enc}_K(N_1, A_1, M_1)$ where $(N_1, A_1, M_1) \leftarrow (N, A_0, M_0)$
2. $Z_0 \leftarrow M_0 \oplus C_0$
3. Parse Z_0 as $Z^* \parallel L^*$ where $|L^*|$ is the key length to compute Step 4
4. $T^* \leftarrow \mathsf{H}_{L^*}(A^*, M^*) \oplus R$
5. $\top \leftarrow$ AEAD-4b.$\mathsf{Ver}_K(N^*, A^*, C^*, T^*)$ where $N^* \leftarrow N$ and $C^* \leftarrow M^* \oplus Z^*$

INT-CTXT attack against DAEAD-2a

1. $(C_0, K') \leftarrow$ DAEAD-2a.$\mathsf{Enc}_K(A_1, M_1)$ where $(A_1, M_1) \leftarrow (A_0, M_0)$
2. $L^* \leftarrow M_0 \oplus C_0$
3. Compute (A^*, M^*) such that $\mathsf{fStr} = \mathsf{H}_{L^*}(A^*, M^*)$ with L^*
4. $\top \leftarrow$ DAEAD-2a.$\mathsf{Ver}_K(A^*, C^*, T^*)$ where $(C^*, T^*) \leftarrow (M^* \oplus \mathsf{msb}_{|M^*|}(L^*), K')$

Fig. 7. INT-CTXT attacks

INT-RUP attack against AEAD-2b

1. $(C, T) \leftarrow$ AEAD-2b.Enc$_K(N_1, A_1, M_1)$ where $(N_1, A_1, M_1) \leftarrow (N, A, M)$
2. Let c be an integer which is at least $|M|$ plus the hash key length of H
3. $Z' \leftarrow$ AEAD-2b.Dec$_K(N_1', A_1', C_1', T_1')$ where $(N_1', A_1', C_1', T_1') \leftarrow (N, A', 0^c, T')$
4. Parse Z' as $Z \parallel L$ where $|Z| = |M|$
5. $R \leftarrow$ H$_L(A, C) \oplus T$
6. Parse Z' as $Z^* \parallel L^*$ where $|Z^*| \le |Z|$
7. $T^* \leftarrow$ H$_{L^*}(A^*, C^*) \oplus R$ where $|C^*| = |Z^*|$
8. $\top \leftarrow$ AEAD-2b.Ver$_K(N^*, A^*, C^*, T^*)$ where $N^* \leftarrow N$

INT-RUP attack against DAEAD-$\{1, 2\}$

1. $M_1' \leftarrow$ DAEAD-$\{1, 2\}$.Dec$_K(A_1', C_1', T_1')$ where $(A_1', C_1', T_1') \leftarrow (A_1', C_1', V_0)$
2. $M_2' \leftarrow$ DAEAD-$\{1, 2\}$.Dec$_K(A_2', C_2', T_2')$ where $(A_2', C_2', T_2') \leftarrow (A_2', C_2', M_1' \oplus C_1')$
3. $\top \leftarrow$ DAEAD-$\{1, 2\}$.Ver$_K(A^*, C^*, T^*)$ where $(A^*, C^*, T^*) \leftarrow (A_0, M_0 \oplus M_2' \oplus C_2', T_2')$

Fig. 8. INT-RUP attacks

Proof. For any distinct $X', X \in \mathcal{D}_H$ and any $Y \in \{0, 1\}^n$, $\varphi(X)$ and $\varphi(X')$ are distinct, and we have

$$\Pr[H_L(X) \oplus H_L(X') = Y] = \Pr[\widetilde{H}_L(\varphi(X)) \oplus c \oplus \widetilde{H}_L(\varphi(X')) \oplus c = Y]$$
$$= \Pr[\widetilde{H}_L(\varphi(X)) \oplus \widetilde{H}_L(\varphi(X')) = Y] \le \epsilon.$$

Therefore, $\{H_L\}$ is also ϵ-AXU. □

There exists an ϵ-AXU hash function $\widetilde{H}_L$ such that $\widetilde{H}_L(A, M) = 0^n$ for $(A, M) = (\epsilon, \epsilon)$, e.g., GHASH function in GCM and Poly1305, and we use the proposition to respect the non-empty plaintext convention of the schemes in [18].

We are now ready to present the details of our attacks.

4.1   AEAD-$\{2a, 4a, 4b\}$ and DAEAD-2a Are Not INT-CTXT Secure

Attack against AEAD-2a. The hash function in AEAD-2a takes associated data A and a ciphertext C as input. Suppose that $\widetilde{H}_L$ is an ϵ-AXU hash function such that $\widetilde{H}_L \colon (\epsilon, \epsilon) \mapsto 0^n$. Let A_0 be any associated data and C_0 be any ciphertext such that $|C_0| = 1$, i.e., C_0 is a bit. We also assume that, given a hash key of length n bits, the adversary can compute the hash value for any input, e.g., Type-I hash functions like GHASH function. Define an injective function φ as follows.

$$\varphi(A, C) = \begin{cases} (\varepsilon, \varepsilon) & \text{if } (A, C) = (A_0, C_0) \\ (A_0, C_0) & \text{if } (A, C) = (\varepsilon, \varepsilon) \\ (A, C) & \text{otherwise} \end{cases} \tag{1}$$

Let $H_L(A, C) = \widetilde{H}_L(\varphi(A, C))$. Then H_L is an ϵ-AXU function from Proposition 1.

Now in the attack in Fig. 7, the adversary receives (C_1, T_1) for the first encryption query $(N_1, A_1, M_1) = (\text{fStr}, A_0, M_0)$, where $|M_0| = 1$. We see that $\Pr[C_1 = C_0]$ is approximately $1/2$. If $C_1 \neq C_0$, then the adversary fails to make a forgery. If $C_1 = C_0$, from $K' = \text{msb}_n(\text{SC}_K(\text{fStr}))$, $\varphi(A_0, C_0) = (\varepsilon, \varepsilon)$, and $\tilde{\text{H}}_L(\varepsilon, \varepsilon) = 0^n$, the adversary receives K' as the tag. Suppose that $K' \neq \text{fStr}$. For the second encryption query $(N_2, A_2, M_2) = (K', A_0, M_0)$, the adversary receives (C_2, T_2). $\Pr[C_2 = C_0]$ is approximately $1/2$, and if $C_2 \neq C_0$, then the adversary fails to make a forgery. If $C_2 = C_0$, from $L = \text{SC}_K(K')$ and $\text{H}_L(A_0, C_0) = 0^n$, the adversary receives the first n bits of the hash key L, called L^*. If $K' = \text{fStr}$, the hash key L^* is fStr. Therefore, the forgery (N^*, A^*, C^*, T^*), where $N^* = \text{fStr}$, is accepted with probability approximately $1/4$.

Attack against AEAD-4a. In AEAD-4a, the hash function takes A and M as input. Let $\tilde{\text{H}}_L$ be an ϵ-AXU hash function such that $\tilde{\text{H}}_L : (\varepsilon, \varepsilon) \mapsto 0^n$. Given a hash key of length n bits, we assume that the adversary can compute the hash value for any input. Let A_0 be any associated data and M_0 be any non-empty plaintext that will be used in the attack. Define an injective function φ as follows.

$$\varphi(A, M) = \begin{cases} (\varepsilon, \varepsilon) & \text{if } (A, M) = (A_0, M_0) \\ (A_0, M_0) & \text{if } (A, M) = (\varepsilon, \varepsilon) \\ (A, M) & \text{otherwise} \end{cases} \tag{2}$$

Let $\text{H}_L(A, M) = \tilde{\text{H}}_L(\varphi(A, M))$. Then H_L is an ϵ-AXU function from Proposition 1.

For the first encryption query $(N_1, A_1, M_1) = (\text{fStr}, A_0, M_0)$, from $K' = \text{msb}_n(\text{SC}_K(\text{fStr}))$, $\varphi(A_0, M_0) = (\varepsilon, \varepsilon)$, and $\tilde{\text{H}}_L(\varepsilon, \varepsilon) = 0^n$, the adversary receives K' as the tag. Suppose that $K' \neq \text{fStr}$. For the second encryption query $(N_2, A_2, M_2) = (K', A_0, M_0)$, the adversary receives the first n bits of the hash key L, which we write L^*, and can compute the tag $T^* \leftarrow \text{H}_{L^*}(A^*, M^*) \oplus K'$ without access to the encryption oracle. Here the length of M^* should be at most the length of M_0. If $\text{fStr} = K'$, then the hash key L^* is fStr. Therefore the forgery (N^*, A^*, C^*, T^*), where $N^* = \text{fStr}$ and $C^* \leftarrow M^* \oplus \text{msb}_{|M^*|}(M_1 \oplus C_1)$, is accepted with probability 1.

Attack against AEAD-4b. The hash function in AEAD-4b takes A and M as input. Suppose that $\tilde{\text{H}}_L$ is an ϵ-AXU hash function such that $\tilde{\text{H}}_L : (\varepsilon, \varepsilon) \mapsto 0^n$. Let A_0 be any associated data and M_0 be any non-empty plaintext. Define an injective function φ as in (2). Let $\text{H}_L(A, M) = \tilde{\text{H}}_L(\varphi(A, M))$. Then H_L is an ϵ-AXU function from Proposition 1. Let $N \in \{0, 1\}^n$ be an arbitrary nonce.

For the encryption query $(N_1, A_1, M_1) = (N, A_0, M_0)$, since we define $R = \text{msb}_n(\text{SC}_K(N))$, $\varphi(A_0, M_0) = (\varepsilon, \varepsilon)$, and $\tilde{\text{H}}_L(\varepsilon, \varepsilon) = 0^n$, the adversary receives R as the tag. Observe that we have $(R, Z_0, L) = \text{SC}_K(N)$. In the attack, we parse Z_0 as $Z_0 = Z^* \| L^*$, and use Z^* as the keystream and L^* as the hash key. Note that $Z_0 = M_0 \oplus C_0$ and hence the adversary can recover Z_0, and given L^*, the adversary can compute T^* for any (A^*, M^*). We remark that the length of L^* to compute Step 4 may depend on $|A^*|$ and $|M^*|$ if Type-II hash function is used, and the length of L^* can be arbitrarily long by using long

M_0. For any $M^* \in \{0,1\}^{|Z^*|}$, the adversary can compute the tag T^*. Hence the forgery (N^*, A^*, C^*, T^*), where $N^* = N$ and $C^* = M^* \oplus Z^*$, is accepted with probability 1.

Attack against DAEAD-2a. Suppose that $\widetilde{H}_L$ is an ϵ-AXU hash function such that $\widetilde{H}_L : (\varepsilon, \varepsilon) \mapsto 0^n$. We also assume that, given a hash key L^* and Y, we can compute some (A^*, M^*) such that $Y = H_{L^*}(A^*, M^*)$. Let A_0 be arbitrary associated data and M_0 be a plaintext. Define an injective function φ as in (2). We have a restriction on $|M_0|$, which is discussed below. Let $H_L(A, M) = \widetilde{H}_L(\varphi(A, M)) \oplus$ fStr. Then H_L is ϵ-AXU from Proposition 1.

For the encryption query $(A_1, M_1) = (A_0, M_0)$, from $\varphi(A_0, M_0) = (\varepsilon, \varepsilon)$ and $\widetilde{H}_L(\varepsilon, \varepsilon) = 0^n$, it follows that $H_L(A_0, M_0) =$ fStr. From $K' = \mathsf{msb}_n(\mathsf{SC}_K(\mathsf{fStr}))$, the adversary receives K' as the tag. From $\mathsf{SC}_K(K') = L$ and $M_0 \oplus C_0$, it obtains the first $|M_0|$ bits of L. Let L^* be the value of $\mathsf{msb}_{|M_0|}(L)$. The length of L^* has to be long enough so that the adversary can compute (A^*, M^*) such that $\mathsf{fStr} = H_{L^*}(A^*, M^*)$. Therefore, (A^*, C^*, T^*), where $(C^*, T^*) = (M^* \oplus \mathsf{msb}_{|M^*|}(L^*), K')$, is always accepted.

Comments. We note that, since the above schemes are not INT-CTXT secure, they are not INT-RUP secure, and these attacks contradict the claims in [18]. All the above attacks use the fixed point of the hash function. For example, given the security proof of AEAD-2, it is tempting to claim that AEAD-2a is also secure. However, the dependence of the generation of K' and (R, Z) within the encryption algorithm allows the adversary to reproduce K' within encryption, and the fixed point of the hash function makes it possible for the adversary to actually learn the value of K'. This type of discrepancy explains the success of the above attacks.

4.2   AEAD-2b and DAEAD-{1, 2} Are Not INT-RUP Secure

Attack against AEAD-2b. Suppose that H_L is ϵ-AXU. The values $N \in \{0,1\}^n$, $A \in \{0,1\}^*$, and $M \in \{0,1\}^*$ can be arbitrarily chosen, where $|M| \neq 0$.

For the encryption query $(N_1, A_1, M_1) = (N, A, M)$, the adversary receives (C, T). For the decryption query $(N'_1, A'_1, C'_1, T'_1) = (N, A', 0^c, T')$, where $A' \in \{0,1\}^*$ and $T' \in \{0,1\}^n$ may be arbitrarily chosen, the adversary receives Z' as the plaintext. Z' can be parsed into the keystream Z and the hash key L. Then the adversary can compute $R = H_L(A, C) \oplus T$ with L. We observe that Z' can also be parsed into another keystream Z^* and another hash key L^*. For any $A^* \in \{0,1\}^*$ and any $C^* \in \{0,1\}^{|Z^*|}$, the adversary can compute the tag as $T^* = H_{L^*}(A^*, C^*) \oplus R$. Therefore, (N^*, A^*, C^*, T^*), where $N^* = N$, is accepted with probability 1. Note that this attack does not rely on the fixed point of the hash function.

Attacks against DAEAD-{1, 2}. Suppose that H_L is an ϵ-AXU hash function such that $H_L(A_0, M_0) = V_0$ for any L, where $A_0 \in \{0,1\}^*$ and $M_0 \in \{0,1\}^n$ denote special input to produce the fixed point V_0. The values $A'_1, A'_2 \in \{0,1\}^*$ and $C'_1, C'_2 \in \{0,1\}^n$ can be arbitrarily chosen.

For the first decryption query $(A_1', C_1', T_1') = (A_1', C_1', V_0)$, the adversary receives the plaintext M_1'. Then the keystream is computed as $M_1' \oplus C_1'$. In fact, it is computed as the tag from $\mathsf{SC}_K(V_0)$. For the second decryption query $(A_2', C_2', T_2') = (A_2', C_2', M_1' \oplus C_1')$, the adversary receives the plaintext M_2'. For the verification query $(A^*, C^*, T^*) = (A_0, M_0 \oplus M_2' \oplus C_2', T_2')$, from $\mathsf{H}_L(A_0, M_0) = V_0$ and $T_2' = \mathsf{SC}_K(V_0)$, the forgery (A^*, C^*, T^*) is accepted with probability 1.

5   Positive Results

5.1   ChaCha20-Poly1305 Is INT-RUP Secure

Let $\mathcal{A}$ be an adversary. Suppose that $\mathcal{A}$ makes q encryption queries (N_1, A_1, M_1), $\ldots, (N_q, A_q, M_q)$, q' decryption queries $(N_1', A_1', C_1', T_1'), \ldots, (N_{q'}', A_{q'}', C_{q'}', T_{q'}')$, and q'' verification queries $(N_1'', A_1'', C_1'', T_1''), \ldots, (N_{q''}'', A_{q''}'', C_{q''}'', T_{q''}'')$. Define the maximum byte length of the message for the encryption queries and the verification queries as

$$16 \left(\max_{\substack{1 \le i \le q \\ 1 \le j \le q''}} \left\{ \left\lceil \frac{|A_i|}{128} \right\rceil + \left\lceil \frac{|M_i|}{128} \right\rceil \right\} \cup \left\{ \left\lceil \frac{|A_j''|}{128} \right\rceil + \left\lceil \frac{|C_j''|}{128} \right\rceil \right\} + 1 \right).$$

The security bound of ChaCha20-Poly1305 is given as follows. We note that we consider the case where CC_K is a random function and focus on the information theoretic case. However, it is standard to derive the corresponding complexity theoretic result. See for example [2].

Theorem 1. *Consider* CC&Poly, *where a random function* $F : \{0,1\}^{32} \times \{0,1\}^{128} \to \{0,1\}^{512}$ *is used as* CC_K. *Let* $\mathcal{A}$ *be an INT-RUP adversary that makes at most* q *encryption queries,* q' *decryption queries, and* q'' *verification queries, and the maximum byte length of the message for the encryption queries and the verification queries is at most* $\ell_{\max}$ *bytes. Then we have*

$$\mathbf{Adv}_{\mathsf{CC\&Poly}}^{\text{int-rup}}(\mathcal{A}) \le q'' \frac{8\lceil \ell_{\max}/16 \rceil}{2^{106}}.$$

A proof is presented in Appendix A. We note that the INT-CTXT security was proved by Procter in [14][1]. The above theorem shows that the security does not change even if the adversary is given access to the decryption oracle. We see that the adversary learns the keystream $M_i \oplus C_i$ by making an encryption query

---

[1] We remark that there is a minor gap in the proof in [14]. The proof introduces a hybrid (E^1, D^1) where the keystream is the output of a random function taking a nonce, and another hybrid (E^2, D^2) where the keystream is completely random for *both* encryption and decryption, and claims both hybrids are equivalent. This does not hold true in general since the keystream in a decryption query can be determined by an encryption query made before. However, as far as we see, the theorem statement stands.

(N_i, A_i, M_i). Intuitively, there is no additional information that the adversary can learn from the decryption oracle, since the decryption oracle simply allows the adversary to learn the keystream, which is already available from the encryption oracle.

5.2 AEAD-$\{1, 2, 3, 4\}$ Are INT-RUP Secure

The following theorem shows the security bounds of AEAD-$\{1, 2, 3, 4\}$. We focus on the information theoretic result, but the corresponding complexity theoretic result can be obtained in a standard way [2].

Theorem 2. *Let* $\mathrm{Rand}(n, \ell)$ *and* H *be the parameters of each AEAD scheme. Suppose that* $\{H_L\}$ *is* ϵ-*AXU. Let* $\mathcal{A}$ *be an INT-RUP adversary that makes at most* q *encryption queries,* q' *decryption queries, and* q'' *verification queries. Then we have the following security bounds:*

$$\mathbf{Adv}^{\text{int-rup}}_{\text{AEAD-1}[\mathrm{Rand}(n,\ell),\mathsf{H}]}(\mathcal{A}) \leq q''\epsilon, \tag{3}$$

$$\mathbf{Adv}^{\text{int-rup}}_{\text{AEAD-3}[\mathrm{Rand}(n,\ell),\mathsf{H}]}(\mathcal{A}) \leq q''\epsilon, \tag{4}$$

$$\mathbf{Adv}^{\text{int-rup}}_{\text{AEAD-2}[\mathrm{Rand}(n,\ell),\mathsf{H}]}(\mathcal{A}) \leq \frac{q + q' + q''}{2^n} + q''\epsilon, \text{ and} \tag{5}$$

$$\mathbf{Adv}^{\text{int-rup}}_{\text{AEAD-4}[\mathrm{Rand}(n,\ell),\mathsf{H}]}(\mathcal{A}) \leq \frac{q + q' + q''}{2^n} + q''\epsilon. \tag{6}$$

A proof is presented in [10].

6 Conclusions

In this paper, we analyzed the integrity of the authenticated encryption schemes that are based on stream ciphers and universal hash functions. Our attacks indicate that the use of fStr to reduce the number of secret keys requires careful handling in the security proof.

It would be interesting clarify the INT-RUP security of the remaining AEAD schemes shown as open in Table 1.

Acknowledgments. We thank the anonymous ProvSec 2016 reviewers and participants of Early Symmetric Crypto (ESC) 2015 for helpful comments. We also thank Palash Sarkar for insightful feedback on an earlier version of this paper. The work by Tetsu Iwata was supported in part by JSPS KAKENHI, Grant-in-Aid for Scientific Research (B), Grant Number 26280045.

A Proof of Theorem 1

We evaluate $\mathbf{Adv}^{\text{int-rup}}_{\text{CC\&Poly}}(\mathcal{A})$ following the game playing proof technique in [5]. Without loss of generality, we assume that $\mathcal{A}$ is deterministic and makes exactly q encryption queries, q' decryption queries, and q'' verification queries. Let

Game G_0
Initialize

1. forge $\leftarrow$ false; $F \xleftarrow{\$} \{f \mid f \colon \{0,1\}^{32} \times \{0,1\}^{96} \rightarrow \{0,1\}^{512}\}$

Oracle Encrypt(N, A, M)

2. $Z \leftarrow \mathbf{KSGen}(N, |M|)$
3. $C \leftarrow M \oplus Z$
4. $T \leftarrow \mathbf{Tag}(N, A, C)$
5. **return** (C, T)

Oracle Decrypt(N, A, C, T)

6. $Z \leftarrow \mathbf{KSGen}(N, |C|)$
7. $M \leftarrow C \oplus Z$
8. **return** M

Oracle Verify(N, A, C, T)

9. $T^* \leftarrow \mathbf{Tag}(N, A, C)$
10. **if** $T^* = T$ **then** forge $\leftarrow$ true; **return** $\top$
11. **return** $\bot$

Subroutine KSGen(N, l)

12. $m \leftarrow \lceil l/512 \rceil$
13. **for** $i \leftarrow 1$ **to** m **do**
14. $\quad Z[i] \leftarrow F(i, N)$
15. $Z[m] \leftarrow \mathsf{lsb}_{l \bmod 512}(Z[m])$
16. $Z \leftarrow \sum_{i=1}^{m} Z[i] \cdot 2^{512(i-1)}$
17. **return** Z

Subroutine Tag(N, A, C)

18. $s \parallel r \leftarrow \mathsf{lsb}_{256}(F(0, N))$ where $|r| = |s| = 128$
19. $l_1 \leftarrow 128\lceil |A|/128 \rceil$
20. $l_2 \leftarrow l_1 + 128\lceil |C|/128 \rceil$
21. $l_3 \leftarrow l_2 + 64$
22. $Y \leftarrow A$
23. $Y \leftarrow Y + C \cdot 2^{l_1}$
24. $Y \leftarrow Y + \lceil |A|/8 \rceil \cdot 2^{l_2}$
25. $Y \leftarrow Y + \lceil |C|/8 \rceil \cdot 2^{l_3}$
26. $T \leftarrow \mathsf{Poly}_{r,s}(Y)$
27. **return** T

Fig. 9. Game G_0 for the proof of Theorem 1

Game G_1
Initialize

1. forge $\leftarrow$ false; $\mathcal{N} \leftarrow \emptyset$

Oracle Encrypt(N, A, M)

2. $Z \leftarrow \mathbf{KSGen2}(N, |M|)$
3. $C \leftarrow M \oplus Z$
4. $T \leftarrow \mathbf{Tag}(N, A, C)$
5. **return** (C, T)

Oracle Decrypt(N, A, C, T)

6. $Z \leftarrow \mathbf{KSGen2}(N, |C|)$
7. $M \leftarrow C \oplus Z$
8. **return** M

Oracle Verify(N, A, C, T)

9. $T^* \leftarrow \mathbf{Tag2}(N, A, C)$
10. **if** $T^* = T$ **then** forge $\leftarrow$ true; **return** $\top$
11. **return** $\bot$

Subroutine KSGen2(N, l)

12. $m \leftarrow \lceil l/512 \rceil$
13. **for** $i \leftarrow 1$ **to** m **do**
14. $Z[i] \xleftarrow{\$} \{0, 1\}^{512}$
15.   **if** $(i, N) \in \mathcal{N}$ **then** $Z[i] \leftarrow F(i, N)$
16.   **else** $\mathcal{N} \leftarrow \mathcal{N} \cup \{(i, N)\}$
17. $F(i, N) \leftarrow Z[i]$
18. $Z[m] \leftarrow \mathsf{lsb}_{l \bmod 512}(Z[m])$
19. $Z \leftarrow \sum_{i=1}^{m} Z[i] \cdot 2^{512(i-1)}$
20. **return** Z

Subroutine Tag2(N, A, C)

21. $U \parallel s \parallel r \xleftarrow{\$} \{0, 1\}^{512}$ where $|r| = |s| = 128$
22. **if** $(0, N) \in \mathcal{N}$ **then** $U \parallel s \parallel r \leftarrow F(0, N)$
23. **else** $\mathcal{N} \leftarrow \mathcal{N} \cup \{(0, N)\}$
24. $F(0, N) \leftarrow U \parallel s \parallel r$
25. $l_1 \leftarrow 128 \lceil |A|/128 \rceil$
26. $l_2 \leftarrow l_1 + 128 \lceil |C|/128 \rceil$
27. $l_3 \leftarrow l_2 + 64$
28. $Y \leftarrow A$
29. $Y \leftarrow Y + C \cdot 2^{l_1}$
30. $Y \leftarrow Y + \lceil |A|/8 \rceil \cdot 2^{l_2}$
31. $Y \leftarrow Y + \lceil |C|/8 \rceil \cdot 2^{l_3}$
32. $T \leftarrow \mathsf{Poly}_{r,s}(Y)$
33. **return** T

Fig. 10. Game G_1. Keystreams and authentication keys are generated at random.

(N_i, A_i, M_i) for $i = 1, \ldots, q$, $(N'_{i'}, A'_{i'}, C'_{i'}, T'_{i'})$ for $i' = 1, \ldots, q'$, and $(N''_j, A''_j, C''_j, T''_j)$ for $j = 1, \ldots, q''$ denote the queries.

We define Game G_0 in Fig. 9. In Fig. 9, Game G_0 simulates the real oracles of ChaCha20-Poly1305 based on the random function F. Then we have

$$\mathbf{Adv}^{\text{int-rup}}_{\text{CC\&Poly}}(\mathcal{A}) = \Pr[\mathcal{A}^{G_0} \text{ sets forge}].$$

We next define Game G_1 in Fig. 10. Game G_1 simulates the oracles using the lazy sampling of F, where F is regarded as an array, and the array $F(X, Y)$ is initially undefined for all $(X, Y) \in \{0, 1\}^{32} \times \{0, 1\}^{96}$. Now since the function F produces the random values and the values are perfectly indistinguishable between Game G_0 and Game G_1, these games are identical. Hence

$$\Pr[\mathcal{A}^{G_0} \text{ sets forge}] = \Pr[\mathcal{A}^{G_1} \text{ sets forge}]. \tag{7}$$

We consider $\Pr[\mathcal{A}^{G_1} \text{ sets forge}]$. In Fig. 9, the authentication keys in verification queries are generated independently of the keystreams in decryption queries, and hence there are two cases to consider. We denote the polynomial hash function in Poly1305 [7] by H_r. If for the j-th verification query, it holds that $N''_j \neq N_i$ for all i, then (r''_j, s''_j) is uniformly distributed and independent of (r_i, s_i). Hence

$$\Pr[T^*_j = T''_j] = \Pr[H_{r''_j}(Y''_j) + s''_j \bmod 2^{128} = T''_j] = \frac{1}{2^{128}}.$$

Suppose that for the j-th verification query, we have $N''_j = N_i$ for some i. Then it follows that $(r''_j, s''_j) = (r_i, s_i)$. The event $T^*_j = T''_j$ is equivalent to

$$H_{r_i}(Y''_j) - H_{r_i}(Y_i) \bmod 2^{128} = T''_j - T_i \bmod 2^{128}. \tag{8}$$

Now if $(A''_j, C''_j) = (A_i, C_i)$, then we necessarily have $T''_j \neq T_i$ and hence (8) cannot hold. Therefore let $(A''_j, C''_j) \neq (A_i, C_i)$. Then, since H_r is ϵ-AΔU [7, Sect. 3], meaning that it has a small differential probability with respect to modulo 2^{128}, we have

$$\Pr[T^*_j = T''_j] = \Pr[H_{r_i}(Y''_j) - H_{r_i}(Y_i) \bmod 2^{128} = T''_j - T_i \bmod 2^{128}] \leq \epsilon.$$

Therefore, for each $j = 1, \ldots, q''$, we have $\Pr[T^*_j = T''_j] \leq \epsilon$. Following [7, Sect. 3], $\epsilon = (8\lceil \ell_{\max}/16 \rceil)/2^{106}$. Hence we have

$$\Pr[\mathcal{A}^{G_1} \text{ sets forge}] \leq q'' \frac{8\lceil \ell_{\max}/16 \rceil}{2^{106}}. \tag{9}$$

The claimed bound is obtained from (7) and (9). □

References

1. Andreeva, E., Bogdanov, A., Luykx, A., Mennink, B., Mouha, N., Yasuda, K.: How to securely release unverified plaintext in authenticated encryption. In: Sarkar, P., Iwata, T. (eds.) ASIACRYPT 2014. LNCS, vol. 8873, pp. 105–125. Springer, Heidelberg (2014). doi:10.1007/978-3-662-45611-8_6

2. Bellare, M., Kilian, J., Rogaway, P.: The security of the cipher block chaining message authentication code. J. Comput. Syst. Sci. **61**(3), 362–399 (2000)
3. Bellare, M., Namprempre, C.: Authenticated encryption: relations among notions and analysis of the generic composition paradigm. In: Okamoto, T. (ed.) ASIACRYPT 2000. LNCS, vol. 1976, pp. 531–545. Springer, Heidelberg (2000). doi:10.1007/3-540-44448-3_41
4. Bellare, M., Rogaway, P.: Encode-then-encipher encryption: how to exploit nonces or redundancy in plaintexts for efficient cryptography. In: Okamoto, T. (ed.) ASIACRYPT 2000. LNCS, vol. 1976, pp. 317–330. Springer, Heidelberg (2000). doi:10.1007/3-540-44448-3_24
5. Bellare, M., Rogaway, P.: The security of triple encryption and a framework for code-based game-playing proofs. In: Vaudenay, S. (ed.) EUROCRYPT 2006. LNCS, vol. 4004, pp. 409–426. Springer, Heidelberg (2006). doi:10.1007/11761679_25
6. Bellare, M., Rogaway, P., Wagner, D.: The EAX mode of operation. In: Roy, B., Meier, W. (eds.) FSE 2004. LNCS, vol. 3017, pp. 389–407. Springer, Heidelberg (2004). doi:10.1007/978-3-540-25937-4_25
7. Bernstein, D.J.: The Poly1305-AES message-authentication code. In: Gilbert, H., Handschuh, H. (eds.) FSE 2005. LNCS, vol. 3557, pp. 32–49. Springer, Heidelberg (2005). doi:10.1007/11502760_3
8. Bernstein, D.J.: ChaCha, a variant of Salsa20 (2008). DocumentID: 4027b5256e14b6796842e6d0f68b0b5e. http://cr.yp.to/papers.html#chacha
9. Black, J., Halevi, S., Krawczyk, H., Krovetz, T., Rogaway, P.: UMAC: fast and secure message authentication. In: Wiener, M. (ed.) CRYPTO 1999. LNCS, vol. 1666, pp. 216–233. Springer, Heidelberg (1999). doi:10.1007/3-540-48405-1_14
10. Imamura, K., Minematsu, K., Iwata, T.: Integrity Analysis of Authenticated Encryption Based on Stream Ciphers (Full version of this paper). Cryptology ePrint Archive, Report 2016 (2016). http://eprint.iacr.org/
11. McGrew, D.A., Viega, J.: The security and performance of the galois/counter mode (GCM) of operation. In: Canteaut, A., Viswanathan, K. (eds.) INDOCRYPT 2004. LNCS, vol. 3348, pp. 343–355. Springer, Heidelberg (2004). doi:10.1007/978-3-540-30556-9_27
12. Namprempre, C., Rogaway, P., Shrimpton, T.: Reconsidering generic composition. In: Nguyen, P.Q., Oswald, E. (eds.) EUROCRYPT 2014. LNCS, vol. 8441, pp. 257–274. Springer, Heidelberg (2014). doi:10.1007/978-3-642-55220-5_15
13. Nir, Y., Langley, A.: ChaCha20 and Poly1305 for IETF protocols. IRTF RFC 7539. https://tools.ietf.org/html/rfc7539
14. Procter, G.: A Security Analysis of the Composition of ChaCha20 and Poly1305. Cryptology ePrint Archive, Report 2014/613 (2014). http://eprint.iacr.org/
15. Rogaway, P.: Authenticated-encryption with associated-data. In: Atluri, V. (ed.), ACM Conference on Computer and Communications Security, pp. 98–107. ACM (2002)
16. Rogaway, P.: Nonce-based symmetric encryption. In: Roy, B., Meier, W. (eds.) FSE 2004. LNCS, vol. 3017, pp. 348–358. Springer, Heidelberg (2004). doi:10.1007/978-3-540-25937-4_22
17. Rogaway, P., Shrimpton, T.: A provable-security treatment of the key-wrap problem. In: Vaudenay, S. (ed.) EUROCRYPT 2006. LNCS, vol. 4004, pp. 373–390. Springer, Heidelberg (2006). doi:10.1007/11761679_23
18. Sarkar, P.: Modes of operations for encryption and authentication using stream ciphers supporting an initialisation vector. Crypt. Commun. **6**(3), 189–231 (2014)
19. Whiting, D., Housley, R., Ferguson, N.: Counter with CBC-MAC (CCM). Submission to NIST (2002). http://csrc.nist.gov/

Secure and Efficient Construction of Broadcast Encryption with Dealership

Kamalesh Acharya[✉] and Ratna Dutta

Department of Mathematics, Indian Institute of Technology,
Kharagpur 721302, Kharagpur, India
kamaleshiitkgp@gmail.com, ratna@maths.iitkgp.ernet.in

Abstract. Broadcast encryption with dealership (BED) has been proposed to achieve more innovative and scalable business models for broadcast services. It has an extensive application future. However, designing secure BED is a challenging task. The only known BED construction so far is by Gritti et al. We aim to raise the profile of BED primitives which has not received much attention despite of its importance. This paper presents a *selectively* chosen plaintext attack (CPA) secure BED scheme supporting *maximum number of accountability* and *privacy* (hides the group of users from broadcaster). Our scheme is a key encapsulation mechanism and practically more efficient. It reduces the parameter sizes and computation cost compared to Gritti et al. More interestingly, the broadcaster does not need to rely on users to detect the dishonest dealer. We provide concrete security analysis of our design under reasonable assumptions.

Keywords: Broadcast encryption with dealership · Chosen plaintext attack · Maximum number of accountability · Privacy

1 Introduction

The increasing interests in the wide application of e-commerce raises issues regarding unauthorised distributions and use of digital content. Broadcast encryption provides enhanced confidentiality in the setting of practical threats against content distribution systems. Broadcast encryption was formally introduced by Fiat and Naor [8] in 1994, followed by a vast literature in various flavours [1–7,9,11–13].

Broadcast encryption with dealership (BED), introduced by Gritti et al. [10], is a promising cryptographic primitive which has been developed very recently. It has greatly facilitated with sufficiently fine grained business model in broadcast environment. The core concept in BED is to enable a dealer to select the set of subscribed users and publishing a group token together with a threshold value on the group size. A broadcaster implicitly verifies the size of the group utilizing the group token without knowing the group explicitly. The broadcaster aborts if the group size exceeds the threshold value, otherwise produces a ciphertext.

Designing BED is not trivial mainly due to the difficulty in achieving the following three security issues:

© Springer International Publishing AG 2016
L. Chen and J. Han (Eds.): ProvSec 2016, LNCS 10005, pp. 277–295, 2016.
DOI: 10.1007/978-3-319-47422-9_16

(i) *Maximum number of accountability:* Dealer should not be able to cheat. If a dishonest dealer selects $k' > k$ users and pays money for k users to the broadcaster, then the business of the broadcaster will be ruined.

(ii) *Privacy:* The dealer should be able to keep the subscribed user set secret from the broadcaster. Otherwise, the broadcaster can directly approach to the subscribers and damage the business of the dealer.

(iii) *Security against illegal users:* Illegal users (including dealers) should not be able to decrypt the encrypted digital content (ciphertext) similar to other broadcast encryption schemes.

Efficiency is always the first priority in obtaining practical BED. Low cost delivery of content is a major challenge in this context apart from achieving the aforementioned security attributes.

Interest in designing BED primitives is due to its applications in the real world. It could solve several problems of security and trust. For instance, suppose a dealer purchases the access of some encrypted digital contents from the service provider (broadcaster) in a bulk and resells them to the subscribers with a better price compared to the broadcaster's price for individual content. The subscribers thus enjoy the cheaper rate. The dealer keeps the identities of these subscribers secret from the broadcaster to protect his business. On the other hand, the dealer should be made incapable of decrypting the digital content to forbid him from rebroadcasting the content. In the light of the above application requirements, BED is useful.

So far as we know, BED has received very little attention despite of its numerous applications in the real world. Our goal is to develop this direction of research further by finding more practical and more efficient solutions towards BED. Principally, a BED makes the existing business model more flexible by creating new business opportunities for the dealers. A local dealer can better explore potentially unknown markets for service provider (broadcaster) and make a strategy according to the market. In addition, the dealer can also help in handling different pricing structures of media in different countries and share with the broadcaster any information on price or demand fluctuation cost. The dealer gets commission from the broadcaster and eventually sale of company increases.

Our contribution: Considering the limited development in the area of broadcast encryption in dealership framework, BED is further studied in this paper. The closest related work to ours is that of Gritti et al. [10]; indeed their work was starting point of ours. However, in the attempt made by [10], the broadcaster does not have the full control to detect illegal behaviour of a dealer as the components of the group token generated by the dealer are not fully binded. A dishonest dealer could easily manipulate some components of a group token $P(G)$ in such a way that the implicit verification of the size of group G by the broadcaster succeeds without following the actual protocol. In fact, in Sect. 2.3 we elaborate this issue. The broadcaster has to release the encrypted content once the verification passes and rely on the response from the user side who has given the power to detect a dishonest dealer on completion of the protocol. This is not a good solution as user may be dishonest themselves, thereby hampering the broadcaster's interest. The construction of [10] is claimed to achieve unconditional privacy. Unfortunately, the argument in the security proof provided to support unconditional privacy allows illegal users to recover messages, thereby leading to a contradiction to semantic security in semi-static security model. We put more light on this in Sect. 2.3. We emphasize that in our scheme, the components of group token are skillfully formed to enable the broadcaster to have full control in detecting the dishonest behaviour of a dealer.

Our BED construction, namely KEMD, adapts key encapsulation mechanism and reduces the parameter sizes and computation cost over the existing scheme [10] significantly. Our construction based upon the identity based encryption scheme of Delerablee et al. [5]. The scheme provides computational *privacy* under the discrete logarithm problem. It is proven to achieve *key indistinguishability* under chosen plaintext attack (CPA) in selective model assuming the hardness of the (f, ϕ, F)-General Decisional Diffie-Hellman Exponent $((f, \phi, F)$-GDDHE) problem. Furthermore, it supports *maximum number of accountability* under the (f, N)-Diffie-Hellman Exponent assumption. In addition, if a user gets revoked from the system, he will be unable to decrypt the ciphertext similar to other broadcast encryption schemes. The dealer can select a new group of users without changing the existing public parameter and secret key.

Organization: The rest of the paper is organized as follows. Section 2 provides necessary definitions and background materials. We describe our main construction in Sect. 3 and its security in Sect. 4. Efficiency and comparison with the existing work is presented in Sect. 5. We finally conclude in Sect. 6.

2   Preliminaries

Notation: We use the notation $x \in_R S$ to denote x is a random element of S and λ to represent bit size of prime integer p. Also, we use $[m]$ to denote integers from 1 to m and $[a, b]$ to denote integers from a to b. Let $\epsilon : \mathbb{N} \to \mathbb{R}$ be a function, where $\mathbb{N}$ and $\mathbb{R}$ are the sets of natural and real number respectively. The function ϵ is said to be a *negligible function* if $\exists\, d \in \mathbb{N}$ such that $\epsilon(\lambda) \leq \frac{1}{\lambda^d}$. Let $|G|$ denotes the cardinality of group G.

2.1   Broadcast Encryption with Dealership

Syntax of KEMD: A key encapsulation mechanism with dealership scheme KEMD = (KEMD.Setup, KEMD.KeyGen, KEMD.GroupGen, KEMD.Verify, KEMD. Encrypt, KEMD.Decrypt) consists of four probabilistic polynomial time (PPT) algorithms - KEMD.Setup, KEMD.KeyGen, KEMD.GroupGen, KEMD.Encrypt and two deterministic polynomial time algorithms - KEMD.Verify, KEMD.Decrypt. Formally, KEMD is described as follows:

- $(\mathsf{PP}, \mathsf{MK}) \leftarrow \mathsf{KEMD.Setup}(N, \lambda)$: The PKGC takes as input the total number of users N in the system and security parameter λ and constructs the public parameter PP and a master key MK. It makes PP public and keeps MK secret to itself.

- $(sk_i) \leftarrow$ KEMD.KeyGen(PP, MK, i): Taking as input PP, MK and a subscribed user i, the PKGC generates a secret key sk_i of user i and sends sk_i to user i through a secure communication channel between PKGC and user i.
- $(P(G), k) \leftarrow$ KEMD.GroupGen(PP, G): The dealer selects a set of subscribed users G and generates a group token $P(G)$ using PP. It outputs a threshold value k, where $|G| \leq k$. The dealer sends G to each subscribed user $u \in G$ through a secure communication channel between them. Subscribed users keep G secret.
- $(0 \vee 1) \leftarrow$ KEMD.Verify($P(G)$, PP, k): The broadcaster verifies implicitly group size $|G| \leq k$ using $P(G)$, PP, k and sets

$$\text{KEMD.Verify}(P(G), \text{PP}, k) = \begin{cases} 1, & \text{if } |G| \leq k \\ 0, & \text{otherwise.} \end{cases}$$

If the verification fails i.e., KEMD.Verify($P(G)$, PP, k) $= 0$, the broadcaster aborts.

- (Hdr, K) $\leftarrow$ KEMD.Encrypt($P(G)$, PP): Taking as input $P(G)$ and PP, the broadcaster produces a header Hdr and a session key K. It makes the header Hdr public and keeps the session key K secret to itself. This session key K can be used to generate a ciphertext for a message using a symmetric key encryption algorithm.
- $(K) \leftarrow$ KEMD.Decrypt(PP, sk_i, Hdr, G): A subscribed user i with secret key sk_i outputs the session key K using PP, Hdr and subscribed user set G.

Correctness: The scheme KEMD is said to be correct if the session key K can be retrieved from the header Hdr by any subscribed user in G. Suppose (PP, MK) $\leftarrow$ KEMD.Setup(N, λ), $(P(G), k) \leftarrow$ KEMD.GroupGen(PP, G), (Hdr, K) $\leftarrow$ KEMD.Encrypt($P(G)$, PP). Then for every subscribed user $i \in G$,

$$\text{KEMD.Decrypt}\Big(\text{PP}, \text{KEMD.KeyGen}(\text{PP}, \text{MK}, i), \text{Hdr}, G\Big) = K.$$

2.2   Security Framework

⟨I⟩**Privacy:** We define the privacy of the subscribed user set G of the protocol KEMD using the game as in Fig. 1 between an adversary $\mathcal{A}$ and a challenger $\mathcal{C}$. We have followed privacy model of [10].

The advantage of the adversary $\mathcal{A}$ in the privacy game is defined as $Adv_{\mathcal{A}}^{\text{KEMD-P}}$ $=|Pr(b^{'} = b) - \frac{1}{2}|$. The probability is taken over random bits used by $\mathcal{C}$ and $\mathcal{A}$.

Definition 1. *The BED scheme* KEMD *is said to be* (T, ϵ)-*secure under group privacy issue, if* $Adv_{\mathcal{A}}^{\text{KEMD-P}} \leq \epsilon$ *for every PPT adversary* $\mathcal{A}$ *with running time at most* T.

Setup: The challenger $\mathcal{C}$ runs KEMD.Setup(N, λ) to generate the public parameter PP and master key MK. It sends PP to $\mathcal{A}$.

Challenge: The adversary $\mathcal{A}$ selects two sets of users G_0, G_1 of same size and submits G_0, G_1 to $\mathcal{C}$. The challenger $\mathcal{C}$ chooses $b \in_R \{0, 1\}$, generates a group token $P(G_b)$ by running KEMD.GroupGen(PP, G_b) and sends $P(G_b)$ to $\mathcal{A}$.

Guess: The adversary $\mathcal{A}$ outputs a guess $b' \in \{0, 1\}$ of b and wins if $b' = b$.

Fig. 1. Privacy of protocol KEMD.

⟨II⟩**Maximum Number of Accountability:** The security game between an adversary $\mathcal{A}$ and a challenger $\mathcal{C}$ addressing maximum number of accountability of the protocol KEMD follows the model in [10] and described in Fig. 2. The adversary $\mathcal{A}$'s advantage in the game for maximum number of accountability is defined as $Adv_{\mathcal{A}}^{\mathsf{KEMD\text{-}M}} = |(Pr(\mathsf{KEMD.Verify}(P(G^*), \mathsf{PP}, k)) = 1) - \frac{1}{2}|$ where $k < |G^*|$. The probability is taken over random bits used by $\mathcal{C}$ and $\mathcal{A}$.

Definition 2. *The BED scheme* KEMD *is said to be* (T, ϵ)-*secure under maximum number of accountability, if* $Adv_{\mathcal{A}}^{\mathsf{KEMD\text{-}M}} \leq \epsilon$ *for every PPT adversary* $\mathcal{A}$ *with running time at most* T.

⟨III⟩**Key indistinguishability of KEMD under CPA**: We have followed [5] to design key indistinguishability against CPA security model. Selective security of the scheme KEMD is measured under the following key indistinguishability game played between a challenger $\mathcal{C}$ and an adversary $\mathcal{A}$:

Initialization: The adversary $\mathcal{A}$ selects a recipient set G and sends to $\mathcal{C}$.

Setup: The challenger $\mathcal{C}$ generates (PP,MK) ← KEMD.Setup(N, λ). It keeps the master key MK secret to itself and makes the public parameter PP public.

Phase 1: The adversary $\mathcal{A}$ sends key generation queries for $i_1, \ldots, i_m \notin G$ to $\mathcal{C}$ and receives the secret key sk_i ← KEMD.KeyGen$(\mathsf{PP}, \mathsf{MK}, i)$ for user $i \in \{i_1, \ldots, i_m\}$.

Challenge: The challenger $\mathcal{C}$ generates (Hdr, K) ← Encrypt$(P(G), \mathsf{PP})$, where $(P(G), k)$ ← KEMD.GroupGen(PP, G). It selects $b \in_R \{0, 1\}$ and sets $K_b = K$, K_{1-b} a random value. Finally, $\mathcal{C}$ returns Hdr, K_0, K_1 to $\mathcal{A}$.

Phase 2: This is similar to Phase 1 key generation queries. The adversary $\mathcal{A}$ sends key generation queries for $i_{m+1}, \ldots, i_q \notin G$ to $\mathcal{C}$ and receives the secret key sk_i ← KEMD.KeyGen$(\mathsf{PP}, \mathsf{MK}, i)$ for $i \in \{i_{m+1}, \ldots, i_q\}$.

Guess: The adversary $\mathcal{A}$ outputs a guess $b' \in \{0, 1\}$ of b and wins if $b' = b$.

Let t be the number of corrupted users and N be the total number of users. Adversary is allowed to get reply up to t key generation queries. In random oracle model t is number of hash queries and key generation queries. The adversary $\mathcal{A}$'s advantage in the above security game is defined as $Adv_{\mathcal{A}}^{\mathsf{KEMD\text{-}INDK}}(t, N) = |2Pr(b' = b) - 1| = |Pr[b' = 1|b = 1] - Pr[b' = 1|b = 0]|$. The probability is taken over random bits used by $\mathcal{C}$ and $\mathcal{A}$.

Definition 3. *Let* $Adv^{\text{KEMD-INDK}}(t, N) = \underset{\mathcal{A}}{max} \left[Adv_{\mathcal{A}}^{\text{KEMD-INDK}}(t, N) \right]$, *where maximum is taken over all PPT algorithm running in poly(λ) (polynomial of λ) time. The BED scheme* KEMD *is said to be* (t, N)- *secure if* $Adv^{\text{KEMD-INDK}} = \epsilon(\lambda)$, *where* $\epsilon(\lambda)$ *is a negligible function in security parameter* λ.

Setup: The challenger $\mathcal{C}$ runs KEMD.Setup(N, λ) and generates public parameter PP and master key MK. It sends PP to $\mathcal{A}$.
Challenge: The challenger $\mathcal{C}$ sends an integer k to $\mathcal{A}$.
Guess: The adversary $\mathcal{A}$ computes $P(G^*)$, with $|G^*| > k$ by running KEMD.GroupGen(PP, G^*) and sends $(P(G^*), G^*)$ to $\mathcal{C}$.
Win: The challenger $\mathcal{C}$ outputs $(P(G^*), G^*)$ if KEMD.Verify($P(G^*)$, PP, k) = 1; otherwise $\mathcal{C}$ aborts.

Fig. 2. Maximum number of accountability of protocol KEMD.

2.3   The Drawbacks of [10]

We provide the overview of the BED construction of Gritti et al. [10] in Appendix A. In BED scheme of [10], the dealer generates the group token as

$$P(G) = \left(w_1, w_2, w_3, w_4, w_5, w_6 \right)$$

$$= \left(u_0^{t_1 \prod_{i \in G}(x_i + \alpha)}, v_0^{t_1 \prod_{i \in G}(x_i + \alpha)}, v_{N-k}^{t_1 \prod_{i \in G}(x_i + \alpha)}, \prod_{i \in G} f_i^{t_2}, g^{t_2}, e(g^\gamma, g)^{t_2} \right).$$

Here $e : \mathbb{G} \times \mathbb{G} \to \mathbb{G}_1$ is bilinear mapping from source group $\mathbb{G}$ with generator g to target group $\mathbb{G}_1$, $u_i = h^{\gamma \alpha^i}$, $v_i = h^{\gamma \beta \alpha^i}$ for $i \in [0, N]$, $\alpha, \beta, \gamma, t_1, t_2 \in_R \mathbb{Z}_p$, $h \in_R \mathbb{G}$, public key of user i is $PK_i = (x_i + \alpha, f_i)$, $x_i \in_R \mathbb{Z}_p$, $f_i \in_R \mathbb{G}$, the group $G = \{i_1, i_2, \ldots, i_{k'}\} \in (\mathbb{Z}_p)^{k'}$, $k' \leq k$. The broadcaster verifies whether group size is $\leq k$ by checking $e(w_2, g_N) = e(w_3, g_k)$. It generates a ciphertext for message $M \in \mathbb{G}_1$ as $(w_5^r, w_4^r, M w_6^r)$ where $r \in_R \mathbb{Z}_p$. Note that the broadcaster does not involve w_1, w_2, w_3 in ciphertext components. A dishonest dealer can generate w_1, w_2, w_3 for less than k users while creating w_4, w_5, w_6 for greater than k users. In decryption phase, a user checks the group size that is received from the dealer during group token generation. If it is greater than k, then the user informs this to the broadcaster. The dealer will be blacklisted and excluded from further business. Consequently, the broadcaster does not have the full control on determining the dishonest dealer and has to rely on user's response to stop release of further encrypted content.

In the *privacy* proof, Gritti et al. [10] argued that group privacy is preserved unconditionally since for each group of receivers G, there is a group G' of same size such that $P(G) = P(G')$. This argument in fact incorrect. It is not sufficient to show that there exists a group G', since the adversary is allowed to choose

G_0 and G_1. It is required to prove that $P(G_b) = P(G_{1-b})$, $b \in \{0,1\}$ for a group G_b. They have proved $P(G_b) = P(G_{b'})$ where $G_{b'}$ may not be equal to G_{1-b}. If unconditional privacy holds, then $P(G) = P(G')$ for all pairs of groups of same size with $G \neq G'$. Then the members of G' would also be able to decrypt the ciphertext generated using $P(G)$ as $P(G) = P(G')$. But if G is the set of legal users, then a user in $G' \setminus G$ is not entitled to decrypt the ciphertext using $P(G)$. This contradicts the semantic security against illegal users.

2.4   Complexity Assumptions

Definition 4 *(Bilinear Map).* *Let* $\mathbb{G}$ *and* $\mathbb{G}_1$ *be two multiplicative groups of prime order* p. *Let* g *be a generator of* $\mathbb{G}$. *A bilinear map* $e : \mathbb{G} \times \mathbb{G} \longrightarrow \mathbb{G}_1$ *is a function having the following properties:*

1. $e(u^a, v^b) = e(u,v)^{ab}$, $\forall\ u,v \in \mathbb{G}$ *and* $\forall\ a,b \in \mathbb{Z}_p$.
2. *The map is non-degenerate, i.e.,* $e(g,g)$ *is a generator of* $\mathbb{G}_1$.
   The tuple $\mathbb{S} = (p, \mathbb{G}, \mathbb{G}_1, e)$ *is called a prime order bilinear group system.*

⟨ A ⟩ The Discrete Logarithm (DL) Assumption:
  Input: $\langle Z = (g^\alpha, g) \rangle$, *where* g *is a generator of* $\mathbb{G}$, $\alpha \in_R \mathbb{Z}_p$.
  Output: α
  Definition 5. *The* (T, ϵ)-DL *assumption holds if for every PPT adversary* $\mathcal{A}$ *with running time at most* T, *the advantage of solving the above problem is at most* ϵ, *i.e.,* $Adv_{\mathcal{A}}^{\mathsf{DL}} = |Pr[\mathcal{A}(Z) = \alpha]| \leq \epsilon(\lambda)$, *where* $\epsilon(\lambda)$ *is a negligible function in security parameter* λ.

⟨ B ⟩ The (f, l)-Diffie-Hellman Exponent $((f, l)$-DHE) Assumption [10]:
  Input: $\langle Z = (\mathbb{S}, g, g^\alpha, \dots, g^{\alpha^l}) \rangle$, *where* g *is generator of* $\mathbb{G}$, $\alpha \in_R \mathbb{Z}_p$.
  Output: $f(x)$ *and* $g^{f(\alpha)}$ *where* $f(x)$ *is polynomial of degree* $l' > l$.
  Definition 6. *The* (f, l)-DHE *assumption holds with* (T, ϵ) *if for every PPT adversary* $\mathcal{A}$ *with running time at most* T, *the advantage of solving the above problem is at most* ϵ, *i.e.,* $Adv_{\mathcal{A}}^{(f,l)-\mathsf{DHE}} = |Pr[\mathcal{A}(Z) = (f(x), g^{f(\alpha)})]| \leq \epsilon(\lambda)$, *where* $\epsilon(\lambda)$ *is a negligible function in security parameter* λ *and* $f(x)$ *is polynomial of degree* $l' > l$.

⟨ C ⟩ The (f, ϕ, F)-General Decisional Diffie-Hellman Exponent $((f, \phi, F)$-GDDHE) Assumption [5]:
  Input: $\langle Z = (\mathbb{S}, f(x), \phi(x), h_0, h_0^\alpha, h_0^{\alpha^2}, \dots, h_0^{\alpha^{t-1}}, h_0^{\alpha f(\alpha)}, h_0^{k\alpha f(\alpha)}, g_0, g_0^\alpha, g_0^{\alpha^2},$
  $\dots, g_0^{\alpha^{2N}}, g_0^{k\phi(\alpha)}), K \rangle$, *where* g_0, h_0 *are generators of* $\mathbb{G}, \alpha \in_R \mathbb{Z}_p, f(x) = \prod_{i=1}^{t}(x + x_i)$, $\phi(x) = \prod_{i=t+1}^{t+N}(x + x_i)$, $x_i \in \mathbb{Z}_p$ *for* $i \in [t + N]$ *are distinct,* K *is either* $e(g_0, h_0)^{F(\alpha)}$ *where* $F(\alpha) = kf(\alpha)$ *or a random element* $X \in \mathbb{G}_1$.
  Output: Yes *if* $K = e(g_0, h_0)^{kf(\alpha)}$; No *otherwise.*
  Definition 7. *The* (f, ϕ, F)-GDDHE *assumption holds with* (T, ϵ) *if for every PPT adversary* $\mathcal{A}$ *with running time at most* T, *the advantage of solving the above problem is at most* ϵ, *i.e.,* $Adv_{\mathcal{A}}^{(f,\phi,F)-\mathsf{GDDHE}} = |Pr[\mathcal{A}(Z, K = e(g_0, h_0)^{kf(\alpha)}) = 1] - Pr[\mathcal{A}(Z, K = X) = 1]| \leq \epsilon(\lambda)$, *where* $\epsilon(\lambda)$ *is a negligible function in security parameter* λ *and* X *is random element of* $\mathbb{G}_1$.

3   Our KEMD Construction

Our key encapsulation mechanism with dealership KEMD = (KEMD.Setup, KEMD. KeyGen, KEMD. GroupGen, KEMD.Verify, KEMD.Encrypt, KEMD. Decrypt) is described as follows:

- $(PP, MK) \leftarrow$ KEMD.Setup(N, λ): Given the security parameter λ and public identity ID $= \{ID_1, ID_2, \ldots, ID_N\} \in (\mathbb{Z}^+)^N$ of a group of N users, the PKGC generates the public parameter PP and a master key MK as follows:
  1. Chooses a prime order bilinear group system $\mathbb{S} = (p, \mathbb{G}, \mathbb{G}_1, e)$, where $\mathbb{G}, \mathbb{G}_1$ are groups of prime order p and $e : \mathbb{G} \times \mathbb{G} \to \mathbb{G}_1$ is a bilinear mapping. Let g, h be generators of group $\mathbb{G}$ and $H : \{0,1\}^* \to \mathbb{Z}_p^*$ be a cryptographically secure hash function.
  2. Selects $\alpha \in_R \mathbb{Z}_p$ and sets a master key MK and public parameter PP as MK $= (\alpha, h)$, PP $= (\mathbb{S}, g, g_1, \ldots, g_N, v = e(g, h), w = h^\alpha, H, \text{ID})$, where $g_i = g^{\alpha^i}$ for $i \in [1, N]$.
  3. Keeps MK secret to itself and makes PP public.

  Note that the public identity of the user i is $ID_i \in \mathbb{Z}^+$ for $i \in [N]$.

- $(sk_u) \leftarrow$ KEMD.KeyGen(PP, MK, u): For each user $u \in [N]$, the PKGC extracts α, h from MK and ID_u from PP, generates a secret key as $sk_u = h^{\frac{1}{\alpha + H(ID_u)}}$ and sends it to user u through a secure communication channel between them.
- $(P(G), k) \leftarrow$ KEMD.GroupGen(PP, G): The dealer selects a group of users $G = \{i_1, i_2, \ldots, i_{k'}\} \subseteq [N]$ and performs the following using PP:
  1. Sets a polynomial $F(x) = \prod_{i_j \in G} (x + H(ID_{i_j})) = \sum_{i=0}^{k'} F_i x^i$, where F_i's are function of $H(ID_j)$ for $j \in G$.
  2. Picks $t_1 \in_R \mathbb{Z}_p$ and generates the group token $P(G) = (w_1, w_2, w_3, w_4)$ by setting

  $$w_1 = w^{-t_1} = h^{-\alpha t_1}, \quad w_2 = \prod_{i=0}^{k'} g_{N-k+i}^{t_1 F_i} = g_{N-k}^{\sum_{i=0}^{k'} t_1 \alpha^i F_i} = g_{N-k}^{t_1 F(\alpha)},$$

  $$w_3 = g^{t_1 F_0} \prod_{i=1}^{k'} g_i^{t_1 F_i} = g^{\sum_{i=0}^{k'} t_1 \alpha^i F_i} = g^{t_1 F(\alpha)}, \quad w_4 = v^{t_1} = e(g, h)^{t_1}$$

  where w, g_i, for $i \in [1, k']$ and v are extracted from PP.
  3. Selects a threshold value k on the group size G where $k \geq k' = |G|$.
  4. Sends G to each subscribed user through a secure communication channel between the user and the dealer. The subscribed users keep G secret to themselves.
  5. Publishes $P(G)$ together with the threshold value k.
- $(0 \vee 1) \leftarrow$ KEMD.Verify$(P(G), PP, k)$: Taking as input the group token $P(G) = (w_1, w_2, w_3, w_4)$, the threshold value k, and g_k, g_N extracted from PP, the broadcaster setsKEMD.Verify$(P(G), PP, k) = \begin{cases} 1, & \text{if } e(w_2, g_k) = e(w_3, g_N) \\ 0, & \text{otherwise.} \end{cases}$

Notice that, $e(w_2, g_k) = e(g_{N-k}^{t_1 F(\alpha)}, g_k) = e\left(\prod_{i=0}^{k'} g^{(t_1 \alpha^{N-k+i} \cdot F_i)}, g^{\alpha^k} \right)$

$$= e(g,g)^{t_1 \alpha^k \left(\sum_{i=0}^{k'} \alpha^{N-k+i} \cdot F_i \right)} = e(g,g)^{t_1 \left(\sum_{i=0}^{k'} \alpha^{N+i} \cdot F_i \right)},$$

and, $e(w_3, g_N) = e(g^{t_1 F(\alpha)}, g_N) = e(g,g)^{t_1 \left(\sum_{i=0}^{k'} \alpha^{N+i} \cdot F_i \right)}$.

If the verification fails i.e., KEMD.Verify$(P(G), \mathsf{PP}, k) = 0$, the broadcaster aborts. We point down here that only two components namely w_2, w_3 of $P(G)$ are used during this verification process.

- (Hdr, K)←KEMD.Encrypt$(P(G), \mathsf{PP})$: Using PP and $P(G) = (w_1, w_2, w_3, w_4)$ with KEMD.Verify$(P(G), \mathsf{PP}, k) = 1$, the broadcaster does the following:
  1. Chooses an integer $r \in_R \mathbb{Z}_p$ and sets a session key K, header Hdr as

$$K = w_4^r = e(g,h)^{t_1 r}, \mathsf{Hdr} = (C_1, C_2) = \left(w_1^r, w_3^r \right) = \left(h^{-\alpha r t_1}, g^{r t_1 F(\alpha)} \right).$$

  2. Finally, publishes Hdr and keeps K secret to itself.

Note that this encryption process utilizes the two components w_1, w_4 of $P(G)$, together with w_3 which has already been used in combination with w_2 and passed the verification in procedure KEMD.Verify successfully.

- (K)←KEMD.Decrypt$(\mathsf{PP}, sk_u, \mathsf{Hdr}, G)$: A subscribed user u with secret key sk_u, uses PP, the header Hdr $= (C_1, C_2)$, the set of subscribed users G and recovers the session key K as $K = \left(e(C_1, g^{P_{u,G(\alpha)}}) e(sk_u, C_2) \right)^{\frac{1}{\prod_{j \in G, j \neq u} H(ID_j)}}$ where $P_{u,G(\alpha)} = \frac{1}{\alpha}\{ \prod_{j \in G, j \neq u} (\alpha + H(ID_j)) - \prod_{j \in G, j \neq u} H(ID_j) \}$.

Observe that $g^{P_{u,G(\alpha)}}$ is computable with the knowledge of G as follows: The expression $\{ \prod_{j \in G, j \neq u} (\alpha + H(ID_j)) - \prod_{j \in G, j \neq u} H(ID_j) \}$ is a polynomial of degree $(k' - 1)$ in α without a constant term where $k' = |G|$ and thus the expression $\frac{1}{\alpha}\{ \prod_{j \in G, j \neq u} (\alpha + H(ID_j)) - \prod_{j \in G, j \neq u} H(ID_j) \} = \sum_{i=0}^{k'-2} a_i \alpha^i$ is a polynomial of degree $(k' - 2)$ in α. Here a_i, $i \in [0, k'-2]$ are constants and are functions of $H(ID_j)$ where $j \in G, j \neq u$. Since $g, g_i = g^{\alpha^i}$ for $i \in [1, k' - 2]$ are all available in public parameter PP,

$$g^{P_{u,G(\alpha)}} = g^{\sum_{i=0}^{k'-2} a_i \alpha^i} = g^{a_0} \prod_{i=1}^{k'-2} g^{a_i \alpha^i} = g^{a_0} \prod_{i=1}^{k'-2} g_i^{a_i}$$

can be computed without the knowledge of α. However, this requires explicit knowledge of group G, which is intimated to each subscriber by the dealer during token generation in the procedure KEMD.GroupGen through a secure communication channel between them.

Correctness of our KEMD: The correctness of KEMD.Decrypt algorithm is as follows:

$$K = \left[e(C_1, g^{P_{u,G(\alpha)}}) e(sk_u, C_2) \right]^{\frac{1}{\prod_{j \in G, j \neq u} H(ID_j)}}$$

$$= \left[e\left(h^{-\alpha r t_1}, g^{\frac{1}{\alpha}\left\{ \prod_{j \in G, j \neq u}(\alpha + H(ID_j)) - \prod_{j \in G, j \neq u} H(ID_j) \right\}} \right) \times \right.$$

$$\left. e\left(h^{\frac{1}{\alpha + H(ID_u)}}, g^{r t_1 \prod_{j \in G}(\alpha + H(ID_j))} \right) \right]^{\frac{1}{\prod_{j \in G, j \neq u} H(ID_j)}}$$

$$= \left[e(g, h)^{-r t_1 \left\{ \prod_{j \in G, j \neq u}(\alpha + H(ID_j)) - \prod_{j \in G, j \neq u} H(ID_j) \right\}} \times \right.$$

$$\left. e(h, g)^{r t_1 \left\{ \prod_{j \in G, j \neq u}(\alpha + H(ID_j)) \right\}} \right]^{\frac{1}{\prod_{j \in G, j \neq u} H(ID_j)}}$$

$$= e(g, h)^{t_1 r}.$$

Remark 1. If a user revokes then the selected user set G will be changed. Accordingly $P(G)$ will be changed. Moreover, a revoked user will not have the information about current subscribed users. Therefore he will unable to recover the session key.

Remark 2. In our scheme dealer can not act dishonestly as we use all the components of our group token

$$P(G) = \left(w_1, w_2, w_3, w_4 \right) = \left(w^{-t_1}, g_{N-k}^{t_1 F(\alpha)}, g^{t_1 F(\alpha)}, e(g, h)^{t_1} \right)$$

either implicitly or explicitly in encryption phase. This property is not achievable in [10].

Remark 3. Note that the decryptor (legitimate subscribed user) needs the explicit knowledge of subscribed users in the decryption procedure. The dealer uses secure communication channel to inform the subscribed user set G while generating the group token $P(G)$. The dealer has to use these secure channels between him and the subscribed user each time a new group token is generated on group membership change. For dynamic group, it is essential to remove the reuse of secure communication channel which can be done by using a suitable public key encryption as follows: The dealer generates (public key, secret key) pair (p_i, s_i) for each user $i \in [N]$ during the procedure KEMD.Setup using a public key encryption mechanism and gives s_i to user i securely. Let at some stage, $j_1, \ldots, j_{k'} \in [N]$ are subscribed users with identities $ID_{j_1}, \ldots, ID_{j_{k'}}$. To represent a user index, we need $s = \log_2 N$ bits for a network with maximum N users. Let message space of the public key encryption scheme $\mathcal{E}$ be at least $(N + 2)s$ bits. The dealer generates ciphertext $y = \left(\left[\mathcal{E}_{p_i}(j_1 || \ldots || j_{k'} || k' || X) \right]_{i=1}^{k'}, \left[\mathcal{E}_{\hat{p}_i}(R_i) \right]_{i=1}^{k-k'}, X \right)$ of size $k + 1$ while generating group token in the procedure KEMD.GroupGen. Here R_i are random messages, $\hat{p}_i$ are random key values for $i \in [1, k - k']$, $||$ denotes concatenation of bits.

Consider $j_1, \ldots, j_{k'}, k', X$ are of s bits. If it is not of s bits, fill up left part by zeros. Last s bits are parity checking bits. The dealer publishes y instead of sending the group G to the subscribed users through secure communication channels. User i decrypts the ciphertext components using the secret key s_i. If it finds a decrypted value whose last s bits matches with X, then it can extract $j_1, \ldots, j_{k'}$ from the decrypted value.

4 Security

Theorem 1. *(Privacy). Our proposed BED scheme KEMD described in Sect. 3 is computationally secure under the hardness of the discrete logarithm problem as per the group privacy issue as described in Fig. 1 in Sect. 2.2.*

Proof. We describe the privacy of KEMD using a game between a challenger $\mathcal{C}$ and an adversary $\mathcal{A}$ as:

Setup: The challenger $\mathcal{C}$ generates the public parameter, $\mathsf{PP} = (\mathbb{S}, g, g_1, \ldots, g_N, v = e(g, h), w = h^\alpha, H, \mathsf{ID})$, and the master key $\mathsf{MK} = (\alpha, h)$ by calling $\mathsf{KEMD.Setup}(N, \lambda)$. Here $g_i = g^{\alpha^i}$ for $i \in [1, N]$, $\alpha \in \mathbb{Z}_p$, g, h are generators of group $\mathbb{G}$, $\mathsf{ID} = \{ID_1, ID_2, \ldots, ID_N\} \in (\mathbb{Z}^+)^N$ is the set of public identities of N users, $H : \{0,1\}^* \to \mathbb{Z}_p^*$ is a cryptographically secure hash function. It keeps MK secret to itself and hands PP to $\mathcal{A}$.

Challenge: The adversary $\mathcal{A}$ selects two sets of users G_0, G_1 of same size and submits G_0, G_1 to $\mathcal{C}$. The challenger $\mathcal{C}$ chooses $b \in_R \{0,1\}$ and generates a group token $P(G_b)$ by running $\mathsf{KEMD.GroupGen}(\mathsf{PP}, G_b)$ as

$$P(G_b) = (w_1, w_2, w_3, w_4) = (w^{-t_1}, \prod_{i=0}^{k'} g_{N-k+i}^{t_1 F_i}, \prod_{i=0}^{k'} g_i^{t_1 F_i}, v^{t_1})$$

$$= (h^{-\alpha t_1}, g_{N-k}^{t_1 F(\alpha)}, g^{t_1 F(\alpha)}, e(g, h)^{t_1})$$

where $t_1 \in \mathbb{Z}_p$, F_i, $0 \le i \le k'$ are coefficient of x^i in polynomial $F(x) = \prod_{j \in G_b}(x + H(ID_j))$. The challenger $\mathcal{C}$ hands $P(G_b)$ to $\mathcal{A}$.

Guess: The adversary $\mathcal{A}$ outputs a guess $b' \in \{0,1\}$ of b and wins if $b' = b$.

Given $P(G_b)$, the adversary $\mathcal{A}$ can predict G_b if it can predict the random number t_1 chosen by the challenger $\mathcal{C}$. As $\mathcal{A}$ has G_0, G_1, he can compute $P(G_0)$ if he can know t_1. If $P(G_0)$ matches with $P(G_b)$, $\mathcal{A}$ predicts $b = 0$, else $b = 1$. Therefore, prediction of b is same as predicting t_1 from $P(G_b)$ i.e., computing t_1 from $w_1 = w^{-t_1}$ where w is available to $\mathcal{A}$ trough PP. So, security depends on the hardness of the discrete logarithm problem. Hence the theorem.

Theorem 2. *(Maximum number of accountability). Our proposed BED scheme KEMD described in Sect. 3 is secure as per maximum number of accountability security model as described in Fig. 2 in Sect. 2.2 under the (f, N)-DHE hardness assumption.*

Proof. Let a PPT adversary $\mathcal{A}$ breaks the maximum number of accountability of our KEMD scheme with non-negligible advantage. We construct an algorithm $\mathcal{C}$ that attempts to solve an instance of the (f, N)-DHE problem using $\mathcal{A}$ as a sub-routine.

$\mathcal{C}$ is given an instance of the (f, N)-DHE problem $\langle Z = (\mathbb{S}, g, g_1, g_2, \ldots, g_N) \rangle$, where $g_i = g^{\alpha^i}$ for $i \in [N]$, $\alpha \in \mathbb{Z}_p$, $\mathbb{S}$ is a bilinear group system, g is a generator of the group $\mathbb{G}$. Now $\mathcal{C}$ plays the role of the challenger in the security game and interacts with $\mathcal{A}$ as follows:

Setup: Using Z, the challenger $\mathcal{C}$ sets public parameter $\mathsf{PP} = (\mathbb{S}, g, g_1, \ldots, g_N, v = e(g, g^x), w = g_1^x, H, \mathsf{ID})$ where $x \in_R \mathbb{Z}_p$, $H : \{0,1\}^* \to \mathbb{Z}_p^*$ is a cryptographically secure hash function, $\mathsf{ID} = \{ID_1, ID_2, \ldots, ID_N\} \in (\mathbb{Z}^+)^N$ is the set of public identities of N users and hands PP to $\mathcal{A}$. It sets $\mathsf{MK} = (\alpha, h = g^x)$. Note that α is not known to $\mathcal{C}$ explicitly and $w = g_1^x = g^{\alpha x} = h^\alpha$, $v = e(g, g^x) = e(g, h)$ as in the real scheme.

Challenge: The challenger $\mathcal{C}$ submits a threshold value $k \in [N]$ on the group size to $\mathcal{A}$.

Guess: The adversary $\mathcal{A}$ computes $P(G^*)$ by running $\mathsf{KEMD.GroupGen}(\mathsf{PP}, G^*)$ where $|G^*| = \hat{k} > k$ as

$$P(G^*) = (\hat{w}_1, \hat{w}_2, \hat{w}_3, \hat{w}_4) = (w^{-t_1}, \prod_{i=0}^{\hat{k}} g_{N-k+i}^{t_1 F_i}, \prod_{i=0}^{\hat{k}} g_i^{t_1 F_i}, v^{t_1})$$

$$= (h^{-\alpha t_1}, g_{N-k}^{t_1 \hat{F}(\alpha)}, g^{t_1 \hat{F}(\alpha)}, e(g, h)^{t_1})$$

where $t_1 \in \mathbb{Z}_p$, F_i, $0 \le i \le \hat{k}$ are coefficient of x^i in polynomial $\hat{F}(x) = \prod_{j \in G^*} (x + H(ID_j))$. The adversary $\mathcal{A}$ sends $(P(G^*), G^*)$ to $\mathcal{C}$.

Note that if the adversary $\mathcal{A}$ outputs a valid $P(G^*)$ for a group G^* of size $\hat{k} > k$ i.e., $\mathsf{KEMD.Verify}(P(G^*), \mathsf{PP}, k) = 1$, then $\hat{F}(x) = \prod_{j \in G^*} (x + H(ID_j))$ is a $\hat{k}(> k)$ degree polynomial and $\hat{w}_2 = g_{N-k}^{t_1 \hat{F}(\alpha)} = g^{t_1 \alpha^{N-k} \hat{F}(\alpha)}$. Let $f(x) = t_1 x^{N-k} \hat{F}(x)$. This is a polynomial of degree $N - k + \hat{k} > N$ as $\hat{k} > k$. Then $(f(x), \hat{w}_2 = g^{f(\alpha)})$ is a solution of the (f, N)-DHE problem. Therefore if $\mathcal{A}$ wins against maximum number of accountability game in Fig. 2, then it can solve the (f, N)-DHE problem. This completes the proof.

Theorem 3. *(Key indistinguishability under CPA) Our proposed BED scheme KEMD described in Sect. 3 achieves selective semantic (indistinguishable under CPA) security in the random oracle model as per the key indistinguishability security game of Sect. 2.2 under the (f, ϕ, F)-GDDHE hardness assumption.*

Proof. Assume that there is a PPT adversary $\mathcal{A}$ that breaks the selective semantic security of our proposed KEMD scheme with a non-negligible advantage. We construct a distinguisher $\mathcal{C}$ that attempts to solve the (f, ϕ, F)-GDDHE problem using $\mathcal{A}$ as a subroutine. Both $\mathcal{A}$ and $\mathcal{C}$ are given N, the total number of users and t, the total number queries for key generation and random oracle. Let $\mathcal{C}$ be given an (f, ϕ, F)-GDDHE instance $\langle Z = (\mathbb{S}, f(x), \phi(x), h_0, h_0^{\alpha}, h_0^{\alpha^2}, \ldots, h_0^{\alpha^{t-1}}, h_0^{\alpha f(\alpha)}, h_0^{k\alpha f(\alpha)}, g_0, g_0^{\alpha}, g_0^{\alpha^2}, \ldots, g_0^{\alpha^{2N}}, g_0^{k\phi(\alpha)}), X\rangle$, where $f(x) = \prod_{i=1}^{t}(x + x_i)$, $\phi(x) = \prod_{t+1}^{t+N}(x + x_i)$ are two co-prime polynomials with pairwise distinct roots i.e., $x_i \in_R \mathbb{Z}_p, i \in [t + N]$ are all distinct, $\mathbb{S} = (p, \mathbb{G}, \mathbb{G}_1, e)$, g_0, h_0 are generators of group $\mathbb{G}$, $X = e(g_0, h_0)^{kf(\alpha)}$ or random element of $\mathbb{G}_1$. The distinguisher $\mathcal{C}$ attempts to output 0 if $X = e(g_0, h_0)^{kf(\alpha)}$ and 1 otherwise, using $\mathcal{A}$ as a subroutine. Let us denote $f_i(x) = \frac{f(x)}{x+x_i}$ for $i \in [t]$, $\phi_i(x) = \frac{\phi(x)}{x+x_i}$ for $i \in [t + 1, t + N]$. Now $\mathcal{C}$ plays the role of a challenger in the security game described in Sect. 2.2 and interacts with $\mathcal{A}$ as follows:

Initialization: The adversary $\mathcal{A}$ selects a target recipient set G of s^* users with identity set $S = \{ID_1^*, \ldots, ID_{s^*}^*\} \subseteq \mathsf{ID} = \{ID_1, ID_2, \ldots, ID_N\} \in (\mathbb{Z}^+)^N$ and declares it to $\mathcal{C}$. Here ID is the set of identities of the group of N users.

Setup: Using Z, the challenger $\mathcal{C}$ first computes $\prod_{i=t+s^*+1}^{t+N}(x + x_i) = \sum_{i=0}^{N-s^*} x^i A_i$ (say), where A_i's, are function of $x_j, j \in [t + s^* + 1, t + N]$ for $i \in [0, N - s^*]$. We note down here that x_j are distinct roots of polynomial $\phi(x)$ which $\mathcal{C}$ can extract from the polynomial. Using these A_i values, $\mathcal{C}$ computes

$$\prod_{i=0}^{N-s^*} (g_0^{\alpha^i})^{A_i} = g_0^{\sum_{i=0}^{N-s^*} \alpha^i A_i} = g_0^{\prod_{i=t+s^*+1}^{t+N}(\alpha+x_i)}$$ by extracting $g_0^{\alpha^i}$ values from

Z and sets $g = g_0^{\prod_{i=t+s^*+1}^{t+N}(\alpha+x_i)}$, $g_j = g^{\alpha^j} = \prod_{i=0}^{N-s^*} (g_0^{\alpha^{i+j}})^{A_i}$.

Note that $\prod_{i=0}^{N-s^*} (g_0^{\alpha^{i+j}})^{A_i} = g_0^{\sum_{i=0}^{N-s^*} \alpha^{i+j} A_i} = g_0^{\alpha^j \left\{ \prod_{i=t+s^*+1}^{t+N}(\alpha+x_i) \right\}} = g^{\alpha^j} = g_j$.

The challenger also computes

$$f(x) \prod_{i=t+s^*+1}^{t+N}(x + x_i) = \prod_{i=1}^{t}(x + x_i) \prod_{i=t+s^*+1}^{t+N}(x + x_i) = \sum_{i=0}^{N-s^*+t} x^i C_i \text{ (say)},$$

where C_i, are function of $x_j, j \in [t + s^* + 1, t + N] \cup [1, t]$ for $i \in [0, N - s^* + t]$. Here x_j are distinct roots of $f(x)$ and $\phi(x)$, which are made available to $\mathcal{C}$ through $f(x), \phi(x)$ provided in Z. Using these C_i values, $\mathcal{C}$ computes

$$\prod_{i=0}^{N-s^*+t} (g_0^{\alpha^i})^{C_i} = g_0^{\sum_{i=0}^{N-s^*+t} \alpha^i C_i} = g_0^{f(\alpha)\left\{ \prod_{i=t+s^*+1}^{t+N}(\alpha+x_i) \right\}} \text{ and}$$

$$e\left(g_0^{f(\alpha)\left\{ \prod_{i=t+s^*+1}^{t+N}(\alpha+x_i) \right\}}, h_0\right) = e(g_0, h_0)^{f(\alpha)\left\{ \prod_{i=t+s^*+1}^{t+N}(\alpha+x_i) \right\}}.$$ Note that, $N - s^* + t \leq 2N$ as $t, s^* \leq N$. Therefore, all $g_0^{\alpha^i}$ values required for the above computation can be extracted by $\mathcal{C}$ from Z. The challenger $\mathcal{C}$ finally sets

$$w = h_0^{\alpha f(\alpha)}, v = e(g_0, h_0)^{f(\alpha)\left\{\prod\limits_{i=t+s^*+1}^{t+N}(\alpha+x_i)\right\}}$$ and gives public parameter

$\mathsf{PP} = (\mathbb{S}, g, g_1, \ldots, g_N, v, w, H, \mathsf{ID})$ to $\mathcal{A}$, where $H : \{0,1\}^* \to \mathbb{Z}_p^*$ is a cryptographic hash function selected by $\mathcal{C}$ himself.

Observe that, $$w = h_0^{\alpha f(\alpha)} = h^{\alpha},$$

$$v = e(g_0, h_0)^{f(\alpha)\left\{\prod\limits_{i=t+s^*+1}^{t+N}(\alpha+x_i)\right\}} = e(g_0^{\prod\limits_{i=t+s^*+1}^{t+N}(\alpha+x_i)}, h_0^{f(\alpha)}) = e(g, h),$$

where $h = h_0^{f(\alpha)}$ is set by $\mathcal{C}$ implicitly. This makes the distribution of PP simulated above identical as in the original scheme. As α or $h_0^{\alpha^t}$ is not known to adversary $\mathcal{A}$ or challenger $\mathcal{C}$, they can not compute h.

Hash queries: The challenger maintain hash list HL that contains at the beginning $\{*, x_i, *\}_{i=1}^t$, $\{ID_{i-t}^*, x_i, *\}_{i=t+1}^{t+s^*}$ ($*$ stands for empty entry) to reply at most $t-q$ hash queries, where q is number of key generation queries. If the queried identity already exists in HL, $\mathcal{C}$ responds with corresponding hash value. Else picks x_i for some $\{*, x_i, *\}$ in HL, returns $H(ID_i) = x_i$ to $\mathcal{A}$, adds $\{ID_i, x_i, *\}$ to HL.

Query Phase 1: The adversary $\mathcal{A}$ issues key generation queries on $\{ID_i\}_{i=1}^m$ with a restriction that $ID_i \notin S$. The challenger generates private key as: If $\mathcal{A}$ already issued a key generation query on ID_i, $\mathcal{C}$ can find an entry (ID_i, x_i, sk_i) in HL and responds to $\mathcal{A}$ with this sk_i.

Else if $\mathcal{A}$ has already issued a hash query on ID_i, then $\mathcal{C}$ can find an entry $(ID_i, x_i, *)$ in HL, uses this x_i to compute $f_i(x) = \frac{f(x)}{x+x_i} = \sum\limits_{i=0}^{t-1} D_i x^i$ (say),

where D_i's are function of the roots x_j, $j \in [1, t]$ of $f(x)$ for $i \in [0, t-1]$, sets

$$sk_i = \prod_{i=0}^{t-1} h_0^{\alpha^i D_i} = h_0^{\sum\limits_{i=0}^{t-1}(\alpha^i D_i)} = h_0^{f_i(\alpha)}, \text{ adds } (ID_i, x_i, sk_i) \text{ to } \mathsf{HL} \text{ and responds}$$

to $\mathcal{A}$ with this sk_i.

Note that $sk_i = h_0^{f_i(\alpha)} = h_0^{\frac{f(\alpha)}{\alpha+x_i}} = h^{\frac{1}{\alpha+x_i}} = h^{\frac{1}{\alpha+H(ID_i)}}$ has the same distribution as in the original scheme.

Else $\mathcal{C}$ sets $H(ID_i) = x_i$, (as in the **Hash queries** phase), computes the corresponding sk_i exactly as above, adds (ID_i, x_i, sk_i) to HL and responds to $\mathcal{A}$ with this sk_i.

Challenge: The challenger $\mathcal{C}$ first extracts $(h_0^{k\alpha f(\alpha)}, g_0^{k\phi(\alpha)})$ from the (f, ϕ, F)-GDDHE instance $\langle Z, X \rangle$ and sets the header Hdr as, $\mathsf{Hdr} = (h_0^{-k\alpha f(\alpha)}, g_0^{k\phi(\alpha)})$.

Observe that, $$h_0^{-k\alpha f(\alpha)} = (h_0^{\alpha f(\alpha)})^{-k} = w^{-k},$$

$$g_0^{k\phi(\alpha)} = g_0^{k\left(\prod\limits_{i=t+1}^{t+s^*}(\alpha+x_i)\prod\limits_{i=t+s^*+1}^{t+N}(\alpha+x_i)\right)} = g^{k\left(\prod\limits_{i=t+1}^{t+s^*}(\alpha+x_i)\right)} = g^{k\prod\limits_{i=1}^{s^*}(\alpha+H(ID_i^*))}$$

are similar to our real construction from $\mathcal{A}$'s point of view.

The challenger $\mathcal{C}$ then computes the polynomial

$$q(x) = \frac{1}{x}\left(\prod_{i=t+s^*+1}^{t+N}(x+x_i) - \prod_{i=t+s^*+1}^{t+N} x_i\right) = \sum_{i=0}^{N-s^*-1} x^i \bar{A}_i \text{ (say), where } \bar{A}_i, \text{ are}$$

function of x_j, $j \in [t+s^*+1, t+N]$ for $i \in [0, N-s^*-1]$. It then generates

$$\prod_{i=0}^{N-s^*-1} g_0^{\bar{A}_i \alpha^i} = g_0^{\sum_{i=0}^{N-s^*-1} \alpha^i \bar{A}_i} = g_0^{q(\alpha)} \text{ by extracting } g_0^{\alpha^i} \text{ from the given instance}$$

$\langle Z, X \rangle$ and sets session key K as, $K = \left[(X)^{\prod_{i=t+s^*+1}^{t+N} x_i}\right] e(h_0^{k\alpha f(\alpha)}, g_0^{q(\alpha)})$, where X is extracted from the (f, ϕ, F)-GDDHE instance. The challenger $\mathcal{C}$ finally chooses $b \in_R \{0,1\}$ and sets $K_b = K$, K_{1-b} as a random element of $\mathbb{G}_1$ and returns $(\mathsf{Hdr}, K_b, K_{1-b})$ to $\mathcal{A}$.

Here $X = e(g_0, h_0)^{kf(\alpha)}$ or random element of $\mathbb{G}_1$, if $X = e(g_0, h_0)^{kf(\alpha)}$ then

$$K = \left[(X)^{\prod_{i=t+s^*+1}^{t+N} x_i}\right] e(h_0^{k\alpha f(\alpha)}, g_0^{q(\alpha)})$$

$$= \left[e(g_0, h_0)^{kf(\alpha)\left\{\prod_{i=t+s^*+1}^{t+N} x_i\right\}}\right]\left[e(g_0, h_0)^{kf(\alpha)\left(\prod_{i=t+s^*+1}^{t+N}(\alpha+x_i) - \prod_{i=t+s^*+1}^{t+N} x_i\right)}\right]$$

$$= e(g_0, h_0)^{kf(\alpha)\left(\prod_{i=t+s^*+1}^{t+N}(\alpha+x_i)\right)} = e(g_0^{\prod_{i=t+s^*+1}^{t+N}(\alpha+x_i)}, h_0^{f(\alpha)})^k = e(g, h)^k = v^k.$$

Hence the simulated session key K has the same distribution as in original scheme.

Phase 2: This is similar to Phase 1 key generation queries. The adversary $\mathcal{A}$ sends key generation queries for $\{ID_i\}_{m+1}^q$ with a restriction that $ID_i \notin S$ and receives back secret keys $\{sk_i\}_{m+1}^q$ simulated in the same manner by $\mathcal{C}$ as in Phase 1.

Guess: Finally, $\mathcal{A}$ outputs a guess $b' \in \{0,1\}$ of b to $\mathcal{C}$ and wins if $b' = b$.

We define $X = e(g_0, h_0)^{kf(\alpha)}$ as real event and X a random element of $\mathbb{G}_1$ as rand event. Therefore

$$Adv_{\mathcal{C}}^{(f,\phi,F)-\mathsf{GDDHE}} = |Pr[b' = b|\mathsf{real}] - Pr[b' = b|\mathsf{rand}]| = |Pr[b' = b|\mathsf{real}] - \frac{1}{2}|$$

$$= \left|(\frac{1}{2}Pr[b' = 1|b = 1 \wedge \mathsf{real}] + \frac{1}{2}Pr[b' = 0|b = 0 \wedge \mathsf{real}]) - \frac{1}{2}\right|$$

$$= \left|\frac{1}{2}Pr[b' = 1|b = 1 \wedge \mathsf{real}] - \frac{1}{2}Pr[b' = 1|b = 0 \wedge \mathsf{real}]\right|.$$

$$[\text{ as } Pr[b' = 0|b = 0 \wedge \mathsf{real}] + Pr[b' = 1|b = 0 \wedge \mathsf{real}] = 1]$$

In real case, the distribution of all the variables agrees with the semantic security game, thereby

$$Adv_{\mathcal{A}}^{\text{KEMD-INDK}}(t, N) = |Pr[b' = 1|b = 1 \wedge \text{real}] - Pr[b' = 1|b = 0 \wedge \text{real}]|.$$

This implies $Adv_{\mathcal{C}}^{(f,\phi,F)-\text{GDDHE}} = \frac{1}{2}Adv_{\mathcal{A}}^{\text{KEMD-INDK}}(t, N)$. Therefore, if $\mathcal{A}$ has non-negligible advantage in correctly guessing b', then $\mathcal{C}$ solves (f, ϕ, F)-GDDHE instance given to $\mathcal{C}$ with non-negligible advantage. Hence the theorem follows.

5 Efficiency

We compare our KEMD construction with the only known work of Gritti et al. [10] in Tables 1 and 2 which exhibit significant improvement in parameter sizes and computation overhead of our scheme over [10].

Table 1. Comparative summaries of storage, communication bandwith and security of BED schemes.

Scheme	$|PP|$	$|PK|$	$|SK|$	$|P(G)|$	$|CT|$	SM	MC	SA
[10]	$(2N + 4)|\mathbb{G}| + 1|\mathbb{G}_1|$	$N|\mathbb{Z}_p| + N|\mathbb{G}|$	$(N+1)|\mathbb{G}|$	$5|\mathbb{G}|+1|\mathbb{G}_1|$	$2|\mathbb{G}|+1|\mathbb{G}_1|$	Semi-static	Semantic	N-DBDHE
Our KEMD	$(N+2)|\mathbb{G}|+1|\mathbb{G}_1|$	0	$1|\mathbb{G}|$	$3|\mathbb{G}|+1|\mathbb{G}_1|$	$2|\mathbb{G}|+1|\mathbb{G}_1|$	Selective	Semantic	GDDHE

$|PP|$ = public parameter size, $|PK|$ = public key size, $|SK|$ = secret key size, $|P(G)|$ = group token size, $|CT|$ = ciphertext size, N = total number of users, $|\mathbb{G}|$ = bit size of an element of $\mathbb{G}$, $|\mathbb{G}_1|$ = bit size of an element of $\mathbb{G}_1$, $|\mathbb{Z}_p|$ = bit size of an element of $\mathbb{Z}_p$, SM = security model, MC = message confidentiality, SA = security assumption, N-DBDHE = N- decisional bilinear diffie-hellman exponent, GDDHE = general decisional diffie-hellman exponent.

Table 2. Comparative summary of computation cost of parameter generation, encryption and decryption algorithm for BED schemes.

Scheme	PP		SK		$P(G)$		Verify	Enc		Dec		
	#exp	#pair	#exp	# inv	#exp	# inv	#pair	#exp	#pair	#exp	#pair	# inv
[10]	$2N+3$ in G	1	$N+2$ in G	1	$k'+4$ in G, 1 in $\mathbb{G}_1$	0	2	2 in G, 1 in $\mathbb{G}_1$	2	0	2	1 in $\mathbb{G}_1$
Our KEMD	$N+1$ in G	0	1 in G	1	$2k'+3$ in G, 1 in $\mathbb{G}_1$	1 in $\mathbb{G}_1$	2	2 in G, 1 in $\mathbb{G}_1$	0	$k'-1$ in G 1 in $\mathbb{G}_1$	2	1 in $\mathbb{G}_1$

PP = public parameter, SK = secret key, $P(G)$ = group token, Enc = encryption, Dec = decryption, N = total number of users, k' = number of users selected by the dealer, #exp = number of exponentiations, #pair = number of pairings, #inv = number of inversions.

Our proposed scheme is essentially a key encapsulation mechanism in dealership framework whereas the construction of [10] is message encryption in dealership framework. Unlike [10], our construction does not require any public key and has constant size secret key. More interestingly, the sizes of the public parameter, secret key, group token and ciphertext are less in our KEMD design than those of [10]. Computation cost in our construction is also favourably comparable with that of [10]. The total number of exponentiation in our scheme is $3k' + N + 9$, whereas in [10] number of exponentiation is $3N + k' + 13$. Here N is the total number of users and k' is the number of subscribed users. As $k' \leq N$, our scheme requires less exponentiation. Our scheme needs 5 pairings whereas [10] needs 7 pairings. While [10] is semi-statically secure in the standard model, our KEMD is selectively secure in the random oracle model.

Remark 4. Session key K is used for message encryption. If we compare with a message encryption scheme, we can consider ciphertext CT as CT $= (\mathsf{Hdr}, MK)$. In our scheme, we can consider ciphertext size as 1 more to the size of header.

6   Conclusion

We have proposed a BED scheme in key encapsulation mode, namely KEMD which significantly reduces the parameter sizes and computation cost compared to the only existing BED scheme constructed by Gritti et al. [10]. The scheme is selectively secure against CPA under reasonable assumption. We have also discussed privacy and maximum number of accountability issues. Furthermore, unlike [10] the broadcaster in our scheme does not have to wait for response from user's side to detect illegal behaviour of a dealer.

References

1. Barth, A., Boneh, D., Waters, B.: Privacy in encrypted content distribution using private broadcast encryption. In: Crescenzo, G., Rubin, A. (eds.) FC 2006. LNCS, vol. 4107, pp. 52–64. Springer, Heidelberg (2006). doi:10.1007/11889663_4
2. Boneh, D., Gentry, C., Waters, B.: Collusion resistant broadcast encryption with short ciphertexts and private keys. In: Shoup, V. (ed.) CRYPTO 2005. LNCS, vol. 3621, pp. 258–275. Springer, Heidelberg (2005). doi:10.1007/11535218_16
3. Boneh, D., Waters, B., Zhandry, M.: Low overhead broadcast encryption from multilinear maps. In: Garay, J.A., Gennaro, R. (eds.) CRYPTO 2014. LNCS, vol. 8616, pp. 206–223. Springer, Heidelberg (2014). doi:10.1007/978-3-662-44371-2_12
4. Chor, B., Fiat, A., Naor, M.: Tracing traitors. In: Desmedt, Y.G. (ed.) CRYPTO 1994. LNCS, vol. 839, pp. 257–270. Springer, Heidelberg (1994). doi:10.1007/3-540-48658-5_25
5. Delerablée, C.: Identity-based broadcast encryption with constant size ciphertexts and private keys. In: Kurosawa, K. (ed.) ASIACRYPT 2007. LNCS, vol. 4833, pp. 200–215. Springer, Heidelberg (2007). doi:10.1007/978-3-540-76900-2_12
6. Delerablée, C., Paillier, P., Pointcheval, D.: Fully collusion secure dynamic broadcast encryption with constant-size ciphertexts or decryption keys. In: Takagi, T., Okamoto, E., Okamoto, T., Okamoto, T. (eds.) Pairing 2007. LNCS, vol. 4575, pp. 39–59. Springer, Heidelberg (2007). doi:10.1007/978-3-540-73489-5_4
7. Dodis, Y., Fazio, N.: Public key broadcast encryption for stateless receivers. In: Feigenbaum, J. (ed.) DRM 2002. LNCS, vol. 2696, pp. 61–80. Springer, Heidelberg (2003). doi:10.1007/978-3-540-44993-5_5
8. Fiat, A., Naor, M.: Broadcast encryption. In: Stinson, D.R. (ed.) CRYPTO 1993. LNCS, vol. 773, pp. 480–491. Springer, Heidelberg (1994). doi:10.1007/3-540-48329-2_40
9. Gentry, C., Waters, B.: Adaptive security in broadcast encryption systems (with short ciphertexts). In: Joux, A. (ed.) EUROCRYPT 2009. LNCS, vol. 5479, pp. 171–188. Springer, Heidelberg (2009). doi:10.1007/978-3-642-01001-9_10
10. Gritti, C., Susilo, W., Plantard, T., Liang, K., Wong, D.: Broadcast encryption with dealership. Int. J. Inf. Secur. **15**, 1–13 (2015)
11. Lewko, A., Sahai, A., Waters, B.: Revocation systems with very small private keys. In: IEEE Symposium on Security and Privacy (SP), pp. 273–285 (2010)

12. Naor, D., Naor, M., Lotspiech, J.: Revocation and tracing schemes for stateless receivers. In: Kilian, J. (ed.) CRYPTO 2001. LNCS, vol. 2139, pp. 41–62. Springer, Heidelberg (2001). doi:10.1007/3-540-44647-8_3
13. Phan, D.H., Pointcheval, D., Shahandashti, S., Strefler, M.: Adaptive CCA broadcast encryption with constant-size secret keys and ciphertexts. Int. J. Inf. Secur. **12**(4), 251–265 (2013)

A   The BED Construction of [10]

The portions in the following scheme of [10] framed by boxes indicates those terms which were added or modified in transition from the syntax of KEMD as described in Sect. 2.1 to the syntax of BED of [10].

$(PP, MK) \leftarrow \mathsf{Setup}(N, \lambda)$: The PKGC chooses a bilinear group system $\mathbb{S} = (p, \mathbb{G}, \mathbb{G}_1, e)$, where $\mathbb{G}, \mathbb{G}_1$ are groups of prime order p and $e : \mathbb{G} \times \mathbb{G} \to \mathbb{G}_1$ is a bilinear mapping. Let g be a generator of $\mathbb{G}$ and $h \in_R \mathbb{G}$. It selects $\alpha, \beta, \gamma \in_R \mathbb{Z}_p$, computes $u_i = h^{\gamma\alpha^i}, v_i = h^{\gamma\beta\alpha^i}$ for $i \in [0, N]$ and sets public parameter PP and master key MK as

$$\mathsf{MK} = (\alpha, \beta, \gamma), \mathsf{PP} = (\mathbb{S}, g, h, e(g^\gamma, g), \{u_i\}_{i=0}^N, \{v_i\}_{i=0}^N).$$

$(sk_i, \boxed{\mathsf{PK}_i}) \leftarrow \mathsf{KeyGen}(\mathsf{PP}, \mathsf{MK}, i)$: The PKGC takes $s_i \in_R \mathbb{Z}_p$, $f_i \in_R \mathbb{G}$ for $i \in [1, N]$ and generates a secret key for user i as $sk_i = (d_{i,0}, \ldots, d_{i,N})$, where $d_{i,0} = g^{-s_i}, d_{i,i} = g^\gamma f_i^{s_i}, d_{i,j} = f_j^{s_i}$ for $i \neq j$. The PKGC additionally generates the public key for user i as $\mathsf{PK}_i = (x_i + \alpha, f_i)$ where $x_i \in_R \mathbb{Z}_p$. It makes PK_i public and sends sk_i to user i securely through a secure communication channel.

$(P(G), k) \leftarrow \mathsf{GroupGen}(\mathsf{PP}, \boxed{\{\mathsf{PK}_i\}_{i=1}^N}, G)$: A dealer selects a group G of $k'(\leq k)$ users and generates a group token $P(G)$ as

$$P(G) = (w_1, w_2, w_3, w_4, w_5, w_6)$$
$$= (u_0^{t_1 \prod_{i \in G}(x_i+\alpha)}, v_0^{t_1 \prod_{i \in G}(x_i+\alpha)}, v_{N-k}^{t_1 \prod_{i \in G}(x_i+\alpha)}, \prod_{i \in G} f_i^{t_2}, g^{t_2}, e(g^\gamma, g)^{t_2})$$

where $t_1, t_2 \in_R \mathbb{Z}_p$, u_i, v_i are extracted from PP, $x_i + \alpha$, f_i are extracted from PK_i for $i \in [N]$. The dealer sends G to each subscribed user through a secure communication channel.

$(0 \lor 1) \leftarrow \mathsf{KEMD.Verify}(P(G), \mathsf{PP}, k)$: The broadcaster implicitly verifies that the size of G does not exceed k by checking the pairing $e(w_2, u_N) = e(w_3, u_k)$. If the verification succeeds, the broadcaster outputs 1 and proceeds; otherwise it outputs 0 and aborts.

$\boxed{C} \leftarrow$ Encrypt$(P(G), \mathsf{PP}, \boxed{M})$: The broadcaster verifies that $w_2 = w_1^\beta$ by checking $e(w_1, v_0) = e(w_2, u_0)$. If the verification succeeds the broadcaster generates a ciphertext C using $P(G) = (w_1, w_2, w_3, w_4, w_5, w_6)$, PP and a message $M \in \mathbb{G}_1$ as

$$C = (C_1, C_2, C_3) = (w_5^r, w_4^r, Mw_6^r) = (g^{rt_2}, \prod_{i \in G} f_i^{rt_2}, M.e(g^\gamma, g)^{rt_2})$$

where $r \in_R \mathbb{Z}_p$.

$\boxed{M} \leftarrow$ Decrypt$(\mathsf{PP}, sk_i, \boxed{C}, G)$: User i checks the cardinality of G which he receives from the dealer. If it is greater than k, then user i informs this to the broadcaster. User i retrieves M by coupling $C = (C_1, C_2, C_3)$ with $d_{i,j}$'s extracted from sk_i as follows:

$$X = e(d_{i,i} \prod_{j \in G, j \neq i} d_{i,j}, C_1)e(d_{i,0}, C_2)$$

$$= e(g^\gamma \prod_{j \in G} f_j^{s_i}, g^{rt_2})e(g^{-s_i}, \prod_{j \in G} f_j^{rt_2}) = e(g^\gamma, g^{rt_2})$$

$$X^{-1}C_3 = e(g^\gamma, g^{rt_2})^{-1}Me(g^\gamma, g^{rt_2}) = M.$$

Towards Certificate-Based Group Encryption

Yili Ren[1,2], Xiling Luo[1,2], Qianhong Wu[1(✉)], Joseph K. Liu[3], and Peng Zhang[4]

[1] School of Electronic and Information Engineering,
Beihang University, Beijing, China
qianhong.wu@buaa.edu.cn
[2] Beijing Key Laboratory for Network-Based Cooperative Air Traffic Management,
Beijing, China
[3] Faculty of Information Technology, Monash University, Melbourne, Australia
[4] ATR Key Laboratory of National Technology,
Shenzhen University, Shenzhen, China

Abstract. Group Encryption (GE) is a recently proposed cryptographic primitive protecting the privacy of the receivers in a communication system. A majority of group encryption schemes are implicitly based on public key infrastructure (PKI) setting in which the management of certificates are complicated. Identity based encryption (IBE) seems to be a good alternative for PKI in GE, but the private key escrow and the user revocation problem are inherent in IBE system. Certificate-based encryption (CBE) overcomes drawbacks of PKI and IBE. In this paper, we propose a new cryptographic primitive, referred to as certificate-based group encryption (CBGE). In this notion, a certificate authority issues the certificate as a part of decryption key corresponding to a user's public key and other information; and the user can register himself as a group member to a group manager. Then anyone can verifiably send confidential messages to a group member whose identity information is hidden within a group of certified users. If required, the group manager (GM) can trace the receiver. Following this model, we propose a scheme towards CBGE, where the roles of the verifier and the GM are taken by a single entity. We formally prove the scheme is secure in the random oracle model. Unlike the users existing in GE schemes, users in our scheme need not to check the certificates. CBGE provides an implicit certification mechanism and allows a periodical update of certificate status.

Keywords: Group encryption · Certificate-based · Knowledge proof

1   Introduction

Privacy leakage has been a critical issue in communication with more and more users frequently accessing to Internet. Communication involves two types of privacy issues, i.e., sender privacy and receiver privacy. Group signature is a well-known cryptographic primitive that guarantees sender privacy. It allows a sender to issue a signature on behalf of a group and the identity authenticity of

L. Chen and J. Han (Eds.): ProvSec 2016, LNCS 10005, pp. 296–305, 2016.
DOI: 10.1007/978-3-319-47422-9_17

the sender is verifiable but hidden from the others. Group signature is introduced by Chaum and van Heyst [3] and developed in subsequent works [2,8].

Group encryption [9] (GE) is the encryption analogue of group signature but designed for the purpose of receiver privacy. It allows a sender to send a cipher-text to a receiver whose identity is hidden within a group of certified users. GE schemes were introduced by Kiayias, Tsiounis and Yung [9] and further developed in a line of works [1,4,10,11]. GE schemes can be used in many important settings, including the scenario where a user wants to hide himself from a trusted third party, Ad-Hoc access structure group signature, as well as secure oblivious retriever storage.

A majority of group encryption schemes are implicitly based on Public Key Infrastructure (PKI). PKI leads to some shortcomings of GE schemes. In public-key cryptosystems, user's public key is a random string unrelated to his identity. When a sender wants to send a message to a receiver, he must obtain the receiver's public key authenticated by a trusted Certificate Authority. So the problem of the PKI-based GE schemes lies in the need of high cost in authenticating and managing the public keys, and the difficulty in managing multiple communities.

One may naturally expect alternative paradigm without the disadvantages of PKI-based GE schemes. Identity-based encryption (IBE) seems a plausible solution. It was introduced by Shamir in 1984 [12]. Its main idea is that the public keys of a user can be easily derived from arbitrary strings corresponding to his identity information. And therefore, certification becomes unnecessary. However, there are still some drawbacks in IBE system. First, the private key escrow is inherent in such systems. A PKG can easily decrypt its users' messages. Second, the secret keys must be sent to the users via a secure channel, which makes the problem of key distribution difficulty. Finally, the user revocation is troublesome if some users' secret keys are leaked.

Recently, certificate-based encryption [7] (CBE) has been proposed to bridge the gap between traditional public key encryption and IBE. CBE provides an efficient implicit certification mechanism as conventional PKI and allows a periodical update of certificate status while eliminating third-party queries for the certificate status in the conventional PKI. In CBE, each user generates his own public/private key pair and requests a long-lived certificate from his certificate authority (CA) as in a conventional PKI system. But, CA generates the long-lived certificate as well as the short-lived certificates. A short-lived certificate is only pushed to the owner of the public/private key pair and acts as a partial decryption key. This additional functionality provides an implicit certification so that the user is required to decrypt the ciphertext using his private key along with an up-to-date certificate from his CA. These desirable features of CBE may allows a new group encryption pardigm without disadvantages in PKI and IBE based ones mentioned before.

1.1 Our Contribution

Motivated by the above scenarios, we propose a new crytographic primitive called certificate-based group encryption (CBGE). In CBGE, a certificate acts as a part of decryption key corresponding to a user's identity information. Anyone can send an encrypted message to an anonymous receiver. The group manager can trace the authentic receiver if the need arises.

We define necessary security notions about CBGE. The first security notion, called anonymity, protects the users from a hostile environment where the attacker may want to extract the identity information about the receivers. The second security notion is semantic security, i.e., indistinguishability against a chosen plaintext attacks. Our model considers adversaries who have oracle access to the certificate functionality of all users. The last security notion is traceability which ensures that tracking dishonest receivers is reliable.

We design a concrete scheme in which the roles of the verifier and group manager are taken by one entity. In order to get an efficient and practical scheme, we use three primitives, i.e., a public-key encryption scheme which satisfies CCA2 security, an CBE scheme which satisfies anonymity and semantic security, and a zero-knowledge proof to guarantee the traceability. And we provide the analysis of successful attack performance of our scheme.

We prove the security of our concrete scheme according to the security definitions. The implementation of the scheme will require less infrastructure since there are no certificates management or certificates revocation problems. The certificates in our scheme are character strings which need not to be checked by the users. Group manager can trace the identity of the receivers. These mechanisms make our scheme easy to be deployed.

1.2 Related Work

Kiayias et al. formalized the notion of group encryption [9]. They provided modular design including zero-knowledge proofs, digital signature schemes, public-key encryption schemes with CCA2 security and key-privacy and commitment schemes. Cathalo et al. [4] proposed a group encryption with non-interactive realization in the standard model. Independently, Qin et al. [11] considered a similar primitive called Group Decryption. The Group Decryption has non-interactive proofs and short ciphertexts. They avoid interaction by explicitly employing a random oracle. Libert et al. proposed a traceable GE [10] which can trace all the ciphertexts encrypted by a specific user without abolishing the anonymity of the others. Aimani and Joye [1] obtain group encryption schemes that support both interactive and non-interactive validity proofs.

The concept of certificate-based encryption (CBE) was proposed by Gentry in 2003 [7]. Several generic constructions [5,13] have been proposed for constructing a certificate-based encryption scheme from an identity-based scheme. In this model, certificates are part of the secret key, so certification is implicit. CBE has two important advantages over IBE. First, there is no key escrow, because certificates are only a part of the secret key, while the other part is owned by the user alone. Second, the approach to user revocation is simple and neat. Specifically, certificates can have an expiry date, which means that the certification is valid for a designated period.

2   Preliminaries

2.1   Bilinear Maps

Our scheme makes use of a bilinear map. Let G_1, G_2 and G_T be cyclic groups of prime order q for some large prime q. g_1 is a generator of G_1. g_2 is a generator of G_2. We say that G_1 and G_2 are admissible bilinear groups if there is a bilinear map $e : G_1 \times G_2 \to G_T$ that satisfies the following properties:

- *Bilinear*. We say that a map $e : G_1 \times G_2 \to G_T$ is bilinear if $e(g_1^a, g_2^b) = e(g_1, g_2)^{ab}$ for all $g_1 \in G_1, g_2 \in G_2$, and all $a, b \in Z_q$.
- *Non-degenerate*. If g_1, g_2 are generators of G_1, G_1, then $e(g_1, g_2)$ is a generator of G_T.
- *Computable*. There is an efficient algorithm to compute $e(g_1, g_2)$ for all $g_1 \in G_1, g_2 \in G_2$.

2.2   Complexity Assumption

Our scheme's anonymity and semantic security are based on the decisional bilinear Diffie-Hellman (DBDH) assumption. Our scheme also relies on the well-know Decisional Diffie-Hellman (DDH) assumption (in G_1 defined below).

Let $e : G_1 \times G_2 \to G_T$ be an admissible bilinear map as defined above. Let g_1 be a generator of G_1 and g_2 be a generator of G_2. The challenger randomly chooses $a, b, c \in Z_q$, $Z \in G_T$, and then flips a coin ξ. If $\xi = 1$ the challenger outputs the tuple $(g_1, g_1^a, g_1^b, g_1^c, g_2, g_2^a, g_2^b, g_2^c, e(g_1, g_2)^{abc})$. Otherwise, the challenger outputs the tuple $(g_1, g_1^a, g_1^b, g_1^c, g_2, g_2^a, g_2^b, g_2^c, Z)$. The adversary output a guess ξ' of ξ.

An adversary, $\mathcal{B}$ has at least an ϵ advantage in solving the DBDH problem if

$$\Pr[\mathcal{B}(g_1, g_1^a, g_1^b, g_1^c, g_2, g_2^a, g_2^b, g_2^c, e(g_1, g_2)^{abc}) = 1]$$

$$-\Pr[\mathcal{B}(g_1, g_1^a, g_1^b, g_1^c, g_2, g_2^a, g_2^b, g_2^c, Z) = 1] \,|\geq \epsilon$$

where the probability is over the random choice of $a, b, c, \in Z_q$, the random choice of $Z \in G_T$, the random choice of $g_1 \in G_1$, the random choice of $g_2 \in G_2$ and the random bits of $\mathcal{B}$.

Definition 1. *The (t, ϵ)-DBDH assumption holds if no t-time adversary has at least ϵ advantage in solving the above game.*

3   Modelling CBGE

3.1   The CBGE System

CBGE system involves five parties: a CA who can generate system parameters and a certificate according to the user's identity and public key, a GM who manages the group and traces the receivers if the need arises, a group of legitimate users who anonymously receive messages from the senders, a sender who might be one of the group members or not and has secret messages to be sent to the legitimate users, and a verifier who can verify whether the encrypted identity and the identity that forms the ciphertext are identical or not. CBGE consists of the following procedures:

- $(Params, SK_{CA}) \leftarrow$ Setup(λ). This is a probabilistic algorithm which takes as input a security parameter λ. It outputs the system parameter $Params$ that includes the description of a string space Λ and a CA's master-key SK_{CA}. This algorithm is run by the CA.
- $(PK_{GM}, SK_{GM}) \leftarrow$ GKGen$(Params)$. This is a probabilistic algorithm which takes as input system parameter $Params$. It outputs the group public key and private key (PK_{GM}, SK_{GM}). This algorithm is run by the GM.
- $(PK_U, SK_U) \leftarrow$ UKGen$(Params)$. This is a probabilistic algorithm which takes as input system parameter $Params$. It outputs the user's corresponding public key and private key pair (PK_U, SK_U). This algorithm is run by a user. Each user can register his public key as a group member to GM.
- $(Cert_{\tau,U}) \leftarrow$ Certificate$(Params, \tau, SK_{CA}, userinfo)$. This is deterministic algorithm which takes as inputs $Params, \tau, SK_{CA}, userinfo$, where $userinfo$ includes the user's public key PK_U and any necessary additional identifying information, while τ is a string identifying a time period. It outputs $Cert_{\tau,U}$ and sends it to the user. This algorithm is run by the CA.
- $(C) \leftarrow$ Encrypt$(M, Params, PK_{GM}, \tau, userinfo)$. This is a probabilistic algorithm which takes as inputs a message M in the structured message space, system parameter $Params$, the $userinfo$, a time period τ, as well as group public key PK_{GM}. It outputs a final ciphertext C in the ciphertext space. This algorithm is run by the sender.
- $(M) \leftarrow$ Decrypt$(Params, C, SK_U, Cert_{\tau,U})$. This is a deterministic algorithm which takes as inputs system parameter $Params$, ciphertext C, user's private key SK_U and the certificate $Cert_{\tau,U}$. It outputs the message M in the message space. This algorithm is run by the receiver.
- $(PK_U) \leftarrow$ Trace(C, SK_{GM}). GM runs a probabilistic algorithm takes as inputs ciphertext C and group private key SK_{GM}, outputs the PK_U of the receiver which indicates the receiver's identity.

3.2   Security Notions of CBGE

We consider the anonymity, semantic security and traceability of a CBGE scheme.

Anonymity. Anonymity of CBGE is defined as follow.

Definition 2. *We say that a CBGE scheme has indistinguishability against a chosen user information attack (IND-CUA) if no polynomially bounded adversary $\mathcal{A}$ has non-negligible advantage in the following game.*

- **Setup.** The challenger takes as input security parameter λ and runs the algorithm Setup(λ) which outputs system parameter $Params$ and masterkey SK_{CA}. The challenger then runs GKGen($Params$) and UKGen($Params$) to obtain the key pairs (PK_{GM}, SK_{GM}) and (PK_U, SK_U). It gives the adversary $Params$, PK_{GM} and PK_U.
- **Phase 1.** The adversary can adaptively issue the certification query of $(\tau, userinfo)$ and the user secret key query. The challenger runs Certificate and returns $Cert_\tau$. The challenger runs UKGen and sends SK_U to adversary.
- **Challenge.** The adversary chooses a message M and two users' information $userinfo_0$, $userinfo_1$ wished to be challenged. The challenger picks a random $b \in \{0,1\}$ and runs Encrypt. Then it returns $(C) = $ Encrypt($M, Params, PK_{GM}, userinfo_b$).
- **Phase 2.** It is similar to Phase 1. One restriction is that in the queries $userinfo \notin \{userinfo_0, userinfo_1\}$. Another is that neither key of the challenging users regarding $userinfo_0$ and $userinfo_1$ can be queried.
- **Guess.** The adversary outputs $b' \in \{0,1\}$. The adversary wins in the game if $b = b'$.

We define adversary $\mathcal{A}$'s advantage with security parameter λ in the above anonymity game as: $Adv_{\mathcal{A}}(\lambda) = \mid \Pr[b = b'] - \frac{1}{2} \mid$.

Semantic security. Semantic security of CBGE is defined as follow.

Definition 3. *We say that a CBGE scheme has indistinguishability against a chosen plaintext attack (IND-CPA) if no polynomially bounded adversary $\mathcal{A}$ has non-negligible advantage in the following game.*

- **Setup.** The challenger takes as input security parameter λ and runs the algorithm Setup(λ) which outputs system parameter $Params$ and masterkey SK_{CA}. The challenger then runs GKGen($Params$) and UKGen($Params$) to obtain the key pairs (PK_{GM}, SK_{GM}) and (PK_U, SK_U). It gives the adversary $Params$, PK_{GM} and PK_U.
- **Phase 1.** The adversary can adaptively issue the certification query of $(\tau, userinfo)$ and the user secret key query. The challenger runs Certificate and returns $Cert_\tau$. Then the challenger runs UKGen and sends SK_U to the adversary.
- **Challenge.** After Phase 1, adversary chooses two equal length plaintexts M_0, M_1 and issues query $(\tau', userinfo', SK'_U, M_0, M_1)$. The challenger runs Encrypt and returns $(C) = $ Encrypt($M_c, Params, PK_{GM}, \tau', userinfo'$).
- **Phase 2.** It is similar to Phase 1. One restriction is that the adversary can at most ask one of two queries of the certification query and the secret query regarding $(\tau', userinfo')$.
- **Guess.** The adversary outputs $c' \in \{0,1\}$. The adversary wins in the game if $c = c'$.

We define adversary $\mathcal{A}$'s advantage with security parameter λ in the above semantic security game as: $Adv_{\mathcal{A}}(\lambda) = |\Pr[c = c'] - \frac{1}{2}|$.

Traceability. Traceability is formally defined as follow.

Definition 4. *We say that an CBGE scheme is traceable if no polynomially bounded adversary has non-negligible probability to win in the following game.*

- **Setup.** The challenger takes as input security parameter λ and runs the algorithm $\mathsf{Setup}(\lambda)$ which outputs system parameter $Params$ and master-key SK_{CA}. The challenger then runs $\mathsf{GKGen}(Params)$ to obtain the key pairs (PK_{GM}, SK_{GM}). It gives the adversary $Params$ and PK_{GM}.
- **Challenge.** The adversary outputs $user_1$ with PK_{U_1}, $user_2$ with PK_{U_2} and an authenticated message M. The challenger returns the corresponding SK_{U_1} and SK_{U_2}.
- **Output.** The adversary outputs a well-formed ciphertext C' and a valid zero-knowledge proof. The adversary wins if the group manager outputs one of the user public keys and decryptions with SK_{U_1} and SK_{U_2} are both valid.

4   The Proposal

In this section, we propose a scheme towards CBGE. The only difference is that the GM and the verifier are identical.

4.1   A Scheme Towards CBGE

Setup. Let $e : G_1 \times G_2 \to G_T$ be a bilinear map as defined in Sect. 2, where G_1 is DDH-hard. The CA picks random generators $g_1, g_2 \xleftarrow{R} G_1$. It picks a random $s_C \xleftarrow{R} Z_q^*$ and sets $g = g_1^{s_C}$. The CA's secret is s_C. It chooses cryptographic hash functions $H_1 : \{0,1\}^* \to G_2$ and H_2 from the family of universal one-way hash functions. The systems paramters are $Params = (q, G_1, G_2, G_T, e, g, g_1, g_2, H_1, H_2)$. The message space is $\mathcal{M} = \{0,1\}^\ell$, where ℓ is the message length.

GKGen. This procedure chooses random $x_1, x_2, y_1, y_2, z \xleftarrow{R} Z_q$, then computes $w = g_1^{x_1} g_2^{x_2}, d = g_1^{y_1} g_2^{y_2}, s = g_1^z$. Group public key and secret key are $PK_{GM} = (g_1, g_2, w, d, s, H_2)$ and $SK_{GM} = (x_1, x_2, y_1, y_2, z)$, respectively.

UKGen. Assume that a user's secret key/public key pair is $(SK_U, PK_U) = (s_U, g_1^{s_U})$, where $s_U \xleftarrow{R} Z_q^*$.

Certificate. The user sends $userinfo$ to the CA, which includes his public key $g_1^{s_U}$ and any necessary additional identifying information, such as his name and email address. The CA verifies the user's information. If satisfied, the CA computes $P_U = H_1(g, \tau, userinfo) \in G_2$ in period τ. The CA then computes $P_U^{s_C}$ as a certificate and sends it to the user via a secure channel. The user also signs $userinfo$, producing $(P_U')^{s_U}$ where $P_U' = H_1(userinfo) \in G_2$. Now, notice that $Cert_{\tau,U} = P_U^{s_C} \cdot (P_U')^{s_U}$ is a two person aggregate signature. The user will use this aggregate signature as his partial decryption key.

Encrypt. This encryption procedure can be divided into two sub-procedures.

- Message encryption. The sender computes $P_U = H_1(h, \tau, userinfo) \in G_2$ and $P'_U = H_1(userinfo) \in G_2$. Then he chooses a random $r \xleftarrow{R} Z^*_q$. Let $g_U = e(g_1^{sc}, P_U)e(g_1^{sU}, P'_U) \in G_T$. Let $M = (M' \| H(M', g_U^r)) \in G_T$, where M' is an appropriate bit string. To encrypt M using $userinfo$, the sender sets the ciphertext to be $C_1 = [C_{10}, C_{11}] = [g_1^r, M \cdot g_U^r]$.
- User's public key encryption. Given the user's public key $g_1^{sU} \in G_1$, the procedure chooses random $n \xleftarrow{R} Z_q$ then it computes $k_1 = g_1^n, k_2 = g_2^n, \psi = s^n g_1^{sU}, \varphi = H_2(k_1, k_2, \psi), v = w^n d^{n\varphi}$. The ciphertext is $C_2 = [k_1, k_2, \psi, v]$.

The sender sends the ciphertext $C = [C_1, C_2]$ to the verifier.

Zero-knowledge proof. We construct a zero-knowledge proof which can prove the encrypted public key and the public key that forms message encryption are identical. It proves the ciphertext has not been tampered as well as the ciphertext is well-formed. This is an interactive protocol between the sender (prover) and the verifier (GM). We denote the protocol as follow.

$$ZK \left\{ M, r, n, PK_U \left| \begin{array}{c} C_{10} = g_1^r, k_1 = g_1^n, k_2 = g_2^n, \\ C_{11} = M \cdot e(g, P'_U)e(PK_U, (P'_U)^r), \\ \psi = s^n PK_U, v = w^n d^{n\varphi} \end{array} \right. \right\}$$

This zero-knowledge proof is difficult to be constructed directly. We compute $T = PK_U^r, \psi' = \psi^r = s^{nr}T, k'_1 = k_1^r = g_1^{nr}$ and set $d^\varphi = d'$. Then we convert the above zero-knowledge proof into an equivalent one as follows.

$$ZK \left\{ M, r, n, T, PK_U \left| \begin{array}{c} C_{10} = g_1^r, k_1 = g_1^n, k_2 = g_2^n,, v = (wd')^n \\ C_{11} = M \cdot e(g, P'_U)e(T, P'_U), \psi' = \psi^r \\ \psi = s^n PK_U, \psi' = s^{nr}T, k'_1 = g_1^{nr}, k'_1 = k_1^r \end{array} \right. \right\}$$

The 3-move protocol is as follows.

1. The prover randomly chooses integers $\bar{r}, \bar{n} \in Z_q$, $P\bar{K}_U, \bar{T} \in G_1$, and $\bar{M} \in G_T$. He computes $\bar{C}_{10} = g_1^{\bar{r}}, \bar{k}_1 = g_1^{\bar{n}}, \bar{k}_2 = g_2^{\bar{n}}, \bar{\psi} = s^{\bar{n}}P\bar{K}_U, \bar{C}_{11} = \bar{M} \cdot e(g, P'_U)e(\bar{T}, P'_U), \bar{\psi}' = s^{\bar{n}\bar{r}}\bar{T}, \bar{k}'_1 = g_1^{\bar{n}\bar{r}}, \bar{v} = (wd')^{\bar{n}}, \bar{\psi}' = \psi^{\bar{r}}, \bar{k}'_1 = k_1^{\bar{r}}$. Then he sends these to the verifier.
2. The verifier challenges the prover with a random element $\bar{c} \in Z_q$.
3 The prover responses with $\sigma = \{\bar{c}, \sigma_1, \sigma_2, \sigma_3, \sigma_4, \sigma_5, \sigma_6\}$, where $\sigma_1 = \bar{M}M^{\bar{c}}$, $\sigma_2 = \bar{r} + \bar{c}r, \sigma_3 = \bar{n} + \bar{c}n, \sigma_4 = P\bar{K}_U PK_U^{\bar{c}}, \sigma_5 = \bar{T}T^{\bar{c}}, \sigma_6 = \bar{n}\bar{r} + \bar{c} \cdot nr$.
4. The verifier who is also the GM computes $PK_U = g_1^{sU} = \psi/k_1^z$. Therefore, it can further compute P_U, P'_U. Then the verifier checks that $g_1^{\sigma_2} \stackrel{?}{=} C_{10}^{\bar{c}}\bar{C}_{10}, g_1^{\sigma_3} \stackrel{?}{=} k_1^{\bar{c}}\bar{k}_1, g_2^{\sigma_3} \stackrel{?}{=} k_2^{\bar{c}}\bar{k}_2, \sigma_1 \cdot e(g, P_U^{\sigma_2})e(\sigma_5, P'_U) \stackrel{?}{=} C_{11}^{\bar{c}}\bar{C}_{11}, s^{\sigma_3}\sigma_4 \stackrel{?}{=} \psi^{\bar{c}}\bar{\psi}, s^{\sigma_6}\sigma_5 \stackrel{?}{=} \psi'^{\bar{c}}\bar{\psi}', g_1^{\sigma_6} \stackrel{?}{=} k_1'^{\bar{c}}\bar{k}'_1, (wd')^{\sigma_3} \stackrel{?}{=} v^{\bar{c}}\bar{v}, \psi^{\sigma_2} \stackrel{?}{=} \psi'^{\bar{c}}\bar{\psi}', k_1^{\sigma_2} \stackrel{?}{=} k_1'^{\bar{c}}\bar{k}'_1$. The verifier outputs 1 if all checks hold and forwards (C, σ) to the anonymous receiver, e.g., in a broadcast way; otherwise it outputs 0 and aborts.

Decryption. To decrypt C, the receiver computes: $M = C_{11}/e(C_{10}, Cert_{\tau,U})$. M can be divided into the form of $M = (M'\|\xi) \in G_T$. The receiver outputs M if $\xi = H(M', g_U^r)$; else, outputs "abort".

Trace. The GM outputs $PK_U = g_1^{s_U} = \psi/k_1^z$. It indicates the receiver's identity.

Correctness of our scheme. We show that the above scheme is correct. We first verify that the ciphertext can be decrypted correctly. $e(C_{10}, Cert_{\tau,U}) = e(g_1^r, P_U^{s_C} \cdot (P_U')^{s_U}) = e(g_1^{s_C}, P_U)^r e(g_1^{s_U}, (P_U'))^r = g_U^r$. We then verify that the receiver can be traced correctly. Since $k_1 = g_1^n, k_2 = g_2^n$, we have $k_1^{x_1} k_2^{x_2} = g_1^{nx_1} g_2^{nx_2} = w^n$. Similarly, we have $k_1^{y_1} k_2^{y_2} = d^n$ and $k_1^z = s^n$. The equation $k_1^{x_1+y_1\varphi} k_2^{x_2+y_2\varphi} = v$ will hold. The output is $g_1^{s_U} = \psi/s^n$.

For the security, we have the following theorems. The proofs are given in the full version of the paper.

Theorem 1. *Our scheme is anonymous against chosen users' information attack in the random oracle model assuming DDH and DBDH are intractable.*

Theorem 2. *Our scheme is semantically secure against chosen plaintext attack in the random oracle model assuming DBDH is intractable.*

Theorem 3. *The probability that the GM outputs a wrong public key of the receiver is $1/q$. Our scheme satisfies traceability.*

4.2   Efficiency

In Table 1, we denote τ_m as one multiplication operation time unit in G_1, G_2 and G_T, τ_e as one exponent operation time unit in G_1, G_2 and G_T, τ_p as one pairing operation time unit. The storage complexity and computational complexity of our schemes are constant. Table 1 shows that our scheme is efficient.

Table 1. Efficiency of our CBGE scheme

PK_{GM} size	5	SK_{GM} size	5
PK_U size	1	SK_U size	1
Ciphertext size	6	Certificate time	$2\tau_e + \tau_m$
Setup time	τ_e	GKGen time	$2\tau_m + 5\tau_e$
UKGen time	τ_e	Encrypt time	$2\tau_m + 8\tau_e$
Decrypt time	$\tau_m + \tau_p$	Trace time	$\tau_m + \tau_e$

5   Conclusion

We formalized a new cryptographic primitive, CBGE, which overcomes the drawbacks of PKI-based and IBE-based group encryption. It allows a sender to send a ciphertext to any group member and the receiver of the ciphertext remains anonymous. The group manager can trace the receiver if the need arises. We propose a concrete construction towards CBGE which achieves anonymity, semantic security and traceability. We leave it as an open question to design a standard CBGE scheme.

Acknowledgment. This paper is supported by the Natural Science Foundation of China through projects 61370190 and by the Science & Technology Plan Projects of Shenzhen (JCYJ20150324140036830, GJHZ20160226202520268).

References

1. Ei Aimani, L., Joye, M.: Toward practical group encryption. In: Jacobson, M., Locasto, M., Mohassel, P., Safavi-Naini, R. (eds.) ACNS 2013. LNCS, vol. 7954, pp. 237–252. Springer, Heidelberg (2013). doi:10.1007/978-3-642-38980-1_15

2. Boyen, X., Waters, B.: Compact group signatures without random oracles. In: Vaudenay, S. (ed.) EUROCRYPT 2006. LNCS, vol. 4004, pp. 427–444. Springer, Heidelberg (2006). doi:10.1007/11761679_26

3. Chaum, D., Heyst, E.: Group signatures. In: Davies, D.W. (ed.) EUROCRYPT 1991. LNCS, vol. 547, pp. 257–265. Springer, Heidelberg (1991). doi:10.1007/3-540-46416-6_22

4. Cathalo, J., Libert, B., Yung, M.: Group encryption: non-interactive realization in the standard model. In: Matsui, M. (ed.) ASIACRYPT 2009. LNCS, vol. 5912, pp. 179–196. Springer, Heidelberg (2009). doi:10.1007/978-3-642-10366-7_11

5. Dodis, Y., Katz, J.: Chosen-ciphertext security of multiple encryption. In: Kilian, J. (ed.) TCC 2005. LNCS, vol. 3378, pp. 188–209. Springer, Heidelberg (2005). doi:10.1007/978-3-540-30576-7_11

6. Cramer, R., Shoup, V.: A practical public key cryptosystem provably secure against adaptive chosen ciphertext attack. In: Krawczyk, H. (ed.) CRYPTO 1998. LNCS, vol. 1462, pp. 13–25. Springer, Heidelberg (1998). doi:10.1007/BFb0055717

7. Gentry, C.: Certificate-based encryption and the certificate revocation problem. In: Biham, E. (ed.) EUROCRYPT 2003. LNCS, vol. 2656, pp. 272–293. Springer, Heidelberg (2003). doi:10.1007/3-540-39200-9_17

8. Kiayias, A., Yung, M.: Secure scalable group signature with dynamic joins and separable authorities. Int. J. Secur. Netw. 2006 1(1/2), 24–45 (2006)

9. Kiayias, A., Tsiounis, Y., Yung, M.: Group encryption. In: Kurosawa, K. (ed.) ASIACRYPT 2007. LNCS, vol. 4833, pp. 181–199. Springer, Heidelberg (2007). doi:10.1007/978-3-540-76900-2_11

10. Libert, B., Yung, M., Joye, M., Peters, T.: Traceable group encryption. In: Krawczyk, H. (ed.) PKC 2014. LNCS, vol. 8383, pp. 592–610. Springer, Heidelberg (2014). doi:10.1007/978-3-642-54631-0_34

11. Qin, B., Wu, Q., Susilo, W., Mu, Y.: Publicly verifiable privacy-preserving group decryption. In: Yung, M., Liu, P., Lin, D. (eds.) Inscrypt 2008. LNCS, vol. 5487, pp. 72–83. Springer, Heidelberg (2009). doi:10.1007/978-3-642-01440-6_8

12. Shamir, A.: Identity-based cryptosystems and signature schemes. In: Blakley, G.R., Chaum, D. (eds.) CRYPTO 1984. LNCS, vol. 196, pp. 47–53. Springer, Heidelberg (1985). doi:10.1007/3-540-39568-7_5

13. Yum, D.H., Lee, P.J.: Identity-based cryptography in public key management. In: Katsikas, S.K., Gritzalis, S., López, J. (eds.) EuroPKI 2004. LNCS, vol. 3093, pp. 71–84. Springer, Heidelberg (2004). doi:10.1007/978-3-540-25980-0_6

Leakage Analysis

Updatable Lossy Trapdoor Functions and Its Application in Continuous Leakage

Sujuan Li[1,2(✉)], Yi Mu[2], Mingwu Zhang[3], and Futai Zhang[4]

[1] School of Mathematical and Physical Sciences,
Nanjing Tech University, Nanjing, China
lisujuan1978@126.com
[2] School of Computing and Information Technology,
University of Wollongong, Wollongong, Australia
[3] School of Computer Science, Hubei University of Technology, Wuhan, China
[4] School of Computer Science and Technology,
Nanjing Normal University, Nanjing, China

Abstract. Lossy trapdoor functions (LTFs) were firstly introduced by Peikert and Waters [2]. Since their introduction, LTFs have found numerous applications. In this paper we focus on the LTFs in the continuous leakage. We introduce the new notion of updatable LTFs (ULTFs) and give its formal definition and security properties. Based on these, we extend the security model of the LTFs to continuous leakage. Under the DDH assumption and DCR assumption respectively, we show two explicit LTFs against continuous leakage in the standard model. We also show the performance of the proposed schemes compared with the known existing continuous leakage resilient LTFs.

Keywords: LTFs · Continuous leakage · ULTFs · DDH · DCR

1 Introduction

Lossy trapdoor functions (LTFs) were firstly introduced by Peikert and Waters [2]. A collection of lossy trapdoor functions can be divided into two computationally indistinguishable families. The first family is the injective functions which can be efficiently inverted using a trapdoor, while the other family is the lossy functions under which the image size of these functions is significantly smaller than the size of their domain. Hence the lossy functions loose a lot of information about their input. Additionally injective and lossy functions are efficiently samplable.

This work was partly supported by the National Natural Science Foundation of China under Grant 61170298, 61370224, 61672010, 61672289, Fujian Provincial Key Laboratory of Network Security and Cryptology Research Fund (Fujian Normal University) under Grant NO. 15006, the Jiangsu Government Scholarship for Overseas Studies (JS-2014-044), the Natural science fund for colleges and universities in Jiangsu Province under Grant 16KJB520018. and the Youth Cultivation Fund of Nanjing Tech University under ZKJ201528.

© Springer International Publishing AG 2016
L. Chen and J. Han (Eds.): ProvSec 2016, LNCS 10005, pp. 309–319, 2016.
DOI: 10.1007/978-3-319-47422-9_18

Actually, lossy trapdoor functions have found numerous applications, which can be used as a tool to construct important cryptographic primitives such as injective one-way trapdoor functions, chosen plaintext secure (CPA) and chosen ciphertext secure (CCA) public key encryptions (PKE) in the standard model and oblivious transfer (OT). In addition, LTFs have already found various other applications, including deterministic PKE scheme [9], OAEP-based PKE scheme, hedged PKE scheme for protecting against bad randomness , selective opening attack (SOA) secure PKE scheme and efficient non-interactive string commitment etc.

The feature of a leakage resilient cryptosystem is that it remains secure even when some secret internal information including the secret key is leaked to the adversary. In the traditional security analysis, security models treat such internal information as perfectly hidden from the adversary. With the development of various side-channel attacks it is clear that the traditional view is inconsistent with some physical realities [16]. The cryptographic researchers have paid much attention to the design of leakage-resilient cryptosystems [5, 17–19].

The continuous leakage resilient (CLR) model was introduced by Dodis et al. [13] and Brakerski et al. [14]. It is a more powerful security model since it allows the adversary to learn unbounded leakage on the system's secret memory along the full time of the system. Such model of invisible key updates was formalized by Alwen et al. [15] where one assumes that there exists a trusted and leak-free device which uses some updatable key uk to continuously refresh the secret key in a way that still satisfies the above two requirements. The leak-free device is only present during the key updates, but not during the normal operations just like decryption when the leakage actually happens. In [1], this CLR model of invisible key updates is referred to the floppy model, where there is assumed an external leak-free storage which is only present for refreshing operations.

OUR MOTIVATION Based on the work of Brakerski et al. [14], Koppula et al. [7] firstly gave the security model of lossy trapdoor functions under continuous leakage and presented the lossy trapdoor functions against continuous leakage which is a base of the deterministic public key encryption against continuous leakage. Their security model is mainly based on the all-but-one (ABO) LTFs of Peikert and Waters in [2]. Under this model their proposal is not concise and efficient in which they utilized many bi-linear parings to encrypt only one bit. Hence their LTFs against continuous leakage is so complicated that it can not be used in practice efficiently. Qin and Liu et al. firstly introduced the leakage resilient lossy trapdoor functions [8]. In their work the structure of LTFs is slightly different from the one introduced by Peikert and Waters in [2]. In [2], the evaluation key of a LTF includes the public parameters. But in [8], they distinguish between the public parameters and the evaluation key with two independent algorithms. Even though, the slight change on the constructure did not has influence on their scheme to satisfy the security properties of LTFs.

Motivated by the work of Qin and Liu et al. [8], we focus on how to construct efficient and practical LTFs against continuous leakage in the floppy model.

OUR CONTRIBUTION In this work, our contribution is described as follows:

1. We introduce the new notion of updatable lossy trapdoor functions (ULTFs) based on the LTFs structure of [8] where the key sample algorithm is divided into two independent steps. At the same time, we also give the security requirements such as the indistinguishability of injective/lossy evaluation key et al. When the evaluation algorithm F is leakage resilient, we can achieve the LTFs against continuous leakage which we denote as CLR-LTFs for short. With the help of the new notion of ULTFs we achieve the security model of CLR-LTFs in the floppy model (Table 1).
2. Based on the ElGamal-like PKE scheme in vector form [1,4,5] which is additively homomorphic and CPA-secure against continuous leakage, we achieve two proposals of CLR-LTFs under the DDH and DCR assumptions respectively. In the two CLR-LTFs schemes, with the public parameters and the evaluation key fixed, we utilize the technology of the matrix kernel to complete the refreshment of the trapdoor.
3. Compared with the other known CLR-LTFs constructions introduced by Koppula et al. [7], we give a efficiency comparison as below.

Table 1. Efficiency comparison.

Scheme	Hardness assumption	Leakage rate	$|m|$	Pairing	Group
[7]	DDH	$1/2$	1-bit	Yes	Prime order
[7]	SXDH	$1 - o(1)$	1-bit	Yes	Prime order
Ours	DDH	$1/n$	n-bit	No	Prime order
Ours	DCR	$1 - o(1)$	$\alpha \log N$-bit	No	Composite order

$|m|$ denotes the length of the encrypted massage; $n \approx \Theta(\kappa)$ where κ is the security parameter; N is a RSA modulus; $\alpha \geq 1$ is a nature number.

2   Preliminaries

Let $[t]$ denote the set $\{1, 2, \cdots, t\}$ where t is a natural number and $\log x$ denote the discrete logarithm of x in base 2. We say that a function $\mathsf{negl}(\kappa)$ is negligible in κ if for all polynomial ploy and sufficiently large $\mathsf{negl}(\kappa) \leq 1/\mathsf{ploy}(\kappa)$. $\mathsf{Rk}_i(\mathbb{Z}_p^{n \times m})$ denotes the uniform distribution on any n-by-m matrices over $\mathbb{Z}_p$ of rank i. We extend the standard DDH assumption to the following form. For a group (G, p, g) and random elements $g_1, g_2, \cdots, g_l \in G$ we define two sets: $L := \{(g_1^r, g_2^r, \cdots, g_l^r) : r \in \mathbb{Z}_p\}$; $X := \{(g_1^{r_1}, g_2^{r_2}, \cdots, g_l^{r_l}) : r_1, r_2, \cdots, r_l \in \mathbb{Z}_p\}$.

If $x \in L$ the corresponding r is called a witness for x. At the same time (X, L) forms a subset membership problem [5] whose hardness is subject to the DDH assumption [4]. On the other hand, Naor and Segev [5] showed that the DDH assumption is equivalent to the assumption that it is hard to distinguish between an n-by-m matrix X with rank $i \geq 1$ and one with rank $j > i$ in the exponent of a generator g of a prime order group G.

Rank Hiding Assumption[14]. Following with the parameters of the DDH assumption. Let $\mathsf{Rk}_i(\mathbb{Z}_p^{n\times m})$ denote the uniform distribution on all n-by-m matrices over $\mathbb{Z}_p$ of rank i. The rank hiding assumption holds iff

$$\mathsf{Adv}_{G,\mathcal{A}}^{\mathrm{rh}} := |\Pr[\mathcal{A}((G,p,g,g^X) : X \leftarrow \mathsf{Rk}_i(\mathbb{Z}_p^{n\times m})) = 1]$$
$$-\Pr[\mathcal{A}((G,p,g,g^X) : X \leftarrow \mathsf{Rk}_j(\mathbb{Z}_p^{n\times m})) = 1]| \leq \mathrm{negl}(\kappa)$$

for any PPT adversary $\mathcal{A}$.

Extended Rank Hiding Assumption[1]. Based on the rank hiding assumption the extended rank hiding assumption states that for any PPT adversary $\mathcal{A}$, the advantage
$\mathsf{Adv}_{G,\mathcal{A}}^{\mathrm{erh}}$
$:= |\Pr[\mathcal{A}((G,p,g,g^X,\boldsymbol{v}_1,\cdots,\boldsymbol{v}_t) : X \leftarrow \mathsf{Rk}_i(\mathbb{Z}_p^{n\times m}); \{\boldsymbol{v}_l\}_{l=1}^t \in \mathsf{kernel}(X)) = 1]$
$-\Pr[\mathcal{A}((G,p,g,g^X,\boldsymbol{v}_1,\cdots,\boldsymbol{v}_t) : X \leftarrow \mathsf{Rk}_j(\mathbb{Z}_p^{n\times m}); \{\boldsymbol{v}_l\}_{l=1}^t \in \mathsf{kernel}(X)) = 1]|$
$\leq \mathrm{negl}(\kappa)$ where $m,n \in \mathbb{N}, j > i \in \mathbb{N}$ and $t \leq \min\{n,m\}-\max\{i,j\}$.

Decisional Composite Residuosity (DCR) Assumption. We assume a group $Z_{N^{\alpha+1}}^*$ is a multiplicative group where $\alpha \geq 1$ is an integer. The integer $N = PQ$ is an RSA modulus which means that P and Q are odd primes of equivalent bit length. Obviously the group $\mathbb{Z}_{N^{\alpha+1}}^*$ is a direct product $\mathsf{G} \times \mathsf{H}$ where G is a cyclic group of order N^α and H is isomorphic to $\mathbb{Z}_N^*$. We define $T := 1 + N(\mathrm{mod}N^{\alpha+1})$, therefore T generates the group H. The decisional composite residuosity (DCR) assumption holds on the group $Z_{N^{\alpha+1}}^*$ iff

$$\mathsf{Adv}_{N,\mathcal{A}}^{\mathrm{DCR}} := |\Pr[\mathcal{A}(N,g) = 1] - \Pr[\mathcal{A}(N,g \cdot T) = 1]| \leq \mathrm{negl}(\kappa)$$

for any PPT adversary $\mathcal{A}$ where $g \in \mathsf{G}$ is chosen at random.

Generalized Leftover Hash Lemma. We write $X \approx_\epsilon Y$ to denote $\mathrm{SD}(X,Y) \leq \epsilon$, and $X \approx Y$ to denote that the statistical distance is negligible. The min-entropy of a random variable X is $H_\infty(X) = -\log(max_x\Pr[X = x])$. We use the notion of average min-entropy which captures the remaining unpredictability of a random variable X conditioned on another random variable Y, formally defined as: $\widetilde{H}_\infty(X|Y) = -\log(E_{y\in Y}[2^{-H_\infty(X|Y=y)}])$ where $E_{y\in Y}$ denotes the expected value over all values of Y.

Definition 2. [6] A function $Ext : \mathcal{X} \times \{0,1\}^t \to \mathcal{Y}$ is an average-case (m,ϵ)-strong extractor if for all pairs of random variables (X,Z) such that $X \in \mathcal{X}$ and $\widetilde{H}_\infty(X|Z) \geq m$ it holds that $\mathrm{SD}((Ext(X,S), S, Z), (U_\mathcal{Y}, S, Z)) \leq \epsilon$. where S is uniform in $\{0,1\}^t$ and $U_\mathcal{Y}$ is uniform over $\mathcal{Y}$.

Lemma 1. [6] *(Generalized Leftover Hash Lemma) Assume that the family $\mathcal{H} = \{H_k : \mathcal{X} \to \mathcal{Y}\}_{k\in\mathcal{K}}$ is a universal hash family. Then for any two random variables X, Z and $k \in \mathcal{K}$, it holds that $\mathrm{SD}((H_k(X), k, Z), (U_\mathcal{Y}, k, Z)) \leq \frac{1}{2}\sqrt{2^{-\widetilde{H}_\infty(X|Z)}|\mathcal{Y}|}$.*

3   Updatable Lossy Trapdoor Function

Though Koppula et al. [7] has introduced a notion of LTFs resilient to continual memory leakage, their notion was mainly based on the all-but-one (ABO) LTFs of Peikert and Waters in [2]. The new notion which will be presented as follows is mainly based on the LTFs structure of Qin and Liu et al. [8] which is slightly different from the one introduced by Peikert and Waters in [2]. In [2], the evaluation key of a LTF includes the public parameters. But in [8], they distinguish between the public parameters and the evaluation key with two independent algorithms. As a result the change on the structure does not do any influence on the security. Based on the new notion, we can extend the ULTFs to CLR-LTFs naturally when the evaluation algorithm is leakage resilient.

We give some related functions about the security parameter κ: $d(\kappa)$: the input length of the polynomial about κ; $k(\kappa)$: the lossiness $k(\kappa) \leq d(\kappa)$.

Definition (Updatable Lossy Trapdoor Functions). A collection of updatable (d, k)-lossy trapdoor functions is a 5-tuple of (possible probabilistic) polynomial-time algorithms (PTAs) $(\mathsf{G}, \mathsf{S}, \mathsf{F}, \mathsf{F}^{-1}, \mathsf{U})$ such that:

1. **Public Parameter.** $\mathsf{G}(1^\kappa)$: It is a probabilistic PTA which takes in the security parameter 1^κ and outputs the public parameter, the trapdoor and the updatable key (pp, td, uk).
2. **Public Parameter.** $\mathsf{S}(\mathsf{pp}, b)$: It is a probabilistic PTA which takes in the public parameter pp and $b \in \{0,1\}$ and samples an evaluation key ek which is also called the function index.
3. **Evaluation.** $\mathsf{F}(ek, x)$: It is a deterministic PTA which takes in the evaluation key ek and $x \in \{0,1\}^d$ and outputs the image y.
4. **Inversion.** $\mathsf{F}^{-1}(td, y)$: It is a deterministic PTA which takes in the image y and the trapdoor td and outputs $x \in \{0,1\}^d$ or $\perp$.
5. **Update.** $\mathsf{U}(uk, td)$: It is a probabilistic PTA which takes in the updatable key uk and the original trapdoor td and outputs the updated trapdoor td' such that $|td| = |td'|$.

Basic Properties. We require that the ULTF $(\mathsf{G}, \mathsf{S}, \mathsf{F}, \mathsf{F}^{-1}, \mathsf{U})$ has some basic properties, indicating its correctness an hardness requirements:

– Correctness. For all $(\mathsf{PP}, td) \leftarrow \mathsf{G}(1^\kappa)$, all $ek \leftarrow \mathsf{S}(\mathsf{pp}, 1)$ and all $x \in \{0,1\}^d$ it holds that $\mathsf{F}^{-1}(td, \mathsf{F}(ek, x)) = x$ which is the preimage of y. On the other hand, it requires that with the fixed public parameter pp and the evaluation key ek the updated trapdoor td' can also recover the preimage x of y correctly in the injective mode i.e. it holds that $\mathsf{F}^{-1}(td', \mathsf{F}(ek, x)) = x$.
– Injective/Lossy. For the third evaluation algorithm $\mathsf{F}(ek, \cdot)$, it requires that for any $ek \leftarrow \mathsf{S}(\mathsf{pp}, 1)$ the function $\mathsf{F}(ek, \cdot)$ is in the injective mode; and for any $ek \leftarrow \mathsf{S}(\mathsf{pp}, 0)$ the function $\mathsf{F}(ek, \cdot)$ is in the lossy mode. The image size of the lossy function $\mathsf{F}(ek, x)$ is at most 2^{d-k}. Even when the evaluation $\mathsf{F}(ek, x)$ is in the injective mode, it requires that it can be inverted to the correct preimage using either the trapdoor td or any of its polynomial many updated trapdoor td'.

– Indistinguishability. For the second public parameter algorithm $\mathsf{S}(\mathsf{pp}, b)$, the two evaluation keys ek respectively produced by $\mathsf{S}(\mathsf{pp}, 1)$ and $\mathsf{S}(\mathsf{pp}, 0)$ are computationally indistinguishable even after the trapdoor updates.

Extension. For the particular structure, the ULTFs can be viewed as a special lossy trapdoor function which serves as a fundamental tool in constructing cryptographic primitives in both leakage-free and leaky settings. If we combine the ULTF with the leakage property efficiently, we can achieve the continuous leakage resilient (CLR) LTFs. Based on the new notion of ULTFs, we give the security model of the CLR-LTFs as follows.

We consider the security model in the floppy model [1]. That means during the trapdoor update there is a leak-free device available and between two trapdoor updates there is bounded leakage about the trapdoor (see [1] for more details).

Definition (Lossy Trapdoor Functions against continuous leakage). We say that ULTFs $(\mathsf{G}, \mathsf{S}, \mathsf{F}, \mathsf{F}^{-1}, \mathsf{U})$ is a collection of continuous λ-bit leakage resilient (d, k)-LTFs (denote λ-CLR-LTFs) in the floppy model if the ULTFs satisfies the basic properties above and for any PPT λ-key leakage adversary $\mathcal{A} = (\mathcal{A}_1, \mathcal{A}_2)$ the advantage

$$\mathrm{Adv}_{\mathrm{ULTF}, \mathcal{A}}^{\lambda-\mathrm{CLR}}(\kappa) := |\Pr[\mathrm{Exp}_{\mathrm{ULTF}, \mathcal{A}}^{\lambda-\mathrm{CLR}}(\kappa, 0) = 1] - \mathrm{Exp}_{\mathrm{ULTF}, \mathcal{A}}^{\lambda-\mathrm{CLR}}(\kappa, 1) = 1]| \leq negl(\kappa)$$

where the experiment $\mathrm{Exp}_{\mathrm{ULTF}, \mathcal{A}}^{\lambda-\mathrm{CLR}}(\kappa, \gamma)$ $(\gamma \in \{0, 1\})$ is described as:

Experiment $\mathrm{Exp}_{\mathrm{ULTF}, \mathcal{A}}^{\lambda-\mathrm{CLR}}(\kappa, \gamma)$:
$(\mathsf{pp}, td_0) \leftarrow \mathsf{G}(1^\kappa)$
For $i = 0, 1, 2, \cdots, t$ where t is polynomial in the security parameter κ
$\{State_i \leftarrow \mathcal{A}_1^{\mathrm{leakage}(td_i)}(\mathsf{pp})$ where $|\mathrm{leakage}(td_i)| \leq \lambda$;
$td_{i+1} \leftarrow \mathsf{U}(uk, td_i)\}$; $ek \leftarrow \mathsf{S}(\mathsf{pp}, \gamma)$; $\gamma' \leftarrow \mathcal{A}_2(State_{i \in [t]}, ek)$
output γ'.

4   ElGamal-Like Public Key Encryption Scheme

Briefly we intrduce the ElGamal-like Encryption scheme which will be elegantly embedded into the following continuous leakage resilient LTFs. We will utilize some good algebraic properties of this cryptographic structure in the following. For the security parameter κ, $\mathbb{G} = (G, p, g) \leftarrow \mathcal{G}(1^\kappa)$. The scheme is run in group G with prime order p. For some negligible $\epsilon = \epsilon(\kappa)$ set $l = 2 + \frac{\lambda + 2\log(1/\epsilon) - 2}{\log p}$. The ElGamal-like PKE (KeyGen, Encrypt, Decrypt) is operated as follows.

1. KeyGen(1^κ): Run $\mathbb{G} = (G, p, g) \leftarrow \mathcal{G}(1^\kappa)$. Choose vector $\boldsymbol{w} \in \mathbb{Z}_p^l$ and $\mathbf{s} \in \mathbb{Z}_p^l$ and let $h = g^{\langle \boldsymbol{w}, \boldsymbol{s} \rangle} \in G$. The public key is $pk = (G, p, g, g^{\boldsymbol{w}}, h)$. The secret key is set to $sk = \boldsymbol{s}$.

2. Encrypt(pk, m): Given a public key $pk = (G, p, g, g^{\boldsymbol{w}}, h)$ along with a message $m \in G$, pick a random scalar $r \in \mathbb{Z}_q$ uniformly at random and output the ciphertext $c = (c_1, c_2) = (g^{r\boldsymbol{w}}, h^r \cdot m)$.
3. Decrypt(sk, c): Given a ciphertext $c = (c_1, c_2)$ along with a secret key $sk = \boldsymbol{s}$ output $m = c_2 \cdot c_1^{-\boldsymbol{s}}$.

The correctness holds directly with $h^r = g^{r\langle \boldsymbol{w}, \boldsymbol{s} \rangle} = g^{\langle r\boldsymbol{w}, \boldsymbol{s} \rangle}$. The above scheme is a variant of the ElGamal public key encryption in vector form. On the other hand, it also can be seen as the BHHO public key encryption [4] when $\boldsymbol{s} \in \{0, 1\}^n$. As we all known that this primitive has some good cryptographic properties. We will use these properties in our LTFs against continuous key leakage.

From the leakage resilient aspect, Naor and Segev [5] showed that given the public key and any λ bits of leakage, $\tilde{H}(sk | (pk, \lambda)) \geq \log p + 2\log(1/\epsilon) - 2$. The leftover hash lemma provides that with overwhelming probability over the choice of $c_1 \in X \setminus L$, it holds that h^r is ϵ-close to the uniform distribution over G.

Lemma 2. *If the DDH assumption is hard in the p-prime order group G, then the above scheme is a λ-LR-CPA secure PKE scheme as long as the leakage parameter $\lambda \leq (l - 2)\log(p) - 2\log(1/\epsilon) + 2$ where $\epsilon = \epsilon(\kappa)$ is some negligible function about the security parameter κ.*

From the continuous leakage resilient aspect, Agrawal et al. [1] showed that with the updated key $\boldsymbol{w} \in \mathbb{Z}_p^l$ we can update the secret key with $sk' = sk + \boldsymbol{\beta}$ where $\boldsymbol{\beta} \in \mathsf{kernel}(\boldsymbol{w})$. With the fixed public key, the updated key sk' can also decrypt the ciphertext correctly. With the above lemma and the help of the (extended) rank hiding assumption, the the above scheme is a λ-CLR-CPA secure PKE scheme.

Lemma 3. *Under the extended rank hinging assumption and the DDH assumption for $\mathcal{G}$, then the above scheme is a λ-CLR-CPA secure PKE scheme in the floppy model as long as the leakage parameter $\lambda \leq (l - 2)\log(p) - 2\log(1/\epsilon) + 2$ where $\epsilon = \epsilon(\kappa)$ is some negligible function about the security parameter κ.*

5   Continuous Leakage-Resilient LTF from the DDH Assumption

In this section, we show how to construct continuous leakage resilient lossy trapdoor function (CLR-LTF) from the continuous leakage resilient CPA-secure ElGamal-like PKE. For some negligible $\epsilon = \epsilon(\kappa)$ set $l = 2 + \frac{\lambda + 2\log(1/\epsilon) - 2}{\log p}$. The construction CLR-TDF=$(\mathsf{G}, \mathsf{S}, \mathsf{F}, \mathsf{F}^{-1}, \mathsf{U})$ is presented as follows.

1. $\mathsf{G}(1^\kappa)$: Run $\mathbb{G} = (G, p, g) \leftarrow \mathcal{G}(1^\kappa)$. Randomly choose $g^{\boldsymbol{w}} = (w_1, w_2, \cdots, w_l) \in \mathbb{Z}_p^l$ and compute $g^{\boldsymbol{w}} = (g_1, g_2, \cdots, g_l)$ where $g_j = g^{w_j}$ for $j \in [l]$. Choose n tuples of secret keys $\boldsymbol{s}_i = (s_{i1}, s_{i2}, \cdots s_{il}) \in \mathbb{Z}_p^l$ for $i \in [n]$. Let $h_i = \Pi_{j=1}^l g_j^{s_{ij}} = g^{\langle \boldsymbol{w}, \boldsymbol{s}_i \rangle}$. Output $\mathsf{pp} = (G, p, g, g^{\boldsymbol{w}}, h_1, h_2, \cdots, h_n), td = (\boldsymbol{s}_1, \boldsymbol{s}_2, \cdots, \boldsymbol{s}_n)$.

2. $S(pp, b)$: Given $b \in \{0, 1\}$. For $i \in [n]$, let $\boldsymbol{R}_i = (g_1^{r_i}, g_2^{r_i}, \cdots, g_l^{r_i}) \in L$ with a witness $r_i \in \mathbb{Z}_p$ independently at random.

$$
\text{Let } R = \begin{pmatrix} \boldsymbol{R}_1 \\ \boldsymbol{R}_2 \\ \vdots \\ \boldsymbol{R}_n \end{pmatrix} = \begin{pmatrix} g_1^{r_1} & g_2^{r_1} & \cdots & g_l^{r_1} \\ g_1^{r_2} & g_2^{r_2} & \cdots & g_l^{r_2} \\ \vdots & \vdots & \ddots & \vdots \\ g_1^{r_n} & g_2^{r_n} & \cdots & g_l^{r_n} \end{pmatrix}_{n \times l}
$$

$$
\text{and } Q = (\boldsymbol{Q}_1, \boldsymbol{Q}_2, \cdots, \boldsymbol{Q}_n) = \begin{pmatrix} h_1^{r_1} \cdot g^b & h_1^{r_2} & \cdots & h_1^{r_n} \\ h_2^{r_1} & h_2^{r_2} \cdot g^b & \cdots & h_2^{r_n} \\ \vdots & \vdots & \ddots & \vdots \\ h_n^{r_1} & h_n^{r_2} & \cdots & h_n^{r_n} \cdot g^b \end{pmatrix}_{n \times n}.
$$

When $b = 1$, we say it is in injective mode; otherwise, let $g^0 = 1_G$ and we say it is in lossy mode. The evaluation key is $ek = (R, Q)$.

3. $F(ek, x)$: Given a message $x = x_1 x_2 \cdots x_n \in \{0, 1\}^n$. Given a function index (R, Q) and then calculate $F_{R,Q}(x) = (c_1, c_2)$ where
   $c_1 = x \cdot R = (c_{11}, c_{12}, \cdots, c_{1l})$, where $c_{1i} = \prod_{j=1}^n g_i^{r_j x_j}, i \in [l]$;
   $c_2 = x \cdot Q = (c_{21}, c_{22}, \cdots, c_{2n})$, where $c_{2i} = \prod_{j=1}^n Q_{ij}^{x_j}, i \in [n]$.
   Output $c = (c_1, c_2) \in G^l \times G^n$.

4. $F^{-1}(td, c)$: Firstly parse c as $(c_1, c_2) = ((c_{11}, c_{12}, \cdots, c_{1l}), (c_{21}, c_{22}, \cdots, c_{2n}))$. If $\prod_{j=1}^l c_{1j}^{s_{ij}} = c_{2i}$, then $x_i = 0, i \in [n]$; if $\prod_{j=1}^l c_{1j}^{s_{ij}} \neq c_{2i}$, then $x_i = 1, i \in [n]$. At last, output the message $x = x_1 x_2 \cdots x_n \in \{0, 1\}^n$.

5. $U(td, uk)$: Input the update key $uk = \boldsymbol{w}$ and the trapdoor is updated into the new one $td' = td + (\boldsymbol{\beta}_1, \boldsymbol{\beta}_2, \cdots, \boldsymbol{\beta}_n) = (s_1 + \boldsymbol{\beta}_1, s_2 + \boldsymbol{\beta}_2, \cdots, s_n + \boldsymbol{\beta}_n)$ where $\boldsymbol{\beta}_i = (b_{i1}, b_{i2}, \cdots, b_{il}) \leftarrow \mathsf{kernel}(\boldsymbol{w})$ (i.e. $s'_{ij} = s_{ij} + b_{ij}$ for $\forall i \in [n], j \in [l]$).

We give the following correctness, consistency and security properties.

– Since the updated trapdoor is $td' = (s_i + \boldsymbol{\beta}_i)_{i \in [n]} = (s_{ij} + b_{ij})_{i \in [n], j \in [l]}$, we have $h'_i = \Pi_{j=1}^l g_j^{s_{ij} + b_{ij}} = g^{\langle \boldsymbol{w}, s_i + \boldsymbol{\beta}_i \rangle} = g^{\langle \boldsymbol{w}, s_i \rangle} = h_i$.

– For any evaluation key ek and $\forall i \in [n]$, we have $c_{2i} = \prod_{j=1}^n Q_{ij}^{x_j} = g^{bx_i} \cdot \prod_{j=1}^n h_i'^{r_j x_j} = g^{bx_i} \cdot h_i'^{\sum_{j=1}^n r_j x_j} = g^{bx_i} \cdot g^{\langle \boldsymbol{w}, s_i + \boldsymbol{\beta}_i \rangle \cdot \sum_{j=1}^n r_j x_j} = g^{bx_i} \cdot g^{\langle \boldsymbol{w}, s_i \rangle \cdot \sum_{j=1}^n r_j x_j}$.

On the other hand,
$$
\prod_{j=1}^l c_{1j}^{s'_{ij}} = c_{11}^{s'_{i1}} c_{12}^{s'_{i2}} \cdots c_{1l}^{s'_{il}} = (\prod_{j=1}^n g_1^{r_j x_j})^{s'_{i1}} (\prod_{j=1}^n g_2^{r_j x_j})^{s'_{i2}} \cdots (\prod_{j=1}^n g_l^{r_j x_j})^{s'_{il}}
$$
$$
= g_1^{s'_{i1} \sum_{j=1}^n r_j x_j} g_2^{s'_{i2} \sum_{j=1}^n r_j x_j} \cdots g_l^{s'_{il} \sum_{j=1}^n r_j x_j}
$$
$$
= g^{w_1 s'_{i1} \sum_{j=1}^n r_j x_j} g^{w_2 s'_{i2} \sum_{j=1}^n r_j x_j} \cdots g^{w_l s'_{il} \sum_{j=1}^n r_j x_j}
$$
$$
= g^{\langle \boldsymbol{w}, s_i + \boldsymbol{\beta}_i \rangle \sum_{j=1}^n r_j x_j} = g^{\langle \boldsymbol{w}, s_i \rangle \cdot \sum_{j=1}^n r_j x_j}.
$$
Since in injective mode (i.e. $b = 1$), $g^{bx_i} = g^{x_i}$ holds and the correctness of F and F^{-1} follows.

Theorem 1. *Under the DDH assumption and the (extended) rank hiding assumption in group G with the prime order p, the proposed scheme is a collection of λ-CLR-LTFs with $\lambda \le (l - 2)\log p - 2\log(1/\epsilon) + 2$ where $\epsilon = \epsilon(\kappa)$ is* *some negligible function of the security parameter κ in the floppy model. There-fore, the leakage rate is $\frac{\lambda}{|td|} = \frac{(l-2)\log p - 2\log(1/\epsilon) + 2}{nl\log p} \approx \frac{1}{n}$. The lossiness is $n - \log p$ bits.*

Remark: In this section we can see that the leakage ratio of the DDH-based CLR-LTF is only $\frac{1}{n}$ where the lossiness is $n - \log p$. This relationship implies that the higher leakage rate, the lower lossiness. Therefore, it is hard to improve the leakage rate in the prime order group. In next section, we present an instantiation in the composite order group which would do some help to improve the leakage rate to $1 - o(1)$.

6 Continuous Leakage-Resilient LTFs from the DCR Assumption

In this section, we show how to construct CLR-LTF under the decisional composite residuosity (DCR) assumption. The group $\mathbb{Z}^*_{N^{\alpha+1}}$ is a multiplicative group where $\alpha \geq 1$ is an integer. The integer $N = PQ$ is an RSA modulus which means that P and Q are odd primes of equivalent bit length. Obviously the group $\mathbb{Z}^*_{N^{\alpha+1}}$ is a direct product $\mathsf{G} \times \mathsf{H}$ where G is a cyclic group of order N^α and H is isomorphic to $\mathbb{Z}^*_N$. We define $T := 1 + N(\mathrm{mod} N^{\alpha+1})$, therefore T generates the group H. In addition, the discrete logarithm with respect to T over group H is efficiently computable. Such an N will be called admissible in the following discussion. The scheme is as follows:

Set $l = 2 + \frac{\lambda + 2\log(1/\epsilon)}{\log N - 3}$ for some negligible $\epsilon = \epsilon(\kappa)$. The construction CLR-TDF=(G, S, F, F^{-1}, U) is operated over the group $Z^*_{N^{\alpha+1}}$ as follows.

1. $\mathsf{G}(1^\kappa)$: On input 1^κ the generation algorithm, chooses an admissible κ-bit RSA modulus $N = PQ$ and a natural number $\alpha \geq 1$. Note that this fixes the groups G where the generator is g and H.

   Choose $\boldsymbol{s} = (s_1, s_2, \cdots, s_l) \in Z^l_{\frac{N-1}{4}}$ at random. Select $g_1 = g^{w_1}, g_2 = g^{w_2}, \cdots, g_l = g^{w_l} \in \mathsf{G}$ uniformly and let $\boldsymbol{w} = (w_1, w_2, \cdots, w_l) \in \mathbb{Z}^l_{\frac{N-1}{4}}$, then $g^{\boldsymbol{w}} = (g_1, g_2, \cdots, g_l)$. Given $h = \Pi^l_{i=1} g_i^{s_i} = g^{\langle \boldsymbol{w}, \boldsymbol{s} \rangle}$. Output $\mathsf{pp} = (N, \alpha, g, g^{\boldsymbol{w}}, h), td = \boldsymbol{s}$.
2. $\mathsf{S}(\mathsf{pp}, b)$: Given $b \in \{0, 1\}$, choose $r \in Z^*_N$ and define $R = g^{\boldsymbol{w}r}, Q = h^r \cdot T^b$. When $b = 1$, we say it is in injective mode; otherwise, we say it is in lossy mode. At last the evaluation key is $ek = (R, Q) \in \mathsf{G}^l \times Z^*_{N^{\alpha+1}}$.
3. $\mathsf{F}(ek, x)$: Given a message $x \in Z_{N^\alpha}$. Given a function index (R, Q), then calculate $F_{R,Q}(x) = (c_1, c_2)$ where $c_1 = x \cdot R = R^x$; $c_2 = x \cdot Q = Q^x$. Output $c = (c_1, c_2) \in \mathsf{G}^l \times Z^*_{N^{\alpha+1}}$.
4. $\mathsf{F}^{-1}(td, c)$: Firstly parse c as (c_1, c_2). In the injective mode, we compute $X = c_2 \cdot (c_1^{-\boldsymbol{s}}) = T^x$. At last, output the message $x = \log_T X$.
5. $\mathsf{U}(td, uk)$: Given the update key $uk = \boldsymbol{w}$ and the trapdoor is updated into the new one $td' = td + \boldsymbol{\beta} = \boldsymbol{s} + \boldsymbol{\beta}$ where $\boldsymbol{\beta} \leftarrow \mathsf{kernel}(\boldsymbol{w})$.

Correctness. The correctness is described as follows.

- For the updated trapdoor is $td' = s + \beta$, we have $h' = g^{\langle w, s+\beta \rangle} = g^{\langle w, s \rangle} = h$.
- For any evaluation key ek, there has $c_2 \cdot (c_1^{-s}) = Q^x \cdot (R^x)^{-s} = h^{rx} \cdot T^{bx} \cdot (g^{w \cdot rx})^{-s} = h^{rx} \cdot T^{bx} \cdot h^{-rx} = T^{bx}$. Since in injective mode (i.e. $b = 1$), $T^{bx} = T^x$ holds and the correctness of F and F^{-1} follows.

Theorem 2. *If the DDH assumption is hard in G and the DCR problem is hard in $Z^*_{N^{\alpha+1}}$, then we can construct a collection of λ-CLR-TDFs. During each time interval the proposed scheme can tolerate at most $\lambda \leq (l-2)(logN - 3) - 2log1/\epsilon$ bits on the trapdoor where $\epsilon = \epsilon(\kappa)$ is some negligible function with the security parameter κ. Therefore, the leakage rate is $\frac{\lambda}{|td|} = \frac{(l-2)(logN-3)-2log1/\epsilon}{l(logN-3)} \approx 1 - o(1)$. The lossiness is at least $\alpha logN - (logN - 2)$ bits.*

7 Conclusion and Future Work

In this paper, we focus on the lossy trapdoor functions in the presence of continuous leakage. Firstly, we introduce the new notion of ULTFs and give the formal definition and security requirements. We extend the notion of ULTFs to CLR-LTFs and give the explicit security model of CLR-LTFs. Under the DDH assumption and DCR assumption respectively, we introduce two concrete lossy trapdoor functions against continuous leakage in the standard model. Our proposed scheme can also be seen as a deterministic public key encryption, we think it is of independent interest in the study of deterministic PKE against continuous leakage which is also an open problem presented in [7].

References

1. Agrawal, S., Dodis, Y., Vaikuntanathan, V., Wichs, D.: On continual leakage of discrete log representations. In: Sako, K., Sarkar, P. (eds.) ASIACRYPT 2013. LNCS, vol. 8270, pp. 401–420. Springer, Heidelberg (2013). doi:10.1007/978-3-642-42045-0_21
2. Peikert, C., Waters, B.: Lossy trapdoor functions and their applications. In: STOC, pp. 187–196 (2008)
3. Wee, H.: KDM-security via homomorphic smooth projective hashing. In: Cheng, C.-M., Chung, K.-M., Persiano, G., Yang, B.-Y. (eds.) PKC 2016. LNCS, vol. 9615, pp. 159–179. Springer, Heidelberg (2016). doi:10.1007/978-3-662-49387-8_7
4. Boneh, D., Halevi, S., Hamburg, M., Ostrovsky, R.: Circular-secure encryption from decision diffie-hellman. In: Wagner, D. (ed.) CRYPTO 2008. LNCS, vol. 5157, pp. 108–125. Springer, Heidelberg (2008). doi:10.1007/978-3-540-85174-5_7
5. Naor, M., Segev, G.: Public-key cryptosystems resilient to key leakage. In: Halevi, S. (ed.) CRYPTO 2009. LNCS, vol. 5677, pp. 18–35. Springer, Heidelberg (2009). doi:10.1007/978-3-642-03356-8_2
6. Dodis, Y., et al.: Fuzzy extractors: How to generate strong keys from biometrics and other noisy data. SIAM J. Comput. **38**(1), 97–139 (2008)

7. Koppula, V., Pandey, O., Rouselakis, Y., Waters, B.: Deterministic public-key encryption under continual leakage. In: Manulis, M., Sadeghi, A.-R., Schneider, S. (eds.) ACNS 2016. LNCS, vol. 9696, pp. 304–323. Springer, Heidelberg (2016). doi:10.1007/978-3-319-39555-5_17

8. Qin, B., Liu, S., Chen, K., Charlemagne, M.: Leakage-resilient lossy trapdoor functions and public-key encryption. In: AsiaPKC, pp. 3–12 (2013)

9. Boldyreva, A., Fehr, S., O'Neill, A.: On notions of security for deterministic encryption, and efficient constructions without random oracles. In: Wagner, D. (ed.) CRYPTO 2008. LNCS, vol. 5157, pp. 335–359. Springer, Heidelberg (2008). doi:10.1007/978-3-540-85174-5_19

10. Li, S., Zhang, F., Sun, Y., Shen, L.: Efficient leakage-resilient public key encryption from DDH assumption. Cluster Comput. **16**, 1–10 (2013)

11. Li, S., Zhang, F.: Leakage-resilient identity-based encryption scheme. Int. J. Grid Utility Comput. **4**(2–3), 187–196 (2013)

12. Li, S., Zhang, F., Sun, Y., Shen, L.: A new variant of the cramer-shoup leakage-resilient public key encryption. In: INCoS 2012, pp. 342–346 (2012)

13. Dodis, Y., Haralambiev, K., Lopez-Alt, A., Wichs, D.: Cryptography against continuous memory attacks. In: FOCS, pp. 511–520 (2010)

14. Brakerski, Z., et al.: Overcoming the hole in the bucket: Public-key cryptography resilient to continual memory leakage. In: FOCS, pp. 501–510 (2010)

15. Alwen, J., Dodis, Y., Wichs, D.: Leakage-resilient public-key cryptography in the bounded-retrieval model. In: Halevi, S. (ed.) CRYPTO 2009. LNCS, vol. 5677, pp. 36–54. Springer, Heidelberg (2009). doi:10.1007/978-3-642-03356-8_3

16. Halderman, J.A., et al.: Lest we remember: Cold boot attacks on encryption keys. In: Proceedings of the 17th USENIX Security Symposium, pp. 45–60 (2008)

17. Akavia, A., Goldwasser, S., Vaikuntanathan, V.: Simultaneous hardcore bits and cryptography against memory attacks. In: Reingold, O. (ed.) TCC 2009. LNCS, vol. 5444, pp. 474–495. Springer, Heidelberg (2009). doi:10.1007/978-3-642-00457-5_28

18. Alwen, J., Dodis, Y., Naor, M., Segev, G., Walfish, S., Wichs, D.: Public-key encryption in the bounded-retrieval model. In: Gilbert, H. (ed.) EUROCRYPT 2010. LNCS, vol. 6110, pp. 113–134. Springer, Heidelberg (2010). doi:10.1007/978-3-642-13190-5_6

19. Brakerski, Z., Goldwasser, S.: Circular and leakage resilient public-key encryption under subgroup indistinguishability. In: Rabin, T. (ed.) CRYPTO 2010. LNCS, vol. 6223, pp. 1–20. Springer, Heidelberg (2010). doi:10.1007/978-3-642-14623-7_1

A Black-Box Construction of Strongly Unforgeable Signature Schemes in the Bounded Leakage Model

Jianye Huang[1], Qiong Huang[1,2(✉)], and Chunhua Pan[1]

[1] College of Mathematics and Informatics,
South China Agricultural University, Guangzhou, China
hjnubys@stu.scau.edu.cn, {qhuang,chpan}@scau.edu.cn
[2] Nanjing University of Information Science and Technology, Nanjing, China

Abstract. Due to the imperfect implementation of cryptosystems, adversaries are able to obtain secret state of the systems via *side-channel attacks* which are not considered in the traditional security notions of cryptographic primitives, and thus break their security. Leakage-resilient cryptography was proposed to prevent adversaries from doing so. Katz *et al.* and Boyle *et al.* proposed signature schemes which are existentially unforgeable in the bounded leakage model. However, neither takes measures to prevent the adversary from forging on messages that have been signed before. Recently, Wang *et al.* showed that any signature scheme can be transformed to one that is strongly unforgeable in the leakage environment with the help of a leakage-resilient chameleon hash function. However, their transformation requires changing the key pair of the signature scheme.

In this work, we further improve Wang *et al.*'s results by proposing a black-box construction of signature schemes, which converts a leakage-resilient signature scheme to one that is both strongly unforgeable and leakage resilient. Our construction does not require adding any element to the signature key pair nor modify the signature scheme at all. It is efficient in the sense that the resulting signature scheme has almost the same computational cost in signing and verification as the underlying scheme.

Keywords: Digital signature · Generic transformation · Strong unforgeability · Leakage-resilient cryptograhpy · Bounded leakage model

1 Introduction

1.1 Side-Channel Attacks

Halderman et al. showed an attack on encryption keys that are stored in memory even when it loses power in their influential paper [13]. It is a kind of *side-channel attacks*, where adversaries are capable of acquiring part of the secret

© Springer International Publishing AG 2016
L. Chen and J. Han (Eds.): ProvSec 2016, LNCS 10005, pp. 320–339, 2016.
DOI: 10.1007/978-3-319-47422-9_19

state (including the secret key and the randomness) from the physical implementation of a cryptosystem. Other side-channel attacks include running-time attack [19], electromagnetic radiation analysis [12,25], power consumption analysis [7,18], fault detection [2,3] and etc. Unfortunately, traditional cryptography does not capture such attacks that craftily bypass the barrier of solving hard problems, which is a threat to practical cryptosystem.

1.2   Leakage-Resilient(LR) Models

To address side-channel attacks, *leakage-resilient cryptography* was introduced [8], which aims to constructing cryptographic schemes that remain secure even if the adversary is able to obtain part of the secret state of the scheme. The first significant issue of leakage-resilient cryptography is how to formalize the *leakage*. Inspired by [1,23], most proposed models define the *leakage* by additionally giving the adversary a leakage oracle $\mathcal{O}^L_{state}(\cdot)$ which outputs a fraction of the cryptosystem's internal state on inputting an adversarially chosen function $f(\cdot)$. However, if the sequence of leakage functions are unrestricted, secure cryptographic schemes are never achievable, i.e. the leakage function simply outputs the whole secret key. The restrictions are listed as follows.

Partial Sate *vs.* Entire State. Inspired by the axiom *only computation leaks information* in [23], [8,24] require that all leakage functions take half of the internal state that is being currently accessed as input and omit the other half. However, [13] showed that the secret information can be leaked as well even if it is not accessed in the computation. Most schemes therefore allow the leakage functions to take the entire internal state as input.

Leakage Resilience *vs.* Fully Leakage Resilience. There are two most common cases in consideration: (1) the internal state is exactly the secret key of the scheme; or (2) additionally containing the randomness used in the computation, e.g. the signing process. The latter is a stronger notion of leakage resilience, called *fully leakage resilience* (FLR).

Output Length. For an arbitrary function f_i that takes the internal state X as input, its output length should satisfy that $\|f_i(X)\| < \|X\|$. Namely, we suppose that any PPT adversary can only get partial information of internal state.

Bounded Leakage *vs.* Unbounded Leakage. Another important issue is whether the amount of the leakage is bounded, i.e. $\sum_{i=1}^{q} \|f_i(X)\| \leq \lambda$ for some bound λ after q leakage queries. If so, the internal state keeps unchanged over time. Otherwise, the internal state should be periodically updated. We call these two models *bounded leakage-resilient* (BLR) model and *continuous leakage-resilient* (CLR) model, respectively.

Polynomial Time. We require that the leakage function should be polynomial-time computable since we only consider the probabilistic polynomial-time adversaries.

1.3   Leakage-Resilient Signature

A leakage-resilient signature remains *existentially unforgeable* even if bounded information about the internal state is leaked. In 2009, Katz and Vaikuntanathan proposed existentially unforgeable signature schemes under bounded leakage model based on standard assumptions [17]. There are also leakage-resilient signature schemes proposed in other LR models like [10,22]. And the fully leakage resilient unforgeability is considered in [6,30]. However, none of these schemes take measures to ensure the *strongly existential unforgeability* (sEUF), i.e. protecting the adversary from forging on messages that have been signed before.

Boneh, Shen, Waters [4] proposed a transformation that converts any existentially unforgeable signature scheme into one that is strongly unforgeable in the non-leakage setting. However, their transformation depends on *partitioned-ness* property of the underlying signature scheme. Not all of the existing signature schemes enjoy this property, e.g. DSA signature [11]. Later works, for example [26], proposed transformations that can convert any signature scheme into a strongly unforgeable one. However, it inevitably modifies key pairs or adds additional randomness in the signing phase. Huang *et al.* proposed another transformation that overcomes this drawback by using a strong one-time signature [15].

1.4   Generic Transformations Under Leakage Models

The black-box construction of strongly unforgeable signature schemes in the leakage-resilient setting, however, is not trivial. The transformations we mentioned above have a common feature. The security proofs are partitioned into several parts, each of which reduces to a different assumption. Consequently, their proofs consist of several reduction games, in each of which the adversary may lack part of secret state and thus may be unable to answer the leakage queries.

Wang *et al.* addressed this issue in [27,28]. They strengthened the definition of Chameleon hash function by giving adversaries a leakage oracle $\mathcal{O}_{td}^l(\cdot)$ where adversaries can adaptively choose leakage functions and learn at most l-bits information on the trapdoor. Utilizing this leakage-resilient Chameleon hash function, any signature scheme can be transformed to one that is strongly existentially unforgeable under bounded leakage model. The intuition of this technique is that if all the reduced objects are leakage-resilient, then the leakage queries can be answered by hard-coding and transmitting the leakage function. Similar to [26], however, the transformation requires changing the key pairs.

1.5   Our Contributions

In this work we further improve Wang *et al.*'s results by introducing a new transformation. Formally, we make the following contributions in the paper.

1. Based on Huang *et al.*'s generic transformation [15], we propose a new black-box construction of strongly unforgeable and leakage-resilient signature scheme, which does not require any special property of the underlying

signature scheme nor adding any element to the public key. The construction makes use of a leakage-resilient strong one-time signature scheme. Briefly, to sign a message m, the signer uses the underlying signature scheme to sign a freshly generated one-time verification key, and then uses the one-time signing key to sign the message. Following the proof technique of [27,28] and [15], we show that if the underlying signature scheme is unforgeable in the leakage setting and the one-time signature scheme is strongly unforgeable in the leakage setting as well, the resulting signature scheme is then strongly unforgeable and leakage-resilient.

2. Moreover, we observe that Katz *et al.*'s one-time signature scheme [17] is actually strongly unforgeable even if $(\frac{1}{4} - \epsilon)|sk|$ bits of the signing key are leaked.

3. To further support our generic construction, we propose another more efficient leakage-resilient strong one-time signature scheme based on cover-free family, which has the same leakage rate $(\frac{1}{4} - \epsilon)$.

Independently, Wang et al. proposed the same construction of leakage-resilient strongly unforgeable signature scheme in [29]. Their work also includes another fully l-leakage-resilient one-time signature scheme which is based on a l-leakage-resilient chameleon hash function.

2   Digital Signature

2.1   Definition of Digital Signature

Digital signature is the analogy of message authentication code (MAC) in the public key setting that ensures the integrity of transmitted messages over public channels. Formally, a signature scheme consists of the following three PPT algorithms (Kg, Sign, Ver).

Kg. The key generation algorithm takes the security parameter n (in unary representation) as input and outputs a key pair (vk, sk), where vk is the verification key (public key) and sk is the signing key (private key). We denote it by $(vk, sk) \leftarrow \mathsf{Kg}(1^n)$.

Sign. The signing algorithm takes the signing key sk and a message $m \in \{0,1\}^*$ as input and outputs a signature σ. We denote it by $\sigma \leftarrow \mathsf{Sign}(sk, m)$.

Ver. The verification algorithm takes the verification key vk, a message m along with a purported signature σ as input and outputs a bit b, which is 1 if σ is a valid signature on m under vk, and 0 otherwise. We denote it by $b \leftarrow \mathsf{Ver}(vk, m, \sigma)$.

Generally, the correctness of a signature scheme requires if a signature is correctly generated, it could always be verified. That is, for any $m \in \{0,1\}^*$, we have that

$$\Pr[\mathsf{Ver}(vk, m, \mathsf{Sign}(sk, m)) = 1] = 1.$$

2.2   Security Models

Let $\Sigma = (\mathsf{Kg}, \mathsf{Sign}, \mathsf{Ver})$ be a signature scheme and $\mathcal{A}$ be an adversary who tries to forge a valid message-signature pair. Consider the following experiment.

Unforgeability Game:

(a) The challenger runs $\mathsf{Kg}(1^n)$ to generate a key pair (vk, sk).

(b) $\mathcal{A}$ is given the verification key vk and accesses to a signing oracle $\mathcal{O}_{sk}(\cdot)$.

(c) $\mathcal{A}$ submits a message to $\mathcal{O}_{sk}(\cdot)$ according to its view and is returned the corresponding signature.

(d) Repeat Step c) $q := q(n)$ times where $q(\cdot)$ is polynomial in n. Denote $\mathcal{Q} := \{(m_i, \sigma_i)\}$ where m_i represents the i-th signing query and σ_i is the corresponding signature.

e) $\mathcal{A}$ outputs a forgery $(\hat{m}, \hat{\sigma})$.

Definition 1 (EUF-CMA Security). *A signature scheme Σ is existentially unforgeable under chosen-message attacks (EUF-CMA secure, in short) if for any PPT adversary $\mathcal{A}$ the probability that $\mathcal{A}$ succeeds in forging a valid signature on a new message in the experiment above is negligible, i.e.*

$$\Pr[\mathsf{Ver}(vk, \hat{m}, \hat{\sigma}) = 1 : (\hat{m}, \hat{\sigma}) \leftarrow \mathcal{A}^{\mathcal{O}_{sk}(\cdot)}(vk); (\hat{m}, *) \notin \mathcal{Q}] \leq \mathrm{nelg}(n).$$

Definition 2 (Strong Unforgeability (sEUF-CMA Security). *A signature scheme Σ is strongly existentially unforgeable under chosen-message attacks (sEUF-CMA secure, in short) if for any PPT adversary $\mathcal{A}$, the probability that $\mathcal{A}$ succeeds in outputting a valid message-signature pair $(\hat{m}, \hat{\sigma})$ in the unforgeability game which is different from all the pairs it has seen, e.g. $(\hat{m}, \hat{\sigma}) \notin \mathcal{Q}$, is negligible, i.e.*

$$\Pr[\mathsf{Ver}(vk, \hat{m}, \hat{\sigma}) = 1 : (\hat{m}, \hat{\sigma}) \leftarrow \mathcal{A}^{\mathcal{O}_{sk}(\cdot)}(vk); (\hat{m}, \hat{\sigma}) \notin \mathcal{Q}] \leq \mathrm{nelg}(n).$$

Leakage Resilience. To model an adversary against a signature scheme, which is allowed to launch side channel attacks, we allow it to submit leakage queries in Steps c) and d) in the unforgeability game. That is, besides the signing oracle $\mathcal{O}_{sk}(\cdot)$, the adversary is also given access to a leakage oracle $\mathcal{O}_{sk}^L(\cdot)$. The adversary submits a leakage function $f_i(\cdot)$ to $\mathcal{O}_{sk}^L(\cdot)$, and is returned $\Lambda_i := f_i(sk)$. Let λ_i be the output length of Λ_i. W.l.o.g., we suppose that the adversary makes a leakage query after a signing query, and it makes at most q queries for each type. We have the following definitions.

Definition 3 (Leakage Resilient Unforgeability). *A signature scheme Σ is λ-leakage resilient and existentially unforgeable under chosen-message attacks (λ-BLR-EUF-CMA) if for any PPT adversary $\mathcal{A}$, the probability that $\mathcal{A}$ succeeds in outputting a valid signature on a new message in the modified game above is negligible, i.e.*

$$\Pr \left[\mathsf{Ver}(vk, \hat{m}, \hat{\sigma}) = 1 : \begin{array}{c} (\hat{m}, \hat{\sigma}) \leftarrow \mathcal{A}^{\mathcal{O}_{sk}(\cdot), \mathcal{O}_{sk}^L(\cdot)}(vk) \\ (\hat{m}, *) \notin \mathcal{Q} \wedge \sum_{i=1}^{q} \|\lambda_i\| \leq \lambda \end{array} \right] \leq \mathrm{nelg}(n).$$

Definition 4 (Leakage Resilient Strong Unforgeability). *A signature scheme Σ is λ-leakage resilient and strongly existentially unforgeable under chosen-message attacks (λ-BLR-sEUF-CMA) if for any PPT adversary $\mathcal{A}$, the probability that $\mathcal{A}$ succeeds in outputting a valid message-signature pair in the modified game above is negligible, i.e.*

$$\Pr \left[\mathsf{Ver}(vk, \hat{m}, \hat{\sigma}) = 1 : \begin{array}{c} (\hat{m}, \hat{\sigma}) \leftarrow \mathcal{A}^{\mathcal{O}_{sk}(\cdot), \mathcal{O}_{sk}^L(\cdot)}(vk) \\ (\hat{m}, \hat{\sigma}) \notin \mathcal{Q} \wedge \sum_{i=1}^{q} \|\lambda_i\| \leq \lambda \end{array} \right] \leq \mathrm{nelg}(n).$$

If the internal state in above experiment consists of the signing key sk and randomness, we replace the leakage oracle $\mathcal{O}_{sk}^L(\cdot)$ with $\mathcal{O}_{state}^L(\cdot)$. Then, we have following definitions:

Definition 5 (Fully Leakage Resilient Unforgeability). *A signature scheme Σ is λ-fully leakage resilient and existentially unforgeable under chosen-message attacks (λ-BFLR-EUF-CMA) if for any PPT adversary $\mathcal{A}$, the probability that $\mathcal{A}$ succeeds in outputting a valid signature on a new message in the modified game above is negligible, i.e.*

$$\Pr \left[\mathsf{Ver}(vk, \hat{m}, \hat{\sigma}) = 1 : \begin{array}{c} (\hat{m}, \hat{\sigma}) \leftarrow \mathcal{A}^{\mathcal{O}_{sk}(\cdot), \mathcal{O}_{state}^L(\cdot)}(vk) \\ (\hat{m}, *) \notin \mathcal{Q} \wedge \sum_{i=1}^{q} \|\lambda_i\| \leq \lambda \end{array} \right] \leq \mathrm{nelg}(n).$$

Definition 6 (Fully Leakage Resilient Strong Unforgeability). *A signature scheme Σ is λ-fully leakage resilient and strongly existentially unforgeable under chosen-message attacks (λ-BFLR-sEUF-CMA) if for any PPT adversary $\mathcal{A}$, the probability that $\mathcal{A}$ succeeds in outputting a valid message-signature pair in the modified game above is negligible, i.e.*

$$\Pr \left[\mathsf{Ver}(vk, \hat{m}, \hat{\sigma}) = 1 : \begin{array}{c} (\hat{m}, \hat{\sigma}) \leftarrow \mathcal{A}^{\mathcal{O}_{sk}(\cdot), \mathcal{O}_{state}^L(\cdot)}(vk) \\ (\hat{m}, \hat{\sigma}) \notin \mathcal{Q} \wedge \sum_{i=1}^{q} \|\lambda_i\| \leq \lambda \end{array} \right] \leq \mathrm{nelg}(n).$$

Leakage Resilient Strong One-Time Signature. We say that Σ is a λ-leakage resilient strong one-time signature scheme in the bounded leakage model (or bounded fully leakage model) if the adversary makes at most $q = 1$ signing query in Definition 4 (or Definition 6).

3   Preliminaries

3.1   Error Correcting Codes

Hamming distance[16] The Hamming distance $d(x, y)$ between two vectors $x, y \in \mathbb{F}_q^n$ is defined to be the number of coordinates in which x and y differ.
Minimum distance[16] The minimum distance of a code $\mathcal{C}$ is the smallest hamming distance between distinct codewords, i.e.

$$d_{min}(\mathcal{C}) := \min\{d(x_i, x_j) | \forall i \neq j, x_i, x_j \in \mathcal{C}\}.$$

Let A be a $k \times l$ matrix over $\mathbb{F}_2$. Then A defines linear error-correcting code $C \subset \{0, 1\}^l$ where the row vector $m \in \{0, 1\}^k$ is mapped to the codeword $m \cdot A$. We have the following lemma.

Lemma 1 ([17]). $\forall \epsilon \in \{0, 1\}, \exists R$ s.t.

$$\Pr\left[d_{min}(m \cdot A) = \left(\frac{1}{2} - \epsilon\right) l : A \xleftarrow{\$} \{0, 1\}^{k \times Rk}\right] \geq 1 - \mathrm{negl}(k),$$

where $\mathrm{negl}(\cdot)$ is a negligible function.

Note that we do not require the efficient decodability in this paper.

3.2   Cover Free Family

Definition 7 (Cover-Free Family[20]). Let U be a universe where $|U| = n$. A family of sets $\mathcal{S} = \{S_1, \cdots, S_N\}$ where $S_i \subseteq U$ and $N = \Omega(2^n)$ is a (k, α)- cover-free family if for all distinct $S, S_1, \cdots, S_t \in \mathcal{S}$,

$$\left| S \setminus \bigcup_{i=1}^{k} S_i \right| \geq \alpha |S|.$$

Lemma 2 ([9]). Given any $N < 0$, there exists (k, α)-cover-free families with N sets s.t. $|S_i| = \mathcal{O}(kn)$ for all i, and $N = \mathcal{O}(k^2 n)$.

3.3   Entropy

Let X be a random variable taking values in $\{0, 1\}^n$. The min-entropy of X is given by

$$H_\infty(X) \overset{\text{def}}{=} \min_{x \in \{0,1\}^n} \{-\log_2 \Pr[X = x]\}.$$

The conditional min-entropy of X given an event E is defined as:

$$H_\infty(X|E) \overset{\text{def}}{=} \min_{x \in \{0,1\}^n} \{-\log_2 \Pr[X = x|E]\}.$$

Lemma 3 (*[17]*). *Let X be a random variable with $H \overset{\text{def}}{=} H_\infty(X)$, and fix $\delta \in [0, H]$. Let f be an arbitrary function with range $\{0, 1\}^\lambda$. Then*

$$\Pr[H_\infty(X|f(X)) \leqslant H - \Delta] \leqslant 2^{\lambda - \Delta}.$$

That is, the probability that knowledge of $f(X)$ decreases the min-entropy of X by Δ or more is at most $2^{\lambda - \Delta}$. Put differently, the upper bound of the probability that given $f(X)$ the residual entropy of X remains at most L is

$$\Pr[H_\infty(X|f(X)) \leqslant L] \leqslant 2^{\lambda - H + L}.$$

4   Generic Transformation to sEUF-CMA Secure in the Leakage Setting

Let $\Sigma = (\mathsf{Kg}, \mathsf{Sign}, \mathsf{Ver})$ and $\Sigma^{OT} = (\mathsf{Kg}^{OT}, \mathsf{Sign}^{OT}, \mathsf{Ver}^{OT})$ be signature schemes. Consider the following construction of a signature scheme $\Sigma' = (\mathsf{Kg}', \mathsf{Sign}', \mathsf{Ver}')$.

Construction 1 $\mathsf{Kg}'(1^n)$. Receive a security parameter n in unary representation, generate the key pairs as follows.
  1. Run $\mathsf{Kg}(1^n)$ to generate a key-pair: i.e. $(vk, sk) \leftarrow \mathsf{Kg}(1^n)$.
  2. Output (vk, sk) as its verification key and signing key, respectively.

$\mathsf{Sign}'(sk, m)$. To sign a message m, run the signing algorithm with signing key sk as follows.
  1. Run $\mathsf{Kg}^{OT}(1^n)$ to generate a key pair, i.e. $(vk^{OT}, sk^{OT}) \leftarrow \mathsf{Kg}^{OT}(1^n)$.
  2. Sign vk^{OT} using sk: $\sigma \leftarrow \mathsf{Sign}(sk, vk^{OT}; w)$ using randomness w.
  3. Sign $\sigma \| m$ using sk^{OT}: $\sigma^{OT} \leftarrow \mathsf{Sign}^{OT}(sk^{OT}, \sigma \| m; w^{OT})$ using randomness w^{OT} (which might be empty if the signing algorithm is deterministic).
  4. Output the signature $\sigma' := (vk^{OT}, \sigma, \sigma^{OT})$.

$\mathsf{Ver}'(vk, m, \sigma')$. Given a message-signature pair (m, σ'), the verification algorithm works as follows.
  1. Parse σ' as $(vk^{OT}, \sigma, \sigma^{OT})$.
  2. Output 1 if $\mathsf{Ver}(vk, vk^{OT}, \sigma) = 1$ and $\mathsf{Ver}^{OT}(vk^{OT}, \sigma \| m, \sigma^{OT}) = 1$, and 0 otherwise.

In ACNS 2007, Huang *et al.* showed the following theorem [15].

Theorem 1 (*[15]*). *If Σ is a EUF-CMA secure signature scheme and Σ^{OT} is a strong one-time secure signature scheme, then the Construction 1 is sEUF-CMA-secure.*

Our construction above extends Huang *et al.*'s result into the leakage setting. We have the following theorem.

Theorem 2. *If Σ is a λ_1-BFLR-EUF-CMA secure signature scheme and Σ^{OT} is a λ_2-BFLR-sEUF-CMA secure one-time signature scheme, then Construction 1 is λ-BFLR-sEUF-CMA secure signature scheme where $\lambda = \min\{\lambda_1, \lambda_2\}$.*

Intuition of proof. Consider a sequence of message-signature pairs $\{(m_i, \sigma'_i = (vk_i^{OT}, \sigma_i, \sigma_i^{OT}))\}_{i=1}^q$ the adversary obtains via signing queries. Let Forge be the event that a PPT adversary $\mathcal{A}$ outputs a valid forgery $(\hat{m}, \hat{\sigma}' = (\hat{vk}^{OT}, \hat{\sigma}, \hat{\sigma}^{OT}))$ s.t. $(\hat{m}, \hat{\sigma}') \notin \{(m_i, \sigma'_i)\}_{i=1}^q$. If Forge occurs, either of following events would occur with non-negligible probability:

- $\overline{\text{Reuse}}$: $\hat{vk}^{OT} \notin \{vk_i^{OT}\}_{i=1}^q$. If $\overline{\text{Reuse}}$ occurs, $(\hat{vk}^{OT}, \hat{\sigma})$ is a valid forgery of Σ;
- Reuse : $\exists i^* \in [q], \hat{vk}^{OT} = vk_{i^*}^{OT}$. We have that $(\hat{\sigma}, \hat{m}, \hat{\sigma}^{OT}) \neq (\sigma_{i^*}, m_{i^*}, \sigma_{i^*}^{OT})$, which gives a forgery $(\hat{\sigma} \| \hat{m}, \hat{\sigma}^{OT})$ against the strong unforgeability of Σ^{OT}.

Obviously, we have that $\Pr[\text{Forge}] = \Pr[\text{Forge}^{\overline{\text{Reuse}}}] + \Pr[\text{Forge}^{\text{Reuse}}]$, where $\text{Forge}^{\overline{\text{Reuse}}} := \text{Forge} \wedge \overline{\text{Reuse}}$ and $\text{Forge}^{\text{Reuse}} := \text{Forge} \wedge \text{Reuse}$. Below we show that each of the terms on the right-hand side is negligible, thus proving the theorem.

Proof. Consider two adversaries $\mathcal{A}_\Sigma$ and $\mathcal{A}_{\Sigma^{OT}}$ attacking the existential unforgeability of Σ and the strong unforgeability of Σ^{OT}, respectively.

Algorithm $\mathcal{A}_\Sigma$:
The challenger runs $\mathsf{Kg}(1^n)$ to generate a key pair (vk, sk). $\mathcal{A}_\Sigma$ is given vk, a signing oracle $\mathcal{O}_{sk}(\cdot)$ and a leakage oracle $\mathcal{O}_{state}^L(\cdot)$. The algorithm $\mathcal{A}_\Sigma$ works as follows.

1. Set the key pair of Σ' as $(vk', sk') := (vk, \perp)$. Notice that the signing key sk' is unknown.
2. Generate q one-time key pairs, i.e., $\forall i \in [q], (vk_i^{OT}, sk_i^{OT}) \leftarrow \mathsf{Kg}^{OT}(1^n)$.
3. Submit $\{vk_i^{OT}\}_{i=1}^q$ to $\mathcal{O}_{sk}(\cdot)$, and obtain the corresponding signatures, i.e. $\sigma_i \leftarrow \mathcal{O}_{sk}(vk_i^{OT}; w_i)$, where w_i is the randomness used to generate σ_i.
4. Run $\mathcal{A}(vk')$, and answer $\mathcal{A}$'s signing and leakage queries as follows.
   Signing Query. The i-th signing query m_i is answered as follows.
   (a) Compute $\sigma_i^{OT} \leftarrow \mathsf{Sign}^{OT}(sk_i^{OT}, \sigma_i \| m_i; w_i^{OT})$.
   (b) Set the state as $\mathcal{S} := \{sk, \{w_j\}_{j=1}^i, \{sk_j^{OT}, w_j^{OT}\}_{j=1}^i\}$. Notice that the adversary $\mathcal{A}_\Sigma$ does not know sk and $\{w_j\}_{j=1}^i$.
   (c) Return $(vk_i^{OT}, \sigma_i, \sigma_i^{OT})$ to $\mathcal{A}$.
   Leakage Query. The i-th leakage query $f_i(\cdot)$ is answered as follows.
   (a) Construct the leakage function $f'_i(\cdot, \cdot) := f_{\{sk_j^{OT}, w_j^{OT}\}_{j=1}^i}(sk, \{w_i\}_{j=1}^i) := f_i(\mathcal{S})$.
   (b) Submit the leakage query f'_i to $\mathcal{O}_{state}^L(\cdot)$ and obtain $\Lambda_i \leftarrow \mathcal{O}_{state}^L(f'_i)$.
   (c) Return Λ_i to $\mathcal{A}$.
5. When $\mathcal{A}$ outputs $(\hat{m}, (\hat{vk}^{OT}, \hat{\sigma}, \hat{\sigma}^{OT}))$, outputs $(\hat{vk}^{OT}, \hat{\sigma})$.

It is clear that if $\mathcal{A}$ succeeds in breaking the fully leakage resilient strong unforgeability, we have that $\mathcal{A}_{\Sigma}$ breaks the fully leakage resilient unforgeability of Σ. Let δ_1 be the probability that $\mathcal{A}_{\Sigma}$ forges a valid signature of Σ. Then we have

$$\delta_1 = \Pr\left[\mathsf{Ver}(vk, \hat{vk}^{OT}, \hat{\sigma}) = 1 \wedge \hat{vk}^{OT} \notin \{vk_i^{OT}\}_{i=1}^q\right] \geq \Pr\left[\mathsf{Forge}^{\overline{\mathsf{Reuse}}}\right].$$

That is, $\Pr[\mathsf{Forge}^{\overline{\mathsf{Reuse}}}] \leq \delta_1 \leq \mathsf{negl}_1(n)$ follows from the fact that Σ is λ_1-BFLR-EUF-CMA secure.

Next, we consider the adversary $\mathcal{A}_{\Sigma^{OT}}$ as follows:

Algorithm $\mathcal{A}_{\Sigma^{OT}}$:
The challenger runs $\mathsf{Kg}^{OT}(1^n)$ to generate a key-pair (vk^{OT}, sk^{OT}). $\mathcal{A}_{\Sigma^{OT}}$ is given vk^{OT}, a signing oracle $\mathcal{O}_{sk^{OT}}(\cdot)$ and a leakage oracle $\mathcal{O}_{state^{OT}}^L(\cdot)$. The algorithm $\mathcal{A}_{\Sigma^{OT}}$ works as follows.

1. Run $\mathsf{Kg}(1^n)$ to generate a key pair (vk, sk) and set the key pair of Σ' as $(vk', sk') := (vk, sk)$.
2. Randomly choose a value $i^* \leftarrow [q]$.
3. Generate q key pairs $\{vk_i^{OT}, sk_i^{OT}\}_{i=1}^q$ where

$$(vk_i^{OT}, sk_i^{OT}) = \begin{cases} (vk^{OT}, \bot) & \text{if } i = i^*, \\ \mathsf{Kg}^{OT}(1^n) & \text{otherwise.} \end{cases}$$

4. Compute signatures on $\{vk_i^{OT}\}_{i=1}^q$, i.e. $\forall i \in [q], \sigma_i \leftarrow \mathsf{Sign}(sk, vk_i^{OT}; w_i)$.
5. Run $\mathcal{A}(vk')$ and answer its signing queries and leakage queries as follows.

   Signing Qeury. Answer the i-th signing query m_i as follows.
   (a) Compute the one-time signature

$$\sigma_i^{OT} = \begin{cases} \mathcal{O}_{sk^{OT}}(\sigma_i \| m_i; w_i^{OT}) & \text{if } i = i^*, \\ \mathsf{Sign}^{OT}(sk_i^{OT}, \sigma_i \| m_i; w_i^{OT}) & \text{otherwise.} \end{cases}$$

   (b) Set the state as $\mathcal{S} := \{sk, \{w_j\}_{j=1}^i, \{sk_j^{OT}, w_j^{OT}\}_{j=1}^i\}$. Notice that $\mathcal{A}_{\Sigma^{OT}}$ does not know $(sk_{i^*}^{OT}, w_{i^*}^{OT})$.
   (c) Return $(vk_i^{OT}, \sigma_i, \sigma_i^{OT})$ to $\mathcal{A}$.

   Leakage Query. Answer the i-th leakage query $f_i(\cdot)$ as follows.
   Case $i < i^*$. Compute $\Lambda_i = f_i(\mathcal{S})$ and return Λ_i to $\mathcal{A}$.
   Case $i \geq i^*$. Return $\Lambda_i \leftarrow \mathcal{O}_{state^{OT}}^L(f_i')$ where
   $f_i'(\cdot, \cdot) := f_{\mathcal{S}/(sk_{i^*}^{OT}, w_{i^*}^{OT})}(sk_{i^*}^{OT}, w_{i^*}^{OT}) := f_i(\mathcal{S})$.

6. When $\mathcal{A}$ outputs $(\hat{m}, \hat{\sigma}' = (\hat{vk}^{OT}, \hat{\sigma}, \hat{\sigma}^{OT}))$, $\mathcal{A}_{\Sigma^{OT}}$ outputs $(\hat{\sigma} \| \hat{m}, \hat{\sigma}^{OT})$.

Let δ_2 be the probability that $\mathcal{A}_{\Sigma^{OT}}$ forges a valid signature on vk^{OT}. Then, we have

$$\delta_2 = \Pr\left[\mathsf{Ver}\left(\hat{vk}^{OT}, \hat{\sigma}\|\hat{m}, \hat{\sigma}^{OT}\right) = 1 \wedge \hat{vk}^{OT} = vk^{OT}\right]$$

$$\geq \Pr\left[\mathsf{Ver'}\left(vk', \hat{m}, \left(\hat{vk}^{OT}, \hat{\sigma}, \hat{\sigma}^{OT}\right)\right) = 1 \wedge \hat{vk}^{OT} = vk_{i^*}^{OT}\right]$$

$$= \Pr\left[\mathsf{Ver'}\left(vk', \hat{m}, \left(\hat{vk}^{OT}, \hat{\sigma}, \hat{\sigma}^{OT}\right)\right) = 1 \wedge \hat{vk}^{OT} = vk_i^{OT} | i = i^*\right] \cdot \Pr[i = i^*]$$

$$= \Pr\left[\mathsf{Forge}^{\mathrm{Reuse}}\right] \cdot \Pr[i = i^*]$$

$$= \frac{1}{q} \Pr\left[\mathsf{Forge}^{\mathrm{Reuse}}\right].$$

Thus we have $\Pr[\mathsf{Forge}^{\mathrm{Reuse}}] \leq q \cdot \delta_2 \leq \mathrm{negl}_2(n)$ follows from the fact that Σ^{OT} is λ_2-BFLR-sEUF-CMA.

From the above we know that $\Pr[\mathsf{Forge}] = \Pr[\mathsf{Forge}^{\overline{\mathrm{Reuse}}}] + \Pr[\mathsf{Forge}^{\mathrm{Reuse}}] \leq \mathrm{negl}_1(n) + \mathrm{negl}_2(n)$, which is negligible as well. This completes the proof. $\square$

Remark 1. Since the amount of the leaked information obtained by $\mathcal{A}$ is bounded by $\lambda = \min\{\lambda_1, \lambda_2\}$, $\mathcal{A}_\Sigma$ and $\mathcal{A}_{\Sigma^{OT}}$ are able to answer all the leakage queries from $\mathcal{A}$.

Remark 2. A reconstructed leakage function based on $\mathcal{A}$'s leakage query can be easily realized thanks to the hard coding technology.

With almost the same proof as above, we can prove the following theorem.

Theorem 3. *If Σ is a λ_1-BLR-EUF-CMA secure signature scheme and Σ^{OT} is a λ_2-BLR-sEUF-CMA secure one-time signature scheme, then Construction 1 is λ-BLR-sEUF-CMA-secure where $\lambda = \min\{\lambda_1, \lambda_2\}$.*

Remark 3. Furthermore, similar with [14], our results above also apply to a weak variant of unforgeability of Σ (weak unforgeability, for short). Namely, the adversary chooses its signing queries $\{m_i\}_{i=1}^q$ before seeing the verification key and submits the queries to the challenger. It is then returned the verification key vk along with all the corresponding signatures $\{\sigma_i\}_{i=1}^q$. The adversary then tries to give a valid forgery. Our construction actually transforms a leakage-resilient and weakly unforgeable signature scheme to a leakage-resilient and strongly unforgeable signature scheme.

5   Leakage Resilient Strong One-Time Signature Schemes

5.1   The First Construction

From Sect. 4 we know that a strong one-time signature scheme in leakage setting is necessary for the generic transformation. In this section, we present a one-time signature scheme that is $(\frac{1}{4} - \epsilon)|sk|$-BFLR-sEUF-CMA secure.

Let $H = \{\mathsf{Kg}_H, h\}$ be a collision-resilient hash function where $h : \{0,1\}^{l_{in}} \to \{0,1\}^{\frac{\epsilon}{2}l_{in}}$ and $\epsilon \in (0, \frac{1}{4})$. Let $A \in \{0,1\}^{\frac{\epsilon}{2}l_{in} \times l}$ be a $\frac{\epsilon}{2}l_{in} \times l$ matrix (viewed as

$\mathbb{F}_2$), then A defines a linear error-correcting code $C \subset \{0,1\}^l$ where the row vector $m \in \{0,1\}^{\frac{\epsilon}{2}l_{in}}$ is mapped to the codeword $m \cdot A$. Consider the following construction of a signature scheme $\Sigma = (\mathsf{Kg}, \mathsf{Sign}, \mathsf{Ver})$, which is a generalization of Lamport's signature scheme.

Construction 2. $\mathsf{Kg}(1^n)$. Receive a security parameter n in unary representation, generate the key pairs as follows.

1. Uniformly sample the matrix $A \xleftarrow{\$} \{0,1\}^{\frac{\epsilon}{2}l_{in} \times l}$.
2. Generate the random seed of collision-resilient hash function h: $s \leftarrow \mathsf{Kg}_H(1^n)$.
3. Randomly select $x_i^b \leftarrow \{0,1\}^{l_{in}}$ and compute $y_i^b := h_s(x_i^b), \forall i \in [l], b \in \{0,1\}$. Set $X := \{x_i^b\}$ and $Y := \{y_i^b\}$.
4. Set the verification key $vk := (A, s, Y)$, and the signature key $sk := X$.

$\mathsf{Sign}(sk, m)$. To sign a message m, run the signing algorithm with signing key sk as follows.

1. Compute the row vector $\overline{m} = m \cdot A$.
2. Return the signature $\sigma = \{x_i^{\overline{m}_i}\}_{i=1}^l$.

$\mathsf{Ver}(vk, m, \sigma)$. Given a message-signature pair (m, σ), the verification algorithm works as follows.

1. Compute the row vector $\overline{m} = m \cdot A$.
2. Parse σ as $\sigma = (x_i)_{i=1}^l$.
3. Output 1 if $\forall i \in [l], y_i^{\overline{m}_i} = h_s(x_i)$, and 0 otherwise.

Theorem 4. *If H is collision-resistant, Construction 2 is a one-time signature scheme that is $(\frac{1}{4} - \epsilon)|sk|$-BFLR-sEUF-CMA secure.*

Intuition. Denote by m, m^* the queried message and the message in forgery, respectively. Let Forge be the event that an PPT algorithm $\mathcal{A}$ forges a valid signature $\sigma^* = \{x_i^*\}_{i=1}^l$ on m^*. The intuition is that if Forge occurs, then either the second-preimage collision resilience or the collision resilience of h would be broken with non-negligible probability.

- $\overline{\text{Reuse}}$: $m^* \neq m$. If $\overline{\text{Reuse}}$ occurs, then $\exists i \in [l]$ s.t. $\overline{m}_i^* \neq \overline{m}_i$, which breaks the second preimage collision resistance of h.
- Reuse : $m^* = m$. If Reuse occurs, then $\exists i \in [l]$ s.t. $x_{i^*} \neq x_i$ which gives a collision of h.

Clearly, we have that $\Pr[\text{Forge}] = \Pr[\text{Forge}^{\overline{\text{Reuse}}}] + \Pr[\text{Forge}^{\text{Reuse}}]$, where $\text{Forge}^{\overline{\text{Reuse}}} := \text{Forge} \wedge \overline{\text{Reuse}}$ and $\text{Forge}^{\text{Reuse}} := \text{Forge} \wedge \text{Reuse}$. Below we show that each of the terms on the right-hand side is negligible, thus proving the theorem.

Proof. Construct two PPT Adversaries $\mathcal{A}_{SPR}$ and $\mathcal{A}_{CR}$ attacking the second-preimage resistance and collision resistance of h, respectively.

Algorithm $\mathcal{A}_{SPR}$:
The challenger runs $\mathsf{Kg}_H(1^n)$ to generate a random seed s of hash function h. $\mathcal{A}_{SPR}$ is given s and a uniformly random value $x \xleftarrow{\$} \{0,1\}^{l_{in}}$. The algorithm $\mathcal{A}_{SPR}$ works as follows.

1. Generate a key pair $(vk, sk) \leftarrow \mathsf{Kg}(1^n)$.
2. $\forall i \in [l], b \in \{0,1\}$, randomly select $x_i^b \leftarrow \{0,1\}^{l_{in}}$, and set $y_i^b = h(x_i^b)$.
3. Choose a random position $i^* \in [l], b^* \in \{0,1\}$ and set $(y_{i^*}^{b^*}, x_{i^*}^{b^*}) = (h_s(x), x)$.
4. Set $vk = \{y_i^b\}_{i \in [l], b \in \{0,1\}}$, and run $\mathcal{A}$ on input vk. Answering $\mathcal{A}$'s signing query and leakage query as follows:
    Signature Query. Given a message m, set $\sigma := \{x_i^{\overline{m}_i}\}_{i=1}^l = \mathsf{Sign}(sk, m)$, and return σ.
    Leakage Query. Given a leakage function f, compute $\Lambda = f(sk)$, and return Λ.
5. When $\mathcal{A}$ outputs $(m^*, (x_1^*, \cdots, x_l^*))$, if $y = h_s(x_{i^*})$, return x_{i^*}; else, return $\bot$.

The event $m^* \neq m$ implies that $\Pr\left[d(\overline{m}^*, \overline{m}) \geq (\frac{1}{2} - \epsilon)l\right] \geq 1 - \mathrm{negl}(n)$ that follows the Lemma 1 where $\mathrm{negl}(n)$ is a negligible function in n. That is, at least $(\frac{1}{2} - \epsilon)l$ bits are opposite between $\overline{m}^*$ and $\overline{m}$ with overwhelming probability if $m^* \neq m$. Define HalfDiff as the event that $d(\overline{m}^*, \overline{m}) \geq (\frac{1}{2} - \epsilon)l$. We have that

$$\Pr[\text{HalfDiff} \mid m^* \neq m] \geq 1 - \mathrm{negl}(n),$$
$$\Pr[\overline{\text{HalfDiff}} \mid m^* \neq m] \leq \mathrm{negl}(n). \tag{5.1}$$

Denote by $I = \{i | \overline{m}_i^* \neq \overline{m}_i\}$ ($|I| \geq (\frac{1}{2} - \epsilon)l$) the positions that $\overline{m}^*$ differ from $\overline{m}$ (i.e. the positions that $\mathcal{A}$ forges on). Let $X' = \{x_i^{\overline{m}_i} | i \in I\}$ be the forged objects. Obviously, the min-entropy of X' is $H_\infty(X') \geq (\frac{1}{2} - \epsilon)l \cdot l_{in}$ bits.

The min-entropy of secret key is $H = 2l \cdot l_{in}$. The verification key will at most leaks $l \cdot \frac{\epsilon}{2}l_{in}$ bits. And the signature and leakage query would leak at most $l \cdot l_{in}$ bits and $(\frac{1}{4} - \epsilon)2l \cdot l_{in}$ bits, respectively. That is, the amount of leakage bits from $\mathcal{A}$'s view is $\lambda = l \cdot \frac{\epsilon}{2}l_{in} + l \cdot l_{in} + (\frac{1}{4} - \epsilon)2l \cdot l_{in} = (\frac{3}{2} - \frac{3\epsilon}{2})l \cdot l_{in}$. Then, we have

$$\Pr[H_\infty(X' \mid \mathcal{A}'s\ View) = 0 \mid m^* \neq m]$$
$$= \Pr[H_\infty(X' \mid \mathcal{A}'s\ View) = 0 \wedge \text{HalfDiff} \mid m^* \neq m]$$
$$\quad + \Pr[H_\infty(X' \mid \mathcal{A}'s\ View) = 0 \wedge \overline{\text{HalfDiff}} \mid m^* \neq m]$$
$$\leq \Pr[H_\infty(X' \mid \mathcal{A}'s\ View) = 0 \wedge \text{HalfDiff} \mid m^* \neq m] + \Pr[\overline{\text{HalfDiff}} | m^* \neq m]$$
$$\leq \Pr\left[H_\infty(X \mid \mathcal{A}'s\ View) \leq l \cdot l_{in} - \left(\frac{1}{2} - \epsilon\right)l \cdot l_{in}\right] + \mathrm{negl}(n) \tag{5.2}$$
$$= \Pr\left[H_\infty(X \mid \mathcal{A}'s\ View) \leq \left(\frac{1}{2} + \epsilon\right)l \cdot l_{in}\right] + \mathrm{negl}(n)$$
$$\leq 2^{(\frac{3}{2} - \frac{3\epsilon}{2})l \cdot l_{in} - 2l \cdot l_{in} + (\frac{1}{2} + \epsilon)l \cdot l_{in}} + \mathrm{negl}(n) \tag{5.3}$$
$$= 2^{-\frac{\epsilon}{2}l \cdot l_{in}} + \mathrm{negl}(n).$$

Equations (5.2),(5.3) follow from Equation (5.1) and Lemma 3, respectively.

Put differently, the forged objects X' are all fixed by $\mathcal{A}$ with negligible probability in the case of $m^* \neq m$. Then there exist at least one bit which is unfixed by $\mathcal{A}$. Let $CorrectGuess$ be the event that an unfixed bit locates at the position (i^*, b^*), i.e. the probability that $\mathcal{A}_{SPR}$ correctly guesses the position of an unfixed bit is $\Pr[CorrectGuess] \geqslant \frac{1}{2l}$.

Let ϵ_1 be the probability that $\mathcal{A}_{SPR}$ succeeds in breaking the second preimage collision resistance, then we have

$$\epsilon_1 = \Pr\left[x \neq x_{i^*} \wedge h_s(x) = h_s(x_{i^*})\right]$$
$$\geqslant \Pr\left[x \neq x_{i^*} \wedge h_s(x) = h_s(x_{i^*}) \wedge m^* \neq m\right]$$
$$\geqslant \Pr\left[x \neq x_{i^*} \wedge \left(\bigwedge_{i=1}^{l} y_i^{\overline{m_i^*}} = h_s(x_i^*)\right) \wedge \overline{m^*} \neq \overline{m}\right]$$
$$= \Pr\left[x \neq x_{i^*} \wedge \overline{\text{Forge}^{\text{Reuse}}}\right]$$
$$\geqslant \Pr\left[x \neq x_{i^*} \wedge \overline{\text{Forge}^{\text{Reuse}}} \wedge H_\infty(X'|\mathcal{A}'s\ View) = 0 \wedge CorrectGuess\right]$$
$$= \Pr\left[x \neq x_{i^*} \wedge \overline{\text{Forge}^{\text{Reuse}}} \wedge H_\infty(X'|\mathcal{A}'s\ View) = 0\right] \cdot \Pr\left[CorrectGuess\right]$$
$$= \Pr\left[x \neq x_{i^*}|\overline{\text{Forge}^{\text{Reuse}}} \wedge H_\infty(X'|\mathcal{A}'s\ View) = 0\right] \cdot$$
$$\left(1 - \Pr\left[H_\infty(X'|\mathcal{A}'sView) > 0|\overline{\text{Forge}^{\text{Reuse}}}\right]\right) \cdot \Pr\left[\overline{\text{Forge}^{\text{Reuse}}}\right] \cdot \frac{1}{2l}$$
$$\geqslant \frac{1}{2}\Pr\left[\overline{\text{Forge}^{\text{Reuse}}}\right]\left(1 - \left(2^{-\frac{\epsilon}{2}l \cdot l_{in}} + \text{negl}(n)\right)\right) \cdot \frac{1}{2l}$$
$$\geqslant \frac{1}{4l}\left(\Pr\left[\overline{\text{Forge}^{\text{Reuse}}}\right] - \left(2^{-\frac{\epsilon}{2}l \cdot l_{in}} + \text{negl}(n)\right)\right).$$

Thus, we have

$$\Pr\left[\overline{\text{Forge}^{\text{Reuse}}}\right] \leqslant 4l \cdot \epsilon_1 + 2^{-\frac{\epsilon}{2}l \cdot l_{in}} + \text{negl}(n) = \text{negl}_1(n)$$

which follows the fact that h is a collision-resilient hash function.
Below we consider the adversary $\mathcal{A}_{CR}$ as follows:

Algorithm $\mathcal{A}_{\mathbf{CR}}$:
The challenger runs $\mathsf{Kg}_H(1^n)$ to generate a random seed s of hash function h. $\mathcal{A}_{CR}$ is given s and works as follows.

1. Compute $(vk, sk) \leftarrow \mathsf{Kg}(1^n)$.
2. Run $\mathcal{A}$ on input vk, and answer $\mathcal{A}$'s signing query and leakage query as follows:
   Signature Query. Given a message m, return $\mathsf{Sign}(sk, m)$ to $\mathcal{A}$.
   Leakage Query. Given a leakage function f, compute $\Lambda = f(sk)$, return Λ to $\mathcal{A}$.
3. When $\mathcal{A}$ outputs $(m^*, (x_1^*, \cdots, x_l^*))$, if $\exists i$ s.t. $x_i^* \neq x_i^{\overline{m_i}}$ and $h_s(x_{i^*}) = h_s(x_i^{\overline{m_i}})$, return (x, x_{i^*}); else, return $\bot$.

Notice that if $m = m^*$ occurs, the forgery refers to positions in σ which have been exposed to $\mathcal{A}$. In this case, $\mathcal{A}$ is not provided with any help from the leakage information.

Let ϵ_2 be the probability that $\mathcal{A}_{CR}$ succeeds in breaking the collision resistance of h, then we have

$$
\begin{aligned}
\epsilon_2 &= \Pr\left[x_i \neq x_{i^*} \wedge h_s(x_i) = h_s(x_{i^*})\right] \\
&\geqslant \Pr\left[x_i \neq x_{i^*} \wedge h_s(x_i) = h_s(x_{i^*}) \wedge m^* = m\right] \\
&\geqslant \Pr\left[x_i \neq x_{i^*} \wedge \left(\bigwedge_{i=1}^{l} y_i^{m_i^*} = h_s(x_i^*)\right) \wedge \overline{m}^* = \overline{m}\right] \\
&= \Pr\left[\mathrm{Forge}^{\mathrm{Reuse}}\right].
\end{aligned}
$$

Thus,

$$
\Pr\left[\mathrm{Forge}^{\mathrm{Reuse}}\right] \leqslant \epsilon_2 \leqslant negl_2(n).
$$

From above, we know that $\Pr[\mathrm{Forge}] = \Pr\left[\mathrm{Forge}^{\overline{\mathrm{Reuse}}}\right] + \Pr\left[\mathrm{Forge}^{\mathrm{Reuse}}\right] \leqslant negl_1(n) + negl_2(n)$, which is negligible as well. This completes the proof. □

5.2   Another More Efficient Construction

Let $H = (\mathsf{Kg}_H, h)$ be a collision-resilient hash function where $h : \{0,1\}^{l_{in}} \rightarrow \{0,1\}^{\frac{1}{2}l_{in}}$ and $\epsilon \in (0, \frac{1}{4})$. Let $\mathcal{S} = \{S_1, \cdots, S_N\}$ be a $(1, \frac{1}{2})$-cover-free family where $U = [l]$, $N = 2^k$ and $\forall i \in [l], |S_i| = \frac{1}{2}l$. Assume that there exists an efficient injective map $f : \{0,1\}^k \rightarrow \mathcal{S}$. Consider the following signature scheme that signs messages of length $l := l(n)$.

Construction 3. $\mathsf{Kg}(1^n)$. Receive a security parameter n in unary representation, generate the key pair as follows.
  1. Sample a random seed $s \leftarrow \mathsf{Kg}_H(1^n)$.
  2. Randomly select $x_i \leftarrow \{0,1\}^{l_{in}}$ and compute $y_i := h_s(x_i), \forall i \in [l]$. Set $X = \{x_i\}_{i=1}^{l}$ and $Y = \{y_i\}_{i=1}^{l}$.
  3. Set $vk := (s, Y)$, $sk := X$.
$\mathsf{Sign}(sk, m)$. To sign a message m, compute $S_m = f(m)$ and return $\sigma = \{x_i\}_{i \in S_m}$.
$\mathsf{Ver}(vk, m, \sigma)$. To verify a given message-signature pair,
  1. Compute $S_m = f(m)$ and Parse σ as $\sigma = \{x_i\}_{i \in S_m}$.
  2. Output 1 if $\forall i \in S_m$, $y_i = h_s(x_i)$ and 0 otherwise.

Theorem 5. *If H is a collision-resilient hash function, Construction 3 is a one-time signature scheme that is $(\frac{1}{4} - \epsilon)|sk|$-BFLR-sEUF-CMA-secure.*

Note that the Construction 3 is a special construction of Bos and Chaum [5] where the one-way function is replaced with a collision-resilient hash function. It is a generalization of Lamport's construction [21] where reduces the size of key pairs to nearly half of their original cost. Actually, it is the special case of the t-time signature given in [17] when $t = 1$.

Intuition of proof. Denote by m, m^* the query message and the forge, respectively. Let Forge be the event that an PPT algorithm $\mathcal{A}$ efficiently forges a valid signature $\sigma^* = \{x_i^*\}_{i \in S_{m^*}}$ on m^*. The initiation of proof is that if Forge occurs, then either the second-preimage collision resilience or the collision resilience of h would be broken with significant probability:

- $\overline{\text{Reuse}} : m^* \neq m$. If $\overline{\text{Reuse}}$ occurs, then $\exists i \in [l]$ s.t. $m_i^* \neq m_i$, which breaks the second preimage collision resistance of h.
- Reuse : $m^* = m$. If Reuse occurs, then $\exists i$ s.t. $x_{i^*} \neq x_i$ which gives a collision of h.

Obviously, we have that $\Pr[\text{Forge}] = \Pr[\text{Forge}^{\overline{\text{Reuse}}}] + \Pr[\text{Forge}^{\text{Reuse}}]$, where $\text{Forge}^{\overline{\text{Reuse}}} := \text{Forge} \wedge \overline{\text{Reuse}}$ and $\text{Forge}^{\text{Reuse}} := \text{Forge} \wedge \text{Reuse}$. Below we show that each of the terms on the right-hand side is negligible, thus proving the theorem.

Proof. Construct two PPT Adversaries $\mathcal{A}_{SPR}$ and $\mathcal{A}_{CR}$ attacking the second-preimage resistance and collision resistance of h, respectively.

Algorithm $\mathcal{A}_{SPR}$:

The algorithm is given s, the seed of collision-resilient hash function h, and a random value $x \xleftarrow{\$} \{0,1\}^{l_{in}}$.

1. Generate key pairs $(vk, sk) \leftarrow \mathsf{Kg}(1^n)$.
2. Choose a random position $i^* \in [l]$ and replace (y_{i^*}, x_{i^*}) with $(h_s(x), x)$.
3. Run $\mathcal{A}(vk)$, answering its signature query and leakage query as follows:
   Signature Query Given the message m, generate the corresponding signature $\{x_i\}_{i \in S_m} \leftarrow \mathsf{Sign}(sk, m)$, and return $\{x_i\}_{i \in S_m}$ to $\mathcal{A}$.
   Leakage Query Given the leakage function f, compute $\Lambda = f(sk)$, return Λ to $\mathcal{A}$.
4. When $\mathcal{A}$ outputs $(m^*, \{x_i^*\}_{i \in S_{m^*}})$,
   - If $y = h_s(x_{i^*})$, return x_{i^*}.
   - Else, return $\bot$.

Denote by $I = \{i | i \in S_{m^*} \setminus S_m\}$ the positions that adversary forges on. Clearly that the event $m^* \neq m$ implies $|I| \geqslant \frac{1}{2} S_{m^*} = \frac{1}{4} l$ follows the Lemma 2. Let $X' = \{x_i | i \in I\}$ be the set of forged objects. Denote H by the min-entropy of sign key, i.e. $H = l \cdot l_{in}$. The secret key is disclosed $\frac{1}{2} l \cdot l_{in}$ bits after the signature query. Additionally, the public key and leakage query leak at most $\frac{1}{2} l \cdot \frac{\epsilon}{2} l_{in}$ bits and $(\frac{1}{4} - \epsilon) l \cdot l_{in}$ of left undisclosed secret key, respectively. Therefore, the amount of leakage is $\lambda = \frac{1}{2}l \cdot l_{in} + \frac{1}{2}l \cdot \frac{\epsilon}{2}l_{in} + (\frac{1}{4} - \epsilon)l \cdot l_{in} = (\frac{3}{4} - \frac{3\epsilon}{4})l \cdot l_{in}$ on $\mathcal{A}$'s view. Then, we have

$$\Pr[H_\infty(X' \mid \mathcal{A}'s\ View) = 0 | m^* \neq m]$$

$$= \Pr[H_\infty(X' \mid \mathcal{A}'s\ View) = 0 | m^* \neq m \wedge |I| \geq \frac{1}{4}l]$$

$$= \Pr[H_\infty(X \mid \mathcal{A}'s\ View) \leq \frac{1}{2}l \cdot l_{in} - \frac{1}{4}l \cdot l_{in}]$$

$$= \Pr[H_\infty(X \mid \mathcal{A}'s\ View) \leq \frac{1}{4}l \cdot l_{in}]$$

$$\leq 2^{(\frac{3}{4} - \frac{3\epsilon}{4})l \cdot l_{in} - l \cdot l_{in} + \frac{1}{4}l \cdot l_{in}} \tag{5.4}$$

$$= 2^{-\frac{3\epsilon}{4}l \cdot l_{in}}$$

The Equation (5.4) follows Lemma 3. In words: the forged objects X' are all fixed by $\mathcal{A}$ with negligible probability in n in case of $m^* \neq m$. That is, there exist at least one bit is unfixed by $\mathcal{A}$. Let $CorrectGuess$ be the event that a unfixed bit locates the position i^*, i.e. the probability that $\mathcal{A}_{SPR}$ correctly guess the position of an unfixed bit is $\Pr[CorrectGuess] \geq \frac{1}{l}$. Let ϵ_1 be the probability that $\mathcal{A}_{SPR}$ succeeds in breaking the second preimage collision resistance, then we have

$$\epsilon_1 = \Pr[x \neq x' \wedge h_s(x) = h_s(x')]$$

$$\geq \Pr[x \neq x_{i^*} \wedge h_s(x) = h_s(x_{i^*}) \wedge m^* \neq m]$$

$$\geq \Pr[x \neq x_{i^*} \wedge \mathrm{Forge}^{\overline{Reuse}}]$$

$$\geq \Pr[x \neq x_{i^*} \wedge \mathrm{Forge}^{\overline{Reuse}} \wedge H_\infty(X' \mid \mathcal{A}'s\ View) = 0 \wedge CorrectGuess]$$

$$= \Pr[x \neq x_{i^*} \wedge \mathrm{Forge}^{\overline{Reuse}} \wedge H_\infty(X' \mid \mathcal{A}'s\ View) = 0] \cdot \Pr[CorrectGuess]$$

$$= \Pr[x \neq x_{i^*} | \mathrm{Forge}^{\overline{Reuse}} \wedge H_\infty(X' \mid \mathcal{A}'s\ View) = 0] \cdot$$

$$(1 - \Pr[H_\infty(X' \mid \mathcal{A}'s\ View) > 0 | \mathrm{Forge}^{\overline{Reuse}}]) \cdot \Pr[\mathrm{Forge}^{\overline{Reuse}}] \cdot \frac{1}{l}$$

$$\geq \frac{1}{2l}(\Pr[\mathrm{Forge}^{\overline{Reuse}}] - 2^{-\frac{3\epsilon}{4}l \cdot l_{in}})$$

Thus,

$$\Pr[\mathrm{Forge}^{\overline{Reuse}}] \leq 2l \cdot \epsilon_1 + 2^{-\frac{3\epsilon}{4}l \cdot l_{in}} \leq negl_1(n)$$

which follows the fact that h is a collision-resilient hash function. Next, we consider the adversary $\mathcal{A}_{CR}$ as follows:

Algorithm $\mathcal{A}_{\mathbf{CR}}$:
The algorithm is given the description of the collision-resilient hash function h, say s.

1. Compute $(vk, sk) \leftarrow \mathrm{Kg}(1^n)$.
2. Run $\mathcal{A}(vk)$, answering its signature query and leakage query as follows:
   Signature Query Given the message m, return $\mathrm{Sign}_{sk}(m)$ to $\mathcal{A}$.

Leakage Query Given the leakage function f, compute $\Lambda = f(sk)$, return Λ to $\mathcal{A}$.

3. When $\mathcal{A}$ outputs $(m^*, \{x_i^*\}_{i \in S_{m^*}})$,
   - If $\exists i$ s.t. $x_i^* \neq x_i$ and $h_s(x_{i^*}) = h_s(x_i)$, return (x, x_{i^*}).
   - Else, return $\bot$.

Notably, if $m = m^*$ occurs, then the forge positions refers to positions in σ which have been exposed to $\mathcal{A}$. In this case, $\mathcal{A}$ is not provided with any help from leakage information resulting from the fact that collisions are independent of the unexposed secret.

Let ϵ_2 be the probability that $\mathcal{A}_{CR}$ succeeds in breaking the collision resistance of h, then we have

$$\begin{aligned}
\epsilon_2 &= \Pr[x_i \neq x_{i^*} \wedge h_s(x_i) = h_s(x_{i^*})] \\
&\geqslant \Pr[x_i \neq x_{i^*} \wedge h_s(x_i) = h_s(x_{i^*}) \wedge m^* = m] \\
&\geqslant \Pr[x_i \neq x_{i^*} \wedge (\bigwedge_{i \in S_{m^*}} y_i = h_s(x_i^*)) \wedge m^* = m] \\
&= \Pr[\text{Forge}^{\text{Reuse}}].
\end{aligned}$$

Thus,

$$\Pr[\text{Forge}^{\text{Reuse}}] \leqslant \epsilon_2 \leqslant \text{negl}_2(n).$$

From above, we know that

$$\Pr[\text{Forge}] = \Pr[\text{Forge}^{\overline{\text{Reuse}}}] + \Pr[\text{Forge}^{\text{Reuse}}] \leqslant \text{negl}_1(n) + \text{negl}_2(n),$$

which is negligible as well. This completes the proof.   □

6   Conclusion

In this paper we proposed a black-box construction of leakage-resilient and strongly unforgeable signature scheme. It uses a leakage-resilient strong one-time signature to transform a leakage-resilient and existentially unforgeable signature scheme to the corresponding strongly unforgeable version. Our construction does not require any special structure or property of the underlying signature scheme, nor add any element to the verification key. To demonstrate our transformation, we further provided two instantiations of leakage-resilient strong one-time signature scheme.

The major drawback of our construction is that the leakage rate of the resulting scheme is restricted by the lower rate of the underlying strong one-time signature schemes, which is $(1/4 - o(1))$ in our instantiation. And leakage rate of strong one-time signature scheme proposed by Wang et al. [29] is $(1/2 - o(1))$. How to construct a leakage-resilient strong one-time signature scheme with high leakage rate e.g. $1 - o(1)$, and thus improving the leakage rate of the leakage-resilient and strongly unforgeable signature scheme, is one of our future work.

Acknowledgements. We would like to thank the anonymous reviewers for their invaluable comments and for referring us to [29]. This work was supported by the National Natural Science Foundation of China (No. 61472146), Guangdong Natural Science Funds for Distinguished Young Scholar (No. 2014A030306021), Guangdong Program for Special Support of Top-notch Young Professionals (No. 2015TQ01X796), Pearl River Nova Program of Guangzhou (No. 201610010037), and the CICAEET fund and the PAPD fund (No. KJR1615).

References

1. Akavia, A., Goldwasser, S., Vaikuntanathan, V.: Simultaneous hardcore bits and cryptography against memory attacks. In: Reingold, O. (ed.) TCC 2009. LNCS, vol. 5444, pp. 474–495. Springer, Heidelberg (2009). doi:10.1007/978-3-642-00457-5_28

2. Biham, E., Shamir, A.: Differential fault analysis of secret key cryptosystems. In: Kaliski, B.S. (ed.) CRYPTO 1997. LNCS, vol. 1294, pp. 513–525. Springer, Heidelberg (1997). doi:10.1007/BFb0052259

3. Boneh, D., DeMillo, R.A., Lipton, R.J.: On the importance of checking cryptographic protocols for faults. In: Fumy, W. (ed.) EUROCRYPT 1997. LNCS, vol. 1233, pp. 37–51. Springer, Heidelberg (1997). doi:10.1007/3-540-69053-0_4

4. Boneh, D., Shen, E., Waters, B.: Strongly unforgeable signatures based on computational Diffie-Hellman. In: Yung, M., Dodis, Y., Kiayias, A., Malkin, T. (eds.) PKC 2006. LNCS, vol. 3958, pp. 229–240. Springer, Heidelberg (2006). doi:10.1007/11745853_15

5. Bos, J.N.E., Chaum, D.: Provably unforgeable signatures. In: Brickell, E.F. (ed.) CRYPTO 1992. LNCS, vol. 740, pp. 1–14. Springer, Heidelberg (1993). doi:10.1007/3-540-48071-4_1

6. Boyle, E., Segev, G., Wichs, D.: Fully leakage-resilient signatures. J. Cryptology **26**(3), 513–558 (2013)

7. Coron, J.-S.: Resistance against differential power analysis for elliptic curve cryptosystems. In: Koç, Ç.K., Paar, C. (eds.) CHES 1999. LNCS, vol. 1717, pp. 292–302. Springer, Heidelberg (1999). doi:10.1007/3-540-48059-5_25

8. Dziembowski, S., Pietrzak, K.: Leakage-resilient cryptography. In: IEEE 49th Annual IEEE Symposium on Foundations of Computer Science, FOCS 2008, pp. 293–302. IEEE (2008)

9. Erdös, P., Frankl, P., Füredi, Z.: Families of finite sets in which no set is covered by the union ofr others. Israel J. Math. **51**(1), 79–89 (1985)

10. Faust, S., Hazay, C., Nielsen, J.B., Nordholt, P.S., Zottarel, A.: Signature schemes secure against hard-to-invert leakage. J. Cryptology **29**(2), 422–455 (2016)

11. Gallagher, P.: Digital signature standard (dss). Federal Information Processing Standards Publications, FIPS, pp. 186–3. Springer, US (2013)

12. Gandolfi, K., Mourtel, C., Olivier, F.: Electromagnetic analysis: concrete results. In: Koç, Ç.K., Naccache, D., Paar, C. (eds.) CHES 2001. LNCS, vol. 2162, pp. 251–261. Springer, Heidelberg (2001). doi:10.1007/3-540-44709-1_21

13. Halderman, J.A., Schoen, S.D., Heninger, N., Clarkson, W., Paul, W., Calandrino, J.A., Feldman, A.J., Appelbaum, J., Felten, E.W.: Lest we remember: cold-boot attacks on encryption keys. Commun. ACM **52**(5), 91–98 (2009)

14. Huang, Q., Wong, D.S., Li, J., Zhao, Y.: Generic transformation from weakly to strongly unforgeable signatures. J. Comput. Sci. Technol. **23**(2), 240–252 (2008)

15. Huang, Q., Wong, D.S., Zhao, Y.: Generic transformation to strongly unforgeable signatures. In: Katz, J., Yung, M. (eds.) ACNS 2007. LNCS, vol. 4521, pp. 1–17. Springer, Heidelberg (2007). doi:10.1007/978-3-540-72738-5_1
16. Huffman, W.C., Pless, V.: Fundamentals of Error-correcting Codes. Cambridge University Press, Cambridge (2010)
17. Katz, J., Vaikuntanathan, V.: Signature schemes with bounded leakage resilience. In: Matsui, M. (ed.) ASIACRYPT 2009. LNCS, vol. 5912, pp. 703–720. Springer, Heidelberg (2009). doi:10.1007/978-3-642-10366-7_41
18. Kocher, P., Jaffe, J., Jun, B.: Differential power analysis. In: Wiener, M. (ed.) CRYPTO 1999. LNCS, vol. 1666, pp. 388–397. Springer, Heidelberg (1999). doi:10.1007/3-540-48405-1_25
19. Kocher, P.C.: Timing attacks on implementations of Diffie-Hellman, RSA, DSS, and other systems. In: Koblitz, N. (ed.) CRYPTO 1996. LNCS, vol. 1109, pp. 104–113. Springer, Heidelberg (1996). doi:10.1007/3-540-68697-5_9
20. Kumar, R., Rajagopalan, S., Sahai, A.: Coding constructions for blacklisting problems without computational assumptions. In: Wiener, M. (ed.) CRYPTO 1999. LNCS, vol. 1666, pp. 609–623. Springer, Heidelberg (1999). doi:10.1007/3-540-48405-1_38
21. Lamport, L.: Constructing digital signatures from a one-way function. Technical report, Technical Report CSL-98, SRI International Palo Alto (1979)
22. Malkin, T., Teranishi, I., Vahlis, Y., Yung, M.: Signatures resilient to continual leakage on memory and computation. In: Ishai, Y. (ed.) TCC 2011. LNCS, vol. 6597, pp. 89–106. Springer, Heidelberg (2011). doi:10.1007/978-3-642-19571-6_7
23. Micali, S., Reyzin, L.: Physically observable cryptography. In: Naor, M. (ed.) TCC 2004. LNCS, vol. 2951, pp. 278–296. Springer, Heidelberg (2004). doi:10.1007/978-3-540-24638-1_16
24. Pietrzak, K.: A leakage-resilient mode of operation. In: Joux, A. (ed.) EURO-CRYPT 2009. LNCS, vol. 5479, pp. 462–482. Springer, Heidelberg (2009). doi:10.1007/978-3-642-01001-9_27
25. Quisquater, J.-J., Samyde, D.: Electro Magnetic Analysis (EMA): measures and counter-measures for smart cards. In: Attali, I., Jensen, T. (eds.) E-smart 2001. LNCS, vol. 2140, pp. 200–210. Springer, Heidelberg (2001). doi:10.1007/3-540-45418-7_17
26. Steinfeld, R., Pieprzyk, J., Wang, H.: How to strengthen any weakly unforgeable signature into a strongly unforgeable signature. In: Abe, M. (ed.) CT-RSA 2007. LNCS, vol. 4377, pp. 357–371. Springer, Heidelberg (2006). doi:10.1007/11967668_23
27. Wang, Y., Tanaka, K.: Generic transformation to strongly existentially unforgeable signature schemes with leakage resiliency. In: Chow, S.S.M., Liu, J.K., Hui, L.C.K., Yiu, S.M. (eds.) ProvSec 2014. LNCS, vol. 8782, pp. 117–129. Springer, Heidelberg (2014). doi:10.1007/978-3-319-12475-9_9
28. Wang, Y., Tanaka, K.: Generic transformation to strongly existentially unforgeable signature schemes with continuous leakage resiliency. In: Foo, E., Stebila, D. (eds.) ACISP 2015. LNCS, vol. 9144, pp. 213–229. Springer, Heidelberg (2015). doi:10.1007/978-3-319-19962-7_13
29. Wang, Y., Tanaka, K.: Generic transformations for existentially unforgeable signature schemes in the bounded leakage model. Secur. Commun. Networks 9(12), 1829–1842 (2016)
30. Yuen, T.H., Yiu, S.M., Hui, L.C.K.: Fully leakage-resilient signatures with auxiliary inputs. In: Susilo, W., Mu, Y., Seberry, J. (eds.) ACISP 2012. LNCS, vol. 7372, pp. 294–307. Springer, Heidelberg (2012). doi:10.1007/978-3-642-31448-3_22

Towards Proofs of Ownership Beyond Bounded Leakage

Yongjun Zhao$^{(\boxtimes)}$ and Sherman S.M. Chow

Department of Information Engineering,
The Chinese University of Hong Kong, Sha Tin, N.T., Hong Kong
{zy113,sherman}@ie.cuhk.edu.hk

Abstract. Cloud servers save their storage cost by applying deduplication. Duplicated copies of the same file uploaded by the cloud service clients can be reduced to a single copy by maintaining a list of clients who own the same file. Nowadays it is a common practice to rely on the message digest of the file for showing its possession. Yet, this property has been exploited to make the cloud storage service effectively become a content distribution network, by sharing a short message digest.

Proof of ownership (PoW) has been proposed to address this problem. PoW is an interactive protocol by which the prover can prove to the verifier about the ownership of a file. Under this setting, the adversary is motivated to leak some knowledge of the file, for helping a non-owner to also claim ownership. We are intrigued to ask, what is the strongest possible form of leakage, such that a PoW protocol can be provably secure?

In this paper, we propose a leakage-resilient PoW under a strong model, such that any adversary who holds leakage derived from a form of one-way function cannot falsely claim the file ownership.

Keywords: Cloud cryptography · Proof of ownership · Leakage-resilience · Bounded retrieval model · Auxiliary input model

1 Introduction

The move to cloud computing is not just a mere slogan but an unstoppable trend for enterprises and personal computer users. Increasing network bandwidth and reliability make outsourcing local data to remote server a more and more attractive option. Compared with personal computing devices, cloud storage systems are considered to be more powerful and reliable. For enterprises, delegating data to cloud storage server could significantly reduce the cost of local data storage and maintenance. Nevertheless, such benefits come at the cost of potential security threats. In fact, researchers have pointed out that many important aspects of information security; including availability, authenticity, and confidentiality are at risk in cloud storage systems. In this paper, we focus on the challenge of achieving authenticity in client-side deduplication system.

S.S.M. Chow—Supported in part by General Research Fund (Grant No. 14201914) and the Early Career Award (439713) from Research Grants Council, Hong Kong.

© Springer International Publishing AG 2016
L. Chen and J. Han (Eds.): ProvSec 2016, LNCS 10005, pp. 340–350, 2016.
DOI: 10.1007/978-3-319-47422-9_20

1.1 Deduplication

Deduplication is a widely used technology in cloud storage systems like Dropbox, Wuala, in order to save space by storing only one copy of duplicated files from different users (or even the same user). That is to say, if multiple users requested the cloud server to store the same file, the server will only store a single copy of that file, and then maintain a list of users who own it.

Deduplication can be classified in different dimensions: *e.g.*, client-side deduplication versus server-side deduplication, cross-user deduplication versus single-user deduplication, *etc.* Server-side deduplication means that the server is in full control of whether to store a file or not by first requiring the clients to always upload the whole file. In contrast, client-side deduplication does not involve always sending the whole file to the server since the deduplication has been done at the client-side before the upload process. For single-user deduplication, only files owned by the same client are deduplicated. Among these variants, client-side cross-user deduplication is most economical in terms of bandwidth and space saving.

The typical work flow of client-side cross-user deduplication is as follows: Instead of uploading the whole file, client sends only the hash of the file. The server then uses this hash as a file identifier, to check whether the file already exists in its database. If so, the server simply adds that client in to the list of file owners. If not, the server asks the client to upload the whole file, and adds the new hash value in its database. In the rest of this paper, deduplication refers to this variant unless otherwise specified.

Client-side deduplication induces security risks for both servers and clients. The root cause of the risk is the lack of authenticity in deduplication: anyone that owns the hash of the file is considered to be its owner by the cloud storage systems. If Alice wants to share a huge file to a larger number of people, she only needs to upload the file to the sever once, and then broadcasts the short hash value to the intended receivers. Since Alice does not need to send the actual huge file to many others, basically Alice uses the cloud storage system as a content distribution network (CDN) almost for free. This impairs the financial interest of the cloud storage system. From the perspective of users, if the short hash value of an important secret file is somehow leaked to an attacker, it essentially means the whole large file is leaked. The above attacks are not just mere speculation but happened in reality already [6,16]. In particular, Dropbox disabled cross-user deduplication due to the CDN attack.

Table 1 summarizes the current state of some popular cloud storage systems. The information in the first three rows comes from an existing study [17] while the last row is based on our own experiment. We notice that client-side cross-user deduplication is still popular.

1.2 Proofs of Ownership

The CDN attack can be somewhat relieved by using a keyed collision-resistant hash function (to be formally reviewed in Sect. 2, despite that it is not used in our

Table 1. Comparison of some popular cloud storage systems

Name	Deduplication	Cross-user
Dropbox	Yes	No (once supported)
SpiderOak	Yes	No
Wuala	Yes	Yes
BaiduYun	Yes	Yes

proposed constructions). By keeping the hashing key secret and encrypting the network traffic using TLS/SSL, the attacker would have a hard time finding the hash value of a file of interest. However, such approach is not very satisfactory. For client-side deduplication, the hashing key has to be stored somewhere within the client-side software program, and the client-side program is always subject to reverse engineering attack. In general, simple use of traditional cryptographic primitives cannot provide a satisfactory solution.

The first solution to the above problem is called "proofs of ownership" (PoW) proposed by Halevi et al. [12]. PoW is an interactive protocol by which the prover can prove to the verifier that the client really owns the file. A trivial approach of realizing PoW is to just send the whole file in clear. Yet, it wastes a lot of bandwidth. All their PoW solutions [12] are based on a Merkle hash tree instead of using a single static digest value as a proof.

Halevi et al. [12] propose three different definitions. The first and the strongest definition parameterizes a PoW scheme with two parameters: slackness s and soundness ϵ. A PoW scheme is said to be (s, ϵ)-secure if the adversary can only convince the server with probability $\mathsf{negl}(s) + \epsilon$ ($\mathsf{negl}(s)$ to be explained in Sect. 2) when the file still has s-bits of entropy after some information of it has been leaked. Their second and third definitions are in the standard bounded-retrieval model (see Sect. 1.3 for details). The security analysis of the last construction of Halevi et al. [12] relies on an assumption that no one knows how to prove yet.

Researchers have been trying to improve efficiency of PoW constructions [1,13,14]. The work of Blasco et al. [1] compresses many cryptographic tags associated to different blocks of the file using Bloom filter [5], resulting in a more efficient scheme (when compared with [12,13]). Yu et al. [19] replaces Bloom filter with *counting Bloom filter* [9] to cope with file deletion and insertion. Recently, Pietro et al. [14] give a very efficient PoW construction that is unconditionally secure by improving their previous work [13]. Unfortunately, the interaction between prover and verifier in the proving protocol of their construction directly leaks the file.

Xu et al. [17] considers the problem of protecting the confidentiality of the file against an honest-but-curious cloud server in the context of PoW. Their solution is a leakage-resilient PoW protocol which is formulated in the following setting. Instead of keeping plaintext on the server as in the tradition notion of PoW, their scheme requires the first uploader to encrypt the file using a randomly selected key and encrypt the selected key by the hash digest of the file. Ciphertexts of the file and the key are uploaded to the server along with an index. For future uploaders of the same file, the server will transmit the ciphertext of the key to the client only if the client passes the PoW challenge. The client can retrieve the encryption key by knowing the hash digest of the file, and then keep the encryption key for future access. One potential problem of this scheme is that it relies on the assumption that the leakage can only happen before a "commit" phase, which may be unrealistic since leakage can happen anytime, anywhere in reality.

1.3 Bounded-Retrieval Model

Bounded-retrieval model (BRM) has been considered as a reasonable model which is widely used in leakage-resilient cryptography. In essence, it bounds the leakage which can be retrieved by the adversary, for example, on the number of bits revealed. A leakage-resilient cryptographic scheme means that the security guarantee still holds even after some information about the secret material (*e.g.*, secret key in an encryption scheme, or the file to be proven in PoW) has been leaked to the adversary.

However, in some applications, BRM might fail to capture necessary security requirements. For example, the work of Halevi *et al.* [12] suggested that the leakage threshold T can be set to be 64 megabytes. But for an attacker who wants to share a 4 gigabytes file, 64 megabytes is less than 2 % of the file size, which means the attacker has a strong incentive to leak a relatively "small" amount of data (64 megabytes in this example). Any security proof in BRM will guarantee nothing in the face of an adversary who receives leakage exceeding the threshold. Constructing PoW beyond BRM is not only of theoretical interest, but also practically necessary.

1.4 Our Contributions

We present a PoW construction in a strong leakage model. Let $\mathsf{Leak}(\cdot)$ be the leakage function supplied by the adversary such that the adversary can learn some information of a file M in the form of $\mathsf{Leak}(M)$. Obviously it is impossible to achieve any security if there is no restriction on $\mathsf{Leak}(\cdot)$. In this work, we choose a more general notion of leakage when compared with BRM, which restricts $\mathsf{Leak}(\cdot)$ to be a one-way function, meaning that we require our proposed PoW construction remains secure as long as it is computationally infeasible to recover M from $\mathsf{Leak}(M)$. In particular, such kind of leakage covers that in existing length-bounded model.

In cryptography, such leakage is often called *auxiliary input* [8,20]. Similar to the benefits of auxiliary input in other cryptographic primitives [8,20], Our result generalizes secure PoW in the dimension of leakage allowed.

2 Background

In this section, we establish some notations that will be used in the rest of the paper, and then introduce some important concepts in cryptography.

2.1 Notation

If S is a finite set, then $|S|$ denotes its size and $s \xleftarrow{\$} S$ denotes picking an element uniformly in S and assigning it to s. If s is a string, then $|s|$ denotes the length of s and $s[i]$ denotes the i-th bit, $s[i,j] = s[i]\ldots s[j]$ for $1 \le i \le j \le |s|$.

By $A(x_1,\ldots) \to y$, we denote the operation of running algorithm A on inputs $x_1,\ldots$ and assigning the output to y. Unless otherwise specified, all algorithms in this paper are randomized. A function is called negligible, denoted by $\mathsf{negl}(\cdot)$, if there exists and N such that for all $n > N$ and for all polynomial function $p(\cdot)$, we have $\mathsf{negl}(n) < 1/p(n)$.

2.2 Hash Functions and Collision-Resistance

A *collision* in a function H is a pair of distinct inputs x and x' such that $H(x) = H(x')$. A function $H(\cdot)$ is said to be *collision-resistant* if it is infeasible for any probabilistic polynomial-time algorithm to find a collision in $H(\cdot)$.

A family of hash functions $\mathsf{H} = (\mathcal{HK}, \mathcal{H})$ is a pair of polynomial-time algorithms, the second being deterministic. The key generation algorithm $\mathcal{HK}$ takes input 1^λ, and returns a hashing key K_h. The hashing algorithm $\mathcal{H}$ takes K_h and a message m and returns its hash $H = \mathcal{H}(K_h, m)$. For simplicity, we refer to H as "hash functions" instead of "a family of hash functions". This should not cause any confusion. We say that H are *"collision-resistant hash functions"* if $\mathcal{H}(K_h, \cdot)$ is collision-resistant for random K_h.

2.3 One-Way Function

A function $f : \{0,1\}^* \to \{0,1\}^*$ is *one-way* [10] if f can be computed in polynomial time, but it is hard to find a preimage of $f(x)$ with success probability noticeably better than a random guess in the domain of x. Typically we only require such computational hardness to hold when x is chosen uniformly at random. For the purpose of this work, we will extend uniform distribution to arbitrary distribution. The reason for this adaptation is that we will model the file as input x, and model the leakage function Leak as a one-way function. It would be unrealistic to assume the file is uniformly distributed. We adopt the definition given by Rosen and Segev [15] which explicitly specifies the input distribution.

Definition 1 (One-way function). *Let $\mathcal{I}$ be a distribution where $\mathcal{I}(1^n)$ is distributed over $\{0,1\}^n$. A polynomial-time computable function $f(\cdot)$ is said to* *be one-way with respect to the input distribution* $\mathcal{I}$ *if for every probabilistic polynomial-time algorithm* $\mathcal{A}$*, it holds that*

$$\Pr[f(\mathcal{A}(1^n, f(x))) = f(x)] < \mathsf{negl}(n)$$

for all sufficiently large n*, where* $x \leftarrow \mathcal{I}(1^n)$*.*

2.4 Hard-Core Predicate and Hard-Core Function

The well-known Goldreich-Levin theorem [10,11] asserts that the exclusive-or of a random subset of the bits of x is hard to approximate when given $f(x)$, if $f(\cdot)$ is a one-way function for uniformly distributed x. Such bit is called *hard-core predicate* of the one-way function $f(\cdot)$. The notion of predicate can be generalized to functions whose output length is not restricted to be 1. Informally, a function $h(\cdot)$ is called a *hard-core function* of the one-way function $f(\cdot)$, if given $f(x)$ it is hard to approximate $h(x)$ with probability noticeably better than a random guess. Moreover, the requirement of uniformly distributed x can be relaxed to consider arbitrary distribution. The hard-core predicate/function exists on the same distribution on which the one-way function is defined.

Definition 2 (Hard-core predicate/function). *Let* $\mathcal{I}$ *be a distribution where* $\mathcal{I}(1^n)$ *is distributed over* $\{0,1\}^n$*. A polynomial-time computable function* $h(\cdot)$ *is said to be a hard-core function of the one-way function with respect to the input distribution* $\mathcal{I}$ *if for every probabilistic polynomial-time algorithm* $\mathcal{A}$*, it holds that*

$$\Pr[\mathcal{A}(1^n, f(x)) = h(x)] < \frac{1}{2^{|h(x)|}} + \mathsf{negl}(n)$$

for all sufficiently large n*, where* $x \leftarrow \mathcal{I}(1^n)$*. When the output of* $h(\cdot)$ *is only 1 bit, namely* $|h(x)| = 1$*,* $h(\cdot)$ *is called a hard-core predicate.*

3 Proof of Ownership

In this section, we introduce the system model of client-side deduplication. In particular, we change the leakage model in existing definitions [12,14,17,18] from bounded-leakage model to auxiliary input model.

3.1 System Model

Cloud Storage Server. The cloud storage server (or the server in short) provides outsourced storage service for users. To save computation and communication cost, the server adopts client-side deduplication technique. As mentioned in Sect. 1.1, the trivial client-side deduplication effectively turns the server into a free content-distribution center, which impairs its financial interest. Therefore, the server wants to make sure that the client indeed holds the claimed file by executing the PoW protocol with the client.

Since it is in the interest of the server to execute the PoW protocol correctly, and the server can learn the file from the client after all, the server does not have any incentive to deviate from the protocol specification.

Cloud Users. Honest users upload files to the cloud server, by following the protocol specification to convince the server that they indeed hold the file. We assume that they do not have any incentive to share their potentially sensitive files to the others. However, adversarial users may obtain partial information about a file (which they do not really have) from elsewhere, say from some side-channel. Compare with other schemes in the literature, we do not restrict the amount of information being leaked. Instead, we model the *knowledge* of the adversary about the file (including some prior knowledge and leakage from side-channel) as a one-way function of the file. Namely, it is computationally infeasible to recover the file from the knowledge of the adversary.

3.2   Syntactic Definition

Definition 3 (Proof of Ownership (PoW)) [12]). *A PoW system comprises the three polynomial-time algorithms* (Challenge, GenProof, CheckProof).
Challenge(M) → c: *The algorithm* Challenge *takes input some file M and outputs a random challenge c for the file M.*
GenProof(c, M) → π: *The algorithm* GenProof *is run by the client to generate a response to a challenge c, in order to prove ownership of the file M.*
CheckProof(π, c, M) → { *"success", "failure"*}: *The algorithm* CheckProof *is run by the verifier, i.e., server, to validate the proof π.*

We mandate the following correctness and security requirements.

Definition 4 (PoW Correctness). *We say that a PoW protocol is correct, if the following condition holds with overwhelming probability: For any file $M \in \{0, 1\}^n$*

$$\text{CheckProof}(\text{GenProof}(c, M), c, M) = \text{``success''}$$

where $c \leftarrow$ Challenge(M).

As for the security of proof-of-ownership, we consider the probability that an adversary can convince the server that it owns the entire file M while it only knows some partial information Leak(M). Based on the auxiliary input modal [7,20], we assume that Leak($\cdot$) is a one-way function.

Definition 5 (PoW Security).   *We say that a PoW protocol is secure if there is no polynomial time adversary who can win the following game with non-negligible probability.*

- *Setup: The challenger generates and sends $\mathcal{A}$ the system parameters P (which includes the security parameter n).*
- *Challenge: The challenger runs $M \leftarrow \mathcal{I}_n$ and sends the proof query c with the auxiliary information Leak(M) to the adversary.*
- *Finally, the adversary outputs the proof π^*. If CheckProof(π^*, c, M) → true, i.e., π^* passes the verification, the challenger outputs 1, otherwise outputs 0.*

We define $\mathcal{A}$'s advantage $\boldsymbol{Adv}^{\mathcal{A}}_{\mathcal{I}_n}$ as the probability that the game outputs 1. A PoW scheme is secure if for any one-way function Leak($\cdot$) on the distribution $\mathcal{I}_n$ and any polynomial time adversary $\mathcal{A}$, the advantage $\boldsymbol{Adv}^{\mathcal{A}}_{\mathcal{I}_n}$ is negligible.

4   Our Constructions

Below we develop our construction step-by-step. The high level idea is that, given that the leakage of the file M is a one-way function $\mathsf{Leak}(\cdot)$ on M, it is hard to approximate some information of M given only $\mathsf{Leak}(M)$ according to the Goldreich-Levin Theorem.

4.1   Our Basic Construction

Before introducing the efficient construction, we first describe the following basic, but inefficient construction.

Let M denote the file of which the adversarial client wants to prove ownership.

$\mathsf{Challenge}(M) \rightarrow c$: The $\mathsf{Challenge}$ algorithm run by the verifier (server) selects a random string r of length $|M|$. The challenge c is set to be r. The verifier sends this random string to the client.

$\mathsf{GenProof}(c, M) \rightarrow \pi$: The $\mathsf{GenProof}$ algorithm run by the client calculates $b = (\sum_{i=1}^{|M|} M[i] \cdot r[i])$ mod 2 and returns b to the verifier. The proof π is set to be b.

$\mathsf{CheckProof}(\pi, c, M) \rightarrow \{\text{"success"}, \text{"failure"}\}$: Upon receiving the proof $b \in \{0, 1\}$, the verifier recomputes $b' = (\sum_{i=1}^{|M|} M[i] \cdot r[i])$ mod 2 and checks $b \overset{?}{=} b'$.

Security and Efficiency. To see the security of the above protocol, let $\mathsf{Leak}(M)$ be the leakage the prover receives. As long as $\mathsf{Leak}(M)$ is a one-way function of M, then b can be viewed as a hard-core predicate of $\mathsf{Leak}'(\cdot, r) = (\mathsf{Leak}(\cdot), r)$ [10]. That means if the prover does not know M in advance, she could only guess b with probability less than $\frac{1}{2} + \mathsf{negl}(n)$.

While achieving strong leakage resilience, this construction is inefficient, because the communication cost is linear in the length of the file. In terms of security, the prover can always pass verification with probability at least $\frac{1}{2}$.

4.2   An Improved Construction

In the more efficient construction, we use hard-core function instead of hard-core predicate to challenge the client. Moreover, instead of sending the random challenge r directly, we use a hash function G to generate r from a short random seed s. We model this function as a random oracle in the security proof. These two improvements significantly reduce the communication cost.

Let $\lambda \in O(\log n)$ be a chosen parameter. Let $M \in \{0, 1\}^n$ be the file of which the client wants to prove ownership. Let $G : \{0, 1\}^\ell \rightarrow \{0, 1\}^{|M|+\lambda-1}, \ell \ll |M|$ be a hash function.

$\mathsf{Challenge}(M) \rightarrow c$: The $\mathsf{Challenge}$ algorithm run by the verifier selects a random string s of length ℓ. The challenge c is set to be s. The verifier sends this random string to the client.

$\mathsf{GenProof}(c, M) \rightarrow \pi$: The client performs the following step:

1. calculates $r = G(s) \in \{0, 1\}^{|M|+\lambda-1}$,

2. calculates $b_j(M, r) = (\sum_{i=1}^{|M|} M[i] \cdot r[i + j - 1]) \bmod 2$ for $1 \le j \le \lambda$,
3. returns $h(M, r) = (b_1(M, r), \ldots, b_\lambda(M, r)) \in \{0, 1\}^\lambda$ as the proof π to the verifier.
   CheckProof$(\pi, c, M) \rightarrow \{\text{"success"}, \text{"failure"}\}$: Upon receiving a λ-bit string π, the verifier recomputes $h(M, r)$ and checks $h(M, r) \stackrel{?}{=} \pi$.

Theorem 1. *If* Leak$(\cdot)$ *is a one-way function of M from the adversary's view, then the advantage $\mathbf{Adv}_{\mathcal{I}_n}^{\mathcal{A}}$ of any probabilistic polynomial time adversary $\mathcal{A}$ breaking the security game in Definition 5 is at most $\frac{1}{2^\lambda}$, when we model G as a random oracle.*

Proof. The core idea of this proof is that $h(M, r)$ is a hard-core function of $f(M) = (\mathsf{Leak}(\cdot))$. This means if the prover does not know M in advance, she could only guess $h(M, r)$ with probability at most $\frac{1}{2^\lambda}$. To formalize the proof, we need to show that replacing r with $G(s)$ would not change the behavior of the adversary. This is can be seen easily from the fact that $G(s)$ is guaranteed to be distributed uniformly random by the definition of a random oracle. $\square$

4.3   Discussions

On the Use of Random Oracle. Note that our use of the random oracle is applying it on a random string s. We did not use the random oracle to take the file M itself, the leakage target which we aim to protect, as an input.

One may ask whether we can simply assume G to be a secure pseudorandom generator (PRG) instead of a random oracle. The answer is probably not because in the standard definition of PRG, it is only ensured that $G(s)$ is computationally indistinguishable from random if the adversary does not know s. However, in our case, the adversary (client) has to know s in order to compute $r = G(s)$. Therefore, it appears that PRG is not very useful in our setting.

Further Reducing $\mathbf{Adv}_{\mathcal{I}_n}^{\mathcal{A}}$. Note that we require $\lambda \in O(\log n)$. This is because we can only extract $O(\log n)$ pseudorandom bits by the Goldreich-Levin Theorem. As a consequence, the winning probability $\mathbf{Adv}_{\mathcal{I}_n}^{\mathcal{A}}$ of an adversary is at most $\frac{1}{n}$, which is still not negligible in n.

Recently it has been shown that by assuming the existence of differing-inputs obfuscation [2,3], we can extract polynomially many pseudorandom bits from any one-way function [4]. Investigating whether such technique can be adapted in our setting to reduce the soundness error is left as a future research direction. We note that to reduce the advantage to negligible, it suffices to extract $\omega(\log n)$ bits instead of polynomially many bits, because $\left(\frac{1}{2}\right)^{\omega(\log n)} = \frac{1}{n^{\omega(1)}} < \mathsf{negl}(n)$.

Preventing Leakage to Outsider Adversary. The execution of the proposed PoW protocol may leak information about the file M to an outsider adversary eavesdropping the communication between an honest server and an honest client. Such leakage can be easily prevented by encrypting all the traffic using a session key established between the client and the server using a standard key exchange protocol. This fix is reasonable since both the server and the client have no intention to leak any information about the files.

5 Conclusion and Future Work

For the first time in the literature, we constructed a leakage-resilient PoW for leakage beyond bounded retrieval model. There are various leakage-resilient models for PoW. A future research direction is to unify the security model. Our basic construction is secure in the standard model, yet it is inefficient. It is interesting to see if a reasonably efficient construction can be obtained by only relying on some of the properties of the random oracle, or getting rid of it altogether.

Acknowledgement. We would like to thank Zongyang Zhang for helpful advice and suggestions. We also want to thank Yu Chen who refers us to the work of Rosen and Segev [15].

References

1. Alís, J.B., Di Pietro, R., Orfila, A., Sorniotti, A.: A tunable proof of ownership scheme for deduplication using bloom filters. In: IEEE Conference on Communications and Network Security, CNS 2014, San Francisco, CA, USA, 29–31 October 2014, pp. 481–489 (2014)
2. Ananth, P., Boneh, D., Garg, S., Sahai, A., Zhandry, M.: Differing-Inputs Obfuscation and Applications. Cryptology ePrint Archive 2013/689 (2013)
3. Barak, B., Goldreich, O., Impagliazzo, R., Rudich, S., Sahai, A., Vadhan, S.P., Yang, K.: On the (im)possibility of obfuscating programs. J. ACM **59**(2), 6 (2012)
4. Bellare, M., Stepanovs, I., Tessaro, S.: Poly-many hardcore bits for any one-way function and a framework for differing-inputs obfuscation. In: Sarkar, P., Iwata, T. (eds.) ASIACRYPT 2014. LNCS, vol. 8874, pp. 102–121. Springer, Heidelberg (2014). doi:10.1007/978-3-662-45608-8_6
5. Bloom, B.H.: Space/time trade-offs in hash coding with allowable errors. Commun. ACM **13**(7), 422–426 (1970)
6. DeFelippi, D.: dropship - Instantly transfer files between Dropbox accounts using only their hashes. github. Accessed 04 June 2016
7. Dodis, Y., Kalai, Y.T., Lovett, S.: On cryptography with auxiliary input. In: Proceedings of the 41st Annual ACM Symposium on Theory of Computing, STOC 2009, Bethesda, MD, USA, 31 May–2 June 2009, pp. 621–630 (2009)
8. Dodis, Y., Vadhan, S., Wichs, D.: Proofs of retrievability via hardness amplification. In: Reingold, O. (ed.) TCC 2009. LNCS, vol. 5444, pp. 109–127. Springer, Heidelberg (2009). doi:10.1007/978-3-642-00457-5_8
9. Fan, L., Cao, P., Almeida, J.M., Broder, A.Z.: Summary cache: a scalable wide-area web cache sharing protocol. IEEE/ACM Trans. Netw. **8**(3), 281–293 (2000)
10. Goldreich, O.: The Foundations of Cryptography - Volume 1, Basic Techniques. Cambridge University Press (2001)
11. Goldreich, O., Levin, L.A.: A hard-core predicate for all one-way functions. In: ACM Symposium on Theory of Computing, STOC 1989, 14–17 May 1989, Seattle, Washington, USA, pp. 25–32 (1989)

12. Halevi, S., Harnik, D., Pinkas, B., Shulman-Peleg, A.: Proofs of ownership in remote storage systems. In: Proceedings of the 18th ACM Conference on Computer and Communications Security, CCS 2011, Chicago, Illinois, USA, 17–21 October 2011, pp. 491–500 (2011)
13. Di Pietro, R., Sorniotti, A.: Boosting efficiency and security in proof of ownership for deduplication. In: 7th ACM Symposium on Information, Computer and Communications Security, ASIACCS 2012, Seoul, Korea, 2–4 May 2012, pp. 81–82 (2012)
14. Di Pietro, R., Sorniotti, A.: Proof of ownership for deduplication systems: a secure, scalable, and efficient solution. Comput. Commun. **82**, 71–82 (2016)
15. Rosen, A., Segev, G.: Chosen-ciphertext security via correlated products. SIAM J. Comput. **39**(7), 3058–3088 (2010)
16. Thomas, K., Dropbox: A File Sharer's Dream Tool? PCWorld, April 2011. Accessed 04 June 2016
17. Xu, J., Chang, E.-C., Zhou, J.: Weak leakage-resilient client-side deduplication of encrypted data in cloud storage. In: 8th ACM Symposium on Information, Computer and Communications Security, ASIACCS 2013, Hangzhou, China, 08–10 May 2013, pp. 195–206 (2013)
18. Xu, J., Zhou, J.: Leakage resilient proofs of ownership in cloud storage, revisited. In: Boureanu, I., Owesarski, P., Vaudenay, S. (eds.) ACNS 2014. LNCS, vol. 8479, pp. 97–115. Springer, Heidelberg (2014). doi:10.1007/978-3-319-07536-5_7
19. Yu, C.-M., Chen, C.-Y., Chao, H.-C.: Proof of ownership in deduplicated cloud storage with mobile device efficiency. IEEE Netw. **29**(2), 51–55 (2015)
20. Yuen, T.H., Chow, S.S.M., Zhang, Y., Yiu, S.M.: Identity-based encryption resilient to continual auxiliary leakage. In: Pointcheval, D., Johansson, T. (eds.) EURO-CRYPT 2012. LNCS, vol. 7237, pp. 117–134. Springer, Heidelberg (2012). doi:10.1007/978-3-642-29011-4_9

Homomorphic Encryption

A Homomorphic Proxy Re-encryption from Lattices

Chunguang Ma[1,2]($\boxtimes$), Juyan Li[1], and Weiping Ouyang[1]

[1] College of Computer Science and Technology, Harbin Engineering University,
Harbin 150001, People's Republic of China
machunguang@hrbeu.edu.cn, lijuyan587@163.com, 185593450@qq.com
[2] State Key Laboratory of Information Security, Institute of Information
Engineering, Chinese Academy of Sciences,
Beijing 100093, People's Republic of China

Abstract. In this paper, we present a unidirectional homomorphic proxy re-encryption (PRE) scheme from learning with errors assumption, which can homomorphically evaluates ciphertexts at input or output side, no matter ciphertexts are fresh or re-encrypted (re-encrypted ciphertexts can come from different identities). Our PRE scheme modify the recent HE scheme of Gentry etc. We also use the approximate eigenvector method to manage the noise level and decrease the decryption complexity without introducing additional assumptions. Furthermore, with the security definition of Nishimai etc., we prove that our homomorphic PRE is indistinguishable against chosen-plaintext attacks, key privacy secure and master secret secure.

Keywords: Homomorphic encryption · LWE · Proxy re-encryption · Key privacy

1 Introduction

Fully-homomorphic encryption marks another milestone in the history of modern cryptography. To put it in a simple way, a fully homomorphic encryption (FHE) scheme is an encryption scheme that allows evaluation of arbitrarily complex programs on encrypted data. Since Regev [1] proved that the learning with errors (LWE) assumption is at least as hard as solving hard problems in general lattices, the FHE scheme is mainly based on LWE. Brakerski et al. [2] established a full homomorphism scheme based on the LWE assumption, which needs modulus $q \approx B^{2L}$, where B is the initial magnitude of noise and L is the levels of multiplication. Brakerski et al. [3] improved [2] by using modulus switching technique. Because [3] can scale down the ciphertext vector after every multiplication, after L levels of multiplication-and-scaling, the noise magnitude is still B, but the modulus is down to $\frac{q}{B^L}$. Therefore it is sufficient to use $q \approx B^{L+1}$. Brakerski [4] proposed a scale-invariant homomorphic encryption scheme, which avoids the utilization of modulus switching technique, considerably simplifying

L. Chen and J. Han (Eds.): ProvSec 2016, LNCS 10005, pp. 353–372, 2016.
DOI: 10.1007/978-3-319-47422-9_21

the scheme [3]. Noise only grows linearly, [4] only depend on the ratio between the modulus q and the initial noise level B, and not on their absolute values. Gentry et al. [5] built a homomorphic encryption scheme by using the approximate eigenvector method. In this scheme, homomorphic addition and multiplication are just matrix addition and multiplication. This makes the scheme asymptotically faster. Zhang et al. [6] presented an effective FHE scheme from Ring-LWE assumption which was obtained by modifying the scheme [7]. They used the re-linearization technique to reduce the length of ciphertext considerably, and used the modulus reduction technique to manage the noise level and decrease the decryption complexity. Furthermore, they extended the FHE scheme to a threshold fully homomorphic encryption scheme, which allows parties to cooperatively decrypt a ciphertext without learning anything but the plaintext. Hiromasa et al. [8] constructed the first FHE scheme that encrypts matrices and supports homomorphic matrix addition and multiplication. This is a natural extension of a packed FHE scheme [5] and thus supports more complicated homomorphic operations.

Proxy re-encryption (PRE) is an extension of public key encryption. In a proxy re-encryption scheme, a server is given re-encryption key from Alice to Bob. The server, given ciphertext for Alice, converts it to ciphertext for Bob with the help of the re-encryption key, without decrypting the ciphertext of Alice [9–11]. The interesting property makes PRE more applicable in many scenarios [9,12,13]. At present, research on PRE over lattices is relatively sparse. Xagawa [14] constructed the first PRE scheme based on lattices, which is a CPA secure with bidirectional and not against collusion attacks. Aono et al. [15] proposed a key-private PRE (KP-PRE) scheme with unidirectional and mulity-hop delegation. A unidirectional proxy re-encryption is said to be key privacy if any adversary cannot distinguish a real re-encryption key from a random re-encryption key even if the adversary is allowed to access to the re-encryption key oracle and the re-encryption oracle which re-encrypts input ciphertexts by using the real re-encryption key. Ateniese et al. [12] introduced master secret security as another security requirement for unidirectional PRE. Master secret security demands that no coalition of dishonest proxy and malicious delegatees can compute the master secret key (private key) of the delegator. Singh et al. [16] showed [15] is not secure under master secret security model and constructed a unidirectional PRE scheme which is secure under master secret security model with multi-use. Nishimak et al. [18] proposed two unidirectional KP-PRE schemes from LWE assumptions, which are CPA secure. Jiang et al. [17] constructed a multi-use unidirectional PRE scheme based on lattices, which is CPA secure and against collusion attacks.

In this paper, we construct a unidirectional homomorphic KP-PRE scheme based on [5,19], which allows users to homomorphically evaluate on the ciphertexts at input or output side, no matter ciphertexts are fresh or re-encrypted (re-encrypted ciphertexts can come from different users). Furthermore, we prove that the homomorphic PRE scheme is indistinguishable against chosen-plaintext attacks, key privacy secure and master secret secure. Our scheme does not use the modulus switching technique, so it is more efficient and easier to understand, operate and analyze.

The rest of this paper is organized as follows. Section 2 is preliminaries. Section 3 describes our homomorphic KP-PRE scheme. Section 4 describes the proof of security. At last, we conclude our work in Sect. 5.

2   Preliminaries

We denote scalars in plain (e.g. x), row vectors in bold lowercase (e.g. $\mathbf{x}$) and matrices in bold uppercase (e.g. $\mathbf{A}$). We use $\lceil x \rfloor$ to indicate rounding x to the nearest integer, and $\lfloor x \rfloor, \lceil x \rceil$ (for $x \geq 0$) to indicate rounding down or up. For an integer q, we define the set $Z_q = [-q/2, q/2) \cap Z$ and $l = \lceil \log q \rceil$. We use the notation [k] for an integer k to denote the set $\{1, 2, \cdots, k\}$. Inner product is denoted by $\langle \mathbf{x}, \mathbf{y} \rangle$, k-dimensional identity matrix is denoted by $\mathbf{I}_k$. For a vector $\mathbf{x}$, $\|\mathbf{x}\|_p$ denote the l_p norm of $\mathbf{x}$.

For two matrices $\mathbf{X} \in Z_q^{m \times n_1}, \mathbf{Y} \in Z_q^{m \times n_2}, [\mathbf{X}|\mathbf{Y}] \in Z_q^{m \times (n_1+n_2)}$ is the concatenation of the columns of $\mathbf{X}, \mathbf{Y}$. For two matrices $\mathbf{X} \in Z_q^{n_1 \times m}, \mathbf{Y} \in Z_q^{n_2 \times m}$, $[\mathbf{X}; \mathbf{Y}] \in Z_q^{(n_1+n_2) \times m}$ is the concatenation of the rows of $\mathbf{X}, \mathbf{Y}$.

For a probability distribution χ, we denote by $x \leftarrow \chi$ the fact that x is sampled according to χ. We overload the notation for a set S, i.e. $x \leftarrow S$ denotes that x is sampled uniformly from S. Two random variables $\mathbf{X}$ and $\mathbf{Y}$ are said to be statistically (and computationally) indistinguishable, denoted by $\mathbf{X} \approx_s \mathbf{Y}$ (and $\mathbf{X} \approx_c \mathbf{Y}$).

A quantity is said to be negligible with respect to some parameter λ, written $negl(\lambda)$, if it is asymptotically bounded from above by the reciprocal of all polynomials in λ.

2.1   Subgaussian Distributions and Random Matrices

For $\delta \geq 0$, we say that a random variable $\mathbf{X}$ (or its distribution) over R is δ-subgaussian with parameter $s > 0$ if for all $t \in R$, the (scaled) moment-generating function satisfies $E[\exp(2\pi t \mathbf{X})] \leq \exp(\delta) \cdot \exp(\pi s^2 t^2)$. If $\mathbf{X}$ is δ-subgaussian, then its tails are dominated by a Gaussian of parameters, i.e. $\Pr[|\mathbf{X}| \geq t] \leq 2\exp(\delta)\exp(-\pi t^2/s^2)$, for all $t \geq 0$. Using the Taylor series expansion of $\exp(2\pi t \mathbf{X})$, it can be shown that any B-bounded symmetric random variable $\mathbf{X}$ (i.e., $|\mathbf{X}| \leq B$ always) is 0-subgaussian with parameter $B\sqrt{2\pi}$.

Subgaussianity is homogeneous, i.e., $\mathbf{X}$ is subgaussian with parameter r, then $c\mathbf{X}$ is subgaussian with parameter cr for any constant $c \geq 0$. Subgaussians also satisfy Pythagorean additivity: if $\mathbf{X}_1$ is subgaussian with parameter r_1, and $\mathbf{X}_2$ is subgaussian with parameter r_2 conditioned on any value of $\mathbf{X}_1$, then $\mathbf{X}_1 + \mathbf{X}_2$ is subgaussian with parameter $\sqrt{r_1^2 + r_2^2}$.

Lemma 1. *([20]) There is a randomized, efficiently computable function g^{-1} : $Z_q \to Z^l$ such that $\mathbf{x} \leftarrow g^{-1}(a)$ is subgaussian with parameter $O(1)$, and always satisfies $\langle \mathbf{g}, \mathbf{x} \rangle = a$, where $\mathbf{g} = (1, 2, 4, \cdots, 2^{l-1}) \in Z_q^l$.*

Notice that for any $\mathbf{A} \in Z_q^{n \times m}$, if $\mathbf{X} \leftarrow G^{-1}(\mathbf{A})$ then $\mathbf{X}$ has subgaussian parameter $O(1)$ and $\mathbf{GX} = \mathbf{A}$, where $\mathbf{G} = I_n \otimes \mathbf{g} = dig(\mathbf{g}, \cdots, \mathbf{g}) \in Z_q^{n \times nl}$.

Definition 1. ([1]) *For security parameter k, let $n = n(k)$ be an integer dimension, let $q = q(n)$ be an integer, and let $\chi = \chi(n)$ be a distribution over Z. The $LWE_{n,q,\chi}$ problem is to distinguish the following two distributions: In the first distribution, one samples $(\mathbf{a}, b) \leftarrow Z_q^{n+1}$. In the second distribution, one first draws $\mathbf{s} \leftarrow \chi^n$ and then samples $(\mathbf{a}, b) \in Z_q^{n+1}$ by sampling $\mathbf{a} \leftarrow Z_q^n$, $e \leftarrow \chi$, and setting $b = \langle \mathbf{a}, s \rangle$. The $LWE_{n,q,\chi}$ assumption is that the problem is infeasible.*

The hardness of $LWE_{n,q,\chi}$ where the entries of the secret are drawn from the subgaussian distribution χ is no easier than for a uniformly random secret [21].

2.2 Definition of PRE Security Model

As [18], we also concentrate on special PRE schemes, there are two PKE schemes and re-encryption converts an input ciphertext of one scheme to an output ciphertext of the other scheme, which is called two-format.

Definition 2. *(Unidirectional PRE Scheme* [18])

A single-hop unidirectional PRE scheme consists of the following eight algorithms:

$Setup(1^k) \rightarrow pp$: Given the security parameter k, output the public parameters pp.

$Gen(pp, i) \rightarrow (ek^i, dk^i)$: Given pp and a user identity i, output an encryption/decryption key pair $\left(\left(ek^i, \widehat{ek^i} \right), \left(dk^i, \widehat{dk^i} \right) \right)$.

$\widehat{Enc}(pp, \widehat{ek}, \mu) \rightarrow \widehat{ct}$: Given pp, $\widehat{ek}$ and a message μ, output an output side ciphertext $\widehat{ct}$.

$\widehat{Dec}\left(pp, \widehat{dk}, \widehat{ct} \right) \rightarrow \mu$: Given output side $\widehat{dk}$ and $\widehat{ct}$, output a plaintext μ or an error symbol $\perp$.

$Enc(pp, ek, \mu) \rightarrow ct$: Given pp, ek and a message μ, output an output side ciphertext ct.

$Dec(pp, dk, ct) \rightarrow \mu$: Given output side dk and ct, output a plaintext μ or an error symbol $\perp$.

$Rekey\left(pp, dk^i, ek^i, \widehat{ek^j} \right) \rightarrow rk^{i \rightarrow j}$: Given a decryption key dk^i, encryption keys ek^i, $\widehat{ek^j}$, output a re-encryption key $rk^{i \rightarrow j}$ from i to j.

$ReEnc\left(pp, rk^{i \rightarrow j}, ct^i \right) \rightarrow \widehat{ct^j}$: Given the re-encryption key $rk^{i \rightarrow j}$ fom i to j and a ciphertext ct^i for the user i, output a ciphertext $\widehat{ct^j}$ for the user j.

We consider indistinguishability of unidirectional PRE against chosen-plaintext attacks, denoted by IND-UniPRE-CPA. We also consider key privacy security and master secret security of unidirectional PRE. The formal definitions appears in Appendix.

3   A Homomorphic PRE Scheme

In this section, we construct a unidirectional homomorphic KP-PRE scheme based on [5,19]. For simplicity of analyses we can assume that χ is 0-subgaussian with parameter $B\sqrt{2\pi}$ (i.e. χ is a B-bound distribution) and the PRE scheme is single-hop. A homomorphic PRE scheme is defined as follows.

$Setup(1^k)$:

1. $\mathbf{A} \leftarrow Z_q^{(n-1)\times nl}$,
2. output $pp = \left(1^k, 1^n, q, \chi, \mathbf{A}\right)$.

$Gen(pp)$:

1. $\mathbf{b} \in Z_q^{nl} \leftarrow -\mathbf{sA} + \mathbf{x}, \mathbf{d} \in Z_q^{nl} \leftarrow -\mathbf{tA} + \mathbf{y}$, where $\mathbf{s}, \mathbf{t} \leftarrow \chi^{n-1}, \mathbf{x}, \mathbf{y} \leftarrow \chi^{nl}$,
2. output $\left(\left(ek, \widehat{ek}\right), \left(dk, \widehat{dk}\right)\right) = ((\mathbf{b}, \mathbf{d}), ([\mathbf{s}|1], [\mathbf{t}|1]))$.

$\widehat{Enc}(pp, \widehat{ek} = \mathbf{d}, \mu \in \{0,1\})$:

1. $\mathbf{C} = [\mathbf{A}; \mathbf{d}]\mathbf{R} + \mu\mathbf{G}$, where $\mathbf{R} \leftarrow \{0,1\}^{nl\times nl}, \mathbf{G} \in Z_q^{n\times nl}$,
2. Output $\widehat{ct} = \mathbf{C} \in Z_q^{n\times nl}$.

$\widehat{Dec}\left(pp, \widehat{dk} = [\mathbf{t}|1], \widehat{ct} = \mathbf{C}\right)$:

Let $\mathbf{c}$ be the penultimate column of $\mathbf{C}$, and output $\mu = \lfloor\langle[\mathbf{t}|1], \mathbf{c}\rangle\rceil_2$, where $\lfloor\cdot\rceil_2 : Z_q \to \{0,1\}$ indicates whether its argument is closer modulo q to 0 or to 2^{l-2}.

$Enc(pp, ek = \mathbf{b}, \mu \in \{0,1\})$:

1. $\mathbf{C} = [\mathbf{A}; \mathbf{b}]\mathbf{R} + \mu\mathbf{G}$, where $\mathbf{R} \leftarrow \{0,1\}^{nl\times nl}, \mathbf{G} \in Z_q^{n\times nl}$,
2. Output $ct = \mathbf{C} \in Z_q^{n\times nl}$.

$Dec(pp, dk = [\mathbf{s}|1], ct = \mathbf{C})$:

Let $\mathbf{c}$ be the penultimate column of $\mathbf{C}$, and output $\mu = \lfloor\langle[\mathbf{s}|1], \mathbf{c}\rangle\rceil_2$, where $\lfloor\cdot\rceil_2 : Z_q \to \{0,1\}$ indicates whether its argument is closer modulo q to 0 or to 2^{l-2}.

$Rekey\left(pp, dk^i = [\mathbf{s}^i|1], ek^i = \mathbf{b}^i, \widehat{ek}^j = \mathbf{d}^j\right)$:

1. $\mathbf{M}^{i\to j} \in Z_q^{n\times n^2 l} \leftarrow [\mathbf{A}\mathbf{R}^{i\to j}; \mathbf{d}^j\mathbf{R}^{i\to j}] + \mathbf{I}_n \otimes \left((\mathbf{s}^i|1)\mathbf{G}\right)$, where $\mathbf{R}^{i\to j} \leftarrow \{0,1\}^{nl\times n^2 l}$,
2. $\mathbf{N}^j \in Z_q^{n\times nl} \leftarrow [\mathbf{A}; \mathbf{d}^j]\mathbf{R}^j$, where $\mathbf{R}^j \leftarrow \{0,1\}^{nl\times nl}$,
3. Output $rk = (\mathbf{N}^j, \mathbf{M}^{i\to j})$.

$ReEnc(rk = (\mathbf{N}^j, \mathbf{M}^{i\to j}), ct = \mathbf{C}^i)$:

Output $\widehat{ct} = \mathbf{C}^j = \mathbf{M}^{i\to j}(\mathbf{I}_n \otimes G^{-1}(\overline{\mathbf{C}}^i)) + \mathbf{N}^j\overline{\mathbf{R}}^j$, where $\mathbf{C}^i = \left[\overline{\overline{\mathbf{C}}}^i \middle| \overline{\mathbf{C}}^i\right]$,

$\overline{\mathbf{R}}^j \leftarrow \{0,1\}^{nl\times nl}, \overline{\mathbf{C}}^i \in Z_q^{n\times l}$.

- Homomorphic addition is defined as $\mathbf{C}_+^i = \mathbf{C}_1^i + \mathbf{C}_2^i$, where $\mathbf{C}_1^i, \mathbf{C}_2^i$ are ciphertexts of user i at input or output side.
- Homomorphic multiplication is defined as $\mathbf{C}_*^i = \mathbf{C}_1^i \cdot G^{-1}(\mathbf{C}_2^i)$, and is right associative, where $\mathbf{C}_1^i, \mathbf{C}_2^i$ are ciphertexts of user i at input or output side.

We show the correctness of the homomorphic PRE scheme below.

Proposition 1. *The scheme is correct at input side if* $nlB < \frac{q}{8}$.

Proof. To decrypt a ciphertext $\mathbf{C} = [\mathbf{A}; \mathbf{b}]\mathbf{R} + \mu\mathbf{G}$ with $[\mathbf{s}|1]$, where $\mathbf{R} \leftarrow \{0,1\}^{nl \times nl}$, $\mathbf{G} \in Z_q^{n \times nl}$, one computes

$$[\mathbf{s}|1]\mathbf{C} = [\mathbf{s}|1][\mathbf{A};\mathbf{b}]\mathbf{R} + [\mathbf{s}|1]\mu\mathbf{G} = \mathbf{x}\mathbf{R} + \mu[\mathbf{s}|1]\mathbf{G}.$$

If the magnitude of the penultimate coordinate $\|\mathbf{x}\mathbf{R}\|_\infty \leq nlB < \frac{q}{8}$. This completes the proof.

Proposition 2. *The scheme is correct at output side if $nlB < \frac{q}{8}$.*

Proof. The proof is similar to Proposition1.

Proposition 3. *The scheme is correct at input side for homomorphic addition and multiplication if $\left(nl + O(n^2l^2)\right)B < \frac{q}{8}$.*

Proof. Let $\mathbf{C}_k = [\mathbf{A}; \mathbf{b}_k]\mathbf{R}_k + \mu_k\mathbf{G}$, $\mathbf{b}_k = -\mathbf{s}_k\mathbf{A} + \mathbf{x}_k$, $\mathbf{s}_k \leftarrow Z_q^{n-1}$, $\mathbf{x}_k \leftarrow \chi^{nl}$, $\mathbf{R}_k \leftarrow \{0,1\}^{nl \times nl}$, $\mathbf{G} \in Z_q^{n \times nl}$, $k = 1,2$.

To decrypt a ciphertext of homomorphic addition $\mathbf{C}_+ = \mathbf{C}_1 + \mathbf{C}_2$ with $[\mathbf{s}|1]$, one computes

$$\begin{aligned}
[\mathbf{s}|1]\mathbf{C}^+ &= [\mathbf{s}|1][\mathbf{A};\mathbf{b}_1]\mathbf{R}_1 + [\mathbf{s}|1]\mu_1\mathbf{G} + [\mathbf{s}|1][\mathbf{A};\mathbf{b}_2]\mathbf{R}_2 + [\mathbf{s}|1]\mu_2\mathbf{G} \\
&= \mathbf{x}_1\mathbf{R}_1 + \mu_1[\mathbf{s}|1]\mathbf{G} + \mathbf{x}_2\mathbf{R}_2 + \mu_2[\mathbf{s}|1]\mathbf{G} \\
&= (\mu_1 + \mu_2)[\mathbf{s}|1]\mathbf{G} + (\mathbf{x}_1\mathbf{R}_1 + \mathbf{x}_2\mathbf{R}_2)
\end{aligned}$$

If the magnitude of the penultimate coordinate of $\mathbf{x}_1\mathbf{R}_1 + \mathbf{x}_2\mathbf{R}_2$ is less than $\frac{q}{8}$, the $Dec\,(pp, dk = [\mathbf{s}|1], ct = \mathbf{C}^+)$ correctly outputs $(\mu_1 + \mu_2)mod2$. We have $\|\mathbf{x}_1\mathbf{R}_1 + \mathbf{x}_2\mathbf{R}_2\|_\infty \leq \sqrt{2}nlB < \frac{q}{8}$.

To decrypt a ciphertext of homomorphic multiplication $\mathbf{C}^* = \mathbf{C}_1 \cdot G^{-1}(\mathbf{C}_2)$ with $[\mathbf{s}|1]$, one computes

$$\begin{aligned}
[\mathbf{s}|1]\mathbf{C}_* &= [\mathbf{s}|1]\mathbf{C}_1 \cdot G^{-1}(\mathbf{C}_2) \\
&= ([\mathbf{s}|1][\mathbf{A};\mathbf{b}_1]\mathbf{R}_1 + [\mathbf{s}|1]\mu_1\mathbf{G})\,G^{-1}(\mathbf{C}_2) \\
&= (\mathbf{x}_1\mathbf{R}_1 + \mu_1[\mathbf{s}|1]\mathbf{G})\,G^{-1}(\mathbf{C}_2) \\
&= \mathbf{x}_1\mathbf{R}_1 G^{-1}(\mathbf{C}_2) + \mu_1[\mathbf{s}|1]\mathbf{C}_2 \\
&= \mu_1\mu_2[\mathbf{s}|1]\mathbf{G} + \mu_1\mathbf{x}_2\mathbf{R}_2 + \mathbf{x}_1\mathbf{R}_1 G^{-1}(\mathbf{C}_2)
\end{aligned}$$

If the magnitude of the penultimate coordinate of $\mu_1\mathbf{x}_2\mathbf{R}_2 + \mathbf{x}_1\mathbf{R}_1 G^{-1}(\mathbf{C}_2)$ is less than $\frac{q}{8}$, the $Dec\,(pp, dk = [\mathbf{s}|1], ct = \mathbf{C}_*)$ correctly outputs $\mu_1\mu_2$. We have

$$\left\|\mu_1\mathbf{x}_2\mathbf{R}_2 + \mathbf{x}_1\mathbf{R}_1 G^{-1}(\mathbf{C}_2)\right\|_\infty \leq \left(nl + O(n^2l^2)\right)B < \frac{q}{8}.$$

This completes the proof.

Proposition 4. *The scheme is correct at output side for homomorphic addition and multiplication if $\left(nl + O(n^2l^2)\right)B < \frac{q}{8}$.*

Proof. The proof is similar Proposition 3

Proposition 5. *The scheme is correct for re-encrypted ciphertexts if* $O(n^2l^2)B + nlB^2 < \frac{q}{8}$.

Proof. Suppose

$$[\mathbf{s}^i|1]\mathbf{C}^i = [\mathbf{s}^i|1]\left[\overline{\overline{\mathbf{C}}}^i|\overline{\mathbf{C}}^i\right] = \mathbf{x}^i\left[\overline{\overline{\mathbf{R}}}^i\middle|\overline{\mathbf{R}}^i\right] + \mu_2[\mathbf{s}^i|1]\left[\,[\mathbf{I}_{n-1};0] \otimes \mathbf{g}|\,[0;1] \otimes \mathbf{g}\right],$$

then $(\mathbf{s}^i|1)\,\overline{\mathbf{C}}^i = \mathbf{x}^i\overline{\mathbf{R}}^i + \mu\mathbf{g}$. To decrypt the re-encrypted ciphertext $\widehat{ct} = \mathbf{C}^j = \mathbf{M}^{i\to j}(\mathbf{I}_n \otimes G^{-1}(\overline{\mathbf{C}}^i)) + \mathbf{N}^j\overline{\mathbf{R}}^j$ with $[\mathbf{t}^j|1]$, where $\mathbf{M}^{i\to j} = [\mathbf{AR}^{i\to j}; \mathbf{d}^j\mathbf{R}^{i\to j}] + \mathbf{I}_n \otimes ((\mathbf{s}^i|1)\,\mathbf{G})$, $\mathbf{C}^i = [\mathbf{A}; \mathbf{b}^i]\,\mathbf{R}^i + \mu\mathbf{G}$, $\mathbf{N}^j = [\mathbf{A}; \mathbf{d}^j]\,\mathbf{R}^j$, $\mathbf{b}^i = -\mathbf{s}^i\mathbf{A} + \mathbf{x}^i$, $\mathbf{d}^j = -\mathbf{t}^j\mathbf{A} + \mathbf{y}^j$, $\overline{\mathbf{R}}^j, \mathbf{R}^i, \mathbf{R}^j \leftarrow \{0,1\}^{nl\times nl}$, $\mathbf{R}^{i\to j} \leftarrow \{0,1\}^{nl\times n^2l}$, $\mathbf{G} \in Z_q^{n\times nl}$, one computes

$$[\mathbf{t}^j|1]\left(\mathbf{M}^{i\to j}\left(\mathbf{I}_n \otimes G^{-1}(\overline{\mathbf{C}}^i)\right) + \mathbf{N}^j\overline{\mathbf{R}}^j\right)$$
$$= [\mathbf{t}^j|1]\left([\mathbf{AR}^{i\to j}; \mathbf{d}^j\mathbf{R}^{i\to j}] + \mathbf{I}_n \otimes ((\mathbf{s}^i|1)\,\mathbf{G})\right)\left(\mathbf{I}_n \otimes G^{-1}(\overline{\mathbf{C}}^i)\right) +$$
$$[\mathbf{t}^j|1]\,[\mathbf{A}; \mathbf{d}^j]\,\mathbf{R}^j\overline{\mathbf{R}}^j$$
$$= \left(\mathbf{y}^j\mathbf{R}^{i\to j} + [\mathbf{t}^j|1]\left(\mathbf{I}_n \otimes ((\mathbf{s}^i|1)\,\mathbf{G})\right)\right)\left(\mathbf{I}_n \otimes G^{-1}(\overline{\mathbf{C}}^i)\right) + \mathbf{y}^j\mathbf{R}^j\overline{\mathbf{R}}^j$$
$$= [\mathbf{t}^j|1]\left(\left(\mathbf{I}_n \otimes ((\mathbf{s}^i|1)\,\mathbf{G})\right)\left(\mathbf{I}_n \otimes G^{-1}(\overline{\mathbf{C}}^i)\right)\right) + \mathbf{y}^j\mathbf{R}^{i\to j}\left(\mathbf{I}_n \otimes G^{-1}(\overline{\mathbf{C}}^i)\right) +$$
$$\mathbf{y}^j\mathbf{R}^j\overline{\mathbf{R}}^j$$
$$= [\mathbf{t}^j|1]\left(\mathbf{I}_n \otimes \left((\mathbf{s}^i|1)\,\mathbf{G}G^{-1}(\overline{\mathbf{C}}^i)\right)\right) + \mathbf{y}^j\mathbf{R}^{i\to j}\left(\mathbf{I}_n \otimes G^{-1}(\overline{\mathbf{C}}^i)\right) + \mathbf{y}^j\mathbf{R}^j\overline{\mathbf{R}}^j$$
$$= [\mathbf{t}^j|1]\left(\mathbf{I}_n \otimes \left(\mathbf{x}^i\overline{\mathbf{R}}^i + \mu\mathbf{g}\right)\right) + \mathbf{y}^j\mathbf{R}^{i\to j}\left(\mathbf{I}_n \otimes G^{-1}(\overline{\mathbf{C}}^i)\right) + \mathbf{y}^j\mathbf{R}^j\overline{\mathbf{R}}^j$$
$$= \mu\,[\mathbf{t}^j|1]\,\mathbf{G} + [\mathbf{t}^j|1]\left(\mathbf{I}_n \otimes \mathbf{x}^i\overline{\mathbf{R}}^i\right) + \mathbf{y}^j\mathbf{R}^{i\to j}\left(\mathbf{I}_n \otimes G^{-1}(\overline{\mathbf{C}}^i)\right) + \mathbf{y}^j\mathbf{R}^j\overline{\mathbf{R}}^j$$

If the magnitude of the penultimate coordinate of

$$[\mathbf{t}^j|1]\left(\mathbf{I}_n \otimes \mathbf{x}^i\overline{\mathbf{R}}^i\right) + \mathbf{y}^j\mathbf{R}^{i\to j}\left(\mathbf{I}_n \otimes G^{-1}(\overline{\mathbf{C}}^i)\right) + \mathbf{y}^j\mathbf{R}^j\overline{\mathbf{R}}^j$$

is less than $\frac{q}{8}$, the

$$Dec\left(pp, \widehat{dk} = [\mathbf{t}^j|1]\,, \widehat{ct} = \mathbf{C}^j = \mathbf{M}^{i\to j}(\mathbf{I}_n \otimes G^{-1}(\overline{\mathbf{C}}^i)) + \mathbf{N}^j\overline{\mathbf{R}}^j\right)$$

correctly outputs μ. We have

$$\left\|\begin{matrix}[\mathbf{t}^j|1]\,(\mathbf{I}_n \otimes \mathbf{x}^i\overline{\mathbf{R}}^i) + \mathbf{y}^j\mathbf{R}^{i\to j}(\mathbf{I}_n \otimes G^{-1}(\overline{\mathbf{C}}^i)) \\ +\mathbf{y}^j\mathbf{R}^j\overline{\mathbf{R}}^j\end{matrix}\right\|_\infty \le O(n^2l^2)B + nlB^2 < \frac{q}{8}.$$

This completes the proof.

Proposition 6. *The scheme is correct for a re-encrypted ciphertext and a fresh ciphertext of identity j with homomorphic addition and multiplication if* $O(n^3l^3)B + O(n^2l^2)B^2 < \frac{q}{8}$.

Proof. Suppose

$$[\mathbf{s}^i|1]\mathbf{C}^i = [\mathbf{s}^i|1]\left[\overline{\overline{\mathbf{C}}}^i\middle|\overline{\mathbf{C}}^i\right] = \mathbf{x}^i\left[\overline{\mathbf{R}}^i\middle|\overline{\mathbf{R}}^i\right] + \mu_2[\mathbf{s}^i|1]\left[[\mathbf{I}n - 1;0] \otimes \mathbf{g}|\,[0;1] \otimes \mathbf{g}\right],$$

then $\left(\mathbf{s}^i|1\right)\overline{\mathbf{C}}^i = \mathbf{x}^i\overline{\mathbf{R}}^i + \mu\mathbf{g}$. Let $\mathbf{C}_1^j = \mathbf{M}^{i \to j}\left(\mathbf{I}_n \otimes G^{-1}(\overline{\mathbf{C}^i})\right) + \mathbf{N}^j\overline{\mathbf{R}}^j$ is a re-encrypted ciphertext form i to j and $\mathbf{C}_2^j = \left[\mathbf{A}; \mathbf{d}^j\right]\mathbf{R}_2^j + \mu_2\mathbf{G}$ is a fresh ciphertext of user j, where $\mathbf{M}^{i \to j} = \left[\mathbf{AR}^{i \to j}; \mathbf{d}^j\mathbf{R}^{i \to j}\right] + \mathbf{I}_n \otimes \left((\mathbf{s}^i|1)\,\mathbf{G}\right)$, $\mathbf{C}^i = \left[\mathbf{A}; \mathbf{b}^i\right]\mathbf{R}^i + \mu_1\mathbf{G}$, $\mathbf{N}^j = \left[\mathbf{A}; \mathbf{d}^j\right]\mathbf{R}_1^j$, $\mathbf{d}^j = -\mathbf{t}^j\mathbf{A} + \mathbf{y}^j$, $\mathbf{R}^{i \to j} \leftarrow \{0,1\}^{nl \times n^2l}$, $\overline{\mathbf{R}}^j, \mathbf{R}^i, \mathbf{R}_1^j, \mathbf{R}_2^j \leftarrow \{0,1\}^{nl \times nl}$, we can decrypt

$$\mathbf{C}_+^j = \mathbf{C}_1^j + \mathbf{C}_2^j, \mathbf{C}_*^j = \mathbf{C}_1^j \cdot G^{-1}(\mathbf{C}_2^j), \widetilde{\mathbf{C}}_*^j = \mathbf{C}_2^j \cdot G^{-1}(\mathbf{C}_1^j)$$

with $\left[\mathbf{t}^j|1\right]$, respectively.

To decrypt a ciphertext of homomorphic addition $\mathbf{C}_+^j = \mathbf{C}_1^j + \mathbf{C}_2^j$ with $\left[\mathbf{t}^j|1\right]$, one computes

$$\begin{aligned}
[\mathbf{t}_j|1]\,\mathbf{C}_+^j &= [\mathbf{t}_j|1]\,\mathbf{C}_1^j + [\mathbf{t}_j|1]\,\mathbf{C}_2^j \\
&= (\mu_1 + \mu_2)\left[\mathbf{t}^j|1\right]\mathbf{G} \\
&+ \left[\mathbf{t}^j|1\right]\left(\mathbf{I}_n \otimes \mathbf{x}^i\overline{\mathbf{R}}^i\right) + \mathbf{y}^j\mathbf{R}^{i \to j}\left(\mathbf{I}_n \otimes G^{-1}(\overline{\mathbf{C}}^i)\right) + \mathbf{y}^j\mathbf{R}_1^j\overline{\mathbf{R}}^j + \mathbf{y}^j\mathbf{R}_2^j.
\end{aligned}$$

If

$$\left\|\left[\mathbf{t}^j|1\right]\left(\mathbf{I}_n \otimes \mathbf{x}^i\overline{\mathbf{R}}^i\right) + \mathbf{y}^j\mathbf{R}^{i \to j}\left(\mathbf{I}_n \otimes G^{-1}(\overline{\mathbf{C}}^i)\right) + \mathbf{y}^j\mathbf{R}_1^j\overline{\mathbf{R}}^j + \mathbf{y}^j\mathbf{R}_2^j\right\|_\infty$$
$$\leq \left(nl + O(n^2l^2)\right)B + nlB^2 = O(n^2l^2)B + nlB^2 < \frac{q}{8},$$

the $Dec\left(pp, \widehat{dk} = \left[\mathbf{t}^j|1\right], \widehat{ct} = \mathbf{C}_+^j\right)$ correctly outputs $(\mu_1 + \mu_2)mod2$.

To decrypt a ciphertext of homomorphic multiplication $\mathbf{C}_*^j = \mathbf{C}_1^j \cdot G^{-1}(\mathbf{C}_2^j)$ with $\left[\mathbf{t}^j|1\right]$, one computes

$$\begin{aligned}
[\mathbf{t}^j|1]\,\mathbf{C}_*^j &= [\mathbf{t}^j|1]\,\mathbf{C}_1^j \cdot G^{-1}(\mathbf{C}_2^j) \\
&= \mu_1\mu_2\left[\mathbf{t}^j|1\right]\mathbf{G} + \mu_1\mathbf{y}^j\mathbf{R}_2^j \\
&+ \left(\left[\mathbf{t}^j|1\right]\left(\mathbf{I}_n \otimes \mathbf{x}^i\overline{\mathbf{R}}^i\right) + \mathbf{y}^j\mathbf{R}^{i \to j}\left(\mathbf{I}_n \otimes G^{-1}(\overline{\mathbf{C}}^i)\right) + \mathbf{y}^j\mathbf{R}_1^j\overline{\mathbf{R}}^j\right)G^{-1}(\mathbf{C}_2^j)
\end{aligned}$$

If

$$\left\|\begin{aligned}&\mu_1\mathbf{y}^j\mathbf{R}_2^j \\ &+ \left(\left[\mathbf{t}^j|1\right]\left(\mathbf{I}_n \otimes \mathbf{x}^i\overline{\mathbf{R}}^i\right) + \mathbf{y}^j\mathbf{R}^{i \to j}\left(\mathbf{I}_n \otimes G^{-1}(\overline{\mathbf{C}}^i)\right) + \mathbf{y}^j\mathbf{R}_1^j\overline{\mathbf{R}}^j\right)G^{-1}(\mathbf{C}_2^j)\end{aligned}\right\|_\infty$$
$$\leq \left(O(n^3l^3) + nl\right)B + O(n^2l^2)B^2 < \frac{q}{8},$$

the $Dec\left(pp, \widehat{dk} = \left[\mathbf{t}^j|1\right], \widehat{ct} = \mathbf{C}_*^j\right)$ correctly outputs $\mu_1\mu_2$.

To decrypt a ciphertext of homomorphic multiplication $\widetilde{\mathbf{C}}_*^j = \mathbf{C}_2^j \cdot G^{-1}(\mathbf{C}_1^j)$ with $\left[\mathbf{t}^j|1\right]$, one computes

$$\begin{aligned}
[\mathbf{t}^j|1]\,\widetilde{\mathbf{C}}_*^j &= [\mathbf{t}^j|1]\,\mathbf{C}_2^j \cdot G^{-1}(\mathbf{C}_1^j) = \left(\mu_2\left[\mathbf{t}^j|1\right]\mathbf{G} + \mathbf{y}^j\mathbf{R}_2^j\right)G^{-1}(\mathbf{C}_1^j) \\
&= \mu_1\mu_2\left[\mathbf{t}^j|1\right]\mathbf{G} + \mu_2\left[\mathbf{t}^j|1\right]\left(\mathbf{I}_n \otimes \mathbf{x}^i\overline{\mathbf{R}}^i\right) \\
&+ \mu_2\mathbf{y}^j\mathbf{R}^{i \to j}\left(\mathbf{I}_n \otimes G^{-1}(\overline{\mathbf{C}}^i)\right) + \mu_2\mathbf{y}^j\mathbf{R}_1^j\overline{\mathbf{R}}^j + \mathbf{y}^j\mathbf{R}_2^jG^{-1}(\mathbf{C}_1^j)
\end{aligned}$$

If

$$\left\|\begin{array}{l} \mu_2\left[\mathbf{t}^j|1\right]\left(\mathbf{I}_n \otimes \mathbf{x}^i\overline{\mathbf{R}}^i\right) \\ +\mu_2\mathbf{y}^j\mathbf{R}^{i\rightarrow j}\left(\mathbf{I}_n \otimes G^{-1}(\overline{\mathbf{C}}^i)\right) \\ +\mu_2\mathbf{y}^j\mathbf{R}_1^j\overline{\mathbf{R}}^j + \mathbf{y}^j\mathbf{R}_2^jG^{-1}(\mathbf{C}_1^j) \end{array}\right\|_\infty \leq O(n^2l^2)B + nlB^2 < \frac{q}{8},$$

the $Dec\left(pp, \widehat{dk} = \left[\mathbf{t}^j|1\right], \widehat{ct} = \widetilde{\mathbf{C}}_*^j\right)$ correctly outputs $\mu_1\mu_2$. This completes the proof.

Proposition 7. *The scheme is correct for re-encrypted ciphertexts from same identity with homomorphic addition and multiplication if $O(n^3l^3)B + O(n^2l^2)B^2 < \frac{q}{8}$.*

Proof. Suppose

$$[\mathbf{s}^i|1]\mathbf{C}_k^i = [\mathbf{s}^i|1]\left[\overline{\overline{\mathbf{C}}}_k^i|\overline{\mathbf{C}}_k^i\right] = \mathbf{x}_k^i\left[\overline{\overline{\mathbf{R}}}_k^i\middle|\overline{\mathbf{R}}_k^i\right] + \mu_2[\mathbf{s}^i|1]\left[\left[\mathbf{I}_{n-1};0\right] \otimes \mathbf{g}\middle|[0;1] \otimes \mathbf{g}\right],$$

then $(\mathbf{s}^i|1)\overline{\mathbf{C}}_k^i = \mathbf{x}_k^i\overline{\mathbf{R}}_k^i + \mu\mathbf{g}$, $k = 1, 2$. Consider the user js re-encrypted ciphertexts $\mathbf{C}_k^j = \mathbf{M}_k^{i\rightarrow j}\left(\mathbf{I}_n \otimes G^{-1}(\overline{\mathbf{C}}_k^i)\right) + \mathbf{N}_k^j\overline{\mathbf{R}}_k^j$ from i to j, where $\mathbf{M}_k^{i\rightarrow j} = \left[\mathbf{A}\mathbf{R}_k^{i\rightarrow j}; d_j\mathbf{R}_k^{i\rightarrow j}\right] + \mathbf{I}_n \otimes ((\mathbf{s}_i|1)\mathbf{G})$, $\mathbf{N}_k^j = [\mathbf{A}; d_j]\mathbf{R}_k^j$, $\mathbf{C}_k^i = \left[\mathbf{A}; \mathbf{b}_k^i\right]\mathbf{R}_k^i + \mu_k^i\mathbf{G}$, $\mathbf{b}_k^i = -\mathbf{s}_k^i\mathbf{A} + \mathbf{x}_k^i$, $\overline{\mathbf{R}}_k^j, \mathbf{R}_k^j, \mathbf{R}_k^i \leftarrow \{0,1\}^{nl\times nl}$, $\mathbf{R}_k^{i\rightarrow j} \leftarrow \{0,1\}^{nl\times n^2l}$, $\mathbf{G} \in Z_q^{n\times nl}$, $k = 1, 2$.

To decrypt a ciphertext of homomorphic addition $\mathbf{C}_+^j = \mathbf{C}_1^j + \mathbf{C}_2^j$ with $\left[\mathbf{t}^j|1\right]$, one computes

$$\left[\mathbf{t}^j|1\right]\mathbf{C}_+^j = \sum_{k=1}^2 \left(\begin{array}{l}\mu_k\left[\mathbf{t}^j|1\right]\mathbf{G} + \left[\mathbf{t}^j|1\right]\left(\mathbf{I}_n \otimes \mathbf{x}_k^i\overline{\mathbf{R}}_k^i\right) \\ +\mathbf{y}^j\mathbf{R}_k^{i\rightarrow j}\left(\mathbf{I}_n \otimes G^{-1}(\overline{\mathbf{C}}_k^i)\right) + \mathbf{y}_k^j\mathbf{R}_k^j\overline{\mathbf{R}}_k^j\end{array}\right)$$

If $\left\|\sum_{k=1}^2\left[\mathbf{t}^j|1\right]\left(\mathbf{I}_n \otimes \mathbf{x}_k^i\overline{\mathbf{R}}_k^i\right) + \mathbf{y}^j\mathbf{R}_k^{i\rightarrow j}\left(\mathbf{I}_n \otimes G^{-1}(\overline{\mathbf{C}}_k^i)\right) + \mathbf{y}_k^j\mathbf{R}_k^j\overline{\mathbf{R}}_k^j\right\|_\infty \leq$ $O(n^2l^2)B + nlB^2 < \frac{q}{8}$, the $Dec\left(pp, \widehat{dk} = \left[\mathbf{t}^j|1\right], \widehat{ct} = \mathbf{C}_+^j\right)$ correctly outputs $(\mu_1 + \mu_2)\bmod 2$.

To decrypt a ciphertext of homomorphic multiplication $\mathbf{C}_*^j = \mathbf{C}_1^j \cdot G^{-1}(\mathbf{C}_2^j)$ with $\left[\mathbf{t}^j|1\right]$, one computes

$$\left[\mathbf{t}^j|1\right]\mathbf{C}_*^j = \left[\mathbf{t}^j|1\right]\mathbf{C}_1^j \cdot G^{-1}(\mathbf{C}_2^j)$$

$$= \left(\begin{array}{l}\mu_1\left[\mathbf{t}^j|1\right]\mathbf{G} + \left[\mathbf{t}^j|1\right]\left(\mathbf{I}_n \otimes \mathbf{x}_1^i\overline{\mathbf{R}}_1^i\right) \\ +\mathbf{y}_1^j\mathbf{R}_1^{i\rightarrow j}\left(\mathbf{I}_n \otimes G^{-1}(\overline{\mathbf{C}}_1^i)\right) + \mathbf{y}_1^j\mathbf{R}_1^j\overline{\mathbf{R}}_1^j\end{array}\right)G^{-1}(\mathbf{C}_2^j)$$

$$= \mu_1\left[\mathbf{t}^j|1\right]\mathbf{C}_2^j$$
$$+ \left(\left[\mathbf{t}^j|1\right]\left(\mathbf{I}_n \otimes \mathbf{x}_1^i\overline{\mathbf{R}}_1^i\right) + \mathbf{y}_1^j\mathbf{R}_1^{i\rightarrow j}\left(\mathbf{I}_n \otimes G^{-1}(\overline{\mathbf{C}}_1^i)\right) + \mathbf{y}_1^j\mathbf{R}_1^j\overline{\mathbf{R}}_1^j\right)G^{-1}(\mathbf{C}_2^j)$$

$$= \mu_1\mu_2\left[\mathbf{t}^j|1\right]\mathbf{G} + \mu_1\left[\mathbf{t}^j|1\right]\left(\mathbf{I}_n \otimes \mathbf{x}_2^i\overline{\mathbf{R}}_2^i\right) + \mu_1\mathbf{y}_2^j\mathbf{R}_2^{i\rightarrow j}\left(\mathbf{I}_n \otimes G^{-1}(\overline{\mathbf{C}}_2^i)\right)$$
$$+\mu_1\mathbf{y}_2^j\mathbf{R}_2^j\overline{\mathbf{R}}_2^j$$
$$+ \left(\left[\mathbf{t}^j|1\right]\left(\mathbf{I}_n \otimes \mathbf{x}_1^i\overline{\mathbf{R}}_1^i\right) + \mathbf{y}_1^j\mathbf{R}_1^{i\rightarrow j}\left(\mathbf{I}_n \otimes G^{-1}(\overline{\mathbf{C}}_1^i)\right) + \mathbf{y}_1^j\mathbf{R}_1^j\overline{\mathbf{R}}_1^j\right)G^{-1}(\mathbf{C}_2^j).$$

If the magnitude of the penultimate coordinate of

$$
\begin{aligned}
&\mu_1 \left[\mathbf{t}^j | 1\right] \left(\mathbf{I}_n \otimes \mathbf{x}_2^i \overline{\mathbf{R}}_2^i\right) + \mu_1 \mathbf{y}_2^j \mathbf{R}_2^{i \to j} \left(\mathbf{I}_n \otimes G^{-1}(\overline{\mathbf{C}_2^i})\right) + \mu_1 \mathbf{y}_2^j \mathbf{R}_2^j \overline{\mathbf{R}}_2^j \\
&+ \left(\left[\mathbf{t}^j | 1\right] \left(\mathbf{I}_n \otimes \mathbf{x}_1^i \overline{\mathbf{R}}_1^i\right) + \mathbf{y}_1^j \mathbf{R}_1^{i \to j} \left(\mathbf{I}_n \otimes G^{-1}(\overline{\mathbf{C}_1^i})\right) + \mathbf{y}_1^j \mathbf{R}_1^j \overline{\mathbf{R}}_1^j\right) G^{-1}(\mathbf{C}_2^j)
\end{aligned}
$$

is less than $\frac{q}{8}$, the $Dec\left(pp, dk = \left[\mathbf{t}^j | 1\right], ct = C_*^j\right)$ correctly outputs $\mu_1 \mu_2$. We have

$$
\begin{aligned}
&\left\| \mu_1 \left[\mathbf{t}_j | 1\right] \left(\mathbf{I}_n \otimes \mathbf{x}_2^i \overline{\mathbf{R}}_2^i\right) + \mu_1 \mathbf{y}_2^j \mathbf{R}_2^{i \to j} \left(\mathbf{I}_n \otimes G^{-1}(\overline{\mathbf{C}_2^i})\right) + \mu_1 \mathbf{y}_2^j \mathbf{R}_2^j \overline{\mathbf{R}}_2^j \right. \\
&\left. + \left(\left[\mathbf{t}_j | 1\right] \left(\mathbf{I}_n \otimes \mathbf{x}_1^i \overline{\mathbf{R}}_1^i\right) + \mathbf{y}_1^j \mathbf{R}_1^{i \to j} \left(\mathbf{I}_n \otimes G^{-1}(\overline{\mathbf{C}_1^i})\right) + \mathbf{y}_1^j \mathbf{R}_1^j \overline{\mathbf{R}}_1^j\right) G^{-1}(\mathbf{C}_2^j) \right\|_\infty \\
&\leq O(n^3 l^3) B + O(n^2 l^2) B^2 < \frac{q}{8}.
\end{aligned}
$$

This completes the proof.

Proposition 8. *The scheme is correct for re-encrypted ciphertexts form different identity with homomorphic addition and multiplication if $O\left(n^3 l^3\right) B + O(n^2 l^2) B^2 < \frac{q}{8}$.*

Proof. Suppose $\left(\mathbf{s}^i | 1\right) \overline{\mathbf{C}}^i = \mathbf{x}^i \overline{\mathbf{R}}^i + \mu_1 \mathbf{g}$, $\left(\mathbf{s}^k | 1\right) \overline{\mathbf{C}}^k = \mathbf{x}^k \overline{\mathbf{R}}^k + \mu_2 \mathbf{g}$, where $\mathbf{C}^i = \left[\overline{\overline{\mathbf{C}}}^i | \overline{\mathbf{C}}^i\right]$, $\mathbf{C}^k = \left[\overline{\overline{\mathbf{C}}}^k | \overline{\mathbf{C}}^k\right]$, $\overline{\mathbf{C}}^i, \overline{\mathbf{C}}^k \in Z_q^{n \times l}$, $i \neq k$. Let

$$
\mathbf{C}_1^j = \mathbf{M}^{i \to j} \left(\mathbf{I}_n \otimes G^{-1}(\overline{\mathbf{C}^i})\right) + \mathbf{N}_1^j \overline{\mathbf{R}}_1^j
$$

is a re-encrypted ciphertext form i to j and $\mathbf{C}_2^j = \mathbf{M}^{k \to j} \left(\mathbf{I}_n \otimes G^{-1}(\overline{\mathbf{C}^k})\right) + \mathbf{N}_2^j \overline{\mathbf{R}}_2^j$ is a re-encryption ciphertext form k to j where $\mathbf{M}^{i \to j} = \left[\mathbf{A} \mathbf{R}^{i \to j}; \mathbf{d}^j \mathbf{R}^{i \to j}\right] + \mathbf{I}_n \otimes \left(\left(\mathbf{s}^i | 1\right) \mathbf{G}\right)$, $\mathbf{C}^i = \left[\mathbf{A}; \mathbf{b}^i\right] \mathbf{R}^i + \mu_1 \mathbf{G}$, $\mathbf{N}_1^j = \left[\mathbf{A}; \mathbf{d}^j\right] \mathbf{R}_1^j$, $\mathbf{C}^k = \left[\mathbf{A}; \mathbf{b}^k\right] \mathbf{R}^k + \mu_2 \mathbf{G}$, $\mathbf{M}^{k \to j} = \left[\mathbf{A} \mathbf{R}^{k \to j}; \mathbf{d}^j \mathbf{R}^{k \to j}\right] + \mathbf{I}_n \otimes \left(\left(\mathbf{s}^k | 1\right) \mathbf{G}\right)$, $\mathbf{N}_2^j = \left[\mathbf{A}; \mathbf{d}^j\right] \mathbf{R}_2^j$, $\mathbf{d}^j = -\mathbf{t}^j \mathbf{A} + \mathbf{y}^j$, $\overline{\mathbf{R}}_1^j, \mathbf{R}^i, \mathbf{R}_1^j, \overline{\mathbf{R}}_2^j, \mathbf{R}_2^j \leftarrow \{0, 1\}^{nl \times nl}$, $\mathbf{R}^{k \to j}, \mathbf{R}^{i \to j} \leftarrow \{0, 1\}^{nl \times n^2 l}$, $k \neq i$.

To decrypt a ciphertext of homomorphic addition $\mathbf{C}_+^j = \mathbf{C}_1^j + \mathbf{C}_2^j$ with $\left[\mathbf{t}^j | 1\right]$, one computes

$$
\begin{aligned}
\left[\mathbf{t}^j | 1\right] \mathbf{C}_+^j &= (\mu_1 + \mu_2) \left[\mathbf{t}^j | 1\right] \mathbf{G} + \left[\mathbf{t}^j | 1\right] \left(\mathbf{I}_n \otimes \mathbf{x}^i \overline{\mathbf{R}}^i\right) + \mathbf{y}^j \mathbf{R}^{i \to j} \left(\mathbf{I}_n \otimes G^{-1}(\overline{\mathbf{C}}^i)\right) \\
&+ \mathbf{y}^j \mathbf{R}_1^j \overline{\mathbf{R}}_1^j + \left[\mathbf{t}^j | 1\right] \left(\mathbf{I}_n \otimes \mathbf{x}^k \overline{\mathbf{R}}^k\right) + \mathbf{y}^j \mathbf{R}^{k \to j} \left(\mathbf{I}_n \otimes G^{-1}(\overline{\mathbf{C}}^k)\right) + \mathbf{y}^j \mathbf{R}_2^j \overline{\mathbf{R}}_2^j
\end{aligned}
$$

If $O\left(n^2 l^2\right) B + nl B^2 < \frac{q}{8}$, the $Dec\left(pp, \widehat{dk} = \left[\mathbf{t}^j | 1\right], \widehat{ct} = \mathbf{C}_+^j\right)$ correctly outputs $(\mu_1 + \mu_2) \bmod 2$.

To decrypt a ciphertext of homomorphic multiplication $\mathbf{C}_*^j = \mathbf{C}_1^j \cdot G^{-1}(\mathbf{C}_2^j)$ with $\left[\mathbf{t}^j | 1\right]$, one computes

$$\left[\mathbf{t}^j|1\right]\mathbf{C}_*^j = \left[\mathbf{t}^j|1\right]\mathbf{C}_1^j \cdot G^{-1}(\mathbf{C}_2^j)$$

$$= \begin{pmatrix} \mu_1 \left[\mathbf{t}^j|1\right]\mathbf{G} + \left[\mathbf{t}^j|1\right]\left(\mathbf{I}_n \otimes \mathbf{x}^i\overline{\mathbf{R}}^i\right) \\ +\mathbf{y}^j\mathbf{R}^{i \to j}\left(\mathbf{I}_n \otimes G^{-1}(\overline{\mathbf{C}}^i)\right) + \mathbf{y}^j\mathbf{R}_1^j\overline{\mathbf{R}}_1^j \end{pmatrix} G^{-1}(\mathbf{C}_2^j)$$

$$= \mu_1 \left[\mathbf{t}^j|1\right]\mathbf{C}_2^j$$

$$+ \left(\left[\mathbf{t}^j|1\right]\left(\mathbf{I}_n \otimes \mathbf{x}^i\overline{\mathbf{R}}^i\right) + \mathbf{y}^j\mathbf{R}^{i \to j}\left(\mathbf{I}_n \otimes G^{-1}(\overline{\mathbf{C}}^i)\right) + \mathbf{y}^j\mathbf{R}_1^j\overline{\mathbf{R}}_1^j\right) G^{-1}(\mathbf{C}_2^j)$$

$$= \mu_1\mu_2 \left[\mathbf{t}^j|1\right]\mathbf{G} + \mu_1 \left[\mathbf{t}^j|1\right]\left(\mathbf{I}_n \otimes \mathbf{x}^k\overline{\mathbf{R}}^k\right) + \mu_1\mathbf{y}^j\mathbf{R}^{k \to j}\left(\mathbf{I}_n \otimes G^{-1}(\overline{\mathbf{C}}^k)\right)$$

$$+\mu_1\mathbf{y}^j\mathbf{R}_2^j\overline{\mathbf{R}}_2^j$$

$$+ \left(\left[\mathbf{t}^j|1\right]\left(\mathbf{I}_n \otimes \mathbf{x}_1^i\overline{\mathbf{R}}_1^i\right) + \mathbf{y}_1^j\mathbf{R}_1^{i \to j}\left(\mathbf{I}_n \otimes G^{-1}(\overline{\mathbf{C}}_1^i)\right) + \mathbf{y}_1^j\mathbf{R}_1^j\overline{\mathbf{R}}_1^j\right) G^{-1}(\mathbf{C}_2^j)$$

If $O\left(n^3l^3\right)B + O(n^2l^2)B^2 < \frac{q}{8}$, the $Dec\left(pp, dk = \left[\mathbf{t}^j|1\right], ct = C_*^j\right)$ correctly outputs $\mu_1\mu_2$. This completes the proof.

Theorem 1. *Let χ be a B-bounded distribution. Suppose that $O\left(n^3l^3\right)B + O(n^2l^2)B^2 < \frac{q}{8}$. Then the homomorphic PRE scheme is correct.*

Proof. The theorem can be easily proved by Proposition 1—Proposition 8.

4 Security

We show the security of the homomorphic PRE scheme in this section. At first, we show the IND-UniPRE-CPA security, and then show the KP-CPA security. At last, we prove the Master secret security.

Proposition 9. *Under the $LWE_{n,q,\chi}$ assumption, the homomorphic PRE scheme is IND-UniPRE-CPA secure at output side.*

Proof. Let us consider the following games for $b \in \{0, 1\}$.

RealPK$_b$: this is the game $Expt_{A,UniPRE}^{Ind-UniPRE-CPA,O}(k)$ with b. Suppose the target public key is $\left(ek^0, \widehat{ek^0}\right) = (\mathbf{b}^0, \mathbf{d}^0)$, where $\mathbf{b}^0 = -\mathbf{s}^0\mathbf{A} + \mathbf{x}^0, \mathbf{d}^0 = -\mathbf{t}^0\mathbf{A} + \mathbf{y}^0, \mathbf{s}^0, \mathbf{t}^0 \leftarrow Z_q^{n-1}, \mathbf{x}^0, \mathbf{y}^0 \leftarrow \chi^{nl}$. The challenger computes the target ciphertext on query $\mu \in \{0, 1\}$ as follows:

- If (b = 0), it returns $\widehat{ct} \leftarrow Z_q^{n \times nl}$.
- If (b = 1), it return $\widehat{ct} \leftarrow [\mathbf{A}; \mathbf{d}^0]\mathbf{R} + \mu\mathbf{G}$, where $\mathbf{R} \leftarrow \{0, 1\}^{nl \times nl}, \mathbf{G} \in Z_q^{n \times nl}$.

The adversary halts after it outputs its decision $b' \in \{0, 1\}$.

FakePK$_b$: In this game, We replace $\mathbf{d}^0$ with $\mathbf{d}_+^0 \leftarrow Z_q^{nl}$, and the challenger computes the target ciphertext as RealPK$_b$. The other parts in this game are the same as RealPK$_b$.

Since in the two games, the challenger does not require the secret $\mathbf{t}^0$, there is $\mathbf{d}^0 \approx_c \mathbf{d}_+^0$ under the $LWE_{n,q,\chi}$ assumption. Furthermore, RealPK$_b \approx_c$FakePK$_b$. In addition, from the leftover hash lemma, we have FakePK$_0 \approx_s$FakePK$_1$. From the above, RealPK$_0 \approx_c$RealPK$_1$ under the $LWE_{n,q,\chi}$ assumption.

Proposition 10. *Under the $LWE_{n,q,\chi}$ assumption, the homomorphic PRE scheme is IND-UniPRE-CPA secure at input side.*

Proof. We consider the following games for $b \in \{0,1\}$.

Game$_0^b$: This is the real game $Expt_{A,UniPRE}^{Ind-UniPRE-CPA,I}(k)$ with b. Suppose the target public key is $\left(ek^0, \widehat{ek^0}\right) = (\mathbf{b}^0, \mathbf{d}^0)$, where $\mathbf{b}^0 = -\mathbf{s}^0\mathbf{A} + \mathbf{x}^0$, $\mathbf{d}^0 = -\mathbf{t}^0\mathbf{A} + \mathbf{y}^0$, $\mathbf{s}^0, \mathbf{t}^0 \leftarrow Z_q^{n-1}$, $\mathbf{x}^0, \mathbf{y}^0 \leftarrow \chi^{nl}$. The other public keys of honest users are $\left\{\left(ek^i, \widehat{ek^i}\right)\right\}_{i=1,\cdots,H} = \left\{(\mathbf{b}^i, \mathbf{d}^i)\right\}_{i=1,\cdots,H}$, where $\mathbf{b}^i = -\mathbf{s}^i\mathbf{A} + \mathbf{x}^i$, $\mathbf{d}^i = -\mathbf{t}^i\mathbf{A} + \mathbf{y}^i$. The challenger computes the re-encryption key from user 0 to user $i \in [H]$ as $\mathbf{M}^{0\to i} \in Z_q^{n\times n^2 l} \leftarrow [\mathbf{AR}^{0\to i}; \mathbf{d}^i\mathbf{R}^{0\to i}] + \mathbf{I}_n \otimes ((\mathbf{s}^0|1)\mathbf{G})$, $\mathbf{N}^i \in Z_q^{n\times nl} \leftarrow [\mathbf{A}; \mathbf{d}^i]\mathbf{R}^i$, where $\mathbf{R}^{0\to i} \leftarrow \{0,1\}^{nl\times n^2 l}$, $\mathbf{R}^i \leftarrow \{0,1\}^{nl\times nl}$. The challenger computes the target ciphertext on query $\mu \in \{0,1\}$ as follows:

- If (b = 0), it returns $\widehat{ct} \leftarrow Z_q^{n\times nl}$.
- If (b = 1), it return $\widehat{ct} = \mathbf{C}^j = \mathbf{M}^{i\to j}(\mathbf{I}_n \otimes G^{-1}(\overline{\mathbf{C}^i})) + \mathbf{N}^j\overline{\mathbf{R}}^j$, where $\mathbf{C}^i = \left[\overline{\overline{\mathbf{C}}}^i \mid \overline{\mathbf{C}}^i\right]$, $\overline{\mathbf{R}}^j \leftarrow \{0,1\}^{nl\times nl}$, $\overline{\mathbf{C}}^i \in Z_q^{n\times l}$.

The adversary finally outputs its guess $b' \in \{0,1\}$.

Game$_1^b$: We replace $\mathbf{d}^i$ with $\mathbf{d}_+^i \leftarrow Z_q^{nl}$ for $i \in [H]$. The challenger computes a re-encryption key from user 0 to user $i \in [H]$ by using $\mathbf{s}^0$ and $\mathbf{d}_+^i$ as Game$_0^b$. The others are the same as in Game$_0^b$.

Since in the two games, the challenger does not require the secret $\mathbf{t}^i$, there is $\mathbf{d}^i \approx_c \mathbf{d}_+^i$ under the $LWE_{n,q,\chi}$ assumption. Furthermore, Game$_0^b \approx_c$Game$_1^b$.

Game$_2^b$: We replace $\mathbf{M}^{0\to i}$, $\mathbf{N}^i$ with $\mathbf{M}_+^{0\to i} \leftarrow Z_q^{n\times n^2 l}$, $\mathbf{N}_+^i \leftarrow Z_q^{n\times nl}$. The others are the same as in Game$_1^b$.

It follows from the leftover hash lemma, we have $\mathbf{M}^{0\to i} \approx_s \mathbf{M}_+^{0\to i}$ and $\mathbf{N}^i \approx_s \mathbf{N}_+^i$. Furthermore, Game$_1^b \approx_s$Game$_2^b$.

Game$_3^b$: We replace $\mathbf{d}^0$ with $\mathbf{d}_+^0 \leftarrow Z_q^{nl}$. The others are the same as in Game$_2^b$.

Since the challenger does not require the secret $\mathbf{t}^0$, there is $\mathbf{d}^0 \approx_c \mathbf{d}_+^0$ under the $LWE_{n,q,\chi}$ assumption. Furthermore, Game$_3^b \approx_c$Game$_2^b$.

Finally, we have that Game$_3^0 \approx_s$Game$_2^1$ from the leftover hash lemma. Combining the above indistinguishabilities, we have shown that Game$_0^0 \approx_c$Game$_0^1$. This completes the proof.

Theorem 2. *Under the $LWE_{n,q,\chi}$ assumption, the homomorphic PRE scheme is IND-UniPRE-CPA secure at both sides*

Proof. It follows from Propositions 9, 10.

Theorem 3. *Under the $LWE_{n,q,\chi}$ assumption, the homomorphic PRE scheme is KP-CPA secure.*

Proof. We start with the original game with b = 1.

$Game_0$: This is the game $Expt^{KP-CPA}_{A,UniPRE}(k)$ with b = 1. The challenger runs the adversary with input pp, public keys

$$\left\{ \left(ek^i, \widehat{ek}^i \right) \right\}_{i=-1,0,\cdots,H} = \left\{ \left(\mathbf{b}^i, \mathbf{d}^i \right) \right\}_{i=-1,0,\cdots,H}$$

for honest users and key pairs

$$\begin{aligned} &\left\{ \left(\left(ek^i, \widehat{ek}^i \right), \left(dk^i, \widehat{dk}^i \right) \right) \right\}_{i=H+1,\cdots,H+C} \\ &= \left\{ \left(\mathbf{b}^i, \mathbf{d}^i \right), \left(\left[\mathbf{s}^i | 1 \right], \left[\mathbf{t}^i | 1 \right] \right) \right\}_{i=H+1,\cdots,H+C} \end{aligned}$$

for corrupted users. The challenger generates the real re-encryption key $\mathbf{M}^{0 \to -1} \in Z_q^{n \times n^2 l} \leftarrow \left[\mathbf{A R}^{0 \to -1}; \mathbf{d}^i \mathbf{R}^{0 \to -1} \right] + \mathbf{I}_n \otimes \left(\left(\mathbf{s}^0 | 1 \right) \mathbf{G} \right), \mathbf{N}^{-1} \in Z_q^{n \times nl} \leftarrow \left[\mathbf{A}; \mathbf{d}^{-1} \right] \mathbf{R}^{-1}$, where $\mathbf{R}^{0 \to -1} \leftarrow \{0,1\}^{nl \times n^2 l}$, $\mathbf{R}^{-1} \leftarrow \{0,1\}^{nl \times nl}$. On the re-encryption query $(0, -1, ct = \mathbf{C}^0)$, it re-encrypts the ciphertext with the real re-encryption key, that is, it returns $\widehat{ct} = \mathbf{C}^{-1} = \mathbf{M}^{0 \to -1}(\mathbf{I}_n \otimes G^{-1}(\overline{\mathbf{C}}^0)) + \mathbf{N}^{-1} \overline{\mathbf{R}}^{-1}$, where $\mathbf{C}^0 = \left[\overline{\overline{\mathbf{C}}}^0 \middle| \overline{\mathbf{C}}^0 \right]$, $\overline{\mathbf{R}}^{-1} \leftarrow \{0,1\}^{nl \times nl}$, $\overline{\mathbf{C}}^0 \in Z_q^{n \times l}$. We summarize the input and the answers to the adversary as follows:

$$\text{RealPK} : \mathbf{d}^{-1}, \text{Challenge} : \mathbf{M}^{0 \to -1}, \mathbf{N}^{-1}, \text{Table} : \mathbf{M}^{0 \to -1}, \mathbf{N}^{-1},$$

$$\text{ReEnc} : \widehat{ct} = \mathbf{C}^{-1} = \mathbf{M}^{0 \to -1}(\mathbf{I}_n \otimes G^{-1}(\overline{\mathbf{C}}^0)) + \mathbf{N}^{-1} \overline{\mathbf{R}}^{-1}.$$

After the learning phase, the adversary outputs its guess $b' \in \{0,1\}$.

$Game_1$: The challenger replace $\mathbf{d}^{-1}$ with $\mathbf{d}^{-1}_+ \leftarrow Z_q^{nl}$, and the re-encryption keys in challenge and the table is constructed from $\mathbf{d}^{-1}_+$ and $\mathbf{s}^0$. The other parters are the same as $Game_0$. The challenger re-encrypts a given ciphertext with the re-encryption key in the table. The challenger answers the queries from user 0 to -1 as follows:

$$\text{RealPK} : \mathbf{d}^{-1}_+, \text{Challenge} : \mathbf{M}^{0 \to -1}, \mathbf{N}^{-1}, \text{Table} : \mathbf{M}^{0 \to -1}, \mathbf{N}^{-1},$$

$$\text{ReEnc} : \widehat{ct} = \widetilde{\mathbf{C}}^{-1} = \mathbf{M}^{0 \to -1}(\mathbf{I}_n \otimes G^{-1}(\overline{\mathbf{C}}^0)) + \mathbf{N}^{-1} \overline{\mathbf{R}}^{-1}.$$

It is easy to verify that $\mathbf{d}^{-1} \approx_c \mathbf{d}^{-1}_+$ under the $LWE_{(n,q,\chi)}$ assumption, since we do not need to know $\mathbf{t}^{-1}$. Furthermore, we have $Game_0 \approx_c Game_1$ by the leftover hash lemma.

$Game_2$: The challenger replaces $\mathbf{M}^{0 \to -1}$, $\mathbf{N}^{-1}$ with $\mathbf{M}^{0 \to -1}_+ \leftarrow Z_q^{n \times n^2 l}$, $\mathbf{N}^{-1}_+ \leftarrow Z_q^{n \times nl}$. The other parts are not changed from the previous game: the challenger re-encrypts a given ciphertext with the random re-encryption key in the table. The challenger answers the queries from user 0 to -1 as follows:

$$\text{RealPK} : \mathbf{d}^{-1}_+, \text{Challenge} : \mathbf{M}^{0 \to -1}_+, \mathbf{N}^{-1}_+, \text{Table} : \mathbf{M}^{0 \to -1}_+, \mathbf{N}^{-1}_+,$$

$$\text{ReEnc} : \widehat{ct} = \widetilde{\mathbf{C}}^{-1}_+ = \mathbf{M}^{0 \to -1}_+(\mathbf{I}_n \otimes G^{-1}(\overline{\mathbf{C}}^0)) + \mathbf{N}^{-1}_+ \overline{\mathbf{R}}^{-1}.$$

It follows from the leftover hash lemma, we have $\mathbf{M}^{0\to-1}\approx_s\mathbf{M}_+^{0\to-1}$ and $\mathbf{N}^{-1}\approx_s\mathbf{N}_+^{-1}$. Furthermore, $Game_1\approx_sGame_2$.

$Game_3$: If the query is $(0, -1, ct = \mathbf{C}^0)$, then it returns $\mathbf{C}_+^{-1} \leftarrow Z_q^{n\times nl}$. The other parts are not changed from the previous game: The challenger answers the queries from user 0 to -1 as follows:

$$\text{RealPK} : \mathbf{d}_+^{-1}, \text{Challenge} : \mathbf{M}_+^{0\to-1}, \mathbf{N}_+^{-1}, \text{Table} : \mathbf{M}_+^{0\to-1}, \mathbf{N}_+^{-1},$$

$$\text{ReEnc} : \widehat{ct} = \mathbf{C}_+^{-1}.$$

It follows from the leftover hash lemma, we have $\widetilde{\mathbf{C}}_+^{-1}\approx_s\mathbf{C}_+^{-1}$. Furthermore, $Game_2\approx_sGame_3$.

$Game_4$: The challenger additionally generates another random re-encryption key $\mathbf{M}_{++}^{0\to-1}$, $\mathbf{N}_{++}^{-1}$ and uses it in the re-encryption oracle. The other parts are not changed from the previous game: As a summary, the challenger answers the queries from user 0 to -1 as follows:

$$\text{RealPK} : \mathbf{d}_+^{-1}, \text{Challenge} : \mathbf{M}_+^{0\to-1}, \mathbf{N}_+^{-1}, \text{Table} : \mathbf{M}_{++}^{0\to-1}, \mathbf{N}_{++}^{-1},$$

$$\text{ReEnc} : \widehat{ct} = \widetilde{\mathbf{C}}_{++}^{-1} = \mathbf{M}_{++}^{0\to-1}(\mathbf{I}_n \otimes G^{-1}(\overline{\mathbf{C}^0})) + \mathbf{N}_{++}^{-1}\overline{\mathbf{R}}^{-1}.$$

We note that the adversary does not know the alternative fake re-encryption key $\mathbf{M}_{++}^{0\to-1}$, $\mathbf{N}_{++}^{-1}$, directly. Even if the adversary knows the alternative, it cannot distinguish the two games since the re-encrypted ciphertext, which is almost uniformly at random in the ciphertext space from the leftover hash lemma. Hence, we have $Game_3\approx_sGame_4$.

$Game_5$: We again modify the re-encryption key in the table and the re-encryption oracle. The challenger additionally generates a fake re-encryption key $\mathbf{M}_*^{0\to-1} \in Z_q^{n\times n^2l} \leftarrow \left[\mathbf{AR}_*^{0\to-1}; \mathbf{d}_+^{-1}\mathbf{R}_*^{0\to-1}\right] + \mathbf{I}_n \otimes \left((\mathbf{s}^0|1)\,G\right)$, $\mathbf{N}_*^{-1} \in Z_q^{n\times nl} \leftarrow \left[\mathbf{A}; \mathbf{d}_+^{-1}\right]\mathbf{R}_*^{-1}$, where $\mathbf{R}_*^{0\to-1} \leftarrow \{0,1\}^{nl\times n^2l}$, $\mathbf{R}_*^{-1} \leftarrow \{0,1\}^{nl\times nl}$. In the re-encryption oracle, the oracle uses the additional fake-re-encryption key $\mathbf{M}_*^{0\to-1}$, $\mathbf{N}_*^{-1}$ instead of $\mathbf{M}_+^{0\to-1}$, $\mathbf{N}_+^{-1}$ that the adversary receives as the challenge. The other parts are not changed from the previous game: As a summary, the challenger answers the queries from user 0 to -1 as follows:

$$\text{RealPK} : \mathbf{d}_+^{-1}, \text{Challenge} : \mathbf{M}_+^{0\to-1}, \mathbf{N}_+^{-1}, \text{Table} : \mathbf{M}_*^{0\to-1}, \mathbf{N}_*^{-1},$$

$$\text{ReEnc} : \widehat{ct} = \widetilde{\mathbf{C}}_*^{-1} = \mathbf{M}_*^{0\to-1}(\mathbf{I}_n \otimes G^{-1}(\overline{\mathbf{C}^0})) + \mathbf{N}_*^{-1}\overline{\mathbf{R}}^{-1}.$$

It follows from the leftover hash lemma, we have $\mathbf{M}_*^{0\to-1}\approx_s\mathbf{M}_+^{0\to-1}$, $\mathbf{N}_*^{-1}\approx_s\mathbf{N}_+^{-1}$ and $\mathbf{C}_*^{-1}\approx_s\mathbf{C}_{++}^{-1}$. Furthermore, $Game_4\approx_sGame_5$.

$Game_6$: This is a final game. We replace the fake public key $\mathbf{d}_+^{-1}$ with the real public key $\mathbf{d}^{-1}$. The other parts are not changed from the previous game: As a summary, the challenger answers the queries from 0 to -1 as follows:

$$\text{RealPK} : \mathbf{d}^{-1}, \text{Challenge} : \mathbf{M}_+^{0\to-1}, \mathbf{N}_+^{-1}, \text{Table} : \mathbf{M}_*^{0\to-1}, \mathbf{N}_*^{-1},$$

$$\text{ReEnc} : \widehat{ct} = \mathbf{M}_*^{0\to-1}(\mathbf{I}_n \otimes G^{-1}(\overline{\mathbf{C}^0})) + \mathbf{N}_*^{-1}\overline{\mathbf{R}}^{-1}.$$

Since $\mathbf{M}_+^{0 \to -1}$, $\mathbf{N}_+^{-1}$ is distributed uniformly at random, this game is equivalent to $Expt_{A,UniPRE}^{KP-CPA}(k)$ with b = 0. We have $Game_5 \approx_c Game_6$ under the $LWE_{(n,q,\chi)}$ assumption, since we only change the random instance $\mathbf{d}_+^{-1}$ with the LWE instance $\mathbf{d}^{-1}$.

Above all, we know $Game_0 \approx_c Game_6$, that is $Expt_{A,UniPRE}^{KP-CPA}(k)$ with b=0 and $Expt_{A,UniPRE}^{KP-CPA}(k)$ with b=1 are computationally indistinguishable under $LWE_{(n,q,\chi)}$ assumption. This completes the proof.

Theorem 4. *Under the $LWE_{n,q,\chi}$ assumption, the homomorphic PRE scheme is master secret security.*

Proof. The proof is similar to Theorem 3 of [16]

5   Conclusion

In this paper, we adopt approximate eigenvector method and the scheme of Gentry etc. to construct a homomorphic PRE scheme. With the approximate eigenvector method, we keep noise that terms in ciphertexts also grow asymmetrically. We also prove that our homomorphic PRE scheme is IND-UniPRE-CPA, KP-CPA and master secret security. We will be devoted to improving the computation efficiency in our future work, so as to make our homomorphic PRE schemes more practical.

Acknowledgements. The authors would like to thank the reviewers for their detailed reviews and constructive comments, which have helped improve the quality of this paper. This work was supported by the National Natural Science Foundation of China (61472097), the Special Research Found for the Doctoral Program of Higher Education of China (20132304110017), and the Open Fund of the State Key Laboratory of Information Security(2016-MS-10).

Appendix

Definition 3. (IND-UniPRE-CPA security at input side [18])

Let UniPRE=(Setup, Gen, $\widehat{Enc}$, Enc, $\widehat{Dec}$, Dec, ReKey, ReEnc) be a single-hop, unidirectional PRE scheme, k a security parameter. Suppose that there exists a PPT algorithm $RandEnc$ which takes pp as input and outputs a random ciphertext at input side. Let H=H(k) and C=C(k) be polynomials of k, which stands for the number of honest users and corrupted users, respectively. Consider the following game, denoted by $Expt_{A,UniPRE}^{IND-UniPRE-CPA,I}(k)$, between challenger and adversary.

Initialization: Given security parameter k and coin $b \in \{0,1\}$, run $pp \leftarrow Setup(1^k)$. Initialize $CU \leftarrow \{H+1, \cdots, H+C\}$, which denote the set of corrupted users. For $i = 0, \cdots, H+C$ generate key pairs $\left(\left(ek^i, \widehat{ek^i} \right), \left(dk^i, \widehat{dk^i} \right) \right) \leftarrow$ Gen (pp, i). Run the adversary on input pp, key pairs of corrupted users

$$\left\{\left(\left(\mathrm{ek}^i, \widehat{\mathrm{ek}^i}\right), \left(\mathrm{dk}^i, \widehat{\mathrm{dk}^i}\right)\right)\right\}_{i=H+1,\cdots,H+C}, \text{ and public keys of honest users}$$
$$\left\{\left(\mathrm{ek}^i, \widehat{\mathrm{ek}^i}\right)\right\}_{i=0,\cdots,H}.$$

Learning Phase: The adversary could issue queries to the following oracles in any order and many times : Oracle REKEY receives two indices $i, j \in \{0, 1, \cdots, H + C\}$. If i = j then it returns $\bot$; if $(i = 0) \cap (j \in CU)$ then the oracle returns $\bot$; otherwise, returns $rk^{i \to j} \leftarrow Rekey\left(pp, dk^i, ek^i, \widehat{ek^j}\right)$.

Oracle REENC receives two indices $i, j \in \{0, 1, \cdots, H+C\}$ and ciphertext ct. If i = j then returns $\bot$; if $(i = 0) \cap (j \in CU)$ then the oracle returns $\bot$; otherwise, it queries (i,j) to REKEY, obtains $rk^{i \to j}$, and returns $\widehat{ct} \leftarrow ReEnc(pp, rk^{i \to j}, ct)$.

Oracle CHALLENGE receives μ. If (b = 0), it returns $ct \leftarrow RandEnc(pp)$. If (b = 1), $ct \leftarrow Enc(pp, ek^0, \mu)$.

Eventually. The adversary halts after it outputs its decision $b' \in \{0, 1\}$.

Finalization: Output 1 if $b' = b$. Otherwise, output 0.

We define the advantage of the adversary as

$$Adv_{A,UniPRE}^{Ind-UniPRE-CPA,I}(k) = \left| \begin{array}{l} \Pr\left[Expt_{A,UniPRE}^{Ind-UniPRE-CPA,I}(k) \to 1 \,|b = 1\right] \\ -\Pr\left[Expt_{A,UniPRE}^{Ind-UniPRE-CPA,I}(k) \to 1 \,|b = 0\right] \end{array} \right|$$

We say that UniPRE is IND-UniPRE-CPA secure at output side if $Adv_{A,UniPRE}^{Ind-UniPRE-CPA,I}(\cdot)$ is negligible for every PPT adversary.

Definition 4. (IND-UniPRE-CPA security at output side [18])

Let UniPRE=(Setup, Gen, $\widehat{Enc}$, Enc, $\widehat{Dec}$, Dec, ReKey, ReEnc) be a single-hop, unidirectional PRE Scheme, k a security parameter. Suppose that there exists a PPT algorithm $\widehat{RandEnc}$ which takes pp as input and outputs a random ciphertext at output side. Let H=H(k) and C=C(k) be polynomials of k, which stands for the number of honest users and corrupted users, respectively. Consider the following game, denoted by $Expt_{A,UniPRE}^{IND-UniPRE-CPA,O}(k)$, between challenger and adversary.

Initialization: Given security parameter k and coin $b \in \{0,1\}$, run $pp \leftarrow Setup(1^k)$. For $i = 0, \cdots, H + C$ generate key pairs $\left(\left(\mathrm{ek}^i, \widehat{\mathrm{ek}^i}\right), \left(\mathrm{dk}^i, \widehat{\mathrm{dk}^i}\right)\right) \leftarrow$ Gen (pp, i). Run the adversary on input pp, public keys of honest users $\left\{\left(\mathrm{ek}^i, \widehat{\mathrm{ek}^i}\right)\right\}_{i=0,\cdots,H}$, and key pairs of corrupted users $\left\{\left(\left(\mathrm{ek}^i, \widehat{\mathrm{ek}^i}\right), \left(\mathrm{dk}^i, \widehat{\mathrm{dk}^i}\right)\right)\right\}_{i=H+1,\cdots,H+C}.$

Learning Phase: The adversary could issue queries to the following oracles in any order and many times :

Oracle REKEY receives two indices $i, j \in \{0, 1, \cdots, H + C\}$. If i = j then it returns $\bot$; otherwise, returns $rk^{i \to j} \leftarrow Rekey\left(pp, dk^i, ek^i, \widehat{ek^j}\right)$.

Oracle REENC receives two indices $i, j \in \{0, 1, \cdots, H + C\}$ and ciphertext ct. If i = j then returns $\bot$; otherwise, it queries (i,j) to REKEY, obtains $rk^{i \to j}$, and returns $\widehat{ct} \leftarrow ReEnc(pp, rk^{i \to j}, ct)$.

Oracle CHALLENGE receives μ. If (b = 0), it returns $\widehat{ct} \leftarrow \widehat{RandEnc}(pp)$. If (b = 1), $\widehat{ct} \leftarrow \widehat{Enc}(pp, \widehat{ek^0}, \mu)$.

Eventually. The adversary halts after it outputs its decision $b' \in \{0, 1\}$.

Finalization: Output 1 if $b' = b$. Otherwise, output 0.

We define the advantage of the adversary as

$$Adv_{A,UniPRE}^{Ind-UniPRE-CPA,O}(k) = \left| \begin{array}{c} \Pr\left[Expt_{A,UniPRE}^{Ind-UniPRE-CPA,O}(k) \rightarrow 1 \,|\, b = 1 \right] \\ - \Pr\left[Expt_{A,UniPRE}^{Ind-UniPRE-CPA,O}(k) \rightarrow 1 \,|\, b = 0 \right] \end{array} \right|$$

We say that UniPRE is IND-UniPRE-CPA secure at output side if $Adv_{A,UniPRE}^{Ind-UniPRE-CPA,O}(\cdot)$ is negligible for every PPT adversary.

Definition 5. (KP-CPA security [18])Let UniPRE=(Setup, Gen, $\widehat{Enc}$, Enc, $\widehat{Dec}$, Dec, ReKey, ReEnc) be a single-hop, unidirectional PRE Scheme, k a security parameter. Suppose that there exists a PPT algorithm *RandRekey* which takes pp as input and outputs a random re-encryption key rk . Let H=H(k) and C=C(k) be polynomials of k, which stands for the number of honest users and corrupted users, respectively. Consider the following game, denoted by $Expt_{A,UniPRE}^{KP-CPA}(k)$, between challenger and adversary.

Initialization: Given security parameter k and coin $b \in \{0, 1\}$, run $pp \leftarrow Setup(1^k)$. Initialize $L \leftarrow \phi$ which is a table containing the re-encryption keys and shared among oracles. For $i = -1, 0, \cdots, H + C$, generate key pairs $\left(\left(ek^i, \widehat{ek^i} \right), \left(dk^i, \widehat{dk^i} \right) \right) \leftarrow Gen(pp, i)$. Run adversary with pp, the public keys of honest users $\left\{ \left(ek^i, \widehat{ek^i} \right) \right\}_{i=0,\cdots,H}$, and the key pairs of corrupted users $\left\{ \left(\left(ek^i, \widehat{ek^i} \right), \left(dk^i, \widehat{dk^i} \right) \right) \right\}_{i=H+1,\cdots,H+C}$.

Learning Phase: Adversary could issue queries to the following oracles in any order and many times except for the constraint in oracle CHALLENGE.

Oracle REKEY receives two indices $i, j \in \{-1, 0, \cdots, H + C\}$. If i=j then it returns $\perp$; if $(i, j) = (0, -1)$, then it returns $\perp$; if there already exists the re-encryption key from i to j, i. e. $(i, j, rk^{i \rightarrow j}) \in L$, then it returns $rk^{i \rightarrow j}$, otherwise, it generates $rk^{i \rightarrow j} \leftarrow Rekey\left(pp, dk^i, ek^i, \widehat{ek^j}\right)$, updates $L \leftarrow L \cup \{(i, j, rk^{i \rightarrow j})\}$, and returns $rk^{i \rightarrow j}$.

Oracle REENC receives two indices $i, j \in \{-1, 0, \cdots, H+C\}$ and a ciphertext ct. if i=j then it returns $\perp$; if there exists no re-encryption key from i to j in the table L, it generates $rk^{i \rightarrow j} \leftarrow Rekey\left(pp, dk^i, ek^i, \widehat{ek^j}\right)$, and updates $L \leftarrow L \cup \{(i, j, rk^{i \rightarrow j})\}$, it finally returns $\widehat{ct} \leftarrow ReEnc(pp, rk^{i \rightarrow j}, ct)$.

Oracle CHALLENGE can be queried only once. On the query, the oracle searches the table L for $(0, -1, rk^{0 \rightarrow -1})$, if such key does not exist, it generates $rk^{0 \rightarrow -1} \leftarrow ReKey\left(pp, dk^0, ek^0, \widehat{ek^{-1}}\right)$ and updates $L \leftarrow L \cup \{(0, -1, rk^{0 \rightarrow -1})\}$.

If b=0 then it returns a random re-encryption key $rk \leftarrow FakeReKey\,(pp)$, which is not contained in L. If b=1, then it returns the real re-encryption key $rk^{0 \rightarrow -1}$ contained in L.

Eventually. Adversary halts after it outputs its decision $b' \in \{0, 1\}$.

Finalization: Output 1 if $b' = b$. Otherwise, output 0.

The advantage of Adversary is

$$Adv_{A,UniPRE}^{KP-CPA}(k) = \left| \begin{array}{l} \Pr\left[Expt_{A,UniPRE}^{KP-CPA}(k) \rightarrow 1\,|b=1 \right] \\ - \Pr\left[Expt_{A,UniPRE}^{KP-CPA}(k) \rightarrow 1\,|b=0 \right] \end{array} \right|$$

We say that UniPRE is KP-CPA secure if $Adv_{A,UniPRE}^{KP-CPA}(\cdot)$ is negligible for every polynomial-time adversary.

Definition 6. (Master secret security [16]) Let UniPRE=(Setup, Gen, $\widehat{Enc}$, Enc, $\widehat{Dec}$, Dec, ReKey, ReEnc) be a single-hop, unidirectional PRE Scheme, k a security parameter. Suppose that there exists a PPT algorithm *RandRekey* which takes pp as input and outputs a random re-encryption key rk . Let H=H(k) and C=C(k) be polynomials of k, which stands for the number of honest users and corrupted users, respectively. Consider the following game, denoted by $Expt_{A,UniPRE}^{MSS}(k)$, between challenger and adversary.

Initialization: The challenger runs $pp \leftarrow Setup\,(1^k)$ and gives the public parameters pp to the adversary.

Challenge: The adversary submits target delegator i.
  Learning Phase :

- The adversary can issue re-encryption key query $rk^{i \rightarrow j}$ corresponding to the public keys ek^i and ek^j.
- The adversary can issue re-encryption query $rk^{i \rightarrow j}$ corresponding to any public keys ek^i and ek^j.

Finalization : Adversary finally outputs a guess x for private key dk^i of target delegator i and wins if $x = dk^i$.

The advantage of adversary is $Adv_{A,UniPRE}^{MSS}(k) = \left| \Pr\left(x = dk^i \right) \right|$, we say that unidirectional PRE is master secret security if $Adv_{A,UniPRE}^{MSS}(\cdot)$ is negligible for every polynomial-time adversary.

References

1. Regev, O.: On lattices, learning with errors, random linear codes, and cryptography. In: STOC, pp. 84–93. ACM (2005)
2. Brakerski, Z., Vaikuntanathan, V.: Efficient fully homomorphic encryption from (standard) LWE. In: Ostrovsky, R. (ed.) FOCS 2011, pp. 97–106. IEEE (2011)

3. Brakerski, Z., Gentry, C., Vaikuntanathan, V.: (leveled) fully homomorphic encryption without bootstrapping. In: ITCS, pp. 309–325. ACM (2012)
4. Brakerski, Z.: Fully homomorphic encryption without modulus switching from classical GapSVP. In: Safavi-Naini, R., Canetti, R. (eds.) CRYPTO 2012. LNCS, vol. 7417, pp. 868–886. Springer, Heidelberg (2012). doi:10.1007/978-3-642-32009-5_50
5. Gentry, C., Sahai, A., Waters, B.: Homomorphic encryption from learning with errors: conceptually-simpler, asymptotically-faster, attribute-based. In: Canetti, R., Garay, J.A. (eds.) CRYPTO 2013. LNCS, vol. 8042, pp. 75–92. Springer, Heidelberg (2013). doi:10.1007/978-3-642-40041-4_5
6. Zhang, X., Xu, C., Jin, C., Xie, R., Zhao, J.: Efficient fully homomorphic encryption from RLWE with an extension to a threshold encryption scheme. Future Gener. Comput. Syst. **36**, 180–186 (2014)
7. Brakerski, Z., Vaikuntanathan, V.: Fully homomorphic encryption from Ring-LWE and security for key dependent messages. In: Rogaway, P. (ed.) CRYPTO 2011. LNCS, vol. 6841, pp. 505–524. Springer, Heidelberg (2011). doi:10.1007/978-3-642-22792-9_29
8. Hiromasa, R., Abe, M., Okamoto, T.: Packing messages and optimizing bootstrapping in GSW-FHE. In: Katz, J. (ed.) PKC 2015. LNCS, vol. 9020, pp. 699–715. Springer, Heidelberg (2015). doi:10.1007/978-3-662-46447-2_31
9. Blaze, M., Bleumer, G., Strauss, M.: Divertible protocols and atomic proxy cryptography. In: Nyberg, K. (ed.) EUROCRYPT 1998. LNCS, vol. 1403, pp. 127–144. Springer, Heidelberg (1998). doi:10.1007/BFb0054122
10. Lu, Y., Li, J.: A pairing-free certificate-based proxy re-encryption scheme for secure data sharing in public clouds. Future Gener. Comput. Syst. doi:10.1016/j.future.2015.11.012
11. Li, J., Zhao, X., Zhang, Y.: Certificate-based conditional proxy re-encryption. In: Au, M.H., Carminati, B., Kuo, C.-C.J. (eds.) NSS 2014. LNCS, vol. 8792, pp. 299–310. Springer, Heidelberg (2014). doi:10.1007/978-3-319-11698-3_23
12. Ateniese, G., Fu, K., Green, M., Hohenberger, S.: Improved proxy re-encryption schemes with applications to secure distributed storage. ACM Trans. Inf. Syst. Secur. **9**(1), 1–30 (2006)
13. Smith, T.: DVD Jon: Buy DRM-less Tracks from Apple iTunes (2005). http://www.theregister.co.uk/2005/03/18/itunes_pymusique/
14. Xagawa, K.: Cryptography with Lattices. Ph.D. thesis. Department of Mathematical and Computing Sciences Tokyo Institute of Technology (2010)
15. Aono, Y., Boyen, X., Phong, T.L., Wang, L.: Key-private proxy re-encryption under LWE. In: Paul, G., Vaudenay, S. (eds.) INDOCRYPT 2013. LNCS, vol. 8250, pp. 1–18. Springer, Heidelberg (2013)
16. Singh, K., Pandu, R.C., Banerjee, A.K.: Cryptanalysis of unidirectional proxy re-encryption scheme. In: Linawati, M.S.M., et al. (eds.) ICT-EurAsia 2014. LNCS, vol. 8407, pp. 564–575. Springer, Heidelberg (2014)
17. Jiang, M., Hu, Y., Wang, B., Wang, F., Lai, Q.: Lattice-based multi-use unidirectional proxy re-encryption. Secur. Commun. Netw. **8**(18), 3796–3803 (2015)
18. Nishimak, R., Xagawa, K.: Key-private proxy re-encryption from lattices, revisiteds. IEICE Trans. Fundam. Electron. Commun. Comput. Sci. **E98**-A(1), 100–116 (2015)
19. Alperin-Sheriff, J., Peikert, C.: Faster bootstrapping with polynomial error. In: Garay, J.A., Gennaro, R. (eds.) CRYPTO 2014. LNCS, vol. 8616, pp. 297–314. Springer, Heidelberg (2014). doi:10.1007/978-3-662-44371-2_17

20. Micciancio, D., Peikert, C.: Trapdoors for lattices: simpler, tighter, faster, smaller. In: Pointcheval, D., Johansson, T. (eds.) EUROCRYPT 2012. LNCS, vol. 7237, pp. 700–718. Springer, Heidelberg (2012). doi:10.1007/978-3-642-29011-4_41

21. Applebaum, B., Cash, D., Peikert, C., Sahai, A.: Fast cryptographic primitives and circular-secure encryption based on hard learning problems. In: Halevi, S. (ed.) CRYPTO 2009. LNCS, vol. 5677, pp. 595–618. Springer, Heidelberg (2009). doi:10.1007/978-3-642-03356-8_35

Preventing Adaptive Key Recovery Attacks on the GSW Levelled Homomorphic Encryption Scheme

Zengpeng Li[1,2], Steven D. Galbraith[3], and Chunguang Ma[1,2(✉)]

[1] College of Computer Science and Technology, Harbin Engineering University,
Harbin 150001, China
{lizengpeng,machunguang}@hrbeu.edu.cn
[2] State Key Laboratory of Information Security, Institute of Information
Engineering, Chinese Academy of Sciences, Beijing 100093, China
[3] Department of Mathematics,
The University of Auckland, Auckland 1142, New Zealand
s.galbraith@auckland.ac.nz

Abstract. A major open problem is to protect levelled homomorphic encryption from adaptive attacks that allow an adversary to learn the private key. The only positive results in this area are by Loftus, May, Smart and Vercauteren. They use a notion of "valid ciphertexts" and obtain an IND-CCA1 scheme under a strong knowledge assumption, but they also show their scheme is not secure under a natural adaptive attack based on a "ciphertext validity oracle".

The main contribution of this paper is to explore a new approach to achieve security against adaptive attacks, which does not rely on a notion of "valid ciphertexts". Instead, our idea is to generate a "one-time" private key every time the decryption algorithm is run, so that even if an attacker can learn some bits of the one-time private key from each decryption query, this does not allow them to compute a valid private key. We demonstrate how this idea can be implemented with the Gentry-Sahai-Waters levelled homomorphic encryption scheme, and we give an informal explanation of why the known attacks no longer break the system.

Keywords: Adaptive key recovery attacks · Lattice-based cryptography · Levelled homomorphic encryption

1 Introduction

It is well-known that access to a decryption oracle can lead to attacks on basic Regev [14] or Gentry-Peikert-Vaikuntanathan (GPV) [7] encryption, as well as various homomorphic encryption schemes [3–5,10,16]. These attacks allow an adversary to learn the private key, and so they are more serious than attacks that learn some information about messages. It is of major interest to obtain secure variants of these schemes, and this problem seems to be very difficult.

© Springer International Publishing AG 2016
L. Chen and J. Han (Eds.): ProvSec 2016, LNCS 10005, pp. 373–383, 2016.
DOI: 10.1007/978-3-319-47422-9_22

Loftus, May, Smart and Vercauteren [10] have considered the security of the private key of Gentry's homomorphic encryption scheme based on ideal lattices [6] (and some variants of it [15]) under adaptive attacks. They show that the private key can be determined if one has access to a decryption oracle. They also give a variant of the Smart-Vercauteren cryptosystem [15] for which the private key seems to be secure even when a decryption oracle is present; this result is based on a notion of "valid ciphertext", which is checked by the decryption algorithm, and the security relies on a very strong knowledge assumption.

Loftus et al. also emphasise the relevance of *ciphertext validity attacks (CVA)*. This model allows an attacker to have access to an oracle that determines whether or not a ciphertext is valid. They show that it is possible for an adversary to decrypt a challenge ciphertext with the help of the CVA oracle (but at least the private key remains secure, and this is not a CCA1 attack but a CCA2 attack). Loftus et al. argue that CCA1 and CVA attacks on homomorphic encryption schemes are realistic in practice (they write in Sect. 6 of [10] that "Such an oracle can often be obtained in the real world by the attacker observing the behaviour of a party who is fed ciphertexts of the attacker's choosing"). For example, if a user is storing an encrypted database in the cloud and making queries to it, then an attacker could send ciphertexts of its choosing in response. If these ciphertexts are invalid then the user might re-send the same query until a valid ciphertext is received in response. Such a situation precisely gives a CVA oracle. Bleichenbacher's use of a CVA oracle to attack certain variants of RSA is well-known [1]. Hence, we believe that this issue is serious and that it is important to develop techniques to secure the private key of homomorphic encryption schemes.

In this paper we consider a different approach to the problem. Rather than relying on a notion of "valid ciphertexts", we avoid the risk of private key exposure by using "one-time" private keys. The idea is that, even if an attacker can learn some bits of the one-time private key from each decryption query, there should be no way for the attacker to combine the information from multiple decryption queries to compute an actual private key. Since there is no check on "valid ciphertexts" there is no risk of an attacker exploiting a CVA attack.

The idea of one-time secret keys can be implemented with many lattice-based cryptosystems but it only gives rise to a somewhat homomorphic scheme. We focus our attention on the Gentry-Sahai-Waters (GSW13) scheme, since it can achieve levelled homomorphic encryption without any key switching. This is important, since it is trivially impossible to achieve CCA1-security for any scheme that uses key-switching or bootstrapping or any other method where the public key contains encryptions of secret information. To argue that our method resists adaptive attacks we use the left-over hash lemma.

The paper is organised as follows. Section 2 recalls some basic notions in the subject. Section 3 presents the Gentry-Sahai-Waters (GSW13) scheme. Section 4 presents our new scheme, while Sect. 5 explains why this scheme is resistant to the known adaptive attack. In the conclusions section we discuss whether our ideas might also be useful in the context of leakage resilience and side-channel protection.

2   Preliminaries

In this section we introduce some notations and recall the learning with errors problem (LWE). Due to lack of space we refer to [11,13] for background details about learning with errors, lattice crypto, and homomorphic encryption.

We use the following variant of the leftover hash lemma [9].

Lemma 1. *(Matrix-vector leftover hash lemma [2] Lemma 2.1) Let $\lambda \in \mathbb{Z}$, $n \in \mathbb{N}$, $q \in \mathbb{N}$, and $m \geq n \log(q) + 2\lambda$. Let $\mathbf{A} \overset{R}{\leftarrow} \mathbb{Z}_q^{m \times n}$ be a uniformly sampled matrix, let $\mathbf{r} \overset{R}{\leftarrow} \{0,1\}^m$ and $\mathbf{y} \overset{R}{\leftarrow} \mathbb{Z}_q^n$, Then:*

$$\Delta\big((\mathbf{A}, \mathbf{A}^T \cdot \mathbf{r}), (\mathbf{A}, \mathbf{y})\big) \leq 2^{-\lambda} \tag{1}$$

where $\Delta(\mathbf{A}, \mathbf{B})$ denotes the statistical distance between the distributions $\mathbf{A}$ and $\mathbf{B}$.

The learning with errors problem is the main computational assumption underlying the GSW13 cryptosystem and our variant of it. Here χ is some distribution on $\mathbb{Z}$.

Definition 1. *(Learning with Errors Distribution) For a vector $\mathbf{s} \in \mathbb{Z}_q^n$ called the secret, the LWE distribution $\mathcal{A}_{\mathbf{s},\chi}$ over $\mathbb{Z}_q^n \times \mathbb{Z}_q$ is sampled by choosing $\mathbf{a} \in \mathbb{Z}_q^n$ uniformly at random, choosing $e \leftarrow \chi$, and outputting $\big(\mathbf{a}, b = \langle \mathbf{s}, \mathbf{a}\rangle + e \pmod{q}\big)$.*

There are two main versions of the LWE problem: search version, which is to find the secret given LWE samples, and decision version, which is to distinguish between LWE samples and uniformly random ones.

Definition 2. *(Search-LWE$_{n,q,\chi,m}$) Given m independent samples $(\mathbf{a}_i, b_i) \in \mathbb{Z}_q^n \times \mathbb{Z}_q$ drawn from $\mathcal{A}_{\mathbf{s},\chi}$ for a uniformly random $\mathbf{s} \in \mathbb{Z}_q^n$ (fixed for all samples), find $\mathbf{s}$.*

Definition 3. *(Decision-LWE$_{n,q,\chi,m}$) Given m independent samples $(\mathbf{a}_i, b_i) \in \mathbb{Z}_q^n \times \mathbb{Z}_q$ where every sample is distributed according to either: (1) $\mathcal{A}_{\mathbf{s},\chi}$ for a uniformly random $\mathbf{s} \in \mathbb{Z}_q^n$ (fixed for all samples), or (2) the uniform distribution, distinguish which is the case (with non-negligible advantage).*

Regev and others [12,14] showed that, when χ is a suitable discrete Gaussian distribution, the LWE problem is as hard as approximating the shortest vector problem in lattices (for appropriate parameters).

The following theorem is a key result used to show the security of our scheme.

Theorem 1. *Let $m > n \in \mathbb{N}$, let $q \in \mathbb{N}$ and let χ be a discrete Gaussian distribution on $\mathbb{Z}$ such that the (n, q, χ, m)-LWE problem is hard. Let t be an integer such that $t = O(\log(n))$. Define two distributions $\mathcal{X}$ and $\mathcal{Y}$ as follows.*

- *$\mathcal{X}$ is the distribution on $m \times (t + n)$ matrices*

$$[\mathbf{b}_1| \cdots |\mathbf{b}_t|\mathbf{B}]$$

where $\mathbf{B} \in \mathbb{Z}_q^{m \times n}$ is chosen uniformly at random and where, for all $1 \leq i \leq t$,

$$\mathbf{b}_i = \boldsymbol{B}\mathbf{t}_i + \mathbf{e}_i \quad (\bmod\ q)$$

where $\mathbf{t}_i$ is sampled uniformly from $\mathbb{Z}_q^n$ and $\mathbf{e}_i$ is sampled from a discrete Gaussian distribution χ.

– $\mathcal{Y}$ is the uniform distribution on $\mathbb{Z}_q^{m \times (t+n)}$.

Then the two distributions $\mathcal{X}$ and $\mathcal{Y}$ are computationally indistinguishable.

Proof. The proof is a straightforward hybrid argument, the details are given in the full version of the paper.

3   Gentry-Sahai-Waters Homomorphic Encryption

In this section we describe the Gentry-Sahai-Waters (GSW13) homomorphic encryption scheme [8], then we sketch the adaptive attack on it due to Chenal and Tang [3]. First we need to recall some terminology and tools from [8] and other previous work.

3.1   Basic Tools

Fix $q, m \in \mathbb{N}$. Let $l_q = \lfloor \log q \rfloor$ and $N = m \cdot (l_q + 1)$. For $\mathbf{v} \in \mathbb{Z}_q^m$ we define

$$Powerof2(\mathbf{v}) = \left(v_1, 2v_1, \cdots, 2^{l_q}v_1, \cdots, v_m, 2v_m, \cdots, 2^{l_q}v_m\right) \in \mathbb{Z}_q^N.$$

For $\mathbf{v} \in \mathbb{Z}_q^m$ we define $BitDecomp(\mathbf{v}) = (v_{1,0}, \cdots, v_{1,l_q}, \cdots, v_{m,0}, \cdots, v_{m,l_q})$ where $v_{i,j}$ is the j-th bit in the binary representation of v_i (ordered from least significant to most significant.) In other words,

$$v_i = \sum_{j=0}^{l_q} 2^j v_{i,j}.$$

For $\mathbf{v} = (v_{1,0}, \cdots, v_{1,l_q}, \cdots, v_{m,0}, \cdots, v_{m,l_q}) \in \mathbb{Z}_q^N$ we define

$$BitDecomp^{-1}(\mathbf{v}) = \left(\sum_{j=0}^{l_q} 2^j \cdot v_{1,j}, \cdots, \sum_{j=0}^{l_q} 2^j \cdot v_{m,j}\right) \in \mathbb{Z}_q^m.$$

Note that the input vectors $\mathbf{v}$ need not be binary, the algorithm is well-defined for any input vector in $\mathbb{Z}^N$. Finally, we define $Flatten(\mathbf{v}) = BitDecomp(BitDecomp^{-1}(\mathbf{v}))$. Note that, for $\mathbf{a}, \mathbf{b} \in \mathbb{Z}_q^m$ and $\mathbf{a}' \in \mathbb{Z}^N$,

$$\langle BitDecomp(\mathbf{a}), Powerof2(\mathbf{b})\rangle = \langle \mathbf{a}, \mathbf{b}\rangle$$

and

$$\langle \mathbf{a}', Powerof2(\mathbf{b})\rangle = \langle Flatten(\mathbf{a}'), Powerof2(\mathbf{b})\rangle.$$

3.2   GSW13 Scheme

Let λ be a security parameter and let L be the number of levels for the some-what homomorphic scheme. We describe the algorithms that form the GSW13 scheme [8]. Due to lack of space, we focus only on the parts relevant for the adaptive key recovery attacks.

- $GSW.Setup(1^\lambda, 1^L)$
    1. Choose a modulus q of $\kappa = \kappa(\lambda, L)$ bits, lattice dimension parameter $n = n(\lambda, L)$, and error distribution $\chi = \chi(\lambda, L)$ appropriately for LWE that achieves at least 2^λ security against known attacks. Choose a parameter $m = m(\lambda, L) = O(n \log(q))$;
    2. Output: $params = (n, q, \chi, m)$.
    We also use the notation $l = \lfloor \log q \rfloor$ and $N = (n+1) \cdot (l+1)$.
- $GSW.KeyGen(params)$:
    1. Sample $\mathbf{t} = (t_1, \ldots, t_n)^T \leftarrow \mathbb{Z}_q^n$ and compute $\mathbf{s} \leftarrow (1, -\mathbf{t}^T)^T \in \mathbb{Z}_q^{n+1}$;
    2. Let $\mathbf{v} = Powerof2(\mathbf{s})$;
    3. Generate a matrix $\mathbf{B} \leftarrow \mathbb{Z}_q^{m \times n}$ uniformly and a vector $\mathbf{e} \leftarrow \chi^m$;
    4. Compute $\mathbf{b} = \mathbf{B} \cdot \mathbf{t} + \mathbf{e} \in \mathbb{Z}_q^m$ and construct the matrix $\mathbf{A}(\in \mathbb{Z}_q^{m \times (n+1)})$ to be the $(n+1)$-column matrix consisting of $\mathbf{b}$ followed by the n columns of $\mathbf{B}$. Observe that

$$\mathbf{A} \cdot \mathbf{s} = (\mathbf{b} \mid \mathbf{B}) \cdot \mathbf{s} = (\mathbf{Bt} + \mathbf{e} \mid \mathbf{B}) \cdot \begin{pmatrix} 1 \\ -\mathbf{t} \end{pmatrix} = \mathbf{Bt} + \mathbf{e} - \mathbf{Bt} = \mathbf{e}.$$

    5. Return $sk \leftarrow \mathbf{v}$ and $pk \leftarrow \mathbf{A}$.
- $GSW.Encrypt(params, pk, \mu)$ where $\mu \in \{0, 1\}$ is a message:
    1. Sample a uniform matrix $\mathbf{R} \in \{0, 1\}^{N \times m}$;
    2. Compute $\mathbf{C} = Flatten(\mu \cdot \mathbf{I}_N + BitDecomp(\mathbf{R} \cdot \mathbf{A})) \in \mathbb{Z}_q^{N \times N}$, where $\mathbf{I}_N$ denotes the N-dimensional identity matrix;
    3. Return the ciphertext $\mathbf{C}$.
- $GSW.Decrypt(params, sk, \mathbf{C})$:
    1. Observe that the first l coefficients of $\mathbf{v}$ are $1, 2, \cdots, 2^l$, among these coefficients, let $v_i = 2^i \in (q/4, q/2]$;
    2. Let $\mathbf{C}_i$ be the i-th row of $\mathbf{C}$. Compute $x_i \leftarrow \langle \mathbf{C}_i, \mathbf{v} \rangle$;
    3. Output $\mu' = \lfloor x_i / v_i \rfloor$.

There is also a variant of the scheme that handles messages in $\mathbb{Z}_q$ when q is a power of two. We refer to [8] for the details.

3.3   Security

A sketch proof is given in [8] of the following theorem.

Theorem 2. *Let (n, q, χ) be such that the $LWE_{(n,q,\chi)}$ assumption holds and let $m = O(n \log(q))$. Then the GSW13 scheme is IND-CPA secure.*

The main step in the proof is showing that $(\mathbf{A}, \mathbf{R} \cdot \mathbf{A})$ is computationally indistinguishable from uniform.

3.4   Key Recovery Attacks

We now briefly review the adaptive key recovery attack due to Chenal and Tang [3]. The adversary recovers the secret key through a number of decryption oracle queries. Note that an attacker can call the decryption oracle on any matrix $\mathbf{C}$ of their choice, and the oracle will return the most significant bit of $\langle \mathbf{C}_i, \mathbf{v} \rangle$ where $\mathbf{C}_i$ is the i-th row of $\mathbf{C}$ (where i is a fixed constant known to the adversary) and $\mathbf{v} = Powerof2(\mathbf{s})$ is a vector containing the entries of the secret key $\mathbf{s} = (1, -\mathbf{t}^T)^T$.

The attack is therefore quite simple: One chooses $\mathbf{C}_i = (0, 0, \ldots, 0, M, 0, \ldots, 0)$ for appropriate values M in appropriate positions and learns the entries of the secret key bit-by-bit. For example, to compute $t_1 \in \mathbb{Z}_q$ one makes a decryption oracle query on a matrix with $\mathbf{C}_i = (0, 0, \ldots, 0, 1, 0, \ldots, 0)$ where the 1 is in the $(l+2)$-th position. Hence

$$\langle \mathbf{C}_i, \mathbf{v} \rangle = -t_1$$

and so one learns the most significant bit of t_1. One can now either re-scale $\mathbf{C}_i$ or put the one in the $(l+3)$-th position to get information about the next most significant bit (one has to correct for modular reduction if the most significant bit was 1). To separate positive and negative values one can use vectors like $\mathbf{C}_i = (M, 0 \ldots, 0, 1, 0, \ldots, 0)$, which provide the most significant bit of $\langle \mathbf{C}_i, \mathbf{v} \rangle = M - 2^j t_i$. We omit further details here, see [3–5] for discussion.

4   Multiple Secret Scheme (MGSW)

We now describe our variant of the GSW13 scheme. First we give some motivation for our design. The adaptive attack exploits the fact that certain queries to the decryption oracle leak one bit of one component of the fixed secret key $\mathbf{s} = (1, -t_1, \ldots, -t_n)^T$. Our main idea is to have a large set of possible secret keys. Each execution of the decryption algorithm will generate a fresh random "one-time" secret key $\mathbf{s}$. The decryption algorithm itself does not change, and we do not introduce any notion of "valid ciphertext", so an attacker can still learn one bit of one component of the key used for decryption. However, the main idea of our approach is that an attacker cannot iterate the attack to learn an "entire" secret key, since each query gives information about a fresh random key and these keys are uncorrelated with each other.

The basic idea is, instead of choosing $\mathbf{A}$ of the form $[\mathbf{Bt} + \mathbf{e}|\mathbf{B}]$ for a uniform $\mathbf{t}$ and a short vector $\mathbf{e}$, to construct

$$\mathbf{A}' = [\mathbf{Bt}_1 + \mathbf{e}_1|\mathbf{Bt}_2 + \mathbf{e}_2|\cdots|\mathbf{Bt}_t + \mathbf{e}_t|\mathbf{B}]$$

where $\mathbf{t}_1, \ldots, \mathbf{t}_t$ are sampled uniformly in $\mathbb{Z}_q^n$ and $\mathbf{e}_1, \ldots, \mathbf{e}_t$ are sampled from the discrete Gaussian distribution χ. It follows that there are now t different secret keys. Further, one can generate exponentially many short vectors that act as secret keys (i.e., satisfy $\mathbf{A}'$s being small) by taking short linear combinations of these t vectors.

We now give the formal details.

4.1 The Scheme

- $params \leftarrow MGSW.Setup(1^\lambda, 1^L)$
    1. Identical to $GSW.Setup$ algorithm except that a parameter $t = O(\log(n))$ is chosen (the number of secret keys);
    2. Output $params = (n, q, \chi, m, t)$ and let $l = \lfloor \log q \rfloor$ and $N' = (t+n) \cdot (l+1))$.
- $(pk, sk) \leftarrow MGSW.KeyGen(params)$:
    1. Sample $\mathbf{t}_i \leftarrow \mathbb{Z}_q^n, i \in [t]$ and output $sk_i = \mathbf{s}_i \leftarrow (0, \cdots, 1, \cdots, 0, -\mathbf{t}_i^T)^T = (0, \cdots, 1, \cdots, 0, -t_{i,1}, \cdots, -t_{i,n})^T \in \mathbb{Z}_q^{n+t}$, where the i-th position is 1;
    2. Choose a matrix $\mathbf{B} \leftarrow \mathbb{Z}_q^{m \times n}$ uniformly and t vectors $\mathbf{e}_i \leftarrow \chi^m$ for $i \in [t]$;
    3. Compute $\mathbf{b}_i = \mathbf{B}\mathbf{t}_i + \mathbf{e}_i \in \mathbb{Z}_q^m$ and $\mathbf{A}' = [\mathbf{b}_1 | \cdots | \mathbf{b}_t | \mathbf{B}] \in \mathbb{Z}_q^{m \times (n+t)}$;
    4. Output $pk \leftarrow \mathbf{A}'$ and $sk \leftarrow \{\mathbf{s}_1, \ldots, \mathbf{s}_t\}$.
- $\mathbf{C} \leftarrow MGSW.Encrypt(params, pk, \mu)$:
    1. To encrypt a message $\mu \in \mathbb{Z}_q$, sample a uniform matrix $\mathbf{R}' \in \{0,1\}^{N' \times m}$;
    2. Compute and output the ciphertext

$$\mathbf{C} = Flatten(\mu \cdot \mathbf{I}_{N'} + BitDecomp(\mathbf{R}' \cdot \mathbf{A}')) \in \mathbb{Z}_q^{N' \times N'},$$

   where the $\mathbf{I}_{N'}$ denotes the N'-dimensional identity matrix;
- $\mu' \leftarrow MGSW.Decrypt(params, sk, \mathbf{C})$:
    1. Choose $\lambda_1, \ldots, \lambda_t$ uniformly from $\{0,1\}$ such that they are not all zero;
    2. Generate one-time key $\mathbf{s}' = \sum_{i=1}^t \lambda_i \mathbf{s}_i$ and set $\mathbf{v}' = Powerof2(\mathbf{s}')$;
    3. Determine an integer $1 \leq I \leq tl$ such that $v_I := 2^I \in (q/4, q/2]$ (note that this value depends on which of the values $\lambda_i = 1$);
    4. Let $\mathbf{C}_I$ be the I-th row of $\mathbf{C}$. Compute $x \leftarrow \langle \mathbf{C}_I, \mathbf{v}' \rangle$ and return $\lfloor x/v_I \rceil \in \{0,1\}$.
- The homomorphic operations are exactly the same as in the original scheme.

4.2 Correctness and Homomorphic Operations

In this section, we will analyze the scheme's correctness and homomorphic operations, following the arguments from [8].

The main change in the scheme is that a secret key is changed from $\mathbf{s} = (1, -\mathbf{t}^T)^T$ to a large set of secret keys of the form $\mathbf{s}' = \sum_{i=1}^t \lambda_i \mathbf{s}_i$ with $\lambda_i \in \{0,1\}$. We have $\mathbf{A}'\mathbf{s}_i = \mathbf{e}_i \pmod{q}$ for all $1 \leq i \leq t$ where $\mathbf{e}_i$ is chosen from a discrete Gaussian distribution. Writing $\mathbf{e}' = \mathbf{A}'\mathbf{s}' \pmod{q}$ for any choice of one-time secret key $\mathbf{s}'$ we have

$$\|\mathbf{e}'\| = \|\mathbf{A}'\mathbf{s}'\| = \left\| \sum_{i=1}^t \lambda_i \mathbf{e}_i \right\| \leq \sum_{i=1}^t |\lambda_i| \|\mathbf{e}_i\|.$$

Since we may assume $\|\mathbf{e}_i\| \leq 2\sqrt{m}\sigma$ it follows that $\|\mathbf{e}'\| \leq 2t\sqrt{m}\sigma$. Gentry, Sahai and Waters consider B-bounded error vectors to show that decryption is correct. If $\|\mathbf{e}_i\|_\infty = \max\{|e_{i,j}|\} \leq B$ then, by the same argument $\|\mathbf{e}'\|_\infty \leq B' = tB$.

To specify parameters we first fix a level L. The parameter n determines a number of parameters $\sigma \geq 2\sqrt{n}$, $t = O(\log(n))$, $B = 10\sigma$, $B' = tB$. It is necessary to choose (l, q) with $2^l < q < 2^{l+1}$ and $q > 8B'((t+n)l+1)^{L+1}$. Finally, one selects a large enough parameter n so that the (n, q, D_σ)-LWE problem is hard with these choices for q and σ. Note that $m > 2n\log(q) > t + n$ and $N' = (t+n)(l+1)$. These are the parameters used in the MGSW key generation.

We say that a ciphertext $\mathbf{C}$ is at *level i* if it has been formed by running the Evaluate algorithm at most i times on encryptions of messages. The Encrypt algorithm outputs ciphertexts of level 0. Lemma 2 shows that our variant of the GSW13 scheme is homomorphic. Due to space restrictions the proof is omitted, but can be found in the full version of the paper.

Lemma 2. *Let notation and parameters be as above. Let $\mathbf{C}$ be any ciphertext at level $i \leq L$. Then the decryption algorithm returns the correct message μ.*

4.3   IND-CPA Security

We show the scheme is IND-CPA secure based on the LWE assumption by using Theorem 1 to show that the scheme is indistinguishable from the original GSW13 scheme, and then applying Theorem 2.

Theorem 3. *Let (n, q, χ, m, t) be such that the $LWE_{n,q,\chi,m}$ assumption holds, $t = O(\log(n))$, and $m = O(n\log(q))$. Then the MGSW scheme is IND-CPA secure.*

Proof. The proof of security consists of two steps:

- Firstly, we apply Theorem 1 to show that, under the LWE assumption, the matrix $\mathbf{A}' = [\mathbf{b}_1, \cdots, \mathbf{b}_t, \mathbf{B}] \in \mathbb{Z}_q^{m \times (n+t)}$ is computationally indistinguishable from a randomly chosen matrix.
- Then we apply the arguments from the proof of Theorem 2, namely that $\mathbf{R}' \cdot \mathbf{A}'$ is indistinguishable from uniform assuming the hardness of $LWE_{n,q,\chi,m}$.

This completes the sketch of the proof.   □

5   Security of the Multiple Secret GSW Scheme Against Adaptive Attacks

In this section we explain how the standard attack on the GSW13 scheme is prevented by our countermeasure. Unfortunately we are not able to prove IND-CCA1 security of our new scheme. Indeed, proving IND-CCA1 security of homomorphic encryption is an extremely challenging problem as one needs to somehow handle the decryption queries. No-one has ever managed to give a proof of such a result, the nearest is the result of Loftus et al. [10], which uses a very strong knowledge assumption.

The crux of our argument is that the one-time keys are distributed uniformly from the point of view of the decryption oracle, and so are independent of the actual secret basis. In terms of linear algebra (assuming for the moment that q is prime), the one-time keys all lie in a vector subspace K of dimension t inside the much larger space $\mathbb{Z}_q^n$. (Not all elements of the space K are valid secret keys; only the ones that correspond to short linear combinations of the basis are allowed.) However, the attacker just gets a single bit of an inner product of the one-time key with the vector coming from the ciphertext. One can think of the inner product with $\mathbf{C}_i$ as giving a projection (linear map) $L_{\mathbf{C}_i} : \mathbb{Z}_q^n \to \mathbb{Z}_q$. So the adversary only sees one bit of one projection of the secret. Even though the subspace K is small, the probability that K lies in the kernel of this projection is equal to the probability that $\mathbf{C}_i$ is chosen in the orthogonal complement $K^\perp$ of K. Since K has dimension t in an n-dimensional space, the dimension of $K^\perp$ is $n - t$. Hence the probability that a randomly chosen $\mathbf{C}_i$ is such that K is in the kernel of the projection $L_{\mathbf{C}_i}$ is $q^{n-t}/q^n = 1/q^t$, which will be negligible. So we can assume that the projection is surjective and it suffices to argue that the distribution of the projected value is close to uniform and so is *independent on the secret vectors*. This is sufficient to prove that the attack cannot work, since the information revealed by the decryption oracle is therefore independent of the choice of secret keys.

First note that the one-time secret key is of the form

$$\sum_{i=1}^{t} \lambda_i \mathbf{s}_i = \begin{pmatrix} \lambda_1 \\ \vdots \\ \lambda_t \\ \hline \sum_i^t \lambda_i \mathbf{t}_i \end{pmatrix} \in \mathbb{Z}_q^n.$$

The first t entries carry no information about the long-term secret $\mathbf{t}_1, \ldots, \mathbf{t}_t$.

We now fix a linear map $L : \mathbb{Z}_q^n \to \mathbb{Z}_q$ (corresponding to an inner product with $\mathbf{C}_i$). We assume that t' of the vectors $\mathbf{s}_1, \ldots, \mathbf{s}_t$ do not lie in $\ker(L)$ where $t' \approx t$ (a random vector lies in $\ker(L)$ with probability $1/q$ so a given set of l vectors lie in $\ker(L)$ with probability $1/q^l$). Re-ordering the vectors we have $\mathbf{s}_1, \ldots, \mathbf{s}_{t'}$ not in $\ker(L)$. When making a decryption oracle query with ciphertext $\mathbf{C}_i$ the adversary gets one bit of information about the value

$$L\left(\sum_{i=1}^{t} \lambda_i \mathbf{s}_i\right) = \sum_{i=1}^{t'} \lambda_i L(\mathbf{s}_i).$$

Since $\mathbf{t}_1, \ldots, \mathbf{t}_t$ are sampled uniformly from $\mathbb{Z}_q^n$ we can model $L(\mathbf{s}_1), \ldots, L(\mathbf{s}_{t'})$ as corresponding to t' non-zero values uniformly sampled from $\mathbb{Z}_q$.

We now apply the left-over hash lemma (Lemma 1) in the one-dimensional case. If $t' \geq \log(q) + 2k$ then the statistical difference between the distribution on $\mathbb{Z}_q$ given by $\sum_{i=1}^{t'} \lambda_i L(\mathbf{s}_i)$ and the uniform distribution is at most 2^{-k}. The adversary does not even see the whole value, but only one bit of it. This means that the value output by the decryption oracle is indistinguishable from a uniform value. Since a uniform value is independent of the long-term secret key $\mathbf{t}_1, \ldots, \mathbf{t}_t$, it follows that the adversary *cannot learn a secret key from making queries of this form.*

To achieve security one can take $t \geq \log(q) + 3k$, but this is likely to be overkill in practice. Since q grows like n^L it is possible to satisfy this inequality while also satisfying the necessary condition $t = O(\log(n))$ for Theorem 1. An open problem is to give a more precise analysis on distribution of a single bit of such a linear projection, and hence obtain a smaller value for t.

6   Conclusion

We have given a variant of the GSW13 scheme and explained why it resists the known adaptive attack that breaks the original version of the scheme. Our ideas may also be useful in the framework of leakage resilience: since we are using a one-time key one could hope that the computations involving the one-time key would not leak information about the long-term secrets. We leave these topics for future research.

Acknowledgments. The authors would like to thank the anonymous reviewers for their helpful advice and comments. This work was supported by the National Natural Science Foundation of China (No.61472097), Specialized Research Fund for the Doctoral Program of Higher Education (No.20132304110017) and International Exchange Program of Harbin Engineering University for Innovation-oriented Talents Cultivation.

References

1. Bleichenbacher, D.: Chosen ciphertext attacks against protocols based on the RSA encryption standard PKCS #1. In: Krawczyk, H. (ed.) CRYPTO 1998. LNCS, vol. 1462, pp. 1–12. Springer, Heidelberg (1998). doi:10.1007/BFb0055716
2. Brakerski, Z., Vaikuntanathan, V.: Efficient fully homomorphic encryption from (standard) lwe. In: Proceedings of the 2011 IEEE 52nd Annual Symposium on Foundations of Computer Science, pp. 97–106. IEEE Computer Society (2011)
3. Chenal, M., Tang, Q.: On key recovery attacks against existing somewhat homomorphic encryption schemes. In: Aranha, D.F., Menezes, A. (eds.) LATINCRYPT 2014. LNCS, vol. 8895, pp. 239–258. Springer, Heidelberg (2015). doi:10.1007/978-3-319-16295-9_13
4. Chenal, M., Tang, Q.: Key recovery attacks against NTRU-based somewhat homomorphic encryption schemes. In: Lopez, J., Mitchell, C.J. (eds.) ISC 2015. LNCS, vol. 9290, pp. 397–418. Springer, Heidelberg (2015). doi:10.1007/978-3-319-23318-5_22
5. Dahab, R., Galbraith, S., Morais, E.: Adaptive key recovery attacks on NTRU-based somewhat homomorphic encryption schemes. In: Lehmann, A., Wolf, S. (eds.) ICITS 2015. LNCS, vol. 9063, pp. 283–296. Springer, Heidelberg (2015). doi:10.1007/978-3-319-17470-9_17
6. Gentry, C.: Fully homomorphic encryption using ideal lattices. In: Proceedings of the Forty-First Annual ACM Symposium on Theory of Computing, pp. 169–169. ACM Press (2009)

7. Gentry, C., Peikert, C., Vaikuntanathan, V.: Trapdoors for hard lattices and new cryptographic constructions. In: Proceedings of the Fortieth Annual ACM Symposium on Theory of Computing, pp. 197–206. ACM (2008)
8. Gentry, C., Sahai, A., Waters, B.: Homomorphic encryption from learning with errors: conceptually-simpler, asymptotically-faster, attribute-based. In: Canetti, R., Garay, J.A. (eds.) CRYPTO 2013. LNCS, vol. 8042, pp. 75–92. Springer, Heidelberg (2013). doi:10.1007/978-3-642-40041-4_5
9. Impagliazzo, R., Levin, L.A., Luby, M.: Pseudo-random generation from one-way functions. In: Proceedings of the Twenty-First Annual ACM Symposium on Theory of Computing, pp. 12–24. ACM (1989)
10. Loftus, J., May, A., Smart, N.P., Vercauteren, F.: On CCA-secure somewhat homomorphic encryption. In: Miri, A., Vaudenay, S. (eds.) SAC 2011. LNCS, vol. 7118, pp. 55–72. Springer, Heidelberg (2012). doi:10.1007/978-3-642-28496-0_4
11. Micciancio, D., Regev, O.: Lattice-based cryptography. In: Bernstein, D.J., Buchmann, J., Dahmen, E. (eds.) Post-Quantum Cryptography, pp. 147–191. Springer, Heidelberg (2009)
12. Peikert, C.: Public-key cryptosystems from the worst-case shortest vector problem. In: Proceedings of the Forty-First Annual ACM Symposium on Theory of Computing, pp. 333–342. ACM (2009)
13. Peikert, C., et al.: Decade of Lattice Cryptography. World Scientific (2016)
14. Regev, O.: On lattices, learning with errors, random linear codes, and cryptography. In: Proceedings of the Thirty-Seventh Annual ACM Symposium on Theory of Computing, pp. 84–93. ACM (2005)
15. Smart, N.P., Vercauteren, F.: Fully homomorphic encryption with relatively small key and ciphertext sizes. In: Nguyen, P.Q., Pointcheval, D. (eds.) PKC 2010. LNCS, vol. 6056, pp. 420–443. Springer, Heidelberg (2010). doi:10.1007/978-3-642-13013-7_25
16. Zhang, Z., Plantard, T., Susilo, W.: On the CCA-1 security of somewhat homomorphic encryption over the integers. In: Ryan, M.D., Smyth, B., Wang, G. (eds.) ISPEC 2012. LNCS, vol. 7232, pp. 353–368. Springer, Heidelberg (2012). doi:10.1007/978-3-642-29101-2_24

A Secure Reverse Multi-Attribute First-Price E-Auction Mechanism Using Multiple Auctioneer Servers (Work in Progress)

Jun Gao[1], Jiaqi Wang[1], Ning Lu[2], Fang Zhu[2], and Wenbo Shi[2(✉)]

[1] Department of Computer Science and Engineering,
Northeastern University, Shenyang, China
[2] School of Computer and Communication Engineering,
Northeastern University at Qinhuangdao, Qinhuangdao, China
swb319@hotmail.com

Abstract. One of the recent focus within the auction field has been multi-attribute auctions where buyer is not restricted to selecting the best option only by price but also other attributes. Due to the increase in the awareness of securing private information, in this paper, we design a secure reverse multi-attribute first-price auction scheme, in which the auction is processed on the bidders' encrypted bids by multiple auctioneer servers. As a result, auctioneer servers can determine the winner without knowing the real value of bids, which let bidder's privacy would not be revealed. At last, an analysis on the privacy of bids is conducted.

Keywords: Secure auction · Threshold homomorphic encryption · Bids privacy · Multiple attributes

1 Introduction

In past decades, e-auction has become a popular form of price determination in e-commerce due to its simplicity and efficiency [7]. Unlike traditional price-only auctions, in multi-attributes reverse (online) auction (MROA) [1,6] describes one such scenario, the buyer organizes an auction for contracts and asks suppliers to submit their bids and attributes through one or a number of different auction agents (servers). Next the auctioneer agents use a kind of scoring rule cooperatively computing and determine the winner of the auction.

In this paper's construction, there is a buyer, n distributed auctioneer servers (calculators) and m bidders with bids $B_i(1 \leq i \leq m)$, which is characterized by a n-length vector of attributes in addition to price: $B_i = \{b_i, \{\alpha_j | 1 \leq j \leq n\}\}$ $(b_i, a_j \in \mathbb{Z}_N)$, b_i is the price and α_j is the value of the j-th non-price attribute submitted by the bidder. To determine the winner, typical linear additive function [3,11] has been used, which takes the following form:

© Springer International Publishing AG 2016
L. Chen and J. Han (Eds.): ProvSec 2016, LNCS 10005, pp. 384–391, 2016.
DOI: 10.1007/978-3-319-47422-9_23

$$Score_i(b_i, AT_i) = -b_i + \sum_{j=1}^{m} w_j * f_j(\alpha_j) \tag{1}$$

AT_i denotes the vector of weighed non-price attributes in ith bids, w_i is the weight indicating the importance given to the attribute in weight set $W = \{w_i | 1 \leq i \leq n\}$. $f_i(\cdot)$ is the valuation function associated with the attribute. So in multi-attribute auctions, to determine the winner is to find:

$$\arg\max_i(Score(b_i, AT_i)) \tag{2}$$

Our goal is to solve the problem: distributed auctioneer servers collaboratively compute the maximum sum of the weighted attribute values while the information of bids should be kept secret.

2   Related Work

In MROA, the computing process is centrally controlled by an auctioneer and bidders are supposed and they are supposed to faithfully reveal their valuations of the goods in the auction, namely auctioneer/bidders could know all the bids information. From the view point of security, it is significant to preserve bids' privacy as once it is revealed to a half-hearted auctioneer, he or she may exploit such knowledge for its own benefit either in future auctions or renege on the sale. To the best our of knowledge, the related research about security issues of MROA is still very lacking. Suzuki *et al.*'s work [13] is the first one about dealing with security in multi-attribute auction. This scheme is applied to Vickrey auction and concentrates on bid privacy, and public verifiability. Shi. *et al.* [10] proposed a new qualitative attribute-based sealed-bid multi-attribute auction scheme under semi-honest model for the first time, which explores the different results in the multi-attribute auction model because of different bid structures, focuses on qualitative attribute-based winner determination auction model. Srinath *et al.* [11,12] proposed two MROA protocols, both use score function to compute the rank of biddings and pseudonym technique to anonymize bidders, however, they all open bids during or after the score computation so that the private information for losing bids will be leaked out.

3   Preliminaries

3.1   Paillier's Homomorphic Cryptosystem

Homomorphic encryption is a form of encryption that enables the decrypted result computed on the ciphertext to match the result calculated on the plaintext. Generally Paillier cryptosystem [8] has three parts: Key Generation, Encryption and Decryption.

Key Generation: Select $n = pq$, where p and q are large primes satisfying $p \nmid q - 1$ and $q \nmid p - 1$. Set $\lambda = lcm(p - 1, q - 1)$ where $lcm()$ represents the least common multiple. Then randomly select $g \in \mathbb{Z}_{n^2}^*$ such that order of g is a multiple of n, this is can be achieved by checking $\gcd(L(g^\lambda \bmod n^2), n) = 1$, in which $L(\cdot)$ is a function defined as $L(\mu) = (\mu - 1)/n$.

Public Key: $S_{pk} = (n, g)$, private Key: $S_{sk} = \lambda$ or (p, q).

Encryption: Given plaintext $m \in \mathbb{Z}_n$ and $r \in_R \mathbb{Z}_n^*$, the ciphertext c is: $c = E(m, r) = g^m r^n \bmod n^2$.

Decryption: Given the ciphertext $c \in \mathbb{Z}_{n^2}^*$, the plaintext m is given by:
$$m = \frac{L(c^\lambda \bmod n^2)}{L(g^\lambda \bmod n^2)} \bmod n.$$

It's necessary to know about its two *homomorphic properties*:

$$D(E(m_1, r_1) * E(m_2, r_2) \bmod n^2) = m_1 + m_2 \bmod n \tag{3}$$

$$D(E(m_1, r_1)^k \bmod n^2) = km_1 \bmod n \tag{4}$$

where $m_1, m_2 \in \mathbb{Z}_n$, $r_1, r_2 \in_R \mathbb{Z}_n^*$.

3.2   Threshold Paillier Cryptosystem

Threshold Paillier cryptosystem (TPC) [5] is utilized in our construction to avoid possible frauds in which a party who knows the secret key decrypts an arbitrary ciphertext and violates the privacy of a participating party. This scheme consists of the following participants: a dealer and a set of n decryption servers U_i.

Key Generation: Each decryption servers could get a share SK_i of the private key which is corresponding to the public key PK through a trusted dealer.

Encryption: Any one of decryption servers can take as input Pk, a plaintext M; it outputs a ciphertext c.

Decrypiton: A decryption server uses its secret key share SK_i to decrypt c to get a partial decryption c_i and forms a proof of its validity $proof_i$.

Recover: If at least a list of $c_1, c_2...c_t$'s $proof_i$ are validated correctly where $t \leq n$, the dealer or any third party can recover the plaintext M using a Lagrange-like combining protocol.

The details will be integrated into proposed protocol and explained in Sect. 4.

3.3   Definition of Security

In this paper, the parties are assumed to be *semi-honest*, i.e., bidders could submit their bids and calculators compute attributes honestly. Moreover, all messages are sent in clear between all participants using a broadcast channel which is public.

Definition 1. *(computationally indistinguishability): Let $\Sigma \subseteq \{0,1\}^*$. Two ensembles (indexed by Σ), $U \stackrel{def}{=} \{U_\sigma\}_{\sigma \in \Sigma}$ and $V \stackrel{def}{=} \{V_\sigma\}_{\sigma \in \Sigma}$ are computationally indistinguishable, if for every family of polynomial-size circuits, $\{X_n\}_{n \in \mathbb{N}}$, there exists a negligible (i.e., dominated by the inverse of any polynomial)function $\mu \colon \mathbb{N} \mapsto [0,1]$ so that*

$$| Pr[X_n(\sigma, U_\sigma) = 1] - Pr[X_n(\sigma, V_\sigma) = 1] | < \mu(| \sigma |)$$

Nextly, let us consider an attacker $\mathcal{A}$ who can actively but non-adaptively corrupts servers to learn both public parameters and private information. The security of protocol π is defined as follows:

Definition 2. *The security of protocol π is defined in terms of the indistinguishability under chosen plaintext attacks (IND-CPA). The security game is executed by a simulator $\mathcal{B}$ and a adversary $\mathcal{A}$ as follows:*

1. **Setup:** $\mathcal{B}$ generates a key pair (S_{pk}, S_{sk}) based on some public parameters. $\mathcal{A}$ chooses t servers to corrupt, he learns all private information of the corrupted servers, and actively controls their behavior.
2. **Query 1:** $\mathcal{A}$ selects a message M and a *partial decryption oracle* gives him l valid decryption shares of the encryption M. This phase can be repeated arbitrary times as $\mathcal{A}$ wishes.
3. **Challenge:** $\mathcal{A}$ submits two distinct messages m_0, m_1 and sends them to $\mathcal{B}$. Then,$\mathcal{B}$ chooses a random bit $b \in \{0,1\}$, and generates the challenge ciphertext c_{m_b}. $\mathcal{B}$ sends it to $\mathcal{A}$.
4. **Query 2:** $\mathcal{A}$ repeats Query 1, asking for decryption shares of encryptions of chosen messages.
5. **Guess:** Finally, $\mathcal{A}$ outputs a bit b'.

The adversary wins the game if $b = b'$ and we define the advantage of $\mathcal{A}$ in this game to be $Adv_\pi(\mathcal{A})$. We say that the protocol π is semantically secure against IND-CPA attack if no polynomially bounded adversary $\mathcal{A}$ has a non-negligible advantage against the simulator in the above game. Namely,

$$Adv_\pi(\mathcal{A}) =| P_r[b = b'] - 1/2 | \approx 0$$

4   Our Proposed Scheme

As introduce in Sect. 1, there is a buyer, l calculators and m bidders in our auction scenario. For the sake of simplicity, we assume a trusted dealer $\mathcal{D}$ as a key generation and distribution center of the underlying threshold Paillier system. Note that the trusted party $\mathcal{D}$ can be removed by using distributed key generation protocols [2,4]. The proposed scheme consists of four stages as 4.1 to 4.4.

4.1   System Initialization and Key Generation

As introduced in Sect. 1, at the beginning of the auction, the buyer publishes the procurement demand which actually is a vector of preferred attributes of goods, and its weight set $\{w_i\}_{i\in[1,l-1]}$ is separately sent to a calculator. Accordingly, each bidder generates his/her own bids $B_i = \{b_i, (\alpha_j | 1 \leq j \leq l-1)\}$ (By default, the attribute with index l is the price attribute) that also are l-length vectors.

Next, $\mathcal{D}$ picks an integer n, a product of two strong primes p and q such that $p = 2p' + 1$ and $q = 2q' + 1$ where p' and q' are large primes. Set $m = p'q'$, $\Delta = l!$, $g = (n+1)^a \times b^n \bmod n^2$ where $(a, b) \in_R \mathbb{Z}_n^* \times \mathbb{Z}_n^*$ and β is randomly selected in $\mathbb{Z}_n^*$. The public key $S_{pk} = (n, g)$ is sent to all bidders, and the secret key $S_{sk} = \beta m$ is shared with the Shamir scheme [9]: selects a polynomial $f(x) = \sum_{i=0}^l a_i x^i$ where $a_0 = \beta m$ and $\{a_i\}_{i=1,\dots,l}$ are random numbers in $\{0, \dots, nm-1\}$, the share s_i for the i-th calculator is $f(i) \bmod nm$.

4.2   Multiple Attributes Encryption and Transmission

In this phase, the bidder starts to send encrypted attribute to calculators. Firstly, when receiving S_{pk}, the bidder encrypts his/her own bids B_i by formula: $E_{S_{pk}}(-b_i) = -g^{b_i} r_1{}^n \bmod n^2$ and $e_j = E_{S_{pk}}(\alpha_j) = g^{\alpha_j} r_2{}^n \bmod n^2$ where $r_1, r_2 \in_R \mathbb{Z}_n^*$. Then sends $E_{S_{pk}}(-b_i)$ and a list of encrypted attributes $\{e_j\}_{j\in[1,l-1]}$ to all calculators $\{AS_k\}_{k\in[1,l]}$.

4.3   Computing Scores of Bids Using Homomorphic Properties

After each calculator $\{AS_k\}_{k\in[1,l-1]}$ receives $\{e_j\}$ from the i-th bidder, AS_k is going to calculate weighted attribute value $w_j * \alpha_j$ with its corresponding weight w_j, by using second Paillier cryptosystem's homomorphic property as described in formula (4), namely: $E_{S_{pk}}(AT_{ij}) = e_j{}^{w_j}$.

Next, each AS_k sends $E_{S_{pk}}(AT_{ij})$ to AS_l, then AS_l calculates the weighted attributes score as formula (1) through executing following operations using (3): $E_{S_{pk}}(AT_i) = \prod_{j=1}^{l-1} e_j{}^{w_j}$, then computes $E_{S_{pk}}(Score_i(b_i, AT_i)) = E_{S_{pk}}(AT_i) * E_{S_{pk}}(-b_i)$. At last of this phase, AS_l sends $E_{S_{pk}}(Score_i(b_i, AT_i))$ to other $l-1$ calculators.

4.4   Share Decryption and Combining

Now, all calculators have $E_{S_{pk}}(Score_i(b_i, AT_i))$, we denote it as c. Next, the i-th calculator $AS_{i,i\in[1,l]}$ computes the decryption share $c_i = c^{2\Delta s_i} \bmod n^2$ using his secret share s_i. Then each AS_i sends c_i to the buyer.

Under the assumption that calculators are semi-honest, the buyer could receive l valid ciphertext shares $\{c_i\}_{i\in[1,l]}$. Let S be the set of these l shares, the buyer could compute the plaintext form of the sum of weighted attributes for j-th bids:

$$Score_j = L(\prod_{k\in S} c_k^{2\Gamma_k} \bmod n^2) \times (4\Delta^2)^{-1} \tag{5}$$

where $\Gamma_k = \Delta \times \prod\limits_{k' \in S \setminus \{k\}} \frac{k'}{k'-k} \in \mathbb{Z}$.

Now, the execution for one bids B_i has been done. After the rest of $m'-1$ bids are computed, the buyer could select one or top-k satisfied bids by sorting $\{Score_j\}_{j \in [1,m']}$ as formula (2).

5   Security Analysis

In this section, we analyze the privacy of bids in proposed auction scheme according to the definition of security in Sect. 3.3. Through the adoption of TPC, the ciphertext is protected by the secret sharing scheme and the *Decisional Composite Residuosity Assumption*(DCRA). Furthermore, under the assumption that the participants are semi-honest, there is no colluding group could decrypt ciphertext to get the real value of the attributes in bids or the final score.

Theorem 1. *During the process of protocol, no participant can disclose B_i even after the bidding procedure is closed, i.e., the computation process is semantically secure under DCRA assumption.*

Proof. As discussed in previous section, only $E_{S_{pk}}(AT_i)$ and $E_{S_{pk}}(b_i)$ having information of B_i are sent during the protocol process. Because all elements of $E(AT_i)$ are the ciphertext forms of $w_j * AT_{ij}$, any party wanting to get the true value of the weighted attribute must decrypt bids, let us consider a adversary $\mathcal{A}$ able to break the semantic security of the threshold scheme. As the Sect. 3.3 defined, in the setup phase, $\mathcal{A}$ obtains the public key (n,g) and chooses two distinct messages (m_0, m_1) which are sent an encryption oracle $\mathcal{B}$, who randomly chooses a bit b and returns the encryption of b to $\mathcal{A}$, namely c_{m_b}. In next phase, called guess phase, $\mathcal{A}$ tries to guess which message has been encrypted.

In the *Setup* phase of the game introduce in Sect. 3.3, the adversary chooses to corrupt t servers and obtain these servers' secret shares $s_1, ..., s_t$. Since our participants are semi-honest, the proposed scheme did not let calculators generate a *proof* for proving that they compute decryption shares rightly as the original TPC does. However, the received data by $\mathcal{A}$ is still indistinguishable to him during the process of *Query 1* to *Query 2*. In these three steps, an encryption of message M is first computed: $c = g_1^M x^n \bmod n^2$. Then the shares of corrupted servers $c_1, ...c_t$ are computed using the secret key $s_1, ...s_t$ as $c_i = c^{2\Delta s_i}$. Finally, the missing c_i's are obtained by interpolation (Sect. 5.2 in [5]), using $c_1, ...c_t$ and the $(t+1)$-th point $c^{m\beta} \bmod n^2$ which we can compute without any secret knowledge since it is equal to $(1 + 2M * n)$. On the other hand, if $E_{S_{pk}}(AT_{ij})$ is instantly modified by a malicious party, this will lead to fail to decrypt the result $Score_i(b_i, AT_i)$ so the tampering activity could be found out.

6   Conclusion and Future Work

In this paper, we propose a secure reverse multi-attribute first-price auction based on *threshold Pallier cryptosystem*, in which multiple servers cooperatively compute the sum of weighted attributes without knowing its real value. In our work, the security definition is under semi-honest model which is a weak model actually. Our future work could undertake to design a more robust scheme to improve the protocol into malicious model, and decrease the cost of communication and computation.

Acknowledgement. The authors thank the editors and the anonymous reviewers for their valuable comments. This research was supported by National Natural Science Foundation of China (Nos.61472074, 61401083), the Doctoral Fund of Northeastern University of Qinhuangdao (Grant No. XNB201410); the Fundamental Research Funds for the Central Universities (Grant No. N130323005, L1523009); the Natural Science Foundation of Hebei Province of China (Grant No. F2014501139, F2015501122); the Doctoral Scientific Research Foundation of Liaoning Province (Grant No. F201501143).

References

1. Bellantuono, N., Ettorre, D., Kersten, G.E., Pontrandolfo, P.: Multi-attribute auction and negotiation for e-procurement of logistics. Group Decis. Negot. **23**(3), 421–441 (2014)
2. Ben-Or, M., Goldwasser, S., Wigderson, A.: Completeness theorems for non-cryptographic fault-tolerant distributed computation. In: Proceedings of the Twentieth Annual ACM Symposium on Theory of Computing, pp. 1–10. ACM (1988)
3. Chen, Y., Qiu, L., Cao, T., Hu, Z.: A multi-attribute reverse auction decision making model based on multi-objective programming. In: Xu, J., Cruz-Machado, V.A., Lev, B., Nickel, S. (eds.) Proceedings of the Eighth International Conference on Management Science and Engineering Management. AISC, vol. 280, pp. 73–81. Springer, Heidelberg (2014). doi:10.1007/978-3-642-55182-6_7
4. Damgård, I., Koprowski, M.: Practical threshold RSA signatures without a trusted dealer. In: Pfitzmann, B. (ed.) EUROCRYPT 2001. LNCS, vol. 2045, pp. 152–165. Springer, Heidelberg (2001). doi:10.1007/3-540-44987-6_10
5. Fouque, P.-A., Poupard, G., Stern, J.: Sharing decryption in the context of voting or lotteries. In: Frankel, Y. (ed.) FC 2000. LNCS, vol. 1962, pp. 90–104. Springer, Heidelberg (2001). doi:10.1007/3-540-45472-1_7
6. Kikuchi, H., Hotta, S., Abe, K., Nakanishi, S.: Distributed auction servers resolving winner and winning bid without revealing privacy of bids. In: Seventh International Conference on Parallel and Distributed Systems: Workshops, pp. 307–312. IEEE (2000)
7. Larson, M., Hu, C., Li, R., Li, W., Cheng, X.: Secure auctions without an auctioneer via verifiable secret sharing. In: Proceedings of the 2015 Workshop on Privacy-Aware Mobile Computing, pp. 1–6. ACM (2015)
8. Paillier, P.: Public-key cryptosystems based on composite degree residuosity classes. In: Stern, J. (ed.) EUROCRYPT 1999. LNCS, vol. 1592, pp. 223–238. Springer, Heidelberg (1999). doi:10.1007/3-540-48910-X_16
9. Shamir, A.: How to share a secret. Commun. ACM **22**(11), 612–613 (1979)
10. Shi, W.: A sealed-bid multi-attribute auction protocol with strong bid privacy and bidder privacy. Secur. Commun. Netw. **6**(10), 1281–1289 (2013)

11. Srinath, T., Kella, S., Jenamani, M.: A new secure protocol for multi-attribute multi-round e-reverse auction using online trusted third party. In: 2011 Second International Conference on Emerging Applications of Information Technology (EAIT), pp. 149–152. IEEE (2011)
12. Srinath, T., Singh, M.P., Pais, A.R.: Anonymity and verifiability in multi-attribute reverse auction. arXiv preprint (2011). arxiv:1109.0359
13. Suzuki, K., Yokoo, M.: Secure multi-attribute procurement auction. In: Song, J.-S., Kwon, T., Yung, M. (eds.) WISA 2005. LNCS, vol. 3786, pp. 306–317. Springer, Heidelberg (2006). doi:10.1007/11604938_24

Author Index